EXPLORING
Health
Care
CAREERS

Editorial Staff

Managing Editor, Career Publications: Andrew Morkes

Senior Editor: Carol Yehling

Editor: Anne Paterson

Assistant Editor: Nora Walsh

Writers: Carole Bolster, Shawna Brynildssen, Mickey Cohen, Felicitas Cortez, Kelly Cronin, Patty Cronin, Tim Cronin, Deborah Douglas, Jennifer Elcano, Laura Gabler, Nic Gengler, Bonnie Griffin, Janyce Hamilton, Kathleen Hayes, Louise Howe, Sally Jaskold, Jane Lawrence, Andrew Morkes, Shar Peters, Kathryn Quinlan, Laurie Sabol, Tim Schaffert, Elizabeth Taggart, Nancy Weatherwax

Proofreaders: Barbara Lightner, Bonnie Needham

Bibliographer: Connie Rockman

Indexer: Sandi Schroeder

Cover Design: Norm Baugher

Book Design Based on Concepts by: Joe Grossmann, Grossmann Design & Consulting

EXPLORING Health Care CAREERS

Second Edition

Ferguson Publishing Company • Chicago

Library of Congress Cataloging-in-Publication Data

Exploring health care careers: real people tell you what you need to know. — 2nd ed.
    p. ; cm.

  Includes bibliographical references and index.

  Summary: Provides information about 115 careers in the health care field including job descriptions, education and licensing requirements, salary, advancement opportunities, and employment outlook.

  ISBN 0-89434-311-4 (alk. paper)

  1. Medicine—Vocational guidance—Juvenile literature.
[1. Medicine—Vocational guidance. 2. Vocational guidance.]

  [DNLM: 1. Health Occupations. 2. Vocational Guidance. 3. Career Choice W 21 E96 2001]
R690 .E97 2001

610.69—dc21

                                                                                        2001001420

Published and distributed by
Ferguson Publishing Company
200 West Jackson Boulevard, Suite 700
Chicago, Illinois 60606
800-306-9941
http://www.fergpubco.com

Printed in the United States of America
Y-8

contents

contents

VOLUME 2

introduction

The health care field has exploded in recent years. One result of that growth is that there are employment opportunities for just about anyone, no matter what your talents, interests, skills, and education levels are.

According to the Bureau of Labor Statistics, four of the 10 occupations with the fastest growth in the next decade are in health care. The number of people employed in health services is expected to increase to 12,600,000—more than 3,100,000 new jobs.

Exploring Health Care Careers focuses on more than 100 jobs that pertain to human health. These jobs include professional careers, such as those of physicians and dentists, and highly skilled positions held by technicians and other specialists. Many health care workers are assistants, providing essential support to other health care workers and, in many cases, working directly with patients themselves.

This second edition includes several new chapters, such as "Health Physicists" and "Myotherapists." All chapters have been revised to include the most recent education, certification, salary, and outlook information available. Organization contact information has been updated, as well as bibliographical material. The most current employment statistics are included in each chapter and some chapters contain new interviews.

A key feature of *Exploring Health Care Careers* consists of interviews with individuals who actually hold health care positions. This personal look reveals that the health care field draws men and women who are not only extremely intelligent, ambitious, and capable but also very caring and compassionate. A common characteristic of many of the persons profiled in these chapters is that they like and want to help people.

Some of the careers discussed in these chapters command very high pay, but they are extremely demanding—in the training and education required, in the hours spent working, in the responsibility of having a person's life depend on what you do. Yet there are many careers in health care that are not so strenuous but are as personally fulfilling. Few are the kinds of jobs in which a person can be as clearly assured of having helped another human being as in health care. Yet death and disease are facts of life, and the health care worker must cope with its disappointments and limitations. In evaluating what type of health care career is right for you, it is important to realize that some jobs, such as working with dying cancer patients, are much more emotionally demanding than others.

If you are drawn to one of the careers that requires attending medical school, it is important to take early steps toward preparation, since admission is highly competitive. Because of the large commitment required in time and money, it is advantageous to gain some exposure to various kinds of health care professions before making a decision to pursue such a career. For medical specialties there is an enormous amount of information to learn initially and then to continue to learn in order to stay up to date. It is not surprising that many health care professionals not only maintain a practice but also are teaching and in research. Participation in professional organizations is also important.

This book includes a number of jobs in nontraditional health care, including acupuncture and hypnotherapy, which many people today seek out for the unique treatments its practitioners have to offer. These practices have varying degrees of acceptance from the traditional medical community, pending scientific verification of their effectiveness.

In many areas of health care there is an increasing reliance on technology, and technicians are needed for operating highly complex equipment. Some technicians work as part of a group of highly trained professionals, such as a surgical team. In some cases, to save costs, technicians are being trained to assume duties once largely held by professionals. Such action has been controversial, since medical professionals argue that the quality of health care may be compromised by using workers with less education.

For some health care jobs the typical workday is fairly predictable; for others, the work is dictated by emergencies. Speed and expertise are essential. Some jobs have unpredictable hours and require working late shifts or being on call during odd hours.

The face of health care in the United States is changing as methods are developed to deal with its ever-rising costs. Health maintenance organizations and other companies have introduced managed care programs in which an insurer offers a company medical insurance for its employees at a fixed cost per person. The company then manages the expenses of providing the health care in order to make a profit. One way it can cut costs is to set up contracts with specific doctors and then limit a patient's coverage to visits to those doctors only. Another way is to require a patient get a referral from his or her primary care physician, such as a general practitioner, before seeing a specialist for more expensive treatment. Medical insurance companies have tried to reduce costs by limiting expensive, and in their view, unnecessary, procedures and tests—especially those performed by specialists.

Critics of managed health care believe that financial considerations are getting in the way of providing good health care and that persons should be free to choose whom they wish to see for treatment. However, managed health care allows employers to plan the cost of providing health care benefits to employees. Many jobs in health care are affected either directly or indirectly by this trend, and its full impact on the industry will not be known for some time.

how to use this book

Each chapter of *Exploring Health Care Careers* is divided into 11 sections (some with subsections) that focus on particular kinds of questions and information about a specific job. An important element of each chapter is an interview with one or more persons who actually have the job. What better way to learn about a job than from someone who actually does it? Some of the persons interviewed are just starting out; others began working many years ago, becoming highly respected individuals in their field. All have experiences and firsthand knowledge of their work that they are here able to share with students and others considering entering health care careers. It is our hope that letting real health care workers describe their work in their own words will help job seekers with their investigation of a career in health care.

the opening

The opening page of each chapter gives the reader an at-a-glance overview of the job being discussed: definition, alternative job titles, lists of high school subjects and personal skills relevant to the specific job, salary range (beginning, experienced, and very experienced), educational requirements, certification or licensing, and outlook. Also given here are the GOE (Guide to Occupational Exploration) subgroup number and the O*NET-SOC (Occupational Information Network-Standard Occupational Classification) group number. Most of the jobs described in this work correspond exactly to a particular GOE and O*NET-SOC category. However, there are some exceptions. When a job does not fit into a specific GOE and/or O*NET-SOC category, a footnote explains the reason.

the introduction

The opening text section of each chapter is an introductory scene showing the profiled person at work. Some introductions are as tense and exciting as a televised medical drama; for example, in the chapter "Neurological Surgeon," the scene begins as the victim of a near-fatal traffic accident is rushed into the emergency room with multiple injuries. Other stories, such as the one in "Physical Therapist," are uplifting. In this case an anxious young man, facing the possibility of back surgery and the loss of his job, has his chronic leg pain dramatically cured in a single visit to his physical therapist. By appealing to readers on an emotional, imaginative level, the introduction involves them immediately and gives them a feeling about the particular type of work.

what does a health care worker do?

This section describes in broad terms the basics of what the health care worker does. Any variations in job duties and titles are covered as well. Actual job duties and titles may vary according to where a health care worker is employed, and an effort is made here to discuss some of the more common ones. Primary duties and secondary duties are also covered.

what is it like to be a health care worker?

In this section, the reader gets a first-person account of what it is like to do the job. This section prompts the reader to ask himself or herself: "Could I really do this?" and, more importantly, "Do I want to?" Here the reader formally meets the profiled person and sees him or her at work on a typical day or series of days. Typical tasks or duties are covered, and a distinction is made between primary duties and secondary ones. As the health care workers describe what their jobs are like, readers can begin asking themselves if this is something they really want to do. For example, jobs that sound glamorous on the surface may seem more monotonous after getting down to the details of the workday; or, conversely, jobs that do not sound too exciting at first glance can be seen as very rewarding when viewed through the eyes of an enthusiastic worker. Readers should remember, however, that these are personal accounts; not all health care workers will have similar situations and experiences.

have I got what it takes to be a health care worker?

In this section, the profiled person tells the reader what personal qualities are important for success in the job and discusses what he or she likes and dislikes about the position. Also discussed are some of the important skills required by health care workers. In addition to the specific skills required for each job, health care workers should have the ability to communicate and relate well to others; they must be able to give—and take—direction and get along with co-workers, patients, clients, and customers. Another important trait is the willingness to commit to lifelong learning. Most of the health care workers interviewed regularly read scientific or trade magazines and books and attend conferences to keep up with new scientific developments and constantly changing technology. Their dedication is demonstrated by the fact that such self-improvement is often done on the health care worker's own time.

how do I become a health care worker?

This section explores the educational path to the job, frequently giving examples from the profiled person's own experiences. A subsection on high school details important classes and activities to take in preparation for the job. It is important to note here that health care workers' jobs are not for academic slouches. High school students will need math and basic science courses such as physics and chemistry, plus English and social studies. Computer courses are strongly recommended.

A subsection on postsecondary training discusses the options of college, medical school, vocational/technical school, apprenticeships, and on-the-job training. Typical courses of study are outlined, including specific courses and practical clinical or internship experience required.

A section on certification or licensing outlines the requirements of the profession, whether voluntary or mandatory. Details about tests and information about contacting certifying or licensing agencies are also given. For most health care workers' jobs that do not formally require certification, many of those interviewed recommended it as a way to show commitment and dedication to the profession.

A section on scholarships and grants highlights any special monies set aside for a particular profession. Readers are reminded to check with their high school guidance counselor and to contact their school's financial aid office for additional information.

A section on internships and volunteerships details options for pre-job experience. Many of the jobs here, or at least their settings, such as hospitals, can be explored first in volunteer situations. Enterprising students can often create their own "internships" by offering to work for experience alone at places such as nursing homes or charitable organizations that cannot afford to hire extra professional help. Finally, a section on labor unions (if applicable) identifies any major unions that are affiliated with the profession.

who will hire me?

This section gives the reader an idea about how to get a job in the particular field, frequently discussing how the profiled person got his or her first job. Identified are the most likely places of employment, such as a hospital, clinic, or government agency. The importance of making and maintaining contacts in one's field is also discussed. Many of the health care workers interviewed here got their first jobs through a personal contact.

where can I go from here?

This section tells the reader about advancement possibilities, illustrated with the profiled person's own goals about where he or she eventually sees himself or herself going in the field. Advancement usually connotes two things: an increase in responsibilities and an increase in pay. In some fields, earning potential for health care workers is virtually unlimited. In other fields, health care workers' salaries eventually top off, so that no matter how many years of experience one has, one is probably not going to earn more than a certain amount. (This scenario is not, of course, limited to health care workers, but is experienced by workers in all types of jobs.) Many health care workers treat their experience in a particular job as a sort of internship for another career; roughly 40 percent of licensed practical nurses, for example, go on to become registered nurses.

what are the salary ranges?

This section gives the reader an idea of the average beginning salary, an experienced worker's salary, and the salary of a very experienced worker. Where available, salaries in particular geographic regions or cities are indicated. When considering salaries, readers should keep the entire benefits package in mind—insurance, retirement plan, tuition reimbursement, and vacation, sick, and holiday pay.

what is the job outlook?

The purpose of this section is to get the reader thinking about the big picture and his or her long-term objectives. It relies heavily on the U.S. Department of Labor's *Occupational Outlook Handbook* to indicate the projected job growth (decline, little change or more slowly than the average, about as fast as the average, faster than the average, and much faster than the average) for the particular job and explains to the reader how the future of the job is tied to the overall economy or subsections of the economy—in short, how it fits into the scheme of things.

how do I learn more?

This section includes two subsections: professional organizations and a bibliography. The organization section lists organizations that provide information to students or their members about the profession, scholarships, employers, or education. The listing includes telephone numbers and Internet addresses. The bibliography lists a sampling of relevant books that students can begin looking through to learn about the profession. Emphasis has been placed on books published in the last five years.

additional material

Each chapter of *Exploring Health Care Careers* also has several sidebars that are quick and fun to read. Sidebars lighten the look of the text, making it visually more inviting. The sidebars also provide useful "for your information" quick facts, "lingo to learn" (glossary of terms relevant to the profession), personal traits necessary for success in the job, related jobs that use similar skills, advancement possibilities, graphs, and in-depth features on history, famous people, and events.

indexes

At the end of volume two are three indexes: GOE, O*NET-SOC, and Job Title. The GOE (*Guide for Occupational Exploration*) index is organized by GOE interest area and work group. Jobs are listed in alphabetical order under their GOE work groups, followed by a page number for easy reference. The O*NET-SOC (Occupational Information Network-Standard Occupational Classification) is organized in a similar fashion by group. Specific jobs are listed in alphabetical order. O*NET-SOC numbers are given for the jobs, as are page numbers so the reader can easily turn to the appropriate page in the set. The Job Title index lists all major jobs discussed in this work and their page numbers, with appropriate cross references.

a final note

It should be obvious from reading the interviews on these pages that people love to talk about what they do. We encourage readers to take this a step further and seek out people who have jobs they are interested in. Talk to them about their work. Find out what they like and do not like and what they would do differently if they had to do it all over again. There is no better teacher than experience. Students would do well to learn from the experiences of those who have been there.

acknowledgements

The editorial staff of Ferguson Publishing Company would like to express its appreciation to all of the individuals profiled here. Your enthusiasm for your work and willingness to share your experiences with others have made this set possible. Also, many thanks to all of the educators, employers, and associations whose additional comments and factual data help make this reference work as up to date as possible.

Acupuncturists

Definition
Acupuncturists insert thin needles into sites on the body to treat various symptoms and disorders.

High School Subjects
Biology
English
Physics

Personal Skills
Helping/teaching
Technical/scientific

Salary Range
$20,000 to $30,000 to $40,000+

Minimum Educational Levels
Bachelor's degree in acupuncture or medical degree, depending on state

Certification or Licensing
Required by certain states

Outlook
About as fast as the average

GOE
02.03.04

O*NET-SOC
NA*

*Not Available.
The O*NET-SOC
does not categorize
the career of
acupuncturist.

Acupuncturist

Michael Boyer is seeing his last patient of the day, a 29-year-old student studying for the bar exam with complaints of cramps, headaches, and chronic lower back pain.

"I'm desperate," she tells him. "I've gone to so many doctors. No one has been able to help me."

Michael nods. "So you've decided to try acupuncture."

"Like I said," the patient repeats, "I'm desperate. I'll try anything. The pain gets so bad I can't move. I can't leave my bed for days. It's been like this since I was 14. But the bar exam is coming up, and I can't afford to be in pain."

Michael finishes his examination and decides she can definitely benefit from some treatments. "I can help. I'd say your liver energy has become stagnant. What I'll do is stimulate that to get it flowing again."

"My liver?" Her look of hope changes to confusion. But she waves her hand. "Whatever. If it'll help."

A month later, Michael's phone rings. It's the patient and she is laughing. "It's amazing!" she says. "I feel great. No cramps, no headaches, no pain at all! I'm on my way to the bar exam now. But I just wanted to thank you first. You've really changed my life!"

lingo to learn

Acupressure, or **shiatsu:** A technique similar to acupuncture but using finger pressure and hand strokes instead of needles.

Herbal medicine: A system of medicine in which herbs are used in various combinations to treat symptoms and promote health. It is often used as a supplement to acupuncture.

Massage therapy: The manipulation of the soft tissues of the body. It is sometimes used in combination with the application of heat or cold.

Moxibustion: A type of treatment in which a cone, called a moxa, of certain plant materials is burnt above the skin to relieve internal pain. Acupuncturists burn moxas on acupuncture needles.

Qi, or **chi:** In traditional Chinese medicine, the energy of the body. It flows along pathways, called meridians, in the body.

Qi gong, or **chi kung:** Exercises meant to improve health, aid in longevity, and promote inner peace and well-being. T'ai chi is a type of qi gong.

T'ai chi: A type of exercise based on a series of more than 100 postures, between which are slow, deliberate movements. It is done to achieve integration of mind and body.

Yoga: A method of achieving physical and mental control by performing a series of poses. The poses are called asanas.

what does an acupuncturist do?

Acupuncture has been practiced for thousands of years; it is one of the ancient Chinese healing arts. *Acupuncturists* treat symptoms and disorders by inserting very thin needles in specific points on the body. Acupuncturists believe that the body has a type of energy, called qi, or chi (both pronounced as "chee"), and that this energy flows along 14 specific pathways, called meridians, in the body. Disease, pain, and other physical and emotional conditions result when the body's qi is unbalanced or when the flow of qi along the meridians is blocked or disrupted. The purpose of acupuncture and other forms of traditional Chinese medicine is to restore balance to the body's qi.

Although acupuncture has been practiced in the United States for more than 150 years, many people in this country are skeptical about its effectiveness. In recent years, however, studies have begun to shed light on the mechanisms involved in acupuncture, and it has seen increased acceptance in the professional medical community. In a move representative of this growing acceptance, in 1996 the U.S. Food and Drug Administration, classified acupuncture needles as medical devices. The World Health Organization has recognized acupuncture's effectiveness since 1979, when it issued a list of more than 40 diseases and other health conditions that acupuncture has helped alleviate. Acupuncture has been most accepted in treating pain and chronic illness, and in helping patients overcome such addictions as smoking and cocaine use. Many physicians now refer patients to acupuncturists. Some physicians practice acupuncture themselves in conjunction with standard medical treatments.

Michael Boyer is in his second year of practicing acupuncture in the state of California. "The first thing I do when I receive a new patient is to get their health history, find out what problems they've had in the past and what problem they're experiencing now. Then I do a physical examination."

During an examination, an acupuncturist tries to determine if a patient's qi is unbalanced and, if so, where the unbalance is located. The acupuncturist tests the patient's pulse at each wrist and examines skin color, body language, and tone of voice. "Observation is important," Michael says. "I can tell a lot from the sound of the patient's voice, for example. I'll also examine the patient's tongue. You can learn a lot about a person's health from the condition of the tongue."

Once the acupuncturist has determined the source of the qi unbalance, he or she will choose the type of needle to be used. There are nine types of acupuncture needles, ranging from just over an inch long to as long as seven inches. Each type of needle is used to treat certain conditions. Most acupuncturists in the United States and other Western countries use only three types of needles, ranging from one to three inches in length. After selecting the type of needle, the acupuncturist determines where the needles will be inserted on the patient's body. There are 365 possible insertion points on the body. Typically, 10 to 12 needles are used in a treatment.

Acupuncture needles are flexible and are much thinner than injection-type needles. They are inserted to a depth of up to one inch. Insertion of the needles is generally painless, though sensitive individuals may feel some slight pain. During treatment, the acupuncturist may stimulate the needles to increase the effect. The needles are stimulated by twirling them or by applying heat or a low electrical current. Treatment sometimes lasts an hour or more, and the patient may have to return for several sessions.

what is it like to be an acupuncturist?

Acupuncturists are trained health practitioners. Many are trained as physicians or chiropractors and use acupuncture in conjunction with other medical treatments. Most acupuncturists work in their own practices or in group practices.

Michael operates his own acupuncture and herbal medicine clinic, with its own herbal pharmacy. His day typically begins at 9 AM and ends between 6 and 7 PM. "I see patients all day," Michael says. "For a new patient, I'll spend half an hour or so with them—taking the medical history and then doing an examination. I take copious notes during an examination. This is partly for legal reasons. But it's also so I can do research into the patient's case, to have a better understanding of what kind of treatment they'll need."

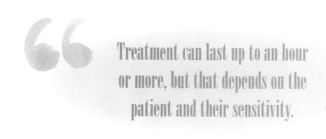

"Treatment can last up to an hour or more, but that depends on the patient and their sensitivity."

Once Michael has determined a patient's treatment, he starts inserting and stimulating the acupuncture needles. "Treatment can last up to an hour or more," he says, "but that depends on the patient and their sensitivity. Some people can take strong stimulation, but others can't."

Michael uses other techniques in conjunction with acupuncture. "We keep a fully stocked herbal pharmacy here with over 100 herbs. We also have herbs in pill form and tinctures [solutions]. I mix and match the herbs to personalize the formula, to individualize the patient's treatment. For some patients, I prescribe only herbs—especially to someone afraid of the needles."

In addition to treating patients, Michael has various administrative duties. "I run my own business, so I have to do all the paperwork myself. That means doing the insurance billing and making sure I get paid. I spend time writing reports, and I also have to order herbs for the pharmacy. Usually I take one day a week just to do all the paperwork. And I also have to market myself; I have to get patients. That's especially important to do during busy times, when I have a lot of patients, so I'll still have business when things are slower." An important source of patients is the medical community. "I get a lot of referrals for patients from physicians," Michael says. "It's important to maintain relationships with physicians. Often they'll refer me patients that they can't do anything for."

Another important aspect of an acupuncturist's job is to remain aware of new types of acupuncture treatments. Michael says, "I take a lot of continuing education programs to keep up with the latest developments in acupuncture."

in-depth

How Does Acupuncture Work?

While there is still a great deal of debate concerning acupuncture's effectiveness in eliminating pain and curing disease, more people are convinced that acupuncture does somehow work. In recent years, research has begun to support some of the claims of acupuncturists and their patients.

Some researchers believe that acupuncture works by increasing the release of endorphins, chemicals that the brain naturally produces in response to pain, stress, and physical exertion. There is some evidence that acupuncture may also help regulate other chemicals in the body.

Other researchers believe that acupuncture needles directly stimulate the nervous system. Yet another way that acupuncture may work is by boosting the body's immune system.

What Is Acupuncture Good For?

The World Health Organization publishes a list of more than 40 diseases and other health conditions for which acupuncture has been shown to be beneficial. The following conditions are among those included on the list.

Acute bronchitis
Bronchial asthma
Common cold
Diarrhea
Duodenal ulcer
Gastritis
Headache
Low back pain
Osteoarthritis
Sciatica
Slight paralysis following a stroke
Toothache

have I got what it takes to be an acupuncturist?

Like any health care practitioner, acupuncturists work with people who are in pain and who have been ill for long periods of time. Because patients often come to acupuncturists only after other medical treatments have failed them, they may be especially pessimistic about finding relief or a cure. "It can be difficult," Michael says. "I listen to people complain all day long about their problems. You have to be compassionate. But at the same time, you have to be able to separate your personal feelings and remain unattached. And this is difficult, because many of my patients come back over and over, and I develop a relationship with them. You have to care for people in order to do this."

Michael finds acupuncture and herbal medicine to be exciting fields. "The challenge is to get people well," he says. "I use all the tools I have to do that. I try to figure out the right treatment plans to get them well. And it's really satisfying when they do get well."

Michael's least favorite part of his career is the paperwork. "I really don't like dealing with the insurance companies. Sometimes it's difficult to get them to pay me. And I also have to make time to market myself, to get patients in. But this is all part of running your own business."

Acupuncture still meets with a great deal of skepticism in the medical community. An acupuncturist must maintain his or her confidence despite that skepticism. An increasing number of physicians, however, are recognizing value in acupuncture. "That's another part of this work," Michael says. "Many doctors refer patients that they can't do anything with. Some of these people have been sick for so long, and they've been pumped so full of drugs, which can cause problems themselves. A lot of what I do is dealing with the adverse effects of Western medicine."

how do I become an acupuncturist?

Because acupuncture has only recently begun to gain acceptance in the United States there are as yet no national guidelines for it in this country, although many states use standards set by the National Certification Commission for Acupuncture and Oriental Medicine(NCCAOM). Requirements vary widely from state to state. In many states, only physicians or doctors of osteopathy can be licensed to practice acupuncture. In a few states, the practice of acupuncture is not regulated at all. You can get information on educational and licensing requirements by contacting the department of health of individual states.

If you are interested in acupuncture as a career, you should be prepared to get at least a bachelor's degree. In states where acupuncturists are required to be licensed physicians, you should be prepared to follow a premedical and medical degree program.

education

High School

If you are interested in acupuncture, take courses that will give you an understanding of the human body and prepare for entry into a college or university. Courses in biology, physiology, and psychology will help you gain an understanding of the body and insight into the mind.

High schools don't generally offer courses that are directly related to acupuncture. Instead, look outside school for experience in alternative medicine techniques. "Acupuncture is so completely different from anything you can study in school," Michael says. "But you can do things like yoga and t'ai chi, ancient methods for achieving control of the mind and body. I worked as a massage therapist for many years, which is similar to acupuncture. I also practiced and taught yoga. And I was going to acupuncturists for years before I realized that I wanted to do this, too."

Apart from these activities, part-time or volunteer work at hospitals, retirement homes, and rehabilitation clinics can offer valuable experience in caring for others.

Postsecondary Training

There are more than 50 schools of acupuncture in the United States. Some of these schools offer only certificate or bachelor's degree programs; others offer master's degree programs. To be admitted into a master's degree program in acupuncture, a student must have at least a bachelor's degree in a related field. Most training programs provide a thorough education in all aspects of traditional Chinese medicine. In states where a medical degree is required to practice acupuncture, students may take acupuncture as part of their medical training.

certification or licensing

Licensing and certification requirements vary widely from state to state. Certification and licensing is usually achieved by meeting educational requirements and passing an examination. Thirty-seven states use NCCAOM standards as an integral part of their licensing process. To become nationally board certified in acupuncture, NCCAOM requires applicants to have followed one of the following: a formal education route, apprenticeship route, professional acupuncture practice route, or combination of training and experience. All applicants are required to complete a Clean Needle Technique course and to pass the NCCAOM Acupuncture Examination, which consists of a written examination and the Point Location Examination.

As mentioned earlier, many states certify only licensed physicians to practice acupuncture, while some states extend this right to chiropractors. In certain states, an acupuncturist is granted the right to practice only after a ruling from the state's board of medical examiners. States that currently have no requirements for practicing acupuncture are considering legislation on the subject.

who will hire me?

Most acupuncturists operate their own private practices. Some acupuncturists form partnerships with other acupuncturists or with people skilled in other areas of Chinese medicine. Michael set up his own clinic after being licensed as an acupuncturist in California. He shares the office with another acupuncturist, although they maintain separate businesses.

There are limited opportunities for acupuncturists in hospitals and university medical schools. However, as acupuncture becomes more accepted, the number of acupuncturists working in these institutions should rise. A few acupuncturists are engaged in medical research, conducting studies on the effectiveness of acupuncture to treat specific health conditions. A small number of acupuncturists work for government agencies, such as the National Institutes of Health.

According to professional organizations' referral lists, more acupuncturists practice in states with large, urban areas than in states with more rural populations. California by far has the most licensed acupuncturists, with over 4,000 registered there (there are about 10,000 in the United States).

where can I go from here?

Acupuncturists advance by establishing their own practices and building large bases of patients. Because an acupuncturist receives referrals from physicians and other health care practitioners, relationships with other members of the medical community can be very helpful in building a patient base.

An acupuncturist may wish to eventually teach acupuncture at a school of Chinese medicine. After much experience, an acupuncturist may achieve a supervisory or directorship position in a school.

There is a great deal of research yet to be done in acupuncture, and an acupuncturist

To be a successful acupuncturist, you should

- Have sensitive hands
- Be very accurate and conscientious
- Be patient and compassionate
- Enjoy working with and helping people
- Be open-minded and interested in alternative viewpoints

can build a rewarding career participating in this effort.

what are the salary ranges?

Acupuncturists can expect starting earnings from $23,058 to $32,817, according to the Economic Research Institute. The average salary of acupuncturists who have worked 10 years or more is about $42,886 per year. Physicians who practice acupuncture as part of their medical practices have incomes that can be well over $100,000 per year. In some cases, starting acupuncturists may earn only $20,000 per year or less, depending on the strength of their practices. As they gain experience and patient referrals, however, they will earn more.

One factor limiting acupuncturists' earnings is the level of acceptance of acupuncture. As acupuncture gains respect, earnings in this field should rise.

what is the job outlook?

In 2000, there were more than 10,000 licensed acupuncturists in the United States. Some in the field estimate that figure will triple by 2015. Each year more than 1,000 new acupuncturists become certified. The number of certified and licensed acupuncturists is expected to grow as additional states establish legal guidelines for acupuncturists to follow.

Twelve million Americans received acupuncture treatments in 1995, and this number has grown every year for the last several years. One of the areas of greatest growth in acupuncture is the treatment of addictions. The U.S. government has provided more than $1 million for research investigating acupuncture's effect on cocaine addiction and alcoholism. Many hospitals and prisons now use acupuncture in their substance abuse programs. A continued interest in the treatment of addictions should bode well for acupuncturists' job opportunities. Besides the treatment of addictions, other areas of growth in acupuncture include the treatment of chronic pain, bronchial asthma, and premenstrual syndrome.

Another factor that favors job growth in acupuncture is an increasing amount of insurance coverage for acupuncture treatments. Following the Food and Drug Administration's 1996 ruling designating acupuncture needles as medical devices Medicare, Medicaid, and private insurance companies are more likely to insure acupuncture treatments for patients. This factor has increased the number of physician referrals to acupuncturists. As a result, there is increasing demand for acupuncturists.

Despite these factors favoring job growth, acupuncture still faces challenges of acceptance. For this reason, conventional medical careers may offer more career opportunities than acupuncture, which many still consider alternative medicine.

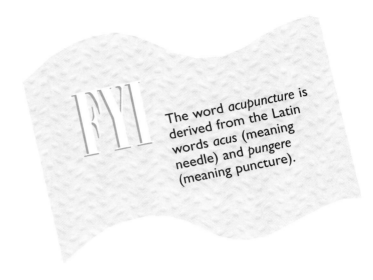

The word *acupuncture* is derived from the Latin words *acus* (meaning needle) and *pungere* (meaning puncture).

how do I learn more?

professional organizations

Following are organizations that provide information on acupuncture careers, accredited schools, and employers.

Acupuncture.com
PO Box 3571
Santa Monica, CA 90408-3571
310-264-6669
http://www.acupuncture.com

American Association of Oriental Medicine
433 Front Street
Catasauqua, PA 18032
888-500-7999
aaom1@aol.com
http://www.aaom.org

Council of Colleges of Acupuncture and Oriental Medicine
7501 Greenway Center Drive, Suite 820
Greenbelt, MD 20770
ccaom@compuserve.com
http://www.ccaom.org

National Acupuncture and Oriental Medicine Alliance
14637 Starr Road SE
Silver Spring, MD 20910
http://acuall.org

National Certification Commission for Acupuncture and Oriental Medicine
11 Canal Center Plaza, Suite 300
Alexandria, VA 22314
703-548-9004
info@nccaom.org
http://www.nccaom.org

bibliography

Following is a sampling of materials relating to the professional concerns and development of acupuncturists.

Flaws, Bob. *Acupoint Pocket Reference.* Boulder, CO: Blue Poppy Press, 1998.

Fleischman, Gary and Charles Stein. *Acupuncture: Everything You Ever Wanted to Know But Were Afraid to Ask.* Barrytown, NY: Barrytown Ltd., 1998.

Johns, Robert and Andrew E. Tseng. *The Art of Acupuncture Techniques.* Berkeley, CA: North Atlantic Books, 1997.

Mole, Peter. *Acupuncture: Energy Balancing for Body, Mind and Spirit.* New York, NY: HarperCollins, 1997.

Sankey, Mikio. *Esoteric Acupuncture: Gateway to Expanded Healing.* Los Angeles, CA: Mountain Castle Publishers, 1999.

Seem, Mark. *Acupuncture Physical Medicine.* Boulder, CO: Blue Poppy Press, 2000.

acupuncturists

Steinfeld, Alan. *Careers in Alternative Medicine.* New York, NY: Rosen Group, 1999.

Williams, Tom et al. *The Complete Illustrated Guide to Chinese Medicine: A Comprehensive System for Health and Fitness.* London, UK: Thorsons Publishers, 1996.

Xinnong, Cheng, ed. *Chinese Acupuncture and Moxibustion.* San Francisco, CA: China Books & Periodicals, 2000.

Zhou, Zhung-ying and Hui De Jin. *Clinical Manual of Chinese Herbal Medicine and Acupuncture.* New York, NY: Churchill Livingstone, 1997.

Allergists/Immunologists

Definition

Allergists/immunologists are doctors who specialize in the treatment of allergic and immunologic diseases. They treat patients with asthma, hay fever, food allergies, AIDS, rheumatoid arthritis, and other diseases.

Alternative Job Title

Allergy and immunology specialists

High School Subjects

Biology
Chemistry
Health

Personal Skills

Leadership/management
Technical/scientific

Salary Range

$50,000 to $164,000 to $200,000

Educational Requirements

Bachelor's degree, medical degree, three years training in internal medicine or pediatrics, two years residency in allergy and immunology.

Certification or Licensing

Required by all states

Outlook

Faster than the average

GOE
02.03.01
O*NET-SOC
29-1063.00

Dr. Costa, an allergist/immunologist, meets in his office with an 11-year-old boy suffering from allergic rhinitis. The doctor has reviewed the patient's medical history and lets the boy talk about his symptoms. "I have difficulty breathing sometimes," the boy says. "I cough sometimes." Dr. Costa takes notes; he knows how important this first meeting is, how important it is to learn as much as possible about the patient and his illness.

Dr. Costa is aware of how much is at stake in treating the illness; rhinitis in children can sometimes develop into asthma. Although fewer people die from asthma in the United States than anywhere else in the world, there is still a great threat. The asthma may persist for the duration of the child's life. The boy was referred to Dr. Costa from another doctor who had been treating the boy with expensive medications. Dr. Costa informs the parents of a less-expensive treatment called immunotherapy, a series of allergy shots that can reduce the symptoms and improve breathing. It can also reduce the chances of the boy developing asthma. Dr. Costa's goal is to treat disease with as little medication as possible to avoid interfering with the child's daily life. This will not only allow the child more freedom but will also keep the cost of treatment low.

what does an allergist/immunologist do?

You finally move out on your own and the first thing you get for your new apartment is a pet dog. Your mother was allergic to dogs, so you never had one when you were a kid. But, after bringing home a puppy from the pound, you're sneezing and coughing, you've got a runny nose and weepy eyes. Well,

lingo to learn

Anaphylaxis: A life-threatening allergic reaction to an insect sting or a drug such as penicillin.

Angiodema: The swelling of the tissues of the throat.

Antihistamines: Drugs designed to relieve allergy symptoms.

Bronchitis: An inflammation of the lung's airways, which causes a persistent cough; controlled with drugs called bronchodilators.

Contact dermatitis: A skin condition, such as an inflammation, or rash, caused by chemicals and plants.

Immune system: A network of cells that protects the body from foreign substances and destroys infected cells.

Rhinitis: Also known as **hay fever;** an inflammation of the membrane in the nose, causing nasal congestion, runny nose, and sneezing.

Urticaria: Also known as **hives;** a skin condition causing itchy lumps and inflammation.

you've just learned that allergies can be inherited. If one of your parents has an allergy, you have a 50 percent chance of having that same allergy. Over 50 million Americans suffer from some kind of allergy. In addition to the fur of animals, a person may be allergic to certain foods, plants, pollen, air pollution, insects, colognes, chemicals, and cleansers. So, many people seek the aid of an *allergist/immunologist,* a doctor who specializes in the treatment of allergic, asthmatic, and immunologic diseases.

Of course, if you are allergic to dogs or cats, the best solution is to avoid dogs and cats. But some allergens (the substance that causes the allergic reaction), like grass, dust, or pollinating plants, can be difficult to avoid. When you visit your family doctor with symptoms of an allergy, the doctor will likely refer you to an allergist/immunologist. Hay fever, also called allergic rhinitis, is a common condition treated by an allergist. A person with hay fever may have symptoms such as congestion, sneezing, and a scratchy throat caused by pollens or molds in the air. Asthma, a respiratory disease, can be more serious. An asthma attack, which is often triggered by an allergic reaction, causes restricted breathing, constricting the air flow to the lungs. Another serious allergic reaction is anaphylaxis. Triggered by a particular food or insect sting, anaphylaxis can quickly restrict breathing, swell the throat, and cause you to lose consciousness. Other allergies treated by an allergist include skin allergies, such as hives and eczema, and food and drug allergies.

Immunologic diseases are those that affect the immune system. Allergists/immunologists treat patients with conditions such as AIDS, rheumatoid arthritis, and lupus. An immunologist will also treat patients who are receiving an organ or bone marrow transplant to help prevent the patient's body from rejecting the transplanted organ.

The allergist/immunologist, in addition to being a licensed doctor, must also be certified by the American Board of Allergy and Immunology.

Allergists/immunologists work in private practice, hospitals, and research laboratories. With their specific knowledge about allergic and immunologic diseases, allergists/immunologists listen carefully to the patient and then develop a treatment plan. The doctor reviews the patient's medical history and background, and may also conduct skin tests and blood tests. Skin tests are often preferred because they are inexpensive and the results are available immediately. Skin tests are also better for identifying more subtle allergies.

Once the diagnosis is made, the doctor will determine a treatment plan. In some cases, the solution may be as simple as avoiding the things that cause the allergic reaction. The allergist will help you find ways to limit your exposure to the allergen.

In other cases, a doctor will prescribe medication. Antihistamines are drugs that relieve allergy symptoms such as nasal congestion, burning eyes, and skin rashes. Antihistamines can have side effects such as dizziness, headaches, and nausea. Should these side effects occur, the allergist will treat them and prescribe a new medication. Sometimes a patient can build up a resistance to an antihistamine and the doctor needs to prescribe a stronger variety.

Immunotherapy (a series of allergy shots) is another kind of treatment for asthma and for allergies to pollen, dust, bee venom, and a variety of other substances. Immunotherapy involves injecting the patient with a small amount of the substance that causes the allergic reaction. The immune system then becomes less sensitive to the substance and reduces the symptoms of allergy. An allergist will give weekly shots over an extended period of time, gradually increasing the dosage; eventually the shots are only necessary once a month.

what is it like to be an allergist/immunologist?

Dr. John Costa, an allergist/immunologist in Massachusetts, divides his time evenly among three areas of practice. He generally works a six-day workweek: two days are spent in private practice in an office-based setting, two days in basic and clinical research, and two days in clinical allergy and immunology in a hospital-based setting. He is currently at the Department of Pathology and Medicine at the Beth Israel Medical Center in Boston.

"Private practice is truly rewarding," Dr. Costa says. "It enables me to provide consultative answers to tough allergy-immunology-asthma questions." When meeting with patients, Dr. Costa listens carefully as they describe their medical history and their symptoms. He then determines a treatment that will

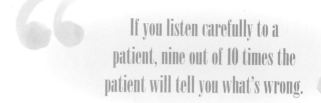

"If you listen carefully to a patient, nine out of 10 times the patient will tell you what's wrong."

do the most good and require the least amount of medication or intervention. He will also perform skin tests and blood tests when necessary. The patients themselves, however, provide the most valuable information. "You should give the patients time to express themselves fully," Dr. Costa says. "If you listen carefully to a patient, nine out of 10 times the patient will tell you what's wrong." He then uses the other tests to confirm what he has already discovered.

"I'm able to follow generations of families long-term," Dr. Costa says. "Because these are chronic diseases, they aren't isolated over time." This allows him to build strong relationships with patients as he sees them frequently over a period of many years. Dr. Costa says, "I am repeatedly able to help people who are truly miserable, to watch them improve and sustain that improvement."

With the research aspect of Dr. Costa's job, he has the opportunity to learn more about specific diseases. "It's why I fell in love with this field," he says. "I have the opportunity to understand, at a molecular and cellular level, how diseases are mediated." His research is focused on the cells of allergic disease and how they are able to produce symptoms. This research helps him learn more about allergies and immunology. "As you understand the mechanisms of the disease better," he says, "you can learn how to apply that understanding more effectively."

His other hours of work are spent in a hospital setting. Though this setting is similar to the office setting, it is more structured, and there is less opportunity for close relationships with patients. "To its detriment, the hospital setting is more impersonal, more formal," he says. "There's less of an opportunity to see multiple members of family units." But, Dr. Costa appreciates the intellectually challenging aspects of hospital work. "The material you're seeing," he says, "is more complex, the problems more severe, chronic. And there have been doctors before you who have attempted to deal with it."

have I got what it takes to be an allergist/immunologist?

Allergist/immunologists should be compassionate and concerned for the well-being of their patients. They should also be careful listeners: a doctor must have a good understanding of a patient's background, environment, and emotional state in order to plan the best treatment. An allergist/immunologist must be prepared to deal with the stress of caring for sick patients; some of these patients may have life-threatening diseases, such as AIDS, cancer, or severe asthma. Despite the many advances in the treatment of allergic diseases and diseases of the immune system, many of them remain incurable. An allergist/immunologist who deals with severe cases must not become too emotionally involved; a doctor too upset by a patient's illness may not be able to provide the best treatment.

In addition to the stress of dealing with life-threatening diseases, Dr. Costa also worries about the toxic effects of medications on some patients. "And there are cases with causes that aren't clear-cut," he says, "so you worry that you've missed the causes." Some patients expect clear-cut answers when such answers aren't available.

Despite stressful situations, Dr. Costa finds most aspects of allergy/immunology very appealing, including applying a basic understanding of science to alleviate a patient's suffering. "I can provide meaningful intervention that improves lives," he says.

how do I become an allergist/immunologist?

It was after taking an immunology course during medical school at Mount Sinai in New York City that Dr. Costa became enthusiastic about allergy/immunology. "I was turned on by the molecular-cellular aspects," he says, "the incredible potency of the system. I was captivated by it." The training was time-consuming and rigorous, "but not difficult," he says, "because I loved it."

education

High School
The science courses offered by your high school will prepare you for a college premedical program. Take biology and chemistry and any health courses offered. Courses that require lab work will help prepare you for the clinical research aspects of allergy/immunology. English composition courses will develop your writing skills for the many papers you'll be writing throughout college and medical school.

Depending on the size of the city in which you live, there may be many volunteer opportunities that can familiarize you with the medical profession. Volunteering in a hospital or nursing home can give you a sense of a doctor's work and responsibilities. Volunteers are often needed to help AIDS and cancer patients in their homes. Part-time work in a retail pharmacy can teach you about the variety of medications prescribed to people with allergies.

Postsecondary Training
To become an allergist/immunologist requires several years of intensive study and training.

FYI

Common allergens

pollen

mold spores

dust mites

animal dander

feathers

insect stings

After high school, you can enter into a pre-medical college program, which usually requires four years of course work. During the second or third year of college you should arrange to take the Medical College Admission Test. The exam covers four areas: verbal facility, quantitative ability, knowledge of the humanities and social sciences, and knowledge of biology, chemistry, and physics. All medical colleges in the country require the test for admission.

After being admitted into a medical school, you begin nine years of intensive training. The first two years of medical school includes course work in human anatomy, physiology, pharmacology, and microbiology. The last two years are then devoted to clinical training: firsthand experience in a hospital setting. These four years of medical school are followed by three years of training in internal medicine or pediatrics, then a minimum of two years of training in an allergy and immunology residency. The American Academy of Allergy, Asthma, and Immunology (AAAAI) publishes a training program directory, which lists accredited training programs and faculty and program information.

certification or licensing

After receiving your medical degree, you are required to take an examination to be licensed to practice. It is conducted through the board of medical examiners in each state. Then, after completing two years of residency, you can apply for certification by the American Board of Allergy and Immunology. To qualify for the certification exam you must have a valid medical license and must show proof that you've completed all the required residency training. You must also provide an evaluation from the director of your training program; the director will review your clinical judgment, attitude, professional behavior, and other work skills and habits.

The certification process consists of an exam that tests the candidate's knowledge of the immune system, human pathology, and the molecular basis of allergic and other immune reactions. The candidate must also show an understanding of diagnostic tests and therapy for immunologic diseases.

I'm able to follow generations of families long-term. Because these are chronic diseases, they aren't isolated over time.

scholarships and grants

Scholarships and grants are often available from individual institutions, state agencies, and special-interest organizations. Many students finance their medical education through the Armed Forces Health Professions Scholarship Program. Each branch of the military participates in this program, paying students' tuitions in exchange for military service. Contact your local recruiting office for more information on this program. The National Health Service Corps Scholarship Program also provides money for students in return for service. Another source for financial aid, scholarship, and grant information is the Association of American Medical Colleges. Remember to request information early for eligibility, application requirements, and deadlines.

Armed Forces Health Professions Scholarship Program
Air Force:
http://hp.airforce.com/training/financial.html
Army:
http://www.sirius.com/~ameddet/hpschps.htm
Navy:
http://nshs.med.navy.mil/hpsp/default.htm

Association of American Medical Colleges
2450 N Street, NW
Washington, DC 20037-1126
202-828-0400
http://www.aamc.org/students/financing/start.htm

National Health Service Corps Scholarship Program
U.S. Public Health Service
4350 East-West Highway, 10th Floor
Bethesda, MD 20814
301-594-4410
http://www.fedmoney.org/grants/93288-00.htm

who will hire me?

Approximately 3,000 allergists/immunologists work in hospitals, private practice, or in clinical research laboratories in the United States. Some, like Dr. Costa, divide their time evenly among the different areas of practice. Before you begin your residency, you will have received your medical degree and license, so your allergy/immunology training is an opportunity to become highly focused.

Dr. Costa advises those going into allergy/immunology to be very careful in selecting a training program (also referred to as a fellowship). "The process of selecting a fellowship is critical," he says. "The clinical exposure available is highly variable, as is the basic science requirement." It is important to learn about the fellowship ahead of time so you can be sure that the program best serves you and your long-term goals. Also, by knowing about the program and faculty, you can impress the people directing the training program.

All this gives you the opportunity to get to know the allergy/immunology field from the inside. You'll have two years of intensive training before going into private practice, so you'll get to know many people and establish many contacts. You'll also attend national meetings for scientific presentations. By the time you complete your residency, you will have had the opportunity to present your own research projects. You may also have published in medical journals, giving you a competitive edge in the job market.

To be a successful allergist/immunologist, you should

- Be compassionate
- Be a careful listener
- Have the ability to manage stress
- Enjoy science
- Be able to inspire trust and confidence in your patients
- Have analytical and problem-solving skills

where can I go from here?

Dr. Costa has developed a career that he is very happy with. "I consider myself very lucky," he says, "to be able to engage in the various components—basic and clinical science, and office and hospital-based practice." He is a member of three professional organizations: AAAAI, the Massachusetts Medical Society, and the New England Society of Allergy.

Once allergists/immunologists have begun a practice, they advance by building a strong reputation and a growing list of patients. It is helpful to have a good business sense since you are responsible for your own advertising, bookkeeping, and bill paying. Continuing education is an important aspect of the job. A doctor must be familiar with new medical findings, medications, and treatments. Some allergists/immunologists, after having a practice for a while, may go into teaching.

what are the salary ranges?

Physicians are rewarded well for their years of intensive study, for their long hours, and for their level of responsibility. Though an allergist/immunologist can make a good living, a number of factors can determine salary. If you practice in a large city you can generally make more money than if you had a practice in a small city. Your background and experience as well as your reputation also play a major role in determining your level of income.

Allergists/immunologists make from about $50,000 to $200,000 a year. Allergists/immunologists who are still in their residencies may make as little as $25,000 a year. The average annual income for all physicians is $164,000, according to the American Medical Association. Allergists/immunologists employed in the East and South generally earn higher median salaries than those employed in the Midwest and West.

what is the job outlook?

With so many Americans suffering from allergies, the allergist/immunologist is in great demand. If you look in your city's phone book, you'll probably see a long list of allergy/immunology practices. Though some doctors remain skeptical about the relationship between allergy and illness, allergy/immunology has become a respected field of medicine. As this acceptance continues to grow, more doctors will refer their patients to these specialists.

Many allergists/immunologists are involved in clinical research that often leads to better treatment for allergies and the causes of allergic reactions. The World Wide Web has proven to be a good forum for promoting the practice and research of allergy/immunology. The Web is inexpensive for doctors to advertise their services and for professional organizations and training schools to publicize the causes and treatment of allergies and to advertise their programs. People with allergies or diseases of the immune system can also find many support groups on the Web.

Good pets for people with allergies

Turtles
Hermit crabs
Fish
Snakes
Iguanas

how do I learn more?

professional organizations

Following are organizations that may provide information about a career as an allergist/immunologist as well as information on education and training.

American Academy of Allergy, Asthma, and Immunology
611 East Wells Street
Milwaukee, WI 53202
http://www.aaaai.org

American Association of Certified Allergists
85 West Algonquin Road, Suite 550
Arlington Heights, IL 60005
847-427-8111

American Association of Immunologists
9650 Rockville Pike
Bethesda, MD 20814-3994
infoaai@aai.faseb.org
http://12.17.12.70/aai/default.asp

American Board of Allergy and Immunology
510 Walnut Street, Suite 1701
Philadelphia, PA 19106-3699
abai@abai.org
http://www.abai.org/

bibliography

Following is a sampling of materials relating to the professional concerns and development of allergists/immunologists.

Brostoff, Jonathan and Linda Gamlin. *Asthma: The Complete Guide to Integrative Therapies.* Rochester, VT: Inner Traditions International Ltd., 2000.

Brostoff, Jonathan and Linda Gamlin. *Food Allergies and Food Intolerances: The Complete Guide to Their Identification and Treatment.* Rochester, VT: Inner Traditions International Ltd., 2000.

Joneja, Janice Vickerstaff. *Dietary Management of Food Allergies & Intolerances.* Burnaby, BC: J.A. Hall Publications, 1998.

Kittel, Mary S., ed. *The Doctor's Book of Home Remedies for Airborne Allergies.* Emmaus, PA: Rodale Press, 2000.

Playfair, J. H. *Immunology at a Glance.* 6th Edition. Cambridge, MA: Blackwell Science, 1996.

Roitt, Ivan, ed. *Immunology.* 5th Edition. St. Louis, MO: Mosby, 1998.

Welch, Michael J. *American Academy of Pediatrics Guide to Your Child's Allergies and Asthma: Breathing Easy and Bringing Up Healthy, Active Children.* New York: Villard Books, 2000.

Related Jobs

The U.S. Department of Labor classifies the career of allergist/immunologist under the headings *Medicine and Surgery* (GOE) and *Healthcare Practitioners and Technical* (O*NET-SOC).

Specific related jobs include:

Anesthesiologists
Cardiologists
Dermatologists
Family practitioners
General practitioners
Gynecologists
Internists
Neurologists
Obstetricians
Occupational physicians
Ophthalmologists
Osteopathic physicians
Otolaryngologists
Pathologists
Pediatricians
Physiatrists
Podiatrists
Police surgeons
Proctologists
Public health physicians
Radiologists
Surgeons
Urologists

Anesthesiologists

Definition

Anesthesiologists are specialists in the medical field who plan, perform, and maintain a patient's anesthesia during surgical, obstetric, or other medical procedures. Using special equipment, monitors, and drugs, the anesthesiologist makes sure the patient feels no pain and remains uninjured during the procedure.

High School Subjects

Biology
Chemistry
Health

Personal Skills

Helping/teaching
Technical/scientific

Salary Range

$199,000 to $232,000 to $272,000

Educational Requirements

Bachelor's degree, medical degree, and specialty training

Certification or Licensing

Required by all states

Outlook

Faster than the average

GOE
02.03.01
O*NET-SOC
29-1061.00

Beneath the lights of an operating room at the Cleveland Clinic, Dr. Thomas Bralliar, an anesthesiologist, and the anesthesia team prepare a patient for surgery. The team, which consists of anesthesiology residents and nurse anesthetists, will perform most of the anesthesia delivery. The Cleveland Clinic is a teaching hospital and Dr. Bralliar directs the team, watching over them as they position the patient and start an IV.

This is not an emergency situation, so everything has been carefully prepared and planned. The team has met with the patient, has reviewed medical records, and has determined the best anesthesia procedure. Because this patient has cardiac problems, a resident inserts a catheter into the patient's neck, leading it down into the right side of the heart. The other residents carefully monitor the response of the patient's body to the surgery. Though everything has been planned beforehand, the anesthesia care team must remain alert and stay focused on the well-being of the patient.

what does an anesthesiologist do?

In medical dramas on TV, an *anesthesiologist* is usually in the background of a surgical scene, maybe holding a mask to the patient's face.

lingo to learn

Ambulatory anesthesia: The use of short-term anesthetic agents and anesthetic techniques for outpatients.

Catheter: A flexible, hollow tube used to drain fluids from the body.

Echocardiograph: A device using ultrasound that shows the activity of the heart.

Electrocardiograph: A device that detects and records the differences in electric potential caused by heart action.

Electroencephalograph: A device used to measure and monitor the electrical activity of the brain (brain waves).

Epidural: Injection of an anesthetic into the spine, sometimes used in childbirth.

General anesthesia: The patient is put to sleep through intravenous and inhaled drugs.

Intravenous: Injected into a vein.

Local anesthesia: The surgeon anesthetizes a specific part of the body while the anesthesiologist monitors a patient's vital signs and maintains sedation with intravenous drugs.

Pharmacology: The science dealing with the preparation, uses, and effects of drugs.

Physiology: The branch of biology dealing with the functions and activities of living organisms and their parts.

Regional anesthesia: Numbing a portion of the patient's body by injecting medication near the nerves of the area requiring surgery.

The patient falls asleep, the surgeons go to work, and it seems the anesthesiologist's job is done. However, in real life, they play a much more active role and must understand a variety of different equipment and techniques. It is their job to make sure the patient's body is not overstimulated or injured by a medical procedure and that the patient feels no pain. Traditionally, anesthesiologists deal mainly in the area of surgery. They may also oversee the administration of anesthetics during other medical procedures and, if needed, during childbirth. This chapter describes the traditional area of an anesthesiologist's work: surgery.

After reviewing a patient's medical history, the anesthesiologist will determine the best form of anesthesia for the patient. Varying medical problems and kinds of surgery require different kinds of anesthesia. The drugs and methods used are determined based on the anesthesiologist's broad background in medicine, which includes an understanding of surgical procedures, physiology, pharmacology, and critical care.

In the operating room, an anesthesiologist may give patients general anesthesia, making them unconscious and numb to pain. They administer drugs, gases, or vapors to put the patient to sleep and then maintain the anesthesia through the duration of the surgery. In some cases only a regional anesthesia is required, numbing only the part of the body on which the surgery is being performed. In more complex cases anesthesiologists may need to prepare special equipment such as blood warming devices. To control the patient's breathing, anesthesiologists use monitoring equipment and insert intravenous lines and breathing tubes. They make sure the mask is secure and allows for proper air flow. In an emergency situation, an anesthesiologist is also part of the cardiopulmonary resuscitation team.

An anesthesiologist pays close attention to the patient's status by monitoring blood pressure, breathing, heart rate, and body temperature throughout surgery. It is also their responsibility to position the patient properly so that the doctor can perform the surgery without injuring the patient. The anesthesiologist also controls the patient's temperature, cooling or heating different parts of the body as needed during surgery.

Anesthesiologists are not limited to the operating room; they also spend time with patients before and after surgery. When meeting the patient beforehand, an anesthesiologist explains the kind of anesthesia that will be used as well as answers any questions the patient might have. This interaction is necessary to put the patient at ease and familiarize the anesthesiologist with the individual patient before surgery. Unlike other doctors, anesthesiologists do not have the opportunity to work closely with their patients for long periods of time.

Anesthesiologists may specialize in a variety of different areas, such as pediatric anesthesia, respiratory therapy, critical care, or cardiovascular anesthesia. An anesthesiologist will often head a team consisting of anesthesiology residents, nurse anesthetists, and anesthesiologist assistants. The anesthesiologist delegates responsibilities to members of the team during a procedure.

While emergency cases require quick decisions, most surgeries are planned in advance and allow anesthesiologists to study medical histories, meet with surgeons and patients, and work on a regular schedule. Most anesthesiologists work in hospitals, though they may actually be part of an individual or group practice. Others direct residents in teaching hospitals or teach at medical schools.

what is it like to be an anesthesiologist?

Dr. Thomas Bralliar has been involved with residency education since his own residency more than 25 years ago. He currently works at the Cleveland Clinic, a multispecialty clinic in Cleveland, Ohio. In addition to his duties as an anesthesiologist, he oversees the training of residents. "Anesthesia," says Dr. Bralliar, "is a different kind of residency. There's all new equipment to deal with, new procedures and techniques."

The day starts around 7:00 AM for Dr. Bralliar, who must set up the operating room and have the patient ready for anesthesia by 7:40 AM. He then preps for surgery at around 7:50 AM. Though the practice of anesthesiology can be broken down into different subspecialties such as cardiovascular, urology, and pediatric anesthesia, Dr. Bralliar works in all areas. "I generally do colon/rectal and ambulatory," Dr. Bralliar says, "but I can cover other services." He covers two operating rooms, each hosting three to five procedures a day.

During the operations, Dr. Bralliar directs a group of residents and nurse anesthetists. The anesthesia team must pay close attention to the patient throughout surgery. This may be routine work, but in the case of complex surgeries and emergencies, an anesthesiologist must be prepared to make important decisions quickly. According to Dr. Bralliar, "anesthesia can be hours of boredom interrupted by moments of sheer panic."

Dr. Bralliar uses many different techniques to perform and maintain anesthesia. "With anesthesiology," he says, "we're trying to depress the patient's system so the body won't be overstimulated by surgery." Complex surgery may require blood transfusions and the use of blood warming devices, ventilators (machines that assist the patient's breathing), and anesthesia machines. Dr. Bralliar may also use blankets and heating devices to keep patients warm.

After positioning the patient to allow the surgeon proper access, Dr. Bralliar will monitor the patient in various ways. He attaches blood pressure cuffs, draws blood samples, and evaluates the oxygen in the blood. Different health problems require different approaches to anesthesia. For a patient with cardiac problems, Dr. Bralliar will insert a catheter into the neck, guiding it down into the right side of the heart. He'll take blood pressure measurements and closely monitor heart activity. For neurosurgery, he'll drain spinal fluid with a catheter. In other cases, Dr. Bralliar may insert a tube into the windpipe and deflate one of the patient's lungs, ventilating through the other lung.

Dr. Bralliar's day ends at around 5:30 PM, or later. He usually works a regular five-day workweek, though about once a month he works "on call," available for emergency cases over a full 24-hour period. Also, three or four times a month Dr. Bralliar is on "late call," requiring

in-depth

The History of Anesthesia

Imagine undergoing surgery or having a tooth extracted without an anesthetic. Ouch! Before the mid-19th century, you would have most likely lived with your affliction or undergone surgery with little or no help for pain. Oftentimes patients would need to be physically restrained during medical procedures. An 18th century French encyclopedia described how to perform bladder surgery by first restraining the patient in a special surgical chair.

Efforts to manage pain have been a constant in medical history. A variety of substances and techniques have been used, including opium, cannabis, alcohol, mandragora root, and hypnotism. None of these proved entirely reliable or completely effective.

Nitrous oxide, developed in the late 18th century, was the first gas recognized to have anesthetic properties. Its effects, which included giddiness, earned it the nickname of laughing gas.

Ether was developed shortly after nitrous oxide. Neither gas, however, was originally used to anesthetize humans. In fact, nitrous oxide was often used for entertainment purposes at laughing gas parties or by sideshow entertainers.

The first successful use of ether as an anesthesia occurred in 1842. Dr. Crawford W. Long used it as an anesthetic to remove a tumor from a friend's neck. Long, however, failed to publicize the event, and a Boston dentist, Dr. William T. G. Morton, became credited with the first use of ether as an anesthesia four years later.

As one would imagine, ether's use spread quickly. During this time, chloroform was also used successfully as an anesthetic. Even Queen Victoria used chloroform giving birth to Prince Leopold and Princess Beatrice.

Anesthesiology continued to advance, and in 1875, the intravenous administration of anesthetics was developed. Greater study of anesthesiology in the 20th century has led to more sophisticated procedures and monitoring devices, revolutionizing the practice of surgery.

---

him to work as late as 9:30 PM. He also works three or four weekends a year.

"Anesthesiology is a wonderful profession," Dr. Bralliar says. "It's enjoyable and rewarding." He is also encouraged by the technological advances that have allowed for safer surgeries. "A lot of our patients are geriatric," Dr. Bralliar points out. "We're doing surgery for those we wouldn't have been able to 20 years ago."

There are many things Dr. Bralliar appreciates about the work. "There is instant gratification," he says. "I like the acute circumstances of the situation, the rapid decisions required." Dr. Bralliar also appreciates the respect of his peers and the ability to provide well for his family. "And there's a consistency of lifestyle," he says. "I have time off; I'm not always on call like some other doctors." As a member of a group practice, Dr. Bralliar can feel confident that work is getting done when he's not around.

"It doesn't get boring," Dr. Bralliar says, citing the constantly advancing medical field. "It's mentally challenging. Each day is a new day."

Though Dr. Bralliar is pleased not to be dealing directly with chronic patients with long, protracted illnesses, he does regret not developing the close relationships general caregivers develop with their patients. "You're helping take care of other people's patients," he says.

have I got what it takes to be an anesthesiologist?

Every surgery calls on an anesthesiologist's ability to pay careful attention to the patient's status and remain alert throughout the procedure. An anesthesiologist sometimes encounters emergency situations, requiring quick, clear-headed responses. But the work can also be slower paced and require patience to comfort those undergoing surgery. Anesthesiologists must be good communicators. They must not only be able to explain a procedure clearly to patients, but also able to precisely direct other members of the anesthesia team.

It's important for an anesthesiologist to care deeply for the health and well-being of others. "I hate to see people hurting," says Dr. Bralliar. "I want to prevent their suffering." He points out that the person going into anesthesiology for the financial reward is making a mistake. "It has to be a vocation," he says. For his success as an anesthesiologist, Dr. Bralliar credits his attention to detail. "I have a compulsive personality," he says. "I'm picky about things."

Like other doctors, becoming an anesthesiologist requires a long period of education and training. A strong dedication to helping others and great perseverance are necessary to successfully complete the rigorous requirements to become licensed and certified.

how do I become an anesthesiologist?

Though Dr. Bralliar did his undergraduate work at the University of Tennessee, he returned to his home state to do graduate study in microbiology at the University of Arizona. After finishing medical school, he began residency training at the Heron Road Hospital in Cleveland, Ohio, one of the oldest residency programs in the country.

"My father was a general surgeon," he says, "and I had aspirations to be the same." Dr. Bralliar had very little experience with anesthesiology so he did a rotating internship that allowed him to work in anesthesiology. "I wanted to know what they'd be doing to my patients," he says. He found anesthesiology exciting and also saw it as an opportunity to be professionally satisfied and still have time to devote to his family.

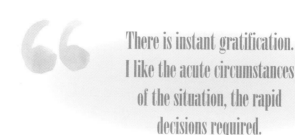

education

High School
Science courses such as biology, chemistry, and health will give you a good foundation for the courses you'll have to take in college and medical school. You may also want to take courses in math, psychology, and sociology. Volunteer work can familiarize you with a hospital or nursing home setting and will also look good on your college applications.

You may want to interview an anesthesiologist at your local hospital or request to spend a day with an anesthesiologist to get firsthand exposure to the doctor's work.

Postsecondary Training
To become an anesthesiologist requires several years of training. First, you must receive an undergraduate degree from a four-year program. Many students major as premed, while others major in biology, chemistry, or some other science. Typically, premed programs require many courses in the sciences, including anatomy, biology, chemistry, and physiology. During the second or third year of college you should arrange to take the Medical College Admission Test (MCAT). The exam covers four areas: verbal facility, quantitative ability, knowledge of the humanities and social sciences, and knowledge of biology, chemistry ,and physics. All medical colleges in the country require the test for admission.

After completing the undergraduate program, students move on to four years of medical school. After receiving a medical degree, the student of anesthesiology begins another four years of training. The first year is spent training in an area of clinical medicine other than anesthesia, such as internal or emergency medicine, pediatrics, surgery, obstetrics, or neurology. The final three years of study are then spent in an anesthesiology residency program accredited by the Accreditation Council for Graduate Medical Education. You can find out more on these programs at the Council's Web site, http://www.acgme.org.

Residency programs cover basic anesthesia training as well as subspecialty training, in areas such as obstetric anesthesia, pediatric anesthesia, cardiothoracic anesthesia, and neuroanesthesia. Residents also spend two months of training in critical care medicine to gain experience with critically ill patients.

certification or licensing

Anesthesiologists are required by state boards of medical examiners to be licensed to practice. To be eligible for licensure, you must first graduate from an accredited medical school, complete one to seven years of graduate medical education, and pass a licensing examination. Most states grant reciprocity licensure to anesthesiologists who move to another state to practice.

After completing a residency and obtaining a license, anesthesiologists can apply for certification from the American Board of Anesthesiology. To be eligible for certification, applicants must first have a Certificate of Clinical Competence. This certificate, filed by the training program, attests to the applicant's clinical competence.

To be a successful anesthesiologist, you should

- Pay close attention to detail
- Have good communication skills with both patients and co-workers
- Be an adept leader
- Make quick, accurate decisions
- Enjoy helping others

scholarships and grants

Scholarships and grants are often available from individual institutions, state agencies, and special-interest organizations. Many students finance their medical education through the Armed Forces Health Professions Scholarship Program. Each branch of the military participates in this program, paying students' tuitions in exchange for military service. Contact your local recruiting office for more information on this program. The National Health Service Corps Scholarship Program also provides money for students in return for service. Another source for financial aid, scholarship, and grant information is the Association of American Medical Colleges. Remember to request information early for eligibility, application requirements, and deadlines.

National Health Service Corps Scholarship Program
Office of Financial Aid
800-221-9393
http://www.fedmoney.org/grants/93288-00.htm

Association of American Medical Colleges
2450 N Street, NW
Washington, DC 20037-1126
202-828-0400
http://www.aamc.org

who will hire me?

After finishing his residency at the Heron Road Hospital, Dr. Bralliar joined the hospital's anesthesiology staff. "I had other offers," he says, "but I liked how Heron Road mixed private practice with residency training." Dr. Bralliar eventually became program director of the hospital as well as vice-chairman of the department. He was happy and satisfied with the work there but some changes in the hospital led him to look elsewhere for employment. He felt he was faced with the choice of being an entrepreneur or an educator. "I didn't want to compromise who and how I trained," he says. Wanting to continue his work with residency training as well as stay in Cleveland, Dr. Bralliar went to work at the Cleveland Clinic in 1987.

In the United States, approximately 23,900 anesthesiologists work in hospitals. Depending on an anesthesiologist's subspecialty, he or she may work by a preplanned schedule of surgery, deal primarily with emergency cases, or may work only with special procedures, as in a pediatric hospital or critical care facility.

Anesthesiologists aren't necessarily employed by the hospitals in which they work. Many have their own practice or are part of a group practice. In smaller hospitals they may be the director of an anesthesia team, or in the case of a teaching hospital, may be responsible for directing residents and nurse anesthetists. Clinics and freestanding surgical centers also employ anesthesiologists to treat people on an outpatient basis.

Jobs are usually concentrated in urban areas where more hospitals and clinics are located. The West and Northeast regions of the United States hire the most medical professionals per capita; the South hires the fewest. Openings are generally advertised nationally in trade publications and through state and national anesthesiology associations.

where can I go from here?

Because of the intensive amount of training required, people usually choose anesthesiology as a lifelong vocation. Some anesthesiologists even stay with the same hospital or clinic for their whole career. Within the profession, however, anesthesiologists can take on new responsibilities as they gain experience. They may become the head of a department or the director of a training program. They may also become involved on a national scale by serving on the committees of professional organizations or by helping to make decisions about education and certification requirements.

Because of the desirable hours and regular work schedule, anesthesiology often attracts doctors from other medical fields.

what are the salary ranges?

Salaries for anesthesiologists vary according to the kind of practice (whether the anesthesiologist works individually or as part of a group practice), geographic location, work experience, how many patients they handle, and the hours they choose to work. Though usually working fewer hours, an anesthesiologist can earn as much as other doctors. According to 2000 Economic Research Institute data, the average annual salary for a first-year anesthesiologist is $199,252. After five years, they average $232,623 a year, and after 10 years, they earn an average of $272,106 annually.

what is the job outlook?

Due to continued growth in the health care industry and a growing elderly population, job prospects for medical professionals are plentiful. The field of anesthesiology is popular due to technological advancements, the regularity of the work, high salaries, and the availability of flexible schedules. Despite the competition, most anesthesiologists find work immediately after finishing their residencies. As medical advances allow for different kinds of treatment facilities, anesthesiologists will find more work outside of a traditional hospital setting. The development of more outpatient clinics, freestanding surgical centers, and respiratory therapy clinics has opened up new opportunities for anesthesiologists.

Managed care organizations have changed the way medicine is practiced and will continue to do so. Because anesthesiology is a hospital-based specialty, anesthesiologists must find ways to work within the guidelines of managed care without compromising the level of care they provide.

how do I learn more?

professional organizations

Following are organizations that provide information about anesthesiologist careers, accredited programs, and certification.

Accreditation Council for Graduate Medical Education
515 North State Street, Suite 2000
Chicago, IL 60610-4322
312-464-4920
http://www.acgme.org

American Board of Anesthesiology
4101 Lake Boone Trail, Suite 510
Raleigh, NC 27607-7506
919-881-2570
http://www.abanes.org

American Society of Anesthesiologists
520 North Northwest Highway
Park Ridge, IL 60068
847-825-5586
mail@asahq.org
http://www.asahq.org

bibliography

Following is a sampling of materials relating to the professional concerns and development of anesthesiologist.

Barash, Paul G. et al. *Clinical Anesthesia*. 4th Edition. Philadelphia, PA: Lippincott Williams & Wilkins, 2000.

Ezekiel, Mark R. *Anesthesiology*. Laguna Beach, CA: Current Clinical Strategies, 1999.

Hurford, William E. et al. eds. *Clinical Anesthesia Procedures of the Massachusetts General Hospital*. Philadelphia, PA: Lippincott Williams & Wilkins, 1998.

Jaffe, Richard A. et al. eds. *Anesthesiologist's Manual of Surgical Procedures*. 2nd Edition. Philadelphia, PA: Lippincott, Williams & Wilkins, 1999.

Nagelhout, John J. and Karen L. Zaglaniczny. *Nurse Anesthesia*. 2nd Edition. Philadelphia, PA: W. B. Saunders, 2001.

Ruskin, Keith et al. *Introduction to Anesthesiology*. New York, NY: McGraw-Hill Textbooks, 2001.

Stoelting, Robert K. and Ronald D. Miller. *Basics of Anesthesia*. 4th Edition. Kent, UK: Churchill Livingstone, 2000.

Vickers, M. D. and I. Power, eds. *Medicine for Anaesthetists*. 4th Edition. Oxford, UK: Blackwell Science, Inc., 1999.

Wiener-Kronish, Jeanine P. and Michael A. Gropper. *Conscious Sedation*. Philadelphia, PA: Lippincott, Williams & Wilkins, 2000.

Zaglaniczny, Karen L. and John Aker. *Clinical Guide to Pediatric Anesthesia*. Philadelphia, PA: W. B. Saunders, 1999.

Audiologists and Speech-Language Pathologists

Definition
Audiologists and speech-language pathologists are members of two distinct but closely related professions that help people with communication problems. Speech-language pathologists identify, evaluate, and treat speech and language disorders. Audiologists identify, evaluate, and treat hearing disorders.

High School Subjects
Biology
Physics
English

Personal Skills
Communication/ideas
Helping/teaching

Salary Range
$27,000 to $43,000 to $80,000+

Minimum Educational Level
Master's degree

Certification or Licensing
Required by certain states

Outlook
Much faster than the average

GOE
02.03.04
O*NET-SOC
29-1121.00
29-1127.00

On the bright yellow bulletin board in the university clinic are red, green, and blue construction paper letters placed next to pictures of objects that use the letters in them. Next to "ch" are pictures of a cheeseburger, a church, and a chicken. Sitting in a circle on the floor are Christine Adkins, a speech-language pathologist at the Bill Wilkerson Center in Nashville, Tennessee, and four preschoolers, squirming and chattering, but focused on the project they are making in their little circle.

The sound they are working on today is "tr", and Christine is passing around colored foam triangles that the children will use to decorate paper tree cutouts. Jill, who is three, tries to ask Jacob for the red triangles in his pile but has trouble pronouncing the "tr" in triangle and instead points to his pile.

"Can I have two twiangles?" she asks him. Christine smiles and gently corrects her. Then all the children repeat the name of the project they are making, "triangle trees" to practice using the tr sound first as a group and then individually.

These children are having fun and learning important skills through their play. While it is common, and sometimes cute or funny, for toddlers who are beginning to speak to mispronounce words, some children have difficulty getting beyond that stage and learning proper word sounds as they prepare to enter the school system. For them, this therapeutic play can redirect their learning and prevent later learning problems that are more difficult to undo, such as reading, writing, and comprehension problems. Professionals that help children with speech/language delays, as well as people of all ages with speech/language disorders are speech-language pathologists.

lingo to learn

Aphasia: Loss of the ability to use speech and language.

Audiometer: Electrical device that measures a person's ability to hear sounds of varying frequency and intensity.

Cleft palate: Congenital condition characterized by a hole in the palate (roof of the mouth) and in the upper lip that interferes with the ability to produce speech sounds.

Delayed language: Slowness in developing age-appropriate language skills.

Dysphagia: Difficulty in swallowing—a problem that speech-language pathologists must sometimes treat.

Fluency disorders: Problems with the flow and rhythm of speech, such as stuttering.

Larynx: Voice box—the portion of the respiratory tract that contains the vocal cords.

Otolaryngology: The medical specialty commonly known as ENT (ear, nose, and throat).

what does an audiologist or a speech-language pathologist do?

Speech-language pathologists identify, evaluate, and treat speech and language disorders. After assessing the problem with various diagnostic procedures, they create and carry out an appropriate treatment program that will improve the client's communication skills.

It is estimated that one out of every 20 Americans has a speech or language disorder. Among common speech problems are fluency, articulation, and voice disorders. Fluency disorders are characterized by difficulties with the flow or rhythm of speech. Stuttering, the most well-known form of fluency disorder, affects over two million Americans. Articulation disorders are problems with the production of specific speech sounds, which result in the omission of certain sounds or the substitution of incorrect sounds—saying "wabbit" instead of "rabbit," for example. Voice disorders involve the vocal cords and are related to difficulties in controlling the pitch, loudness, or quality (too nasal, harsh, hoarse, or breathy) of the voice. Language disorders are problems with the comprehension and/or use of language. Such disorders include delayed development of normal language skills in children or the loss of formerly normal language and speech skills. Aphasia, the loss of the ability to use speech and language, strikes about 80,000 Americans annually as the result of stroke or serious head injury.

Speech and language disorders have many origins and affect people of all ages. Problems may be caused by stroke or brain injury, hearing impairment, or disease, such as cerebral palsy. Other problems may be caused by structural abnormalities (such as cleft palate) or mental retardation. About 30,000 Americans have had their larynx (voice box) removed as a result of laryngeal cancer.

The speech-language pathologist must first determine the precise nature and extent of the problem. Tests are administered to assess language comprehension, vocabulary, and the ability to produce various sounds. The course of treatment depends on the type of speech or language disorder present.

Patients with articulation disorders are taught how to produce speech sounds correctly. Those who stutter are taught techniques for enhancing speech fluency. People with voice disorders need to learn how to use their vocal and respiratory systems to produce speech of more appropriate pitch, quality, or loudness. Therapy for children with delayed speech or language often takes the form of group play; the speech-language pathologist chooses toys and directs activities that teach specific communication skills.

Speech-language pathologists teach patients who have had their larynx removed how to produce esophageal speech. People with aphasia can relearn language and speech skills. Modern technology offers assistance to persons who are physically unable to produce speech sounds. Speech-language pathologists can teach these clients to use a computer or other device to communicate. Counseling the families of people with speech-language disorders is also an important part of the speech-language pathologist's job.

Because many, though not all, speech-language disorders are related to hearing disorders, audiologists often work closely with speech-language pathologists. *Audiologists* administer tests to identify and measure hearing loss. They then design and implement rehabilitation programs that instruct clients in the use of hearing aids and other devices to maximize their hearing ability. Audiologists also train people in lip-reading techniques. Counseling clients and their families is an important part of the audiologist's work, since a hearing disorder has an impact on the life of everyone in close contact with the hearing-impaired individual.

Hearing loss affects people of all ages and has many causes. Some hearing disorders are genetic or the result of structural problems. Others are caused by viral infection or exposure to hazardous noise levels. The incidence of hearing loss increases with age. Nearly one-third of Americans aged 65 and over have hearing loss that is serious enough to interfere with their ability to communicate.

Audiologists use highly sophisticated equipment to evaluate a client's hearing. It is essential to determine not only the degree of loudness required for the person to begin hearing sounds, but also to assess the person's capacity to distinguish between various sounds, since the ability to understand speech depends on the ability to recognize many different sounds.

It is important to identify hearing problems as early as possible in a child's life so that assistance with the development of communication skills can begin. Modern technology makes it possible for an audiologist to test auditory brain-stem response in a sleeping

You need to be a good listener and definitely have good communication skills to counsel patients on what they can expect.

baby by fastening electrodes to the infant's head in order to discover whether sound is traveling through the nerve to the brain.

In addition to working directly with people who have hearing problems, many audiologists are also involved in the prevention of hearing loss. They are employed as consultants in industry and government to evaluate and advise on occupational and environmental noise levels.

what is it like to be an audiologist or a speech-language pathologist?

Christine Adkins has been on the staff of the Wilkerson Center ever since completing her M.S. in speech pathology at Vanderbilt University in 1989. After 11 years, she continues to find every day's work both challenging and rewarding.

Although Christine has some experience in working with speech and language problems in persons of all ages, her work at the center is exclusively with young children and their parents. Displaying her weekly schedule blocked out on a large desk calendar, she explains that she currently has a caseload of 25 children, nearly all of whom are preschoolers.

Christine is responsible for two groups of two-year-olds with speech and language delays (problems expressing thoughts and comprehending language). Each group of five includes one child with "normal" speech and language skills, who serves as peer model.

Christine's task is to enable the children to develop age-appropriate speech and language skills through participation in group activities, such as playing, eating, and making things. The toys for each session are chosen to elicit the speech sounds or language techniques being worked on that week. The children learn communication skills by taking part in activities they enjoy. The parents also have a very important role, as Christine emphasizes. They watch all the group sessions, and she trains them in the observational skills and techniques they will need for helping their children develop speech and language skills at home between sessions at the center.

Christine also works, mostly in individual sessions, with preschool children who have problems with stuttering—a condition known as "disfluency." As she explains, there is an ongoing controversy in the field concerning the spelling of the word—should it be "dysfluency" or "disfluency"? Since many words beginning with "dys" (such as "dysfunctional") have negative connotations, many parents prefer that the more neutral "dis" spelling be used to describe their children's speech problem. Christine is careful to use the "disfluency" spelling in her work.

In addition to her sessions with the children, Christine also works with their parents, teaching them strategies to employ at home to enhance their children's speech fluency. Her weekly schedule also includes a staff meeting, smaller team meetings with colleagues, report writing, and supervision of graduate students doing their required clinical fellowship year at the center.

Audiologist Jennifer Sangston has an equally busy and rewarding work schedule at the Riverside Medical Center in Kankakee, Illinois. She has been an audiologist for over four years and splits her days between working with hearing aid clients in the morning and with patients of an otolaryngologist (ear, nose, and throat doctor) in the afternoon. On a typical morning, Jennifer sees several clients for hearing aid fittings, evaluations, and adjustments. Learning to get the full benefit out of a hearing aid is a complicated and sometimes frustrating process that frequently requires a number of follow-up visits with the audiologist.

"Usually I set up a 30-day trial period for someone getting a hearing aid and I'll see them every week or two within that time," Jennifer says. A great deal of the time she spends with hearing aid clients is educating them how to get the most out of their hearing aid. "It's a lot of step-by-step repetition of making sure they can take the hearing aid in and out and change the battery. Some of my older clients have arthritic hands, so it can definitely be a challenge for them. They also need to get used to hearing sounds they haven't heard in a while and even to adjust to the different way their own voice sounds."

In the afternoons, Jennifer works with a wider age group, ranging from infants to adults who have been referred to the otolaryngologist. Children with earaches or fluid in their ears are frequent patients, and Jennifer administers hearing tests to help the doctor determine if there is hearing loss. She uses an audiometer, which emits tones to measure the patient's ability to distinguish different tones and sounds.

In addition to the basic hearing tests, there are more sophisticated techniques for monitoring hearing-nerve responses. One test uses electrodes that are hooked up to the forehead and ears. The ears are also checked for structural defects by a process called odoacoustic emissions testing. After a child's hearing is evaluated and the results are discussed with the parents (and often with teachers in the case of school-age children), he or she begins work with a speech-language pathologist. Some need to begin using hearing aids.

Like Christine, Jennifer spends a portion of her time keeping records and notes on hearing aid clients and submitting test results to the otolaryngologist.

have I got what it takes to be an audiologist or a speech-language pathologist?

Similar qualities are essential for success as either an audiologist or speech-language pathologist. "You need to be flexible and open to the unexpected," advises Christine. Jennifer adds, "You need to be a good listener and definitely have good communication skills to counsel patients on what they can expect. Sometimes there is a lot of hand-holding to help them adjust."

Patience is especially necessary when working with people who have communication problems. Therapy is often a long, slow process that makes demands on both the client and the therapist. The rewards, however, are also great. Audiologists and speech-language pathologists express deep satisfaction with a profession that enables them to help people improve the speech, language, and hearing abilities that make such a difference in the quality of life.

Since careers in these fields require a master's degree, future audiologists and speech-language pathologists need to have good academic skills and enjoy studying, especially the sciences.

Christine discovered the field of speech pathology while taking a 10th grade class called Career and Life Planning. For her research paper topic, she chose speech pathology. She had long known that she wanted a career that involved some combination of teaching, social service, health or medicine, and work with children, and she found that speech pathology would offer her an opportunity to bring all of those interests together. She characterizes her career as one that combines the qualities she was attracted to in her parents' careers; her father is a social worker and her mother an English teacher.

Jennifer had also identified a strong interest in the field while she was in high school. She was first exposed to the field by doing secretarial work in the office where her mother worked for an otolaryngologist.

how do I become an audiologist or a speech-language pathologist?

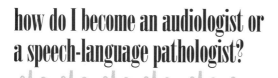

education

High School

Future audiologists and speech-language pathologists should take well-balanced college preparatory course work in high school. Mathematics and the sciences, especially biology and physics, are important for developing a scientific orientation as well as for providing a foundation for the work you will do later in human anatomy and acoustics (the scientific study of sound).

If your high school offers an introduction to psychology, that would be a helpful course. Classes that improve communication skills (both written and oral), such as composition and public speaking, are also important.

Volunteer work at hospitals, clinics, or speech and hearing centers would give you some idea of what it is like to work with people who have communication problems. Of course, baby-sitting is good experience for any career involving work with children.

Postsecondary Training

It is not necessary to major in speech-language pathology at the undergraduate level in order to enter a master's degree program in that field. Audiology is not offered as an undergraduate major, although basic courses in audiology are available in departments of speech and hearing or communication sciences.

The American Speech-Language-Hearing Association (ASHA) recommends that college students planning careers in speech-language pathology or audiology take a liberal arts program that includes courses in biology, anatomy, physiology, human development, psychology, speech and hearing, linguistics, phonetics, and semantics (the study of the relationships between signs and symbols and what they represent). Students who do not take these basic speech, language, and science courses as undergraduates will need to do extra work in their master's degree programs.

There are a few positions available in special education for individuals with only a bachelor's degree in speech-language pathology. A position known as a speech aide seems to be evolving within the profession for bachelor's level speech-language graduates, but the standard credential for entering the profession is a master's degree.

There are currently about 235 colleges and universities that offer an M.S. in speech-language pathology and/or audiology. You should make sure that the programs to which you are applying are accredited by the Educational

Standards Board of ASHA; a list of accredited programs is available from the association. Because audiology and speech-language pathology are popular and growing fields, getting into a good M.S. program is competitive.

Master's degree programs last one and a half to two years; they require course work and 300 to 375 hours of supervised clinical experience. The course work is in such areas as advanced anatomy and physiology of speech, language, and hearing; acoustics; psychological aspects of communication; and techniques for evaluating and treating speech, language, and hearing disorders. Persons who are interested in research and teaching at the college or university level or going into private practice usually need to earn a doctoral degree. The audiology doctoral degree is known as the Au.D. The American Academy of Audiology offers information on Au.D. programs.

certification or licensing

Nearly all states require audiologists and speech-language pathologists to be certified. To receive the ASHA Certificate of Clinical Competence (CCC), it is necessary to complete an M.S. program, do a nine-month clinical fellowship, and pass a national examination. All states recognize the CCC as the basic professional credential. Some states also require continuing education hours for license renewal. In addition, some states require that speech-language pathologists who work in the public schools have a teaching certificate or at least have taken a certain number of education courses. You should check with the state board

To be a successful audiologist or speech-language pathologist, you should

- Have strong academic skills, with emphasis on the sciences
- Be able to counsel parents and teachers of school-age patients
- Have the organizational skills to keep up with a considerable amount of paperwork

of education of the state where you expect to be employed.

scholarships and grants

There are numerous sources of financial aid—grants, scholarships, loans, work-study programs—for students in audiology and speech-language pathology. Consult the financial aid office of the school that you plan to attend for further information. Graduate students should consult their academic department as well as the financial aid office. ASHA also can provide information on funding sources for students in audiology and speech-language pathology. There are some scholarships targeted for specific racial/ethnic groups; for example, there is a scholarship program for Native American students planning to enter the health professions. When applying for any type of financial aid, be sure to begin the process early enough to meet the deadlines.

Fellowships (required training that generally pays a stipend or covers expenses) are a required part of most master's programs and require some type of competitive application process. People doing their clinical fellowships receive salaries in the upper $20,000s a year.

who will hire me?

About half of all speech-language pathologists and audiologists work in public and private schools where they screen students for speech, language, and hearing problems and provide therapy to improve communication skills. You may remember having had hearing tests several times during elementary school. At that time, you probably were not aware that the person administering the tests was a professional expert called an audiologist.

The other half of speech-language pathologists and audiologists work in a wide range of settings: hospitals (where they often work closely with ENT specialists, physicians with advanced expertise in ear, nose, and throat problems); rehabilitation centers; nursing homes; adult day care centers; hearing and speech centers (like the Wilkerson Center); community centers; home health care agencies; federal, state, and local government agencies and health departments; centers for the developmentally disabled; private practice offices (either solo or group practice); colleges and universities; research laboratories; industry; institutes and private agencies.

The clinical fellowship year may turn into a permanent position for a beginning speech-language pathologist or audiologist. Your supervisors and other professional colleagues are also very useful sources of information for job leads elsewhere. Professors in your M.S. program may know of job openings; some departments post information about positions on a central bulletin board. You might try contacting local hospitals and rehabilitation centers. Job openings are also listed in professional publications.

where can I go from here?

Some experienced audiologists and speech-language pathologists decide to go into private practice (either on their own or as part of a group), acting as service providers and consultants for schools, health and medical facilities, and industry. Those with an interest in administration might move into supervisory positions in public school systems or agencies. Some become specialists in certain areas, such as the rehabilitation of patients with aphasia.

One of the things about speech-language pathology that attracted Christine to the field is the opportunities for advancement and flexibility. "It provides more opportunities than something like teaching might. I have been able to advance to more administrative work within the field without having to go back to school for business classes," she says. "And it's quite flexible. I know people who work out of their homes, or who work only a few days a week."

Audiologists and speech-language pathologists with an interest in research and/or teaching at the college level usually need to earn a Ph.D. Research in communications disorders focuses on many areas, ranging from the physiological processes involved to the psychological factors. It may lead to collaboration with engineers in the development of high-tech aids, such as electronic voice boxes and computer-assisted communication devices. Some researchers are employed by universities; others work in industry.

what are the salary ranges?

According to the U.S. Department of Labor's *Occupational Outlook Handbook*, the lowest paid 10 percent of speech-language pathologists and audiologists earned $27,460 a year. This represents those early in their careers. Most speech-language pathologists and audiologists earn between $34,580 and $55,260 in a year, with a median salary of $43,080 reported.

Individuals with an Av.D. tended to have higher salaries than those with an M.S. Those with many years of experience in leadership positions also earned higher salaries. According to the *Occupational Outlook Handbook*, the highest paid 10 percent of speech-language pathologists and audiologists earned more than $80,720 a year.

what is the job outlook?

There are approximately 105,000 audiologists and speech-language pathologists employed in the United States. Jobs in these fields are expected to increase much faster than the average for all occupations through the next decade, according to the *Occupational Outlook Handbook*. Several factors are involved in this prediction.

As the population continues to age, an increasing number of people will be in the over-65 age group that is most likely to experience hearing loss or strokes that interfere with the ability to communicate. More people of all ages are surviving traumatic head injuries and will need rehabilitative therapy to regain language and speech abilities. More premature infants with disabilities are surviving and will need expert therapy to develop communication skills.

Greater public awareness of the importance of identifying and treating language, speech, and hearing problems is expected to increase the demand for audiologists and speech-language pathologists. The employment of speech-language pathologists and audiologists in the public schools, which began expanding with the passage of the Education for All Handicapped Children Act of 1975, is expected to continue growing. Other recent laws mandating services for the disabled should also increase the demand. Private practice is expected to be an expanding field for audiologists and speech-language pathologists who contract to provide services.

Despite this overall positive outlook, future audiologists and speech-language pathologists should keep in mind that cutbacks by health care providers could have a negative impact on the field's growth.

Economic factors also play a role in people's ability to purchase services not covered by health insurance. Hearing aids, for example, are generally not paid for by insurance.

how do I learn more?

professional organizations

For additional information about careers in audiology and speech-language pathology, contact the following organizations:

American Academy of Audiology
8300 Greensboro Drive, Suite 750
McLean, VA 22102
703-790-8466
http://www.audiology.org

American Auditory Society
512 East Canterbury Lane
Phoenix, AZ 85022
602-789-0755
http://www.amauditorysoc.org

American Speech-Language-Hearing Association
10801 Rockville Pike
Rockville, MD 20852
301-897-5700
http://www.asha.org

bibliography

Following is a sampling of materials relating to the professional concerns and development of audiologists and speech-language pathologists.

Quick Guide to the Internet for Speech-Language Pathology & Audiology. 2nd Edition. Reading, MA: Addison-Wesley Publishing Co., 1998.

Flexer, C. *Facilitating Hearing and Listening in Young Children.* San Diego, CA: Singular Publishing, 1999.

Gelfand, Stanley A. *Essentials of Audiology.* New York:, NY: Thieme Medical Publishers, 1997.

Hall, James W., III. *Handbook of Otoacoustic Emissions.* San Diego, CA: Singular Publishing, 2000.

Hall, James W. and Gustav Mueller, III. *Audiologists' Desk Reference.* Albany, NY: Delmar Publishers, 1996.

Hicks, Patricia Larking. *Opportunities in Speech and Language Pathology Careers.* Lincolnwood, IL: VGM Career Horizons, 1996.

Martin, Frederick N. and John Greer Clark. *Introduction to Audiology: A Review Manual.* 5th Edition. Needham Heights, MA: Allyn & Bacon, 2000.

Martin, Frederick N. *Introduction to Audiology.* 7th Edition. Needham Heights, MA: Allyn & Bacon, 1999.

Shprintzen, Robert J. Syndrome *Identification for Audiology: An Illustrated Pocket Guide.* San Diego, CA: Singular Publishing Group, 2001.

Silverman, Franklin H. *Fundamentals of Electronics for Speech-Language Pathologists and Audiologists.* Needham Heights, MA: Allyn & Bacon, 1998.

Warren, Richard M. *Auditory Perception: A New Analysis and Synthesis.* New York, NY: Cambridge University Press, 1999.

Biofeedback Therapists

Definition

Biofeedback therapists are health care professionals who specialize in monitoring a patient's heart rate, skin temperature, and muscles. Using test results, they aim to teach their patients how to better regulate their physical responses to stress.

High School Subjects

Biology
Health
Psychology

Personal Skills

Helping/teaching
Technical/scientific

Salary Range

$50,000 to $90,000 to $200,000+

Educational Requirements

Bachelor's degree; biofeedback training; advanced degree recommended

Certification or Licensing

Recommended

Outlook

Faster than the average

GOE
NA*
O*NET-SOC
NA*

*Not Available. The U.S. Department of Labor does not classify biofeedback therapists as such, but rather classifies the therapist's primary profession (e.g., registered nurse).

No pills, no tongue depressors, and no examining tables. Though Andrea Sime treats many different health problems, her office doesn't look like a typical doctor's office. Along one wall is her desk and chair, along the other sits the only examining equipment she uses: what looks like boxes with switches, lights, and wires hooked up to a computer.

Andrea sits with the computer screen turned away from the patient so only she can see it. The patient, a woman complaining of tension headaches, has sensors attached to her hands.

"I have trouble relaxing at work," the woman says. As she speaks, the sensors monitor her muscle responses and Andrea reads the feedback. She asks the woman specific questions about her workplace, trying to identify tensions that may be causing her headaches. By the end of the session,

Andrea will have a printout of the biofeedback results and can determine a treatment plan.

This session is the start of a learning process for the patient; she can study the causes of her headaches and try to alter her behavior to prevent them. In further sessions, patients learn how to interpret and manipulate their biofeedback results to get their minds and bodies in better synch.

what does a biofeedback therapist do?

It's late at night and you're walking alone down a dark city street. No one else is around. Then you hear what sounds like the soft shuffling of feet coming up quickly from behind you. What do you do first? Shout for help? Run? Put up your fists? Actually, before you do anything voluntarily, your body has several automatic reactions: your muscles tense up, the hair bristles at the back of your neck, your heart beats faster, you lose your breath. Your mind, which perceives a threat, sends fight-or-flight mes-

sages to your body, preparing for battle or to run away. Then, when you turn around to discover that the noise was only a newspaper blowing down the street, your body relaxes. A *biofeedback therapist* works with this relationship between the mind and the body. Biofeedback is about training your body to react to stress and illness in certain ways to prevent headaches, stomach pain, and other disorders.

Or think of it this way: you're in a theater watching a horror movie. The main character is suddenly stabbed in the stomach with a knife. The entire audience is startled; stomach muscles tighten and people gasp or scream. Then, the brain reminds the body that you are all actually just watching a movie. Everyone relaxes, amused by their dramatic reaction.

Biofeedback therapists helps patients learn about their natural reactions to the things around them. A student may have tension headaches every time he or she takes a test or gets an upset stomach when talking to his or her parents. The biofeedback therapist, using a variety of technical tools, can study a patient's response to stress and instruct the patient on how to manipulate that response.

Biofeedback therapists come from a variety of backgrounds. Social workers, nurses, physical therapists, psychiatrists, and other professionals who work in health care or counseling may pursue biofeedback training. They may choose to focus on biofeedback therapy or incorporate it into other methods of treating patients.

A biofeedback therapist uses equipment such as an electromyograph (EMG). The therapist places sensors on the patient's skin and the EMG monitors muscle tension. When the muscles tense up, they send out electrical signals that the EMG picks up and records.

Therapists can also monitor a patient's skin temperature. Skin temperature is determined by blood flow, which can be affected by stress. When a person is tense, blood vessels narrow, limiting the flow of blood in the body and causing skin temperature to drop. Biofeedback therapists usually place sensors on the hands or feet to determine blood flow.

The amount a patient sweats can also be monitored by biofeedback equipment. Electrodermal response (EDR) of the fingers and palms is monitored by biofeedback instruments. Studying these responses can help the therapist treat excessive sweating and other skin conditions.

As in most areas of health care, the methods of biofeedback treatment are constantly developing. Electroencephalograms (EEGs)

lingo to learn

Biofeedback: The immediate feedback of information about heart rate, blood flow, tension, sweating response, and other body processes.

Electrodermal feedback: A measure of skin conductivity used in relaxation training and in the treatment of dermatological conditions.

Electroencephalograph: A record of brain waves used to develop treatment for such conditions as hyperactivity, epilepsy, and alcoholism.

Electromyograph: A device that measures muscle tension for relaxation training and treatment of headaches and chronic pain.

Thermal feedback: A measure of blood flow. The temperature of a person's fingertip is taken to determine his or her stress level.

are being used by biofeedback therapists to monitor brain waves. EEGs are used in the treatment of such disorders as epilepsy, alcoholism, and attention deficit disorder.

Biofeedback therapists treat many other disorders. Biofeedback is used to help with back and neck pain, headaches, urinary stress incontinence, anxiety, ulcers, and many other health problems.

what is it like to be a biofeedback therapist?

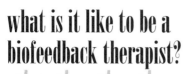

In an office composed mostly of psychologists, Andrea Sime practices biofeedback therapy. Like her colleagues, Andrea uses counseling skills to treat her patients. Before becoming certified in biofeedback therapy, Andrea worked for many years as a clinical social worker, offering clients counseling and psychotherapy. Now she treats a different group of clients, offering a very different kind of treatment. "I think of myself as more of a teacher," she says. "I tell my clients, I teach skills, I don't give pills."

What she does give her clients is the ability to regulate their bodies by learning the relationship between their minds and their physical health. Her patients have a variety of different health disorders, including headaches, chronic pain, high blood pressure, and arthritis. Using equipment to monitor and record a patient's physical reactions, Andrea often uncovers stress in a patient's life that may be causing illness. She uses equipment that monitors muscles, skin temperature, and sweat gland activity through sensors placed on the patient's body.

Each client will usually come in about once a week for eight to 12 weeks, for sessions lasting about 50 to 60 minutes. Andrea arranges her schedule so she does not see more than six patients a day.

"Biofeedback can be so effective in the things that it treats, we don't see people a lot," she says. By reducing treatment to fewer sessions, Andrea is able to limit the cost of a patient's health care. However, some patients may require longer treatment, particularly those who have suffered some kind of traumatic injury such as a car accident.

Before the first session, the patient must fill out a long questionnaire covering health problems, symptoms, stresses, and medical history. Andrea discusses the responses with the patient before beginning any biofeedback procedure.

Andrea uses all the biofeedback equipment on most patients. The instruments are hooked up to a central computer, providing information on the patient's muscle reactions, hand temperature, heart rate, and blood pressure. "I turn the computer [monitor] so they can't see it," she says. "Sometimes people will figure out the process right away, and I want to keep it objective."

While the equipment is monitoring the patient's responses, Andrea talks to the patient about his or her symptoms. She asks about what brought them to therapy, what stresses are in their lives, and what medication they're taking. Their answers help her to develop what is called a "psychophysiological profile," a portrait of a patient's mental and physical state. As the equipment gathers data, Andrea pays close attention to the patient, taking notes to develop a treatment plan. "At the end of the session," she says, "I hit the print bar and get a nice printout of everything in their physiology."

Andrea then gives patients an audiotape directing them to become aware of the tension in their bodies. She offers a series of taped instruction, including programs on stress, self-esteem, assertiveness, and self-confidence. She also gives patients articles on stress and on how it affects the body and immune system. "They have no idea how much tension they're holding in," she says.

During the second session, Andrea teaches patients how to interpret and manipulate the biofeedback reports. She moves the sensors around to different muscle groups, showing patients how to react differently to change their biofeedback reading. Andrea instructs patients to pay attention to their behaviors and monitor them throughout the day through coping and stress management skills.

She also listens to a patient's personal problems, calling on past experience in clinical therapy. However, biofeedback therapists with different backgrounds approach therapy in different ways; a physical therapist, for example, will use less counseling and rely more on physical exercise to repair such problems as muscle damage.

During the last session, Andrea reviews the patient's initial questionnaire. She asks if the problems reported before the treatment still exist. "A lot of times," Andrea says, "a person will say, 'Oh, that's right, I was having trouble with sleep when I first came to see you. I've been sleeping so well I kind of forgot about it.' So they recognize that they've made a lot of changes."

In addition to treating patients, a biofeedback therapist is required to complete a large amount of paperwork to keep the practice going. Managed care and insurance companies require Andrea to fill out many forms. Also, because biofeedback is relatively new, she must field many phone calls, answering questions by people interested in pursuing biofeedback treatment but unsure of what it entails.

have I got what it takes to be a biofeedback therapist?

Biofeedback therapists must be good listeners. If they are going to determine what is causing a patient's illness, they must be able to listen for things that may be causing stress. Teaching patients how to improve their coping and stress management skills is also an important part of biofeedback therapy, so therapists must be good communicators. A genuine empathy for patients is also important. Biofeedback therapists spend many hours a week working one-on-one with people, listening to their problems. They have to enjoy being around a variety of people.

It is important that biofeedback therapists practice the very things they teach. They should have an understanding of the relationship between the mind and the body and be able to control their own tensions.

Good business sense is also valuable. Therapists have to build up their own practice, deal with insurance and managed care companies, hire staff, purchase and maintain equipment, and handle other concerns of a small business.

It is the business aspect of the job that is the most frustrating for Andrea. Managed care

requires a lot of additional paperwork, often causing Andrea problems getting paid for treatment. "I would much rather just work with people," she says.

Instead, she has to keep extensive records, writing treatment summaries and letters to doctors and insurance firms. Balancing both the practice and the record keeping can make her schedule tight. Keeping regular hours can be difficult; often Andrea's patients want to schedule sessions in the evening or on the weekend.

"Sometimes people come in with really sad stories," she says, speaking of the more stressful aspects of the job. Andrea sometimes works with patients whose health is not likely to improve much, such as patients with multiple sclerosis, terminal cancer, or other serious diseases. However, her training in psychotherapy taught her how to handle the stressful parts of her job to avoid becoming burned out.

Because Andrea likes her work so much, there are few negative aspects for her. "There are a lot of psychic benefits to the work," she points out. "Patients usually say, 'I have learned so much. I feel so much different.'" She likes being able to see these good results quickly.

how do I become a biofeedback therapist?

Most biofeedback therapists start out in other areas of counseling or health care. Nurses, psychologists, and physical therapists will use biofeedback as a specialty within their regular practices. Andrea worked for many years as a clinical social worker. While exploring relaxation techniques, she took a workshop in biofeedback and found it interesting. She had become tired of counseling and was fascinated with the interaction between the mind and body. She continued to take biofeedback courses and eventually became certified to practice as a biofeedback therapist.

education

High School
Any science-related courses can help you prepare for a health care career. Biology, anatomy, and health will give you some back-

ground in the physical aspect of biofeedback therapy. Counseling skills are also valuable, so take psychology and sociology classes if available.

Postsecondary Training

Most people who practice biofeedback therapy first become licensed in another area of health care, such as nursing or psychology; biofeedback therapy is often studied later in a career as an area of specialization.

According to the guidelines set by the Biofeedback Certification Institute of America (BCIA), a biofeedback therapist must have a bachelor's degree or higher in social work, psychology, nursing, medicine, physical therapy, or other approved field. After receiving his or her degree (which may take up to 10 years for those studying medicine), an individual can then choose to continue training in biofeedback therapy through an accredited training program. The BCIA publishes a list of approved programs that offer the training and education necessary to practice. Though many other institutions offer workshops or training programs in biofeedback, not all of them are approved by the certifying board. Some biofeedback therapists choose to practice without certification; these therapists are not recognized by the BCIA.

certification or licensing

Biofeedback therapists become certified through the Biofeedback Certification Institute of America. After completing 200 hours of training, an applicant takes a comprehensive exam covering both the applicant's knowledge of biofeedback and his or her ability to use and understand the equipment.

Andrea has been certified for 15 years. She describes the exams as the toughest tests she has ever taken. "It's designed for multiple disciplines," she says, "designed to test psychologists, social workers, physical therapists, physicians, and nurses." Despite the degree of difficulty involved, she believes that the examination is necessary to create quality standards of practice.

Biofeedback Benefits

Biofeedback is an effective treatment for migraine and tension headaches among both children and adults. This has been proven by numerous controlled studies with follow-ups of up to 15 years. The American Association for Headache cites biofeedback as an acceptable treatment for these conditions.

Eighty percent of individuals with essential hypertension who underwent biofeedback training in one study reduced their prescription medications or no longer needed them at all, even after years of taking medication.

More than 700 groups worldwide are using EEG biofeedback therapy for treatment of attention deficit hyperactivity disorder (ADHD). Clinicians have reported patients who experienced a 60 to 80 percent improvement in the condition and marked reduction in medication requirements.

Studies on women with PMS have shown biofeedback can help reduce the symptoms.

In more than 90 percent of children under the age of 12 with sleeping problems such as bedwetting, recovery is expected within the first two months of biofeedback treatment.

Numerous studies have shown that people with panic and anxiety disorders who begin biofeedback training gain significantly in their ability to control these states, such that they no longer interfere with their daily life.

scholarships and grants

Scholarships and grants are often available from individual institutions, state agencies, and special-interest organizations. Additionally, your high school or college counselor can help you find sources of financial aid. Your local library and the Internet are other sources of information about funding for medical school.

Many students finance medical education through programs that exchange military service for tuition coverage. The National Health Service Corps Scholarship Program and the Armed Forces Health Professions Scholarship Program are two opportunities to help finance medical education.

Another source for financial aid, scholarship, and grant information is the Association of American Medical Colleges. Remember to request information early for eligibility, application requirements, and deadlines.

National Health Service Corps Scholarship Program
Department of Health and Human Services
4350 East-West Highway, 10th Floor
Bethesda, MD 20814
800-638-0824
http://www.fedmoney.org/grants/93288-00.htm

Armed Forces Health Professions Scholarship Program
Air Force:
http://hp.airforce.com/training/financial.html
Army:
http://www.sirius.com/~ameddet/hpschps.htm
Navy:
http://nshs.med.navy.mil/hpsp/default.htm

To be a successful biofeedback therapist, you should

- Be a good listener
- Have good teaching skills
- Be an effective communicator
- Have empathy for others
- Have a good business sense
- Have good counseling skills

Association of American Medical Colleges
2450 N Street, NW
Washington, DC 20037-1126
202-828-0400
http://www.aamc.org

who will hire me?

After tiring of work as a clinical social worker, Andrea explored biofeedback therapy. Her brother had also become interested in biofeedback at the time and he suggested they work together. He held a Ph.D. in exercise physiology. "I had more of a clinical background," Andrea says, "and he had more of the physiological background." This original partnership was a good combination of skills and knowledge since biofeedback therapy uses a blend of both body and mind concepts. In time, Andrea eventually built up her own practice.

Most biofeedback therapists work in private practice, though some work in hospitals and clinics. Others teach in biofeedback training programs. In addition to seeing patients, Andrea occasionally speaks to classes, support groups, and businesses about biofeedback.

Typically, biofeedback therapy becomes a specialization within another area of health care; most individuals gradually develop their biofeedback practice within their own established careers.

After receiving BCIA certification, biofeedback therapists invest in the necessary equipment and begin to promote the benefits of biofeedback therapy to their current patients and to the larger community.

where can I go from here?

Once biofeedback therapists have established their own practices, they generally do not advance in the typical way. Continuing education is important to any health care professional, so biofeedback therapists advance within their practices by developing their skills and learning about new methods of treatment.

Andrea is happy with her current situation. "I've reached a balance in my life," she says. "When I started out in private practice, it involved a lot of long hours. Now it's going well, and I'm as busy as I want to be." There are more areas of biofeedback that Andrea would like to explore, such as brain wave biofeedback, or neurofeedback.

what are the salary ranges?

Biofeedback therapists generally charge from $50 to $125 per session, according to EEG Spectrum International, a research institute that specializes in the study of EEG feedback. Depending on the level of experience and client base, a biofeedback therapist can earn as much as a physician.

However, because they come from different professional backgrounds, salaries vary among biofeedback therapists. A psychologist with a Ph.D. is going to make more money practicing biofeedback than will a nurse or clinical social worker. Location also affects earnings; therapists working in more urban areas generally make more money than those in smaller communities. In more rural areas, therapists may make around $50,000, while those working in larger communities, often handling more patients, may make up to $200,000 a year.

what is the job outlook?

Employment of biofeedback therapists is expected to grow faster than the average for all occupations. According to the U.S. Department of Labor, the field of health care is expanding faster than any other industry. The U.S. population is growing, as is the number of Americans aged 65 and over. This growth will increase the demand for most health care industry workers, including biofeedback therapists. Also, because most individuals have some sort of medical insurance, the costs of care, including nontraditional courses of treatment such as biofeedback therapy, have become more affordable. According to EEG Spectrum International, many insurance plans cover biofeedback therapy for treatment of certain conditions.

According to the Association for Applied Psychphysiology and Biofeedback, revenues for alternative medicine are almost equal to that of traditional medicine. In many cases, patients seek the assistance of biofeedback therapists after more traditional medical treatment has failed. On the other hand, some people choose to look first to alternative forms of health care to avoid medications or invasive surgery.

In addition, continued research within the field of biofeedback should allow for the treatment of more disorders. Currently, the study of brain waves in cases involving alcoholism, attention deficit disorder, insomnia, epilepsy, and traumatic brain injury point to new biofeedback treatment methods.

Some conditions, such as incontinence and chronic headaches, are often better treated through biofeedback therapy than through more invasive medical treatment.

how do I learn more?

professional organizations

Following are organizations that provide information about training for careers in biofeedback therapy.

Association for Applied Psychophysiology and Biofeedback
10200 West 44th Avenue, Suite 304
Wheat Ridge, CO 80033-2840
303-422-8436
aapb@resourcenter.com
http://www.aapb.org

Biofeedback Certification Institute of America
10200 West 44th Avenue, Suite 304
Wheat Ridge, CO 80033-2840
bcia@resourcenter.com
http://www.bcia.org

EEG Spectrum International
16500 Ventura Boulevard, Suite 418
Encino, CA 91436-2505
818-789-3456
http://www.eegspectrum.com

biofeedback therapists

bibliography

Following is a sampling of materials relating to the professional concerns and development of biofeedback therapists.

Berger, Stanley A. et al. *Introduction to Bioengineering.* 2nd Edition. New York, NY: Oxford University Press, 2000.

Bronzino, Joseph D., ed. *The Biomedical Engineering Handbook.* 2nd Edition. Boca Raton, FL: CRC Press, 1999.

Evans, James R. and Andrew Abarbanel, eds. *Introduction to Quantitative EEG and Neurofeedback.* Burlington, MA: Academic Press, 1999.

Mappes, Thomas A. and David DeGrazia, eds. *Biomedical Ethics.* 5th Edition. New York, NY: McGraw-Hill, 2000.

Robbins, Jim. *A Symphony in the Brain: The Evolution of the New Brain Wave Biofeedback.* Boston, MA: Atlantic Monthly Press, 2000.

Schwartz, Mark S. and Frank Andrasik. *Biofeedback.* 2nd Edition. New York, NY: Guilford Press, 1998.

Biomedical Engineers

Definition

Biomedical engineers apply engineering principles to problems in medical research and health care.

High School Subjects

Biology
Mathematics
Physics

Personal Skills

Helping/teaching
Technical/scientific

Salary Range

$36,000 to $61,000 to $92,000+

Educational Requirements

Bachelor's degree, advanced degree recommended

Certification or Licensing

Voluntary

Outlook

About as fast as the average

GOE
02.02.04
O*NET-SOC
17-2031.00

Wrapping up the report he is working on, Mike Vonesh is ready to go home. He is checking his planner to see what he has scheduled for the next day when his phone rings.

"There's a Dr. John Mackey for you on line one," says his secretary. "Do you want to take it?" Mike remembers the name. Dr. Mackey is a surgeon working in Denver. They had met at a convention the year before.

"Put him through. Hello, Dr. Mackey, how are you?"

"Mike! I'm glad I caught you. I remember we spoke about blood vessel technology, and I just thought. . . ." There is a long pause. When Dr. Mackey continues, he sounds tired. "I lost a patient today. Aortic aneurysm. He was only 60, but he had diabetes and previous heart attacks, so we just couldn't operate. Mike, I don't ever want to look a patient like this in the eye again and tell them there is nothing I can do. There has to be a way to treat this without opening them up."

They talk for a while—the doctor who wants to save lives and the engineer who wants to help him. Mike tells Dr. Mackey about the advisory group of surgeons he works with and asks the doctor to join. Dr. Mackey agrees and by the time they say good night, Mike has a page of notes and a new member on his team. As he leaves the office, his mind is filled with possible solutions and ways to test those ideas. He knows that with the right tools, doctors like John Mackey could save many more lives. Mike's job is to give them those tools.

what does a biomedical engineer do?

Biomedical engineers, in cooperation with doctors, technicians, and other engineers, bridge the gap between the mechanical world and the world of flesh and blood. They use their understanding of engineering to develop and test machines, materials, and techniques that give patients hope for longer, fuller lives.

On the surface, the fields of engineering and medicine seem far apart. Engineers work with steel, fluids, and mathematical principles to create new and better things. Doctors work with the most amazing machine: the human body. However, ever since the first artificial limb was used to replace a missing leg, engineering and medicine have worked together. Engineers use their knowledge of physical laws to study the operations of the natural world. Better understanding of how systems within the body work can lead to new treatments and tools for doctors. The wonders of modern medicine, from the simplest artificial limbs to an artificial heart, are due in part to the work of biomedical engineers.

There are a number of subfields within biomedical engineering. Some people in these fields work in basic research, exploring theories and broad concepts. Others use theories to build, test, and eventually market products or equipment such as titanium hip joints or ultrasound machines. Engineers also work in adapting these new devices to the medical environment, customizing software and training personnel.

Whatever their role, biomedical engineers work closely with people from many different fields. They need the input and cooperation of doctors and medical scientists, but they also work with marketing and sales departments, grant foundations, and machinists that build prototypes of new devices.

Though they are specialists to some extent, biomedical engineers are also generalists who know something about a variety of disciplines. Biomedical engineers can work in a number of different environments depending on their specialty. For example, clinical engineers work mostly in hospitals, while engineers who have moved into sales or marketing may spend more time traveling.

lingo to learn

Bioinstrumentation: Building machines for the diagnosis and treatment of disease.

Biomaterials: Anything that replaces natural tissue, such as artificial materials or living tissues grown for implantation.

Biomechanics: Developing mechanical devices like the artificial hip, heart, and kidney.

Cellular, tissue, and genetic engineering: Application of engineering at the cellular and subcellular level to study diseases and design intervention techniques.

Clinical engineering: Application of engineering to health care through customizing and maintaining sophisticated medical equipment.

Systems physiology: Using engineering principles to understand how living systems operate.

what is it like to be a biomedical engineer?

Mike Vonesh works in artificial blood vessel product design for W. L. Gore and Associates in Flagstaff, Arizona. Before that, he worked at Northwestern Memorial Hospital in Chicago. His days vary, but there is one constant: "There is a lot of interaction with other specialists," he says. "That's a big part of the job—working with other people."

Some of this communication is with other engineers working on related products or doctors seeking (or giving) advice, but not all of it. "You have to be able to talk with all kinds of people, from CEOs to the machinists who help build the models."

Mike estimates that about 75 percent of his time is spent doing hands-on work— running tests, performing animal studies, or working on models. The remaining 25 percent of his time is spent in meetings or other administrative duties. "I have a lot of long telephone conversations," he says.

Mike divides his job into four phases. Phase one is problem identification. What exactly is the nature of the problem? Doctors may approach him about a problem, as Dr. Mackey did. Or, Mike's company may identify a problem that it hopes to remedy.

Once the problem is isolated, the second phase, problem solving, begins. "I spend a good percentage of my time in problem-solving sessions," Mike says. "I'm a fairly creative person; engineering is really like an art form in the conceptual phase." Much of this phase is devoted to making sure the solutions that are proposed are feasible. Mathematical models are created, often with the aid of computers.

If the theories are sound, the process moves on to the next phase: turning the ideas into reality. Prototypes are built and tested in laboratories. Some of the tests are on animals. Data is collected, modifications are made, and new models are built and tested.

Once the concepts are tested and proven to work, the final phase begins: new devices or procedures are tested on humans under carefully supervised conditions. If the company decides that there is a market, and government regulatory agencies like the Food and Drug Administration approve, the new device can go into production. The whole process takes between 18 months and two years.

These steps can overlap. At W. L. Gore and Associates, for example, steps are taken to keep regulatory agencies abreast of developments during each phase of development. "We have a long history of cultivating relationships with regulators," explains Mike. That way, problems can be identified early, before they become serious. Engineers working in basic research would not be involved in product design, as Mike is, but the essential goals of their work are the same as his.

You have to be able to talk with all kinds of people, from CEOs to the machinists who help build the models.

have I got what it takes to be a biomedical engineer?

Engineering and medicine are among the most demanding fields of study, attracting the highest-caliber students. "If you aren't dedicated, you won't make it through," Mike says. Those interested in biomedical engineering must be good students and be prepared to study hard.

Interest in math and science is important. You must be able to solve problems using an inquisitive mind. Problem solving often requires a new approach, so the ability to think creatively is critical. As Mike puts it, "The big hurdle is translating ideas into reality. You have to be able to think 'outside the box.' I think tinkering, inventor-type skills are very important."

Biomedical engineers often serve as the link between very different areas of expertise. For this reason, it is necessary to learn about other fields, such as electrical, material, and chemical engineering. Because they spend so much time talking with other professionals, biomedical engineers need to be excellent communicators.

Technical skills aside, Mike feels that the key element needed to being a successful biomedical engineer is compassion. "You can see a real difference between biomedical engineers and other types of engineers," he says. "They have the philosophy that they want to give something back."

As with any job, there are difficulties. Working within a number of different fields means there is always more to learn. "I wish I had more knowledge," Mike admits. "It's frustrating, but you can never know everything about every field." Biomedical engineers face challenges other engineers do not. Instead of dealing strictly with materials that have known properties, engineers like Mike must grapple with biological systems that are never the same. "Engineers tend to be perfectionists. It's difficult to have optimal solutions. You have to make compromises."

how do I become a biomedical engineer?

education

Mike graduated second in his class from the University of Illinois, one of the best engineering schools in the country. Despite this accomplishment, he was unable to find a job in biomedical engineering. To become more attractive to employers, Mike decided to go to the University of Arizona for more education. After spending two years there, he landed his first job at Northwestern University. He earned his Ph.D. while working full-time.

High School
The course of study for biomedical engineering is very demanding. High school students should take as much math and science as possible, including trigonometry, calculus, biology, physics, and chemistry. In addition, communication and problem-solving classes (using logic) will also be helpful. If you live near a facility that does biomedical work, you

To be a successful biomedical engineer, you should

- Have good problem-solving skills
- Be a good communicator
- Be able to get along with many types of people
- Be compassionate
- Have an aptitude for math and science
- Have an inquisitive mind

may wish to arrange a tour or talk to workers to see if biomedical engineering interests you.

Postsecondary Training
The minimum degree required for working in biomedical engineering is a bachelor's degree, but most engineers obtain an advanced degree as well. Many biomedical engineers have a bachelor's degree in biomedical engineering or a related science field and a Ph.D. in a biomedical engineering specialty.

Undergraduate study is divided into two concentrations. In addition to studying the core curriculum, bioengineering students devote their first two years to theoretical subjects like abstract physics and differential equations. The third and fourth years are spent on more applied science instruction. "I didn't like the theory very much," Mike admits. "The hands-on classes were more interesting to me—and I got better grades."

There are a number of excellent graduate-level programs available. For example, the biomedical engineering department at the University of Arizona, where Mike went for two years, helped to develop the first artificial heart implanted in a human—the Jarvic 7.

In addition to classroom work, students in graduate programs work on research projects headed by permanent faculty. Mike was able to work on projects in partnership with some of the best-known companies in the field, like Boston Scientific and Baxter. In the past, basic research was done at universities and product development was done by private companies. "I think there are more combined efforts now," Mike says. "A lot of the cutting-edge research is being done by small companies that may have money but lack the kind of intellectual resources you find in universities."

certification or licensing

All engineers who work in health care must become registered as professional engineers through their state boards of technical registration. To become registered, you must graduate from an engineering program accredited by the Accreditation Board for Engineering and Technology, have four years of work experience, and pass a state examination.

Certification or licensing is voluntary for biomedical engineers. However, obtaining advanced credentials will make you more attractive to employers and certify that you have been trained as a qualified professional.

Mike obtained his certification through his state board of technical registration. Candidates must have a bachelor's degree in engineering, after which they serve a five-year residency before taking a comprehensive exam.

internships and volunteerships

It stands to reason that the more "real world" research experience you have, the better your chance of finding a job after school. Internships are one way of getting that type of marketable experience, as well as a way to network with possible employers. "W. L. Gore and Associates sponsors about a dozen interns every summer, and other major companies have similar programs," Mike says.

The American Society for Engineering Education offers information on internship opportunities, such as the Research Science Institute program, and also lists engineering competitions for high school students. Visit its Web site, http://www.asee.org, for more information.

who will hire me?

Biomedical engineers work in universities, hospitals, government agencies, and in private industry, depending on the type of engineering practiced. Rehabilitative and clinical engineers find more opportunities in hospitals, for example. Research and product development engineers usually work with private companies such as Boston Scientific, Johnson & Johnson, and Baxter.

Universities hire biomedical engineers to work in their labs with professors and graduate students. However, government funding for basic research done at universities has been one of the victims of budget cuts in recent years. Some of this loss has been replaced by research done in private industry through cooperative partnerships.

Biomedical engineers also work for federal and state regulatory agencies that approve new devices and procedures before they are marketed. The Food and Drug Administration is the primary employer of biomedical engineers at the federal level.

where can I go from here?

Biomedical engineers have a number of career paths. They can continue researching, move into management, or enter into government service. The interdisciplinary nature of biomedical engineering allows for flexibility. Many in the field often have the background and experience to move easily into other business jobs in marketing or sales. Established professionals may choose to become consultants. As new technologies are developed, opportunities arise for entrepreneurs to go into business for themselves. Bioengineering is a field where there are new developments all the time.

Mike plans to stay with product development, at least for now. "I may decide to leave at some point," he says. "There's a lot of mentoring in this profession, and I feel like that's where I am now—where I want to do that myself."

what are the salary ranges?

Salaries vary greatly depending on education, experience, and place of employment. According to a 2000 salary survey by the National Association of Colleges and Employers, the average starting offer for bioengineers with a bachelor's degree was $44,863. For those with advanced training and a master's degree, the average salary offer was $50,433.

The U.S. Department of Labor, which classifies biomedical engineers under the designation *All Other Engineers,* reports that the 1998 median salary was $61,690. The lowest paid 10 percent earned less than $36,070, and the highest paid 10 percent earned over $92,320 a year.

In addition, those with established research credentials can earn substantially more as consultants to business and government.

what is the job outlook?

Employment for biomedical engineers is expected to grow about as fast as the average for all occupations, according to the U.S. Department of Labor. The best opportunities may be found in large hospitals; biomedical engineers are needed to ensure the safety of all medical equipment. Opportunities in research, increasingly within private industry, will also be plentiful. Job prospects will be the most promising for those with advanced degrees.

As the population ages and the health care industry continues to grow, more opportunities will arise for biomedical engineers. Older people require more tests and procedures than do younger people. And while the industry is changing rapidly as managed care assumes a more dominant role, the search for better (and cheaper) ways of treating patients will continue to drive bioengineering research and development. The use of MRIs, ultrasound equipment, CAT scans, PET scans, artificial hearts, kidney dialysis, tissue replacement technology, artificial joints and limbs, and dozens of other advances in medicine are the products of bioengineering. Biomedical engineers and the professors to train them will be needed to produce the tools for the next generation of treatments.

how do I learn more?

professional organizations

The following organizations provide additional information on the career of biomedical engineer.

American Society for Engineering Education
818 N Street, NW, Suite 600
Washington, DC 20036-2479
http://www.asee.org

Biomedical Engineering Society
8401 Corporate Drive, Suite 110
Landover, MD 20785-2224
301-459-1999
http://www.bmes.org

Junior Engineering Technical Society
1420 King Street, Suite 405
Alexandria, VA 22314
703-548-5387
jets@nae.edu
http://www.jets.org

bibliography

Following is a sampling of materials relating to the professional concerns and development of biomedical engineer.

Berger, Stanley A. et al. *Introduction to Bioengineering.* 2nd Edition. New York, NY: Oxford University Press, 2000.

Bronzino, Joseph D., ed. *The Biomedical Engineering Handbook.* 2nd Edition. Boca Raton, FL: CRC Press, 1999.

Enderle, John D., ed. *Introduction to Biomedical Engineering.* Burlington, MA: Academic Press, 1999.

Mappes, Thomas A. and David DeGrazia, eds. *Biomedical Ethics.* 5th Edition. New York, NY: McGraw-Hill, 2000.

Biomedical Equipment Technicians

Definition

Biomedical equipment technicians install, maintain, repair, and calibrate biomedical equipment used in hospitals, clinics, and other medical or laboratory facilities.

Alternative Job Titles

Biomedical electronics technicians
Biomedical engineering technicians
Biomedical instrumentation technicians
Clinical engineering technicians

High School Subjects

Chemistry
Mathematics
Physics

Personal Skills

Mechanical/manipulative
Technical/scientific

Salary Range

$25,000 to $33,000 to $40,000

Minimum Educational Level

Associate's degree

Certification or Licensing

Voluntary

Outlook

About as fast as the average

GOE
05.05.11
O*NET-SOC
49-9062.00

Responding to a request for assistance, Brent Doyen walks into the operating room to find a roomful of medical professionals staring in his direction. He's steered toward the faulty equipment—an aortic balloon pump designed to assist the heart if it is not functioning correctly. Brent can't very well take the machine apart in the operating room, but he has diagnosed the problem. He exits the operating room, runs down two floors, grabs a new set of cables, and rushes back up. He plugs one end of the new cables into the machine, and it starts pumping as it should. He breathes a sigh of relief and leaves the operating room as the surgery team hurriedly resumes the operation. Brent heads back down to the equipment shop. Saving lives is all in a day's work for a biomedical equipment technician.

what does a biomedical equipment technician do?

Biomedical equipment technicians (BMETs) are responsible for the maintenance, installation, calibration, and repair of biomedical equipment, electronic equipment designed to diagnose and treat medical conditions. This equipment may include anesthesiology machines, cardiac monitors, infusion pumps, defibrillators, radiology equipment, and ventilators and may range in size from a handheld unit to a machine that takes up an entire hospital room. BMETs, with their highly specialized training in electronics, are important links between technology and medicine.

lingo to learn

Biomechanics: Explores the response of living matter to physical forces, such as how the knee of a jogger responds to repeated impact on the pavement.

Calibrate: To adjust or set a device so that it records and measures accurately.

Defibrillator: An electronic device that creates an electric shock designed to restore the rhythm of a fibrillating heart.

Fibrillation: Irregular, rapid contractions of the heart muscles that cause the heartbeat and pulse to fall out of synchronism.

Heart-lung machine: A machine used to divert blood from the heart during heart surgery and to keep it oxygenated and in circulation.

Metabolic imaging: Noninvasive methods of seeing inside the body, such as positron emission tomography (PET), magnetic resonance imaging (MRI), X-ray computed tomography (CT or CAT scan), and ultrasound.

Pulmonary function machine: A machine that examines and measures a patient's breathing efficiency and analyzes the gases throughout the lungs.

Biomedical equipment technicians spend a considerable amount of time on preventive maintenance. All biomedical equipment must undergo regularly scheduled preventive maintenance checks to ensure that everything is in top working condition. Maintenance includes cleaning and calibrating, or adjusting the machine so it works in a standardized manner, and conducting operational verification tests to make sure the machine is operating as designed. Technicians may test circuits, clean and oil components, and replace worn parts. BMETs use tools such as voltmeters, oscilloscopes, spectrum analyzers, and computers to make sure equipment is functioning properly. Detailed records of all preventive maintenance checks must be kept by biomedical equipment technicians as well.

When equipment malfunctions, it's the job of the biomedical equipment technician to diagnose the problem and repair it. The BMET must determine whether the problem is due to operator error or whether the equipment is in need of actual repair. If the machine or instrument must be repaired, the BMET may refer to product manuals, test the equipment to try to pinpoint the problem, or speak with manufacturers about possible causes. The problem may be as elementary as a loose wire or as major as a defective motor. BMETs often take apart equipment and replace or repair parts, such as transistors, switches, or circuit boards.

Installing or upgrading equipment is also the responsibility of biomedical equipment technicians. BMETs follow manufacturer's guidelines to set up machinery, then inspect and test it to make sure it complies with safety standards.

Technicians often train those who will operate the equipment, such as nurses, doctors, and other health care personnel. They also answer questions regarding equipment usage.

Biomedical equipment technician I is a junior-level or entry-level technician. These technicians generally work under heavy supervision, and the majority of their work is maintenance-oriented. They are also capable of carrying out basic repairs on less-complicated equipment such as infusion pumps or defibrillators.

The *biomedical equipment technician II* is a senior-level technician and evenly splits time between preventive maintenance checks and repair work. These technicians work on equipment that is technically more demanding than the machinery entry-level technicians repair, including radiology equipment, laboratory analyzers, which involve robotics, pneumatics, and hydraulics, and anesthesiology equipment. Senior-level technicians may also oversee the installation of systems, such as nurse stations or heart monitor systems, while the junior-level technicians perform the physical tasks of installation. Technician IIs also evaluate new equipment and make purchasing recommendations.

The biomedical equipment technician who specializes in a particular area or type of equipment is known as a *biomedical equipment technician specialist.* Areas of specialization can include the catheter lab, pulmonary function machines, ultrasound, respiratory care, or X-ray equipment. Specialists must gain a solid foundation in biomedical equipment technology before focusing on a specialty. Many biomedical equipment technicians work in hospitals or clinics, taking care of all the equipment needs. Other BMETs work for third-party companies or manufacturers. Those working for manufacturers service and install equipment made by the manufacturing company. Frequent travel may be involved, and some technicians may be assigned a region covering several states.

what is it like to be a biomedical equipment technician?

The first thing Brent Doyen, clinical engineering supervisor, does when he arrives at work at St. Joseph's Medical Center in Tacoma, Washington, is to check the work orders that have been generated over the course of the night.

The orders are prioritized according to type of equipment and urgency. For example, life support equipment will take precedence over a piece of equipment that is not in use or not being used to keep someone alive. Once the work orders are handed out, the biomedical equipment technicians disperse to take care of repairs and routine preventive maintenance checks. Smaller equipment may be brought back to the shop area, while the large machinery will stay put. Brent and the other technicians wear pagers and frequently respond to calls throughout the day. "You stay pretty darn busy," Brent admits.

At St. Joseph's, preventive maintenance checks are conducted on a monthly basis and require thoroughness and precision. When Brent checks a heart monitor, he first walks into the room and observes the overall condi-

tion of the monitor. Is the screen brightness at an acceptable level? Can he read everything clearly on the monitor? Is it in focus? If the monitor passes this initial check, Brent conducts an operational verification test. This entails hooking up a test device called a chicken heart to the machine. The test device simulates heart rate, blood pressure, temperature, and cardiac output and allows Brent to make sure the machine is functioning within specifications.

Brent then removes the heart monitor from the power source and prepares to examine the inside of the machine. He takes off the cover and cleans the inside, which attracts quite a bit of dust due to the heat of the components.

"That's one of your biggest enemies when it comes to electronics," explains Brent. "The dust and the dirt generate heat and cause components to overheat and burn out. So we keep them clean." Brent also checks the power supplies for proper voltage levels, examines the wires to make sure none are loose, and looks for any signs of wear, such as discoloration of components. If everything looks in order, Brent reassembles the unit and performs an electrical safety check, which tests for leakage of current, resistance, and line voltage using an electrical safety analyzer. "Any time we open up a piece of equipment," Brent says, "the last thing we do after it's all completed, before we give it back, is electrical safety." The entire preventive maintenance check can take anywhere from 30 minutes to an hour to complete.

If the equipment does not pass all of the tests and is determined to be faulty, Brent removes it from service and transports it to the shop. He troubleshoots and evaluates the unit to determine the cause of the problem. Brent tries to narrow down the problem to a specific circuit board or component and then must decide how to remedy the problem. "You have to constantly be thinking about what you're doing," says Brent. "Is it cost effective to put my time into this to try and repair this, or is it more cost effective to just buy a board? That's the big question: Which is the best way to go so it's cost effective?" As long as Brent considers the most economical approach to fixing problems and keeps the biomedical equipment in top working condition, his employer is happy.

Although Brent generally works a 40-hour workweek, he is on call on a rotational basis and may have to report to the hospital on weekends or holidays. He may also have to stay late on occasion to repair equipment that

in-depth

Biomedical technology began in the 1970s, when consumer advocate (and recent presidential candidate) Ralph Nader publicized a document that suggested that people were being killed by microshock, the leakage of an electrical current whose level is below the sensation of feel and is therefore almost impossible to detect. The leakage can be caused by improper grounding, a loose wire inside the instrument, or leaking components. According to the document, microshock was occasionally causing patients' hearts to fibrillate, which is similar to a heart attack. The awareness of microshock and its potential hazards created a need for technicians who could test the electronic equipment to ensure proper grounding and minimal leakage of current.

is needed for the following morning, but this doesn't happen very often, and Brent feels the hours balance out.

have I got what it takes to be a biomedical equipment technician?

If you are interested in becoming a biomedical equipment technician, you should have technical aptitude for working on a variety of electronic equipment. You must also be detail oriented, enjoy working with your hands, and have excellent troubleshooting skills. Stamina and patience are also important, and you must be able to see projects through to the finish. There are times you may be stumped by a problem, but you need to persevere and follow through.

Although biomedical equipment technicians are trained to fix and service electronic equipment, they must also communicate and work with others, so people skills are crucial. You have to be adept at listening to others as they explain problems with machinery, and you need to be able to communicate clearly and tactfully when you are training people or correcting operator error.

"You shouldn't be in this job if you can't handle stress," Brent adds. "You're quite often the front line for life support. When the equipment fails, you're it." A person's life may depend on whether or not biomedical equipment is functioning properly, and occasionally you may be called upon to repair life-sustaining machinery on the spot, so you must be able to work under pressure. And if you have a

weak stomach, you might want to consider another job. "You do see a lot of blood," Brent says. "There's equipment that has, shall we say, high-protein substance on it." You may also be exposed to hazardous substances, including chemicals and blood, so you must be careful and take precautions.

If you can handle the pressure and enjoy working with electronic equipment, however, biomedical technology can be very rewarding. One thing Brent particularly enjoys is the continuing education. "You're staying current with technology," explains Brent. "As technology advances, so does your education. You're always learning something new." He also enjoys the nationwide camaraderie with other biomedical equipment technicians and notes, "It's kind of like we're a big family."

how do I become a biomedical equipment technician?

Brent was an electronics technician before he became a biomedical equipment technician. He worked on repairing and servicing amusement games and equipment, such as video games and jukeboxes. Brent had been working on a pinball machine in a bar one evening. "I came across a person who was having a beer watching me work on stuff, and he said, 'Hey, I do the same thing you do, but I get paid more.' It turns out he was a biomed tech," Brent recalls. The prospect of earning more money and being able to work indoors instead of moving pool tables in the snow appealed to

Brent, and he looked into biomedical equipment technology.

education

High School

If you're thinking about becoming a biomedical equipment technician, it's never too early to start preparing. In high school, you should take mathematics classes as well as science courses. Brent advises, "I would recommend taking any kind of electronics classes offered in high school, as well as math classes." He stresses that students shouldn't be scared off by the math; if math is not your forte, don't worry. Math can help your understanding of electronic processes and equipment, but it is not crucial to be a successful biomedical equipment technician. Shop classes can help you develop skills working with various tools, and if an electronics shop class is available, you should definitely enroll.

Computer science classes are helpful as well. As biomedical equipment becomes increasingly computerized, having an understanding of how computers function is important. Health science classes will acquaint you with medical terminology and basic anatomy, both very important in the realm of the BMET. Not only must you understand the electronic equipment, but you must also know how the equipment affects or works with the patient.

If there is an opportunity to join an electronics club in your school or community, you should. Many high schools also participate in statewide or nationwide technical or science fairs, which give students an opportunity to build various objects and compete against other schools. These fairs are an excellent opportunity for you to gain some experience seeing projects through to the end, working with hand tools, and troubleshooting.

Postsecondary Training

Although a college degree is not absolutely mandatory to become a biomedical equipment technician, it is highly recommended, and many employers list a degree as a hiring requirement. Brent believes, "You would definitely have to have an associate's degree in biomed to pursue a good job." According to the Association for the Advancement of Medical Instrumentation (AAMI), there are currently 65 accredited two-year programs in biomedical

Advancement Possibilities

Biomedical engineers design medical apparatus, including pacemakers, artificial organs, and ultrasonic imaging devices, by applying engineering principles.

Clinical engineers design and evaluate biomedical systems and are involved with technology management.

Regional service managers represent manufacturers or third-party companies. They supervise field offices and teams of technicians and may also develop customer relations and provide training to customers.

Customer service representatives handle queries from customers about all aspects of the particular type of biomedical equipment their company sells.

technology offered in the United States. These two-year programs are available at both community colleges and technical schools. Training is also available through the armed forces.

A two-year degree in electronics is sometimes acceptable, but because biomedical technology is rather specialized, it is preferable to find a biomedical technology program. Brent already had an electronics degree when he decided to pursue biomedical technology. He thought he could waive some of the classes in the biomedical technology program at Spokane Community College in Spokane, Washington, but decided not to after speaking with the advisor. Brent is glad he decided to start from scratch when he entered the program, explaining, "Those classes are something you definitely have to be dedicated to. We started out with 24 students in the first year. By the time we finished the second year, there were only 10 of us left. The courses that he covers are very in-depth, and there's no time for monkeying around."

Courses in biomedical technology programs can include safety, including hospital and patient safety, medical terminology, medical instrumentation, physiology, circuits and devices, and digital electronics.

certification or licensing

Certification is generally not required, but some institutions only hire certified biomedical equipment technicians. At Brent's workplace, you cannot become a senior technician without certification. Brent also believes that certified technicians command higher wages and that certification is important for the field. "It's a way for the biomedical community to police themselves."

Operating under the direction of the International Certification Commission for Clinical Engineering and Biomedical Technology (ICC), the Board of Examiners for Biomedical Equipment Technicians, which is affiliated with AAMI, maintains the certification programs. Certification as a certified biomedical equipment technician (CBET) can be attained after passing a rigorous examination and meeting the education and experience requirements.

The candidate must have an associate's degree and/or proper work experience to meet the eligibility requirements. The examination tests the applicant's knowledge of anatomy and physiology, safety in the health care facility, electricity and electronics, medical equipment function and operation, and medical equipment problem solving. Two areas of specialization are also available: the certified radiology equipment specialist (CRES) and the certified clinical laboratory equipment specialist (CLES).

scholarships and grants

Technical schools and community colleges with biomedical technology programs may have scholarship opportunities available. These schools may also have general scholarships open to the entire student population that you may wish to explore. Contact the financial aid office or your department advisor for further information.

Other avenues to investigate include professional associations involved in the biomedical or health care fields, manufacturing companies, or large health care organizations. Companies that manufacture medical instruments and equipment may offer scholarships to aspiring biomedical equipment technicians. Professional associations such as AAMI may either sponsor scholarships or provide lists of award opportunities to members. Large hospitals and health care organizations may also grant scholarships. Searching on the Internet and contacting organizations directly may lead you to some promising possibilities.

internships and volunteerships

Internships are an excellent way to gain experience, skills, and connections in the biomedical field. Internships are often required for students in associate's degree programs and can lead to job opportunities after graduation. They are usually set up through the placement department and are without pay. "You're compensated slightly somehow," says Brent. "I know one facility that will give interns living quarters. Here you get a lunch every day." Compensation varies from facility to facility.

Volunteer opportunities in medical facilities are plentiful as well. Brent usually brings in an intern from one of the two biomedical technology programs in Washington, but, he recalls, "This last summer I had a high school student come to me and ask me if he could work with us, stay out of the way and just observe. And I said sure, and he turned out to be a real help." The student recently paid Brent a visit and told him that much of what he observed over the summer hadn't made sense to him, but now that he is taking chemistry and physics, things are starting to click. Volunteering can give you some exposure to the industry and to the health care field in general. Brent suggests, "Call and ask if you can volunteer a few hours a week."

Employers are fond of internships because it provides them a chance to teach aspiring technicians about the field. It is also a means to seek job candidates. Brent is involved with hiring personnel at St. Joseph's, and many of the former interns are now employees. "What I use it for is to look at potential employees in the future," Brent explains. "It's kind of like a three-month interview."

labor unions

Union membership depends on the employer. Brent believes that there are currently more nonunion biomedical equipment technicians. There is no union specifically for biomedical equipment technicians, which means that technicians must usually join the union that represents the majority of the other health care workers in the facility. Some of the unions BMETs can join include the International Brotherhood of Electrical Workers, the International Union of Operating Engineers, and the Service Employees International Union.

who will hire me?

When Brent graduated from Spokane Community College's biomedical technology program, St. Joseph's Medical Center, where he had completed an internship, did not have a job opening. Brent sent out 100 resumes and found a job working for a third-party company that overhauled ventilators. He worked there for about a year when a position opened up at St. Joseph's. "Because of the internship," Brent feels, "they knew I would mix with the other employees there, so the internship did get me my job."

Many biomedical equipment technicians are employed by hospitals of all sizes. The federal government is another employer of BMETs, primarily through the Veterans' Administration Hospitals and medical centers on army bases. Technicians working for manufacturers often specialize in the repair of machinery. It is commonplace for manufacturing companies to provide maintenance agreements on new equipment, and biomedical equipment technicians are equipped to service the machinery. They may also install the equipment and train the operators or in-house technicians on its functions.

Independent service companies, or third-party companies, also service equipment. Hospitals that do not employ in-house biomedical equipment technicians may use the services of these third-party companies for repair, maintenance, and installation of equipment. Research and development departments within companies may also employ technicians to help test new equipment.

You may have to move a few times to find work as a biomedical equipment technician. "Basically, you probably won't find a job where you think you want to find a job," says Brent. Trade journal publications are an excellent source for job prospects. Magazines such as *Biomedical Instrumentation and Technology* and *Journal of Clinical Engineering* list job opportunities. Brent also suggests becoming involved with local biomedical associations and attending the meetings to find out about what is happening in the biomedical community and to develop some relationships and connections.

The Internet may provide some leads on job openings, and looking through the classified advertisements in the newspaper might be helpful as well. Many large hospitals, manufacturers, and health care organizations have job hotlines that announce new openings. These are often updated weekly. You might also send resumes and cover letters to all the facilities in the state you wish to live in to inquire about job possibilities.

where can I go from here?

Brent is content with his current job as a supervisor, but he thinks a regional position at some point in the future might be interesting. His employer is now part of a nationwide network of medical facilities, and if Brent's boss moves into a national position, there might be an opportunity for Brent to assume a regional administrative position. If there's one thing Brent is sure of, it's that he would like to stay with his current employer. "I really, really like working for the company I work for. They're very aggressive in their technologies and the business side of it, too. They're not asleep at the wheel. They're aware of what's happening within health care, and it's a real honor to work for them."

As biomedical equipment technicians gain more experience, they begin working more independently and on more technically demanding equipment. They may move into supervisory positions, training entry-level technicians and overseeing the daily operation of facilities. Experienced technicians may also choose to specialize in one type of equipment.

With a four-year degree in biomedical engineering, technicians may become biomedical or clinical engineers and assist in the research and design of new equipment and processes. Clinical engineers are engineers who assess and repair biomedical systems and may be involved in technology management. They are more concerned with the big picture than with individual pieces of equipment. Biomedical engineers, on the other hand, design medical equipment and instruments by applying engineering principles.

Biomedical equipment technicians who enter the industry as field service technicians with manufacturers or third-party companies can move into regional service management positions. Regional service managers supervise biomedical equipment technicians and other staff and may oversee a number of field offices or service centers. Managers may also provide training to customers and solicit new clients.

what are the salary ranges?

According to the Center for Health Careers in Pennsylvania, starting salaries for biomedical equipment technicians average about $25,000 annually. With certification and experience, technicians can expect to earn about $33,000. Medical equipment specialists with several years' experience earn over $40,000 a year.

Biomedical equipment technicians generally receive generous benefits packages with medical benefits, pension plans, and more. Employers may also finance continuing education courses and seminars.

what is the job outlook?

The *Occupational Outlook Handbook* indicates that jobs for biomedical equipment technicians will grow about as fast as the average. Technological advances will affect the health care industry, and qualified biomedical equipment technicians will be needed to install, maintain, and repair equipment, as well as train operators on proper usage and care. Equipment will rely more heavily on microprocessors and computers, which will also create a need for skilled technicians. New instruments and machines are developed and manufactured on a regular basis, and technicians are qualified to evaluate, test, and make recommendations from both the purchasing end and the design end.

The state of health care may influence the outlook for biomedical equipment technicians. As the trend toward health maintenance organizations (HMOs) increases, medical facilities will be persuaded to adopt cost-cutting measures. Biomedical equipment technicians will therefore be in demand to keep the existing equipment in top working condition.

Brent has noticed that many technicians who entered the field in the 1970s are nearing retirement, which means job openings will arise. And though he feels the biomedical community should have been more aggressive about presenting itself as a cost-saving option, he feels the future looks good. "Institutions like ours that realize there's a significant value in biomedical and clinical engineering are expanding the role there and developing it, so there are things on the horizon that will keep it going," Brent believes.

how do I learn more?

professional associations

For information on health care engineering, contact:
American Society for Healthcare Engineering
One North Franklin, 27th Floor
Chicago, IL 60606
ashe@aha.org
http://www.ashe.org

To learn more about certification, contact:
Association for the Advancement of Medical Instrumentation
1110 Glebe Road, Suite 220
Arlington, VA 22201-4795
certifications@aami.org
http://www.aami.org

To learn about careers in biomedical engineering, contact:
Biomedical Engineering Society
8401 Corporate Drive, Suite 110
Landover, MD 20785-2224
http://www.mecca.org/BME/BMES/society/

bibliography

Following is a sampling of materials relating to the professional concerns and development of biomedical equipment technicians.

Bronzino, Joseph D., ed. *The Biomedical Engineering Handbook.* Boca Raton, FL: CRC Press, 1999.

Careers in Focus: Medical Technicians. 2nd Edition. Chicago, IL: Ferguson Publishing Company, 2001.

Cardiologists

Definition
A cardiologist is a physician who diagnoses and treats diseases of the heart.

High School Subjects
Biology
Health

Personal Skills
Helping/teaching
Technical/scientific

Salary Range
$147,000 to $212,000 to $300,000

Educational Requirements
Bachelor's degree; medical degree; residency program

Certification or Licensing
Recommended (certification)
Required by all states (licensing)

Outlook
Faster than the average

GOE
02.03.01
O*NET-SOC
29-1063.00

Something is wrong. It isn't just the results of the patient's electrocardiogram that leads Dr. Stuart Greenfield to that conclusion, but a combination of test results, physical appearance, and discussions he has had with the patient.

Dr. Greenfield orders an angiogram: a diagnostic procedure that uses catheters (small tubes), dyes, and X rays of blood vessels to reveal any cardiac problems. The angiogram shows a 90 percent blockage of the left main artery in the patient, a condition that could potentially cause immediate death. The patient undergoes bypass surgery and after just two days is able to leave the hospital. In Dr. Greenfield's words, the patient "is doing wonderfully."

what does a cardiologist do?

Cardiologists practice in the subspecialty of internal medicine that diagnoses and treats heart disease. In most instances, cardiologists treat patients on a consultative basis to determine if the symptoms the patients are exhibiting are signs of heart disease. For example, if an internist has a patient who is complaining of chest pain, the doctor will refer the patient to a cardiologist. It is the cardiologist's job to determine if the chest pain the patient is experiencing is the result of a serious heart condition or perhaps only the result of indigestion.

During an initial interview, a cardiologist reviews the patient's medical history. Dr. Stuart Greenfield, a cardiologist at Chicago's Northwestern Memorial Hospital, believes that this information is critical. "The cardiologist's job really starts with the medical history. A cardiol-

lingo to learn

Angiogram: Also called an **arteriogram,** this diagnostic procedure uses catheters, dyes, and X rays to examine blood vessels. Dye is injected into an artery to make them visible in X rays and determine if there is any blockage.

Echocardiography (ECG): A diagnostic procedure in which ultrasound waves are sent into the body. The echoes are plotted to create an image of the heart.

Electrocardiogram (EKG): A measurement of the electrical activity of the heart.

Heart catheterization: A diagnostic procedure in which a small tube is inserted into the heart to view the chambers and surrounding structures.

Heart murmur: An abnormal heartbeat.

Stress echocardiogram: A diagnostic procedure that measures the supply of blood going to the heart muscles before and after exercise.

ogist will take a history from a patient a lot differently than an internist will take a history. We have a group of questions that are specific to our specialty that give us insight into what is wrong with the patient."

A cardiologist will ask the patient to try to describe the quality of the pain. Does the patient experiences this pain during an activity, such as grocery shopping or making a bed? How often do they experience the pain? How long have they been experiencing discomfort?

After taking the medical history, the cardiologist performs a physical examination. This is their first opportunity to listen to the patient's heart. Often, a cardiologist can tell if there is a problem just by listening to the rhythm of the heartbeat. "There are things that we listen to, that we are attuned to, that other people aren't . . . and it gives us a lot of information as to whether or not there is a problem," Stuart says. For example, when examining a patient for a heart murmur (an abnormal heartbeat), cardiologists will be able to tell if it is benign, (innocent murmur) or whether it could cause problems.

If warranted, a cardiologist will send the patient for specific tests that will aid in evaluation and diagnosis. The most common test is the electrocardiogram (EKG), which is used to detect abnormal heart activity. An EKG measures the electrical activity produced by the heart. Electrodes are attached to different parts of a patient's body to record electrical impulses caused by heart contractions. These impulses are plotted into a graph to illustrate the patterns.

Another common procedure used by cardiologists is echocardiography (ECG). This test uses ultrasonic waves to illustrate the structures and motions of the heart. Using high-pitched soundwaves, an instrument called a transducer measures any echoes produced and translates them into a graphic picture of the heart. ECGs are used to detect heart valve problems and tumors.

Cardiac catheterization is another type of test. In this procedure, a small tube, or catheter, is inserted through a blood vessel into the heart. Dye is injected into the catheter to be traced in an X ray. These images are used to measure the amount of pressure found in the heart's chambers or to detect any defects or obstructions blocking circulation.

Cardiologists are often called in to assist other doctors. Cardiac surgeons often request cardiologists to consult in the preoperative phase of treatment. Stuart explains, "Surgeons may need to clear their patients preop to make sure they don't have any cardiac problems that may interfere with either the surgical or the postsurgical periods." If a patient is known to have a preexisting heart problem, a surgeon will consult a cardiologist before, during, and after a surgery to track the patient's cardiac health.

Cardiologists do more than treat existing problems. They also provide information and advice to their patients regarding the prevention of cardiac disease. This advice is best known early on; many of the patients who see cardiologists are advanced in age and find it difficult to change their behavior. Stuart believes that the earlier a patient is reached, the better chance preventive measures such as a healthy diet and daily exercise can be adapted into that patient's lifestyle.

what is it like to be a cardiologist?

Unlike other medical specialties that may require a physician to be called in at any time, cardiologists tend to keep more regular working hours. During a full week, Stuart will see approximately 50 patients. In addition to his time at his office, he also spends time at Northwestern Memorial Hospital supervising stress tests. Because of the extensive research constantly being conducted in his field, Stuart tries to devote as much time as he can to reading up on the latest developments. He also works as an internist, diagnosing and treating patients for medical problems not requiring surgery.

Stuart feels that one of the greatest rewards of being a cardiologist is the ability to help people feel better and live healthier, longer lives. "I think the main reward is that no matter how serious a problem a patient has, a cardiologist almost always makes them feel better very quickly by doing something very simple. The return on your intervention is quick and it's large and the patients tend to be very grateful because of that."

However, one of the more stressful aspects of his career is the fact that he often treats patients who could have avoided developing problems altogether. Stuart says, "I think probably the most stressful or the most disappointing aspect of my job is that in many respects,

It's kind of nice knowing that a lot of patients that are coming to you are 60, 70, or 80 years old and you're buying them a little extra time.

most of the diseases I treat are preventable. If you could get patients to adopt healthier lifestyles you could greatly reduce the number of patients who end up with coronary artery disease."

The relationship between a cardiologist and a patient may be short or long term, depending on the situation. For example, a cardiologist may be called in for consultation by a primary care physician. The cardiologist may make a diagnosis and give recommendations for treatment, but then returns the patient to the care of the original physician. On the other hand, the referring physician may ask the cardiologist to remain on the patient's team for a longer period of time. Stuart explains, "Very often we will give advice to the referring physician as to what they can do to treat the particular patient. And very often they will ask us to follow the patient with them, and so we become their physician for the cardiology problem. These days, it happens more and more often that the referring physician is comfortable taking over the patient's care and then we just send them back and don't see them again . . . unless there is another problem."

Unfortunately, not all cardiac patients survive their battle with heart disease. It may become the responsibility of the cardiologist to inform the family of a death, a duty that is always difficult. When a young person dies it is especially tragic. Stuart finds some comfort in the fact that he has been able to help his patients with their struggle. "It's kind of nice knowing that a lot of patients that are coming to you are 60, 70, or 80 years old and you're buying them a little extra time. You're not offering them immortality, you're just telling them you can make their lives a little more comfortable for a few years more."

in-depth

Some Milestones in the History of Cardiology

1749: Jean Baptiste Sénac publishes a comprehensive study of the heart, marking the beginning stage of the development of modern cardiology.

1816: René Laënnec invents the stethoscope, which by the middle of the century was refined and routinely used as a diagnostic tool for the heart.

1838: Carlo Matteucci illustrates that the heart generates a measurable electrical charge.

1903: William Einthoven modifies a string galvanometer to record electrical impulses of the heart, marking the beginnings of electrocardiography.

1924: Einthoven refines his device and invents the electrocardiograph, winning the Nobel Prize for his achievement.

1929: Werner Forssman invents the technique of cardiac catheterization.

1956: Forssman, Dickinson Richards, and André F. Cournand win the Nobel Prize for their use of the catheter to study the circulatory system and heart.

have I got what it takes to be a cardiologist?

Success as a cardiologist demands a high level of dedication and discipline. As an intern, Stuart worked very hard to develop the skill and expertise necessary to succeed in this field. In time, he came to enjoy and appreciate the intellectual challenges presented to him.

It takes a great deal of hard work and perseverance to be accepted into a medical school. After completing a medical program, prospective doctors still need to complete a residency program before they are allowed to practice as a cardiologist. Therefore, anyone interested in a career as a cardiologist must be willing to dedicate many years to the study of medicine.

Additionally, cardiologists need a nurturing personality. The needs of the patient must always come first. Cardiologists must be willing to put aside their own concerns while they are responsible for the care of a patient.

Because cardiologists often detect a heart problem just by listening to the rhythm of the heart beating, they must possess excellent hearing. In addition to being able to hear the heartbeat, cardiologists must also be able to listen to the questions or worries of their patients. Good communication skills are necessary. Patients often mask their symptoms when talking to their cardiologist. According to Stuart, patients will talk about their unhappiness or anger when actually they should be addressing an illness. "They use anger a lot as a substitute for feeling sick about things."

Also, some patients will magnify their symptoms when they talk to their cardiologist because they may want attention. Cardiologists must be sensitive to this possibility and treat the patients with the patience necessary to help them.

how do I become a cardiologist?

Stuart knew he wanted to be a doctor from the time he was a child. "I was one of those kids who one day said, 'I'm going to be a doctor when I grow up.'" And he never changed his mind. While in high school, his course work included biology, chemistry, and math. He majored in physiology in college, a degree that helped him when he entered medical school. He attended medical school in Canada and is board certified in internal medicine and cardiology.

education

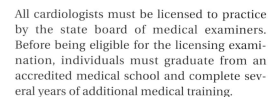

High School

Since acceptance into medical school is extremely difficult, it is never too early to begin preparing yourself. For Stuart, attending a high school with a rigorous curriculum, including classes in Latin, math, and science, helped prepare him for the academic demands of college and medical school.

If you are interested in a career as a cardiologist, you should enroll in as many science classes as possible. These should include classes in biology, chemistry, and anatomy. If possible, enroll in these classes at an advanced level.

English and speech courses will also come in handy since good communication skills will help you throughout your academic and professional careers. These skills will also help you, as a future physician, interact with staff and patients.

Postsecondary Training

After graduation from high school, prospective cardiologists must attend college and earn an undergraduate degree. Even though many medical schools accept students with liberal arts degrees, college freshmen interested in a medical career should consider earning a bachelor's degree in the sciences or entering a premed program. Stuart majored in physiology. "Three of the first eight courses I took my first year in medical school were repetitions of things I had taken as an undergrad."

During the second or third year of college, students should arrange to take the Medical College Admission Test (MCAT). The exam covers four areas: verbal facility, quantitative ability, knowledge of the humanities and social sciences, and knowledge of biology, chemistry, and physics. All medical colleges in the country require the test for admission.

Competition for acceptance into medical school is intense. Therefore it is important to maintain a high grade point average, score well on the MCAT, and show involvement in extracurricular activities.

After medical school, prospective cardiologists must take several more years of specialized training. On average, cardiologists spend three years in a residency program studying internal medicine and another three years in the subspecialty of cardiology.

certification or licensing

All cardiologists must be licensed to practice by the state board of medical examiners. Before being eligible for the licensing examination, individuals must graduate from an accredited medical school and complete several years of additional medical training.

Most cardiologists choose to become board certified, first in a specialty (e.g., internal medicine, pediatrics, or surgery) and then in their chosen subspecialty (e.g., cardiology, pediatric cardiology, or thoracic surgery). To become certified in their specialty, individuals must graduate from an accredited medical school, complete at least three years of additional training, and pass a rigorous examination. Subspecialty certification requires at least three more years of accredited cardiology training and proven clinical competence through examination. According to the American Board of Medical Specialists, board certification in most specialties must be renewed after six to 10 years. Certification renewal ensures that all certified doctors maintain a high level of competency. For continuing medical education, cardiologists can attend conferences, lectures, or specialized readings.

Many cardiologists choose to become members of the American College of Cardiology. Membership is a sign of a high level of professionalism and competence. To be considered for various levels of membership, the College takes into account the physician's length of service, board certifications, and scientific accomplishments. The highest level, fellow, is bestowed upon professionals with high credentials and expertise. These cardiologists carry the title F.A.C.C. (Fellow of the American College of Cardiology).

scholarships and grants

Scholarships and grants are often available from individual institutions, state agencies, and special-interest organizations.

Many students finance their medical education through programs that exchange military service for tuition coverage. The National Health Service Corps Scholarship Program and the Armed Forces Health Professions Scholarship Program are two opportunities to help finance medical education.

Another source for financial aid, scholarship, and grant information is the Association of American Medical Colleges. Remember to request information early for eligibility, application requirements, and deadlines.

Armed Forces Health Professions Scholarship Program
Air Force:
http://hp.airforce.com/training/financial.html
Army:
http://www.sirius.com/~ameddet/hpschps.htm
Navy:
http://nshs.med.navy.mil/hpsp/default.htm

Association of American Medical Colleges
2450 N Street, NW
Washington, DC 20037-1126
202-828-0400
http://www.aamc.org

National Health Service Corps Scholarship Program
Department of Health and Human Services
4350 East-West Highway, 10th Floor
Bethesda, MD 20814
800-638-0824
http://www.fedmoney.org/grants/93288-00.htm

internships and volunteerships

If you are interested in the field of cardiology, you should consider volunteering at a local hospital. This provides an excellent opportunity to gain practical experience and insight into various medical careers. Volunteering also offers the opportunity to observe how different departments within a hospital interact.

To be a successful cardiologist, you should

- Be highly disciplined
- Be dedicated to helping others
- Have a nurturing personality
- Have excellent hearing
- Be an effective communicator
- Work well with a variety of other people

It is not necessary to work at a hospital to gain experience serving others. Local nursing homes and medical clinics may also offer volunteer opportunities to allow you to discover whether a medical career is right for you.

who will hire me?

Most cardiologists work either within a group practice or as solo practitioners. Many physicians open up their practices in the area in which they have completed their residency in order to develop a reputation and make contacts within their communities. Stuart, however, came to work in the Chicago area almost by accident.

Stuart wanted to study stress echocardiography, which at the time was a new specialty in the field of cardiology. Unfortunately, only two programs offered this new specialty in Canada—Toronto and Montreal—neither of which he could attend. Because of family connections in the Chicago area, he decided to try Northwestern Memorial Hospital. Through networking and hard work, he was given an interview. Originally Stuart meant to spend a year in training in stress echocardiology and then return to practice in Montreal. But by the time his year was up he was asked to stay on. He agreed to stay and has been developing his own practice ever since.

Many doctors prefer the academic world to the professional. These cardiologists may choose to teach medical students or conduct cardiac research in university labs.

where can I go from here?

Once cardiologists have completed their residency programs, they are ready to either open their own offices or share a practice with other physicians. For cardiologists, success is measured by the number of patients they have been able to treat successfully. Because they often treat their patients on a consultative basis, cardiologists must build up their reputations to become known in the medical community and gain referrals from other physicians. One way many gain recognition is through conducting research and publishing their results.

what are the salary ranges?

According to a survey conducted by the American Medical Association, the median net income for internal medicine physicians in 1997 was $147,000. Cardiologists can expect a higher income considering it is a subspecialty of internal medicine and demands a higher level of training. According to the Medical Group Management Association, salaries for cardiology specialties are on the rise. The starting salary for invasive cardiology jumped from $195,630 in 1998 to $212,044 in 1999. Starting salaries in cardiovascular surgery jumped from $214,193 in 1998 to $291,292 in 1999.

Other factors that can affect a physician's income include the area of the country they work in and their level of experience. Physicians who work for themselves tend to earn a higher median income than those working within a group. However, solo practitioners are responsible for the cost of the administrative staff that maintains their office, as well as the rent for the office space, property insurance, and malpractice insurance. One reason doctors chose to work in a group practice is to share the costs of running an office.

what is the job outlook?

According to the U.S. Department of Labor, the employment of physicians in general is expected to increase faster than the average for all occupations. The expansion of the health care industry, the aging of the population, and the continued advancements in technology and procedure, all contribute to the demand for qualified medical personnel.

The influence of managed care is being felt in the field of cardiology. The usual inpatient time for someone who has suffered a heart attack has been greatly reduced. Years ago, it was common for heart attack patients to remain in the hospital for a month. When Stuart was an intern, the usual inpatient time was approximately 10 days. Today, it is not uncommon for patients to stay only two to five days.

According to Stuart, another effect of managed care is that before its introduction it wasn't unusual for a patient with chest pain to

I think what you're going to see is a return to cardiologists who actually listen to patients, who examine patients more carefully before deciding what tests to give them.

automatically have an angiogram. Angiograms, however, are costly and doctors are not prescribing them as quickly as before. "I think what you're going to see is a return to cardiologists who actually listen to patients, who examine patients more carefully before deciding what tests to give them," Stuart explains.

Trends in cardiology are dictated by the constant research that is being performed in the field. With the steady influx of new information, the practice of cardiology is continually evolving. Medical breakthroughs have allowed for more intensive care; physicians can and will continue to treat cases previously thought untreatable.

how do I learn more?

professional organizations

Following are organizations that provide information on the field of cardiology.

American Board of Internal Medicine
510 Walnut Street, Suite 1700
Philadelphia, PA 19106-3699
800-441-2246
http://www.abim.org

American College of Cardiology
9111 Old Georgetown Road
Bethesda, MD 20814-1699
800-253-4636
http://www.acc.org

bibliography

Following is a sampling of materials relating to the professional concerns and development of cardiologists.

Alpert, Joseph S. *Cardiology for the Primary Care Physician.* 2nd Edition. New York, NY: McGraw-Hill, 1998.

Drake, William M. et al. *Cardiology Explained.* New York, NY: Chapman & Hall, 1997.

Michaels, Andrew D. and Craig Frances. *Saint-Frances Guide to Cardiology.* Philadelphia, PA: Lippincott Williams & Wilkins, 2001.

Nash, Ira S. *The Cardiologist's Managed Care Manual.* Boston, MA: Total Learning Concepts, 1998.

Oz, Mehmet and Lisa Oz. *Healing from the Heart: A Leading Surgeon Combines Eastern and Western Traditions to Create the Medicine of the Future.* New York, NY: Plume, 1999.

Park, Myung K. *Pediatric Cardiology for Practitioners.* St. Louis, MO: Mosby-Year Book, 1996.

Cardiovascular Technologists

Definition

Cardiovascular technologists support physicians in the diagnosis and treatment of heart and related blood vessel ailments.

Alternative Job Titles

Cardiac monitor technicians
Cardiology technologists
Echocardiography technologists
Electrocardiograph (EKG) technicians and technologists
Holter monitor and stress test technologists
Vascular technologists

High School Subjects

Biology
Health

Personal Skills

Leadership/management
Technical/scientific

Salary Range

$23,000 to $35,000 to $50,000

Educational Requirements

Some postsecondary training

Certification or Licensing

Voluntary

Outlook

About as fast as the average

GOE
10.03.01

O*NET-SOC
29-2031.00

A major vessel in the patient's heart is blocked, potentially endangering the patient's life. He must undergo a special procedure that involves forcing a tube through the artery to unblock the obstruction. A team of health care professionals that specializes in diagnosis and treatment of heart ailments is assembled to carry out the procedure. On hand are a cardiologist (heart doctor), nurse, and various tech support people, including a highly trained cardiology technologist, which is a type of cardiovascular technologist.

After the patient is prepped, this special team begins its work. The physician begins by inserting a tube into the patient's leg. Slowly, carefully, the fine tube is woven up through the arteries and into the patient's heart. As she works, the physician watches a video monitor that shows an internal view of the tube making its way to the heart. The cardiology technologist is standing by, all senses alert, checking the view on the monitor, making adjustments to the camera as needed, entering information about the procedure into a computer, and providing other support. Afterward, she will process the film obtained from the camera for use by the doctor.

This procedure is not without risk; sometimes it doesn't work, and about 2 percent of patients—primarily older patients, weak patients, or those with very bad heart disease—may suffer from an infection, heart attack, or stroke while undergoing it. However, this patient is lucky: The obstruction is successfully cleared, and he is spared the need for open-heart surgery.

lingo to learn

Angioplasty: Procedure involving insertion into the heart of a catheter (tube) with a balloon at one end to widen a blocked blood vessel.

Cardiologist: Physician who specializes in the heart. The prefix "cardio" means "heart."

Cardiology: Of or relating to the heart.

Cardiopulmonary: Of or relating to the heart or lungs.

Cardiovascular: Having to do with the heart ("cardio") and the vessels around it ("vascular").

Catheter: Small tube.

Catheterization: Procedure involving insertion of a catheter (tube).

Congenital: Condition or opportunity for condition that has existed since birth.

Diagnostic: Disease—or condition—identifying (such as "diagnostic tests").

Echocardiography: Procedure for studying the structure and motion of the heart using ultrasound technology.

Electrocardiogram: The paper printout showing the results of the EKG test.

what does a cardiovascular technologist do?

Congenital heart disease. Acquired heart disease. Coronary artery disease. Peripheral vascular disease. Heart disease of all kinds is still the leading killer of men and women in this country, despite increased awareness in recent years of the ill effects on the heart of stress, poor diet, lack of exercise, smoking, and other unhealthy behaviors. As the Baby Boomer generation ages, health professionals are expecting to see the number of coronary patients increase.

Technologists who assist physicians in the diagnosis and treatment of heart disease are known as *cardiovascular technologists*. ("Cardio" means heart, "vascular" refers to the blood vessel/circulatory system.) They include *electrocardiograph (EKG) technologists, Holter monitoring and stress test technologists, cardiology technologists, vascular technologists and echocardiographers* (both ultrasound technologists), *cardiac monitor technicians,* and others. As the services of EKG technologists may be required throughout the hospital, such as in cancer wards or emergency rooms, there may be a separate department for these EKG professionals. Increasingly, however, hospitals are centralizing cardiovascular services under one full cardiovascular "service line," all overseen by the same administrator. According to a spokesperson at the American Academy of Medical Administrators, "This is because cardiology services is the hottest area in health care today. At the present time, it is continuing to emerge, unfold, and expand."

In addition to cardiovascular technologists, the cardiovascular team at a hospital may include radiology (X-ray) technologists, nuclear medicine technologists, nurses, physician assistants, respiratory technologists, and respiratory therapists. For their part, the cardiovascular technologists contribute by performing one or more of a wide range of procedures in cardiovascular medicine, including invasive (enters a body cavity or interrupts normal body functions), noninvasive, peripheral vascular, or echocardiography (ultrasound) procedures. In most facilities they use equipment that's among the most advanced in the medical field; drug therapies also may be used as part of the diagnostic imaging procedures or in addition to them. Technologists' services may be required when the patient's condition is first being explored, before surgery, during surgery (cardiology technologists primarily), and/or during rehabilitation of the patient. Some of the work is performed on an outpatient basis.

Depending on their specific area of skill, some cardiovascular technologists are employed in nonhospital health care facilities. For example, EKG technologists may work for clinics, mobile medical services, or private doctor's offices. Their equipment can go just about anywhere. The same is true for the ultrasound technologists.

Some of the specific duties of cardiovascular technologists are described in the next sections. Exact titles of these technologists often vary between medical facilities because there is no standardized naming system.

Electrocardiograph (EKG) Technologists

Electrocardiograph (EKG) technologists use an electrocardiograph (EKG) machine to detect the electronic impulses that come from a patient's heart during and between a heartbeat. The EKG machine then records these signals on a paper graph called an electrocardiogram. The electronic impulses recorded by the EKG machine can tell the physician about the action of the heart during and between the individual heartbeats. This in turn reveals important information about the condition of the heart, including irregular heartbeats or the presence of blocked arteries, which the physician can use to diagnose heart disease, monitor progress during treatment, or check the patient's condition after recovery.

To use an EKG machine, the technologist attaches electrodes (small, disk-like devices about the size of a silver dollar) to the patient's chest. There are wires attached to the electrodes that lead to the EKG machine. Up to 12 leads or more may be attached. To get a better reading from the electrodes, the technologist may first apply an adhesive gel to the patient's skin that helps to conduct the electrical impulses. The technologist then operates controls on the EKG machine or (more commonly) enters commands for the machine into a computer. The electrodes pick up the electronic signals from the heart and transmit them to the EKG machine. The machine registers and makes a printout of the signals, with a stylus (pen) recording their pattern on a long roll of graph paper.

During the test, the technologist may move the electrodes in order to get readings of electrical activity in different parts of the heart

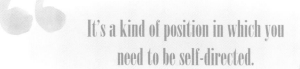

It's a kind of position in which you need to be self-directed.

muscle. Since EKG equipment can be sensitive to electrical impulses from other sources, such as other parts of the patient's body or other equipment in the room, the technologist must watch for false readings.

After the test, the EKG technologist takes the electrocardiogram off the machine, edits it or makes notes on it, and sends it to the physician (usually a cardiologist, or heart specialist). Physicians may use computers to help them use and interpret the electrocardiogram; special software is available to assist them with their diagnosis.

EKG technologists don't have to repair the EKG machine, but they do have to keep an eye on it and know when it's malfunctioning so they can call someone to fix it. They also may keep the machine stocked with paper.

Holter Monitor Technologists and Stress Test Technologists

Holter monitoring and stress testing may be performed by Holter monitor technologists or stress test technologists, respectively, or may be additional duties of some EKG technologists. In Holter monitoring, electrodes are fastened to the patient's chest and a small, portable monitor is strapped to the patient's body, at the waist, for example. The small monitor contains a magnetic tape or cassette that records the heart during activity, as the patient moves, sits, stands, sleeps, etc. The patient is required to wear the Holter monitor for 24 to 48 hours while he or she goes about normal daily activities. When the patient returns to the hospital, the technologist removes the magnetic tape or cassette from the monitor and puts it in a scanner to produce audio (sound) and visual representations of heart activity. (Hearing how the heart sounds during activity can help the physician diagnose a possible heart condition.) The technologist reviews and analyzes the information revealed in the tape. Finally, the tech-

in-depth

History

EKG machines are very high tech, and equipment manufacturers are constantly coming up with new improvements to these vital parts of cardiology care. However, electrocardiography can be traced back 300 years to the work of the Dutch anatomist and physiologist Jan Swammerdam, who in 1678 demonstrated that a frog's leg will contract when stimulated with an electrical current. It was not until 1856, however, that two German anatomists, Albert von Kolliker and Heinrich M. Mueller, showed that when a frog's heart contracted, it produced a small electrical current. In succeeding years, the electrical behavior of beating hearts was extensively studied, but always with the chest open and the heart exposed.

In 1887, Augustus Desire Waller discovered that the electrical current of the human heart could be measured with the chest closed. He was able to do this by placing one electrode on a person's chest and another on the person's back and connecting them to a monitoring device.

The first EKG was invented in 1902 by a Dutch physiologist, Willem Einthoven (1860-1927). Before that, physicians had to rely mainly on their stethoscopes and their own perceptions. With the EKG, they now had a whole new insight into heart problems, especially irregular heartbeats and severe blockages.

The invention of the EKG came on the heels of the discovery of X rays just seven years earlier, in 1895. Together, they made detecting and diagnosing heart ailments much more of a science, with objective data to help in the process, and much less of a hit-and-miss proposition.

Even today, EKGs can't spot everything. With women, for example, the breast tissue may make a reading more difficult, and a positron-emission tomography (PET) scan may be more useful. Also, EKGs still can't pick up subtle heart problems, although researchers are working on improving the EKG's ability to make more accurate and detailed readings of the heart. However, EKGs will continue to be in wide use in routine physicals, presurgical physicals, in diagnosing disease, and in monitoring the effects of surgery or drug therapy.

---

nologist may print out the parts of the tape that show abnormal heart patterns or make a full tape for the physician.

Stress tests record the heart's activity during physical activity. In one type of stress test, the technologist hooks up the patient to the EKG machine, attaching electrodes to the patient's arms, legs, and chest, and first obtains a reading of the patient's resting heart activity and blood pressure. Then, the patient is asked to walk on a treadmill for a certain period of time while the technologist and the physician monitor the heart. The speed of the treadmill is increased so that the technologist and physician can see what happens when the heart is put under higher levels of exertion.

Cardiology Technologists

Cardiology technologists specialize in providing support for cardiac catheterization (tubing) procedures. These procedures are classified as invasive because they require the physician and attending technologists to enter a body cavity or interrupt normal body functions. In one cardiac catheterization procedure, an angiogram, a catheter (tube) is inserted into the heart (usually by way of an artery in the leg) in order to diagnose the condition of the heart blood vessels, such as whether there is a blockage. In another procedure, known as angioplasty, a catheter with a balloon at the end is inserted into an artery to widen it.

Unlike some of the other cardiovascular technologists, cardiology technologists are actually in on surgical procedures. They may assist in surgery by helping to secure the patient to the table, setting up a 35 millimeter video camera or other imaging device under the instructions of the physician (to produce images that assist the physician in guiding the catheter through the cardiovascular system), entering information about the surgical procedure (as it is taking place) into a computer, and providing other support. After the procedure, the tech may process the angiographic film for use by the physician. Cardiology technologists may also assist during open-heart surgery by preparing and monitoring the patient, and may participate in placement or monitoring of pacemakers.

Vascular Technologists and Echocardiographers

These technologists are specialists in noninvasive cardiovascular procedures using ultrasound equipment to obtain and record information about the condition of the heart. Ultrasound equipment is used to send out sound waves to the part of the body being studied; when the sound waves hit the part being studied, they send back an echo to the ultrasound machine. The echoes are read by the machine, which creates an image on a monitor, permitting the technologist to get an instant picture of the part's condition.

Vascular technologists are specialists in the use of ultrasound equipment to study blood flow and circulation problems. Echocardiographers are specialists in the use of ultrasound equipment to evaluate the heart and its structures such as the valves. (Ultrasound also is used in other medical procedures, perhaps most familiarly in capturing images of a fetus to check its condition and learn what sex it is (see the chapter "Diagnostic Medical Sonographers").

Cardiac Monitor Technicians

Cardiac monitor technicians are similar to, and sometimes perform some of the same duties as, EKG technologists. Usually working in the intensive care unit (ICU) or cardio-care unit of the hospital, cardiac monitor technicians keep watch over all the screens that are monitoring the patients to detect any sign that a patient's heart is not beating as it should.

Cardiac monitor technicians begin their shift by reviewing patients' records to familiarize themselves with the patient's normal heart rhythms, the current pattern, and what types

more lingo to learn

Electrocardiograph (EKG) machine: Detects the electronic impulses that come from a patient's heart during or between a heartbeat, which may reveal heart abnormalities, and records that information in the form of a paper graph called an electrocardiogram.

Electrode: Device that conducts electricity.

Holter monitor: Cardiac-function monitoring device.

Invasive: A medical procedure that penetrates into a body cavity or interrupts normal body functions; examples in cardiology include cardiac catheterization procedures.

Noninvasive: A medical procedure that does not penetrate into a body cavity or interrupt body functions; examples in cardiology include ultrasound tests.

Phonocardiograph: Sound recordings of the heart's valves and of the blood passing through them.

Radiographs: X rays.

Vascular: Relating to the blood vessels. Vascular technologists are concerned about the blood vessels around the heart.

of problems have been observed. Throughout the shift, the cardiac monitor technician watches for heart rhythm irregularities that need prompt medical attention. Should there be any, he or she notifies a nurse or doctor immediately so that appropriate care can be given.

In addition to these positions, there may be other cardiovascular technologists, depending on the specific health care facility. For example, a *cardiopulmonary technologist* specializes in procedures for diagnosing problems with the heart and lungs. He or she may conduct electrocardiograph, phonocardiograph (sound recordings of the heart's valves and of the blood passing through them), echocardiograph, stress testing, and respiratory test procedures.

Cardiopulmonary technologists also may be in on cardiac catheterization procedures, measuring and recording information about the patient's cardiovascular and pulmonary system during the procedure and alerting the cardiac catheterization team of any problems.

Nuclear medicine technologists, who use radioactive isotopes in diagnosis, treatment, or studies, may be in on diagnosis or treatment of cardiology problems. *Radiology, respiratory,* and *exercise technicians* and *therapists* also may assist in patient diagnosis, treatment, and/or rehabilitation.

what is it like to be a cardiovascular technologist?

Ted Christman has been working as a technologist for 15 years. As lead tech at a hospital in Fort Collins, Colorado, Ted did echocardiograms and vascular work. "Taking care of patients was number one in doing the ordered tests for the physicians," he says. He performed echocardiograms on a variety of patients, from children to adults. This involved using ultrasound instruments to record vascular information such as heart rate and blood pressure. The equipment transmits sound waves and records the resulting echos on a computer screen. Ted also performed stress tests, which involved documenting a patient's vascular information while the patient was resting, then again while the patient was walking on a treadmill, in order to see the effect that the activity had on the body. Pharmaco-

logical stress tests involved injecting a chemical to increase the heart load.

"The echocardiographic technologist, or echo-tech, is the first filter," he says. "You go in and assess the patient, then perform the echo, and as you're doing the echocardiogram, you have to be able to look at it to determine what further parts of the echo need to be done. In other words, if a patient has a bad valve, then you need to know you have to do more Doppler, per se. You need to explore all the aspects you can about that valve."

When with a patient, Ted relied a great deal on his clinical knowledge. "You have to know when you're seeing something that's bad," he says. "If you go in there and the patient is at threat because of their disease state, then you have to be smart enough to tell somebody, 'You need to get in here and look at this right now.' That happens more often than you'd like to think. So the echo-tech is really the eyes and ears of the cardiologist at the first level." Ted says it is important for the echo-tech and the cardiologist to work as a team. The echo-tech does the study, then creates a preliminary report for the cardiologist. The tech then works alongside the cardiologist in interpreting the patient's situation to assure that everything is seen and done.

"The smart cardiologists respect their echo-techs because they help them quite a bit," Ted says. "A good tech can make a good doctor better. When I made a good call, when I saw something that was serious on a patient and let people know about it, I was rewarded with respect. It's a very responsible position."

In a hospital setting, the hours can be long and may also involve mobile service, requiring the tech to move from location to location. Ted adds that, for all the job's rewards, the work could also be frustrating because he was unable to see the patient's case all the way through. "I didn't get to sign off on reports," he says. "I wasn't the doctor."

Currently, Ted is using his experience as a technologist for a company called Agilent Technologies. Ted explains that, for a tech, industry work is often a natural next step in career advancement. "I'm implementing systems that read echocardiograms," he says. "A lot of techs do go into industry as people who know everything there is to know about a particular ultrasound machine. They're able to demonstrate all the features, plus train customers, techs, in the utilization of that instrument." This computer system works with the echo machine. "The images on the echo machine are recorded digitally," Ted explains,

---

To be a cardiovascular technologist, you should

- Have mechanical/technological aptitude and feel comfortable using computers
- Be able to empathize with others and project a calm and reassuring manner
- Have analytical and problem-solving skills; be able to measure, calculate, reason, evaluate, and synthesize information; and demonstrate good judgment
- Be detail-oriented
- Be flexible and adapt well to change
- Be able to work under pressure, if necessary

"and we download this into the system, and the system is able to read the images offline and actually create the tech's report and do the dictation without the tech ever having to pick up the phone. It's a digital echo lab."

Cardiovascular technologists usually work five-day, 40-hour weeks, but some may be on 24-hour emergency call, and almost all work occasional evenings or weekends. Cardiology departments may be closed or run only a skeleton crew on the weekends. Technologists whose tests usually are scheduled in advance—such as stress tests or Holter monitoring—usually don't face emergency work loads and the need for overtime. Some of the other types of cardiovascular technologists, such as the catheterization professionals, may work longer hours and evenings, and also be on call for emergencies.

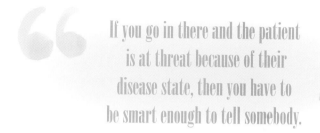

If you go in there and the patient is at threat because of their disease state, then you have to be smart enough to tell somebody.

have I got what it takes to be a cardiovascular technologist?

"It's a kind of position in which you need to be self-directed," Ted says. "There's a lot of work to be done during the day. Labs are not very often managed at the level where someone directs you. You pick up your own work, you pace yourself, you do the work that's scheduled."

Cardiovascular technologists need a combination of mechanical/technological, analytical, and people skills. They should be able to follow instructions and communicate what they know to others. Cardiovascular technologists should be detail oriented; test results are very important to accurate diagnoses. The ability to work under pressure, including during medical emergencies, also is helpful for some of these positions.

Mechanical/technological aptitude is helpful because the technologists in many of these positions use sophisticated diagnostic imaging equipment. Almost all of this equipment is computerized, so it helps to feel comfortable with the computer. Technologists also may have to calibrate or run tests on their equipment to make sure it is operating correctly.

All of the technologists need analytical skills. They have to be able to measure, calculate, reason, evaluate, and synthesize information. Problem-solving ability, flexibility, and good judgment are crucial. Technologists must be able to handle "out-of-the-ordinary" patients or problems (those that don't fit the "textbook case" mold) and use alternative methods when the regular ones won't work.

The ability to think spatially—that is, comprehend two-dimensional or three-dimensional relationships, for example, or visualize the relationships between the imaging equipment and the part of the body being studied—also is very useful for the imaging technologists.

At the same time, human skills—the ability to empathize with patients, calming their fears, explaining the procedure, and answering any questions—also are important for the technologist. Patience and a calm, reassuring, confident manner are helpful.

Finally, cardiovascular technologists should be able to adapt well to change. Every day brings different patients with different specific problems. Employers may tinker with positions or departments as they strive to find a good balance between services and cost-efficiency. Constant medical advances mean that the technologist has to be flexible and keep up with changes in equipment and procedures.

how do I become a cardiovascular technologist?

After completing a degree and working in a variety of jobs, Ted decided to take technical courses at a community college. "I thought I would go into medicine in some way or another," he says. "Maybe work as an OR tech, or something." A counselor at the college introduced him to echocardiography and to the many jobs available at the time.

"A person who has an interest in math, physics, medicine, and diagnoses," Ted says, "would do well in the job."

education

In the past, EKG operators may have simply been trained on the job by an EKG supervisor. This still may be true for some EKG technician positions. However, increasingly, EKG technologists get postsecondary education before they are hired. Holter monitoring and stress testing may be part of the student's EKG training, or they may be learned through additional training. Ultrasound and cardiology technologists tend to have the most postsecondary schooling (up to a four-year bachelor's degree), and to have the most extensive education and experience requirements for credentialing purposes.

People can get into these positions without having had previous health care experience. However, it certainly doesn't hurt to have had some previous exposure to the business or even training in related areas. People with academic training or professional experience in nursing, radiology science, or respiratory science, for example, may be able to make the move into cardiology technology, if they wish.

High School

At a minimum, cardiovascular technologists need a high school diploma or equivalent to enter the field. Although no specific high school classes will directly prepare you to be a technologist, learning problem-solving skills and getting a good grounding in basic high school subjects are important to all technologist positions.

During high school, take English, health, biology, and typing (data entry). Also consider

When does a physician order an echocardiogram?

- In the event of a heart attack
- When there is abnormality in the rhythm or the pumping action of the heart
- When the patient shows symptoms such as shortness of breath or swelling of extremities
- When the physician suspects that the heart may be enlarged
- When there is a suspected infection or leaking of the heart valve

courses in the social sciences to help you understand patients' social and psychological needs.

Postsecondary Training

As a rule of thumb, the medical profession values postsecondary schooling that gives real hands-on experience with patients, in addition to classroom training. At many schools that train cardiovascular technologists, you will be able to work with patients in a variety of health care settings and train on more than one brand of equipment. The Commission on Accreditation of Allied Health Education Programs (CAAHEP) provides a listing of accredited cardiovascular technology programs.

EKG. With some employers, EKG technicians are still simply trained on the job by a physician or EKG department manager. Length of time for this training varies, depending on the employer and the trainee's previous experience, if any; it is usually at least one month long and may be up to six months. The trainee learns how to operate the EKG machine and produce and edit the electrocardiogram, along with related tasks.

EKG/Holter/stress. Some vocational, technical, and junior colleges have one- or two-year training programs in EKG, Holter monitoring, or stress testing; otherwise, EKG technologists may obtain training in Holter and stress procedures after they've already started working, either on the job or through an additional six months or more of education. The formal academic programs give you more preparation in the subject than available with most on-the-job training and allow you to earn a certificate (one-year programs) or associate's degree (two-year programs). The American Medical Association's *Allied Health Directory* has listings of accredited EKG programs.

Cardiology technologists. These technologists tend to have the most stringent education requirements of all; for example, a four-year bachelor of science degree or two-year associate's degree or certificate of completion from a hospital, trade, or technical cardiovascular program for training of varying length. A two-year program at a junior or community college might include one year of core classes (math, science, etc.) and one year of specialized classes in cardiology procedures.

Ultrasound (vascular and echocardiography). These technologists usually need a high school diploma or equivalent plus one, two, or four years of postsecondary schooling in a trade school, technical school, or community college. Vascular technologists also may be trained on the job. Again, a list of accredited programs can be found in the American Medical Association's *Allied Health Directory.* Also, a directory of training opportunities in sonography is available from the Society of Diagnostic Medical Sonographers (SDMS).

Cardiac monitor. These technicians need a high school diploma or equivalent, plus education similar to that of the EKG technician.

Cardiology is a cutting-edge area of medicine, with constant advancements, and medical equipment relating to the heart is always being updated. Therefore, keeping up with new developments is vital. Technologists who add to their qualifications through continuing education also tend to earn more money and have more opportunities. The major professional societies encourage and provide the opportunities for professionals to continue their education (see "How Do I Learn More?").

certification or licensing

Right now, certification or licensing for cardiovascular technologists is voluntary, but the move to state licensing is in the air. Many credentialing bodies for cardiovascular and pulmonary positions exist, including American Registry of Diagnostic Medical Sonographers (ARDMS), Cardiovascular Credentialing International (CCI), and others, and there are more than a dozen possible credentials for cardiovascular technologists. For example, sonographers can take an exam from the ARDMS to receive credentialing in sonography. Their credentials may be registered diagnostic medical sonographer, registered diagnostic cardiac sonographer, or registered vascular technologist. Especially at the level of cardiology technologist or ultrasound technologist, the credentialing requirements may include test-taking plus formal academic and on-the-job experience requirements. Professional experience or academic training in a related field—such as nursing, radiology science, respiratory science—may be acceptable as part of these formal academic/professional requirements. As with continuing education, certification is a sign of interest and dedication to the field and is generally looked upon more favorably by potential employers.

Related Jobs

The U.S. Department of Labor classifies EKG technologists and other cardiovascular technologists under the headings *Child and Adult Care: Data Collection* (GOE) and *Healthcare Practitioners and Technical* (O*NET-SOC).

Specific related jobs include:
Biochemistry technologists
Cardiopulmonary technologists
CT scan technologists
Dialysis technologists
Electroencephalographic (EEG) technologists
Electromyographic (EMG) technologists
Magnetic resonance imaging (MRI) technologists
Nuclear medicine technologists
Ophthalmic technologists
Perfusionists
Pulmonary function technicians
Radiation-therapy technologists
Radiologic (X-ray) technologists

internships and volunteerships

An internship as an EKG assistant is possible. Check local hospitals to learn of opportunities. Some employers prefer to hire a person who has already worked in the health care field, such as a nurse's aid. If you are interested in health care positions, consider being a volunteer at a hospital, which will give you exposure to patient-care activities. Or you might visit a hospital, clinic, or doctor's office where EKG or other cardiovascular procedures are used and ask to talk to a cardiovascular technologist.

who will hire me?

EKG technologists work in large and small hospitals, clinics, health maintenance organizations (HMOs), cardiac rehabilitation centers, cardiologists' or other physicians' offices, long-term care facilities, and nursing homes. Other types of cardiovascular technologists may work primarily in either community hospitals or teaching hospitals, in industry, for mobile medical service clinics, in academia, or in government hospitals (VA, armed forces, public health services, etc.). Another possibility is finding employment with a manufacturer of EKG or other equipment.

EKG technicians, by far, outnumber the other specialists. There are fewer ultrasound technologists at this time, for example, because of the expertise required and the lower frequency of these tests. "Even in a large-size hospital where there may be a large radiology department with 15 rooms and a 20- to 30-person staff, the ultrasound department may have a staff of six and maybe two rooms," notes Dennis King, chairman of the diagnostic medical imaging program at Wilbur Wright College, Chicago. "However, sonography is a growing profession nationally, even if some areas are 'soft' for new hires, or oversaturated, from time to time."

Check the want ads (under "health care professionals" and related sections), contact national associations, and check with hospitals or other health care facilities in your area to learn of opportunities.

where can I go from here?

Rather than move into upper management, Ted chose to go into industry work. "I'm working with Agilent," he says, "which is providing the digital solution, and my clinical background makes me unique within the computer group." He hopes to expand his computer skills and go into consulting. As a consultant, Ted would go into a lab and evaluate workflow and the problems that could be solved by the technology company.

Opportunities for advancement are best for EKG technologists who learn to do or assist with more complex procedures, such as Holter monitoring, stress testing, echocardiography, and cardiac catheterization. With proper training and experience, they may become cardiology technologists or cardiopulmonary technologists, another type of heart-related technology specialist. Besides specialist positions, opportunities may be found in supervisory or teaching positions. At some hospitals there may be a *chief cardiopulmonary technologist,* for example, who coordinates the activities of technologists who perform diagnostic testing and treatment of patients with heart, lung, and blood vessel disorders. The *chief*

radiologic technologist coordinates activities of the radiology or diagnostic imaging department in the hospital or other medical facility.

Besides those mentioned, areas of special experience for cardiovascular technologists may include infant pulmonary function testing, blood gas studies, sleep disorder studies, pacemaker procedures, and other related procedures. Nuclear medicine, which uses radioactive isotopes in diagnosis, treatment, or studies, also is applied to cardiology problems.

what are the salary ranges?

According to the *Occupational Outlook Handbook,* the median annual salary for cardiovascular technologists and technicians was $35,770 in 1998. The lowest 10 percent earned less than $23,010 annually, and the highest 10 percent earned more than $49,780. The Society of Diagnostic Medical Sonographers (SDMS) reports that the starting salary for sonographers is $15 to $18 an hour. An SDMS survey released in 2000 reported that the medial annual income for sonographers is between $40,000 and $50,000. According to the report, 75 percent of the sonographers responding to the survey earned between $30,000 and $65,000 annually.

Cardiovascular technologist positions are typically salaried, but overtime pay (or extra time off in lieu of overtime) may be available. Technologists in large hospitals may work one of three shifts and may receive a higher rate of pay for taking second- or third-shift work.

Hospital benefits generally are good, including health and hospitalization insurance, paid vacations, sick leave, and possibly educational assistance and pension benefits.

what is the job outlook?

The job outlook for cardiovascular technologists is a mixed bag. Sources say the employment of EKG technologists is on the decline because the equipment and procedures have grown increasingly efficient and fewer technologists are required to do the work. Also, the equipment is increasingly easy to use, so hospitals can train other personnel, such as registered nurses or respiratory therapists, to do the job. EKG technologists who have experience with Holter monitoring or stress testing should fare better, though. Their multiple skills make them more attractive to employers trying to improve efficiency. According to the *Occupational Outlook Handbook,* employment of cardiovascular technicians is expected to grow as fast as the average for all occupations.

Ultrasound technologists should see slow but steady growth into the next century. Some areas of the country currently have few openings for new hires, partly because of low turnover in the job, but in general this is a growing specialty. Self-employment provides lucrative opportunities for experienced sonographers. The 2000 SDMS survey found that self-employed sonographers have the highest incomes, with 28.6 percent of them earning over $80,000 a year.

Cardiology technologists should fare the best of all, as more hospitals create cardiac catheterization units and as new procedures and drug treatments are developed. Some of the procedures in which cardiology technologists assist—notably, angioplasties—are still the subject of some controversy and ongoing research. This shouldn't hurt cardiology technologists' opportunities for employment, but you should be aware that procedures are constantly changing and that what you study in school now may need updating in the near future. Because of the demand for skilled technologists, educational opportunities are expected to become more plentiful.

how do I learn more?

professional organizations

To learn about certification and accredited programs:
American Registry of Diagnostic Medical Sonographers
600 Jefferson Plaza, Suite 360
Rockville, MD 20852-1150
800-541-9754
http://www.ardms.org

Advancement Possibilities

Chief cardiopulmonary technologists coordinate the activities of technologists who perform diagnostic testing and treatment of patients with heart, lung, and blood vessel disorders.

Chief radiologic technologists coordinate activities of the radiology or diagnostic imaging department in the hospital or other medical facility.

Medical technologist teaching supervisors teach one or more phases of medical technology to students of medicine, medical technology, or nursing arts, or to interns; organize and direct medical technology training programs.

Nuclear medicine chief technologists supervise and coordinate activities of nuclear medical technologists engaged in preparing, administering, and measuring radioactive isotopes in diagnosis, treatment, or studies.

For a list of accredited programs:
Commission on Accreditation of Allied Health Education Programs
35 East Wacker Drive, Suite 1970
Chicago, IL 60601-2208
312-553-9355
caahep@caahelp.org
http://www.caahep.org

For career and conference information and job listings, contact:
Society of Vascular Technology
4601 President's Drive, Suite 260
Lanham, MD 20706
301-459-7550
info@svtnet.org
http://www.svtnet.org

For information on credentials, contact:
Cardiovascular Credentialing International
4456 Corporation Lane, Suite 120
Virginia Beach, VA 23462
800-326-0268
http://www.cci-online.org

cardiovascular technologists

For a career brochure:
Society of Diagnostic Medical Sonography
12770 Coit Road, Suite 708
Dallas, TX 75251
972-239-7367
http://www.sdms.org

bibliography

Following is a sampling of materials relating to the professional concerns and development of cardiovascular technologists.

Careers in Focus: Medical Technicians. 2nd Edition. Chicago, IL: Ferguson Publishing Company, 2001.

Snook, Donald I., and Lee D'Orazio. *Opportunities in Health and Medical Careers.* Lincolnwood, IL: VGM Career Horizons, 1997.

Child Life Specialists

Definition

Child life specialists work in health care settings to help children, adolescents, and their families through illness or injury. They are members of the health care team in hospitals and ambulatory care facilities.

High School Subjects

Health
Psychology
Sociology

Personal Skills

Communication/ideas
Helping/teaching

Salary Range

$19,000 to $35,000 to $49,000+

Educational Requirements

Bachelor's degree

Certification or Licensing

Voluntary

Outlook

Faster than the average

GOE
10.01.02
O*NET-SOC
21-1021.00

"**Create a picture** which expresses a feeling. It can be a feeling you're having now, or a feeling you've had before, a good feeling or a bad feeling, it's up to you." Melissa Deifer, a child life specialist at an Atlanta children's hospital, offers these instructions as well as paper and crayons to a group of kids gathered in a playroom.

A few of the children immediately begin drawing; a few others sit back and think a moment. Another has to be coaxed from his stillness, and Melissa helps him choose colors. But soon, they're all hunched over their paper, some scribbling hurriedly, others slowly and carefully drawing lines and circles. When they've all finished, Melissa asks them to talk about their drawings.

"Why is this blue?" she asks one child. She says to another, "This is an interesting design. What does it mean?" The children describe the choices they've made, the feelings they represent, and when they last had these feelings. Melissa listens carefully to them, learning much about their emotions and attitudes concerning their illnesses and hospitalization.

what does a child life specialist do?

If, as a kid, you ever spent any time in a hospital, you know it's not all Jell-O and puppet shows. For some kids, a night in the hospital is their first night away from home. They may have to go through a series of tests, or perhaps even have an operation. Some kids have to be prepared for a long stay, or a long series of stays. *Child life specialists* explain medical procedures to help children and their parents relax. They may do this through crayons and toys or through introducing them to other children in the hospital.

Whether working in a hospital that provides care for both adults and children or in a hospital committed primarily to child care, the child life specialist is an important member of the health care team. As more and more health care professionals come to understand the connection between mind and body, more child life specialists are called upon to ease a child's hospital stay. A positive experience can contribute to a child's attitudes toward health care throughout his or her life.

To be effective, child life specialists must be prepared to work with a variety of age groups. Most children's hospitals care for infants, toddlers, preadolescents, and teenagers. Specialists don't just work with the hospitalized kids; they also work with the child's parents and siblings. Parents sometimes need counseling in how to deal with their child's illness, as well as advice on how best to relate to the child.

A good child life program is composed of people with diverse backgrounds. People with experience in nursing, psychology, child development, and social work all bring unique skills that can benefit a program. Someone with training in psychology or social work can offer counseling skills to help children and their families through emotional situations. Someone with a background in special education understands how to work with children in instructional groups. The main thing child life specialists have in common is an interest in the well-being of children.

Sometimes very young children don't understand why they can't stay at home or why they're being poked and prodded with needles and medical instruments. A child life specialist must use tact and creativity to explain medical procedures, such as using a doll to demonstrate the nature of a test or operation.

Adolescent children may withdraw from their families, choosing to endure the experience alone. In this case, the child life specialist counsels both the patient and family, helping them to understand the emotional impact of the hospitalization.

From the first hour that a child is admitted into a hospital, a child life specialist is dedicated to making the stay as pleasant as possible. Child life specialists start their day by reviewing the chart of admittances and discharges, then set up a schedule of priorities. When working with a newly admitted child, child life specialists make an assessment to determine how to best help the young patient. This usually means setting up open lines of communication with parents and getting them involved in the planning stage. When the parents feel comfortable, they can help make their child feel comfortable. Child life specialists may need to make special visiting arrangements so that parents can have unrestricted visitation and even stay overnight if they choose.

Specialists may initiate individual or group play activities that encourage free expression so that the child can speak openly

lingo to learn

Art therapy: Helping a child express feelings through painting, drawing, and sculpting.

Bibliotherapy: Introducing a child to books and stories that promote discussion of the child's own feelings.

Play behavior: The behavior of a child during play activity that gives insight into a his or her fears and concerns.

Play therapy: Enjoyable activities that allow children to express themselves openly and comfortably.

Therapeutic recreation: Teaching language, motor, and socialization skills though recreational activities.

of fears and concerns. If the child is hospitalized during a holiday or birthday, child life specialists may arrange a party. In some situations, such as emergencies or cases of terminal illness, they may need to work more intensely with the child and family, helping them to prepare for a difficult illness or the possibility of death.

In addition to working directly with children and families, a child life specialist also maintains toys and games, trains nursing and medical students, writes reports and evaluations, and attends meetings and conferences. Every duty is performed with empathy, compassion, and support, always keeping the child's best interest in mind.

what is it like to be a child life specialist?

Melissa Deifer works as a child life specialist at the AFLAC Cancer Center at Egleston Children's Hospital in Atlanta, Georgia. She rarely has a typical day. "You have to remain flexible," she says. "Things are always changing."

When she arrives for work, she looks over the list of patients and the reports from the charge nurse. Based on this information and the medical procedures planned, she determines which patients will require more of her time and plans her day accordingly.

Every morning, group play time for the children is organized and led by volunteers, but Melissa often likes to participate. She involves children in exercises that encourage them to express their feelings. For example, she may invite the kids to finish the sentence, "Things that I treasure are. . . ." Group play is a good opportunity for Melissa to determine a child's fears and misconceptions.

"You have to listen to them," she says. "A child may say, 'I'm sick because I'm bad,' or they may think nurses will be stabbing them with needles." Through careful observation, Melissa can learn what's bothering the child and offer support and information.

She also works one-on-one with the children. This often involves preparing a child for a medical procedure. The older the child, the more concrete information he or she needs. A child who is familiar with the procedure already has particular coping skills. Melissa will talk to the child and find out how he or she

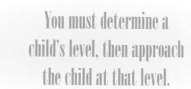

You must determine a child's level, then approach the child at that level.

feels about the procedure and what can make it easier for them to handle. "You have to be very careful with younger kids," Melissa warns. "You can't just tell them that they are going to be asleep while doctors perform the needed surgery; you might not get them into the operating room."

In addition to working with hospitalized children, Melissa initiates community outreach projects. This sometimes involves visiting a school and educating a patient's classmates about the child's illness.

Child life departments also require administrators. Sharon McLeod works as an administrator of a children's hospital in Cincinnati, Ohio. Though her duties don't involve her directly with the children, she is closely involved with the staff and volunteers of the child life program. "Direct care has more tangible rewards," she says, "but can also have a lot of pain along with it, particularly if a child is doing poorly." She points out that everyone in a child life program must be conscious of maintaining professional boundaries and must not become too personally involved in a child's crisis. These lessons, which Sharon learned after several years of experience in various children's hospitals, come in handy when managing staff and giving presentations to medical students and volunteers.

Sharon's daily routine includes many different administrative tasks. In addition to attending management meetings, she meets with individuals about donations, presentations, and parties. She screens entertainers and other visitors to make sure they are appropriate for the children. She is also in charge of the budget, supply needs, and the hiring and supervising of staff. To keep her department running smoothly, Sharon makes a point to meet regularly with staff members to address individual thoughts and concerns.

have I got what it takes to be a child life specialist?

As with most caregivers, empathy and compassion are important personal qualities for child life specialists. They must have genuine interest in the well-being of every patient and family and treat every child as a unique individual. It's important for a child life specialist to understand the psychology and concerns of children and adolescents.

Sharon McLeod emphasizes the importance of flexibility. "No day is ever the same as the one before," she says. "You have to be ready to roll with the punches." Specialists must plan each day according to the admissions and procedures schedule. "Children are hospitalized 365 days a year," Sharon says, "so child life provides services 365 days a year."

Also, because they often work in hospitals, child life specialists may have to deal with emergency or traumatic situations. Child life specialists may be required to explain a new, unanticipated procedure to a child and to prepare him or her emotionally in a short amount of time. Sometimes the specialist must also deal with the unexpected death of a patient, a tragedy that not only affects the family but the entire health care unit as well.

Sharon likes working with colleagues because they are caring individuals. "The profession attracts that type," she says, "as does the pediatric setting." Sharon also likes feeling that she can make a difference in the lives of children and families by helping them through a crisis. And though, for Sharon, the pros outweigh the cons, she does not thrive on the job's high degree of stress.

There are over 30 colleges and universities in the United States that offer degrees or curriculums in child life.

"It's especially stressful in intensive care," she says, "where grief and loss are more common. It's a challenge to keep a balance and not burn out." She does point out that administrators experience less burnout than the front-line clinical staff.

Melissa Deifer emphasizes that a child life specialist must avoid approaching the child as if he or she were an adult. "You must determine a child's level," she says, "then approach the child at that level." Melissa finds it rewarding to see a child develop good coping skills. "You're helping build a foundation for the child's future," she says. She also appreciates the special relationships that she develops with children and their families. "Being with people during a stressful time affects a relationship," she says. Working with young children during times of adversity allows Melissa the opportunity to see patients mature before her very eyes. Often she has a surprising impact on their lives. A former patient of hers recently told her he was going to major in adolescent therapy in college. "I think that's great," she says. "And he'll be great at it."

how do I become a child life specialist?

As an undergraduate, Melissa studied physical therapy, but she was interested in something that incorporated the physical with the psychological. She spent a summer in a local hospital, spent some time working in England, then came back to intern at Johns Hopkins, which included a combination of clinical study and lectures.

Sharon received her undergraduate degree in early childhood education from the University of North Carolina at Chapel Hill. After student teaching she decided she did not want to be in a classroom year-round. She then pursued a master's degree in therapeutic recreation, thinking she would like to work with adults and children with disabilities. A field program in pediatric play therapy at Duke University changed her mind. "It was my first experience working with hospitalized children," she said, "and it clicked."

education

High School

To develop a basic understanding of human behavior, take courses such as psychology, sociology, and child development. Many high schools offer home economic courses that include lessons in parenting, relationships, and family study. In addition to courses about the human mind and lifestyles, biology, health, anatomy, and other science courses can be valuable. You may also want to develop skills in art and physical education since child life specialists use a variety of different therapies, including play, art, and recreation in their work.

High school students should also look for part-time work that involves child care. Day care centers, after-school programs, and children's hospitals sometimes employ high school students or offer volunteer opportunities.

Postsecondary Training

A bachelor's degree is required for work as a child life specialist. A variety of different academic programs, including social work, psychology, and special education, can prepare you for a child life internship. The Child Life Council (CLC), a professional organization for child life specialists, advises students to look for a program that has a sufficient faculty, a variety of field opportunities, and positive student evaluations.

"Diversify your skills and talents as much as possible," Sharon encourages students, "so that you're not just focused on hospitals. You can play a role in many different arenas. You must think beyond the hospital walls to clinics, hospices, and camps. Be thinking about ways to look at prevention, to promote health and wellness. Look at degrees that will give several options." For example, she recommends students focus on therapeutic recreation or special education before taking an internship in a child life program. "It's good to have richness of experience in a child life program," she says.

Sharon believes the training process has improved over the years. When she first began studying child life in the mid-1970s, not much had been written on the subject. "There was very little to pick up in textbooks or journal articles," Sharon says. "Now there are more resources. Universities now offer courses in hospitalization, in stress and [its] effects on children and families. Back then, I had to do independent studies in those areas."

Advancement Possibilities

Child life administrators or **directors** manage child life programs for hospitals and clinics. An advanced degree is usually required.

Child psychologists study the psychosocial aspects of childhood and counsel children in a variety of ways. An advanced degree is required.

Pediatricians are doctors who specialize in the treatment of children. A medical degree and residency are required.

certification or licensing

Certification, offered through the Child Life Council, is voluntary for specialists. However, according to CLC staff member Joana Mota, more hospitals are requiring their child life specialists to become certified. In order to be eligible for the certification examination, applicants must have a bachelor's degree, have taken 10 courses in child life, child development, family studies, or other related areas, and have accumulated 450 hours of clinical child life work. To remain certified, individuals must pass the certification exam at least once every 10 years.

internships and volunteerships

In the mid-1970s, Sharon did an internship at an Easter Seal Camp, which, she says, "would still be an appropriate setting for a child life internship."

Melissa also supports working in an internship. "If it's for you," she says, "you'll know it's for you."

To pursue an internship, you should narrow your search to a geographic area and locate nearby pediatric facilities. The Child Life Council encourages you to consider all patient settings, including chronic, acute, rehabilitative, inpatient, and outpatient. The best internships can be found at institutions that have well-established services for family-centered care, good child life facilities, resource libraries, and clear goals and objectives. Contact the CLC (see How Do I Learn More?) for a checklist to help you determine the quality of an internship site.

who will hire me?

After Sharon finished her internship, she consulted the Child Life Council's Standards for Academic and Clinical Preparations Programs in Child Life to consider her options before sending out resumes. Ultimately, it was a classified ad in the newspaper that directed her to apply for a job in Rockford, Illinois. The job was in a community hospital where she worked in a 24-bed pediatric unit for eight years. There she gained both clinical and administrative experience and, in time, supervisory experience.

Her extensive work skills developed on the job proved valuable to other institutions. Sharon was hired to develop a child life department in a hospital in Nashville, Tennessee. Her ultimate goal, however, was to work in a freestanding children's hospital. After nine years in Nashville, she moved to Cincinnati, Ohio, to work for a hospital that cares only for children and adolescents. "It's a big leap," Sharon says. "The administration, physicians, nurses, everyone is focused on children and families."

Today there are child life programs in more than 380 hospitals in the United States and Canada, according to figures provided by CLC. Most programs are in children's hospitals and university-affiliated academic medical centers.

You can approach finding a job in a child life program in the same way that you approach finding an internship. Once you have determined where you would like to live, examine the pediatric settings available. For an internship, you want to choose a well-established program; for a job, you may be interested in helping to develop a less-established child life program. A good resource for job openings is the CLC's Job Bank. To receive this semimonthly listing of advertised child life jobs, you must first become a member of the CLC.

where can I go from here?

Melissa wants to continue to work in child life, but she would like to work exclusively one-on-one with children in a private practice. She's aware of a few specialists who practice privately. She plans on pursuing grants and other resources in order to make this transition.

Because Sharon has been a child life specialist since the 1970s, she has worked her way up to a management position. "I'm open to other possibilities," she says, "but I have no plans to do anything majorly different." One opportunity she has considered is teaching at the University of Cincinnati.

A good guide towards career advancement is participating in professional organizations. "At annual professional conferences," Sharon says, "you can network, share experiences, and absorb information. Also, by subscribing to a professional journal, you can keep up to date on continuing education opportunities.

"Continuing education is tremendously important to the job," Sharon says. "There is so much changing in health care that it's important to stay aware of the climate. It's important to be politically aware, as well as be aware of the latest advancements and procedures." Sharon also emphasizes that there's always room to grow and learn. "I get concerned when people see themselves as a finished product. Specialists should be open to growth and change."

To be a successful child life specialist, you should

- Enjoy working with children
- Be naturally compassionate
- Be able to communicate effectively with children as well as adults
- Enjoy teaching
- Be good at organizing activities
- Be emotionally stable when facing tragic situations

what are the salary ranges?

Salary ranges vary widely for child life specialists. Some of the factors that influence earning potential are location, work experience, degrees or credentials obtained, and size of the program.

According to 1997 U.S. Department of Labor data, the median annual salary for medical social workers employed by hospitals was $31,500. Those working in medical offices or clinics made on average $33,700. The lowest paid 10 percent of all social workers earned less than $19,250 a year; the highest paid 10 percent earned over $49,080.

According to an independent study by the Department of Human Development and Family Studies at the University of Alabama, the average salary of child life specialists was $35,593 in 2000. Certified professionals earned an average annual salary of $36,256, about $5,510 more than those who did not have the credential. The survey also found that child life specialists who had earned a master's degree earned an average of $38,904 a year, approximately $6,000 more than those with a bachelor's degree.

Because earnings can vary greatly simply by location, a general rule of thumb, according to the Children's Hospital Medical Center in Cincinnati, Ohio, is that the salary range for child life specialists is often comparable to that of teachers in the area.

Sharon notes that one of the potential downsides of working as a child life specialist is the comparatively low salary. "But people don't take helping positions to get rich," Sharon says. "It's work of the heart."

what is the job outlook?

The U.S. Department of Labor predicts the demand for all social workers will increase much faster than the average for all occupations in the next decade. More hospitals are recognizing the need for individualized care for children and adolescents. In addition, job openings will become available as workers retire or move into other professions.

Many child life specialists are also exploring alternative job opportunities, considering all the options available for special projects and programs. "You have to be creative," Melissa says about seeking out grants and

> "Continuing education is tremendously important to the job. There is so much changing in health care that it's important to stay aware of the climate."

other resources to fulfill her dream of working in a private practice. "You have to sell your idea, you have to really advocate."

how do I learn more?

professional organizations

The following organization provides information on the field of child life, including career and educational information and certification requirements.
Child Life Council
11820 Parklawn Drive, Suite 202
Rockville, MD 20852-2529
clcstaff@childlife.org
http://www.childlife.org

For general information on social work careers, contact:
National Association of Social Workers
750 First Street, NE, Suite 700
Washington, DC 20002-4241
800-638-8799
info@naswdc.org
http://www.naswdc.org

bibliography

Following is a sampling of materials relating to the professional concerns and development of child life specialists.

Eberts, Marjorie and Margaret Gisler. *Careers in Child Care.* 2nd Edition. Lincolnwood, IL: VGM Career Horizons, 2000.

Hobday, Angela M. and Kate Ollier. *Creative Therapy with Children & Adolescents*. Atascadero, CA: Impact Publishers, Inc., 1999.

Kaduson, Heidi G. and Charles Schaefer, eds. *Short-Term Play Therapy for Children*. New York, NY: Guilford Press, 2000.

Kaduson, Heidi G. and Charles Schaefer, eds. *101 Favorite Play Therapy Techniques*. Northvale, NJ: Jason Aronson, 1997.

Landreth, Garry L. et al. eds. *Play Therapy Interventions with Children's Problems*. Northvale, NJ: Jason Aronson, 1996.

Lowenstein, Liana. *Creative Interventions for Troubled Children & Youth*. Vancouver, WA: Champion Press, 1999.

McCue, Kathleen and Ron Bonn. *How to Help Children Through a Parent's Serious Illness*. 3rd Edition. New York, NY: St. Martin's Press, 1996.

Peterson, Carol Ann and Norma J. Stumbo. *Therapeutic Recreation Program Design: Principles and Procedures*. 3rd Edition. Needham Heights, MA: Allyn & Bacon, 1999.

Ross, Carol. *Something to Draw On: Activities and Interventions Using an Art Therapy Approach*. London, UK: Jessica Kingsley Publishers, 1997.

Straus, Martha B. *No-Talk Therapy for Children and Adolescents*. New York, NY: W. W. Norton & Company, 1999.

Chiropractors

Definition

Chiropractors use conventional and alternative therapies to diagnose and treat patients whose medical problems may be caused by disturbances of the nervous, muscular, and skeletal systems.

Alternative Job Titles

Chiropractic physicians
Doctors of chiropractic

High School Subjects

Biology
Business
Health

Personal Skills

Helping/teaching
Technical/scientific

Salary Range

$36,000 to $86,000 to $110,000+

Educational Requirements

High school diploma; two-years of pre-chiropractic study; four years of study at accredited chiropractic college.

Certification or Licensing

Required by all states

Outlook

Faster than the average

GOE
02.03.04

O*NET-SOC
29-1011.00

Mangled by surgical failures, the man's spine was unrecognizable in X rays. Dr. Teri Reinke of the National University of Health Sciences Clinic, in Lombard, Illinois, didn't give up. "I remember taking his history and thinking, 'We're going to be lucky if we can do anything for this poor guy.'" Working with her interns, she developed a treatment plan that incorporated many chiropractic techniques to help her patient. These techniques included massage therapy, acupuncture, and dietary advice. Although she could not undo the damage already done to his lower back, she could begin to control the patient's pain. When Teri's chiropractic treatments succeeded, the patient's life turned around. "I mean from head to toe, inside and out, everything in his life was broken and this man is now unbelievably happy. He's working again, his boss can't believe it. It's done wonders for him."

what does a chiropractor do?

Chiropractors use treatments such as spinal manipulation, physiotherapy, acupuncture, and massage to help treat their patients. They do not use drugs or surgery. Instead, an important aim of chiropractic medicine is to encourage and enable the body to heal itself. Instead of treating only a particular injury or medical complaint, chiropractors consider the whole body and its interrelated internal systems.

Chiropractors believe that the relationship between the structure and function of the human body can affect a person's health and well-being. For example, asthma (a function problem with the lungs), can lead to such structural problems as problems with the joints of the ribs and the spine. The ligaments and muscles connected to these joints can in turn become affected, as well. In other words, when a patient has an internal condition that has compromised the function of the body, it will also affect the structure of the body. Conversely, the condition of the structure of the body can also affect the internal functions of the body.

Chiropractors believe that disturbances of the nervous system can impair the health of other systems in the body. As Dr. James Win-terstein, president of The National University of Health Sciences explains, "all of the systems in your body are integrated, you can't take apart, for example, the digestive system and the pulmonary system. They are all integrated and the integrator is the nervous system, so when something goes wrong in the nervous system then those others begin to reflect that abnormality."

Chiropractors call one type of disturbance of the nervous system a subluxation. A subluxation interferes with the normal neurological activity of the body and may affect the function of the body. Subluxations can be created by many different things. For example, prolonged bad posture can create an imbalance in the body and eventually a subluxation will form. Other factors that can directly or indirectly create a subluxation include a bad fall or asymmetric repetitive action. To correct the subluxations a chiropractor performs a treatment called a spinal adjustment.

Spinal adjustment, sometimes referred to as spinal manipulation, is one of the best known of the chiropractic treatments. When chiropractors adjust a patient's spine, they are manipulating the joints to remove the subluxation and return them to normal functioning levels.

Because chiropractors treat the whole person they also instruct their patients on the importance of good nutrition. Proper diet and nutrition can help the body's healing process and prevent the development of certain dysfunctions. By the time patients complete their treatment, they will have been educated in the way to make appropriate food choices and maintain proper diets.

Chiropractors may also use physiotherapy during and after treatment. Physiotherapy can include the use of ultrasound, electrostimulation, exercise, or traction. Once patients complete their treatment, the chiropractor may send them to a physical therapist who will design an exercise program created especially for their needs. Chiropractors may also use supportive devices or acupuncture and massage therapies to help develop the most effective treatment for their patients.

lingo to learn

Acupuncture: For centuries the Chinese have practiced this treatment, which involves inserting needles into the skin at certain points to treat pain or illness.

Physiotherapy: Treatment by physical and mechanical means that use the therapeutic properties of heat, cold, electricity, massage, and ultraviolet radiation.

Postural analysis: A study of a patient's posture and how it can affect overall health.

Spinal adjustment: A chiropractic technique where the doctor uses his or her hands to apply pressure to a spinal joint or group of joints to restore the proper alignment of the spine.

Subluxation: A misalignment of the spine.

what is it like to be a chiropractor?

For Dr. Teri Reinke, no two days of practicing chiropractic medicine are the same. In addition to treating patients she is also responsible for helping to train new interns. Her current class contains 17 students. She began teaching in 1993 when she left private practice to begin work at the National University of Health Sciences.

Most patients who are seen at the clinic have scheduled visits, but that isn't always the case. Because of the clinic's size and reputation, many emergency cases are sent there. There are also many walk-ins who come to the clinic because they need immediate attention. The frantic atmosphere often creates teaching opportunities for Teri, as she explains, "When the patients come in, it's similar to an emergency room around here. I never know who's going to walk in or what I'll have to be dealing with or teaching my students."

New patients take part in a comprehensive interview with the chiropractor. The patient interview is an opportunity for the chiropractor to gain a clear and comprehensive understanding of the patient's current health status and medical history. "We pretty much get an idea of their health status from birth to the present: diseases, surgeries, accidents, all their health care issues," Teri says. It is very important for the chiropractor to know the patient's medical history because that information may shed light on his or her current medical problems.

After taking the medical history, the chiropractor gives the patient a thorough physical exam. The chiropractor may also order neurological and orthopedic examinations and postural or spinal analysis. These examinations can help determine the basis for the patient's medical complaint.

During the interview, Teri will work with the patient to develop a treatment plan. For every patient there is a different treatment plan and each treatment plan contains short- and long-term goals. When these goals have been met, the treatment is considered complete.

For example, if a young, relatively healthy person comes into the clinic complaining of back pain, Teri's long-term goal for that patient would be 100 percent pain relief. Teri measures the patient's pain relief and returning function of the body as the treatment continues until the patient's back pain is gone.

However, chiropractic medicine does not promise complete success for every case. For example, if an elderly woman with an arthritic spine comes into the clinic complaining of back pain, the treatment goals for this patient are different from the treatment goals for the younger patient. Perhaps the back pain has

> When the patients come in, it's similar to an emergency room around here. I never know who's going to walk in or what I'll have to be dealing with.

prevented the patient from working in her garden. The treatment plan would then be completed and considered a success when the patient could comfortably plant flowers and pull weeds again.

Teri has heard the complaint that patients become dependent on their chiropractors and never leave treatment. She believes, however, that this complaint is based on a misunderstanding of the role of chiropractic medicine. Patients do need to return regularly to the chiropractor but this is for checkups, just as patients return regularly to see their dentists. However, patients returning for regular checkups are not the same as patients who see their chiropractor weekly while they are in treatment. As she explains, "What we do is maintain a certain aspect of a patient's health, but it doesn't mean they come in and see us every week for a treatment."

Sometimes patients do not respond to chiropractic therapies. In those cases, the chiropractor may have to refer the patient to medical doctors, such as neurosurgeons or orthopedic surgeons, who may be able to help them. However, when treatments are effective, it can be very rewarding for the chiropractor. As Teri describes, "A patient comes in with, literally, tears in their eyes thanking us for turning something in their life around. Even if it is as simple as pain relief. It's nice when you get a thank you from a patient, and you realize 'I really changed the quality of this patient's life.'"

have I got what it takes to be a chiropractor?

Good people skills are necessary to be a successful chiropractor. According to Dr. Winter-

in-depth

A Short History of Chiropractics

The origin of chiropractic philosophy dates to ancient times. Prehistoric cave paintings in southeastern France clearly illustrate spinal manipulation practices. Other evidence indicates spinal manipulation practices were present in ancient China, India, Egypt, Greece, and Rome. Also, Native American peoples, including the Aztecs, Creeks, Incas, Mayas, Sioux, and Winnebagos, used spinal manipulation to treat illness and back pain.

Chiropractic medicine declined during the early Middle Ages, largely because it was often associated with superstitions and the occult. During the latter Middle Ages and the Renaissance, however, chiropractic practitioners gained greater acceptance. People often known as "bone setters" enjoyed a considerable reputation as healers.

Modern chiropractic medicine did not reach the United States until the late 19th century. Dr. Daniel David Palmer is credited with developing modern chiropractics in this country in 1895. It was then, in Davenport, Iowa, that Dr. Palmer successfully restored the hearing of a janitor by repositioning a misaligned vertebra. Two years later Dr. Palmer opened the nation's first chiropractic school.

Since then, chiropractic medicine has expanded, often coming into conflict with the field of traditional medicine. Nonetheless, chiropractic today is a constantly growing field that continues to attract practitioners and patients.

---

stein, "Chiropractic is very much a people profession." Compassion is also very important. Chiropractors must have the ability to care about their patients' overall health and well-being, from their initial visit to completion of treatment.

Another important aspect is the ability to listen closely to their patients. A patient once broke down during an interview with Teri saying, "You're the first doctor to ever take such a complete history on me and I've been going to all different medical doctors and nobody wants to seem to tie all my body together. I go to the guy for my thyroid problem, I go to the guy for my diabetes, I go to the guy for my knee problem, and nobody seems to care about the other parts of my body." Knowing that their chiropractor cares and is listening to them often makes a significant difference in effective treatments.

Many people assume that chiropractors need a great deal of physical strength for spinal manipulations; however, rather than physical strength, the chiropractor needs a combination of dexterity, finesse, and speed. In fact, patients have commented to Teri before their treatments that they thought she was too small to manipulate their spine only to be pleasantly surprised when she adjusted their spine and they felt better.

Finally, the ability to recognize their own limitations and the limitations of chiropractic medicine is one of the most important characteristics of good chiropractors. They must know when chiropractic therapy cannot help anymore and refer patients to other health specialists who may be able to help them.

how do I become a chiropractor?

education

High School

If you are interested in the study of chiropractic as a career, take as many science classes as possible, including advanced biology and chemistry.

Most chiropractors working in private practice are responsible for the administration of their offices, so in addition to science classes, business courses like bookkeeping or business law are also important.

Since communication between the chiropractor and the patient is so important, such communication classes as English and speech are very useful. These courses provide an opportunity for you to learn the skills chiropractors need to express themselves clearly to their patients as well as learn to listen attentively to what their patients are saying to them.

Postsecondary Training

Applicants must complete the pre-chiropractic educational requirements before they can be considered for acceptance into an accredited chiropractic college. There are 16 accredited chiropractic programs located throughout the United States. (A list is available from the Council on Chiropractic Education and the American Chiropractic Association. See How Do I Learn More? at the end of this article.) Nearly one-third of all chiropractors are graduates of the largest program, Palmer College of Chiropractic, which has campuses in Iowa and California. Currently, most colleges require 60 to 75 hours of postsecondary study. Furthermore, the applicant needs a grade point average of at least 2.25 on a 4.0 scale. Academic standards at some colleges may be higher. Anyone interested in attending a specific college should inquire as to what the pre-chiropractic requirements are for that college.

Some colleges may require that incoming students have a bachelor's degree. Students need all the standard required science classes but also need courses in the humanities and social sciences. In addition to benefiting from a fuller educational experience, earning a bachelor's degree is an opportunity for students to develop the people skills that are so important for success as a chiropractor.

During the first two years at a chiropractic college, students take classes covering the basic sciences, including anatomy, biochemistry, microbiology, pathology, physiology, nutrition, and public health. The second two years focus on clinical studies, where students develop the skills needed to diagnose and treat patients effectively.

A small percentage of chiropractors have advanced degrees. In 1998, 5 percent of chiropractors surveyed by the National Board of Chiropractic Examiners had master's degrees and 2.3 percent had doctorates. Over half (53.8 percent) of respondents had bachelor's degrees. Postgraduate specialization is available for chiropractors in areas such as family practice, sports chiropractic, industrial consulting, orthopedics, pediatrics, and rehabilitation.

FYI

Chiropractic medicine is the single largest alternative method of healing in the country. There are between 55,000 and 70,000 chiropractors in the United States and each year more than 19 million people are treated by chiropractors.

certification or licensing

After graduating from an accredited chiropratic college, students must pass a licensing board examination in their state before they can begin to practice. Most state chiropractic licensing boards accept certificates of the examination offered by the National Board of Chiropractic Examiners in place of passing a state exam. Some states require also passing a basic science exam.

Chiropractic doctors can receive special clinical certifications, called "diplomates," in the areas of neurology, nutrition, sports medicine, orthopedics, diagnostic imaging, diagnosis, and internal disorders. Diplomate certification is awarded after the passage of an examination written by a board set up for each specialty. Not every college offers diplomate programs and not all programs cover every specialty.

To retain their licenses, chiropractors are required to earn a minimum of 50 hours of continuing education every year. Some chiropractic colleges have entire departments devoted to continuing education.

internships and volunteerships

One way to gain practical experience in a chiropractor's office is to contact a local chiropractor and ask about any possible volunteer opportunities. Most chiropractors are eager to explain their profession to anyone who is interested. They may allow the student to work as an assistant or file clerk to gain a better understanding of the responsibilities of a chiropractor.

Outreach programs also offer practical experience. Some chiropractic colleges offer introduction programs for high school students in their area. During the visitations, students may have the opportunity to attend a dissection seminar or see demonstrations of chiropractic and acupuncture therapies. Persons interested in visitation programs should contact the chiropractic college in their vicinity and speak to the director of admissions. Not all chiropractic colleges offer this program.

who will hire me?

Presently, the majority (63 percent, according to the National Board of Chiropractic Examiners) of chiropractors work on their own in private practice. Nearly one-third share an office with one or more chiropractors, and a small percentage practice in multidisciplinary offices.

Most new graduates find it easiest to begin their careers by working as an associate. Many chiropractic colleges have placement offices that keep records of doctors who have called the college looking for a new associate. The placement office will put the doctor and the graduate together.

Another way a chiropractor may begin his or her career is by buying the practice of an older, more established doctor. When someone buys a practice, they are purchasing several things. Among these are the physical assets of the practice (e.g. office, equipment,

To be a successful chiropractor, you should

- Have good people skills
- Be compassionate
- Be a very good listener
- Have the ability to concentrate
- Have dexterity
- Be able to realize limitations

etc.), patient files, and, usually, a "covenant not to compete." This means that the doctor who is selling promises not to set up a new practice and begin to compete with the buyer.

New chiropractors may find it easier to set up their own practice by moving to areas that are currently in need of chiropractors. In a study done by the American Chiropractic Association, it was found that there are hundreds of towns across the country that do not have any chiropractors. Furthermore, there are cities and larger towns that do not have enough chiropractors.

Some chiropractors prefer to engage in research or teach. Teri knew she wanted to teach as soon as she graduated. However, she felt that she should work in private practice first to gain practical experience before returning to the college to teach. She felt strongly that her real world experience would benefit her students. She worked for years in private practice, or as she describes it, "in the trenches." However, she knew it was time to go back to college and start to teach when she found herself trying to explain to her patients how to read their own X rays.

where can I go from here?

For most chiropractors, advancement in their field means successfully treating as many patients as possible. However, the career path for many chiropractors means beginning by working as associates for other chiropractors. Once they build up their reputation and client base, they may decide to open their own offices.

Some chiropractors, like Teri, were born to be teachers. After working in private practice they feel unfulfilled. By teaching students to become competent chiropractors, they often feel the satisfaction and gratification they never felt in private practice.

Research is a highly valued part of chiropractic medicine. Some chiropractors feel it is important to learn and study as much about the human body as possible so they can develop new and better ways to help treat patients. Chiropractors also have the option of attaining diplomate status through a specialty board, council, academy, college or association.

what are the salary ranges?

Self-employed chiropractors usually earn more than salaried chiropractors, such as those working as an associate with another chiropractor or doctor. According to the American Chiropractic Association, average income for all chiropractors was about $86,500, after expenses, in 1997. Expenses for a chiropractor can include, but are not limited to, equipment costs, staff salaries, and health insurance. A survey by the California Labor Market Information Division showed that national median earnings for chiropractors were $70,000 for a 40-hour workweek.

Length of experience and geographic location can affect annual salary. Chiropractors at the lower end of the pay scale had a median net income of $36,820, while chiropractors at the highest end of the scale earned $110,000 a year or more.

what is the job outlook?

In 1998, the Federation of Chiropractic Licensing Boards reported between 55,000 and 70,000 practicing chiropractors in the United States. The future of chiropractic medicine is very bright and is expected to continue to grow. One of the factors influencing this growth is the relatively low cost of chiropractic care. For example, chiropractic medicine has always offered people a reasonably affordable treatment that can still be very effective. Even when health insurance companies or managed care programs do not cover chiropractic treatments, many people still are able to afford chiropractic care. A 1999 study by Landmark Healthcare Inc. found that coverage of chiropractic care is offered by nearly two-thirds of all HMOs.

Another factor that points to a healthy future for chiropractors is the growing acceptance of chiropractic treatment by the conventional medical establishment. Residents in radiology and orthopedics from the National University of Health Sciences now go to area hospitals for their rotations. Furthermore, a number of chiropractic doctors have been granted formal hospital privileges.

Chiropractic medicine is also seen as a form of alternative medicine by many people who are looking for holistic ways of healing.

Interest in alternative care has grown and is expected to continue to grow. In 1990, visits to nonmedical care providers, including chiropractors, totaled 425 million. By 1997, that number had grown to 629 million. Visits to chiropractors exceeded visits to any other practitioner of alternative health care.

how do I learn more?

professional organizations

Following are organizations that provide information on chiropractic medicine and training and education.

American Chiropractic Association
1701 Clarendon Boulevard
Arlington, VA 22209
800-986-4636
http://www.amerchiro.org

Council on Chiropractic Education
7975 North Hayden Road, Suite 1-210
Scottsdale, AZ 85258
602-443-8877
CCEoffice@aol.com

National Board of Chiropractic Examiners
901 54th Avenue
Greeley, CO 80634
970-356-9100
nbce@nbce.org
http://www.nbce.org

bibliography

Following is a sampling of materials relating to the professional concerns and development of chiropractors.

Huff, Lew and David M. Brady, eds. *Instant Access to Chiropractic Guidelines and Protocols.* St. Louis, MO: Mosby-Year Book, 1999.

O'Neill, Arthur. *Enemies Within & Without: Educating Chiropractors, Osteopaths and Traditional Acupuncturists.* Portland, OR: International Specialized Book Service, 1995.

Rondberg, Terry A. *Chiropractic First: The Fastest Growing Healthcare Choice Before Drugs or Surgery.* Chandler, AZ: Chiropractic Journal, 1996.

Steinfeld, Alan. *Careers in Alternative Health Care.* New York, NY: Rosen Group, 1996.

Tierney, Gillian. *Opportunities in Holistic Health Care Careers.* Lincolnwood, IL: VGM Career Horizons, 1999.

Clinical Nurse Specialists

Definition
Clinical nurse specialists are registered nurses (R.N.s) who have advanced education and expertise in a specific area of nursing.

High School Subjects
Biology
Chemistry
Physics

Personal Skills
Helping/teaching
Technical/scientific

Salary Range
$47,000 to $59,000 to $67,000

Minimum Educational Level
Master's degree

Certification or Licensing
Licensing is mandatory for all R.N.s; additional certification in advanced practice specialties is available.

Outlook
Much faster than the average

GOE
10.02.01
O*NET-SOC
29-1111.00

After a few minutes in the hospital room, Matt Brayton could tell the woman was upset about something other than her medical condition. Brayton, a clinical nurse specialist at Vanderbilt University Medical Center, finishes taking her blood pressure and then asks gently if there is anything about her care she wants to discuss. The woman, a 48-year-old, otherwise healthy teacher who had been admitted after suffering a slight heart attack, visibly relaxes and even manages a small smile. "You are the first person to ask me that. Everyone here seems so busy and no one seems to know what will happen next or when I might be able to go home or back to work."

Matt smiles back, "That's my job. Let's take a look at your chart again and I'll tell you some of the things that might happen over the next few days. We are waiting now for some of your labs to come back."

They discuss her care options, and Matt tells her her blood pressure is still a bit high and suggests some breathing exercises and relaxation techniques to help her through this stressful time.

what does a clinical nurse specialist do?

Clinical nurse specialists are advanced practice nurses, which means that they have education and expertise beyond the level required for registered nurses (R.N.s). The key word in the definition of the clinical nurse specialist is expert. Clinical nurse specialists have expert knowledge in a defined area of nursing, such as medical-surgical, gerontological (older adult), or mental health. They function as expert clinicians, consultants, educators, case managers, researchers, and administrators.

The National League of Nursing Education first drew up a plan to create the clinical nurse specialist role in the 1940s. The first master's degree level program opened in 1954 at Rutgers University; the only specialty offered at that time was psychiatric nursing. By 1970, clinical nurse specialty certification had become available in a number of fields in response to the increased specialization in health care, the development of new technolo-

lingo to learn

ANA: American Nurses' Association, an important professional society for nurses.

ANCC: American Nurses Credentialing Center, the ANA's separately incorporated national certification exam-administering organization.

Change agent: The term often used to characterize the clinical nurse specialist's role as an identifier, analyst, and solver of health care problems.

Direct care: The part of the clinical nurse specialist's work that involves actual interaction with patients and their families.

gies, and the need to provide alternative cost-efficient health care during the physician shortage of the 1960s.

The nurse practitioner role was also developed during the 1960s, principally to provide cost-efficient health care in rural and inner-city areas where there were few physicians. *Nurse practitioners* usually focus on primary health care and prevention of health problems; they are more likely to work from various sites in the community than solely in a hospital. In light of the current direction taken by the U.S. health care industry (e.g. shorter hospital stays, more procedures done in outpatient settings, emphasis on efficient management and cost containment), many nursing educators believe that the roles of the nurse practitioner and clinical nurse specialist are gradually merging. (The other two advanced practice nursing categories are nurse-midwife and nurse anesthetist.)

The details of a clinical nurse specialist's job depend on the setting in which he or she is employed (e.g. hospital, nursing home, community clinic, mental health facility, home health care, industrial setting, or other). Working as part of an interdisciplinary health care team, which can include doctors, psychologists, physical therapists, or social workers, is basic to virtually any clinical nurse specialist position.

The clinical nurse specialist is expected to be able to see the "big picture" in a way that the staff nurse who is focused on delivering direct care cannot. Patients and their families need an expert guide and advocate in order to make the most constructive use of today's immensely complex health care delivery system.

In addition to making sure that the patient receives the most appropriate state-of-the-art nursing care while in the hospital, the clinical nurse specialist has an important role as an educator and consultant. Educating patients and their families is the most obvious part of the teaching role but far from the only part. The clinical nurse specialist is also involved in the professional development of the other members of the nursing staff and the nursing students by teaching them about new concepts and techniques in nursing.

Clinical nurse specialists may be involved in the planning and development of nursing school courses or continuing education programs either in the hospital or academic setting. They may be called on to provide an expert nursing perspective for students in other disciplines, such as social work or medical ethics. Clinical nurse specialists are frequently called on to provide health care education for the community at large or for specific sectors of the community (such as manufacturers of medical equipment).

what is it like to be a clinical nurse specialist?

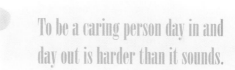

Matt Brayton has been a clinical nurse specialist in general internal medicine at Vanderbilt University Medical Center in Nashville, Tennessee, for over two years. He became an R.N. three years ago, after deciding that the stories his wife told about her work as a nurse were more interesting than the reports he was writing for a local newspaper.

Matt sometimes says that he has a "nonspecialty specialty," since general internal medicine covers such a broad range of medical conditions: infections, heart diseases, lung problems, gastrointestinal problems, and more.

As a clinical nurse specialist case manager, Matt works with the patient, the patient's family, and other members of the health care team to assess the patient's condition and to create an appropriate plan for hospital care.

Most of Matt's day is spent in one-on-one work with patients. All of the Vanderbilt clinical nurse specialists have been given the role of case manager, which means that they are responsible for quality control and efficiency in the handling of each patient's hospital stay. The clinical nurse specialist assesses every person who is admitted: How sick is the patient? How long will the hospital stay last? What kind of financial resources are available? Will the patient need a referral to a social worker, a psychiatrist, or other mental health professional?

Is the patient here because of a chronic illness that is not being managed well? If a problem is caught at an early stage, it can often be handled without hospitalization. An important part of Matt's job is to educate patients in the management of their illness. Asthma attacks can be avoided, for example, if the patient is taught to use a peak-flow monitor every day to measure lung capacity. Simply relying on "how you feel" is inadequate, as Matt explains, since people can lose 25 percent of lung capacity without experiencing any symptoms. Then an asthma attack catches them unprepared and may result in admission to the hospital.

Likewise, Matt teaches diabetics to use a glucometer daily to check their blood sugar. People with high blood pressure are shown how to use a blood pressure cuff at home to monitor their condition; those with congestive heart failure are taught the importance of weighing themselves daily to find out if they are retaining fluid, which would be an indication that the heart condition is worsening.

Anne Luther has similar responsibilities as the clinical nurse specialist in otolaryngology (ear, nose, and throat), the position she has held since 1988. (Before that, she was a clinical nurse specialist in general surgery.) She usually begins her day by talking with the intern. who did early rounds. Sometimes she finds that her first task of the day is "putting out fires": a medical crisis, a postoperative patient whose condition has suddenly deteriorated, or an unhappy family member.

Because Vanderbilt is a tertiary care facility (a hospital that treats illnesses requiring specialized procedures such as coronary artery bypass surgery), many of Anne's patients have come from neighboring states to undergo surgery not available in their local hospitals. Anne meets with the patients and their families before surgery to prepare them for what they will experience. She continues to meet with them during their hospital stay and makes postdischarge arrangements. As case manager, an important part of her role is acting as the liaison among the health care team members.

Extensive preop education is essential: Otolaryngological surgery often means that the patient will wake up with a tracheostomy, an opening through the neck into the trachea into which a tube has been inserted. A patient with a tracheostomy is unable to speak or swallow.

If the patient will be leaving the hospital with the tracheostomy in place, the patient and family need to be taught self-care (the management of artificial airways, for example). Arrangements need to be made for ongoing home health care and physical therapy. Anne arranges for speech-language pathologists to come to the hospital to begin teaching alternative methods of swallowing and speaking, but therapy generally needs to continue after discharge. Removal of a cancerous larynx (voice box) does not mean that the person will never be able to talk again; it means that he or she will need to learn compensatory techniques for producing speech. Anne is the nurse adviser for the New Voice Club, a monthly support group for people developing "new voices."

Surgical patients have the advantage of learning in advance what to expect. Accident victims are less fortunate. Another important part of Anne's job is working with patients who have suffered injuries that unexpectedly require them to have their jaws wired shut, a highly traumatic experience, especially when accompanied by other injuries that make it difficult or impossible to speak or breathe normally. Anne delivers oral care and teaches the patient and family how to do the self-care they will need to perform after the patient is discharged.

When Anne first started graduate school (after serving as a staff nurse in surgery and rehabilitation and as a clinical instructor of nursing students), her intention was to go into teaching after finishing her degree. When she realized how much she enjoyed working with patients and their families, however, she decided to apply her expertise in the hospital setting instead, a decision that she has not regretted.

have I got what it takes to be a clinical nurse specialist?

Anyone going into nursing needs to have a caring attitude and a strong commitment to helping people. Emotional maturity, a well-balanced personality, and excellent communication skills are vital. "You need to be able to forget your personal stuff while you focus on the patient's problem," said one clinical nurse specialist, adding frankly, "to be a caring person day in and day out is harder than it sounds."

A nurse needs to have the ability to remain calm in an emergency and to accept frequent interruptions in the daily work routine. "You have to be able to juggle and reprioritize and have a high tolerance for delayed gratification" is the way Anne Luther puts it.

In addition to possessing the qualities shared by all good nurses, clinical nurse specialists need to develop the leadership skills and expert competence necessary for advanced practice nursing. Because the clinical nurse specialist role is still not understood by some doctors and nurses, the clinical nurse specialist must have the professional self-confidence to educate colleagues as well as patients and families. Physicians may be reluctant to recognize the qualifications of the clinical nurse specialist, and staff nurses may be resistant to what they perceive as criticism or interference with their work. A clinical nurse specialist also needs to have the academic interest and ability to do graduate study. A master's degree is required, and a doctorate is becoming increasingly necessary for top-level positions involving research, teaching, and policy making.

In today's health care environment, clinical nurse specialists often find themselves spending a large amount of time trying to sort out problems with cost-conscious insurance companies. Many people, especially those with low incomes, often have trouble getting the health care that they need, and trying to work within such situations can be difficult for nurses, who recognize the need for cost-effective care but do not want to see the quality of care suffer.

more lingo to learn

Indirect care: The part of the clinical nurse specialist's work that is aimed at improving nursing care by interaction with other care providers rather than with the patients themselves.

Nursing service director: The administrator in charge of a hospital's total nursing services.

Preventive care: Health care with the goal of maintaining health and preventing illness (or identifying and treating problems at the earliest possible stage).

Tertiary health care: The high-tech specialized diagnoses and treatment available only in large research and teaching hospitals.

An important part of nursing, especially in advanced practice roles, is helping patients to help themselves keep healthy. Empowering people this way is often one of the most satisfying aspects of a nurse's job. Yet, when people persistently refuse to make the effort to take care of themselves, it can be very frustrating for the nurse who spent hours educating them only to see them back in the hospital with a medical crisis that could have been avoided.

how do I become a clinical nurse specialist?

education

High School

If you are interested in a nursing career, it is a good idea to take good college-preparatory course work that includes biology, chemistry, physics, and mathematics. If a course on human anatomy and physiology is offered as a follow-up to basic biology, that would be a good elective. English and speech classes that emphasize communication skills (both written and oral) are also important.

You may find opportunities to do volunteer work at a local hospital, nursing home, or clinic. You might also take a Red Cross first aid course or join a chapter of the Future Nurses Club to learn more about the nursing profession.

Postsecondary Training

Before becoming a clinical nurse specialist, you must become an R.N. There are three ways to become an R.N.: a two-year associate's degree (A.D.N.) program at a junior or community college, a two- or three-year diploma program at a hospital, or a bachelor's degree (B.S.N.) program at a college or university. All the programs include supervised hands-on training in a hospital setting. Since a clinical nurse specialist needs a master's degree (M.S.N.), the B.S.N. is the most appropriate educational route to choose. People who are already practicing nursing with an A.D.N. or diploma and decide to upgrade their qualifications generally need to do additional course work to receive a bachelor's degree before they can enter an M.S.N. program.

Courses in a nursing degree program include human anatomy and physiology, microbiology, chemistry, nutrition, and psychology, as well as nursing theory and practice. Students in a bachelor's degree program will also take classes in English, humanities, and social sciences.

Graduate programs for clinical nurse specialists offer more advanced work in nursing theory, research, and clinical practice, giving you the opportunity to develop an area of in-depth nursing expertise. Usually clinical nurse specialists have been R.N.s in staff positions for several years before deciding to enter graduate programs, but that is not always the case. It sometimes happens that individuals in other professions decide to become clinical nurse specialists.

There are various routes of professional transition. Matt Brayton, for example, earned an undergraduate degree in journalism and worked in that field for several years before deciding to become a nurse. He entered a "bridge" program at a university nursing school that allowed him to move into an M.S.N. program without earning a B.S.N. first.

After completing his M.S.N., passing his licensing exam to become an R.N., and working for several years as a staff nurse, he was eligible to take certification exams to become a clinical nurse specialist. Since he already had his M.S.N., further graduate study was not necessary.

certification or licensing

To become a clinical nurse specialist, you must first become a licensed R.N. by passing a national examination after graduating from an approved nursing program. All states require R.N. licensing before a nurse is allowed to practice.

National certification exams are offered by the American Nurses Credentialing Center (ANCC) in various clinical specialties, although not all states require these examinations or recognize clinical nurse specialist status.

The ANCC offers clinical nurse specialty examinations in areas including adult psychiatric and mental health nursing, child and adolescent psychiatric and mental health nursing, medical-surgical nursing, community health, home health, and gerontological nursing.

ANCC certification is valid for five years; recertification can be obtained by exam or continuing education.

scholarships and grants

There are numerous sources of financial assistance for people interested in nursing careers. Your state nurses' association (for info, see http://www.nursingworld.org/snaaddr.htm), the National Student Nurses' Association, nursing honor societies, state departments of education, the federal government, private agencies, civic and alumni organizations, and the U.S. military are all possible sources of grants or scholarships. You may also be eligible for scholarship aid targeted for members of

To be a successful clinical nurse specialist, you should

- Be able to handle stress and remain calm in emergencies
- Be strongly committed to helping people
- Enjoy solving problems
- Be able to handle a heavy workload
- Have strong communication skills
- Be well organized

specific racial/ethnic groups. An annual guide to financial aid, *Scholarships and Loans for Nursing Education,* is published annually by the National League for Nursing. Some scholarship sponsors require recipients to work for their agencies for a specific length of time afterward, generally at full salary.

If you are already an R.N. employed by a health care organization and you want to take graduate courses to prepare to become a clinical nurse specialist, you may be eligible for tuition assistance or reimbursement from your employer. Some hospitals and agencies encourage the nursing staff's professional development.

For additional information about assistance, consult the financial aid office of the school you plan to attend.

who will hire me?

Clinical nurse specialists work in a wide range of health care settings, depending on their particular area of specialization and interest. They are employed in hospitals, clinics, community health centers, mental health facilities, nursing homes, home health care agencies, veterans affairs facilities, industrial organizations, nursing schools and other educational institutions, physicians' offices, and the military. A few are in private or independent practice.

Information about job openings for clinical nurse specialists is available from many sources. Your nursing school placement office is the best place to start; other avenues include nursing registries, nurse employment agencies, and state employment offices. Positions are often listed in professional journals and newspapers. Information about government jobs is available from the Office of Personnel Management for your region. Contacts you have made through clinical work or involvement in professional societies can be helpful sources of information. The organization that formerly employed you as a staff nurse may be eager to rehire you as a clinical nurse specialist now that you have received your M.S.N. and are certified in an advanced practice specialty.

where can I go from here?

As clinical nurse specialists gain experience, they become qualified for positions that involve greater responsibility and give them opportunities to have a greater impact on nursing practice. Some people choose to broaden their base of expertise by adding nurse practitioner qualifications to their credentials.

Many clinical nurse specialists become involved in nursing education, research, publishing, and consulting. Additionally, some may want to make their voices heard in the current debate on the future of health care.

Moving into faculty or administrative positions is the form of advancement chosen by some clinical nurse specialists, while others prefer to remain in positions that are more direct-care oriented.

A Ph.D. in nursing is becoming increasingly necessary for advancement into high-level research, teaching, administrative, and policy-making positions.

what are the salary ranges?

Clinical nurse specialists have more education and may have more experience and thus tend to earn higher salaries than traditional R.N.s According to a survey of members of the National Association of Clinical Nurse Specialists, annual earnings were $47,374 for a clinical nurse specialist with two to four years of clinical experience in 2000. Median earnings were $59,114, and clinical nurse specialists with supervisory positions or years of experience on the higher end of the scale earned $67,191.

In comparison, R.N.s in 1998 had median annual earnings of $40,690, according to the *Occupational Outlook Handbook*. Salaries may also vary by geographic location. Clinical nurse specialists who work in large urban areas where the cost of living is higher tend to be on the higher end of the earnings scale. Those who practice in smaller cities or rural areas would likely have earnings at the lower end.

what is the job outlook?

The job outlook for advanced-practice nurses is excellent, since they are winning increasing recognition for their ability to provide high-quality, cost-effective health care. As discussed earlier in this chapter, the roles of the clinical nurse specialist and the nurse practitioner may be merging in the near future as many clinical nurse specialists move beyond the traditional hospital setting into outpatient settings with an emphasis on preventive health care. (Outpatient health centers and a focus on prevention are important cost-cutting measures.)

The fact that the role of the clinical nurse specialist is evolving means that people entering the field should be flexible in their expectations and open to further education to broaden their areas of competency.

Areas of practice that are likely to grow especially fast are those involving home health care (in keeping with the emphasis on getting the patient out of the hospital as quickly as possible) and care for the elderly (since the percentage of the U.S. population in the over-65 age group is steadily increasing). Rehabilitation and outpatient surgery are also growing fields.

how do I learn more?

professional organizations

To learn more about becoming a clinical nurse specialist, contact the following organizations:

American Nurses Association
600 Maryland Avenue, SW, Suite 100 West
Washington, DC 20024-2571
http://www.ana.org

National Association of Clinical Nurse Specialists
3969 Green Street
Harrisburg, PA 17110
info@nacns.org
http://www.nacns.org

National League for Nursing
61 Broadway, 33rd Floor
New York, NY 10006
800-669-1656
http://www.nln.org

bibliography

Following is a sampling of materials relating to the professional concerns and development of clinical nurse specialists.

Chang, Cyril F. et al. *Economics and Nursing: Critical Professional Issues.* Philadelphia, PA: F. A. Davis Company, 2000.

Collier, J. A. et al. *The Oxford Handbook of Clinical Specialties.* 5th Edition. New York, NY: Oxford University Press, 1999.

Coulehan, John L. and Marian R. Block. *The Medical Interview: Mastering Skills for Clinical Practice.* 4th Edition. Philadelphia, PA: F. A. Davis Company, 2001.

Dunphy, Jill E. and Lynne M. Winland-Brown, eds. *Primary Care: The Art and Science of Advanced Practice Nursing.* Philadelphia, PA; F. A. Davis Company, 2001.

Ferri, Fred F. *Practical Guide to the Care of the Medical Patient.* St. Louis, MO: Mosby, Inc. 2001.

Kumar, Parveen. *Clinical Medicine.* San Diego, CA: Harcourt Brace, 1998.

Prickett-Ramutkowski, Barbara et al. eds. *Clinical Procedures for Medical Assisting: A Patient-Centered Approach.* New York, NY: Glencoe McGraw-Hill, 1998.

Related Jobs

Jobs related to clinical nurse specialists are other registered nurses, especially other advanced practice nurses (nurse practitioners, nurse-midwives, and nurse anesthetists). The U.S. Department of Labor classifies clinical nurse specialists and other registered nurses with people in the *Health Assessment and Treating Occupations,* a subcategory of the much broader *Professional Specialty Occupations* field. Also under the *Health Assessment and Treating Occupations* heading are dietitians and nutritionists, pharmacists, occupational therapists, recreational therapists, respiratory therapists, physician's assistants, audiologists and speech-language pathologists.

Colon and Rectal Surgeons

Definition

A colon and rectal surgeon diagnoses and treats disorders of the intestinal tract, rectum, anal canal, and perianal area and can also surgically repair organs affected by primary intestinal disease.

Alternative Job Title

Proctologists (Although this title is frequently used by the general public, it is not used professionally.)

High School Subjects

Biology
Chemistry
Mathematics

Personal Skills

Mechanical/manipulative
Technical/scientific

Salary Range

$80,000 to $100,000 to $350,000+

Educational Requirements

Bachelor's degree, M.D., five years of general surgery, and a minimum one year fellowship in colon and rectal surgery

Certification or Licensing

Recommended (certification)
Required by all states (licensing)

Outlook

Faster than the average

GOE
02.03.01
O*NET-SOC
29-1067.00

Sleds fly down the hill in the moonlight, soaring over bumps, as their riders scream with excitement in the chilly Minnesota air. College students riding in one sled turn off the main path and head in a direction that takes them down a narrow pass along the side of the slope. The sled zips down the shorter, but steeper incline while the riders hoot and howl with delight at the incredible speed they're achieving when, suddenly, the sled veers out of control and runs straight into a branch embedded in the ice and snow. Shaken, but unharmed, several students pull themselves out of the snow and gaze around. One rider, however, remains motionless in the sled. The girl, lying unconscious, has been impaled on the branch that the sled struck.

"Call an ambulance! Hurry!" shouts one of the students.

Somewhere on the other side of town, Dr. David Rothenberger answers the coded page: emergency surgery. Within moments he's dressed and headed for the hospital where he meets the paramedics who are just bringing the girl in to the hospital.

"Perineal trauma. Bunch of college students going for a night sled ride. We left the stick in," one paramedic says as they wheel her into the emergency room. "Didn't want to risk having her bleed out on us. Looks like it pierced the rectum and came out through her abdomen."

David, a colon and rectal surgeon, quickly examines the girl and nods to the paramedic. "Good thing you didn't move that stick. It looks pretty close to a major vein. Let's get her prepped."

David operates for several hours to repair and reconstruct the girl's torn rectum, vagina, and abdomen. Fearing infection, the surgeon also temporarily brings her colon out to the skin in a colostomy so that the rectum can heal properly. David has saved the girl's life.

what does a colon and rectal surgeon do?

A *colon and rectal surgeon* is responsible for the diagnosis and treatment of diseases of the intestinal tract, rectum, anal canal, and perineal area. This doctor can also surgically repair organs and tissues secondarily affected by primary intestinal disease. The colon and rectal surgeon has special skills in the performance of endoscopic procedures of the rectum and colon. Endoscopy involves the passage of lighted tubes into the body to evaluate and treat problems such as cancer, polyps (precancerous growths), and inflammatory conditions. Many of the diseases treated by colon and rectal surgeons are related to the lower gastrointestinal tract, which is involved in digestion.

The colon and rectal surgeon has the expertise to diagnose and often manage anorectal conditions such as hemorrhoids, fissures (painful tears in the anal lining), abscesses, and fistulae (infections located around the anus and rectum). These conditions are often diagnosed and treated in the colon and rectal surgeon's office.

The colon and rectal surgeon also treats problems of the intestine and colon and performs endoscopic procedures to detect and treat conditions of the bowel lining. Some of these endoscopic procedures include proctoscopy (examination of the rectum), sigmoidoscopy (examination of the rectum and sigmoid colon), and colonoscopy (examination of the colon lining). Polyps can often be removed during endoscopy without subjecting the patient to highly invasive abdominal surgery. If cancers are detected, the colon and rectal surgeon is able to plan the surgical treatment program based on his or her first hand visualization of the tumor and follow up with endoscopic techniques.

A colon and rectal surgeon performs abdominal surgical procedures involving the small bowel, colon, and rectum. These include treatment of inflammatory bowel disease, such as ulcerative colitis, as well as diverticulitis and cancer. Because of their expertise, colon and rectal surgeons are often able to treat cancer of the rectum without a colostomy (removal of the colon). The colon and rectal surgeon also treats intestinal infections resulting from, for example, intestinal parasites.

Training in colon and rectal surgery also provides the specialist with the in-depth knowledge of intestinal and anorectal physiology required for the evaluation and treatment of problems such as constipation and incontinence (loss of bowel or bladder control).

lingo to learn

Anorectal: Involving the anal and rectal areas of the large intestine.

Diverticulitis: A painful condition in which diverticulum or diverticula, especially in the colon, become inflamed.

Diverticulum (plural, diverticula): A sac that can occur on the wall of an organ or canal area.

Hemorrhoidal disease: Inflammation of veins in the anal area.

Polyps: Precancerous tissue growths that can become cancerous or remain benign. Some type of biopsy is usually necessary to determine whether or not the polyps are cancerous.

Pilonidal cyst: A hairy cyst, which is a sac in or under the skin.

Ulcerative colitis: A painful inflammatory disease of the large intestine and rectum.

what is it like to be a colon and rectal surgeon?

"People just love you," says Dr. Susan Briley, a colon and rectal surgeon practicing in Nashville, Tennessee. "You develop a real rapport with your patients and the great thing is that you can really help them. Sometimes, you fix them instantly and without surgery. A patient coming out of gall bladder surgery might not even remember his surgeon, but a patient with hemorrhoids is really grateful when you get rid of his pain."

As for many physicians and surgeons, a typical day for a colon and rectal surgeon begins early and ends late. "I start seeing patients at 6:45 AM as part of my rounds at the hospital," explains Dr. Charles Littlejohn, a colon and rectal surgeon in Stamford, Connecticut. "By 7:30 I'm in the operating room, usually until lunch. I perform an average of 14 to 16 operations each week. Then, from about 1 PM to 6 PM I'm in my office, seeing patients. After that I spend an hour to two hours on the telephone, informing patients of test results, answering patients' questions, and explaining upcoming surgeries." Charles continues, "Then I either attend an educational meeting to keep up with new general surgical techniques and issues or I go home and have dinner. Later, I read a medical journal or I go online to present a problem. I also write articles for the publications of the various organizations to which I belong."

Colon and rectal surgeons see patients of varying ages and with a variety of problems. "This is not something that is confined to old people," says Dr. David Rothenberger. "I see a lot of teenage patients with inflammatory bowel disease, ulcerative colitis, pilonidal cysts, and women suffering from birthing injuries. Women giving birth sometimes tear the tissue between the rectum and the vagina; it's only a half inch to an inch thick. If that tears, the woman becomes incontinent and needs to have surgery."

Charles realized during a rotation in colon and rectal surgery that he enjoyed the combination of skills involved in the treatment of colon and rectal conditions and diseases. "I especially liked it because you got to talk to people and you didn't always have to treat with surgery." He adds, "Not that many surgical fields allow you to practice medicine and surgery."

David has similar sentiments. In addition to being Chief of Colon and Rectal Surgery at the University of Minnesota and the president of the largest private or university group practice of colon and rectal surgeons in the world, he is a past president of the American Society of Colon and Rectal Surgeons. "This specialty is wonderful, that's why I chose it. It's such a nice mix that satisfies a lot of different interests. You spend a lot of time with patients, perform complex surgeries, endoscopies. Simple things, complex things, it's all there in this specialty."

During an office visit, the colon and rectal surgeon first takes the patient's history, which actually consists of several steps: assessing the patient's present illness (What are the patient's symptoms? How long has the patient felt this way?) and reviewing the patient's past medical history (Previously, what other illnesses, conditions, allergies, or diseases did the patient have?), social history (Does the patient smoke? Drink? Abuse substances?) and family history (Did anyone else in the patient's family have cancer? heart disease?).

"It is so crucial to be able to understand what patients are saying, what they're telling you. There's a lot of misunderstanding and embarrassment in this area. A total stranger walks into your office and you have to immediately put him or her at ease," explains David, "because you're going to ask questions of a very intimate nature and you want honest answers. You really need to be a good clinician, and by that I mean you need to be a good listener and observer."

After taking the patient's history, the colon and rectal surgeon then runs several diagnostic tests, including a physical examination, to determine if other aspects of the patient's health and functions have been affected. The physician begins by listening to the patient's heart and lungs and then performs an abdominal exam by gently pressing the abdomen in various places, searching for the presence of any masses or tenderness.

The colon and rectal surgeon then puts on surgical gloves to perform a general rectal examination of the patient. During this exam, the doctor observes the condition of the perineal area and feels the rectum for any irregular masses that might be signs or symptoms of the patient's problem. Subsequent examinations may involve the use of scopes, which are lighted video tubes that are passed into these cavities to provide the colon and rectal surgeon with greater visualization of potential or existing problems.

"Every once in a while," says Susan, "someone asks me, 'how can you do that all day long?'" She says that she calmly explains that she doesn't give general rectal exams all day but spends most of her time in surgery or talking to patients in order to best help them with their problems.

David puts it plainly: "When I tell someone I'm a colon and rectal surgeon, the conversation usually stops," he chuckles. Then he adds, "Seriously, if answering that question is going to make you feel uncomfortable or embarrassed, this isn't the field for you. I think it has a lot to do with ego. If someone has a huge ego and can't handle what someone else might think of their work, they shouldn't go into this specialty."

Following the physical examination, the colon and rectal surgeon explains the diagnosis to the patient and methods for treating the problem and perhaps preventing it in the future. Charles stresses the importance of this communication between physician and patient. He believes listening to what patients say is just as crucial as getting across the message that a nonsurgical solution or preventive method might work.

"Community awareness is a large part of my job," he says, explaining that many diseases and conditions can be treated or prevented entirely by a change in diet, such as reducing the intake of fat and red meat. In addition to advising his own patients on the importance of diet, Charles sometimes gives talks at schools, hospitals, and nursing homes.

have I got what it takes to be a colon and rectal surgeon?

Colon and rectal surgeons should like working with people, enjoy both surgery and diagnostic medicine, and have a strong interest in pro-

moting good health through preventive measures, like diet and exercise. Surgery is a demanding field requiring considerable time, energy, intellect, and stamina.

Surgeons, in general, do not have flexible hours and a lot of free time. A lot depends, however, on whether the surgeon is a solo practitioner or is one of several colon and rectal surgeons in a practice. "I'm in practice with one other surgeon," says Dr. Susan Briley. "Which means I'm on call half the time. A solo practitioner is on call all the time. But, you never know. For example, today is my day off and I've got to go and see a patient in the hospital. Your patients come first, always."

Colon and rectal surgeons, like other physicians, need to stay up to date with developments in their field. For colon and rectal surgeons this means constantly adding to their knowledge of general surgery, as well as topics and issues in colon and rectal surgery. "Medicine is a self-motivating field," says Dr. Charles Littlejohn. "The purpose of reading is to keep up with my field and apply this research to my patients. I might also present a problem online. Four years ago I couldn't do that. Once the technology was there, I had to learn how to do it. In addition to medical knowledge, I have had to educate myself about computers and the Internet." Those students interested in colon and rectal surgery must like the learning process since it never ends. "Surgery is so demanding of your time," Susan says. "If you're not with patients or in surgery, you're reading about it."

Technology has greatly enhanced the colon and rectal surgeon's ability to diagnose and treat diseases of the intestinal tract and colon, thus technical expertise has become increasingly important. The introduction of optical scopes allowed physicians and surgeons to actually see the interior of the intestinal tract, eliminating guesswork and invasive exploratory surgeries. "We're developing new ways of handling, managing, and treating cancer. It's very exciting," says Dr. David Rothenberger. "Colostomies used to be performed on a fairly high number of patients. Now, they're much more rare."

Technology is not limited to the actual procedures and equipment, themselves, Charles is quick to add. "How we use technology to better improve patient care also includes using the Internet, MEDLINE, and maybe one day, telemedicine." Charles, for example, uses the Internet to present problems to physicians halfway around the world. "I have a colleague in England with whom I often consult," he says. MEDLINE is an online database of medical

To be a successful colon and rectal surgeon, you should

- Be a good clinician
- Enjoy helping and working with people
- Have good hand-eye coordination and manual dexterity
- Be able to listen and communicate well
- Be able to put people at ease and talk about subject matter some might find embarrassing

information that is stored at the U.S. National Library of Medicine in Bethesda, Maryland. Many physicians routinely access it to research treatments, illnesses, and medical studies. Through telemedicine, a surgeon in Rome, for example, could lead a surgeon in New York through a procedure via simultaneous computerized images of the surgery in progress.

Like many doctors, Charles sits on several committees for his specialty and at the hospital where he works. This work is rewarding, he says, but it can be time-consuming and sometimes requires travel. Charles, for example, routinely travels to other cities for lectures, presentations, consultations, and medical conferences.

Part of being a physician means studying, treating, and discussing bodily functions such as breathing, giving birth, or metabolizing calories, and working with substances and fluids that run the gamut from blood to vomit. Without losing sight of the patient as a person, physicians must develop a certain clinical detachment from the functions of the body that might seem embarrassing or unsuitable for conversation.

The truth is, most people are uncomfortable or embarrassed discussing many aspects of their personal health care, and topics involving the intestinal tract and colon probably top the list. The typical response to embarrassment is to deflect it with humor. So, students interested in the medical specialty of colon and rectal surgery should be prepared for the occasional joke at the expense of the profession. Says David, "The same people who like to make jokes about our work are awfully glad to see us when something happens to them." As always, it is best to combat ignorance with education: the more people know and understand about the profession, the human body, and good health, the less likely they are to feel embarrassment.

how do I become a colon and rectal surgeon?

education

High School

A career as a surgeon requires years of schooling. High school courses that are college preparatory are a must. Classes in biology and chemistry as well as mathematics are important. These courses will not only prepare you for college but also help you determine your aptitude in these areas. In addition, it will be beneficial to take courses in social sciences and English, since working with people and communicating effectively will be a large part of your career. When the time comes to choose a college or university, look for one that offers a strong core of science classes that will benefit you in your premedical school studies. You might also want to consider attending an undergraduate institution where you could continue on in its graduate medical school.

Postsecondary Training

"I like people, a lot," explains Charles. "When I was in my first year in college, I knew I wanted to help people with emotional and social issues, but I also wanted to help with physical problems. I thought about going into social work, but I knew I would be frustrated because the funding wasn't always there. Medicine was attractive to me because I could fix things." University or college courses that may help prepare the prospective physician are math, biology, chemistry, and physics. Non-science courses, however, are equally prized by medical school admissions committees. "They like people to have a balance of interests," says Charles. David is a strong advocate of learning more than just medical knowledge. "My philosophy is that you need a broad-based liberal arts education just to be a better person and enjoy life to its fullest."

After receiving an undergraduate degree, someone planning to become a doctor must then apply and be accepted to medical school. Admission is competitive. Applicants must undergo a fairly extensive and difficult admissions process, which considers grade point averages, scores on the Medical College Admission Test (MCAT), and recommendations from professors. Most students apply to several medical schools early in their senior year of college. Only about one-third of the applicants are accepted.

Susan almost didn't become a doctor. After taking an incredibly heavy load of 17 semester hours in her first semester of college at Vanderbilt, she received straight A's, with the exception of a B in general chemistry. She will never forget what happened next. "My chemistry professor knew I wanted to go to medical school and he told me I'd never get in with a grade like that. He said I should just give up." She almost did but then decided to transfer to

Vanderbilt's four-year nursing program. Upon completing nursing school, she worked for two years as an intensive care nurse. Her father encouraged her to keep pursuing her dream and, eventually, her perseverance paid off. "I couldn't apply to medical school on time, so I applied late and didn't get in the first time. But the second time I applied, I got in."

In order to earn the degree of doctor of medicine (M.D.), you must complete four years of medical school study and training. The first two years of medical school consists of lectures and classes and lab work. You learn to take patient histories, perform routine physical examinations, and recognize symptoms of diseases. The third and fourth years involve more practical studies. You work in clinics and hospitals supervised by residents and physicians and you learn acute, chronic, preventive, and rehabilitative care. You go through rotations (brief periods of study) in such areas as internal medicine, obstetrics and gynecology, pediatrics, dermatology, psychiatry, and surgery.

Upon graduating from an accredited medical school, physicians must pass a standard examination given by the National Board of Medical Examiners. Most physicians complete an internship, also referred to as a transition year. The internship is usually one year in length, and helps graduates to decide on an area of specialization.

Following the internship, the physicians begin what is known as a residency. Physicians wishing to pursue the surgical specialty of colon and rectal surgery must first complete a residency in general surgery. Residents begin their training by assisting on and then performing basic operations, such as the removal of an appendix. As the residency years continue, residents gain responsibility through teaching and supervisory duties. Eventually the residents are allowed to perform complex operations.

After satisfactory completion of a general surgical residency, physicians must enter a residency program in colon and rectal surgery for a minimum of one year. The colon and rectal residency program is designed to produce a specialist who has gained extra knowledge, expertise, and skill in treating patients with diseases of the colon, rectum, and anus. Because of the brevity of the program, no rotations in other areas are required. Close interaction with radiology, pathology, and gastroenterology is part of the normal study. Most colon and rectal programs are small, which allows for very close, one-on-one interaction with staff.

Residents are primarily devoted to advanced training in patient care but are expected to develop a research project during their year of training.

certification or licensing

In the United States, licensing is required before a doctor can practice medicine. In order to be licensed, doctors must have graduated from medical school, passed the licensing test of the state in which they will practice, and completed their residency.

Certification for a colon and rectal surgeon is highly recommended. Board certified colon and rectal surgeons have successfully completed at least a five-year training program in general surgery and one additional year in a colon and rectal surgery residency approved by the Accreditation Council for Graduate Medical Education. They have then passed both the written (qualifying) and oral (certifying) examinations given by the American Board of Colon and Rectal Surgery (ABCRS). The ABCRS requires certification by the American Board of Surgery for all candidates entering the examination process. The requirements of residency programs take into account those standards so that residents can best prepare for the certifying examinations.

scholarships and grants

Scholarships and grants are often available from individual institutions, state agencies, and special-interest organizations. Many students finance their medical education through the Armed Forces Health Professions Scholarship Program. Each branch of the military participates in this program, paying students' tuitions in exchange for military service. Contact your local recruiting office for more information. The National Health Service Corps Scholarship Program also provides money for students in return for service. Another source for financial aid, scholarship, and grant information is the Association of American Medical Colleges. Remember to request information early from these organizations for eligibility, application requirements, and deadlines.

American College of Surgeons

(Maintains Surgical Research Clearinghouse on research grants and fellowships.)

633 North St. Clair Street

Chicago, IL 60611-3211

postmaster@facs.org

http://www.facs.org

Association of American Medical Colleges

2450 N Street, NW

Washington, DC 20037

http://www.aamc.org

National Health Service Corps Scholarship Program

U.S. Public Health Service

1010 Wayne Avenue, Suite 240

Silver Spring, MD 20910

nhsc@matthewsgroup.com

http://www.fedmoney.org/grants/93288-00.htm

who will hire me?

In general, surgeons can choose to work in a number different settings. They may open a private practice, be employed at a teaching hospital, military hospital, or other long-term care institution, work in an HMO (Health Maintenance Organization), or work at a combination of sites. For example, a surgeon with a private practice may also have privileges at a hospital. In this environment the colon and rectal surgeon may work with other physicians, nurses, and hospital staff on diagnosis and treatment. A colon and rectal surgeon may also be asked to consult on a case that involves other complications outside of the colon and rectal specialty.

David has his own private practice in Stamford, Connecticut. Opening a private practice can be expensive. Also, opening a practice limited only to colon and rectal surgery is not always feasible in less populated areas. "You need to be in a fairly large urban area, a community that has a population of between 50,000 and 100,000," he says. "This is because to support a practice you need a number of people who will have problems related to the specialty of colon and rectal surgery."

Unless a recently certified colon and rectal surgeon can afford the expenses associated with opening up a private practice—such as purchasing equipment and office furniture, paying for a rental property, and buying liability insurance—the most common route for a new doctor is to join a more established practice or to open a practice with several others. "Most of the colon and rectal surgeons I know went into practice with one to two other surgeons," says Susan. "I went into practice with one other doctor and, as result, I'm on call half the time."

where can I go from here?

David has already been practicing for over 13 years, but he sees a change in his work in the next five years. In addition to developing his own private practice, he has begun publishing original papers on topics in colon and rectal surgery. Publishing is an excellent way for a physician to advance his or her career. He explains, "The longer a doctor is in practice, the more he learns and knows, and the best way to pass that information on is through publications and research."

Of special interest to David is patient care, how it has changed, how it has remained the same, and what that means for the patient. "I'm interested in evaluating whether or not the way we practice is valid. Outcomes research is a combination of science and statistics, a way of looking at what you're doing and determining what the impact of that is on the patient."

Research and teaching are two other options for the colon and rectal surgeon. Many colon and rectal surgeons combine research and/or teaching with a private practice. According to David, this makes the specialty all the more appealing. "In this specialty, you can easily do all three—research, teach, and practice. If I weren't already in the field, I would be tempted," he adds with a smile.

what are the salary ranges?

The national average salary for first-year residents in 1998 was $34,100. That average increased to $42,100 by the final residency year. Salaries vary depending on the kind of residency, the hospital, and the geographic area.

Colon and rectal surgeons just opening their own practices or in the early stages of their careers can expect to make between $80,000 and $120,000. More experienced colon and rectal surgeons can expect to earn between $150,000 and $250,000, while a very few may earn close to $300,000 or $350,000. Individual incomes vary according to the type of practice, amount of experience, and geographic location.

what is the job outlook?

The health care industry is thriving and the employment of physicians in almost all fields is expected to grow faster than the average for all occupations through the next decade. Although advancements in technology and an increasing public awareness of the importance of a healthy diet will continue to improve the general health of patients, people will continue to need the specialized skills and expertise of the colon and rectal surgeon.

"I think the future looks great," says David. "Managed care [through an HMO] has put the emphasis on cost. The trend right now is to try and keep patients with the generalist as long as possible, the idea being that the specialist is too expensive. In reality, keeping patients with the generalist for too long has resulted in inappropriate testing and expensive delays," he says. "But I think the pendulum will soon swing back in favor of the specialist. What is being discovered is that generalists should do triage and then send the patients on to the specialist as soon as possible. I firmly believe that specialty care will increase in the future, not decrease."

To David, managed care represents an increasing responsibility for physicians to protect their patients. "It used to be that we needed to make sure we protected our patients by maintaining or improving the quality of care," he explains. "Now, instead of focusing solely on the quality, we also have to focus on the economics of patient care, and make certain the economics doesn't detract from the quality."

The future of colon and rectal surgery holds great promise for women surgeons. Currently, there are approximately 1,280 board certified colon and rectal surgeons in the United States, according to the American Board of Colon and Rectal Surgery. The board certifies approximately 50 to 60 new surgeons each year. Of the 1,280 board certified colon and rectal surgeons, only 85 are women. David believes that colon and rectal surgery is a smart career move for women surgical residents looking for a specialty. He notes, "Diseases of the colon and rectum affect both genders equally. More women need help with problems in the pelvic floor area, problems with defecation, incontinence, and prolapse." Susan heartily agrees with this assessment. "Colon and rectal surgery is a good choice for women. Women like to be seen by women doctors."

how do I learn more?

professional organizations

Following are organizations that provide information on the residency, certification, and profession of colon and rectal surgeons.

American Board of Colon and Rectal Surgery
20600 Eureka Road, Suite 713
Taylor, MI 48180
admin@abcrs.org
http://www.abcrs.org

American Society of Colon and Rectal Surgeons
85 West Algonquin Road, Suite 550
Arlington Heights, IL 60005
ascrs@fascrs.org
http://www.fascrs.org

bibliography

Following is a sampling of materials relating to the professional concerns and development of colon and rectal surgeons.

Corman, Marvin L. *Handbook of Colon and Rectal Surgery.* Philadelphia, PA: Lippincott Williams & Wilkins, 2001.

Gordon, Philip H. and Santhat Nivatvongs. *Neoplasms of the Colon, Rectum and Anus.* St. Louis, MO: Quality Medical Publishing, Inc., 2000.

Gordon, Philip H. and Santhat Nivatvongs. *Principles and Practice of Surgery for the Colon, Rectum and Anus.* 2nd Edition. St. Louis, MO: Quality Medical Publishing, 1998.

Hicks, Terry C. et al. eds. *Complications of Colon & Rectal Surgery.* Philadelphia, PA: Lippincott, Williams & Wilkins, 1996.

Soreide, O. *Rectal Cancer Surgery: Optimisation-Standardisation-Documentation.* New York, NY: Springer-Verlag Inc., 1997.

Wexner, Steven D. and Anthony M. Vernava, III. *Clinical Decision Making in Colorectal Surgery.* Philadelphia, PA: Lippincott Williams & Wilkins, 1995.

Creative Arts Therapists

Definition

Creative arts therapists use the arts as rehabilitation to help people heal from physical, developmental, and emotional illness.

Alternative Job Titles

Art therapists
Music therapists
Drama therapists
Dance therapists
Poetry therapists
Recreation therapists

High School Subjects

Art
Speech

Personal Skills

Artistic
Helping/teaching

Salary Range

$25,000 to $35,000 to $81,000

Educational Requirements

Bachelor's degree

Certification or Licensing

Required by all states

Outlook

About as fast as the average

GOE
10.02.02

O*NET-SOC
29-1125.00

"**Hello,** Mrs. Taylor, are we ready to begin?"

The 72-year-old woman nods wanly. It has been a tough road to recovery since her stroke four months ago. She has lost use of most of the left side of her body, and had to leave her apartment in the high rise where she had lived since her husband died five years ago. Now she is a resident of Pleasant View Manor, a nursing home where she can get the physical therapy and rehabilitation she needs to someday be able to return to her apartment.

Alan Bumanis strums his guitar and together they hum the first refrains of one of her favorite hymns. They sing the next verse, Alan carefully enunciating the words over the music. Mrs. Taylor works very hard to get her tongue around the familiar words that she sang so many times in the church choir.

Alan is pleased. As a music therapist, he knows recovering speech is a slow, frustrating process for stroke victims, but he is encouraged by Mrs. Taylor's quick progress over the last eight weeks.

"Wonderful," Alan says. "I know it may be hard for you to notice, but I can tell your breath support is stronger than it was last time, and I was able to understand more of that second verse. Let's try again."

what does a creative arts therapist do?

Creative arts therapy uses visual art, dance and movement, drama, music, and poetry to treat a wide range of mental, emotional, physical, and developmental problems. The creative process, not the end product, promotes healing. *Creative arts therapists* combine their arts

lingo to learn

Acting out: Uncontrolled behavior in which a client responds in the present in a way determined by previous experiences. It is usually aggressive in nature.

Bibliotherapy: Use of books to help people solve problems or adjust behavior.

Creativity coach: A person hired by a company or individual to help nurture the creative process.

Integrative medicine: Combines conventional Western medicine with mind-body-spirit alternative and complementary techniques.

Portfolio: A collection of personal work that shows examples of an artist's skills and techniques.

Psychodrama: Guided dramatic action used in therapeutic settings to clarify emotions and enhance well-being.

Treatment plan: The documentation and discussion of a client's goals and the services necessary for the client to achieve them, guided by a treatment team.

expertise with knowledge of therapeutic techniques. To reach their patients, they can use a variety of mediums, including visual art, dance, music, drama, or poetry or other kinds of creative writing. They usually specialize in one medium.

Alan Bumanis, was using music therapy as a physical rehabilitation tool with Mrs. Taylor in the nursing home. But music and other art therapies can be used to facilitate emotional healing as well. For example, Barbara Fish, Director of Activity Therapy for the Illinois Department of Mental Health and Developmental Disabilities, Chicago Metropolitan Child and Adolescent Services, has a patient who has been sexually abused. The patient is extraordinarily frightened because of the traumatic abuse and is slow to trust Barbara. This may be the first time in the patient's life that she is in an environment of acceptance and support. It may take months or even years before the patient begins to trust the therapist, "come out of the woods," and begin to heal.

It is important to note that creative arts therapy sessions are not classes. In the case of visual arts, for example, it is not important if the patients ever learn perspective or color theory. The therapist is not there to teach art history. What is important is that the patients begin to open up their imaginations, become more vital and energetic, and begin to heal.

Creative arts therapists may use many tools in their sessions, including clay, chalk, paint, musical instruments, puppets, or paper. Therapists themselves, are perhaps the most important tool. They have to use their eyes and ears to pay constant attention to the behavior of patients before, during, and after the session. That behavior is as significant as the artistic work they create. In Alan's case with the elderly stroke victim, music therapy was being used to help in the physical healing process. A side benefit of music therapy is the feeling of comfort Mrs. Taylor may have drawn from hearing and singing a familiar hymn at a time when her own body and disability may seem foreign to her.

Similar to dreaming, creative arts therapy taps into the unconscious and gives people a way to express themselves in an uncensored environment. This is important because before patients can begin to heal, they must first identify their feelings. Once they recognize their feelings, they can begin to develop an understanding of the relationship between their feelings and their behavior.

"In my groups we use poetry and creative writing," Barbara explains. "We do all kinds of things to get at what is going on, at an unconscious level." When the patients begin to realize that the creative arts therapist is accepting of their feelings, they begin to accept their own feelings and start to heal.

Within the context of Barbara's job, patients can create images and artwork as powerful as they want and not be afraid of the consequences. "An art therapist helps people to learn about themselves and accept themselves and begin to heal," Barbara explains. "The first way the therapist does this is by creating an environment where it is safe to create." For many patients this level of acceptance is something they have never known before.

In some cases, especially when the patients are adolescents, they may have become so detached from their feelings that they can physically act out without consciously knowing the reasons for their behavior. This detachment from their emotions creates a great deal of psychological pain. With the help of a creative arts therapist, patients can begin to communicate their unconscious feelings nonverbally. They can express their emotions in a variety of ways without having to name them.

Creative arts therapists work with children, adolescents, adults, and senior citizens. They can work in individual, group, or family sessions. The approach of the therapist, however, depends on the specific needs of the patient or group. For example, if a patient is feeling overwhelmed by too many options or stimuli, the therapist may give him or her only a plain piece of paper and a pencil to work with that day.

what is it like to be a creative arts therapist?

Creative arts therapy is a popular second career choice for people in many related professions. Alan says that nurses and teachers with some artistic talent are among professionals who make a career change when they see how creative arts therapy can benefit people. The work is rewarding for someone who has the patience to notice and encourage small increments of slow improvement in their patients.

A creative arts therapist working in a nursing home setting is part of a treatment team assigned to each patient. The team may be headed by a doctor or nurse and include an occupational or physical therapist and a social worker. The patient may or may not be included in treatment planning. For a stroke victim like Mrs. Taylor, the team assesses her current level of functioning and physical and mental health before and after the stroke and, given her age, establishes short-term and long-term goals to regain and improve functioning.

For therapists who work with elderly patients, getting used to the fact that many of your patients will never recover fully or will show only marginal improvement is an important lesson to learn early in your career. "In geriatrics, it is much harder to regain the health you once had, be it physical or mental, so many of our goals are maintenance goals," Alan says. "But it can be dramatic in the sense that a person with Alzheimer's can't communicate, but music may bring them out of their shell. As a quality of life issue, music therapy is a powerful tool."

The pace of treatment is slow and measured in psychiatric settings as well. The adolescents who are in the long-term unit at the Chicago Metropolitan Child and Adolescent Services Center are there because they have failed in other placements. The patients at this facility are very disturbed. Some patients have impulse disorders, some have been abused, and some have become abusers. To be allowed into the creative arts therapy sessions, patients must agree to follow Barbara's three ground rules: respect yourself, respect other people, and respect property. The therapy groups are limited to five patients per group.

Barbara is also part of a treatment team. The team includes a psychologist, psychiatrist, social worker, nurse, and a representative of the center's school. They meet once a week to discuss the direction and progress of each patient's treatment.

Barbara begins the session by asking each person in the group how he or she is feeling that day. By carefully listening to their responses, a theme may emerge that will determine the direction of the therapy. For example, if anger is recurring in their statements, Barbara may ask them to draw a line down the center of a piece of paper. On one side she asks them to draw how anger looks and on the other side how feeling sad looks. Then, once the drawing is complete, she will ask them to compare the two pictures and see that their anger may be masking their feelings of sadness, loneliness, and disappointment. As patients begin to recognize their true feelings, they develop better control of their behavior.

Creating an environment of acceptance and support, however, does not mean creating a space where the patients can do whatever they want. It must be a safe space both emotionally and physically. Patients are not allowed to laugh at or criticize another patient's work. Furthermore, patients can be unpredictable and capable of violence. For that reason, a creative arts therapist must always, on some level, be on guard. In her desk Barbara keeps the knife that a troubled adolescent pulled on her when she was an intern. It is a reminder to always be careful.

Rewards for a creative arts therapist can come in unexpected ways. Fifteen years ago, as an intern, Barbara gave one of her patients a sketch pad. He had been hospitalized for the first time suffering from a psychotic episode. In the years that followed he became a chronic patient, moving in and out of hospitals. Three years ago Barbara was supervising an intern who brought in a patient's sketchbook. She recognized the work as that of the man she had given a sketch pad to 15 years earlier. His mental illness is incurable but his art has become a source of comfort for him.

have I got what it takes to be a creative arts therapist?

To work successfully in the field of creative arts therapy, you must have a high level of maturity. That includes a strong understanding of personal strengths and weaknesses. If a patient, especially an adolescent, realizes that certain behavior will trigger a particular reaction from the therapist, the patient may use this knowledge to manipulate the session. Alan describes the profession as "a more mature profession that requires some life experience" and empathy for a patient's situation.

For example, if the therapist is accustomed to having a certain amount of control during the session, the patient may decide to challenge the therapist. At this point the therapist must realize what the patient is doing and change the approach of the session to prevent a power struggle from developing. As Barbara explains, "You can't win a power struggle, so you have to know yourself well enough and step sideways and move around it."

Another important characteristic of a good creative arts therapist is a very high level of sensitivity. It is important that the therapist respect the risks that patients take when they create something. They are expressions of the deepest part of themselves. The therapist must be incredibly careful to validate what the patient is trying to communicate. It takes a great deal of courage for patients to reveal themselves to someone else and the reaction of the therapist can have a major impact on the patient and the progress of the therapy.

Sometimes therapists must allow patients to work issues out for themselves but be there as a guide if they are needed. Patients may be trying to communicate desperate thoughts through their work and the therapist must know when to step in and when to leave the patient alone. Knowing the difference between the two is the tightrope a creative arts therapist walks everyday.

One of the most helpful skills a creative arts therapist can develop is the ability to appear calm even in the most difficult situations. While working with emotionally troubled patients, the therapist often listens to disturbing and painful patient accounts of life experiences. It is extremely important that therapists control their reactions to what is being said. Barbara explains, "If you start to seize up, the patient will sense that and they will stop and move further away."

The ability to relinquish the lead and let patients work at their own pace is very important. Standing by and letting a patient draw with the same color marker, filling in the paper with the same image, day after day, for months can take incredible patience. But the therapist must recognize that there has been progress when the patient asks for a different colored marker.

how do I become a creative arts therapist?

education

High School
A high school diploma or a GED equivalent is mandatory to become a creative arts therapist. Depending on what type of creative arts therapy you want to pursue, you must become as proficient as possible with the methods and tools of the trade. For example, if you want to become involved in music therapy, you need to become familiar with musical instruments as well as music theory. A

good starting point for a music therapist is to study piano or guitar. It is helpful to begin studying any applicable art forms as soon as possible. When you work with patients you must be able to concentrate completely on the patient rather than on learning how to use tools or techniques.

In addition to courses such as drama, art, music, and English, consider taking an introductory class in psychology if one is offered. Also, you should take a communication class to gain an understanding of the various ways people communicate, both verbally and nonverbally.

Postsecondary Training

To become a creative arts therapist you must have earned at least a bachelor's degree, usually in an the area in which you wish to specialize. However, to be certified, many nationally recognized associations require a graduate degree from a university with an accredited program. For instance, the American Association for Art Therapy requires a master's degree for certification. The association lists 31 schools with approved graduate degree programs in art therapy.

Accredited graduate programs for creative arts therapists vary according to the discipline pursued. As an example, graduate programs in art therapy require applicants to submit a portfolio of original artwork. The portfolio should demonstrate a high level of competence with art materials and not necessarily a certain degree of talent.

Once accepted into a program, classroom instruction for art therapy students includes at least 15 semester hours of studio art and 12 semester hours of psychology. It is a requirement of the program that these hours of study be completed within a year of beginning the program. In addition to class work, you must participate in 600 hours of supervised art therapy practice, half of which is in individual sessions and half in group sessions. Finally, the core curriculum includes 21 graduate credit hours, which you must complete within two years or four full-time semesters.

Alan describes college training for music therapists as an intense degree program. In addition to the demands of the music program, which includes skill on guitar, piano, and/or voice, students take courses in psychology, anatomy and physiology, and education. Requirements in graduate programs for most of the other areas of creative arts therapy are similar to those for art therapists. There are over 70 colleges with bachelor-level degrees in music therapy

According to a survey conducted by the American Music Therapy Association, the typical musical therapist is female, has an advanced degree in music therapy, and earned an average salary of $34,893 in 2000.

certification or licensing

Most creative arts therapists must be certified or registered by the nationally recognized association specific to their field of choice. For example, the Art Therapy Credentials Board, Inc. (ATCB) offers registration and certification separately. To become registered, applicants must document their graduate education and postgraduate supervised experience. Once art therapists are registered, they must pass a written examination administered by the ATCB to become board certified. To retain this status, therapists must maintain their continuing education.

Certification for most other creative arts therapists also requires passing a national examination. For instance, a music therapist must pass an exam administered by the Certification Board for Music Therapist. The examination tests competence in individual skills and knowledge, and the practical application of professional music therapy. The American Dance Therapy Association offers the D.T.R. designation (dance therapist registered), which means the therapist has a master's degree and is qualified to treat clients, and the A.D.T.R. designation, which means the therapist has met additional requirements and is qualified to teach and supervise dance therapists.

Many registered creative arts therapists also receive additional licenses as social workers, educators, mental health professionals, or marriage and family therapists. They often are also members of other professional associations, including the American Psychological Association, the American Association of Marriage and Family Therapists, and the American Counseling Association.

scholarships and grants

There are few scholarships specifically for creative arts therapy students. However, the field covers two disciplines, so you may qualify for the many allied health or arts scholarships offered nationwide. Many states have a health professions education foundation to encourage students to enter the health care field in their states. In addition, most communities have local music or art appreciation groups that might offer small scholarships.

The various creative arts therapy associations do have charitable giving foundations; however, most of their work is in the promotion of their therapy, which can include research and publishing support, as well as travel and lecture support for their members.

The American Association for Art Therapy sponsors research grants for members working towards a master's or doctoral degree in art therapy. The American Therapeutic Recreation Foundation awards educational scholarships for students to attend recreation therapy conferences and forums. Visit http://www.atra-tr.org or call 703-683-9420.

internships and volunteerships

Beyond your artistic talent, practical experience in sharing it with others will give you an edge in applying for admission to college arts therapy programs. Cities of every size have local hospitals, clinics, and nursing homes that generally welcome volunteers to share their creative talents.

To be a successful creative arts therapist, you should

- Be a good listener
- Be very observant
- Enjoy working with people
- Have a lot of patience
- Be even-tempered and have the ability to adapt quickly
- Have a great deal of sensitivity

There are professional creative arts therapy associations that may be able to identify volunteer programs by regions. Speaking to members of an association is also a great opportunity to talk to someone who is active in the field.

who will hire me?

As the medical community realizes the positive effects that mental health can have on physical well-being, the demand for creative arts therapists will grow. Many people in the medical field have begun to look at creative arts therapy as an enhancement to traditional treatment. In addition, the demand for creative arts therapists in nursing homes is expected to grow as more of the baby-boom generation enters old age.

Employment opportunities for creative arts therapists vary greatly across the profession. The work settings can include psychiatric facilities, private practices, schools, and medical, correctional, and geriatric facilities. Most creative arts therapists, however, work in psychiatric or mental health settings.

The breakdown of responsibilities within the different work settings can include individual therapy, group therapy, administrative work, workshops, and training.

Universities employ creative arts therapists to conduct research and teach. Therapists often present their research findings at conferences or workshops. Workshops and conferences are good opportunities for therapists to discuss new ideas and developments with other therapists. Creative arts therapists working at universities with accredited programs may also be employed to supervise graduate students.

Almost a third of all creative arts therapists work in private practices. Private practices allows therapists to treat a wider range of patients. Working from their own studios, therapists can treat adolescents, adults, and seniors. They can also conduct sessions in individual, group, and family settings. Some therapists work only part-time in a private practice but maintain a staff position at a mental health facility.

In addition to her work at the state facility, Barbara sees patients in a private practice. One of her patients is a photographer who uses art therapy as a means of becoming more creative. As Barbara explains, "Art therapy is not just art for pain but art for growth."

where can I go from here?

As therapists gain more experience they can move into supervisory, administrative, or teaching positions. Often, the supervision of interns can resemble a therapy session. The interns will discuss their feelings and ask any questions that they may have regarding their work with patients. How did they handle their patients? What were their reactions to what their patients said or did? What could they be doing to help their patients more? The supervising therapist helps the interns answer these and other questions as they help the interns become competent creative arts therapists.

Many therapists have represented the profession internationally. Barbara was invited to present her paper, "Art Therapy with Children and Adolescents." at the University of Helsinki. Additionally, Barbara spoke in Finland at a three-day workshop exploring the use and effectiveness of art therapy with children and adolescents. Raising the public and professional awareness of creative arts therapy is an important concern for many therapists. There are areas where it is desperately needed.

Alan worked as a music therapist in nursing homes and psychiatric settings for many years before becoming the director of communications and conferences for the American Music Therapy Association. Now his job is to raise public awareness and promote knowledge of music therapy.

what are the salary ranges?

A therapist's annual salary depends on experience, level of training and education. Working on a hospital staff or being self-employed also affects annual income. In 1998, the American Association for Art Therapy reported that entry-level creative arts therapists earned $25,000. The median annual salary was in the $28,000 to $38,000 range, with top earnings for salaried administrators reported at $40,000 to $60,000. Those who had Ph.D.s and were licensed for private practice reported charging between $75 and $90 per hour for their services; however, professional expenses such as insurance and office rental must be paid by those in private practice.

The American Music Therapy Association reported average annual salaries for music therapists as $34,893 in 2000. Salaries varied from

Places where creative arts therapists work
Hospitals
Schools
Universities
Mental health centers
Nursing homes
Prisons
Rehabilitation centers

that average by region, most by less than $2,000 a year, with the highest average salaries reported in the New England states at $41,600. Salaries reported by its members ranged from $15,000 to $81,000. The average annual earnings for music therapists with more than 20 years of professional experience was $43,306 in 2000.

The annual salary for therapists working for the government is determined by their level of education and responsibilities. It can be as high as $50,000.

what is the job outlook?

The job outlook for creative arts therapists depends on the setting where you work, but the creative arts therapy field is expected to grow as fast as the average. Anticipated expansion in long-term care, physical and psychiatric rehabilitation, and services for people with disabilities will keep employment opportunities steady in this field. Also, the rapidly growing number of older adults is expected to create job growth in this field, and creative arts therapists may find that opportunities in gerontology settings may grow faster than the average.

Managed care and the resulting tightening of insurance reimbursement for some therapies could adversely affect this field. However, consumer demand seems to be working against any reductions. The American Music Therapy Association reports that 23 percent of its members received some sort of insurance reimbursement in 1999 for music therapy services. That number has continued to rise, the association reports, as government agencies and insurance companies respond to increased market demand for interventions such as music therapy that meet quality of life needs.

Therapists are beginning to redefine their roles and their responsibilities to reach a new segment of the population. For example, some have begun to refer to themselves as creativity coaches. They use creative arts therapy to help healthy people become more creative. Clients enroll in creative arts therapy to help themselves open up and become more creative, to grow emotionally, and to experience a fuller life.

Corporate America has recognized the important uses of intuitive thinking, creating a new employment opportunity for creative arts therapists. A former intern of Barbara's now works for IBM in its creative services department. By helping executives think on a more intuitive level, they may be able to approach old problems from different perspectives and discover new solutions.

how do I learn more?

professional organizations

Following are organizations that provide information on the field of creative arts therapy and on careers in the field.

American Association for Art Therapy
1202 Allanson Road
Mundelein, IL 60060
847-949-6064
arttherapy@ntr.net
http://www.arttherapy.org

American Dance Therapy Association
2000 Century Plaza
10632 Little Patuxent Parkway, Suite 108
Columbia, MD 21044
410-997-4040
info@adta.org
http://www.adta.org

Art Therapy Credentials Board, Inc.
3 Terrace Way, Suite B
Greensboro, NC 27403
877-213-2822
atcb@nbcc.org
http://www.atcb.org

National Association for Drama Therapy
5505 Connecticut Avenue, NW, #280
Washington, DC 20015
nadt@danielgrp.com
http://www.nadt.org

National Association for Music Therapy, Inc.
8455 Colesville Road, Suite 1000
Silver Spring, MD 20910-3392
301-589-3300
info@musictherapy.org
http://www.musictherapy.org

National Association for Poetry Therapy
5505 Connecticut Avenue, NW, #280
Washington, DC 20015
202-966-2536
napt@danielgrp.com
www.poetrytherapy.org

bibliography

Following is a sampling of materials relating to creative arts therapy.

Allen, Pat B. *Art Is a Way of Knowing*. Boston, MA: Shambhala Publications, 1995.

Bertman, Sandra L., ed. *Grief and the Healing Arts: Creativity as Therapy*. Amityville, NY: 1999.

Hervey, Lenore Wadsworth. *Artistic Inquiry in Dance/Movement Therapy: Creative Research Alternatives*. Springfield, IL: Charles C. Thomas Publisher, Ltd., 2000.

Johnson, David Read. *Essays on the Creative Arts Therapies: Imaging the Birth of a Profession*. Springfield, IL: Charles C. Thomas Publisher, Ltd., 1999.

Makin, Susan R. *A Consumer's Guide to Art Therapy for Prospective Employers, Clients, and Students*. Springfield, IL: Charles C. Thomas Publisher, Ltd., 1996.

Malchiodi, Cathy A. *The Art Therapy Sourcebook*. Los Angeles, CA: Lowell House, 1998.

Parsons, Vicki. *Simple Expressions: Creative & Therapeutic Arts for the Elderly in Long-Term Care Facilities*. Andover, MA: Venture Publishing, 1998.

Riley, Shirley, et al. *Contemporary Art Therapy with Adolescents*. London, UK: Jessica Kingsley Publishers, 1999.

Rogers, Natalie. *The Creative Connection: Expressive Arts as Healing*. Palo Alto, CA: Science & Behavior Books, 1997.

Cytotechnologists

Definition

Cytotechnologists study cells. They assist in the collection of body cells, prepare slides, and examine cells using microscopes. Cytotechnologists search for cell abnormalities in order to aid in the diagnosis of disease.

High School Subjects

Biology
Chemistry
Computer science

Personal Skills

Following instructions
Technical/scientific

Salary Range

$19,000 to $32,000 to $48,000

Minimum Educational Level

At least one year of professional instruction in cytotechnology after or included in a bachelor of science degree.

Certification or Licensing

Required by certain states

Outlook

About as fast as the average

GOE
02.04.02
O*NET-SOC
29-2012.00

The room is quiet, the lights bright. Bill Crabtree positions a glass slide under the microscope lens and studies the collected cell sample. He's on the lookout for abnormal growth patterns. A cytotechnologist and director of the Indiana University School of Medicine's Cytotechnology Program, Bill spends the majority of his day at the bench, peering through the microscope and picking out cell samples that appear to be cancerous. "We're cell detectives," says Bill. "We really affect people's lives. What we do can be a matter of life or death."

Like good detectives, cytotechnologists are careful and precise. They are laboratory specialists who search cell specimens, seeking out abnormalities. Some forms of cancer, a tumor growing on someone's liver, for instance, can be seen with the naked eye, but other types of cancer are not so easily detected. Cytotechnologists are particularly effective at finding cancer of the cervix. Much of their work involves diagnosing Pap smears, cell samples that are taken during routine gynecological exams. Because of the detective skills cytotechnologists bring to their profession, the death rate from cancer of the cervix is 25 percent lower than what it was 40 years ago.

"Cytotechnology is a challenging field," says Bill, "but it's a good one if you like laboratory work. Plus it's a field where you can really make a difference."

what does a cytotechnologist do?

Cytotechnologists perform the majority of their work by looking through a microscope at prepared slides. They study cell growth patterns

lingo to learn

Bronchoscopy: The taking of tissue samples from the bronchi (in the lungs) with the use of a bronchoscope.

Cell: The structural unit of which all body tissues are formed. The human body is composed of billions of cells differing in size and structure.

Cervix: The hollow end of a woman's uterus that forms the passageway to the vaginal canal.

Gastrointestinal: Relating to the digestive system.

Gynecology: The branch of medicine that deals with the reproductive system of women.

Needle aspiration: The taking of tissue with the use of a long, syringe needle.

Pathologist: A doctor who specializes in the study of diseases.

Sputum: Expectorated matter, usually from the lungs.

Tumor: A swelling in or on a particular area of the body, usually created by the development of a mass of new tissue cells having no function. Tumors may be benign (noncancerous) or malignant (cancerous).

and check to see whether the specimens under the lens have normal or abnormal patterns. Abnormal patterns can indicate the presence of disease. Cytotechnologists search for changes in cell color, shape, or size. A change in any one of these can be cause for concern. In any single slide there may be more than 100,000 cells, so cytotechnologists must be patient and thorough in order to make accurate evaluations.

Cytotechnologists do more than peer through microscopes. When they are away from the laboratory, they may work at patients' bedsides assisting doctors in the direct collection of cell samples. The respiratory system, urinary system, and gastrointestinal tract are some of the body sites from which cells may be gathered. Cytotechnologists also assist physicians with bronchoscopies and with needle aspirations, a process that uses very fine needles to suction cells from many locations within the body. Needle aspirations sometimes replace invasive surgeries as a means of gathering microscopic matter for disease detection. Once cells are collected, cytotechnologists may prepare the slides so that the cell samples can be examined under the microscope. In some laboratories, medical technicians prepare slides rather than cytotechnologists.

Another part of the cytotechnologist's day is spent keeping records, filing reports, and consulting with co-workers and pathologists on cases. Cytotechnologists can issue diagnoses on Pap smears if the diagnosis is normal. However, if cell examination indicates any abnormalities, Pap smear results as well as other cytological results are sent on to supervising cytotechnologists or to pathologists for review.

Most of the time cytotechnologists work independently. They may share lab space with other personnel, but the primary job of a cytotechnologist is to look through the microscope and search for evidence of disease. Most cytotechnologists work for private firms that are hired by physicians to evaluate medical tests, but many cytotechnologists also work for hospitals or university research institutions.

what is it like to be a cytotechnologist?

"Where I work," says Bill, "it's routine for cytotechnologists to spend 50 or 60 percent of their day at the microscope. Like all cytotechnologists, we see a lot of Pap smears, but at the Indiana University School of Medicine we also look at cell samples that are nongynecological, too. We look at material collected from any kind of solid tumor, at abdominal fluids, thoracic fluids, urine samples, sputum, brushes and washes of the lungs and bronchial passages, lesions from the gastrointestinal tract, scrapings from the mouth or skin, and spinal fluid. Occasionally we can identify microbiological infections, bacteria, fungus, and such, but principally we're diagnosing cancer or its precursors."

Cytotechnologists usually work a standard eight-hour day, five days a week. They also do a lot of work on computers. They enter and retrieve information using computers. Diagnostic results are entered into computers so that pathologists can directly access the information and make the results available to patients.

"Since I'm at a university medical school," says Bill, "part of my day is involved with the education program for cytotechnology students and part of my day is involved with research. Another part of my time is spent working on quality control and going through quality assurance procedures. I also file reports and keep records using the computer."

Susan Dingler also works at a teaching hospital. "Simply working in a laboratory can be repetitive," she says, "but here at the School of Cytotechnology at Henry Ford Hospital in Detroit, cytotechnologists rotate job duties. One week I might work in the preparation area, extracting cells and preparing slides. We use various methods, depending on the source of the cells and the amount of sample available. Another week I might assist with needle aspirations. Or I could be working in the CAT scan room. Then again, I could be involved with coordinating our education program.

"Everybody's cells and every single tumor is different," says Susan. "There are similarities—otherwise we wouldn't be able to do our work—but because no two cells look exactly the same, I'm never bored when I'm looking through the microscope. Cytotechnology is an especially challenging field."

Bernadette Inclan works for a private company in Phoenix, Arizona. Unlike Bill and Susan, she does not teach students or perform research. She does not work for a university. As a quality insurance inspector, she oversees the work done in several private laboratories located across the Southwest and along the West Coast.

I'm never bored when I'm looking through the microscope. Cytotechnology is an especially challenging field.

Because the diagnoses that cytotechnologists make can literally be matters of life and death, the profession is governed by a system of checks and balances. Bernadette and other supervisors help make sure that the medical tests cytotechnologists perform are accurate. For example, she does second screenings to assure quality control and to confirm test results on high-risk patients.

When specimens are hard to screen because the sample itself is very small or because the cells are obscured by too much blood, Bernadette is also called upon to give her expert opinion. In fact, any time any cytotechnologist in her company's laboratories marks a sample "Please Check" (meaning that the cytotechnologist is unable to make an unequivocal decision about the contents of the cell sample), Bernadette or one of the other supervisors double-checks the work.

Bernadette is also involved in managing people. "It's an exciting time for us," she says. "My firm is merging with another health lab and so that means a lot of changes. I'll do a lot of traveling between company sites and help make sure that the merger goes well for our cytotechnology team. I'll also make sure that the work continues successfully in the lab."

Teamwork is an important feature of cytotechnology. "Sure, we're behind individual microscopes a lot of the time," says Bill. "But really we're rather unique in the health care field. Cytotechnologists work more closely with physicians, especially with pathologists, than do most laboratory workers. Plus we work together as cytotechnologists, consulting with each other and with our supervisors on unusual cases."

have I got what it takes to be a cytotechnologist?

"The person who gets straight A's does not necessarily make the best cytotechnologist. Our job involves more than learning facts and memorizing information. You need to know how to apply what you learn when you look through the microscope. You need a knack for detail," Bill says. "Cytotechnologists are very art-oriented really." He goes on to explain that cytotechnologists must be good observers. Like artists they search for subtleties in color, shape, and size. "Cytotechnology is an art as well as a science," Bill says.

"If you like to work jigsaw puzzles, cytotechnology just might be the career for you," suggests Susan. "Like jigsaw puzzle fans, cytotechnologists enjoy comparing the shapes and sizes of small objects, scanning a lot of similar objects as they try to detect subtle differences. Both puzzles and microscope work require hard concentration, patience, and observation of acute detail."

Bernadette adds, "You must be meticulous and able to make your own decisions. The supervisor is there to back you up, but a lot of your original work will be done at the bench, working alone at the microscope. Cytotechnologists use worksheets and must follow the printed orders exactly. In addition, you must be able to sit for long periods of time without moving from the bench. It's not like working with a computer keyboard. You can't shift positions and place the microscope on your lap."

To be a successful cytotechnologist, you should

- Be patient and precise
- Be detail oriented
- Be a problem solver
- Enjoy working at a microscope
- Be a responsible decision-maker
- Be willing to stay seated for long periods of time

"One big advantage of working in cytotechnology," says Bernadette, "is that you can come to work, do your job, and then go home. It is literally impossible to take your work home with you. Oh, you may go home and mull over an interesting case sometimes, but that's all you can do. Plus, if you're ever unsure about a diagnosis, there's always another set of eyes there to help you out. Still, cytotechnology can get monotonous at times, especially if you're working in a huge lab and doing nothing but processing Pap smears."

Cytotechnology is a good field for someone who is less people oriented but who still enjoys working in the medical field. "I wanted a job with stability and lots of opportunities," says Bill, "where I could make good money and work at an interesting job in a laboratory."

"It's an especially challenging field," Susan says. "The best thing for me is that cytotechnologists are involved in patient diagnosis. We don't just handle specimens and pass on the results. We're the first to evaluate. We get to give our opinion. Cytotechnology appeals to people who want to be responsible and who want to be involved in something that will have a direct effect on patient care."

how do I become a cytotechnologist?

Bill fell into the career of cytotechnology by accident. "I always enjoyed studying biology," he says. "I was interested in disease, but I knew that I didn't want to become a physician. Then I stumbled across a brochure that described laboratory careers, including cytotechnology. It sounded good." He attended school at the University of Tennessee and then had the chance to work on a large research project, the National Bladder Cancer Project. He's been in the field for 18 years and now directs a program to train new cytotechnologists.

Susan entered the field of cytotechnology after studying medical technology for two years. She'd taken seven chemistry classes already and didn't look forward to taking any more. She enjoyed studying the biological sciences, however, and began searching for a new course of study that could take her in that direction. Cytotechnology fit what she was looking for, and, 32 years later, she still enjoys her work as a cytotechnologist.

education

High School

Biology, chemistry, and other science courses are necessary for students wishing to become cytotechnologists. Math, English, and computer literacy classes are also important. In addition, you should be sure to fulfill the entrance requirements of the college or university you plan to attend.

Postsecondary Training

There are two routes you may take to become a cytotechnologist. One route involves obtaining a bachelor's degree in biology, life sciences, or a related field. Following this, you can enter a one-year, postbaccalaureate certificate program sponsored by a hospital or university accredited by the Commission on Accreditation of Allied Health Education Programs (CAAHEP).

The second route involves transferring into a cytotechnology program during your junior or senior year of college and earning a bachelor of science degree in cytotechnology. In both cases, you earn a college degree and complete at least one year of training in cytotechnology.

General college course work includes biology, microbiology, parasitology, cell biology, physiology, anatomy, zoology, histology, embryology, genetics, chemistry, computer science, and mathematics. Additional courses include cytochemistry, cytophysiology, diagnostic cytology, endocrinology, medical terminology, the study of inflammatory diseases, and the history of cytology. You learn how to prepare slides, use microscopes, and follow safe laboratory procedures.

certification or licensing

Cytotechnology graduates (from either degree programs or certificate programs) may register for the certification examination given by the Board of Registry of the American Society of Clinical Pathologists. Most states require cytotechnologists to be certified, and most employers insist that new employees be certified. Usually it is a requirement for advancement in the field.

Many continuing education programs exist for professionals working in the field of

Cytotechnology and the Pap Smear

The field of cytotechnology is only a half century old. It began in the 1940s, more than 10 years after Dr. George N. Papanicolaou (1883–1962), a Greek-American physician, developed a procedure for early diagnosis of cancer of the uterus in 1928. Dr. Papanicolaou collected cell samples by scraping the cervixes of female patients. He placed these cell samples on glass slides. The slides were then stained so that individual cell differences and abnormalities could be studied more easily. Using microscopes, medical laboratory workers then compared cells known to be healthy against those known to be diseased. As the value of the "Pap smear" (the term used for the test Dr. Papanicolaou developed) became more widely accepted, demand for laboratory personnel trained to read Pap smears grew, and the career of cytotechnologist was born. Over time, the field of cytotechnology expanded to include examination of other cell specimens besides gynecological samples.

cytotechnology. It is important that practicing cytotechnologists remain current with new ideas, techniques, and medical discoveries.

scholarships and grants

Most colleges and universities offer general scholarships. Institutions with specific cytotechnology programs are most likely to have scholarships available for students interested in the field.

In exchange for a promise of two to three years of staff work at a private laboratory, some employers offer scholarships to students.

internships and volunteerships

Colleges and universities, along with professional organizations, are sources of information on work-study projects and student internships. For more information, contact the program director at individual teaching institutions. A list of accredited cytotechnology programs may be obtained through the American Society of Cytopathology (see "How Do I Learn More?").

who will hire me?

Like many veteran cytotechnologists, Susan now directs a teaching program. More than 50 hospitals and universities have CAAHEP-approved programs in cytotechnology. Other cytotechnologists are involved in research. Some cytotechnologists work for federal and state governments and some work in private industry, nursing homes, public health facilities, or businesses. The majority of cytotechnologists work for either hospitals or for private laboratories.

Demand for cytotechnologists is high, and recruiters often visit universities and teaching hospitals in the months prior to graduation. Professional journals also list advertisements for employment.

Advancement Possibilities

Teaching supervisors in medical technology teach one or more phases of medical technology to students of medicine, medical technology, or nursing arts.

Chief medical technologists direct and coordinate activities of workers engaged in performing chemical, microscopic, and bacteriologic tests to obtain data for use in diagnosis and treatment of diseases.

Cytology supervisors supervise and coordinate activities of staff in cytology laboratories.

Pathologists are medical doctors who specialize in the study and diagnosis of diseases.

where can I go from here?

Cytotechnologists who work in larger labs may move up to supervisory positions. However, cytotechnologists seeking managerial or administrative positions in smaller labs may find limited opportunities for advancement. Another career move might be to enter the teaching field and direct classes or oversee research.

Some cytotechnologists join forces with medical directors and open their own laboratories. One creative cytotechnologist opened his own business by concentrating on his expertise at staining cells. He developed his own line of chemicals and is now a leader in the staining industry.

what are the salary ranges?

According to the American Society of Clinical Pathologists (ASCP), the national average annual salary for cytotechnologists is $32,000. Supervisors average $48,000 annually. A 1998 wage survey of medical laboratories conducted by ASCP found that the median annual salary for those starting out as medical technologists was $27,040. The median top rate for these technologists was $38,480 annually. According to the *Occupational Outlook Handbook*, the median annual earnings of clinical laboratory technologists were $32,440 in 1998. The lowest 10 percent earned less than $19,380 annually, while the top 10 percent earned more than $48,290. Those employed by the federal government earn slightly less overall. Cytotechnologists working in private laboratories earn slightly more than those working in hospitals. Geographically, salaries are highest in the West.

what is the job outlook?

The U.S. Department of Labor reports that employment of clinical laboratory workers is expected to grow about as fast as the average for all occupations. Competition to enter cytotechnology programs is keen and shortages still exist for qualified graduates. The demand for cytotechnologists is especially

Related Jobs

The U.S. Department of Labor classifies cytotechnologists under the headings *Occupations in Laboratory Technology: Life Sciences* (GOE) and *Healthcare Practitioners and Technical* (O*NET-SOC). Also under these headings are medical technologists who perform laboratory tests and analyze data for diagnosis, treatment, and prevention of disease; orthotic assistants who help with the fabrication and fitting of orthopedic braces for patients with disabling conditions; and pheresis specialists who collect blood components and provide therapeutic treatments, such as replacement of plasma.

Specific related jobs include:

Biochemistry technologists
Biomedical technicians
Cardiopulmonary technologists
CT scan technologists
Dialysis technologists
Electroencephalographic (EEG) technologists
Electromyographic (EMG) technologists
Embalmers
Food testers
Laboratory testing technicians
Magnetic resonance imaging (MRI) technologists

Medical laboratory technicians
Microbiology technologists
Nuclear medicine technologists
Ophthalmic technologists
Orthotic assistants
Perfusionists
Pheresis specialists
Public health microbiologists
Pulmonary function technicians
Radiation-therapy technologists
Radiologic (X-ray) technologists
Special procedures technicians
Veterinary laboratory technicians

high in private industry. As more and more hospitals contract with private companies to perform work formerly done inside hospitals, more jobs will open up. Additional governmental regulations now limit the number of slides cytotechnologists may work with each day and this adds to the shortage of qualified personnel.

In the future, the demand for cytotechnologists may be slowed somewhat by advances in laboratory automation, but for now demand remains very high.

Vacancy rates for cytotechnologists are highest in the southern United States and in the mountain states of the West. Vacancy rates are lowest in areas closest to universities or teaching hospitals with cytotechnology programs, but shortages in this field exist in every geographical area.

how do I learn more?

professional organizations

For information about training programs and educational materials, contact the following organizations:

American Society for Cytopathology
400 West 9th Street, Suite 201
Wilmington, DE 19801
asc@cytopathology.org
http://www.cytopathology.org

American Society for Cytotechnology
1500 Sunday Drive, Suite 102
Raleigh, NC 27607
919-787-5181
info@asct.com
http://www.asct.com

FYI

Preparing a Slide

To prepare a slide, cells are spread, or "fixed," in the center of narrow glass rectangles. Following this, colored dye is added to emphasize cell structure and make disease detection easier. Finally, using a smaller piece of glass, the specimens are covered and sealed in order to preserve them.

Contact ASCP for information on educational courses and a career brochure about cytotechnology and other clinical technology careers:

American Society of Clinical Pathologists
2100 West Harrison Street
Chicago, IL 60612
info@ascp.org
312-738-1336
http://www.ascp.org

To learn about accredited cytotechnology programs, contact:

Commission on Accreditation of Allied Health Education Programs
35 East Wacker Drive, Suite 1970
Chicago, IL 60601-2208
312-553-9355
caahep@caahep.org
http://www.caahep.org/

bibliography

Following is a sampling of materials relating to the professional concerns and development of cytotechnologists.

Bibbom, Marluce, ed. *Comprehensive Cytopathology.* St. Louis, MO: W. B. Saunders, 1996.

Keebler, Catherine M. *The Manual of Cytotechnology.* Chicago, IL: American Society of Clinical Pathologists, 1993.

Dental Assistants

Definition

Dental assistants help dentists treat and examine patients. They clean, sterilize, and disinfect equipment and prepare dental instrument trays. They pass the proper instruments to the dentist, take and process X-rays, prepare materials for making impressions and restorations, and instruct the patient in oral health care. They also make appointments, maintain patient records, and handle billing.

High School Subjects

Biology
Chemistry
Health

Personal Skills

Helping/teaching
Technical/scientific

Salary Range

$14,000 to $22,000 to $32,000

Minimum Educational Level

Some postsecondary training

Certification or Licensing

Required by certain states

Outlook

Much faster than the average

GOE
10.03.02

O*NET-SOC
31-9091.00

The boy is screaming, his face red from the effort and streaked with tears. He hasn't even met the dentist, and he's already terrified of having his teeth examined. While his mother tries desperately to pull him out of the waiting room chair he's gripping with both hands, his older brother sits nearby, smiling smugly after having filled his brother's head with horror stories about the dentist.

Although the job of a dental assistant entails many duties such as cleaning and sterilizing the dental office and performing clerical tasks, a major part of the work is calming nervous patients. The assistant walks over to the boy and after a few soothing words and her promise that he can tour the office first and then decide whether or not to see the dentist, the little boy takes the assistant's hand and together they walk through the office. By the time he meets the dentist, his face is dry of tears and he's smiling as he waves a pack of sugar-free gum at his older brother.

Dental assisting requires a lot of attention to detail and repetition throughout the day. Dental assistants must clean up after each patient, making sure the dental operatory is clean and sterilized for the next, they must wear proper protective equipment, and must follow very specific industry guidelines for cleaning the dentist's instruments. Speed and efficiency are of utmost importance. The most valuable quality for patients who are often afraid to visit the dentist, however, is the dental assistant's ability to be personable.

what does a dental assistant do?

Looking forward to your next visit to the dentist? For many people, the very mention of a check-up brings to mind sharp, noisy equipment, pain, and lots of discomfort. But the talents of a good dental assistant can keep you from associating your dentist with pure misery. Dental assistants perform a variety of duties in the dental office, including helping the dentist examine and treat patients, performing office and laboratory duties, and making patients feel comfortable in the dentist's chair.

Individual states regulate what assistants are allowed to do. Usually assistants are involved in the sterilization and preparation of equipment, and in preparing trays for individual procedures. They retrieve and update patient records, and prepare rooms. They help patients get comfortable before dental treatment, as well as explain the treatment to them. They may anesthetize patients and administer nitrous oxide (laughing gas). In such cases, the dental assistant will stay with the patient while waiting for the dentist. They may also place rubber dams in the mouth or on the teeth to protect the patient and to isolate areas for treatment. An assistant serves as an extra set of hands during treatment, helping the dentist by operating suction machinery that keeps the mouth clear of blood and saliva so the dentist can see himself or herself work. Dental assistants also take and develop X-rays, ask medical history questions before an examination, and take patients' blood pressure, pulse, and temperature. Following a procedure, an assistant will instruct the patient on oral care and how to take any medications required. Assistants also make appointments for patients with referred specialists such as orthodontists and oral surgeons. Assistants may also provide patients with floss, toothbrushes, and other dental care supplies, and instruct in their proper use.

Many dental assistants perform office duties, such as scheduling appointments, answering telephones, handling billing, and working with vendors to replenish office and clinical supplies. Dental laboratory duties may include making impressions of a patient's teeth so the dentist can use the models to study the patient's condition and monitor progress, or they may make temporary crowns. They may also process X-ray film.

A dental assistant's tasks can be divided into categories. An *administrative assistant* acts as a receptionist, handles appointments, manages patient records, and may be responsible for inventory control, and handling correspondence and bookkeeping. A *chairside assistant* works directly with the dentist by seating patients, preparing the instrument tray, operating the suction devices while the dentist works, performing X-rays, and educating patients. (The majority of dental assistants work chairside.) A *coordinating assistant* may

lingo to learn

Amalgam: An alloy containing silver, mercury, and other metals used as a dental filling material.

Gypsum: Powdered material used to make models, dies, and denture molds that help the dentist diagnose patients and develop a treatment plan.

Operatory: Patient treatment room which contains an electronically controlled reclining chair and a dental unit containing an overhead light, a small sink, a saliva ejector, an instrument tray, and air hoses.

Periapical films: An X-ray that helps detect those suspected diseases that show no physical symptoms.

Saliva ejector: A small suction pump used to keep the patient's mouth dry and free of blood or saliva during treatment.

work where needed, such as processing X-ray film and performing laboratory procedures. Dental assistants often act as business managers who perform all nonclinical responsibilities such as hiring auxiliary help, scheduling and terminating employees, and overseeing accounting, supply ordering, and records management.

An assistant may work for only one dentist, or may work in a group practice where he or she may assist two or more dentists. Some assistants work full-time, while some either work part-time or on a temporary, self-employed basis, filling in at more than one office over a period of time. Some assistants work in the offices of specialists. There are also opportunities outside of the dentist's office: some assistants visit schools and community centers to instruct in proper dental care; they may teach in dental school clinics; and they may visit hospitals and nursing homes to assist dentists caring for bed-ridden patients.

Dental offices typically are clean, modern, quiet, and pleasant. They are also well lighted and well ventilated. In small offices, dental assistants may work solely with dentists, and in larger offices and clinics they may work with dentists, other assistants, dental hygienists, and laboratory technicians.

Although dental assistants may sit at desks to do office work, they spend a large part of the day beside the dentist's chair where they can reach instruments and materials. Taking X-rays poses some physical danger if handled incorrectly because regular doses of radiation can be harmful. However, all dental offices must have lead shielding and safety procedures that minimize the risk of exposure to radioactivity.

what is it like to be a dental assistant?

Dawn Ashcraft works in a two-doctor office, assisting both doctors as the need arises. Her responsibilities have expanded over the years as she has gained more experience and as the job has become more demanding. "Initially, dental assistants were referred to as 'spit suckers,' because that was basically all they did," she says. Now, in addition to seating patients and assisting with the four-handed passing of instruments, Dawn's responsibilities include restorative procedures, impres-

sions, placing deposit fillings, making temporaries, assisting in crown and bridge procedures, and taking X-rays.

The practice for which Dawn works follows a trend in dentistry: it is open only Monday through Thursday, with additional hours on Thursday night. She is usually the first one to the office in the morning, and she starts the work day by preparing the sterilization units. She also starts the X-ray machine. Dawn then goes through the patients' charts. "I make sure that what's on the schedule for the day goes along with the charts." At a start-up meeting with the other assistants and hygienists, Dawn discusses any problems or discrepancies between the schedule and the charts. She then begins to prepare trays and rooms. "Usually we'll set up basic trays for the whole morning's procedures."

In the case of root canals, for example, Dawn brings patients back, seats them, and helps them get comfortable. "As you know," she says, "most people don't like coming to the dentist. You have to try to soothe them and calm them." Dawn takes a starting film X-ray, then prepares the patient for the procedure. "We use topical anesthetic before the doctor gets the patient numb with the injection. We put them on nitrous oxide, if necessary." After the doctor has made the injection and the mouth is numb, Dawn then places the rubber dam. During the procedure, Dawn and the doctor pass the instruments back and forth as needed. Following the procedure, Dawn takes a final X-ray, then releases the patient.

In a crown and bridge procedure, Dawn places a temporary crown or cap over the top of the tooth. The crown may be made of acrylic materials, silver, or metal, and is fit with resin. "Sometimes we do a preliminary impression," she says, "so that we can put the material in the preliminary impression and place it back in the patient's mouth. Or we have to do a ball impression, which means making a big ball of acrylic material, placing it over the tooth, then forming it to look like a tooth."

Throughout any procedure, Dawn may be required to check on other things that need to be done as well. There may still be instruments that need sterilizing, or another patient who needs attention. "You have to know when the doctor's ready to start," she says, "and where he is at all times. So if you go into central sterilization to help out there, you have to know when you're needed right back."

Dawn's office has three assistants and three to four hygienists at any given time. Though Dawn likes the stability of the job, working for

exploring health care careers

125

two different dentists and managing their different personalities can be difficult. "I like the expanded duties of the work," she says, "because you're not doing the same thing every day."

have I got what it takes to be a dental assistant?

"Assistants should have an easiness about them," Dawn says, "so they can calm the patient." It's also important for assistants to be able to work well with all the other employees in their offices. "The number one thing doctors want is teamwork within their staff," Dawn says. Dawn is also expected to handle a variety of tasks at any given moment. Not only must you be able to learn quickly, but you must be capable of managing multiple duties. Assistants must remain alert, and must be able to recognize when they can move onto another task. "When I see help needed elsewhere, I go."

how do I become a dental assistant?

Part of Dawn's training involved a nine-month dental assisting course at a community college. Since then, she has had to take continuing education courses in order to maintain certification. "If you get in with a good prac-

FYI

Dental implants are a new alternative to dentures. To meet the demand for more permanent and stable dental replacements, dentists are placing implants, which involves placing a metal screw into the jaw. A prosthetic tooth or set of teeth are attached to the screw. The specialty areas that offer implant surgery are prosthodontics, oral and maxillofacial surgery, and periodontics.

tice," Dawn says, "they'll be willing to teach you and train you." Dawn feels fortunate for having had the opportunity to work for doctors dedicated to their assistants. "I've worked for five different dentists through the years. Each one of them has been very helpful as far as my expanded duties are concerned. They've helped me grow."

education

High School
If you are considering a career as a dental assistant, take science courses, such as biology and health, and obtain office skills such as typing and bookkeeping. With an increasing number of small businesses using computers, one or more computer courses are also recommended. In addition, some dental assisting programs require you to pass physical and dental examinations and have good high school grades.

Postsecondary Training
Students who attend two-year college programs receive associate's degrees, while those who attend trade and technical school programs earn a certificate or diploma after one year.

Graduating from an accredited school ensures that you learn all necessary information required to successfully practice dental hygiene. There are approximately 252 accredited programs in the United States that are approved by the American Dental Association's Commission on Dental Accreditation (CDA). The commission is responsible for setting standards for dental assisting programs.

certification or licensing

Some states require dental assistants to become licensed or registered, but even if you practice in states that don't require it, certification helps boost knowledge and earning power. Graduates from CDA-approved schools are automatically eligible to take examinations required to become certified. The certification process evaluates a dental assistant's knowledge. The Dental Assisting National Board (DANB), which offers a national certification, requires that an assistant have completed an accredited dental assisting program, or have completed two years of full-time work as a dental assistant. There are approximately 30,000 Certified Dental Assistants (CDAs) nationwide.

who will hire me?

Since the dental community is rather small in most cities and towns, many positions are learned about by word of mouth. High school and college guidance counselors, family dentists, dental schools, dental employment agencies, and dental associations are ways to learn about job openings. Also, many dental assisting training programs offer job placement assistance.

Dental assisting associations also help you gain a foothold into the field and help you cultivate knowledge and skills while developing a local and national network of friends and colleagues. The American Dental Assistants Association keeps assistants up to date on all aspects of their profession by offering home study courses, monitoring local and national legislation that affects dental assistants, and publishing a newsletter identifying clinical and practice trends in dental assisting.

Most dentists work in private practices, so that's where an aspiring dental assistant will most likely end up working. An office may have a single dentist or may be a group practice with several dentists, assistants, and hygienists. Other places to work include dental schools, hospitals, public health departments, and U.S. Veterans and Public Health Service hospitals.

where can I go from here?

Dental hygiene is a natural step for an assistant looking to advance in the dental field, but Dawn feels that the work of a hygienist is too repetitive. Dawn would prefer to go into teaching in a dental assisting program. She'd also like to go on the market as a temporary, filling in at offices in her area. "I think I'm capable of picking up on anything in any office," she says.

Becoming a dental hygienist requires taking more courses and taking state and national licensing exams designed for hygienists.

Dental hygienists perform many of the same skills as dental assistants, but they also take more courses and certification exams in order to assume some of the responsibilities of a dentist.

Assistants to specialists study the procedures of a dental specialist, such as an orthodontist or pediatric dentist, to assist in complicated or specialized techniques or oral surgeries.

Dental office managers schedule appointments, maintain business records, and depending on the size of the dental office and its staff, manage staff schedules. In addition, they are responsible for maintaining and ordering the proper clerical and dental supplies.

Dental assistants advance in their careers by moving to larger dental practices where they can take on more responsibility. An assistant's ability to command higher pay is tied to the prestige of the dentist for whom the assistant works. By upgrading skills, continuing education, and achieving national certification, dental assistants may achieve higher pay in small offices. Specialists in the dental field, who typically earn higher salaries than general dentists because of their specialized knowledge, often offer higher salaries to their assistants.

Dental assistants also may use their dental knowledge to obtain sales jobs at dental product companies or work for placement services or insurance companies.

what are the salary ranges?

Although wages for assistants have not kept up with inflation, salaries naturally increase with experience. Working for a specialist, such as a pediatric dentist or orthodontist, often results in higher pay. According to the *Occupational Outlook Handbook,* dental assistants working full-time earned a median salary of $22,600 a year in 1998. Those in the lower 10 percent earned less than $14,600, while those in the higher 10 percent earned more than $32,600. Salary.com figures in 2000 found that assistants had a median base pay of $21,722 a year.

Benefits may include health and disability insurance, dues for membership in professional organizations, paid vacations, and provision of uniforms. Assistants may have to work more than 30 hours per week to be eligible for these benefits.

what is the job outlook?

The employment outlook for dental assistants looks bright. Employment for dental assistants is expected to grow much faster than all occupations, according to the U.S. Department of Labor. As the median age of the U.S. population rises, and people become more aware that they can keep all of their teeth and be healthy, more people will seek dental services for preventive care and cosmetic improvements. Moreover, younger dentists who earned their dental degrees in the 1970s and '80s are more likely than other dentists to hire one or more assistants. As dentists increase their clinical knowledge of innovative techniques, such as implantology and periodontal therapy, they will delegate more routine tasks to assistants so they can make the best use of their time and increase profits. Job openings also will be created through attrition as older assistants retire and others assume family responsibilities, return to school, or transfer to other occupations.

To be a successful dental assistant, you should

- Be cheerful; you're the patient's first impression of the dentist
- Have compassion and understanding for people with fears about dental procedures
- Be patient, calm, and flexible
- Be able to anticipate the dentist's needs
- Be able to sit still and remain alert for several hours through longer procedures

how do I learn more?

professional organizations

Following are organizations that provide information on dental assisting careers, accredited schools and scholarships, and possible employers.

American Dental Association
211 East Chicago Avenue
Chicago, IL 60611
312-440-2500
http://www.ada.org

American Dental Education Association
1625 Massachusetts Avenue, NW, Suite 600
Washington, DC 20036-2212
202-667-9433
adea@adea.org
http://www.adea.org

American Dental Assistants Association
203 North LaSalle Street, Suite 1320
Chicago, IL 60601-1225
312-541-1550
adaa1@aol.com
http://www.dentalassistant.org

For information about certification, contact:
Dental Assisting National Board
676 North Saint Clair, Suite 1880
Chicago, IL 60611
312-642-3368
danbmail@dentalassisting.com
http://www.dentalassisting.com

bibliography

Following is a sampling of materials relating to the professional concerns and development of dental assistants.

Anderson, Pauline C., and Alice Pendleton. *Dental Assisting Essentials* (Dental Assisting Procedures). Albany, NY: Delmar, 2000.

Ehrlich, Ann B., and Hazel O. Torres. *Essentials of Dental Assisting.* 2nd ed. Philadelphia, PA: W. B. Saunders, 1996.

Dental Hygienists

Definition
Dental hygienists provide preventive dental care by performing clinical tasks such as cleaning and scaling teeth to remove tartar and plaque, instructing patients in proper oral care, taking X-rays, administering anesthesia, and assisting dentists.

High School Subjects
Biology
Chemistry
Mathematics

Personal Skills
Helping/teaching
Technical/scientific

Salary Range
$25,000 to $45,000 to $80,000

Minimum Educational Level
Associate's degree

Certification or Licensing
Required by all states

Outlook
Much faster than the average

GOE
10.02.02

O*NET-SOC
29-2021.00

Hectic isn't the word for Mary Hafner Myers' morning—more like controlled chaos. After getting her kids dressed and dropping them off at the babysitter's, she has to dash off to the office to be in time for a 9:00 AM appointment.

Fortunately, Mary is an organized woman. She won't have to set up her dental instrument trays this morning because she normally does that at the end of each day, after she has cleaned and sterilized all of the instruments required to clean and scale debris from her patients' teeth. Once in the office, she takes off her jogging pants and walking shoes and slips into freshly laundered "scrubs," her uniform as a dental hygienist, and then pulls on rubber soled shoes comfortable enough to stand in all day. Mary's daily goal in a fast-paced environment of seeing eight or nine patients a day is to be relaxed enough to put patients at ease and spend enough time educating them about proper oral care and good nutrition.

After getting dressed, Mary glances down at her watch and smiles. She still has 10 minutes to spare before her appointment with Mr. Vincenzo. She washes her hands and dons rubber gloves for her and her patients' protection. She slips a clear plastic shield over her head to block any saliva or blood that may splatter while peering inside her patients' mouths. She is ready for her first patient.

what does a dental hygienist do?

Dental hygienists perform clinical tasks, serve as oral health educators in private dental offices, work in public health agencies, and promote good oral health by educating adults and children.

lingo to learn

Calculus: The hard deposit of mineralized plaque that forms on the crown or root of the tooth.

Curette: A spoon-shaped blade on a long handle used for extensive tartar removal on teeth and below the gum line.

Mouth mirror: A small round mirror on a long handle that allows the hygienist to see hard-to-reach areas of a patient's mouth.

Probe: A tapered, rodlike blade on a long handle. The probe is inserted under the gum line to measure gum depth, an indicator of gum disease.

Scaler: A sickle, chiseled, or hoe-shaped blade instrument on a long handle used to remove "tartar" from the tooth surface. A scaler is also used to smooth the tooth surface so it will resist reaccumulation of deposits that cling to rough surfaces.

Sealant: A composite material used to seal the decay-prone pits, fissures, and grooves of children's teeth.

In clinical settings, hygienists help prevent gum diseases and cavities by removing deposits from teeth and applying sealants and fluoride to prevent tooth decay. They remove tartar, stains, and plaque from teeth, take X-rays and other diagnostic tests, place and remove temporary fillings, take health histories, remove sutures, polish amalgam restorations, and examine head, neck, and oral regions for disease.

Hygienists' main responsibility is to perform "oral prophylaxis," a process of cleaning teeth by using sharp dental instruments, such as scalers and prophy angles. With these special instruments they remove stains and calcium deposits, polish teeth, and massage gums. They teach patients proper home dental care, such as choosing the right toothbrush or how to use dental floss. Their instruments include hand and rotary instruments to clean teeth, syringes with needles to administer local anesthetic (such as Novocaine), teeth models to explain home care procedures, and X-ray machines to take pictures of the oral cavity that the dentist uses to detect signs of decay or oral disease.

A hygienist also provides nutritional counseling and screens patients for oral cancer and high blood pressure. More extensive dental procedures are done by dentists. In some states, a dental assistant is permitted to perform some of the same tasks as a dental hygienist, such as taking X-rays, but a hygienist has more extensive training and has received a license to perform the job.

Like all dental professionals, hygienists must be aware of federal, state, and local laws that govern hygiene practice. In particular, hygienists must know the types of infection control and protective gear that, by law, must be worn in the dental office to protect workers from infection. For example, dental hygienists must wear gloves, protective eyewear, and a mask during examinations. As with most health care workers, hygienists must be immunized against contagious diseases, such as hepatitis.

Dental hygienists also are required by their state and encouraged by professional associations to continue learning about trends in dental care, procedures, and regulations by taking continuing education courses. These courses may be held at large dental society meetings, colleges and universities, or in a more intimate setting such as a nearby dental office. These meetings also foster comradery among fellow dental professionals, which is important in a field where the majority of people work in offices with small staffs.

In some private dental offices, a dental hygienist may perform office duties, such as answering phones, ordering dental supplies, keeping patient records, scheduling appointments, and processing dental insurance claims. Hygienists also visit local schools to perform oral prophylaxis on students and to teach them how to properly brush and floss their teeth. While most hygienists in clinical practice work in private dental offices, others may work in hospitals, correctional facilities, health maintenance organizations, and school systems.

Hygienists also carry out administrative, educational, and research responsibilities in private and public settings. They hold administrative positions in education, public health, hospitals, and professional associations. They sell dental products and supplies and evaluate dental insurance claims as consultants to insurance companies. Dental hygienists may teach in dental hygiene schools, present seminars, conduct clinical research, write grant proposals, and publish scientific papers.

what is it like to be a dental hygienist?

Mary Hafner Myers, a registered dental hygienist with a bachelor of science degree (R.D.H., B.S.), works full-time, about 30 hours in a four-day workweek. On average, she sees five or six patients in the morning, and she takes an hour lunch. During the remaining three hours, she sees the rest of her patients.

Most patients are on a regular recall schedule, such as every six months, to get a checkup, cleaning, and to have their health history updated. "I clean their teeth and go over special areas they need to pay attention to, such as plaque or tartar accumulating in certain areas," Mary says. "I spend a lot more time with new patients, and I show kids their X-rays. They're always excited about that."

Most hygienists work in private dental offices. Dental hygienists must be flexible to accommodate varying patient schedules, which includes working evenings or Saturdays. Approximately 50 percent of all hygienists work full-time, about 35 to 40 hours a week. Full-timers and part-timers may work in more

> **Hygienists must have patience to work on really tight schedules, be organized, and able to work on a team.**

than one office because dentists typically only hire hygienists to work two or three days a week. Many piece together part-time positions at several different dental offices and substitute for fellow hygienists who take days off.

Flexibility is key for hygienists. Before Mary got married, she worked in many dental offices as a substitute for the staff hygienist. Fortunate to have an annual eight-week vacation at her present job, Mary can easily fill up her schedule subbing at nearby dental offices whenever she wants the extra work and money. Usually, she prefers to enjoy her vacation. "If I didn't want to take a week off, there are at least four dentists I could call to fill a schedule for me," Mary says. "I can make good money doing that because as a sub they aren't paying my benefits, so the hourly rate is a little higher."

Work conditions for the dental hygienist in a private office, school, or government facility are pleasant with well-lit, modern, and adequately equipped facilities. The hygienist usually sits while working. State and federal regulations require that hygienists wear masks, protective eyewear, and gloves as well as follow proper sterilizing techniques on equipment and instruments to guard against passing infection or disease, such as hepatitis or AIDS.

Mary wears scrubs in the dental office because they are designed to protect her from transmitting or getting an infection from patients, particularly those who have infectious diseases. She doesn't wear any jewelry, such as earrings or her wedding band. She used to launder her work clothes at home, but new government infection control procedures for health care workers require her to change into her street clothes and leave her work clothes at work. Some dentists have a washer and dryer on site to launder clothes according to government guidelines. Mary's dentist pays a laundry service to pick up all his employees' uniforms and launder them. "I used to wear short sleeves, but now I'm covered from head to toe," Mary says.

in-depth

Endodontics

Dental hygienists work in every dentist's office, from the orthodontist to the endodontist.

Endodontists treat diseased inner tooth structures, such as the nerve, pulp, and root canal. Every tooth has the same basic structure. The outer covering of the tooth exposed above the gum line is called the enamel, the hardest substance in the human body. Beneath the enamel is another layer of hard material, dentin, that forms the bulk of the tooth. Cementum, a bonelike substance, covers the root of the tooth. Finally, a generous space within the dentin contains the pulp, which extends from just beneath the crown, or top of the tooth, to down through the root. The pulp contains blood vessels that supply the tooth and the lymphatic system.

Not so long ago, if a tooth was diseased, that was it; yank—no more tooth. Things have changed. Modern preventive endodontic techniques now make it possible to save many teeth that would have been extracted once decay spread into the pulp canal. These specialized procedures include root canal therapy, pulp capping, and pulpotomy.

In root canal therapy, the endodontist first examines the pulp to determine the extent of infection. Using rotary drills and other instruments, the pulp is removed and the empty canal surrounding the root is sterilized and filled with gutta-percha (a tough plastic substance) or silver, or a combination of the two.

Pulp capping consists of building a cap over the exposed pulp with layers of calcium hydroxide paste and zinc oxide. These layers are then topped with a firm dental cement.

Pulpotomy involves removing the pulp within the crown while leaving intact the pulp within the root canal. A pulp-capping procedure is used to seal and restore the crown of the tooth.

As a licensed health care worker, Mary knows all the laws governing infection control, and she knows how to properly clean and sterilize her instruments. The dentist pays for all of her instruments and the machinery necessary to keep them clean and safe. He buys all the barrier items, such as plastic to cover chairs and trays. Whenever Mary needs a new instrument, she just asks her employer and he orders it because he wants her to do the best job she can.

Government hygienists work hours regulated by the particular agency. For a salaried dental hygienist in a private office, a paid two- or three-week vacation is common. Part-time or commissioned dental hygienists in private offices usually have no paid vacation. Benefits will vary, however, according to the hygienist's agreement with the employer.

When Mary was pregnant with her two children, the dentist accommodated her schedule and always understands when family emergencies arise. "My dentist was super with both of my pregnancies. I could take off as much time as I needed," she says. "I also like that he's very much for continuing education, and I have full-time benefits, health insurance, and pretty much everything that I need."

have I got what it takes to be a dental hygienist?

"There's a lot of blood in dentistry, but it's not the life-and-death kind that you find in medical careers," Mary says. Dental hygienists operate in a more controlled atmosphere, and that appeals to her.

However, being a hygienist requires grace under pressure, Mary says. Although patient schedules are often full with one patient after another, hygienists must possess the manual dexterity to properly clean and scale below the patients' gum lines, answer the patients' questions, and make them feel so relaxed that they feel they're all that matters. Fortunately, Mary has a dental assistant who helps her in the afternoons to usher in patients, clean up after every appointment, adjust the chair, and make patients feel comfortable.

"Hygienists must have patience to work on really tight schedules, be organized, and able to work on a team," Mary says. Dental hygiene school prepared her for real practice because in that strict atmosphere, she learned discipline. Mary had to find her own patients and learn to talk to strangers. Skipping a class was unheard of. "You have to really feel bad not to go to work," Mary says. "Patients will be there waiting for you and they depend on you. School definitely prepared me for that."

As an oral care educator, hygienists must be capable of communicating with patients because if they don't understand, they won't come back, Mary says. She also tells patients what she's doing and what instrument she's using because if they haven't been to the dentist in a while, sharp instruments can startle them if they don't understand their purpose.

how do I become a dental hygienist?

Mary was naturally drawn to college prep courses in high school because challenging herself provided personal satisfaction. She knew she wanted to do something related to health and education, and the comradery among dental workers at her family dentist's office convinced her to seek a career in dental hygiene.

education

High School

Dental hygiene programs vary, but all require you to have a high school diploma or general educational development (GED), also known as general equivalency degree. Recommended high school courses include mathematics, chemistry, biology, and English. College entrance test scores are needed, and some dental hygiene programs require prerequisite college courses in chemistry, English, speech, psychology, and sociology.

To be a successful dental hygienist, you should

- Enjoy working with people of all ages
- Be patient, flexible, and calm in stressful situations
- Be articulate and organized
- Work well as part of a team
- Be willing to follow strict safety and health guidelines

Math and science courses proved to be most helpful as Mary first worked to earn an associate's degree in dental hygiene science and later a bachelor's degree in public health, which gave her teaching experience on top of her clinical skills.

Postsecondary Training

Dental hygiene education takes a minimum of two years in an accredited two-year program that offers a certificate or associate's degree, or an accredited four-year program offering a bachelor's degree. A master's degree may be an option for those seeking opportunities in education, research, or administration. Thirty percent of hygienists have a bachelor's or master's degree.

The dental hygiene curriculum generally consists of approximately 1,000 clock hours of instruction, including more than 600 hours of clinical experience that involves working on patients. Courses include chemistry, anatomy, physiology, biochemistry, dental anatomy, radiology, pain control, dental materials, and pharmacology. Dental hygiene science courses include oral health education and preventive counseling, patient management, clinical dental hygiene, and ethics.

Mary earned an associate's degree and immediately went to work for a private dental office almost 50 miles from her home. She completed her studies toward a bachelor's degree in dental hygiene so she could teach and increase her earning power.

"Dental hygiene school was tough because I worked full-time to pay for school," Mary says. "The instructors are very strict, and you have to be very attentive and disciplined. There is so much responsibility because you have to set up your own schedule, find your own patients."

certification or licensing

A state or clinical examination is required for licensing, as is a written national dental examination that is required by all states and the District of Columbia. Upon passing required exams, a dental hygienist becomes a Registered Dental Hygienist (R.D.H.). Other designations include Licensed Dental Hygienist (L.D.H.), and Graduate of Dental Hygiene (G.D.H.). If a hygienist moves to another state, he or she must pass that state's licensing exam and requirements. In Alabama, for example, hygienists may forego college and obtain on-the-job training in a dentist office that has been approved by the state. This is called preceptorship.

Mary's dentist supports her need to update her education and pays for her continuing education courses. To maintain her license, she must take a certain number of continuing education courses. She takes others to keep up to date and because she finds them quite interesting.

Advancement Possibilities

Dental school instructors teach college-level dental hygiene courses. This includes assigning and grading papers and administering exams.

Directors of public dental programs administer and carry out the policies of agencies whose mission is to educate the public about the importance of dental care and maintenance as well as provide free or affordable dental care.

Dentists try to maintain the dental health of their clients through preventative and restorative practices, such as cleaning or replacing teeth, filling cavities, and performing extractions. With additional years of schooling, a hygienist could advance to become an endodontist, periodontist, prosthodontist, pedodontist, oral pathologist, or oral surgeon.

who will hire me?

Once hygienists pass national board exams and licensing exams for their particular state, they must decide where to work, such as a private dental office, a school system, or a public health agency. Hospitals, industry, and the armed forces also employ a small number of dental hygienists. Graduating students have little difficulty finding a satisfactory position. Most dental hygiene schools maintain placement services, and dentists make announcements at local dental hygiene meetings. Often, temporary services match hygienists with dentists.

Upon earning an associate's degree, Mary had no trouble finding a job. As a matter of fact, the job found her. A dentist from a small community 50 miles from her home asked her school for a list of new graduates, and she was invited for an interview. She was hired to work three days a week, and the dentist paid her an extra dollar for each hour worked to compensate for travel expenses.

"I liked it because it was a small office and it just seemed like a real homey atmosphere," Mary says. "I thought even if I just worked there one year, it would be fun to get out of my general area and meet new people. Who would have thought I'd end up living there?"

where can I go from here?

Opportunities for advancement, other than salary increases and benefits that accompany experience in the field, usually require postgraduate study and training. Educational advancement may lead to a position as an administrator, teacher, or director in a dental health program or in a more advanced field of practice. Only a small number of dental hygienists have continued their education to become practicing dentists.

With her bachelor's degree, Mary is qualified to teach college-level dental hygiene courses, which she has done. She plans to earn a master's degree in a different field, although she hasn't quite figured out what field that will be. "I'll probably branch out more into teaching," Mary says.

what are the salary ranges?

A dental hygienist's income is influenced by such factors as education, experience, geography, and type of employer. Most dental hygienists who work in private dental offices are salaried employees, though some are paid a commission for work performed, or a combination thereof.

According to the *Occupational Outlook Handbook,* the median hourly earnings of dental hygienists were $22.06 in 1998 (or approximately $45,000 annually). Those in the lowest 10 percent earned less than $12.37 an hour (around $25,000 annually); those in the highest 10 percent earned more than $38.81 an hour (over $80,000 annually).

Dental hygienists working in research, education, or administration may earn higher salaries. Another factor affecting earning power is the hygienist's level of responsibility. In addition, an increased demand for dental care and higher wages has provided incentives for hygienists to work in the field longer or to return to the field.

what is the job outlook?

The *Occupational Outlook Handbook* reports that employment for dental hygienists is expected to grow much faster than the average for all occupations. The demand for dental hygienists is expected to grow as younger generations who grew up receiving better dental care, keep their teeth longer. For example, 69.3 percent of dentists employed a hygienist in 1996 compared to 53 percent in 1983 and 66 percent in 1990, according to the American Dental Association.

Older dentists, who are less likely to hire one hygienist, let alone more than one, will retire, and younger dentists will hire one or more hygienists to perform preventive care so they can have more time to perform more profitable, medically complex procedures. Population growth, increased public awareness of proper oral home care, and the availability of dental insurance should result in more dental hygiene jobs. Moreover, as the population ages, there will be a special demand for hygienists to work with older people, especially those who live in nursing homes.

Dental hygienists clean teeth of plaque and calculus deposits to prevent gum damage, or periodontal disease. Untreated teeth cause gums to become inflamed and infection to spread to the roots of the teeth. Regular cleanings help prevent the disease.

Because of increased awareness about caring for animals in captivity, hygienists are also among a small number of dental professionals who volunteer to help care for animals' teeth and perform annual examinations. Dental professionals are not licensed to treat animals, though, and must work under the supervision of veterinarians.

how do I learn more?

professional organizations

Following are organizations that provide information on dental hygienist careers, accredited schools and scholarships, and possible employment.

American Dental Hygienists' Association
444 North Michigan Avenue, Suite 3400
Chicago, IL 60611
312-440-8900
mail@adha.net
http://www.adha.org

American Association of Dental Examiners
211 East Chicago Avenue, Suite 760
Chicago, IL 60611
312-440-7464
info@aadexam.org
http://www.aadexam.org

American Dental Education Association
1625 Massachusetts Avenue, NW
Washington, DC 20036
adea@adea.org
http://www.aads.jhu.edu

American Dental Association
211 East Chicago Avenue
Chicago, IL 60611
http://www.ada.org

bibliography

Following is a sampling of materials relating to the professional concerns and development of dental hygienists.

Alvarez, Kathleen H. *Williams & Wilkins' Dental Hygiene Handbook.* New York, NY: Lippincott Williams & Wilkins, 1998.

Kendall, Bonnie L. *Opportunities in Dental Care Careers.* Discusses the job of dental hygienist. Lincolnwood, IL: VGM Career Horizons, 2000.

Requa-Clark, Barbara S. *Applied Pharmacology for the Dental Hygienist.* Chicago, IL: Year Book Medical Publishing, 2000.

Wilkins, Esther M. *Clinical Practice of the Dental Hygienist.*. 8th Edition. New York, NY: Lippincott Williams & Wilkins, 1999.

Related Jobs

The U.S. Department of Labor classifies dental hygienists under the headings *Rehabilitation* (GOE) and *Healthcare Practitioners and Technical* (O*NET-SOC).

Working as a dental assistant may serve as a stepping stone to a hygiene career and be a source of insight and information about the field. As a dental assistant, you may closely observe the work of dental hygienists, assess the personal aptitude required for this work, and discuss any questions with other hygienists before enrolling in dental hygiene school (see chapter "Dental Assistants").

Other related occupations include: prosthodontists, orthodontists, medical assistants, ophthalmic medical assistants, podiatric assistants, radiologic technicians, and surgical technologists.

Dental Laboratory Technicians

Definition
Dental laboratory technicians make and repair dental appliances and replacements for missing, damaged, or poorly positioned teeth according to dentists' orders. Appliances include dentures, inlays, bridges, crowns, and braces made with materials such as plastic, ceramics, and metals.

Alternative Job Titles
Crown and bridge specialists
Dental ceramists
Orthodontic technicians

High School Subjects
Chemistry
Technical/Shop

Personal Skills
Artistic
Technical/scientific

Salary Range
$14,000 to $25,000 to $45,000+

Minimum Educational Level
High school diploma

Certification or Licensing
Voluntary

Outlook
Little change or more slowly than the average

GOE
05.05.11

O*NET-SOC
51-9081.00

What's in a smile?

Everything, if you're a dental laboratory technician. Gerson Shapiro owns a dental laboratory, and every day he and his staff of 22 create and repair a whole slew of dental appliances so they can keep people smiling. Gerson, as the owner, focuses on the big picture, such as managing employees, insuring quality control, planning complicated cases, and communicating with and keeping his dentist-customers happy.

But it's the details that have made Gerson a success in the business of fabricating dental appliances to help dentists improve their patients' oral health and outlook. Since high school, Gerson's daily routine has revolved around sitting at a workbench equipped with a Bunsen burner and tools, such as wax spatulas, wax carvers, and grinding and polishing equipment. As a dental technician, he fills a dentist's prescription for dentures, braces, bridges, crowns, and inlays. It takes a lot of time, patience, and artistic skills to create durable, lifelike teeth. Gives you something to think about next time you brush your teeth, doesn't it?

what does a dental laboratory technician do?

Dental laboratory technicians work in the trenches, filling dentists' prescriptions for crowns, dentures, bridges, braces, and other dental prosthetics and devices. Technicians spend several hours a day working at a bench making and perfecting these dental appliances. Dentists send the laboratory impressions, or molds, of the patient's teeth or mouth. Using knowledge of oral anatomy and restoration, the technician then creates a model of the mouth or teeth by pouring plaster into the mold from the dentist. After the

lingo to learn

Articulator: A device that mimics the movement of the mouth; used to make dental laboratory models.

Artificial crown: A restoration that reproduces the entire surface of the natural crown of a tooth.

Bridge: An artificial appliance that replaces lost teeth and is held in place by attachments to nearby natural teeth.

Denture: An artificial or prosthetic replacement for natural teeth and adjacent tissues.

Implant: A foreign object, such as a metal root, set into the jaw bone to support an artificial tooth or set of teeth.

Inlay: A tooth filling shaped and cemented into place.

Occlusion: How the upper and lower teeth fit together when the mouth is closed.

Prosthodontics: Dentistry involving artificial replacements and devices.

plaster sets, the technician places the model on an articulator, a device that mimics the movement of the jaw opening and closing. After studying the model and determining the best position so the upper and lower teeth will fit together when the mouth is closed (known as occlusion), the technician builds up wax over the model using wax spatulas and carvers. A lathe equipped with polishing wheels is used to clean and buff the model.

Once the wax model is complete, the dental laboratory technician pours a mold and casts a metal framework. The technician uses small, hand-held tools to prepare the metal surface so it will bond with porcelain. Porcelain layers are applied layer by layer to accurately create the shape and color of a real tooth. The dental appliance is then baked in a porcelain furnace so the porcelain will adhere to the metal framework. The technician touches up the appliance by shaping, grinding, and removing excess porcelain or adding more porcelain, and voila—a precise replica of the patient's tooth or teeth.

While some dental laboratory technicians perform all stages of the work, others specialize as they gain more experience in the field. There are five areas of specialization: full dentures, partial dentures, orthodontic appliances, crowns and bridges, and ceramics.

Technicians specializing in complete dentures not only create dentures, but also repair them. When repairing dentures, technicians cast plaster models of replacement parts and match the new tooth's color and shape to the adjacent teeth. They cast reproductions of gums, fill cracks in dentures, and rebuild linings using acrylics and plastics. They may also bend and solder wire made of gold, platinum, and other metals. Occasionally, technicians fabricate wire using a centrifugal casting machine.

Partial dentures restore missing teeth for patients who have some teeth remaining on the jaw. Technicians use the same techniques as those used to make full dentures, but partials require metal clasps to secure them to remaining teeth. The clasps also facilitate removal of the partials for cleaning.

Orthodontic technicians bend wire into intricate shapes and solder them into complex positions to make and repair frames and retainers for positioning teeth. In other words, the technicians make braces, something most teenagers are familiar with. The tasks include shaping, grinding, polishing, carving, and assembling metal and plastic appliances.

Crown and bridge specialists restore the missing parts of a natural tooth. Crowns and bridges are made of plastics and metal and are sometimes called fixed bridgework because they are permanently cemented to the natural part of the tooth. Crown and bridge specialists are adept at melting and casting metals and must also wax and polish the finished product.

Dental laboratory technicians who specialize in porcelain are known as *dental ceramists* and are involved primarily with cosmetic dentistry. They make natural-looking replacements to fit over natural teeth or to replace missing ones, including crowns, bridges, and tooth facings. Ceramists apply multiple layers of mineral powders or acrylic resins to a metal framework then fuse the materials in an oven. This process is repeated until the product is exactly as specified. Ceramists must possess natural creative abilities and understand all phases of dental technology. They are, therefore, generally the highest paid of dental laboratory technicians.

what is it like to be a dental laboratory technician?

On a typical day when Gerson makes an implant prosthesis, he situates himself at his workbench to begin a process that will take several days to complete. He attaches a model of the patient's mouth to an articulator and fashions a wax pattern of teeth in preparation for a metal casting.

He puts the wax pattern into a mold and heats the mold to get rid of the wax pattern. A metal alloy, the substance that will make the metal casting, the basis of the prosthesis, is cast into the mold. The metal fills the void that had been filled by the wax pattern. When the cast has filled the space left by the melted wax, it is allowed to cool and become a solid mass. This process takes place in a furnace with a special exhaust fan that sucks out fumes. "It takes about two hours, but we put it in the oven overnight, and a timer turns on the oven so that we can cast the metal when we start work in the morning," Gerson says. "You can't let the metal get too hot because it will burn out the ingredient that makes the metal, but you also have to make it hot enough so it flows into the cast. When it cools, we break it out of

the mold and finish the metal. We grind it and take out the scratches and polish it, like you would a ring."

The next step is adding "teeth" to the metal appliance. Gerson uses a porcelain paste that matches the color of the patient's real teeth and forms the teeth using his bare hands, instruments, and knowledge of tooth anatomy. He also uses a color guide and a description from the dentist to help him match the teeth perfectly. "It's like an art. You have to pick the right colors. It's the same porcelain used to make a bathtub, but it's finer and translucent. It's almost the quality of a fine China dish."

Forming teeth takes expert artistic skill, Gerson says. He molds the porcelain to tooth shapes and then puts them into a furnace to go through a heating and drying process. This only takes about five to 10 minutes.

"You have to file and shape it," he says. "We use dental hand pieces and different types of grinding stones and diamond stones, very similar to what a dentist uses. Then we have to stain and glaze the porcelain so it has a sheen to it."

When complete, the implant prosthesis will either be attached with tiny screws to the metal roots that have been implanted into the patient's jaw bone or attached to a connective bar. The prosthesis is then polished, checked, and sent out to the dentist.

Each procedure takes a day or two, and the dentist has the patient try on the prosthesis to make sure he or she can speak, eat, and swallow properly. Gerson makes as many adjustments as needed to achieve the right fit for the patient.

Dental lab technicians generally work five days a week, eight hours a day with required overtime if a special order needs to be filled. "You can't be a clock watcher," Gerson says. "When your normal assignment is done, try another assignment. Most laboratory owners would be pleased to have someone like that."

Wages tend to be low when a person first starts working as a lab technician because of the high potential to easily damage a product, Gerson says. Dental laboratory technicians must prove themselves over time by mastering small tasks and progressively accepting more responsibility. Trainees generally start by performing simple tasks, such as mixing plaster and pouring molds. Making dental appliances well requires years of hands-on experience. Whether trained on the job or graduated from a two-year applied science or arts program, it generally takes three to four years before a trainee is formally considered a full-fledged technician. Experience is reflected in salaries. "We have technicians who make $30,000 to $50,000 or more a year, but that doesn't happen overnight," Gerson says.

have I got what it takes to be a dental laboratory technician?

Lab technicians must be creative and artistic, says Gerson, who went into dental laboratory technology because he wanted to do something health-related and liked working with his hands. Precision, patience, and dexterity are the key skills required if you want to be a successful dental laboratory technician. You must understand and carry out verbal and written instructions according to the dentist's prescription. You must have good color vision to be able to distinguish between innumerable shades of "pearly white," and you must have

Advancement Possibilities

Dental laboratory supervisors supervise and coordinate activities of workers engaged in fabrication, assemblage, and repair of full or partial dentures, crowns, bridges, inlays, and orthodontic appliances.

Dentists are medical doctors who treat diseases, injuries, and malformations of teeth and gums and related oral structures.

Dental and medical equipment and supplies sales representatives sell medical and dental equipment and supplies, except drugs and medicines, to doctors, dentists, hospitals, medical schools, and retail establishments.

the ability to perform delicate and intricate tasks with your fingers. A friendly personality helps a lot, Gerson adds, and a good command of dental terminology is essential.

Lab technicians must also be able to sit for several hours while producing an appliance. "This can get very boring," Gerson admits. If you like to sit in one place and do routine work, you will have a better chance at success, he says. If you are considering dental laboratory technology, you should also like to learn new things because the only way to improve technique and skill is to tackle more challenging assignments in school or during on-the-job training.

how do I become a dental laboratory technician?

Gerson attended a vocational-technical high school, and that was where he began learning about dental laboratory technology. In the mornings, he would take traditional high school courses such as English and math, and in the afternoons, Gerson learned dental anatomy, dental chemistry, biology, and fabrication of dental appliances, such as dentures, partial dentures, and crowns and bridges. He also learned how to make a model from a patient's impression taken by a dentist. "We had to make a positive of the patient's mouth from the negative sent over by the dentist," Gerson explains. "The dentist would tell the lab what his plans were, and we'd fill the prescription."

education

High School
Dental laboratory technicians must have a high school diploma. Science and math courses are essential to future success as a lab technician. Chemistry, biology, anatomy, shop, mechanical drawing, and ceramics are all useful courses you should take in preparation for a career as a lab technician.

Metallurgy courses, which teach the science of metals and working with them, are also helpful. Metals have certain properties that make them less effective if they are not prepared properly, Gerson explains. If certain metals are overheated, the dentist wouldn't get medically acceptable results, and the metal would be harmful to patients.

Any other courses or activities that would allow you to gain skills practiced by dental laboratory technicians should be taken advantage of. If you can learn how to solder or mold or learn about the chemistry of plastics, seize the opportunity.

Part-time or summer jobs as laboratory helpers may be available. You may also want to visit a local dentist or dental laboratory to see firsthand what the work entails.

Postsecondary Training

There are primarily two ways to get training to be a dental laboratory technician: on-the-job training or earning an associate's degree or certificate in a two-year applied science or arts training program at a community college, technical college, vocational school, or dental school. Many dental lab technicians have been successfully trained on the job under the supervision of veteran technicians. It generally takes three to four years of on-the-job training to achieve the same level of knowledge as someone trained formally in school. Trainees start with simple tasks and work their way up to more complex tasks.

The American Dental Association's Commission on Dental Education has approved more than 30 dental laboratory technology programs. Programs consist of classroom instruction in chemistry, dental materials science, oral anatomy, fabrication procedures, ethics, metallurgy, and more. Students gain hands-on experience at school or at an associated dental laboratory.

Although classroom training provides a good introduction into the field, dental laboratory technician trainees must undergo additional training and practice to acquaint them with their lab's specific procedures. Students of dental laboratory programs, regardless of whether they have graduated, are considered good candidates for training because of their previous exposure in class.

The military is a third, less common route for students to obtain dental laboratory technology training. After high school, Gerson joined the U.S. Air Force where he was able to continue his training and do more concentrated work. "Because of my previous education, I was able to get a good position," Gerson says. "In high school, I wasn't really able to work on my own. Students had to have complete supervision." In the Air Force, Gerson

mastered the art and science of fabricating crowns and bridges, got advanced training in inlays, and learned to understand contour and how to properly use materials. He also learned how to fabricate various connecting devices and precision attachments.

"The more knowledge you have, the more the dentist will consult with you because they have very limited training in laboratory technology," Gerson says. "In dental schools of the past, dentists spent a great deal of time learning dental lab technology. Now they learn more oral medicine and don't have time to be dental lab technology experts."

certification or licensing

Certification is an option but not a requirement for dental laboratory technicians. Certification signifies that you have attained a high level of academic and practical achievement in dental technology. It also may be an advantage when you apply for a job.

Technicians who have five years' experience or an associate's degree with two years' experience are eligible for certification. The certification exams are administered by the National Board for Certification, a division of the National Association of Dental Laboratories (NADL), and include written and practical (an exam where you have to prove that you can actually do the work) examinations for five laboratory specialties: crowns and bridges, ceramics, complete dentures, partial dentures, and orthodontic appliances. Technicians who successfully pass certification tests earn the right to put the initials CDT after their names, signifying that they are Certified Dental Technicians. Courses taken during dental technology training may count toward certification.

Every year, certified dental technicians must take a certain number of continuing education courses to maintain their status and to further master skills. Gerson says he originally sought certification for "my own self-respect." Continuing education courses are easy to attend as they are usually held at nearby schools or a large dental laboratory, Gerson says. Local dental societies offer many of these dental laboratory technology courses.

One of the biggest benefits of taking continuing education courses is meeting with other dental laboratory technicians to share tips and discuss the pluses and minuses of different products, Gerson says.

To be a successful dental laboratory technician, you should

- Have manual dexterity and mechanical aptitude
- Be artistically inclined and like to make things with your hands
- Be patient
- Be able to sit in one place for long hours
- Take orders well and understand instruction

scholarships and grants

The American Dental Association Endowment and Assistance Fund, Inc. offers the Allied Dental Health Scholarship for students studying to become dental laboratory technicians. For requirements, details, and deadline information, contact the American Dental Association (ADA). (See "How Do I Learn More?")

Scholarship and grant opportunities may also be available through one of the accredited dental laboratory technology programs or dental schools. Check with your financial aid office or counselor.

Other sources for possible scholarship opportunities include state and local dental societies or large commercial dental laboratories. The ADA may be able to point you in the right direction.

internships and volunteerships

While some internship opportunities may exist, the common route for aspiring dental laboratory technicians is to start as trainees. Trainees, regardless of whether or not they graduated from a dental laboratory technology program, begin with simple tasks such as mixing plaster and pouring it into molds. Trainees with no formal training in the field may spend three to four years mastering the techniques of an accomplished technician. Graduates of dental laboratory technology programs may progress more rapidly out of the trainee ranks and become fully qualified technicians in a few years.

who will hire me?

Although Gerson worked in dental laboratories throughout high school as part of his diploma requirements, his first official job was in the Air Force where he was fortunate to get a good position because of his prior education. The Air Force also sent him to advanced courses, which he used to his advantage to get a job when he left the service.

New graduates of dental laboratory technology programs should make use of school placement offices to find a job, or they may apply directly to dental laboratories and dentists' offices, which sometimes have on-site labs. Private and state employment agencies may be helpful in finding employment. Networking at dental laboratory association meetings is also a good way to find out about job opportunities.

Government opportunities may be found by applying at regional offices of the U.S. Veterans Administration or at the Office of Personnel Management. Many Department of Veterans Affairs hospitals provide dental services and may have the need for technicians.

Experienced technicians may contact dental supply houses and salespeople they meet on the job for potential leads. Sales representatives often know about staffing needs because they are in constant contact with dentists and dental laboratories.

New technicians usually start off with small jobs performing several routine tasks, such as making and trimming models, making minor denture repairs, or polishing dentures. Those working in large commercial laboratories may be assigned to various departments. The average dental laboratory, however, employs fewer than five technicians.

where can I go from here?

Gerson originally wanted to be a dentist, but eventually changed his mind and decided to become a laboratory tech instead. He spent several years working in a dental laboratory, working his way up to be a manager. "A lot of that had to do with my experience in the service and working in clinical environments with dentists," Gerson says. He spent six years managing a laboratory for three prominent big-city dentists. He had to know more about supervising people, scheduling cases, and communicating directly and effectively with dentists. "As you prove your ability, you can advance," says Gerson, noting that some people are more content sitting and doing one thing all day than being responsible for the running of a laboratory.

As dental technicians improve their skills and techniques, they can work on more complex or special assignments. They also can become supervisors or managers like Gerson, which involves resolving problems with prescriptions, establishing costs and delivery arrangements, and training new workers. Lab supervisors also inspect work and order materials and supplies. Managers may be assigned to a specific department, covering single areas such as dentures, partial dentures, or porcelain.

Technicians also may become teachers in dental laboratory programs or become technical representatives or salespeople for dental product companies. Outstanding technicians also may teach continuing education courses.

After Gerson built a reputation for being accurate and personable, he was able to start his own dental laboratory. According to the *Occupational Outlook Handbook*, one in five technicians is self-employed, a higher proportion than in other occupations. Dentists also call Gerson when they want to try a new technique and need to have a laboratory technician help them plan the case. For example, Gerson worked on some of the first cases of modern tooth implants with a group of university-based dentists. Implantology is one of the new techniques used by dentists to replace patients' teeth in a more permanent manner than dentures. "It's one of the most dynamic things going on in the dental field," Gerson says. Planning implant cases requires technicians to make study models and discuss plans for tooth placement with the dentist. Technicians also give dentists an indication of how much the laboratory work will contribute to the overall cost of the procedure.

what are the salary ranges?

Wages usually are low for beginning technicians because they have to fully develop skills and techniques to obtain higher pay. Earnings also vary depending upon the laboratory size, geographic location, and responsibilities of the technician.

The 1998 Wage and Price Survey conducted by *Laboratory Management Today* found that the average starting wage was $7.05 an hour for dental laboratory technicians. According to the *Occupational Outlook Handbook,* the median annual salary for dental laboratory technicians in 1998 was $25,660. The lowest 10 percent earned less than $14,720, while the highest 10 percent earned more than $45,980. Salary.com estimates for 2000 found that dental laboratory techs made between $24,500 and $31,441, with a median base of $26,695.

Self-employed technicians generally have higher salaries, but must provide their own insurance. Full-time employees of laboratories may receive insurance and retirement benefits, continuing education assistance, and paid vacation.

what is the job outlook?

According to the *Occupational Outlook Handbook,* opportunities for dental laboratory technicians should be favorable, although little or no change in the employment of technicians is expected in the next decade. This is attributed to the improvement in the overall dental health of the population. People are taking better care of their teeth and are suffering from fewer cavities because of fluoridated drinking water. Full dentures are therefore often unnecessary.

According to the NADL, demand for highly skilled dental laboratory technicians will increase as restorative and cosmetic dentistry become more sophisticated and more popular. The NADL also notes that the job outlook should be positive for skilled technicians because fewer people are entering the field. This decrease may be due to the low entry-level wages and the fact that many are unaware of the field of dental technology.

how do I learn more?

professional organizations

For a career brochure on dental laboratory technicians, contact:
American Dental Association
211 East Chicago Avenue
Chicago, IL 60611
312-440-2500
http://www.ada.org

Related Jobs

The U.S. Department of Labor classifies dental laboratory technicians under the headings *Craft Technology: Scientific, Medical, and Technical Equipment Fabrication and Repair* (GOE) and *Production* (O*NET-SOC).

Also listed under these headings are opticians, ophthalmic laboratory technicians, artificial plastic eye makers, instrument makers, taxi meter repairers, watch repairers, glass blowers, biomedical equipment repairers, orecision printing workers, arch-support technicians, orthotics technicians, prosthetists (artificial limbs), and camera repairers. Jobs that require similar skills also include biological technicians, dental assistants, dental hygienists, jewelers and jewelry repairers, and museum exhibit technicians.

For career and certification information, contact:
National Association of Dental Laboratories
1530 Metropolitan Boulevard
Tallahassee, FL 32308
800-950-1150
nadl@nadl.org
http://www.nadl.org

bibliography

Following is a sampling of materials relating to the professional concerns and development of dental laboratory technicians.

Basic Sciences: A Working Reference for Dental Laboratory Technicians. Bowling Green Station, NY: Gordon Press Publishers, 1997.

Careers in Focus: Medical Technicians. 2nd Edition. Chicago, IL: Ferguson Publishing Company, 2001.

Kendall, Bonnie L. *Opportunities in Dental Care Careers.* Lincolnwood, IL: VGM Career Horizons, 2000.

Dentists

Definition
Dentists help maintain the teeth through cleaning, filling, extraction, and replacement procedures. They also help maintain the gums and other tissues of the mouth.

High School Subjects
Biology
Chemistry
Health

Personal Skills
Helping/teaching
Technical/scientific

Salary Range
$58,000 to $125,000 to $202,000

Educational Requirements
Bachelor's degree; Doctor of Dental Surgery (D.D.S.) or Doctor of Dental Medicine (D.D.M./D.M.D.) degree

Certification or Licensing
Required by all states

Outlook
Little change or more slowly than the average

GOE
02.03.02
O*NET-SOC
29-1021.00

The accident, when Joyce was very young, had knocked out four of her front teeth. As a result, she had worn a partial denture for years. But it was poorly fitted, and now, in her late twenties, she was too ashamed to smile.

"I told them it didn't feel right but they wouldn't listen to me," she said. "I don't want to go through the rest of my life like this."

Mitchell Cohen, D.D.S., nodded. "It's going to take a few months. I'm sending you to an orthodontist to be fitted with braces. Then we're going to remove the old denture inserts and give you new ones. And then we're going to build new teeth. They'll look natural enough, but you won't ever have a movie star's smile. It's important that you realize that."

"That's not what I want," Joyce said. "I just want to be able to smile again and to be able to speak clearly."

Mitchell lowered the dentist chair. There were tears in his patient's eyes.

"It's silly, isn't it?" Joyce said. "All I want for Christmas is my two front teeth."

"It's not silly," Mitchell said. "It's exactly what we're going to do."

what does a dentist do?

Many people associate *dentists* with filling cavities and pulling teeth. But dentists play an important role in maintaining our oral hygiene. Problems with our teeth and gums can cause significant complications that affect our lives. Dentists help prevent tooth decay and such infections as gingivitis and periodontal disease, and can recognize the early signs of oral cancer and other serious diseases. Incorrect alignment of the teeth can cause a variety of problems, including poor digestion, loss of sleep, headaches, and other health conditions that may seem unrelated to our mouths. Our

lingo to learn

Bicuspids: The side teeth between the cuspids and the molars. They are used for tearing and grinding food.

Caries or **cavities:** Tooth decay; the progressive destruction of a part of a tooth generally caused by bacteria in the mouth.

Cementum: A thin covering at the roots of the teeth that attaches the teeth to the surrounding tissues.

Crowns: The parts of the teeth that are above the gumline.

Cuspids: Also called **canine teeth,** the four fang-shaped side teeth used for tearing food.

Dentin: The hard, yellowish material that forms the bulk of a tooth and supplies support and nourishment to the enamel.

Enamel: The substance that covers the crown of a tooth. Enamel is the body's hardest substance.

teeth play a major role in our facial appearance and in our ability to speak clearly.

Dentists use a variety of equipment, including X-ray machines, dental drills, ultrasound devices, mirrors, probes, forceps, and scalpels, to examine and repair teeth and gums. A dentist must be proficient in many areas of dentistry. Dentists clean teeth, identify and fill cavities, extract diseased teeth, and fit patients with dentures or artificial teeth. They are skilled in administering anesthesia to reduce or eliminate the pain associated with many dental procedures. Dentists treat patients suffering from bruxism (grinding of the teeth), which can have serious health consequences if not recognized and stopped. Some dentists perform root canal surgery to repair damage to the pulp and roots of the teeth. Dentists also look for changes in mouth tissues that may signal the onset of oral cancer and other diseases. When these diseases are detected and treated early, the chance of recovery is greatly increased.

The majority of dentists are independent practitioners who either operate their own private practices or work in partnerships with other dentists. They hire *dental hygienists* and *dental assistants* to help them treat patients. A dental hygienist is responsible for cleaning teeth, instructing patients in dental care, and taking X rays. Dental assistants help by preparing patients for exams, handing the dentist instruments during exams, and performing clerical tasks. A dentist may also hire an *office manager* to ensure the smooth operation of the business of the practice.

The dentist is usually responsible for maintaining the practice's equipment, arranging for repair of broken equipment, and making certain that the practice is properly supplied with tools and other dental devices. Because the dentist owns the practice, he or she is responsible for establishing office procedures and for maintaining employee satisfaction. The dentist must also ensure that the practice complies with a multitude of federal, state, and local regulations and with the requirements of health insurers.

While general practitioners make up the majority of dentists, many dentists choose to specialize in particular areas of dentistry. *Orthodontists* specialize in problems with the development of the teeth and jaws. These dentists use equipment such as braces and retainers to correct positioning of the teeth. *Oral and maxillofacial surgeons* perform surgery on the teeth, gums, jaws, and related structures in the head and neck. They perform difficult tooth extractions, remove tumors, and repair damage caused by accidents, injuries, and birth defects. *Endodontists* treat diseased tissues inside the teeth, such as nerves, pulp, and root canals. *Pedodontists,* or *pediatric dentists,* specialize in children's dental care. *Periodontists* work with diseased gums and other support tissues. *Prosthodontists* make artificial teeth and dentures.

Like general practitioners, specialists may operate their own practices. Some specialists work as part of hospital staffs. Other specialists are involved with governmental organizations working to promote dental education and public policy affecting dental health. Still others perform research into the causes and development of dental diseases.

what is it like to be a dentist?

Dr. Mitchell Cohen has been a dentist for more than 12 years. He's a partner in Bordentown Family Dental, in Bordentown, New Jersey. "Both of my partners are more or less retired, though," Mitchell says. "So while we make major decisions together, I'm pretty much in charge of running the actual practice."

Mitchell generally works a 45-hour week. "Only about 38 hours or so are actually involved with seeing patients. The rest of the time I'm dealing with all the other things that need to get done. Usually, I get here by 7:30 AM, and most days I leave around 5 in the evening. But we're open late one day a week, so I'll stay until 9 PM, and we're open Saturdays, too. In all, I work four and three-quarter days a week because I take Fridays off."

Mitchell is often the first to arrive in the morning. "I'll go to the different rooms, turning on the lights and the equipment. Then I'll review the charts of the patients I'll be seeing that day. There's often things on my desk that I'll need to respond to, like ordering supplies and equipment. Usually, I'll have 15 minutes or so to have coffee and read the newspaper. Then I'll set up for my first patient."

Mitchell sees a variety of patients during the course of a day. "I'll have anywhere from five to 10 patients in my chair. And I'll see anywhere from zero to 20 hygienists' patients. Those are patients who are just here for routine cleaning, so I just do quick checks on their teeth. But it's difficult to talk about a typical day because there really isn't one. Every patient is different, really. I may perform part

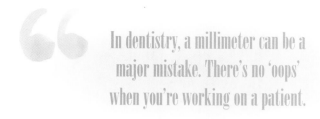

In dentistry, a millimeter can be a major mistake. There's no 'oops' when you're working on a patient.

of the root canal process on one patient, do a filling for the next, fit dentures for another patient, and maybe construct a crown for the patient after that."

Mitchell's workday can become very hectic. "Sometimes, I'll have a patient in the chair, another in the reception room, two hygienists waiting for me to check their patients, and someone on the phone. But there are other times when things calm down. I'll get my work done and have a chance to relax a bit. It really varies from day to day."

In addition to seeing patients, Mitchell has many responsibilities related to running the practice. "One of my employees may request a review of office procedure, so we'll sit down and discuss that in between patients. I may have to fight with an insurance company to make certain they'll cover a treatment or meet with government regulators. Meanwhile, I have to inspect and maintain the equipment. If something breaks down, I'm usually able to repair it myself. Otherwise, I'll have to call a repair service.

"I'm also responsible for this building. I'll do some maintenance or I'll hire contractors for the work. Also, I have to make sure we have enough supplies at all times."

Financial concerns are an important aspect of running the business. "My office manager takes care of routine billing and other matters. And I have a good accountant providing me with financial reports. But I'm in charge of things like hiring employees, setting salaries and raises, and determining bonuses. I keep a weekly check on our revenues, and I also approve any expenditures.

"I also have to make sure all our licenses are current and that we're complying with the different regulations," Mitchell says. "I also keep track of our business trends. For example, I wanted to see if having patients from HMOs [health maintenance organizations] was good for the practice. I came to the conclusion that we would actually be losing money accepting these kinds of patients."

have I got what it takes to be a dentist?

Mitchell chose dentistry as a career out of a desire to be a health professional. "Dentistry attracted me because it has less of an emergency component than the other health professions," Mitchell says. "And it's more technical in nature, which appealed to me. I liked the hands-on aspects of the career."

A dentist must be very precise in his or her work. Mitchell says, "In dentistry, a millimeter can be a major mistake. There's no 'oops' when you're working on a patient. This job requires strong hand-eye coordination skills. You have to have a steady hand, and you need good visual abilities. Depth perception and the ability to conceptualize in three dimensions are both important parts of my work. Without good vision and hands, you just can't be a dentist. This is something you really don't find out about until you're already in dental school. I've known people who got really good grades, but when it came time to do laboratory work, they just couldn't handle it."

Dentists must have strong people skills as well. "In a way, I'm performing all day," Mitchell says. "The patient in my chair deserves friendly, cheerful service, no matter what else may be going on in my life. And a lot of patients are nervous about being there. I have to understand what they're going through and try to make it a positive experience for them. It's also important to be able to communicate with patients. A lot of times, a patient's expectation of his or her treatment may not match the reality. I have to communicate to the patient exactly what to expect as an outcome."

Another career requirement of this career is the ability to concentrate. "You really need incredible focus. I usually speak to the patient or to one of my assistants while I'm working, because this helps to put the patient at ease. But at the same time, I have to really concentrate on my work."

Owning his own practice is a strong source of satisfaction for Mitchell. "I wanted to be my own boss. No one can fire me. You really have control over your own destiny. You have the ability to set the rules and the tone of the whole office, which makes working easier." But the real source of Mitchell's satisfaction comes from the work itself. "I like it that I'm actually making something. I'm producing and accomplishing something with my own hands. There's this satisfaction of a job well done. Like when a 10 year-old gets out of my chair saying, 'Gee, that felt great!' after I've just given him a filling. You know, there's kind of a high you get when your patient thinks you're the greatest."

A dentist needs to recognize his or her own limits, however. "I think a lot of people going into dentistry are highly competitive. They're just not used to failure," Mitchell says. "But you're dealing with living tissue here. And that means it's inevitable that you're going to fail. And that's part of the job too. You have to be able to allow yourself to be human. It really requires that you have a strong self-image and that you have a good feeling about yourself. Then you can make your patients feel good too."

how do I become a dentist?

education

High School
High school students should begin preparing for this career with a course load emphasizing math and science subjects, including chem-

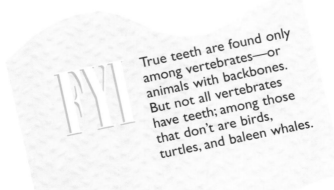

FYI True teeth are found only among vertebrates—or animals with backbones. But not all vertebrates have teeth; among those that don't are birds, turtles, and baleen whales.

istry, biology, physics, and health. Students should also work on developing their communication skills. "I did a lot of drama," Mitchell says, "and I think that really helps me when I'm dealing with my patients. Basically, when I come into the examination room, I'm on stage. It's my time to perform."

Because of the precision work involved in being a dentist, Mitchell also recommends courses and activities that can help develop these skills. "I liked to work with electronics, and I used to build model airplanes. And this comes in handy in a lot of ways. For instance, I can usually repair my equipment when it breaks down. And that saves a lot of money, because repair services can be very expensive." Also, because dentists usually own their own practices, Mitchell recommends taking some business courses as well. "It's helpful to at least understand the basics of running a business. Though a lot of it you'll learn just from encountering it."

Postsecondary Training

Before entering dental school, you must have completed three to four years of undergraduate education. Entry into a postgraduate dental program is highly competitive, so students should maintain a strong grade point average while in college. A bachelor's degree, while not strictly required, significantly increases an applicant's chance of gaining admission into a dental school. While in college, students should continue to emphasize math and science courses but should not neglect liberal arts courses. "I recommend taking psychology courses as well," says Mitchell. "This will help in understanding the patient and in understanding yourself. You want to be very comfortable with yourself, because each patient is, in a way, a test of your ego. The patient's standards can be very different from your own. They may judge you by how their teeth look or by how much pain they might have felt. But they'll never notice the real precision of the work you've done. So, in a way, you'll always be underappreciated. It helps to be aware of the reasons for that and to be strong enough to accept it."

In order to be admitted into a dental program, a student must first pass the Dental Admissions Test. Dental schooling usually lasts four years and includes classroom and laboratory courses in the basic sciences, such as anatomy, biochemistry, microbiology, and physiology, as well as courses in the clinical sciences, such as laboratory technique. Many dental programs offer interdisciplinary programs in which the dental student attends basic science courses with students preparing for careers in general medicine and other health professions. Clinical practice at a dental clinic is emphasized during the last two years of the program, giving students the opportunity to treat patients under faculty and professional supervision. Graduates receive a degree of Doctor of Dental Surgery (D.D.S.) or, in some states, the equivalent Doctor of Dental Medicine (D.D.M. or D.M.D.).

certification or licensing

All states and the District of Columbia require new graduate to pass a licensing exam before being allowed to practice dentistry. Depending on the state, students may also be required to continue their education by studying a specialty within dentistry (usually an additional two to four years) and obtain a specialized license. "I did a year of general residency," says Mitchell, "and then I did a year's residency in anesthesiology. That field interested me because it was actually founded by a dentist who discovered that nitrous oxide could limit the patient's ability to feel pain."

more lingo to learn

Incisors: The front teeth used for cutting and gnawing food.

Molars: The back teeth used for grinding and crushing food.

Plaque: A film composed of bacteria on the surface of the tooth that leads to tooth decay.

Pulp: The substance that lies in the central cavities of the teeth. It contains the nerves and blood vessels of the teeth and provides nourishment to the dentin, enamel, and cementum.

Roots: The parts of the teeth that are below the gumline. They attach the teeth to the jaws.

Wisdom teeth: The molars furthest back in the jaws that may or may not break through the gums.

All dentists should expect to continue their education throughout their careers. By reading professional journals, attending seminars, and taking short-term graduate courses, dentists will keep current with the latest advances in procedure and technology.

who will hire me?

According to the U.S. Department of Labor, there are more than 160,000 dentists in the United States and approximately 90 percent of them are in private practice. Because of the cost involved with setting up a practice, however, few dentists begin their careers owning their own practices.

Mitchell's career path is somewhat typical of many dentists. "I got my first job through the New Jersey Dental Association's matching service. They matched me with a private practice in Old Bridge, New Jersey. After working there for a while, I joined a dental clinic as an employee. But what I really wanted was my own practice. Eventually, I found this one. One of the original partners was retiring, so I bought his share of the partnership."

Although most dentists are in private practice, they are not limited to this area. Dentists may enter military service as commissioned officers, or they may apply for positions with various government agencies. Public health dentistry is a growing specialty area of dentistry. Dentists also work in hospital settings, dental clinics, or in schools. Some pursue careers in dental research or education and work in laboratory settings.

To be a successful dentist, you should

- Enjoy working with people
- Have excellent communication and people skills
- Be able to work independently
- Be detail-oriented
- Have excellent visual perception and steady hands
- Be able to perform under pressure

where can I go from here?

The primary career path for most dentists in private practice is to build the reputation of the practice and attract a large clientele. Most dentists continue practicing dentistry long after the normal retirement age. Many of these dentists are semi-retired and choose to practice part-time.

Dentists who work for others may choose to form or join their own private practice. Other dentists may shift from general dentistry to specialty dentistry, returning to school to achieve the necessary additional training and certification.

what are the salary ranges?

Earnings vary depending on level of experience and specialty. According to 1999 Economic Research Institute data, after one year of experience, dentists earned between $58,844 and $104,543 a year. After 11 years, they earned between $90,531 and $160,840. With over 20 years of experience, dentists earned between $113,797 and $202,175 a year. Specialized dentistry pays higher salaries than general practice. In the first year of practice, endodontists earned an average annual salary of $89,684; periodontists, $92,210; oral surgeons, $117,132; and orthodontists, $136,931.

The location of a dentist's practice also plays a role in determining income. Dentists located in affluent suburban areas will generally earn more than dentists in urban or rural areas. However, a dentist's income is also affected by the number of other dental practices operating in the area. In an area with fewer dentists, a dental practice will find it easier to develop a large client base.

what is the job outlook?

According to the U.S. Department of Labor, the field of dentistry is expected to grow more slowly than the average in the next decade. Dentistry continues to be highly competitive. The number of admissions to dental schools declined significantly between 1978 and 1994 and only recently has begun to increase. Setting up a private practice has also become more difficult, as costs for equipment and other supplies have been rising. And, since most dentists continue to practice until well after the normal retirement age, the number of openings that normally arise from the need to replace an aging workforce are limited.

Yet, despite the slower growth, the demand for dentists is expected to remain strong. People will always have a need for dentists and the growing availability of dental insurance makes it easier and more affordable to visit them regularly.

The aging of the population is also expected to increase the need for dentists because the elderly require more complex services for their teeth and gums.

However, the *Occupational Outlook Handbook* notes that employment of dentists is not expected to grow as quickly as demand; instead of hiring fellow dentists, those who own their own practice will hire lower-paid dental hygienists and assistants to handle more routine care.

how do I learn more?

professional organizations

Following are organizations that provide information on dental careers, accredited schools, and employers.

American Dental Association
211 East Chicago Avenue
Chicago, IL 60611
312-440-2500
http://www.ada.org

American Dental Education Association
1625 Massachusetts Avenue, NW, Suite 600
Washington, DC 20036-2212
202-667-9433
adea@adea.org
http://www.aads.jhu.edu

Canadian Dental Association
1815 Alta Vista
Ottawa, ON K1G 3Y6 Canada
613-523-1770
reception@cda-adc.ca
http://www.cda-adc.ca

Feelin' no pain

Though people had been extracting defective teeth for hundreds of years, it wasn't until 1844 that a method was found to extract teeth painlessly. In that year, Horace Wells, an American dentist, used nitrous oxide, or laughing gas, as an anesthetic. Two years later, William Morton, another American dentist, used ether as an anesthetic. Both of these anesthetics made patients unconscious. The first anesthetic used to minimize pain without causing unconsciousness was cocaine, in 1884. Novocaine was first used in 1905.

For information from a dentist on careers in dentistry, visit this Web site:
So, You Want to Be a Dentist?
http://www.vvm.com/~bond/home.htm

bibliography

Following is a sampling of materials related to the professional concerns and development of dentists.

Hall, W. *Decision Making in Dental Treatment Planning.* St. Louis, MO: Mosby-Yearbook, Inc., 1998.

Homoly, Paul. *Dentists, An Endangered Species: A Survival Guide for Fee-For-Service Care.* Tulsa, OK: PennWell Publishing, 1996.

Kendall, Bonnie L. *Opportunities in Dental Care Careers*. Revised Edition. Chicago, IL: NTC Publishing Group, 2000.

Mitchell, David A. and Laura Mitchell. *Oxford Handbook of Clinical Dentistry*. 3rd Edition. New York, NY: Oxford University Press, 1999.

Ord, R. *Oral Cancer: Dentist's Role in Diagnosis, Management, Rehabilitation, and Prevention*. Chicago, IL: Quintessence Publishing, 2000.

Dermatologists

Definition

Dermatologists are physicians who diagnosis and treat benign and malignant disorders of the skin and related tissues of the mouth, hair, and nails. They also advise on caring for normal skin.

High School Subjects

Biology
Chemistry
Physics

Personal Skills

Helping/teaching
Technical/scientific

Salary Range

$120,000 to $228,000 to $337,000

Educational Requirements

Bachelor's degree, M.D., four or more years of post-graduate training

Certification or Licensing

Recommended (certification)
Required by all states (licensing)

Outlook

Faster than the average

GOE
02.03.01
O*NET-SOC
29-1062.00

Sharp odors of sweat and aftershave hang in the air of the men's locker room. The walls and lockers are damp with the steam issuing from the showers. A group of six wrestlers waits anxiously with their coach as the team physician examines the last of the young men. These six wrestlers all have the same inexplicable rash behind their ears, on their foreheads, and all over their scalps.

"What have we got?" one of the wrestlers finally asks, unable to contain his worry.

"Will they be able to wrestle at the meet next week?" asks the coach.

The doctor pulls off the plastic gloves he is wearing and tosses them into a nearby trash can.

"I don't know, and I don't know," the doctor answers. He shakes his head and jots down a few notes on a pad of paper. "I haven't got a clue. I've never seen anything like this before." A dejected silence settles on the group. "But we're not out of options just yet," he assures them. "If there's one guy who can figure out what's wrong here, it's Basler. I'll give him a call right away."

"Who's Basler?" demands the coach.

Dr. Rodney Basler, a dermatologist specializing in sports-related skin diseases, has just been given another medical mystery to unravel.

lingo to learn

Abscess: A pus-filled cavity resulting from a bacterial infection that has destroyed or displaced the healthy tissue.

Antigen: A protein or carbohydrate substance that stimulates an immune response.

Biopsy: Removal of a small piece of tissue for microscopic examination.

Cryosurgery: A type of surgery in which liquid nitrogen is applied to a skin growth to freeze and kill abnormal cells.

Immunofluorescence: A diagnostic procedure involving fluorescent dye that is used to detect an antigen. If the antigen is present, injected tissue will glow under microscopic examination with a fluorescent light source.

MEDLINE: Computer link to the U.S. National Library of Medicine in Bethesda, Maryland, which allows health professionals to search for and retrieve specific medical bibliographic information.

Mohs' surgery: A technique used to remove skin cancers when the shape and depth of a tumor are difficult to determine. Layers of skin are shaved off one at a time until the entire tumor is gone.

Tinea: Latin for worm, *tinea* is commonly called ringworm. Despite its name, ringworm has nothing to do with worms but is a fungal infection. *Tinea capitis* is ringworm of the scalp. *Tinea pedis* is ringworm of the foot, which is commonly known as athlete's foot.

what does a dermatologist do?

A *dermatologist* studies, diagnoses, and treats the diseases, conditions, and disorders of the skin, hair, nails, mucous membranes, and related tissues and structures. Dermatologists begin their work by first diagnosing the patient's problem. The first and most important step in the diagnosis is a physical examination of the patient. This examination, combined with a thorough review of the patient's history, is often enough to solve a patient's problem. The dermatologist usually can identify common problems by sight and then trace the source of the problem to a recent event or change in the patient's life or habits. A mysterious rash, for example, may have a mundane origin, such as the patient's use of a new perfume or soap.

Beyond a visual inspection of the problem area, the dermatologist may perform many diagnostic procedures, including taking blood samples and skin-cell smears (scrapings that are examined on microscopic slides) from the affected area. These specimens are then sent to a laboratory for chemical and biological analyses. Since skin disorders are frequently caused by the presence of fungi or bacteria, the dermatologist also may order fungus cultures and other microbiologic examinations of the skin scrapings and secretions. Sometimes it is also necessary to excise (cut out) a portion of the affected tissue for analysis. Biopsies conducted on such tissue specimens can reveal whether or not the tissue is cancerous. If the dermatologist suspects allergic or immunologic diseases, he or she may perform patch and photosensitivity testing.

The diagnosis of skin diseases and disorders is not limited to the surface of the skin. Dermatologists may evaluate bone marrow, lymph nodes, and endocrine glands in their search for the source of a patient's problem.

After they determine the cause of the condition or identify the disease, dermatologists may treat their patients with a variety of methods. Certain conditions, such as eczema, dermatitis, acne, and impetigo, are treated with topical solutions that are applied to the skin. Other disorders are treated with prescribed oral medications or injections, including antibiotics. Ultraviolet light treatments are prescribed for some conditions, such as psoriasis. Radiation therapy is sometimes used to treat keloids (scar tissue). Still other disorders and diseases require surgical treatment.

Dermatologists are trained in surgical techniques to treat everything from warts to skin cancer. Skin cancers may be removed by laser surgery, frozen through cryosurgery, cauterized (burned) through electrosurgery, or destroyed through radiation therapy.

Dermatologists perform skin grafts to repair wounds too large to be stitched. For a skin graft, a dermatologist removes a portion of skin from another area of the patient's body and transplants it to the wounded area. In time, the transplanted skin begins to grow over the wound, helping the area to heal.

Dermatologists treat cosmetic defects through techniques such as dermabrasion, chemical face peels, and hair transplants. They also reduce or revise the appearance of scars or birthmarks through injections or laser surgery.

Many of the surgical procedures practiced by dermatologists are minor enough to be handled on an outpatient basis. A patient might come into the clinic early in the morning, receive a local anesthetic, undergo the procedure and, in some cases, recover quickly enough to drive home in time for lunch.

Many diseases seemingly unrelated to the skin and tissues manifest themselves in skin conditions. Itchy skin or rashes can be caused by the chemicals in new clothes or by a severe allergy. The common boil can indicate the onset of diabetes mellitus. As a result, dermatologists are frequently asked to consult on cases by other physicians or specialists. Likewise, when dermatologists discover that a skin condition is an indication of an illness in another part of the patient's body, they will refer the patient to a specialist for further treatment.

Many professionals choose to specialize, obtaining additional training and certification. Two subspecialties within the field of dermatology are immunodermatology and dermatopathology. *Dermatoimmunologists* have additional training in the diagnosis and treatment of skin diseases involving the immune system, including allergies. They may use a procedure called immunofluorescence to diagnose and characterize these skin disorders. *Dermatopathologists* have received extensive training in the evaluation of tissue specimens from patients. These evaluations include the examination and interpretation of microscopic slides of thin tissue sections and smears, and scrapings from lesions of the skin or related tissues. The dermatopathologist has expertise in light and electron microscopy, immunohistochemistry, and laboratory management.

In addition to these recognized subspecialties, many dermatologists may also develop expertise in specific areas of dermatology through their own experiences and research. A dermatologist may have a general practice, for example, but be uniquely qualified in women's skin disorders and diseases. *Dermatologic surgeons* are only involved in surgical cases. *Pediatric dermatologists* treat skin disorders in children. *Occupational dermatologists* study and treat those skin disorders associated with various occupations, such as contact dermatitis caused by exposure to chemical irritants.

what is it like to be a dermatologist?

"No emergencies, no deaths, and no cures," jokes Dr. Rodney Basler. He should know. With two thriving practices in Lincoln, Nebraska, Rodney sees a lot of skin every day. "And what's more fun than skin?" he says.

Most of Dr. Basler's time is spent at one of his two offices where he sees patients. The broad-based patient range is part of what he loves about his job. "The diversity of cases has tremendous appeal for me. There's such a nice balance of diagnostic—or medical—and surgical cases."

He ticks off a list of common skin disorders and diseases that he encounters every day. "Of the diagnostic cases, you see rashes, hives, acne, and contact dermititis. Of the surgical cases, you see warts, moles and, unfortunately, lots and lots of skin cancer." The bulk of cases he sees also break down by age. Understandably, he treats acne for a large group of patients who fall between the ages of 13 and 20. The other large patient group is made up of individuals between the ages of 70 and 90 who suffer from skin cancer.

Rodney is also the team physician for the University of Nebraska Cornhuskers. Athletes come directly to his campus office when they have a skin problem or if their coach refers them to him. His hard work for the various athletic teams over the years has turned into something more than another job. "My personal experiences and all the research I did resulted in my expertise in the area of sports-related skin diseases," he explains. Now, coaches and team physicians for college and professional sports teams all over the country call Rodney for consultations and advice on

in-depth

Derm Surgeons: What Do They Do?

Dermatologic surgery, commonly called derm surgery, involves a variety of procedures and a vast knowledge of the skin. Derm surgeons perform skin cancer surgeries, such as Mohs' surgery, and cosmetic procedures. Derm surgeons are trained to do sclerotherapy (injecting fluid into spider, or varicose, veins to make them less visible), dermabrasion (planing the surface skin cells using sandpaper, wire brushes, or other abrasive materials), and chemical skin peels (applying chemicals to the skin to remove wrinkles or other defects).

Dr. Geoff Basler, son of Dr. Rodney Basler, is training to be a derm surgeon. "The stuff I was really interested in—head/neck surgeries, skin cancer resections, and all of the pioneering techniques—was being done by derm surgeons," he says. Geoff also discovered that many of the techniques used by plastic and reconstructive surgeons were pioneered by derm surgeons. "Because of their background in dermatology, derm surgeons have a greater appreciation of the biology of the skin than plastic and reconstructive surgeons," he says.

Geoff is most interested in skin cancer resections and the reconstructive surgery used to close and repair these surgical sites. He remembers the experience that helped him decide on this specialty. "It was in the middle of a lecture on skin cancer," says Geoff. "Part of the lecture was a slide show, and the derm surgeon projected these pictures of skin cancers in middle-aged and younger women. After the tumors were removed, the resections were big, potentially a cosmetic disaster. But this surgeon showed us how to do it, using flaps and grafts. And that was it—I knew this was what I wanted to do."

Like dermatologists, derm surgeons must have a bachelor's degree, graduate from an accredited medical school, and successfully complete an approved residency program in dermatology. At that point, someone interested in becoming a derm surgeon goes on to complete a one- to two-year fellowship in dermatologic surgery. The residency programs are extremely selective. Geoff notes, "While it's true that derm surgery is the easiest in terms of hours in the hospital—50 to 60 hours as compared to 100 for a thoracic surgeon—with no emergencies and no call, intellectually, it's just as challenging as other specialties, if not more." Prospective derm surgeons should be aware, however, that office hours are equal to the other specialties.

"My advice to future med students," says Geoff, "would be to look carefully at all the different specialties. Because my father was a dermatologist, I had the advantage of knowing what dermatology was all about." Although managed care is affecting the choices many doctors make about what specialty to go into, Geoff is optimistic about the future of health care professionals. "The important thing," he says, "is that you're doing what you like, so that no matter what happens, you're happy in your work."

sports-related skin diseases. In addition, he estimates that every week he gives somewhere between three and five interviews to popular magazines and daily newspapers on subjects ranging from athlete's foot to weird rashes—just like the one afflicting the six wrestlers.

After a consultation with their team doctor, Rodney diagnosed their case as *tinea capitis,* or ringworm of the scalp. "Wrestlers do get a lot of strange skin conditions, which makes sense, though, once you think about it," Rodney says. "Unlike other athletes who make little contact, they may brush up against each other or something, wrestlers are on that mat for a relatively long time in extremely close contact.

"That's what a lot of my work is like—someone calling up, describing a strange rash. And I've got to figure out what it is," Rodney adds. Fortunately, he enjoys solving a good mystery.

Like Dr. Basler, Dr. Iris Aronson is intrigued by a medical riddle. "There are so many skin diseases," says Iris, a Chicago-based immunopathologist certified in dermatologic immunology. "I like the puzzle of it. I enjoy trying to figure it out." Iris spent her internship at Michael Reese Hospital in Chicago and discovered her niche during a dermatology rotation. "The world opened up to me when I realized how the skin is related to the immunological mechanisms of diseases." Currently, Iris divides her time between the laboratory, seeing patients, and teaching dermatology residents and medical students at the University of Illinois, Chicago.

"Disease can occur anywhere in the skin," she says. "The skin is made up of three layers: the outer layer, or epidermis; the inner layer, or dermis, which contains the nerves, veins, hair follicles, sweat glands, and blood vessels; and the bottom layer, which contains subcutaneous tissue, mainly fat. Different diseases will cause changes in any of these areas or combinations of areas. By looking for these changes or patterns in biopsied skin, you can determine and differentiate between diseases. Psoriasis, eczema, lupus—these all have pathological features that allow us to differentiate between them."

Typically Iris spends two days a week in her clinic seeing patients. The rest of the week is spent preparing for lectures, participating in meetings, working in her laboratory, and fulfilling other duties associated with teaching.

Most of her time spent in the laboratory is used to review slides of tissue samples sent by other dermatologists and physicians seeking consultation. Her associate usually runs the laboratory tests, including immunofluorescence testing, which can take up to two hours to complete. Iris then spends several days "reading" the slides through a special immunofluorescent microscope, looking for signs of patterns specific to a particular disease or disorder. If she identifies a problem after reviewing the samples and consulting the patient's medical history, she can prescribe the best therapy option.

Iris's many teaching duties include giving lectures and monitoring guest lectures. She enjoys going to other physicians' lectures because she continues to learn, too. Another rewarding aspect of teaching is attending clinical conferences with her students, clinic staff, and other physicians. A clinical conference is an informal presentation of a complex patient case, offered up for discussion by a patient and his or her doctor. "We discuss the diagnosis and alternative treatments, among other things," Iris says.

have I got what it takes to be a dermatologist?

Dr. Marianne O'Donoghue is one of the leading dermatologic experts in the country. She has been in private practice since 1970 and sits on countless boards, including the American Academy of Dermatology. She has written and published extensively on dermatologic issues such as skin cancer and preventive skin care. The media regularly seeks out her opinion on such topics as the effectiveness of sunscreen and other skin-related issues.

But Marianne is the first to confess that her original reasons for choosing dermatology couldn't be further from the limelight. "I just loved it on my rotation, the diagnosing, all of it. But from a very practical point of view, I knew that I wanted to have a family and be able to see them. A dermatologist's hours are as close to nine to five as you get in the medical profession," she explains. "In that sense, it's a great field for women. Sixty percent of those entering are women—and it's largely because of the hours."

Each and every dermatologic practice will have differing demands on the physician's time and skills. Long hours and a large patient load are common to most practices. Dermatologists need to be able to work with many patients who are of diverse ages and have different problems. Rodney, for example, is one of only a few dermatologists in the Lincoln area, and he is genuinely sympathetic to the patient who has driven four or five hours to see him. "There's a lot of pressure and responsibility to help people who have become your patients," he admits. "But I can't tell that guy to go home and come back the next day. You learn to be efficient, that's for sure. You have to be able to make quick decisions, diagnose and treat."

Rodney says he usually puts in 55-hour workweeks. "I try and break it down into long days and short days. That seems to make it more bearable." For example, on Mondays, Tuesdays, and Thursdays, he and his staff work from 8 AM to 7:30 PM, but on Wednesday and Friday, they leave the office around 2 or 2:30 in the afternoon. "And yes," he groans with mock disgust, "Saturday is a workday, too." Rodney and his staff come in regularly on Saturdays from 8 AM until noon. "The reward," says Rodney, "what makes dermatology a great job, is that everyone likes you because you can help them. Patients tell you that you're great all the time. People are so grateful for helping them feel better about themselves."

The number of patients who want to see a dermatologist can create tight schedules. "A typical day for me is six patients an hour. I've got a high-volume practice," says Marianne. "And one of the greatest frustrations of the job is getting behind. Good scheduling is crucial to doing this job well and to fitting everyone in. If a patient needs more of my time, of course he or she gets it, but it's going to cut into my time with the next patient."

Besides patience and time management skills, a dermatologist also needs to be able to adapt to quickly changing situations. Rodney notes, "You need to have a pretty flexible personality. One patient might be a 12 year-old and the next patient might be 64. You talk to so many people of every age and socioeconomic level, you better be flexible."

Not all dermatologists work in private practices. Many work as faculty members in teaching hospitals or medical schools. These individuals must possess more than just dermatology expertise, they must also have quali-

ties unique to academic life, such as effective communication skills and the desire to continue research. Iris, a faculty member at the University of Illinois since 1978, says her job has its frustrations, but those are overshadowed by the larger pleasure she takes from teaching. "Since I'm in charge of teaching residents and medical students, I have to be up on the latest research. I love that. To me, that's not a job, that's a learning process. But there's so much to learn, there's no way one person can keep up with it, which makes it difficult and, yes, frustrating."

To keep abreast of developments in technology and technique, Iris subscribes to multiple journals and is constantly reading. Computer skills are also important; Iris often uses the World Wide Web to search for information. One Internet resource available to all health professionals is MEDLINE. "I use MEDLINE when I'm looking for the latest medical research," she says. "You don't have to go anywhere to get a tremendous amount of knowledge. To access the data I now receive online, I used to have to go to the library and spend hours looking for what I needed."

how do I become a dermatologist?

education

High School

If you are interested in pursuing a medical degree, a high school education emphasizing college preparatory classes is a must. Math and science courses, including biology, chemistry, and physics, are necessary. These classes will not only provide you with basic science and math concepts, but also allow you to determine your own aptitude in these areas. Since college will be your next educational step, it is also important to take English courses to develop researching and writing skills. A foreign or classical language, such as Latin, can also be helpful. In addition, it is important to gain a familiarity with using computers. Many medical resources are now available online, and doctors need to know how to access this information.

To be a successful dermatologist, you should

- Enjoy working with a wide variety of people
- Be interested in diagnostic medicine as well as surgical medicine
- Enjoy researching and constant learning
- Be sensitive to the way people feel about their appearance

Postsecondary Training

Following high school you will need to earn a bachelor's degree from an accredited four-year college or university. Suggested premedical courses include physics, biology, and organic and inorganic chemistry. Courses in English and the humanities, mathematics, and the social sciences are also highly recommended.

Many colleges and universities that have medical schools often have accelerated programs for high school seniors who plan to attend medical school. These programs typically reduce or consolidate the number of years spent as an undergraduate, thereby speeding up the student's entrance into medical school. Special restrictions and qualifying requirements apply. Interested students should contact schools early on in the application process.

Born in Israel, Iris emigrated to Chicago with her parents when she was still a young girl. She credits her parents with encouraging her to study hard for college. Though she won numerous scholarships to a number of schools, the funding wasn't adequate. In order to defray the cost, she stayed in Chicago and attended the University of Illinois, graduating in only three years. With no break, she immediately entered medical school at the same university. "The focus was to do everything as quickly as possible." Iris admits. "If I could tell kids today anything, it would be to go slowly and appreciate the experiences and diversity of college."

After receiving an undergraduate degree, a student then must apply and be accepted to medical school. Admission is competitive and applicants must undergo a fairly extensive and difficult admissions process that takes into consideration grade point averages, scores on the Medical College Admission Test, and recommendations from professors. Some schools may also require an interview before final selections are made. Most students apply to several medical schools early in their senior year of college. Only about one-third of the applicants are accepted.

In order to earn the doctor of medicine degree, a student must complete four years of medical school study and training. For the first two years, students attend lectures and classes and spend time in laboratories. Courses include anatomy, biochemistry, physiology, pharmacology, psychology, microbiology, pathology, and medical ethics. Students learn to take patient histories, perform routine physical examinations, and recognize symptoms of diseases. In their third and fourth

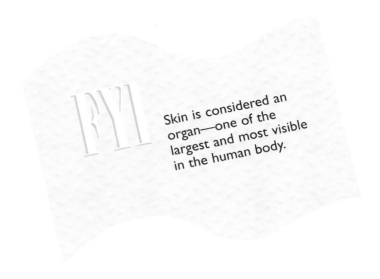

FYI Skin is considered an organ—one of the largest and most visible in the human body.

years, students are involved in more practical studies. Under the supervision of residents and physicians, students work in clinics and hospitals to learn acute, chronic, preventive, and rehabilitative care. They go through what are known as rotations. Rotations are brief periods of study in a particular area, such as internal medicine, obstetrics and gynecology, pediatrics, dermatology, psychiatry, and surgery. Rotations allow students to gain exposure to the many different fields within medicine and to learn firsthand the skills of diagnosing and treating patients.

"At a very basic level, you really have to like scientific subjects," Iris explains, "and it helps if you have a good memory. If you can't remember what you read, medical school isn't a good idea. A lot of medical school is pure memorization," she says. "There's really nothing that intuitive about it. That comes later."

Upon graduating from an accredited medical school, physicians must pass a standard examination given by the National Board of Medical Examiners. Most physicians complete an internship, also referred to as a transition year. The internship helps graduates decide on their area of specialization.

Following the internship, physicians begin what is known as a residency. Dermatology residency programs usually last four years. The first year is a general overview of internal medicine, family practice, pediatrics, or general surgery. The other three years are spent in training related to the direct care of dermatologic patients, including consultations, clinical conferences, and patient rounds. Residents study skin pathology, bacteriology, mycology, radiology, surgery, biochemistry, allergy and immunology, and other basic studies. Intensive laboratory work in mycology (the study of the fungi that infect humans) is usually required.

The residency years are as filled with stress, pressure, and physical rigor as medical school—perhaps even more. Residents are given greater responsibilities than medical students, working 24-hour shifts, easily clocking in 80 hours or more per week.

Additional training, research, and certification is required for subspecialties such as immunodermatology and dermatopathology. The duration of these programs is generally at least a year.

Rodney received his undergraduate degree from the University of Nebraska and went on to study medicine at the Nebraska Medical Center. Like many physicians, it was while on a rotation in dermatology that he was first impressed by the extensive range of skills and knowledge necessary to the profession. After finishing medical school, Rodney went on to a residency in dermatology at the University of Michigan, and then spent several years at St. Joseph's Hospital in Phoenix, Arizona.

"What students considering dermatology should know," he says, "is the kind of commitment they will be making. There's a lot of time and money invested in a dermatologist's career," says Rodney. The average length of schooling for those studying to become dermatologists is 12 years, and the costs of these programs are on the rise. According to the American Medical Association, the average tuition and fees associated with medical schooling have increased 312 percent at public schools and 221 percent for private institutions between 1981 and 1999. The average tuition in 1999 for one year of medical school was $11,375 at public schools (for in-state residents) and $28,733 at private schools.

certification or licensing

Dermatologists must pass an examination by the board of medical examiners in order to receive a license from the state in which they intend to practice. Certification by dermatological associations, on the other hand, is voluntary and affirms that dermatologists are qualified to practice the specialty of dermatology. The phrase, "board certified" refers to the certification of a dermatologist by the American Board of Dermatology.

After finishing her studies in clinical dermatology at the University of Chicago, Iris won a fellowship—a year of special training—in dermatopathology. The fellowship included work in surgery and general pathology. However, she didn't take the boards, or certifying examinations, in dermatopathology, but chose instead to become certified in dermatologic immunology. "I never wanted or intended to be a pathologist and just read slides, but I believed the only way to truly understand the pathology of skin was to study it in depth," she says.

scholarships and grants

Scholarships and grants are often available from individual institutions, state agencies, and special-interest organizations. Many students finance their medical education through military service. The Armed Forces Health Professions Scholarship Program and the National Health Service Corps Scholarship both offer students the opportunity to pay for tuition in exchange for military service. Contact your local recruiting office for more information on these programs.

Other sources of financial aid are available to those currently in residency programs. Individual medical schools, residency programs, and even pharmaceutical companies may fund individual and departmental research projects in dermatology. The American Academy of Dermatology annually sponsors awards for clinical research conducted by outstanding dermatological residents. This recognition, called The Award for Young Investigators, offers the prize amount of $5,000 to be divided between the individual resident ($2,000) and his or her residency department ($3,000). Other organizations that offer scholarships and grant opportunities are the Dermatology Foundation and the Association of American Medical Colleges.

American Academy of Dermatology
Department of Professional Education
930 North Meacham Road
Schaumburg, IL 60173-4965
http://www.aad.org

Armed Forces Health Professions Scholarship Program
Air Force: http://hp.airforce.com/training/ financial.html
Army: http://www.sirius.com/~ameddet/ hpschps.htm
Navy: http://nshs.med.navy.mil/hpsp/default.htm

Association of American Medical Colleges
2450 N Street, NW
Washington, DC 20037-1126
202-828-0400
http://www.aamc.org

The Dermatology Foundation
1560 Sherman Avenue
Evanston, IL 60201-4808
info@dermfnd.org
http://www.dermfnd.org

National Health Service Corps Scholarship Program
Department of Health and Human Services,
4350 East-West Highway, 10th Floor
Bethesda MD 20814
800-638-0824
http://www.fedmoney.org/grants/93288-00.htm

According to Dr. Marianne O'Donoghue, most skin damage from overexposure to the sun occurs before the age of 17. Of course, you can still further damage your skin past that age. Marianne recommends using a sunscreen to help prevent skin cancer and premature aging.

who will hire me?

Dermatologists work in a variety of settings, from private practices to laboratories to industrial environments. A recently certified dermatologist may not be able to afford the expense of opening up his or her own private practice. Often the most common route for a young dermatologist interested in private practice is to join an existing one. A second option is to take over the practice of a dermatologist who is retiring or relocating. In this case, the new practitioner has the added benefit of a previously established patient base. Some dermatologists join a group practice or enter into partnership with a related medical specialist, such as an allergist, an immunologist, or a plastic surgeon. Other dermatologists take salaried positions in clinics or health maintenance organizations (HMOs). After several years, they may decide to open their own practice.

Dermatologists may also choose to combine a private practice with a teaching position at a medical school or a teaching hospital. Some are involved in laboratory research, studying skin disorders to develop new treatments and therapies. Dermatologists also work in the business world, studying the effects of a variety of products on the skin or developing new products for the consumer market, such as lotions and cosmetics that contain sunscreen and anti-aging properties.

Opportunities also exist for dermatologists with federal or state agencies, including the military. Interested physicians should contact these agencies directly.

where can I go from here?

Dermatologists with their own private practice can increase their earnings or improve their clinical status by expanding their patient population, moving to a larger city, or developing an area of expertise. In addition to treating patients, dermatologists may also become teachers at medical schools or go into research.

A dermatologist can improve his or her professional status by publishing scholarly articles in respected journals of the field, such as *Cutis*. Frequent and influential publications can lead to offers to speak on a lecture circuit. Marianne thoroughly enjoys lecturing, although the strain of travel can take its toll. "It's a real honor," she says of her frequent speaking engagements, which are both financially and intellectually rewarding.

Many physicians also enhance their professional status by participating in the activities of national organizations, such as the American Dermatological Association, where they can serve on committees and in elected offices.

what are the salary ranges?

Salaries depend on the size and scope of a dermatologist's practice, the geographic area, level of skill and experience, and hours worked. According to a 2000 salary survey by Physicians Search, the average starting salary for practicing dermatologists was $150,000. The lowest paid group earned an average of $120,000; the highest paid earned $200,000. For those working three or more years, the average salary was $232,000. The lowest paid group earned an average of $168,988; the highest earned $337,000.

what is the job outlook?

The health care industry is thriving. According to the U.S. Department of Labor, the employment of physicians in almost all fields is expected to grow faster than the average rate for all occupations. Approximately 1.2 percent of all physicians are dermatologists—a figure that is expected to grow in the coming years.

Marianne is confident that dermatologists will always be able to make a healthy living doing what they love. "Since I entered the field people are much more concerned with their physical appearances. They want to look younger, cleaner, better," she asserts. "Even if insurance were to drop off and no longer cover dermatologic care, people would pay out of their own pockets."

Demand for dermatologists has increased because of the growing awareness of and concern about skin damage from the sun and other airborne pollutants and irritants. Increasingly, men and women strive to improve their appearance through preventative skin care that takes advantage of new technology and anti-aging products and techniques.

"Women tend to notice things earlier," says Rodney. "Men tend to wait until it's almost too late—but that's changing as awareness about skin cancer grows. I'll see patients who have a problem that's been bothering them for years, and in one visit I can really affect their quality of life."

how do I learn more?

professional organizations

Following are organizations that provide information on accredited schools, careers, and the certifying process.

American Academy of Dermatology
Department of Professional Education
930 North Meacham Road
Schaumburg, IL 60173-4965
http://www.aad.org

American Board of Dermatology
Henry Ford Health System
1 Ford Place
Detroit, MI 48202-3450
http://www.abderm.org

American Society for Dermatologic Surgery
930 North Meacham Road
Schaumburg, IL 60173-6016
http://www.asds-net.org

bibliography

Following is a sampling of materials relating to the professional concerns and development of dermatologists.

Fitzpatrick, Thomas B. et. al. *Color Atlas and Synopsis of Clinical Dermatology*. New York:, NY: McGraw-Hill, 2000.

Habif, Thomas P. and James L. Campbell. *Skin Disease: Diagnosis and Treatment*. St. Louis, MO: Mosby, Inc., 2000.

Lookingbill, Donald P. and James G. Marks, Jr. *Principles of Dermatology*. 3rd Edition. Philadelphia, PA: W. B. Saunders, 2000.

Sahn, Eleanor. *Dermatology Pearls*. Philadelphia, PA: Lippincott Williams & Wilkins, 1999.

Shelley, Walter B. and E. Dorinda. *Advanced Dermatologic Therapy*. Philadelphia, PA: W. B. Saunders, 2001.

Turkington, Carol A. and Jeffrey S. Dover. *Skin Deep: An A-Z of Skin, Skin Disorders, Treatments, and Health*. New York, NY: Checkmark Books, 1998.

Diagnostic Medical Sonographers

Definition

Diagnostic medical sonographers use advanced technology, in the form of high-frequency sound waves, to produce images of the internal body for analysis by radiologists and other physicians.

Alternative Job Title

Ultrasound technologists

High School Subjects

Biology
Chemistry

Personal Skills

Helping/teaching
Technical/scientific

Salary Range

$24,000 to $33,000 to $48,000

Minimum Educational Level

Associate's degree, hospital certificate program, or bachelor's degree

Certification or Licensing

Required

Outlook

Faster than the average

GOE
02.04.01
O*NET-SOC
29-2032.00

The young expectant mother waits on an examination table, her forehead creased with lines. It seems like weeks since she last felt the sharp kick of her baby from within her body. She is worried that something has gone wrong with the development of her child.

Carol Seguin maintains a steady dialogue with the frightened woman in order to distract her from her anxiety; she calms her patient with gentle humor as she coats her stomach with ultrasound gel. She then explains the procedure and positions the woman in order to assure optimum scanning.

Using a device called a transducer, Carol directs high-frequency sound waves toward the unborn baby. These waves will reflect off the body tissue to form a two-dimensional, real-time image on a video monitor. She is careful to observe the screen as she moves the transducer, aware of the need for a high-quality ultrasound image.

An image of a baby, a healthy, breathing boy, appears. Carol quickly points to the baby's beating heart on the monitor. She also points out the baby's head and other body parts; and the mother is overwhelmed with happiness and relief.

Carol is extremely happy for the young woman, yet also knows there is a job to complete. She finishes recording the images of the baby and prepares the film to be taken to a physician for further analysis. This high degree of professionalism, combined with compassion, allows diagnostic medical sonographers like Carol to be prepared and able to do their jobs in the event of good news, as with the young mother, or bad news. The image of another young mother whose baby girl did not survive still lingers in her memory.

Carol wishes the young woman well and readies her equipment for the next patient. In the course of her day she will complete procedures that test for cysts, abdominal tumors, and impeded function of blood vessels and heart valves.

what does a sonographer do?

Diagnostic medical sonographers (DMSs), sometimes known as *ultrasound technologists,* or simply *sonographers,* use high-frequency sound waves, which are an offshoot of World War II SONAR technology, to produce images of the internal body. A picture is obtained when these sound waves bounce off internal structures, becoming echoes that are then displayed as two-dimensional gray images on a video screen. The recorded images are used by a physician in diagnosing disease and in studying the malfunction of organs.

Diagnostic medical sonographers, working under the supervision of a qualified physician, are responsible for the selection and the setup of the proper ultrasound equipment for each specific examination. They also explain the procedure to the patient, record any additional information that may help in the diagnosis, and help the patient into the proper physical position so the test may begin.

When the patient is properly aligned, the sonographer applies ultrasound gel to the specific test area. He or she is responsible for selecting the transducer and adjusting controls in relation to the depth of field, organ or structure examined, and other factors. The sonographer physically moves the transducer, a microphone-shaped device that sends high-frequency sound waves into the area to be imaged. At the same time, the sonographer watches the video monitor to be sure that a quality ultrasonic image is being produced. The sonographer must also be aware of subtle differences between healthy and diseased areas in order to be able to record the correct image.

Once the target area is located and a quality image appears consistently on screen, the sonographer then activates the equipment that begins to record images on magnetic tape, a computer disc, strip printout, film, or videotape. The sonographer is responsible for filming individual views or sequences of real-time images in affected areas. When a procedure is completed, the sonographer removes the film and prepares it for analysis by a specially trained physician. The sonographer may also be asked to discuss the test with a supervisor or attending physician.

In addition to diagnostic procedures, DMSs must also maintain patient data relating to each test, and check and adjust their equipment to ensure that readings are accurate. They may also, after considerable experience, have a role in preparing work schedules and evaluating potential equipment purchases.

lingo to learn

Doppler: A stethoscope-like instrument that is used to measure blood flow velocity.

Megahertz: The degree of strength for a sound wave in an ultrasound procedure.

M mode: A reading that determines the fetal heart rate.

Sonography: A diagnostic procedure that uses sound waves, instead of radiation, to create an image of the human body.

Transducer: A technologist-controlled device that directs high-frequency sound waves to a specific body part in order to create a two-dimensional moving image for analysis.

what is it like to be a sonographer?

Diagnostic medical sonographers work in a variety of settings such as hospitals, imaging centers, health maintenance organizations (HMOs), physicians' offices, mobile imaging clinics, industry, and clinical research labs. They may also work in departments of cardiology, radiology, obstetrics, and vascular surgery.

Carol has been a diagnostic medical sonographer since 1971. She received her training at Rush-Presbyterian-St. Luke's Medical Center, which is a teaching hospital in Chicago. In addition to X-ray techniques, she also learned magnetic resonance imaging (MRI), CT scan, and ultrasound, which became her career choice.

Carol's day begins at 8:00 AM and ends at 5:00 PM. There is no overtime for DMSs at Meyer Medical, her current employer. She sees 20 to 25 patients in the course of those nine hours and describes her day as, "busy, busy, busy." There is no typical day for DMSs like Carol, in that they complete a wide variety of sonographic examinations. Among the most frequent exams done are fetal ultrasounds, gynecological (e.g., uterus, ovaries) and abdominal (e.g., gallbladder, liver, and kidney) tests.

Carol has a lot of expertise in dealing with patients, many of whom are frightened. "We have to exercise a lot of patience and understanding," she explains. "We have to talk to the patients, explain the procedure . . . reassure them so we can successfully complete the examination."

Carol's secondary duties include setting up her work area for each new patient and checking her equipment for malfunction, although she is quick to declare, "We have excellent equipment. Our machines are never down." Actual maintenance and monthly preventive programs are taken care of by an outside firm. Carol does little paperwork except what is done during actual tests. "We leave that to our receptionist-helper," she says, "so we can concentrate on our patients." She is also required in her off-hours to maintain her certification by completing 30 hours of continuing education over a three-year period.

Carol is a member of the Society of Diagnostic Medical Sonographers (SDMS), whose main goal is to organize seminars for continuing education and keep members updated about new technology and the ultrasound field throughout the country and the world. Carol

Types of Sonography

Abdominal: Evaluation of all the soft tissue structures in the abdomen and retro-peritoneal space (liver, spleen, kidneys, pancreas, aorta, vena cava).

Echocardiography: Evaluation of the heart and its structures such as the valves.

Neurosonology: Examination of the contour and inner structures of the brain.

Obstetrics/Gynecology: Evaluation of the pregnant and non-pregnant female pelvis.

Ophthalmology: Examination of the eye, including orbital structures and muscles.

Vascular Sonography: Evaluation of the peripheral vascular structures including Doppler.

reads trade magazines such as the *Journal of Diagnostic Medical Sonographers,* which she receives as a member of SDMS. "A trade magazine like JDMS is beneficial," she explains, "because it keeps us aware of any new ideas that may be out there, as well as updates on the latest technology."

Aspiring DMSs should take to heart Carol's comment that, "there are many highs and lows in this job." The good parts of being a DMS may include the opportunity to help people. Carol likes the idea that when she goes home at night she feels that she has helped both patient and physician with her imaging expertise. The most exciting or rewarding part of Carol's job is her opportunity to work with pregnant women. "We get to show couples, especially first-time parents, their healthy babies. We get to share in their excitement."

On the other hand, there are significant downsides to her job. Her work may reveal cancer, untreatable disease, even fetal death. "If you want to work in this field," Carol counsels, "you'll have to learn how to handle tragedy and the devastating effects of disease on patients." It is important for prospective DMSs to acquire a professional demeanor to be able to confront tragedy and still do their jobs.

Carol cautions students to be aware of the repetitive nature of the job, the long hours on one's feet, and the patience and good nature

in-depth

Ultrasonics

Ultrasonics is the branch of physics and engineering dealing with high-frequency sound waves. The waves are produced by objects vibrating more than 20,000 times a second, creating sound that is beyond the range of human hearing—ultrasound.

Ultrasonic vibrations may be created electronically, by passing alternating current through a quartz or ceramic crystal; mechanically, with special sirens; or magnetically, by the action of an alternating magnetic field on a hollow metal rod.

Pierre Curie discovered how to produce ultrasonic vibrations in 1890. By World War II their first practical application—the detection of submarines underwater—had been developed (i.e., sonar).

Today ultrasonic waves have many important applications. In addition to the medical imaging uses discussed in this chapter, ultrasonic energy is also used in medicine to heat deep tissues. The method has been used to treat arthritis, bursitis, muscular dystrophy, and other diseases. High-energy ultrasonic waves can also be focused into a pinpoint "scalpel" for bloodless brain surgery.

In dentistry, ultrasonic devices are sometimes used to remove calcium deposits from the surface of teeth.

Ultrasonic vibrations in a liquid cause millions of bubbles to form and collapse thousands of times a second. This process, called cavitation, blasts clean the surface of objects immersed in the liquid. Applications of this process include sterilization of surgical instruments and the scouring of precision metal parts. Diamonds, tungsten carbide, and tool steel are readily carved and drilled by ultrasonic techniques. The material to be machined is fixed in place and the cutting tool is lowered until it is in contact with the surface. Then a liquid abrasive is poured over the material in a steady stream. The tool vibrates at an ultrasonic frequency and drives tiny particles of the abrasive against the material with tremendous impact. This bombardment, together with cavitation, grinds an exact counterpart of the tool face into the material being machined. Odd-shaped cuts not possible with other methods can be made.

Sound waves beamed into solid materials will not readily cross air barriers such as cracks. When a crack or other defect is encountered, the sound waves are reflected to a measuring instrument. This form of inspection has replaced the use of X rays in many industries.

Ultrasound is used in some types of burglar alarms and remote-control television tuners. It is also sometimes used in welding and soldering metals, mixing liquids, and dyeing and bleaching textiles.

---

one must possess to succeed in the field. "This is hard, grueling work. It's not easy," Carol warns. Students should be aware of the physical and mental energy that this job requires, and also keep in mind the amount of outside work, in the form of continuing education, that they will be responsible for.

Royceanne Faggins works as an echocardiographer in the Veterans Administration Medical Center in Stillwater, Oklahoma, focusing exclusively on the heart. She has been with the center for several years, before which she worked in an outpatient clinic and in a private hospital. "I didn't really like the clinic," she admits. "There's a wider variety of cases in a hospital." Royceanne had done some vascular work in the past, primarily general circulatory system tests.

She prefers working on the heart. "It just clicked with me," she says. "At the time I was getting into echocardiography, it seemed to be the area that was changing the fastest." Many labs do not differentiate between echocardiography and vascular sonography, she adds, but the lab at the Veterans Administration Hospital works just on hearts.

The work for the day is arranged with the most serious cases first. "Once the schedule is set, you just move from case to case," says Royceanne. Doctors order a standard series of tests, called a protocol. The protocol has been established by the American Society of Echocardiography.

"You have a series of views you have to give, but to be good, you have to go beyond that to give the doctor the best possible information," Royceanne says. The full heart series takes about an hour, so Royceanne sees about seven or eight patients a day. Other kinds of sonographers may handle up to 25 patients a day.

Working with patients means talking—explaining procedures, telling them when and how to move, etc.—but it also means listening. "Sometimes patients will tell you things they haven't even told their doctors," she says. She will pass that information to the doctor along with the test results. The results are recorded on VHS tape. Still pictures are available, but the beating heart requires a moving record.

have I got what it takes to be a sonographer?

DMSs should be technically adept and possess a thorough knowledge of medical terminology. They must have a superior understanding of human physiology, combined with an artistic approach in order to visualize human anatomy. Kathy Radcliffe, Carol's supervisor, comments, "You have to see the body and conceptualize the image-taking."

DMSs must also have good communication skills in order to understand and implement physicians' orders, and also to instruct and guide patients into the proper position. They must also learn how to respectfully deflect any questions that they are unauthorized to answer. Carol explains, "Most bad news must be handled by the doctor, so that he or she can answer the many questions the patient might have." Like other members of the diagnostic field, DMSs must learn to be objective and unemotional in order to accomplish their duties. DMSs must also possess good people skills such as compassion, patience, kindness, and empathy in order to help very ill, scared, young, or very old patients understand and complete a procedure.

Although diagnostic sonography does not involve harmful radiation, DMSs should be aware that they will be exposed to sick people who might carry communicable diseases. Universal standards do exist to ensure safety for both patient and technologist. The only hazardous material that sonographers are exposed to is waste from invasive procedures. "We wear gloves and dispose of the waste in special containers to maintain safety," Carol explains.

DMSs can assure continuing safety by keeping updated on current hazardous waste disposal methods and being diligent in applying universal safety standards to every procedure.

how do I become a sonographer?

Carol, after completing her two-year hospital certificate, "lucked out," as she puts it, in terms of finding a job. On the first day of her job search she found employment at the second of three hospitals at which she applied, Little Company of Mary. She clearly had the educational and practical experience to qualify for immediate employment.

Royceanne was a high school senior when she first discovered sonography. "I was headed for radiology [X-ray technician]," she says. "My school counselor got me thinking about ultrasound. I was able to observe a sonography lab at a local medical center, and that convinced me."

education

High School
Students intent on a career in diagnostic medical sonography should take courses in chemistry, biology, physics, anatomy and physiology, mathematics, speech, and technical writing. Carol counsels students still in high school to take four years of science, when possible, especially chemistry, since it is a main component of the state boards which grant licensure.

Postsecondary Training
Instruction in diagnostic medical sonography is offered at technical schools, colleges, and universities in the form of four-year bachelor's programs, two-year associate's programs, in teaching hospitals in the form of a two-year hospital certificate, and also in the armed forces.

Carol characterizes the training she received as excellent, yet harder than she expected. "We were on call at any time, after an eight-hour work/school day." Carol's curriculum included instruction in medical technology and procedures, patient care and medical ethics, general and cross-sectional anatomy and physiology, principles and techniques of diagnostic soundwave imaging, and others. Carol encourages prospective students to thoroughly check school accreditation before investing time and money. A list of accredited programs can be obtained through the Society of Diagnostic Medical Sonographers (see "How Do I Learn More?").

certification or licensing

All medical employers of DMSs require certification by the American Registry of Diagnostic Medical Sonographers (ARDMS). After completion of educational requirements, DMSs must register with ARDMS and take and pass the National Boards to obtain their license. Carol is certified in radiology by the American Registry of Radiologic Technologists (ARRT), and in ultrasound technology by the ARDMS, which certifies technologists in the United States and Canada. ARDMS administers examinations and awards credentials in the areas of diagnostic medical sonography, diagnostic cardiac sonography, vascular technology, and ophthalmic biometry. Licensing requirements may exist at the state level also, although requirements vary from state to state. The Department of Health and the Food and Drug

To be a successful diagnostic medical sonographer, you should

- Have good communication skills, oral and written
- Have patience for sometimes monotonous or repetitious procedures
- Enjoy helping and working with people as part of a team
- Be technically adept and detail-oriented
- Have a compassionate nature

Administration also have a role in regulating the sonographic industry.

In addition to standard licensing, Carol must also complete 30 hours of continuing education in three years to keep her certification current. Carol comments, "Many hospitals and ultrasound equipment companies sponsor continuing-education programs so we can earn our credits. If we don't keep updated, we could possibly lose our license."

scholarships and grants

Information regarding scholarships and grants can be accessed through national and regional trade organizations, trade periodicals such as the *Journal of Diagnostic Medical Sonography*, local lending institutions, government programs, and technical, university, and hospital programs that offer training in diagnostic sonography.

internships and volunteerships

Although no one except a licensed DMS may actually work in the field, experience and insight may be gained from dialogue with a DMS, visiting a job site, or for those still in high school, arranging informational exchanges between student groups and a local employer of diagnostic medical sonographers. Another possibility for experience is to speak with a teacher at an accredited ultrasound program. Carol gained valuable internship experience and enjoyed informative interaction with professionals during her practical student hours at Rush-Presbyterian.

who will hire me?

Some may not find a job as quickly as Carol did. Certified technologists should seek out the publications of professional organizations, such as the SDMS which maintains a list of job openings (see "How Do I Learn More?"). Other avenues include employment agencies specializing in the health care field, "headhunters," or direct application to the personnel officers of potential health care employers.

Hospitals are the main employers of diagnostic medical sonographers. Career opportunities also exist in HMOs, private physicians' offices, imaging centers, research labs, educational institutions, and industry.

Rural areas and small towns may offer the best employment opportunities for those willing to relocate and accept lower wages and compensation as compared to jobs in larger cities.

where can I go from here?

There are many avenues of advancement open to experienced DMSs, yet technologists and prospective students should be aware that advancement can only occur through further education. Those with a bachelor's degree stand the best chance for promotion or advancement. Advanced education can be obtained through technical programs, colleges and universities, teaching hospitals, and sometimes through in-house retraining. Further education will allow DMSs to become certified in nuclear medicine technology, radiation therapy, magnetic resonance imaging, CT scan, computer tomography, or special procedures.

With considerable experience, DMSs can rise to teaching positions in sonography education programs, or train other technologists in-house or at another location. Other DMSs may become involved in the sales and marketing aspect of their profession, working as equipment demonstrators and instructors for the medical industry. In a hospital setting, DMSs with advanced degrees can become clinical supervisors, administrators, or assume other managerial positions.

Carol, while aware of the vast assortment of advancement opportunities open to her, plans to stay for now in her position at Meyer. She enjoys the diagnostic part of her job and her chance to help physicians and patients alike.

what are the salary ranges?

According to the U.S. Department of Labor, radiologic technologists (which includes diagnostic medical sonographers) earned a median annual income of $32,880 in 1998. The lowest paid 10 percent of this group, which included those just beginning in the field, made approximately $23,650. The highest paid

Advancement Possibilities

Chief technologists and administrators are sonographers who, as a result of advanced education and experience, have risen to supervisory positions in hospitals and other medical settings.

Sonography instructors teach in technical programs, teaching hospitals, and university settings.

Sales representatives for ultrasonic equipment sell electronic devices that clean, test, or process materials by means of high-frequency sound waves, such as disintegrators for cleaning surgical instruments, electronic guns for bonding plastics, and sonic devices for detecting flaws in metals, cutting steel and diamonds, and separating fossils from rocks.

10 percent, which included those with experience and managerial duties, earned roughly $47,610 annually.

Hospital DMSs earn more on average than those technologists employed by HMOs, private physicians' offices, and other employers. As always, pay scales and compensation vary based on education level, experience and responsibilities, and location of employers, with urban employers offering more financial compensation than rural or small town employers. The American Society of Radiologic Technologists reports that the most financially lucrative areas for sonography in the United States are the Northeast and Pacific regions. Beyond base salaries, sonographers can expect to enjoy many fringe benefits, including paid vacation, sick and personal days, and health and dental insurance.

what is the job outlook?

Although not as big as the radiology field, diagnostic sonography offers excellent prospects. Ultrasound technology will enjoy even more widespread use, especially in the expanding fields of obstetrics/gynecology and cardiology. Demand for qualified DMSs exceeds the supply in some areas of the country, especially in rural areas and small towns. Those who are flexible about pay scales and compensation will find ready employment in these areas. Increased employment opportunities also exist in California and the Southeast region of the United States.

Those interested in the diagnostic field should be aware of potential roadblocks to future employment. The health care industry currently is in a state of great potential change as the government and public debate future health care policy and the role of third-party payers in the system. Some procedures may not be readily used due to their cost to insurance companies and the government. Job opportunities and growth may be limited as a result.

Hospitals will also continue to downsize, causing some procedures to be done on weekends, nights, or on an outpatient basis. Future DMSs should be aware of the growth of imaging centers, HMOs, and physicians' offices as significant employers of their profession. These employers will compete with hospitals for the most qualified DMSs.

According to the U.S. Department of Labor, employment of diagnostic medical sonographers should grow faster than the average. One reason for this growth is that sonography is a safe, nonradioactive imaging process. In addition, sonography has proved successful in detecting life-threatening diseases and in analyzing previously nonimageable internal organs. Sonography will play an increasing role in the fields of obstetrics/gynecology and cardiology. "It's a good field," Carol says. "Nothing is becoming obsolete. All of our specialty fields are growing." She sees CT scan and magnetic resonance imaging as areas with great growth potential.

Prospective sonographers need to be aware that stiff competition exists for good jobs. Those with advanced education, experience, and certification in other specialized areas such as CT scan, mammography, radiation therapy, nuclear medicine technology, and other fields stand to prosper in future job markets.

how do I learn more?

professional organizations

Following are organizations that provide information on careers, accredited schools, and employers.

American Institute of Ultrasound in Medicine
14750 Sweitzer Lane, Suite 100
Laurel, MD 20707-5906
301-498-4100
http://www.aium.org

American Medical Association
515 North State Street
Chicago, IL 60610
312-464-5000
http://www.ama-assn.org/home.htm

American Registry of Diagnostic Medical Sonographers
600 Jefferson Plaza, Suite 360
Rockville, MD 20852-1150
800-541-9754
http://www.ardms.org/

National Foundation for Non-Invasive Diagnostics
103 Carnegie Center, Suite 311
Princeton, NJ 08540
609-520-1300

Society of Diagnostic Medical Sonographers
12770 Coit Road, Suite 708
Dallas, TX 75251-1319
972-239-7367
http://www.sdms.org/

bibliography

Following is a sampling of materials relating to the professional concerns and development of diagnostic medical sonographers.

Berman, Mimi, and others. *Diagnostic Medical Sonography: A Guide to Clinical Practice*. Philadelphia, PA: Lippincott-Raven, 1991.

Fleischer, Arthur C., and Donna M. Kepple. *Diagnostic Sonography: Principles and Clinical Applications*. 2nd ed. Philadelphia, PA: W. B. Saunders Company, 1995.

Sanders, Roger C. *Clinical Sonography: a Practical Guide*. 3rd ed. New York, NY: Lippincott Williams & Wilkins, 1998.

Dialysis Technicians

Definition

Dialysis technicians set up and operate hemodialysis (artificial kidney) machines. These machines filter the blood of patients whose kidneys no longer function. Dialysis technicians also maintain and repair this equipment.

Alternative Job Titles

Hemodialysis technicians
Nephrology technicians
Renal dialysis technicians

High School Subjects

Biology
Chemistry
Mathematics

Personal Skills

Helping/teaching
Technical/scientific

Salary Range

$16,000 to $32,000 to $48,000

Minimum Educational Level

High school diploma

Certification or Licensing

Required by certain states

Outlook

About as fast as the average

GOE
10.02.02
O*NET-SOC
NA*

*Not Available. The O*NET-SOC does not categorize the career of dialysis technician.

After setting up the dialysis machine, technician Robert Kinnecom prepares for his first patient of the day. Two weeks ago, this patient had arrived at the dialysis unit having put off care too long. She'd stopped eating because of a loss of appetite, but her extremities had swollen. "A few weeks ago," he reminds his patient, "if I were to push my finger in your arm and pull it away, the indentation would have stayed for a minute or two." She had also had to rely on a walker, which she has left at home today.

"I'm eating again too," she tells Robert, smiling. "I have more energy. I feel better." Though she doesn't express it, she clearly credits Robert with helping her to get her health back. Robert attaches the blood pressure cuff, reminded of why he finds the work so inspiring. He feels that he has helped this patient find some hope.

what does a dialysis technician do?

The kidneys are vital organs; they remove the waste products of daily living that accumulate in the bloodstream and are normally eliminated from the body as urine. Many people, particularly those who are diabetic or suffer from undetected high blood pressure, develop a condition known as chronic renal failure (CRF) in which their kidneys no longer function properly. Before artificial kidney machines were developed in the 1940s, such patients would die of uremic poisoning as toxic products built up in their bloodstream.

lingo to learn

Anticoagulant: A chemical substance that prevents blood from clotting.

Artificial kidney: A dialysis machine used to filter impurities and waste products from the blood of patients whose kidneys do not function properly.

Chronic renal failure (CRF): Long-term kidney disease.

Continuous ambulatory peritoneal dialysis (CAPD): A form of dialysis that takes place within the patient's body.

Dialysate: A solution used in artificial kidney machines; impurities and waste products pass from the patient's blood to the dialysate through a semipermeable membrane.

Dialysis: The process of removing waste products from the blood.

Dialyzer: The part of a kidney dialysis machine in which impurities and waste products are removed from the patient's blood.

End stage renal disease (ESRD): Kidney disease so severe that the patient can only be kept alive by dialysis or a kidney transplant.

Hemodialysis: The process of removing waste products from the blood using an artificial kidney machine.

The use of artificial kidney machines is called hemodialysis. In the process of hemodialysis, blood is pumped from the body through a dialyzer, where it passes through tubes constructed of artificial membranes. The outer surfaces of these membranes are bathed with a solution called the dialysate; body waste chemicals pass from the blood through the membrane into the dialysate, but blood cells and other vital proteins do not. The cleansed blood is returned to the patient's body without the harmful waste products. The rate of waste removal depends on the extent of the patient's kidney failure, the concentration of waste products in the blood, and the nature and strength of the dialysate.

The National Association of Nephrology Technicians/Technologists recognizes three types of dialysis technician, although in some hospitals and dialysis centers the responsibilities may overlap. These are the patient-care technician, the biomedical equipment technician, and the dialyzer reprocessing (reuse) technician. Dialysis technicians always work under the supervision of medical personnel, usually nurses.

Patient-care technicians are responsible for setting up the dialysis machine and connecting it to the patient's body, for measuring the patient's vital signs (including weight, pulse, blood pressure, and temperature), and for monitoring the process of dialysis. They must be able to administer cardiopulmonary resuscitation (CPR) or other life-saving techniques if an emergency occurs during a dialysis session. In some states, including Illinois, technicians are not permitted to administer drugs to patients; this can only be done by nurses.

Biomedical equipment technicians are responsible for maintaining and repairing the dialysis machines (see chapter "Biomedical Equipment Technicians"). *Reuse technicians* care for the dialyzers—the apparatus through which the blood is filtered. Each one must be cleaned and bleached after use, then sterilized by filling it with formaldehyde overnight so that it is ready to be used again for the next patient's treatment. To prevent contamination, a dialyzer may only be reused with the same patient, so accurate records must be kept. Some dialysis units reuse plastic tubing as well; this too must be carefully sterilized.

The spread of hepatitis and the growing risk of HIV infection have necessitated extra precautions in the field of hemodialysis, as in all fields whose procedures involve possible contact with human blood. All patient-care personnel must observe universal precautions, which include the wearing of a protective apron, foot covers, gloves, and a full face shield.

While most hemodialysis takes place in a hospital or a free-standing dialysis center like BMA, the use of dialysis in the patient's home is becoming more common. In this case, technicians may travel to patients' homes to carry out the dialysis procedures or to instruct family members in assisting with the process.

Another form of dialysis is continuous ambulatory peritoneal dialysis (CAPD). In CAPD, the membrane used is the peritoneum (the lining of the abdomen), and the dialysis process takes place within, rather than outside, the patient's body. Dialysis technicians are not needed for this form of treatment.

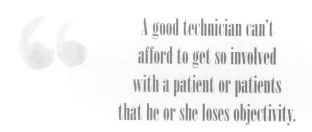

> A good technician can't afford to get so involved with a patient or patients that he or she loses objectivity.

what is it like to be a dialysis technician?

Robert Kinnecom works as a dialysis technician in two different settings: in a Navy facility and at the University of California at San Diego (UCSD). In the Navy setting, Robert performs a number of procedures, processes that include removing one component of the blood, such as platelets or plasma; suctioning someone's blood from his or her own surgery and "cleaning" it with saline and reinstilling the blood; and dialysis using the abdomen, in which fluid is put into the abdomen, allowing the body to perform the exchange through diffusion. "Any of these modalities may be activated on a daily basis here [in the Navy unit] because we're an acute unit," Robert says. "We only do patients in the hospital and some patients from our clinic. So, day to day it can be very different here, versus UCSD where it's more mass productive." At UCSD, Robert is assigned three to four outpatients a day. He checks a patient's vital signs, puts them on the machine, monitors them during treatment, then prepares for the next patient. With the Navy unit, Robert functions more as a nurse, with more responsibilities. "We work directly with the doctors," he says. "We can go to the intensive care unit. We can do all kinds of things that we wouldn't be able to do in the civilian world, as far as giving heart medications, transfusing blood, responding to our patients in ways to continue the treatment in the other modes, and respond to low blood pressure or high blood pressure."

In the Navy setting, the dialysis unit consists of seven machines, while the UCSD unit consists of 17 machines. Most units have many more machines. "If you can picture 30 to 50 machines in a big room," Robert says, "even though it's clean with white floors, it's still like a factory setting." When the patient arrives, Robert takes the patient's weight. When the kidneys fail, a patient tends to gain fluid; Robert checks the patient's current weight against the "dry weight," or the weight at which the patient would be without the excess fluids. Robert enters the figures into a palm pilot which calculates how much time will be needed for gradual fluid removal. Robert then takes the patient's blood pressure. "We take a standing and sitting blood pressure because this tells us the fluid balance inside the body," he says. "Often if your fluid is imbalanced, and you're dehydrated, your fluid pressures will be 20 to 30 degrees different in standing to sitting. Then we take a temperature, because that way if they have a fever at the end of treatment, we know it's isolated to whatever they come into contact with during dialysis."

Typically, a patient will have a surgically placed access, usually in the arm—either a graft, which is a piece of surgical rubber connecting a vein to an artery, or a fistula, which is a surgical connection between a vein and artery without using a foreign object. "That's for the purpose of having arterial blood flow and not grabbing and returning to the same line. So, if we pull from the artery and return to the vein, then we've effectively opened up the system circulatory." Robert inserts two needles into the patient's access, one connected to an outflow tube and the other to an intake tube. "The bigger the needle, the better the blood flow," Robert says. Because of poor blood vessels, some patients are unable to have these accesses. In such cases, the patient has a catheter in the jugular or another major vein in order to circulate the blood system. "It has two tubes in it," Robert explains. "One of the tubes is further downstream than the other, so we pull from the tube closest to us and we return further downstream so that we don't reclean the same blood over and over again."

Once the tubes have been connected to the patient, the cleansing process starts. "We start the bloodflow, and their blood is cleansed through the machine through what looks like any other filter, but is of course a sterile filter built for dialysis. After three to four hours, we rinse all their blood back to them. We pull needles out and hold pressure for 10 minutes." Robert again takes the patient's blood pressure to assure that the machine didn't remove too much fluid. He also takes the patient's temperature again to rule out an infection that may have occurred during the run, and he also weighs the patient to determine if the patient is now at the desired weight.

The work is extremely dangerous, which is of concern to Robert. "The biggest concern to anyone in the medical field is hepatitis," he says. "Hepatitis can survive on a droplet of dried blood for one to two weeks and still infect someone." But such dangers don't prevent Robert from appreciating the rewards of helping patients. "You have such an impact on a life," he says. "I literally see people start dialysis hesitantly where they are in wheelchairs because they've let themselves get so symptomatic, where they didn't have any energy, or

they had so much fluid around their lungs that they couldn't breathe. Within a two week period, you can see their whole lives turn around."

have I got what it takes to be a dialysis technician?

The ability to talk easily with patients and their families is essential. Kidney patients, especially those who are just beginning dialysis, are confronting a major—and permanent—life change. The technician must be able to help them deal with the emotional as well as the physical effects of their condition. Good interpersonal skills are crucial not only in the technician-patient relationship but in working with other team members. "You have to be a people person to an extreme extent," Robert says. At the same time, a good technician can't afford to get so involved with a patient or patients that he or she loses objectivity. "You have to care about people's feelings and be able to put your own aside. You can't be too timid. Some people have problems with needles, or doing any kind of medical care that could cause harm to someone if it's done wrong. If you draw blood, even if it's done right, it still causes pain. So if you don't have the type of personality that can relax your patient and reassure them and give them confidence in you, it could give them a negative experience."

A good head for mathematics and familiarity with the metric system are required. Technicians must be able to calibrate machines and calculate the correct amounts and proportions of solutions to be used, as well as quickly determine any necessary changes if there are indications that a patient is not responding to the treatment appropriately.

Technicians keep logs and fill out daily reports; their signature on the log verifies the accuracy of its content.

FYI

NephroWorld
(http://www.nephroworld.com) serves as an online community for professionals, technicians, organizations, and companies related to nephrology. Among the site's features are news reports about dialysis treatment, detailed information about kidney disease and dialysis, links to job postings, directories of related Web sites, and information of specific interest to technicians.

how do I become a dialysis technician?

After graduating from high school, Robert enrolled in the Navy where he studied dialysis. Robert's six month training in the Navy was in-depth, preparing him for a number of aspects of dialysis treatment. "Our training is more extensive in theory, response, medication, and knowledge," he says. During his training, he worked in intensive care and in the emergency room. "That was very exciting compared to working on the ward where you're doing basically routine things every day." To prepare for the career, Robert recommends courses in mathematics and science. "You should take the same basic things you would take if you were interested in becoming a doctor."

education

High School

Interested high school students should study general science, chemistry, biology, mathematics, and communication. Volunteering in a hospital, nursing home, or other patient care facility can give you a taste of what it's like to interact with patients in a health care setting.

Postsecondary Training

If you are interested in the requirements for becoming a dialysis technician, you can obtain job descriptions from the National Association of Nephrology Technicians/Technologists (NANT). If you are interested in nursing, contact the American Nephrology Nurses Association (ANNA). (See "How Do I Learn More?" for contact information.) Until there are a greater number of organized and accredited training programs, those who are interested in this career must seek information about educational opportunities from local sources such as high school guidance centers, public libraries, and occupational counselors at technical or community colleges. Specific information is best obtained from dialysis centers, dialysis units of local hospitals, home health care agencies, medical societies, schools of nursing, or individual nephrologists (physicians who specialize in treating kidney disease).

Advancement Possibilities

Biomedical equipment technicians repair, calibrate, and maintain medical equipment and instrumentation used in health care.

Counseling psychologists provide individual and group counseling services in universities, schools, clinics, rehabilitation centers, Veterans Administration hospitals, and industry to assist individuals in achieving more effective personal, social, educational, and vocational development and adjustment.

Registered nurses provide general medical care and treatment to patients in medical facilities, under the direction of physicians.

Other ways to enter this field are through schools of nurse assisting, practical nursing, or nursing and programs for emergency medical technicians. In these programs you learn basic health care and elementary nursing. After that, you must gain the specific knowledge, skills, and experience required to become a dialysis technician. The length of time required to progress through the dialysis training program and advance to higher levels of responsibility should be shorter if you first complete a related training program.

certification or licensing

The Board of Nephrology Examiners—Nursing and Technology (BONENT) offers a voluntary program of certification for nurses and technicians. The purposes of the program are to identify safe, competent practitioners, to promote excellence in the quality of care of kidney patients, and to encourage study and advance the science of nursing and technological fields in nephrology. You must be a high school graduate to become certified. You must either have at least one year of experience and be currently working in a hemodialysis facility or have completed an accredited dialysis course.

The certification examination contains questions related to anatomy and physiology, principles of dialysis, treatment and technology related to the care of patients with end stage renal disease, and general medical knowledge. Certified technicians use the title CHT (Certified Hemodialysis Technician) after their names (See "How Do I Learn More?").

Recertification is required every four years. To be recertified, you must continue working in the field and present evidence of having completed career-related continuing education units.

States have their own regulations for certification of dialysis technicians. Some states require that you take a training program through the state's health department, that you be certified by BONENT, or that you graduate from the training program of an accredited college.

who will hire me?

Dialysis technicians are employed by most major hospitals and by free-standing dialysis units. Many of these are listed under "Clinics" in the local Yellow Pages. Health care chains that provide home dialysis, either independently or in conjunction with a clinic, also employ larger numbers of technicians.

where can I go from here?

Dialysis technicians who have gained knowledge, skills, and experience advance to positions of greater responsibility within their units and can work more independently. The

To be a successful dialysis technician, you should

- Like working with people
- Be comfortable dealing with the chronically ill
- Be able to follow directions and procedures exactly
- Be familiar with the metric system and able to do calculations
- Keep cool in emergency situations

NANT guidelines encourage a distinction between technicians and technologists, with the latter having additional training and broader responsibilities. Not all dialysis units make this distinction.

"At one point," Robert says, "I did want to be a physician, but I have a family and I really feel I would dedicate more time to the hospital than to my family." Though he's not sure he wants to stay in dialysis because of the standardization that is occurring, he does want to continue to work with patients. "Anything where I can get this feeling," he says. "It's addicting once you're able to help people on this personal level. It's hard to feel the same gratification and impact doing anything else."

A technician looking for career advancement in the patient-care sector may elect to enter nurses' training; many states require that supervisory personnel in this field be registered nurses. Social, psychological, and counseling services may appeal to others who find their greatest satisfaction in interacting with patients and their families.

Someone interested in advancement in the area of machine technology may elect to return to college and become a biomedical engineer. Technical support and equipment maintenance is of major importance, and biomedical/equipment technicians may go on to become management personnel in this field.

what are the salary ranges?

According to the *Occupational Outlook Handbook,* clinical laboratory technologists and technicians had median earnings of $32,440 in 1998. The lowest 10 percent earned less than $19,380, while the highest 10 percent earned more than $48,290. The National Kidney Foundation estimates that salaries for dialysis technicians range from $16,000 to $33,280. Whereas experienced technicians could once make upwards of $30 an hour, standardization in the field has resulted in lower wages.

Technicians receive the customary benefits of vacation, sick leave or personal time, and health insurance. Many hospitals or health care centers not only offer in-service training but pay tuition and other education costs as an incentive to further self-development.

what is the job outlook?

According to the *Occupational Outlook Handbook,* employment of clinical laboratory workers is expected to grow about as fast as the average for all occupations. The need for dialysis in particular is growing at a rate of about 6 percent per year. The average wait for a kidney transplant is two to three years. In 1998, there were 12,166 transplants according to the National Kidney Foundation; as of February 27, 2000, there were 44,350 registrants on the waiting list. More than 2,000 new patients are added to the waiting list each month. For those waiting for a transplant, dialysis is necessary. Technicians make up the largest proportion of the dialysis team, since they can care for only a limited number of patients at a time (the ratio of patient-care technicians to nurses is generally about four to one). In addition, there is a shortage of trained dialysis technicians in most locales and a high turnover rate in the field.

As medical technology advances, dialysis becomes more standardized and refined. As a result, the work of a dialysis technician is becoming more routine. Hourly wages have decreased in recent years as the work has become less demanding of technicians. Increasingly, the manufacturers of the dialysis machines are investing in dialysis units and staffing them.

Dialysis Facts

The 1999 Data Report of the United States Renal Data System found that:

- There were over 3,200 dialysis facilities in the United States.
- The estimated annual cost of treating end stage renal disease (ESRD) in the United States was $15.64 billion.
- There were over 304,000 patients treated for ESRD.
- The estimated growth of new ESRD was 6 percent per year.
- There has been a progressive improvement in first-year survival among dialysis patients, credited to the changes in dialysis therapy over the previous 10 years.

For career information, contact:
National Association of Nephrology Technicians/Technologists
PO Box 2307
Dayton, OH 45401-2307
937-586-3705
nant@nant.meinet.com
http://www.nephroworld.com/nant

how do I learn more?

professional organizations

To learn about nephrology nursing, scholarship opportunities, publications, and educational programs:
American Nephrology Nurses Association
East Holly Avenue, Box 56
Pitman, NJ 08071-0056
http://anna.inurse.com

To learn about certification:
Board of Nephrology Examiners—Nursing and Technology
PO Box 15945-282
Lenexa, KS 66285
http://www.applmeapro.com/bonent/

bibliography

Following is a sampling of materials relating to the professional concerns and development of dialysis technicians.

Daugirdas, John T. *Handbook of Dialysis.* New York:, NY: Lippincott Williams & Wilkins, 1994.

Gutch, C. F., Martha H. Stoner, and Anna L. Corea. *Review of Hemodialysis for Nurses and Dialysis Personnel.* St. Louis, MO: Mosby, Inc., 1999.

Henrich, William L. *Principles and Practice of Dialysis.* New York, NY: Lippincott Williams & Wilkins, 1999.

Nissenson, Allen R., and Richard N. Fine. *Clinical Dialysis.* New York, NY: McGraw-Hill Professional Publishing, 1996.

Related Jobs

The U.S. Department of Labor classifies dialysis technician under the heading *Therapy and Rehabilitation* (GOE).

Specific related jobs include:
Audiometrists
Biomedical equipment technicians
Cardiology technologists
Cardiopulmonary technologists
Clinical laboratory technologist
Dental hygienists
Electrocardiograph technicians
Health service coordinators
Medical laboratory technologists
Medical records technicians
Nuclear medicine technologists
Occupational health and safety
  specialists
Occupational therapy assistants
Optometric and ophthalmic
  technicians
Orthotists and prosthetists
Pheresis technicians
Physical therapist assistants
Radiation therapists
Radiologic technologists
Surgical technologists
Transplant coordinators

Dietetic Technicians

Definition

Dietetic technicians usually work under the supervision of a dietitian on a food service or health care team. Their responsibilities include taking dietary histories, planning menus, supervising food production, monitoring food quality, and offering dietary counseling and education.

High School Subjects

Biology
Chemistry
Family and consumer science

Personal Skills

Leadership/management
Technical/scientific

Salary Range

$20,000 to $30,000 to $40,000

Minimum Education Level

Associate's degree

Certification or Licensing

Voluntary

Outlook

About as fast as the average

GOE
05.05.17

O*NET-SOC
29-2051.00

Karen Lucas stops in front of Room 203 in the Cardiovascular Services wing and taps lightly on the door, glancing down at the chart in her hand. After pausing a moment, she pushes the door open and smiles broadly at the elderly woman in the bed nearest her. "Good afternoon, Mrs. Breeden. How are you feeling today?" She pulls a chair nearer the bed and sits down. "Oh, pretty good, honey," the woman responds weakly. "It looks like you get to go home tomorrow, right?" Karen asks, as she organizes the papers on her lap. Mrs. Breeden's face brightens. "Dr. Whiting says I do. I'll be glad to sleep in my own bed."

Smiling, Karen nods. "Now, Mrs. Breeden, you know Dr. Whiting has put you on a salt-restricted diet for your heart. We don't want you to end up in here again." "I always watch my salt, honey." "Good! Good for you. You're a step ahead, then. I'm just going to give you this list of foods that are high in sodium to take home." Karen pauses to hand Mrs. Breeden a printed sheet. "The doctor says you should be getting no more than four grams a day. Now, what that means is . . ."

what does a dietetic technician do?

Dietetic technicians work in a variety of different settings, such as hospitals, nursing homes, community programs and wellness centers, public health agencies, weight management

lingo to learn

Diet history: A background of eating habits, diet restrictions, appetite fluctuations, and weight gain, or loss that is used to help assess nutritional status and prescribe diet changes.

Four-gram sodium diet: Usually called a "no added salt" diet, restricts patients from adding salt to already prepared foods and from eating such high-sodium foods as bacon and ham.

Health screening: A battery of tests, including blood pressure, cholesterol, weight-appropriateness, and body fat percentage, used to detect any potential health concerns.

Low-fat diet: A diet which restricts fat intake to between 30 and 40 grams per day.

Practicum: A period of supervised practice experience in various health care and food service facilities, and community programs.

Two-gram sodium diet: A stricter diet than the four-gram, allows patients only 2,000 milligrams of sodium daily.

Wellness: From a dietetic standpoint, a lifestyle that promotes good health in terms of diet and exercise.

clinics, schools, day care centers, correctional facilities, and food companies. They may work independently, or in partnership with a dietician, depending on their employer and what they do.

Dietetic technicians work in food service administration and clinical nutrition, which is the nutritional care of individuals. Technicians in smaller facilities may be involved in both areas of work, while in a larger facility they will probably have more specific duties in one area or the other.

Dietetic technicians working in food service administration will probably be involved in the management of other food service employees. They develop job descriptions, plan work schedules, and help train staff members in methods of food production and equipment operation. They may also work directly in the kitchen, supervising actual food preparation, or in the cafeteria, supervising the workers who assemble and serve the food. In some cases, dietetic technicians are responsible for meeting standards in sanitation, housekeeping, and safety.

Another area of responsibility for the technician in food service administration can be diet and menu planning. Technicians may help modify existing recipes, or create new menus to meet the particular needs of individuals or institutions. They may also be in charge of monitoring the quality of the food and service. Finally, some dietetic technicians are involved in purchasing supplies and equipment, keeping track of the inventory, supervising food storage, and budgeting for cost control measures.

Dietetic technicians working in clinical nutrition at hospitals and nursing homes observe and interview patients to obtain diet histories and food preferences. Using this information, they work with a dietician to determine each patient's nutritional status and dietary needs, and to develop diets that meet these needs. They also counsel and educate the patients and their families on good nutrition, food selection and preparation, and healthy eating habits. Some dietetic technicians make follow-up contacts with these patients to monitor their progress and offer them further help.

Technicians employed by a community program, such as a public health department, clinic, youth center, or home health agency, have many of the same counseling duties as the technicians in patient care facilities. They provide health screenings and dietary education for low-income families, elderly persons, parents of small children, or any groups of people who might have special questions about nutrition and health care. In some cases, they make follow-up visits to their clients' homes to check on their progress, or make permanent arrangements for continuing care for the needy, such as hot meals for the housebound, or school lunch programs for children.

Dietetic technicians in a community program may also be in charge of developing and coordinating community education efforts. Technicians may help create brochures and teaching materials, or plan classes in nutrition, weight loss, and other health-related topics. Some diet techs teach or co-teach the classes. They may also work with other community groups, corporations, or schools to promote an interest in health and nutrition.

what is it like to be a dietetic technician?

Karen Lucas and Joan Shaw are both dietetic technicians working in the area of clinical nutrition at the same hospital, and their duties are almost exactly the same. Because one of them must be there every day, during the hours meals are served, they do not work together.

"We have 10-hour days," Joan says, "and we alternate weekends. It works out so that we work eight days and have six days off in a two-week period." Although this particular schedule is not the most common for dietetic technicians, the 40-hour workweek is standard.

For Karen and Joan, the typical day at work begins at 6:30 AM. "The first thing that must be done is to check the breakfast tray line for completeness and accuracy, because at 6:45, the first wave of breakfast trays goes upstairs to the patients." According to Joan, it usually takes about an hour to check all the trays.

The diet tech on duty then has the responsibility of collecting all of the patient menus for the next day. Each day, the patients are given menus that contain all of their food options, and they are instructed to mark their choices on the menu form. Every morning, Karen or Joan goes to each floor to collect all menus that have already been completed. After taking the completed forms back to the department to be processed, she checks a

computer printout to see which patients still need to make up menus.

"We try to get everyone to fill out a menu," Karen says, "so we go to each patient's room. If they haven't already done it, we try to help them make the choices." Because patients may be sleeping, out of the room, being bathed, or receiving doctors' visits, seeing every one of these patients may take a number of trips, and often lasts until nearly lunch time.

Afternoons are mostly reserved for nutrition assessment and education, according to Karen and Joan. After conferring with one of the three dietitians to determine which patients need attention, and receiving diet orders for these patients, the dietetic technician checks each individual's chart to find out if he or she needs nutrition education. Not everyone on a special diet needs the training. "Sometimes they already know what they're supposed to be eating," Joan says. "Maybe they've had the counseling before, or have been on the diet for a long time already."

If the patient does need dietary counseling, Joan or Karen makes a personal visit to explain the prescribed diet and to go over the restricted foods. "We talk through it with them," Karen says, "and we have printed material, also, for them to take home."

There are different diets that the technicians must understand and be able to explain, such as two- and four-gram sodium, bland, low-fat, low-residue or low-fiber, and no sugar. "We don't usually see the diabetic patients," Karen says. According to her, the dietitians do the counseling for those patients, because the education is much more extensive and time consuming. Many of the patients Joan and Karen see are on low-salt and low-fat diets because of heart problems.

Although most of the days follow the same routine, Karen's duties do vary slightly on one day each week. On these days, she works for the Wellness Center, which is an offshoot of the hospital. "I do on-site health screenings for corporations and organizations," she says. The Wellness Center also offers on-site classes in better nutrition, stopping smoking, weight loss, and other health-related issues. Karen helps teach some of these classes. "It is a part of the hospital," she says, "but it serves the whole community." She enjoys her time at Wellness, as she calls it, because it adds variety to her job.

have I got what it takes to be a dietetic technician?

The duties of individual dietetic technicians vary widely from person to person, depending both on workplace and area of service. Likewise, the personal qualities necessary to excel depend somewhat on the responsibilities of the particular job.

Karen and Joan agree that one of the most important skills is being able to communicate and deal well with people. "You have to really like people," Joan says. "We have to deal with patients all the time. A large part of our day is spent with them." Although the majority of patients she sees are very friendly and cooperative, she acknowledges that some of them are difficult to communicate with. "Sometimes, you walk into a room and the patient won't talk to you," she says. "Sometimes it's because of medication, or they're groggy, or they're depressed. Occasionally, but not often, they are unpleasant and argumentative." Because the technician has to deal with all sorts of people

in all different circumstances, compassion and a desire to serve others are important. "The personal interaction can be a positive point about the job," Karen says. "You really feel like you're helping, and that's very satisfying."

Interpersonal skills are significant for the dietetic technicians who work in food service administration, as well as for those who, like Karen and Joan, work in nutrition and counseling. Food service administration may involve managing, scheduling, training, and evaluating other employees. Communication skills and an aptitude for dealing with people are essential for this area.

For the dietetic technicians who work in food service administration, it is also extremely important to be well organized, efficient, and able to deal with stress. Both Karen and Joan worked previously in food service supervision, and they say it's very different than the jobs they now perform. "Supervising is stress times ten," Karen says. "I was always swamped with work. Staffing the department, making sure the employees are there, and finding replacements for the ones who cancel at the last minute can be especially taxing." On the other hand, she says, she did enjoy the challenge of the job, and the duties she now performs, while much less stressful, can sometimes be a bit too routine.

Finally, the dietetic technicians say that an interest in nutrition and health care is important to being a success in this job. Joan has a long-time interest in cooking and home economics, while Karen has always been interested in health and fitness. "I think you need to be interested in some aspect of nutrition," Joan says. "I don't think you'd be in this field if you weren't."

FYI

The concept of dietetics is by no means a new one. Guidelines about food have existed for thousands of years in religious beliefs, and ancient and folk traditions.

how do I become a dietetic technician?

Karen and Joan took different paths to becoming dietetic technicians. Joan has a four-year bachelor of science degree in home economics, and was a high school teacher before deciding to move into dietetics. Karen, on the other hand, enrolled in the two-year dietetic technician program at her college, after learning that such a degree was offered. "I'd always been interested in nutrition and wellness, and

I wanted a two-year degree, so it seemed like a natural choice," she says.

education

High School

To become a dietetic technician, you need at least a two-year college degree. The American Dietetic Association (ADA) suggests that students who are considering a technician career should emphasize science courses in their high school studies. Biology, anatomy, and chemistry will provide a very important background for success both in college classes and in the course of a career. High school math and business courses will also be good training, since the college requirements for this degree include some accounting and purchasing classes. Finally, the ADA recommends sociology and psychology classes, to broaden the student's understanding of people, as well as English to improve communication skills.

You might also want to check in your area to see if there are summer or part-time jobs, or volunteer opportunities available in the field of dietetics. Actually working in the field can provide valuable experience, as well as insight into what the jobs are like.

Postsecondary Training

In order to become a dietetic technician, you must enroll in one of the more than 70 colleges offering the ADA's approved program. The program is a combination of classroom training and a set number of hours of supervised practical experience, usually called a practicum. The classes generally include a number of science courses, such as biology, anatomy, and chemistry, and some business and administrative courses, such as accounting and institutional administration. General education classes, such as English and psychology, are also part of the curriculum. The technical, specialized dietetic training may include classes in food preparation, therapeutic diets, meal management, community nutrition, quantity food purchasing, and nutritional management of disease.

Over the two-year period, you also get a certain amount of supervised practical experience in various health care and food service facilities. The type of field experience a student dietetic technician might receive includes practicums in clinical nutrition; food service planning, purchasing, equipment use, sanitation, and training; and management. You may

Advancement Possibilities

Clinical dietitians, also known as **therapeutic dietitians,** plan menus and oversee preparation of meals for patients in hospitals or nursing homes, consult with doctors to determine diet needs and restrictions, and instruct patients and families in nutrition and diet planning.

Community dietitians coordinate food services for public health care organizations, evaluate nutritional care, instruct individuals and families in diet and food selection and provide follow-up, and conduct community dietary studies.

Administrative dietitians, also known as **dietetic department directors,** or **chief dietitians,** direct food service and nutritional care departments of institutions, establish policies and procedures, hire and supervise staff members, and are responsible for menu planning, meal preparation, purchasing, sanitation, and finances.

be assigned to a patient care facility for practicum, where you help prepare schedules, order food, cook, or instruct patients. If you are assigned to a community agency, you might go on home visits with a nutritionist, help teach individuals, or assist in demonstrations and classes.

Karen especially enjoyed the practicums. "You really get a feel for what the job is like in practicum," she says. She doesn't remember the classes being extremely difficult, although she did have to study. Overall, she felt like her college program left her well prepared to enter the dietetics field.

certification or licensing

After successfully completing a dietetic technician program approved by the ADA, you are eligible to take the ADA's registration examination for dietetic technicians. The exam is given in October each year and consists of 240 multiple choice questions broken down into four subject areas.

Technicians who have passed the registration exam are known as Dietetic Technicians, Registered, and are allowed to use the initials DTR after their names. They are also eligible to become members of the American Dietetic Association.

It is not a requirement that dietetic technicians be licensed or certified. However, many do choose certification. As a newly graduated dietetic technician, it is a good credential to have, since it indicates that you have met a certain standard of competence. While it may not be necessary to be registered in order to get a job, it might provide a competitive edge in some cases.

Registered dietetic technicians are required to earn 50 hours of continuing education every five years to maintain the credential. You can do this by attending hospital programs, symposiums, or college classes. You can also perform approved self-studies or self-assessment modules for credit.

scholarships and grants

Students in the dietetics field have a number of possibilities for financial aid to help pay for schooling. In addition to federal grants, the ADA also offers aid, in the form of scholarships, to encourage eligible students to enter the field. Students in the first year of a dietetic technician program may apply (see "How Do I Learn More?").

Finally, qualified students might be able to obtain a grant or scholarship from corporations, community or civic groups, religious

organizations, or directly from the college or university they plan to attend.

who will hire me?

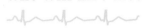

When Karen graduated from college, she sent her resume out to several hospitals, nursing homes, and food service companies. Her first dietetics job was as manager of a corporate cafeteria for a vending and food service company. After four years in that position, she decided she'd like to work in a clinical setting, because of her interest in therapeutic nutrition. She applied at a hospital near her home, and was hired as the assistant director of the food service department.

The majority of dietetic technicians are employed by hospitals. Technicians who work in long-term patient care facilities, such as nursing homes, make up the second largest group. A smaller percentage of dietetic technicians work in community health care programs or outpatient clinics. Finally, some dietetic technicians work in settings that are not directly related to health care, such as schools, colleges, hotels, or, as in Karen's case, employee cafeterias.

Graduates of a dietetic technician program who are looking for a first job should check the placement office of their school. Also, since they have spent a considerable amount of time in various dietetic workplaces to complete practicums, they may have excellent contacts in the field, which can serve as job leads. Applying directly to the personnel offices of all area hospitals, nursing homes, and public health programs is another possible route to finding a position. Finally, the classified ads of local newspapers, private and public employment agencies, and job listings in health care journals are all potential employment sources.

In some locations, the labor market for dietetic technicians may be flooded, particularly in areas near schools that offer the training program. In such cases, you might have more luck by broadening your search to include less competitive areas, and by looking for creative job opportunities. Karen advises that the dietetic technician who is looking for a job should keep an open mind about the possibilities. "Anywhere a dietician is, a dietetic technician could investigate," she says. Joan agrees. "Look for situations where

To be a successful dietetic technician, you should

- Have a desire to serve people
- Be a good communicator
- Have an interest in health care and nutrition
- Be able to follow instructions well
- Be a good planner and organizer

there's too much work for one dietician, but not enough for two," she counsels.

where can I go from here?

Karen is currently in the process of finishing her bachelor's degree in business administration. She hopes that the extra schooling in administration, combined with her training and experience in dietetics, will help her obtain a managerial position. "I'd like to get more into the Wellness Center type of work," she says. "I'd like a supervisory job in something like that."

Beginning technician positions are usually closely supervised, but after spending some time on the job, the dietetic technician may be able to take on more responsibilities. Many technicians, after proving their abilities, are allowed to perform some of the same functions as entry-level dietitians, such as diagnosing nutrition problems, prescribing diets, helping develop educational materials, and being involved in the financial management of the department. With the expanded range of duties, technicians may then earn higher pay, while either keeping the same title, or officially changing positions. For example, a dietetic technician could be promoted to kitchen manager.

A very common means of advancement in the field of dietetics involves further schooling. The dietetic technician who wants to attain a higher position, such as dietician, may decide to pursue a bachelor's degree. A major in dietetics, nutrition, food science, or food service systems management, plus a year of internship, are the requirements for becoming a dietician. Although earnings vary widely with employer and amount of experience, the salary range for dietitians is $28,000 to $45,000 annually.

Further advancement possibilities for experienced dietitians include assistant, associate, or director of a dietetic department. With a graduate degree, the dietician could move into research or an advanced clinical position.

what are the salary ranges?

According to the ADA's 1997 Membership Database, dietetic technicians earned between $20,000 and $30,000 annually. Those with more experience reported incomes of between $30,000 and $40,000 annually.

Aside from the amount of experience a dietetic technician has, a significant factor affecting salary level is the area of work he or she has chosen. For those employed in clinical nutrition, which involves patient assessment and counseling, the overall median salary was $35,500 in 1997, according to the ADA. For those who work in food and nutrition management, which involves the supervision of food service employees and the overseeing of food production, the median was $44,900.

Most technicians are offered a benefits package by their employers, usually including health insurance, paid vacations and holidays, and meals during working hours.

what is the job outlook?

Although the *Occupational Outlook Handbook* indicates that the outlook for dietitians is expected to be average, it appears as though opportunities for dietetic technicians may be better than average. Because the position is a fairly new one, dating back only to the early 1970s, the demand for technicians has previously been unsteady and patchy. Now, however, as employers are becoming more aware of the advantages of hiring dietetic technicians, the need is increasing yearly and is expected to continue to expand.

One major reason for the positive job forecast is that hiring dietetic technicians is cost-effective for employers. Many functions that dietitians used to perform can be done easily by dietetic technicians, leaving the dietitians free to concentrate on the work that only they can do. Since dietitians are expensive to hire, it makes sense for employers to supplement their nutrition or food service team with technicians who can do many of the same tasks but do not earn as high a wage. This method of reducing expenses may become even more popular, with the increasing public and governmental concern over health care costs.

The emphasis on nutrition and health in today's society is another reason for the positive outlook for dietetic technicians. In future years, more health services, some of them involving nutrition, diet training, and monitoring, will be used. The population is growing, and with it, the percentage of older people who have the greatest health care demands. The increasing need for health care services translates into an increasing need for workers.

how do I learn more?

professional organizations

The following organization provides information on dietetic technician careers, accredited schools and scholarships, and possible employers.
The American Dietetic Association
216 West Jackson Boulevard, Suite 800
Chicago, IL 60606-6995
312-899-0040
education@eatright.org
http://www.eatright.org/careers.html

Related Jobs

Dietetic technicians use the principles of nutrition, working under the supervision of a dietician, in a variety of ways. They must have an understanding of food science, menu planning, and dietary needs, and may have, as well, a special aptitude for making food look and taste good.

The U.S. Department of Labor classifies dietetic technicians under the headings *Craft Technology: Food Preparation* (GOE) and *Healthcare Practitioners and Technical* (O*NET-SOC). All types of dietitians are, likewise, classified in these categories. Also under these headings are people who prepare, test, decorate, and analyze various foods and beverages, or who supervise others in performing these activities.

Specific related jobs include:
Clinical dietitians
Community dietitians
Consultant dietitians
Cooks
Farm and home management advisors
Food and beverage analysts
Food products tasters
Home economists
Research dietitians

To learn about advancement opportunities in nutrition:
American Society for Nutritional Sciences
9650 Rockville Pike, Suite 4500
Bethesda, MD 20814
301-530-7050
http://www.faseb.org/asns/

bibliography

Following is a sampling of materials relating to the professional concerns and development of dietetic technicians.

Caldwell, Carol Coles. *Opportunities in Nutrition Careers.* Lincolnwood, IL: VGM Career Horizons, 1999.

Careers in Focus: Medical Technicians. 2nd Edition. Chicago, IL: Ferguson Publishing Company, 2001.

Kane, Michael T., ed. *Role Delineation for Registered Dietitians and Entry-Level Dietetic Technicians.* Chicago, IL: American Dietetic Association, 1990.

Dietitians

Definition
Dietitians use the principles of nutrition to develop diet programs and supervise the preparation and serving of meals.

Alternative Job Title
Nutritionists

High School Subjects
Biology
Chemistry
Health

Personal Skills
Communication/ideas
Helping/teaching

Salary Range
$20,000 to $35,000 to $51,000+

Educational Requirements
High school diploma; bachelor's degree in dietetics, nutrition, or related area

Certification or Licensing
Required by certain states

Outlook
About as fast as the average

GOE
02.02.04
05.05.17
11.02.02
11.02.03
O*NET-SOC
29-1031.00

The lab results on her desk show good news and Merrianne Myers-Zietlow smiles encouragingly at the patient sitting across from her. The patient, an overweight man in his forties who has just been diagnosed as diabetic, looks skeptical, but returns the smile.

"Okay, Bill. As you know, Dr. Briggs has ordered a special diet for you," Merrianne says. The patient nods gloomily, and Merrianne continues. "Before we start talking about what you should and shouldn't be eating, I'd like to get some idea of what your eating habits are currently."

As she questions Bill about what he eats in the course of an average day, Merrianne makes notes on an assessment sheet. Bill's current sugar intake is far too high. Following a diabetic diet will require major lifestyle changes—difficult changes to make. Merrianne knows that Bill will have to work very hard to improve his eating habits. She also knows that she will have to work very hard to help him.

what does a dietitian do?

For centuries, people have realized that there is a correlation between diet and health. Consider the old adages "you are what you eat" and "an apple a day keeps the doctor away." However, dietetics became widely recognized as a profession only about 50 years ago.

Dietitians are experts in food and nutrition. They help promote good health through proper eating. They may also supervise the preparation and service of food, develop modified diets, participate in nutrition research, and educate individuals and groups on good nutritional habits. The specific duties of a

lingo to learn

Antioxidant: A substance that helps protect healthy cells from damage by free radicals. Found in leafy vegetables, tomatoes, carrots, sweet potatoes, and broccoli.

Fad diet: A diet that encourages rapid, unhealthy weight loss, often by promoting or completely restricting one food or food group, suggesting that food can change body chemistry, or blaming specific hormones for weight problems.

Fiber: A substance found only in plants, such as fruits, vegetables, and grains, which is essential to a healthy diet. Eating 20 to 35 grams daily promotes regular digestion and reduces cholesterol levels and the risk of heart disease.

Food guide pyramid: Established by the USDA, this guide divides foods into their basic food groups and the recommended servings for each: grains, six servings; vegetables, three servings; fruits, two servings; meat, two servings; dairy, two servings; fats and sweets, eat sparingly.

dietitian depend largely on what area of practice he or she works in.

The majority of dietitians are *clinical,* or *therapeutic, dietitians.* Working as a member of a health care team, this type of dietitian develops diets and oversees the preparation of meals for patients in hospitals and nursing homes.

The clinical dietitian reviews medical charts and talks with patients, their families, and various health care professionals to determine both current diet patterns and nutritional needs for each individual. After determining a patient's dietary needs, the clinical dietitian develops an appropriate nutrition program and explains it to the patient and his or her family. The clinical dietitian periodically evaluates the effectiveness of the nutrition program during the hospital or nursing home stay.

Some clinical dietitians specialize in a particular area of nutrition, such as the nutrition of children, diabetics, or critically ill patients.

Community dietitians work for various organizations, including public health agencies, daycare centers, and health clubs. They counsel families and individuals about proper nutrition, and develop diet plans for clients with special needs, such as pregnant women, cancer patients, and the elderly.

The community dietitian may instruct clients on how to grocery shop and prepare food. He or she may plan and participate in community programs designed to educate people about nutrition. Finally, he or she may work in cooperation with different agencies to coordinate health care for clients.

Consultant dietitians usually work in their own private practices or under contract with health care facilities. In some cases, they are employed by wellness programs, sports teams, food companies, or schools. Consultant dietitians perform nutrition screenings on clients by talking with them about diet and health. They develop appropriate diets and offer advice on food selection and preparation. They also follow up with clients periodically to see how they are doing with their diets and to make any necessary modifications.

Administrative dietitians, also called *management dietitians,* are trained in the administration and management of large-scale food preparation. They may work in schools, prisons, company cafeterias, or restaurants. The administrative dietitian hires, trains, schedules, and supervises other dietitians, such as *dietetic technicians,* who help dietitians plan nutrition and education programs, and *food service workers,* who prepare and serve food. The administrative dietitian creates budgets for his or her department and is responsible for planning menus, purchasing food and equipment, and enforcing sanitation and safety regulations.

Teaching or *educator dietitians* instruct courses in dietetics at colleges, universities, and technical schools.

Business dietitians work in industries related to food and nutrition and are involved in product development, sales and marketing, advertising, public relations, and purchasing.

Dietitians who choose to pursue advanced degrees may specialize in nutritional research. *Research dietitians* work for government agencies, food and pharmaceutical companies, major universities, and medical centers. They conduct experiments to further public knowledge of nutrition and health.

what is it like to be a dietitian?

The duties of a dietitian can vary widely from one position to the next. Merrianne Myers-Zietlow has had many different jobs; she has worked as a food service supervisor for a dormitory, as a dietitian for a community health program, and as a clinical dietitian for a hospital. Currently she is a consultant dietitian under contract with a hospital.

"One of the things that a career in dietetics allows you to do is to be a lot of different things," Merrianne says. "I think one of the reasons I've been happy with my career for so long is that I've managed to have several different kinds of jobs."

As a consultant dietitian, Merrianne works a regular 40-hour week. The bulk of each day is spent meeting with clients in her office. "I do one-on-one nutrition counseling with individuals for whatever reasons they might need it," says Merrianne. Her clients, who have been referred to her by their doctors, have a wide variety of nutritional needs. Some have been diagnosed with diabetes, hypertension, cancer, or allergies. Others have been referred to her because of heart or kidney problems. Many are overweight and need to modify their eating habits to achieve a healthier weight.

For each patient, Merrianne develops a diet plan that meets specific nutritional needs and fits into that patient's lifestyle. She begins by reviewing the results of any laboratory tests that the patient has had, such as blood tests that check glucose and cholesterol levels.

She then talks with the patient about his or her current eating patterns. "When the patient first comes in, I get his or her weight, height, and diet history," says Merrianne. "I ask what he or she usually eats for breakfast, lunch, dinner, and snacks. That usually tells me a lot and gives me a kind of trigger to help me get started."

Merrianne also asks the patient about his or her medical history and the history of family. Finally, she asks for a list of medications that the patient is taking. "There are many links between medication and what lab results look like," she says.

Once she has the necessary information, Merrianne starts to figure out what modifications need to be made to the patient's diet. "After I have the patient's height and weight, I calculate how that compares to the norms for that person's age and sex," she says. "If weight is an issue, which it is in about 40 percent of my patients, I calculate how many calories that person needs to maintain his or her weight." When Merrianne has determined how many calories her patient should be taking in daily, she plans a diet that distributes the calories among the food groups for a balanced diet.

In cases in which patients don't need to lose weight, calories are not important. "If a patient has allergies, I try to get that person to eat a balanced diet while staying away from things he or she can't eat," Merrianne says. "I try to help patients find things they can tolerate without causing allergic reactions."

Merrianne must help some patients learn how to restrict salt, sugar, or fat in their diets. This often involves first teaching them how to read recipes and food labels. "Sometimes, I actually pull out examples of food labels and go through them with my clients so they can learn how to do it on their own at home," Merrianne says.

in-depth

In the early 20th century, Mary Swartz Rose became known as the "First Lady of Nutrition" for furthering the cause of health and dietetics in the United States.

Rose was born in 1874 in Ohio. After graduating from college and spending three years as a high school home economics teacher, she resumed her education at Columbia University Teachers College, then went on to receive a Ph.D. in physiological chemistry from Yale in 1909.

In 1910, Rose returned to Columbia's Teachers College to found a department of nutrition and became its first full-time instructor in dietetics. Under her direction, the department became the first nationally recognized center for the training of nutrition teachers.

In 1933, Rose became a member of the Council on Foods of the American Medical Association; two years later, she became a member of the nutrition committee of the Health Organization of the League of Nations. In 1937 and 1938, she served as president of the American Institute of Nutrition, of which she had been a founder. Finally, a year before her death in 1941, she served as an advisor on nutrition to the Council of National Defense.

Each patient that Merrianne sees is given a personalized meal plan that is based on the results of her calculations, what a doctor has ordered, and what the patient has told her. "Each of our meal plans is personalized to fit a patient's lifestyle and food preferences," Merrianne says.

For each meeting with a client, Merrianne fills out a report for the referring doctor. "The reports delineate what information we've given the patients," she says. "We might also share reports with other members of the health care team, such as diabetic educators." The dietitians in Merrianne's office are also responsible for filling out forms for insurance carriers and keeping track of referrals and types of diets prescribed.

have I got what it takes to be a dietitian?

"To succeed in most dietitian positions, it is important to enjoy working with people," Merrianne says. Whether dealing directly with patients, working with colleagues, or supervising food service workers, most dietitians spend a great deal of time communicating with others.

Merrianne says that it is particularly important to be flexible when working with patients. "You're working with a wide variety of people. You might get a client that can't read, or you might have someone with a really short attention span," she says. "You have to be able to switch gears and figure out how you're going to present the information to best educate that person."

Patients are occasionally difficult to deal with. For example, a patient may be depressed from just having been diagnosed with an illness; another patient may simply be resistant to any dietary changes. "Some people sit and cry. Sometimes they're negative about having to go on a diet," Merrianne says. "Sometimes you have to be as much of a social worker as a dietitian." She notes that depression and resistance are even more common in clinical settings, where a patient doesn't have much time to adjust to a diagnosis.

For Merrianne, the opportunity to work closely with people is one of the job's perks. "I get a lot of personal satisfaction," she says. "When people are motivated and they really follow through with diets, I feel like I did a good job of educating them and that I did something positive."

In addition to being good with people, the successful dietitian should be highly motivated. "Because there may not be someone standing over you all the time, you have to be accountable to yourself," Merrianne says. "You need to be an organized self-starter." This is especially important for administrative dietitians, who must supervise other workers, keep meal services on a time schedule, and plan menus and food purchases in advance.

It is beneficial to dietitians to be interested in math and science, according to Merrianne. "Those are the skills you'll use every day, especially in a clinical setting," she says.

how do I become a dietitian?

Merrianne discovered she wanted to be a dietitian while in high school. "When I was in school, I took four years of home economics to get out of taking health," she laughs. "I can remember being a sophomore in home economics and thinking, I want to be a dietitian."

education

High School

All dietitians must first complete high school. The American Dietetic Association (ADA), which is the largest group of dietetic professionals in the world, suggests that high school students considering careers as dietitians emphasize science courses in their curriculum. Biology, anatomy, and chemistry classes will provide a good base of knowledge that will be beneficial both during college and for your future career.

Because dietitians often use math to calculate nutritional needs, recipe modifications, and amounts of food to be purchased, mathematics courses will also prove useful.

In addition, you should take classes to improve your communication skills, such as English or speech. Finally, the ADA recommends sociology, psychology, and business classes to round out a curriculum that will prepare you for college courses in dietetics.

While still in high school, you should start looking at college dietetics programs and talk to local dietitians about their job experiences and training. You might also want to consider a part-time job or volunteer position in a local hospital, nursing home, or community program to gain more insight into the field of dietetics.

Advancement Possibilities

Chief dietitians direct food service departments in hospitals, nursing homes, colleges, universities, school systems, company cafeterias, and prisons. They establish department procedures, develop menus, and oversee budgeting, purchasing, food preparation, and service. They hire, train, and supervise all dietetic staff members.

Research dietitians conduct nutritional research in major universities, medical centers, and hospitals. They plan and implement experiments in nutrition to discover ways to improve the public's welfare.

Teaching dietitians work in colleges, universities, and technical schools to educate future dietitians, dietetic technicians, nursing students, and other medical professionals. They develop curriculums, conduct classes, and evaluate students on performance.

Postsecondary Training

To become a dietitian, you must earn a bachelor's degree in dietetics, foods and nutrition, food service systems management, or a related concentration. Undergraduates in these majors take classes in nutrition, chemistry, biology, microbiology, physiology, and bacteriology. Other classes include mathematics, business, statistics, psychology, sociology, and economics.

certification or licensing

Although not required, many dietitians choose to become registered by the American Dietetic Association to indicate to their clients that they have achieved a high level of professionalism.

To become a Registered Dietitian (R.D.), a student without a bachelor's degree can enroll in one of 51 accredited programs that combine classroom work with on-the-job experience. If the individual already has obtained a bachelor's degree, he or she can become an R.D. by completing 900 hours of supervised experience through one of the 225 accredited internship programs. Internships may be full-time, lasting nine to 12 months, or part-time, lasting up to two years. The R.D. credential awarded by the ADA is a separate and distinct title from any state licensure or registration.

The Commission on Dietetic Registration, the credentialing agency of the ADA, states that 41 states have laws that regulate the practice of dietetics. Twenty-seven states require licensure, 13 require certification, and one requires registration. These limitations are in place to ensure only qualified professionals provide nutritional counseling. Since requirements vary, individuals should contact the board of licensure and certification for the state in which they plan to practice.

scholarships and grants

Through its many association groups, the ADA offers various scholarships and stipends to eligible students who are interested in the field of dietetics. Some awards require membership in the ADA or another dietetic association, or require residency in a particular state. Contact the American Dietetic Association Foundation, the scholarship arm of the ADA, for more information.

Dietetic students seeking financial aid should also check with community or civic groups, philanthropic or religious organizations, the colleges or universities they will be attending, and state and federal governments for additional financial aid opportunities.

To be a successful dietitian,
you should

- Be good at communicating with people
- Have an interest in health care and nutrition
- Be organized and detail-oriented
- Be self-motivated and able to work independently
- Have an aptitude for science and math

American Dietetic Association Foundation
216 West Jackson Boulevard
Chicago, IL 60606-6995
312-899-0040, ext. 4752
adaf@eatright.org
http://www.eatright.org/foundation.html

U.S. Department of Education
Federal Student Aid Information Center
800-433-3243
http://www.ed.gov

who will hire me?

Merrianne's first job was as a food service supervisor for a dormitory at a state university. "After my supervised work experience, I started looking for a job," she says. "There was an opening at the university, I applied, and that was it."

There are approximately 54,000 dietitians currently employed in the United States. More than half work in hospitals, doctors' offices, or nursing homes. Roughly 16 percent are employed in state and local government agencies and other public health-related organizations.

Other dietitian jobs are found in social service agencies, residential care facilities, physical fitness facilities, public and private schools, colleges and universities, and the federal government. A small number of dietitians are self-employed, providing consulting services to facilities or to individuals.

There are, increasingly, new and diverse employment options for dietitians as the public's interest in nutrition grows. "I think that there's just been an explosion in the types of careers people can have in dietetics," says Merrianne. "You see dietitians in the media, in sales, on the World Wide Web, designing software, all over the place."

Where to look for a dietitian position depends upon the type of work in which you are interested. A good starting point may be the career placement service of the college or university you attend. Newspaper classified advertisements are another source for job leads.

In addition, prospective dietitians can apply directly to area hospitals, nursing homes, and community nutrition-related programs. Local school systems, colleges and universities, and correctional facilities are also employment possibilities. Even if a facility does not have a current position available, the personnel office often keep resumes on file for future openings.

Finding a less conventional job in dietetics may require more creativity and time. Food and nutrition-related businesses, pharmaceutical companies, large grocery store chains, and sports facilities are all potential employers to contact. Some of these employers, however, may require prior work experience or an educational background that includes more business courses.

where can I go from here?

Merrianne plans on remaining in consulting work. "In a fairly short career, I've explored a lot of avenues that fit my dietetics degree," she says. "I think that, for the time being, I'm in a holding pattern."

There are several ways that a dietitian can further his or her career. They may be promoted to a position with more responsibilities and higher pay, such as head dietitian, chief director of a food service department, or director of a community program.

Some dietitians advance by specializing. Clinical and consultant dietitians may decide to become specialists in nutritional care for certain types of clients, such as heart or kidney patients, diabetics, children, or people with weight disorders.

Yet another path to advancement is to return to school for a master's or doctoral degree in dietetics. An advanced degree can open up more opportunities in the fields of research and teaching. It can also command a higher salary.

what are the salary ranges?

Salaries vary by practice area, years of experience, educational level, and location. In general, administrative, self-employed, and business dietitians earn more than their clinical and community counterparts.

According to the U.S. Department of Labor, the median annual salary for dietitians was $35,020 in 1998. The lowest paid 10 percent earned less than $20,350; the highest paid 10 percent earned over $51,320 a year.

more lingo to learn

Free radical: A substance that attacks healthy cells; free radicals are naturally produced by normal body functions (such as breathing and physical activity) and lifestyle choices (such as smoking).

Lactose intolerance: A set of symptoms affecting 30 to 50 million Americans resulting from the body's inability to digest the milk sugar called lactose. Can be easily managed through dietary limits or substitutions.

Registered Dietitian (R.D.): A food and nutrition expert who has met certain educational and work standards established by the American Dietetic Association.

Wellness: A lifestyle that promotes good health through a balanced diet and regular exercise.

The American Dietetic Association reports the following 1997 salary levels for Registered Dietitians based on area of practice: community nutrition, $34,900; clinical nutrition, $35,500; food and nutrition management, $44,900; education and research, $45,200; and consultation and business, $46,000.

In addition to salary, most employers also offer dietitians benefits packages including health and life insurance, paid vacations and holidays, and a pension or profit-sharing plan.

what is the job outlook?

Career opportunities for dietitians are expected to increase about as fast as the average for all occupations over the next decade, according to the U.S. Department of Labor. One reason for this expected increase is the growing elderly population. As more people live longer, there is more need for nutritional counseling and meal preparation in nursing homes and home health agencies.

Another cause for employment growth is an increase in public awareness of healthy eating habits. In recent years, the medical profession has placed more emphasis on the role of nutrition in preventing disease. In response, the public has shown an increased interest in good eating habits and a demand for easily accessible nutrition information. As health, nutrition, and fitness continue to grow in public interest, the number of jobs for dietitians will increase.

Positions will also arise from the need to replace dietitians who are retiring or changing occupations.

The rate of growth in dietitians' job opportunities will vary from field to field. Employment in hospitals is expected to grow more slowly due to the growing practice of contracting out food service operations. However, as a result of this trend, demand for dietitians in food service providers will increase. Employment of dietitians in nursing homes, residential care facilities, and social service organizations is also expected to grow.

The demand for dietitians is limited by employer hiring practices. Some employers substitute other workers such as dietetic technicians, health educators, or food service managers for more highly paid dietitians. Growth is also limited by the restrictions that some insurance companies place on reimbursement for dietetic services.

how do I learn more?

professional organizations

Following are organizations that provide information on dietitian careers, accredited schools, internships, and employers.

American Dietetic Association
216 West Jackson Boulevard
Chicago, IL 60606-6995
312-899-0040
http://www.eatright.org

American Society for Nutritional Sciences
9560 Rockville Pike, Suite 4500
Bethesda, MD 20814
http://www.faseb.org/asns

Center for Food Safety and Applied Nutrition
U.S. Food and Drug Administration
200 C Street, SW
Washington, DC 20204
http://vm.cfsan.fda.gov

FYI

The word *diet* comes from the Greek *diaita*, meaning "manner of living."

Dietitians Online
dieteticscom@aol.com
http://www.dietetics.com

Dietitians of Canada
480 University Avenue, Suite 604
Toronto, ON M5G 1V2 Canada
416-596-0857
http://www.dietitians.ca

bibliography

Following is a sampling of materials relating to the professional concerns and development of dietitians.

Caldwell, Carol C. *Opportunities in Nutrition Care.* Chicago, IL: NTC Publishing Group, 1999.

Endress, Jeanette Brakhane. *Community Nutrition: Challenges and Opportunities.* Upper Saddle River, NJ: Prentice-Hall, 1998.

Hurwitz, Sue. *Choosing a Career in Nutrition.* New York, NY: Rosen Group, 1996.

Sadler, M. J. et al., eds. *Encyclopedia of Human Nutrition.* Albany, NY: Academic Press, 1999.

Sims, Charles and Gary Roderick. *Introductory Food Science.* Dubuque, IA: Kendall/Hunt, 1995.

Dispensing Opticians

Definition
Dispensing opticians are health professionals who fit eyeglasses and contact lenses using prescriptions written by eye doctors.

High School Subjects
Biology
Mathematics
Physics

Personal Skills
Helping/teaching
Mechanical/manipulative

Salary Range
$14,000 to $22,000 to $37,000

Minimum Educational Level
Apprenticeship

Certification or Licensing
Required by certain states

Outlook
As fast as the average

GOE
05.10.01

O*NET-SOC
29-2081.00

By 3:30 on a Tuesday afternoon, Carla Hawkins has been at work for several hours. She's had to send back a young man's contact lenses because he couldn't adjust to them. She spent an hour helping an elderly woman who didn't want glasses in the first place to find a pair of frames she liked, and that was no easy task. A shipment of new display frames arrived damaged, and one of her co-workers called in sick. Carla hopes that the rest of her day will be easy. Instead she sees a little girl, around eight years old, nearly dragged in by her mother.

"We need glasses," the mother says when Carla approaches them with a smile. She hands Carla a prescription. The little girl is pouting.

"Not too excited to get glasses, huh?" Carla says, leaning down. The little girl doesn't answer. "Come over here with me," Carla says, and leads her to a stool where she can sit. Carla and the mother sit, too.

"You might feel like the only one," she says, "but I see kids your age and much younger every day who come in here and don't want glasses, feel mad or disappointed, or just that they're not going to look good, and I've had nearly everyone leave pretty happy with what they've chosen." The little girl is starting to show some interest.

"Maybe you're afraid you can't play ball as well with glasses or that you're going to stick out, but I will show you some frames you'll like. We can even make you some sunglasses."

"None of my friends have glasses," the little girl says finally.

"They will sometime," Carla says. "I promise you, it's going to feel good to see properly. Tell me about what you do after school."

A little while later they've found some frames the little girl likes, and she and Carla are looking for a chain for them to hang from around her neck. "I think it was the idea of the chain that won her over," her mother says to Carla as her daughter tries one on in the mirror.

what does a dispensing optician do?

With 70 percent of the work force needing corrective eyewear, *dispensing opticians* are in demand. Carla is one of many people throughout this country as well as throughout the world, who help customers find glasses or contact lenses that fit their needs and their lifestyles. Customers count on dispensing opticians to guide them through their eyewear process, and even the most experienced customer needs to be sure that her glasses or contacts fit and correct her vision.

Glasses were widely used in the 1500s when printed matter for reading first became readily available, and the use of corrective lenses continued over the next several hundred years. From the start, dispensing opticians have been necessary to ensure the accuracy of the corrective eyewear prescribed. The optician needs to be sure that eyeglasses or contacts are made according to the optometrist's prescription specifications. They need to be certain of the placement of the lenses in relation to the pupils of the eyes. Dispensing opticians are valuable in helping customers select lenses or frames appropriate for their lifestyle. They also prepare work orders for the optical laboratory workers.

Dispensing opticians work around people all day long. Once a customer has obtained a prescription from the optometrist or ophthalmologist, he or she gives the prescription to an optician and begins the selection process. The optician asks the customer about what he or she does. Will the glasses be for everything? Just for reading? Will they be needed while playing sports or engaging in hobbies? What types of jobs does the customer have? What kinds of hobbies? The optician can tell from the prescription whether the customer will require thick or thin lenses in the glasses, and can therefore advise certain frames. They offer suggestions as needed to the customer regarding the style and color of the frames.

Dispensing opticians are responsible for making certain that glasses fit the customer's face once the glasses have returned from the lab. While the process of finding and fitting glasses used to take some time, it has been turned into a one- or two-hour process thanks to the optical superstores with in-store labs.

Regardless of the time period, however, the optician fits the glasses for the customer when they return from the lab. They use small tools and instruments to make minor adjustments to the frames.

When fitting contact lenses, opticians must be precise and skilled. The optician measures the curvature of the cornea and prepares very specific directions for the optical mechanic who will make the lenses. They must be very careful and patient when placing the lenses on the customer's eyes and when teach-

lingo to learn

Astigmatism: A vision problem caused by an irregularly shaped cornea.

Diopter: Measurer of visual deficiency.

Hyperopia: Scientific term for farsightedness, or inability to see close up.

Myopia: Scientific term for nearsightedness, or inability to see far away.

Presbyopia: Latin for "old eyes"; the process of vision deterioration that occurs in most people once they pass the age of 40.

Refractometry: The process by which visual accuity is measured.

Visual accuity: The measurement of how well an individual is able to see.

ing the customer to insert and remove the lenses.

what is it like to be a dispensing optician?

Carla Hawkins has been a dispensing optician for the past five years. "I started because I needed a job I'd be interested in," she says. "I'd just decided that I'd had enough of community college and wanted to take a break because without knowing what I wanted to do, I was wasting time." Carla found a job with Lenscrafters, an optical superstore where customers can have their glasses made for them, on-site, in less than an hour. She started at minimum wage. "The funny thing is that I mainly needed to earn money," she says. "I learned more about the work and liked it a lot. I ended up deciding to go back to school for opticianry."

Like most dispensing opticians who work in retail stores, Carla works a mix of shifts. She is in school so she doesn't work full-time, but dispensing opticians who work a full-time schedule generally put in a 40-hour week, and often evening and weekend shifts are worked into that schedule. Salaried employees are sometimes asked to work overtime, but not regularly. Dispensing opticians who are paid by the hour get paid time-and-a-half for overtime work. Retail opticians are usually expected to work some holidays.

Dispensing opticians work in pleasant surroundings—clean, well-lit areas, whether in retail stores or in doctors' offices. They spend their time alternately sitting and standing. To aid customers in finding suitable frames, the dispensing optician generally points out several frames in different parts of the store. Customer information and medical history is generally taken sitting down. Fitting glasses and contacts involves sitting.

Carla works with a variety of people all day every day. Her job is to make sure the customers who walk into her store feel that they've received the best possible service and care. "People like to feel taken care of," Carla says. "For many people, buying glasses is a new experience. It's not just any purchase—people have to feel comfortable with their choice of frames because they're going to wear them. I know from experience that the customer is very grateful if they feel you've spent a lot of time with them, getting to know them a bit so that you can make suggestions. People feel vulnerable when it comes to glasses."

The work Carla does requires a lot of patience because of the different people she encounters every day, but the work is not physically difficult. Before the store opens in the morning, she makes sure that the store is neat and attractive, that new merchandise has been registered on the computer, that the customer records are up to date. There is behind-the-scenes work that allows the dispensing optician to devote her full attention to the customer when the customer is there.

Once the initial duties have been taken care of and the store is open, Carla's day revolves around the people she serves. "Some days it's all people who have never worn a pair of glasses before," she says. "This happens a lot with older people who need corrective eyewear as they age. Some days it might be all older people and little kids. Other days I get people who have all been wearing glasses for years. It's easier to help people who know what it's like to wear them, but I like to help people get over the hump of adjusting to themselves in glasses."

Carla finds out about the customers' lifestyle: what type of work they do, what type of hobbies, whether or not they play sports. "Unless they're getting two pairs of glasses or glasses and contacts, you need to do your best to make the glasses fit their lifestyle. For someone really active and involved in contact sports, you can't suggest some small delicate frame. It'll never survive." Carla works to make the customer at ease. Once she knows a bit about what they're looking for, she is ready to suggest some frame options. She goes through the store selection, suggesting frames she thinks suit the customer's needs and appearance. "It's important to find a style that's flattering to the face of the person," she says.

Some dispensing opticians spend time on the phone talking with the labs that make their glasses and contacts, but at Lenscrafters where Carla works, the lab is on-site. "I know a lot of places call you up when your glasses are ready and you go in for a fitting or a lesson in how to wear contacts," she says, "and sometimes people come back for their glasses here, but mostly I deal with same-day service since we can make most prescriptions in an hour."

Like every dispensing optician, Carla is meticulous about the prescription she gets for glasses or contact lenses. Lenscrafters has an on-site optometrist, the doctor who prescribes the strength of corrective eyewear, but

in-depth

Transforming Light Energy into Vision

If you could look through the opening in the front of your eye (the pupil), and see to the very back surface, you would see your retina. On your retina are all the sense receptor cells that enable us to see. There are none anywhere else in the body.

On the paper-thin retina are two distinct sense receptors (nerve endings) called rods and cones. The cones are concentrated at a tiny spot on the retina called the fovea. If the focusing machinery of the eye (cornea, lens, etc.) is working just right, light rays from the outside have their sharpest focus on the fovea. Surrounding the fovea is a yellowish area called the macula lutea. Together, the fovea and macula lutea make a circle not much bigger than the head of a pin.

The cones are responsible for all color vision and fine detail vision, such as for reading. Beyond the circumference of the macula lutea, there are fewer and fewer cones, and rods become the dominant structures on the retina. It is estimated that there are roughly 10,000,000 cones on each retina, but more than 10 times as many rods. The rods are responsible for vision in dim light and peripheral vision. Because the rods are not sensitive to colors, our night vision is almost completely in black and white.

The momentary interval after the cones stop working but before the rods begin to function is explained by a curious pigment in the eye called visual purple. This substance is manufactured constantly by the rods, and must be present for them to respond to dim light, but it is destroyed when exposed to bright light. Thus, after entering a darkened room, it takes a few moments for visual purple to build up in the retina. One of the principal constituents of visual purple is vitamin A, which is why this vitamin is said to increase our capacity to see in the dark.

Every nerve ending is part of a larger unit, a neuron or nerve cell, and the rods and cones are no exception. Like all nerve cells, each rod and cone sports a long nerve fiber leading away from the site of reception. In each eye, the fibers converge at a certain spot just behind the retina, forming the optic nerve. There are no rods or cones at the point where the optic nerve exits from behind the retina at the back of the eyeball. That is why everybody has a "blind spot" at that point. An image passing through that spot completely disappears.

From the retina, each eye's optic nerve goes almost directly to the middle of the brain, and the two converge a short distance behind the eyes. The optic nerve trunk then proceeds toward the rear of the head where the occipital lobes, the brain's "centers for seeing," are located. Just before reaching the occipital lobes, the optic nerve splits again into thousands of smaller nerve bundles that disappear into the visual cortex or "outer bark" of the occipital lobes. Only at this point are the bits of light energy that have stimulated our rods and cones transformed into images that our brain can "see."

just as many people come with prescriptions from their own doctors. Because of the importance of the accuracy of prescriptions, Carla tests the customer's eyes before sending the prescription to the lab, and then later fits the customer with the glasses or contacts and has them do a reading test. "You have to be certain that they can see," she says. "After all, this is the reason they've come in the first place." She laughs.

have I got what it takes to be a dispensing optician?

"Dispensing opticians have to like people," says Carla. "All day long you are interacting with people, and you can't get upset or impatient if things get frustrating. You need to be able to adjust yourself to get along with anyone." Children can be the most frustrating to deal with, but also the most rewarding, she says. "Kids come in here dragging their feet and it's not like we transform them into great fans of glasses every time," she says, "but it is very rewarding to watch their faces when they put their glasses on and you know they can really see. It's the best part of the job."

Opticians need to have steady hands and good hand-eye coordination for the tiny, tedious tightening and adjustment jobs that need to be done to glasses. They need to be patient and meticulous when it comes to measuring the cornea for contact lenses or making sure by checking their lens machine that someone's prescription is exactly right. A soothing and confident manner is beneficial for an optician. "People are very sensitive when it comes to their eyes," Carla says. "When you're asking someone to sit still for a few minutes so you can check the accuracy of their prescription through the lensometer, they feel more at ease with a quiet voice. I've been told that." Opticians touch their customers, when checking the fit of frames, when checking their eyes, when adjusting the finished glasses, or inserting someone's contacts for them initially. A fine sense of touch is an attribute of a good dispensing optician.

Since dispensing opticians very often play a large role in a customer's frame selection, it is important that the optician has a good sense of color and feels comfortable advising the customer. Taking hair and skin color as well as face shape into account is what helps the optician to point out flattering and practical frames for the customer. "You wouldn't believe how many people want your opinion on the frames they choose," says Carla. "Some people have very strong ideas, but there are just as many who almost want you to choose for them. I guess they figure that since you work with eyewear, you must know best."

There are many qualities important to a dispensing optician, but perhaps the most important of all is good communication skills. To be able to obtain the information needed to

help customers through the eyewear process, to make them feel at ease and in a friendly environment, to have a nonthreatening and efficient manner: these are the crucial skills.

how do I become a dispensing optician?

education

High School

A high school diploma is preferred but not absolutely mandatory in the field of opticianry. While it's necessary to have completed high school to go on to a program offered by a community college, it is not impossible to work as an apprentice without a high school diploma. Students interested in entering the field will find it much easier having earned their diploma, simply because employers tend to attribute a higher level of knowledge and competency to students who have successfully completed their high school studies.

Courses such as algebra, geometry, and physics will help the aspiring optician later, as well as any course work in mechanical drawing. Communications classes are also valuable, because opticians need to be able to relate to a variety of people on all different levels.

Postsecondary Training

There are two ways of entering the field of opticianry. One is through a two-year associate's degree in optical dispensing from a community college. The other is by serving a supervised multi-year apprenticeship with an optician or optical association. Once you finish a program, you can sit for licensing (that is, if you live in one of the 21 states that require licensing to practice opticianry). If there is no licensing requirement, you take an exam with the American Board of Opticianry.

Community colleges and trade schools concentrate on mechanical and geometric optics, ophthalmic dispensing procedures, contact lens practices, business concepts, communications, and mathematics, as well as lab work in grinding and polishing lenses.

Opticians who work as apprentices learn all aspects of the business by following in the footsteps of another optician and gradually working up to taking on tasks and responsibilities individually. The apprenticeship process tends to take longer than the community college or technical school training; however, apprentices are paid while they learn, while students of opticianry must pay for the training they receive.

certification or licensing

Twenty-one states require dispensing opticians to have a state license. The requirements for these licenses vary from state to state, but all require passing a written examination. Opticians who work in doctors' offices are not required to have state licensing.

Regardless of the requirements of the states in which they live, many opticians choose to be certified at the national level by

To be a successful dispensing optician, you should

- Genuinely enjoy working with people
- Have steady hands
- Possess good eye-hand coordination
- Have a calm, soothing manner of touching and speaking
- Pay scrupulous attention to detail and accuracy

either the American Board of Opticianry (ABO) or the National Contact Lens Examiners (NCLE). Certification is achieved after successful completion of examinations and is maintained by attending continuing education classes that meet with the approval of the associations. Opticians are expected to renew their certification every three years. Examinees are not required to have had formal training or experience to sit for these examinations, but some experience or education improves your chances of passing. According to the ABO-NCLE, well over half of the estimated number of dispensers in the United States are certified by the organizations. ABO certifies approximately 28,000 opticians, and NCLE certifies about 8,000 contact lens dispensers. A survey found that 28 percent of employers required certification of their opticians, and 75 percent preferred to hire certified applicants.

Many opticians choose to become members of professional organizations, such as the Opticians Association of America. These organizations offer the dispensing optician good resources for professional networking, continuing education, and career enhancement, as well as possible sources of employment (see "How Do I Learn More?").

who will hire me?

More than half of the dispensing opticians in the United States work in the offices of optometrists and ophthalmologists, and in hospitals and eye clinics. Others work in small retail optical stores, in optical departments of department stores and large discount chains, and in optical superstores that have laboratories on-site and offer to make the customer's glasses in an hour.

In urban areas, employment opportunities are particularly good because of the number of eyewear stores and departments in the area. There are also more hospitals and more doctors' offices in larger urban areas than in smaller towns or rural areas.

Community colleges and technical schools with programs in opticianry generally have good career placement centers to help their graduates find work. Apprenticeships often turn into full-time, well-paying jobs for the certified optician. The Opticians Association of America and other professional organizations also help opticians find work in their field (see "How Do I Learn More?").

History of Lenses

The early history of lenses is unknown. In 1845 an archeologist uncovered in what is now Iraq an ancient rock crystal ground to form a small convex lens, but there is no evidence that lenses were widely known or used in ancient times.

An early investigation of the principles of lenses was made in the 11th century by Alhazen, a Persian physician. Spectacles with convex lenses were in common use both in Europe and in China as early as the thirteenth century.

Zacharias Janssen, a Dutch optician, is credited with combining lenses to make a compound microscope about 1590. Another Dutchman, Hans Lippershey, built the first telescope in 1608. The art of designing and manufacturing lenses has progressed steadily since that time.

With certain exceptions, the lenses in conventional eyeglasses sold in the United States are required by federal law to be either plastic or specially treated impact-resistant glass. Frames are generally plastic or metal.

Eyeglasses are used primarily to correct refractive errors of vision. Defects in the size and shape of the eye cause various kinds of vision problems because they interfere with the normal refraction, or bending, of light rays passing through the various parts of the eye and coming to a focus on the retina. Two common disorders of refraction for which corrective eyeglasses are needed are nearsightedness (myopia) and farsightedness (hyperopia).

Contact lenses, which are worn directly on the eyeball, are usually more expensive than ordinary eyeglasses, and they must be removed from time to time to prevent irritation to the eye. Contact lenses are used primarily for correcting nearsightedness.

where can I go from here?

When Carla began working at Lenscrafters, she was taking a break from community college. Once she realized that she loved what she was doing, she went back to school full-time and graduated with a bachelor's degree in health sciences. She is presently enrolled in graduate school for optometry. "It's a four-year degree," she says. "It's been great working at Lenscrafters. I started knowing nothing. They are good about promoting you. I've been promoted as I've been going to school. I'm a day manager now, while I'm becoming an optometrist."

Why did she decide to go into optometry? "I became very interested in the field and realized that I could go a lot further as a doctor," she says. "I guess I always knew I'd finish school, but I didn't know I'd go this far. It's been incredible." Carla's schedule is anything but easy. She works 25 hours a week at Lenscrafters, attends school full-time, studies, and works on campus at the eye clinic. "Working at an eye clinic is interesting," she says, "but since it's on campus, nothing we see is very serious. People who are working in the inner city or in poor areas of the country get a lot of exposure to serious eye problems."

Will she stay on at Lenscrafters once she has her degree? "I don't know," Carla says. "If there's an opening here for an optician, I may stay for a while. I'm most interested in going into private practice. That's when you have the most freedom and make the most money." She laughs. "I have to get some patients first, though. Right now I don't have any patients. It'll probably be slow going for the first few years."

what are the salary ranges?

According to the *Occupational Outlook Handbook,* the median annual earnings of dispensing opticians were $22,440 in 1998. Those opticians in the lowest 10 percent earned less than $14,240 annually, while those in the highest 10 percent earned more than $37,080. A survey by ABO-NCLE found that 75 percent of employers offered higher beginning salaries to certified applicants. The survey also found that, after 10 years of experience, certified opticians can earn about $6,000 more per year than non-certified opticians. Full-time employees may receive health and retirement benefits.

what is the job outlook?

According to the *Occupational Outlook Handbook,* job opportunities for dispensing opticians are expected to increase as fast as the average for all occupations. As the population grows older due to advances in medical technology, and as baby boomers move into their 50s and 60s, there are more people around who need glasses. One out of every four children aged five to 12 requires corrective eyewear. Many employers across the nation are adding eyecare allowances to their benefits packages offered to employees. Also, with the increased use of computers in the workplace, more workers are complaining of eye strain and blurred vision. Special prescriptive eyewear for use by those who spend many hours staring at a computer screen has also been developed, and may be covered by employer insurance plans.

The optics industry will also grow because of the influence of fashion. With a wider selection of colors and styles and materials of frames to choose from than ever before, people are interested in owning more than one pair of glasses. The optical superstores repeatedly offer specials encouraging people to buy two pairs of glasses, or contacts and glasses, for a price barely higher than the price of one pair.

Demand in the industry will also increase because of innovative ideas along the lines of special lens treatments and new lens and protective materials, as well as innovations relating to contact lenses, such as extended wear and disposable lenses.

To be competitive for the future of opticianry, students are encouraged to follow a course of study through a community college or tech school, and to become certified. The future holds good jobs for dedicated dispensing opticians.

how do I learn more?

professional organizations

For information about certification:
American Board of Opticianry/National Contact Lens Examiners
6506 Loisdale Road, Suite 209
Springfield, VA 22105
703-719-5800
mail@abo-ncle.org
http://www.ncleabo.org

For information about accredited opticianry programs:
Commission of Opticianry Accreditation
7023 Little River Turnpike, Suite 207
Annandale, VA 22003
703-941-9110
coa@erols.com
http://www.coaccreditation.com

For information about education, training, and career preparation, contact the following organizations:
National Academy of Opticianry
8401 Corporate Drive, Suite 605
Landover, MD 20785
301-577-4828
http://www.nao.org

Opticians Association of America
7023 Little River Turnpike, Suite 207
Annandale, VA 22003
703-916-8856
oaa@oaa.org
http://www.opticians.org

bibliography

Following is a sampling of materials relating to the professional concerns and development of dispensing opticians.

Belikoff, Kathleen M. *Opportunities in Eye Care Careers.* Lincolnwood, IL: VGM Career Horizons, 1998.

Trobe, Jonathon D. *The Physician's Guide to Eye Care.* 2nd Edition. San Francisco, CA: American Academy of Ophthalmology, 2000.

Ear-Nose-Throat Specialists

Definition
Ear-nose-throat (ENT) specialists are physicians who provide medical and surgical care for diseases involving the ears, nose, throat, and related structures of the head and neck.

Alternative Job Titles
Otolaryngologists
Otolaryngologist-head and neck surgeons
Otorhinolaryngologists

High School Subjects
Biology
Chemistry

Personal Skills
Mechanical/manipulative
Technical/scientific

Salary Range
$40,000 to $206,000 to $260,000+

Educational Requirements
Medical degree

Certification or Licensing
Recommended (certification)
Required by all states (licensing)

Outlook
Much faster than the average

GOE
02.03.01

O*NET-SOC
29-1063.00

Surgical drapes and sheets covers the patient completely, except for the site of the surgical procedure, where the antiseptic solution used to clean the skin stains the patient's throat a deep orange-yellow. Dr. Marcella Bothwell, prepped and ready, stands next to the operating room table. She has read the patient's chart and history, so she knows the patient's vital statistics. Still, Dr. Bothwell can't help but stare for a moment. The small, fine bones of the patient's neck and jawline give away her gender, but the lined and leathery condition of her skin makes the question of the woman's age more difficult. Dr. Bothwell shakes her head slowly, then says to the other members of the surgical team, "Let's get started."

The next day, Dr. Bothwell visits the woman to check up on her. The surgery has been a success. The woman is resting comfortably and will soon begin physical therapy to learn how to speak through the hole in her throat that Dr. Bothwell has created. A young doctor joins Dr. Bothwell outside of the patient's room. "Yours?" he asks.

"Yes," she says, noticing the pack of cigarettes in the chest pocket of the doctor's lab coat. "Thirty-six-year-old woman with throat cancer."

The young doctor blinks. "She's only 36?" he repeats incredulously. Unconsciously, his hand goes to his own throat and hovers there for an instant. He tries to recover from his shock, but his voice shakes slightly. "She looks 50," he says.

Dr. Bothwell nods. "Thirty-six and a chronic smoker. Yesterday, I removed her voice box, gave her a tracheoesophageal puncture and stoma. The prosthetist and physical therapist will be in tomorrow to talk to her about living the rest of her life with a hole in her throat and, of course, the possibility of fitting her with a prosthetic tube she can talk through."

what does an ENT specialist do?

Ear, nose, and throat (ENT), or otolaryngology, is the oldest medical specialty in the United States. Fifty percent of all physician office visits are for ear, nose, and throat illnesses. Problems as varied as adenoid infections, allergies, earaches, earwax buildup, hay fever, snoring, and swallowing difficulties are treated by *ear-nose-throat (ENT) specialists*, as well as many far more serious conditions or diseases. An ENT specialist, or *otolaryngologist*, has special expertise in managing diseases of the ears, nose, nasal passages, sinuses, larynx (voice box), and oral cavity and upper pharynx (mouth and throat), as well as structures of the neck and face.

Ear problems are the unique domain of the ENT specialist. Hearing disorders, ear infections, balance disorders, facial nerve or cranial nerve disorders, as well as management of congenital and cancerous disorders of the outer and inner ear are among the problems that ENT specialists treat, both medically and surgically. ENT specialists also manage disorders of the nasal cavity, paranasal sinuses, allergies, sense of smell, and nasal respiration (breathing), as well as the external appearance of the nose, from its aesthetic appearance to the skin that covers it. The ENT specialist also has unique expertise in treating diseases of the larynx and the upper aerodigestive tract (esophagus), including disorders of the voice, respiration (breathing), and swallowing. In the head and neck area, ENT specialists are trained to treat infectious diseases, tumors (benign and malignant), facial trauma, and facial deformities. They perform plastic surgery on the face and neck for both cosmetic and reconstructive purposes.

The expertise of the ENT specialist involves knowledge of more than nine other medical disciplines: neurosurgery (in treating skull base disorders), plastic and reconstructive surgery (in correcting cosmetic and traumatic deformities), ophthalmology (in treating structural abnormalities near the eye), oral

lingo to learn

Adenoid: Tissue located at the top of the throat. Bacteria and viruses entering through the nose pass through the adenoids, causing this tissue to produce antibodies that help the body fight infections.

Adenoidectomy: The surgical removal of the adenoids. This surgery used to be the most common remedy for infected adenoids. Now, such infections are treated with antibiotics.

Sinusitis: An infection of the sinus cavities caused by bacteria. When the infection lasts for three months or longer, it is said to be chronic sinusitis.

Snoring: Obstruction to the flow of air through the passages at the back of the mouth and throat, where the tongue and throat meet the soft palate and the uvula. Snoring occurs when these structures strike each other and vibrate during breathing.

Tonsil: Glandular tissue located on both sides of the throat that catch bacteria and viruses entering through the throat, and produce antibodies to fight infections.

Tonsillectomy: The surgical removal of the tonsils. Once, this surgery was a common practice. Now, antibiotics are usually used to fight off the infection.

Tonsillitis: An infection of the tonsils.

surgery (in treating jaw and dental trauma), allergy (in managing sinus disease), dermatology (in caring for skin cancers), oncology (in managing head and neck cancers), and pediatrics and family practices (in caring for common infectious, congenital, traumatic, and malignant diseases and disorders in the pediatric and general populations).

The well-trained ENT specialist has a thorough knowledge of all of the organs and physical structures in the head and neck region. Virtually all ENT specialists routinely handle adenoidectomies, tonsillectomies, nosebleeds, earaches, hearing loss, dizziness, hoarseness, and sinus disease. Patients either seek out the expertise of an ENT specialist on their own or are referred to one by another physician. The physical examination given by the ENT specialist may vary slightly, depending on the doctor's subspecialty and the patient's problem. For someone experiencing pain in his jaw, for example, the physical examination might include examination and testing of the ear, a common focus of pain for patients who are suffering from temporomandibular joint dysfunction. Many ENT specialists are generalists; others specialize in one of seven major subspecialties, limiting their practice to that area.

what is it like to be an ENT specialist?

"I told my sister about that woman whose voice box I had to remove," Dr. Marcella Bothwell admits a little mischievously, but her voice is full of pride with her next words. "She quit smoking after hearing it. Now, she's almost got too much energy." Currently a pediatric otolaryngologist and assistant professor at the University of Missouri-Columbia University Hospital, Marcella specializes in the ear, nose, and throat problems of infants to 18 year olds. A typical day for her begins early; she works about 80 hours a week. Next to the family practice service, the otolaryngology service at the University of Missouri is the largest clinic there. Speaking of her work at the university clinic, Marcella says, "Unlike most private practices, the academic practice is a more end-of-the-line situation for the patient. Either we fix it, or it's not fixable."

The physical evaluation is a focused exam of the head and neck, eyes, ears, nose, and

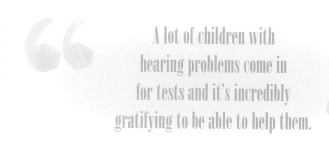

throat. Again, depending on the patient's complaint, the ENT specialist looks for different signs. "I might be looking for anything from edema, or swelling, to polyps, fluid in the ear, or red cobblestones on the back of the throat, which might indicate an allergy," explains Marcella. The ENT specialist also takes a past and present medical history of the patient, with the goal of trying to figure out the patient's problem. "Part of the patient/physician discussion during the clinic visit includes talking about smoking and alcohol," says Marcella. "It's something we like to stress."

The operating service begins at 7:00 AM. "The surgeries performed each day depend on the schedule," Marcella explains. While still in her residency a few years ago, she was exposed to all types of surgery and still performs pediatric surgeries. "Beyond that, a simple hierarchy determines who's in line for what surgery. If a tonsillectomy was up, a first-year resident would be assigned to it. On the other hand, a head/neck dissection, in which all the lymph nodes in the neck are removed, would be performed by a third-year resident." ENT residents learn special skills associated with the different procedures. "The details of each surgery differ, of course, on where the tumor is," says Marcella. "If it's a malignant tumor in the sinuses, we might have to remove the eye." Or, a patient with cancer of the ear might need to have what is known as a temporal bone resection. "We drill through the mastoid, and remove the external and middle ear structure," Marcella says. Part of the ENT's work also includes reconstructing the site of the surgery. Grafts and flaps are used to fill in the void created by the removal of the tumor. Flaps can be skin, vein, muscle, bone, or any combination of these, which are taken from the arm, leg, or shoulder blade.

ENT specialists work closely with other physicians. "ENTs work with endocrinologists a lot," says Marcella. Endocrinologists have specialized knowledge of gland systems. "I check the thyroid—palpate the neck and feel the thyroid—but, if I think that's the problem, I send the patient to the endocrinologist. We can treat it, but we feel that's their forte," she says. Asthma is also a problem that might be referred to a different specialist. "I usually send patients with asthma to see the pulmonologist." In the operating room, the story is slightly different. The ENT specialist shares common ground with many other physicians: neurological surgeons, plastic surgeons, general surgeons, allergists, and oncologists. Occasionally, some disagreement will occur over which doctor should be treating the problem. For example, the ENT who specializes in facial plastics will be performing some of the same procedures as a plastic and reconstructive surgeon, just as the ENT who specializes in the head and neck area will perform procedures that a general surgeon also performs. Most often, however, the ENT specialist works in concert with other medical specialists to solve single or multiple issues.

"It's the greatest thing in the world," says Marcella of her work as a pediatric ENT. Obviously, she doesn't mind the thought of spending the next two years surrounded by children with earaches and stuffy noses. "Fifty percent of an otolaryngologist's practice is pediatrics," she says, and then describes some problems or disorders common in the child population. "Have you ever heard a child with wheezing breathing?" She demonstrates, taking several rapid, labored breaths. "We call that a strider, and we correct that by opening up the trachea and putting in a piece of cartilage to open up the airway. It's called a laryngotracheal reconstruction." She continues, "A lot of children with hearing problems come in for tests and it's incredibly gratifying to be able to help them." Marcella then proceeds to describe what is called a cochlear implant. "By putting a 20-channel, programmable electrode into the inner ear, you can make a deaf child hear. Hearing, it's everything," Marcella says. "For children and the elderly, it's how they communicate with the world, how they interact with it."

Dr. Ira Papel, a Baltimore-based ENT specialist, concentrates his practice on facial plastic surgery, one of the subspecialties of otolaryngology. Typical procedures that Ira performs include face-lifts, skin cancer resections, and repairing broken noses, chins, and jawbones. He describes removing a large skin cancer from a patient's face. "I work with a dermatologic surgeon to remove the tumor. What remains is often a large gap that needs to be closed, basically a three- to four-inch hole. I use local skin flaps or grafts from the chest skin to try and close the hole." When asked why he chose to go into otolaryngology instead of plastic and reconstructive surgery, Ira answers, "When I was in medical school, I knew I liked surgery, but I disliked general surgery. The ENT specialists were all nice people. I saw that they were having a good time. There wasn't a lot of bellyaching. And there were lots of opportunities to be creative."

have I got what it takes to be an ENT specialist?

"I love what I do," says Dr. Lee Eisenberg, an ENT specialist with a private practice in Englewood, New Jersey. "It's a tough specialty, I won't kid you. You're working with both sexes, with children and adults of all ages." Although 75 percent of his practice is pediatric, he doesn't hold a subspecialty certificate in pediatric otolaryngology. Maintaining a positive relationship with his patients is extremely important to Lee and, he believes, vital to creating a solid practice. "You have to treat patients with respect. You have to listen to them and give them the chance to tell you what's the problem. Good listening and communication skills are essential," he stresses. "Sometimes, you may be the only doctor the patient sees. I can tell you, I've had a number of patients break down in my office, upset because they can't talk to their physician, or they feel he doesn't listen to them. Lawsuits," Lee says, "come from patients who don't have a good rapport with their physicians." Marcella agrees with the need to communicate. "You need to be able to converse with patients," she says. "If you don't have those skills, you need to develop them."

Ira believes that imagination and flexibility are also desirable qualities. "You need to be able to think on your feet," he says. "You have to decide right there, in the OR, what to do next. Being imaginative and resourceful helps." Due to his work in facial plastic surgeries, Ira also thinks it helps to be an individual who pays close attention to detail.

As in all of medicine, there are difficult moments, and there are stressful moments. Egos abound, schedules conflict, pagers go off, and sometimes there are disagreements among professionals. Whenever an overlap in expertise occurs, disagreements can occur as to which specialty should treat the problem. Prospective ENT specialists should be aware of the potential for these rifts. How these disagreements are resolved largely depends on the temperaments of those involved, as well as the context. So-called turf wars seem to occur with greater frequency in academic/university settings than in private practice. Although turf wars occasionally happen between surgical specialties, disagreements need to be worked out responsibly. "It all depends on the egos involved," comments Marcella. "For example, we have an amicable relationship with the neurological surgeons. We do the access [opening procedure] and then they come in and do their thing."

Prospective ENT specialists should also know that while the field is growing, it is one of the more competitive specialties. Marcella estimates that one of three students won't get the ENT residency they request and adds that the field tends to look at extracurricular activities as well as consistently good grades across the board. "We pick people a lot on personality; you need to be well-rounded and like people because of the high patient contact."

In the battle against infections, tonsils and adenoids are especially important defense mechanisms for infants and young children. As a child grows, tonsils and adenoids shrink. By puberty, tonsils are about the size of almonds and adenoids have almost disappeared.

how do I become an ENT specialist?

Dr. Marcella's decision to pursue a career in medicine stemmed from an early affinity for science. "My brother is a research scientist, and I always enjoyed science, too," she explains. "But I really enjoy working with people and, to me, the scientific lab setting is too cold and detached. When I went to medical school, I was thinking about holistic medicine, but then surgery really fit my personality." She adds, "I like to size up a problem and solve it."

education

High School

If you are considering a career in otolaryngology, taking high school courses that are college preparatory is a must. Classes in biology and chemistry as well as mathematics are important. These courses will not only prepare you for college but also help you determine your aptitude in these areas. In addition, it will be beneficial to take courses in social sciences and English, since working with people and communicating effectively will be a large part of your career. When the time comes to choose a college or university, you may want to consider attending an undergraduate institution where you could continue on in its graduate medical school.

Postsecondary Training

Receiving an undergraduate bachelor of arts (B.A.) degree or bachelor of science (B.S.) degree is the next step in your education. During the college years you will probably major in a science field and continue to study math, biology, and chemistry in preparation for medical school. You should note, however, that medical schools, like colleges and universities, seek well-rounded candidates— people with more than one interest.

After receiving an undergraduate degree, you must then apply and be accepted to medical school. Admission is competitive, and applicants undergo a fairly extensive and difficult admissions process that considers grade point averages, scores on the Medical College Admission Test (MCAT), and recommendations from professors. Most students apply to several schools early in their senior year of college. Only about one-third of the applicants are accepted.

In order to earn the doctor of medicine (M.D.) degree, you must complete four years of medical school. For the first two years of medical school, you attend lectures and classes and spend time in laboratories. Courses include anatomy, biochemistry, physiology, pharmacology, psychology, microbiology, pathology, medical ethics, and laws governing medicine. You learn to take patient histories, perform routine physical examinations, and recognize symptoms of diseases and disorders.

"I had a wonderful time in medical school," says Marcella. "I think it was the first time I was challenged. I met people who had the same interests, the same motivations, even the same study habits." She smiles. "Even though I was athletic, I was always the egghead. Suddenly, it was like we were all the same. I wasn't the egghead, anymore." Marcella credits part of her success to her ability to adapt her study habits to the demands of medical school.

In the third and fourth years, you are involved in more practical studies. You work in clinics and hospitals supervised by residents and physicians and you learn acute, chronic, preventive, and rehabilitative care. You go through rotations (brief periods of study) in such areas as obstetrics and gynecology, pediatrics, dermatology, psychiatry, and surgery. Rotations allow you to gain exposure to the many different fields within medicine and to learn firsthand the skills of diagnosing and treating patients.

Upon graduating from an accredited medical school, physicians must pass a standard examination given by the National Board of Medical Examiners. Most physicians complete an internship, also referred to as a transition year. The internship is usually one year in length and helps graduates decide on an area of specialization. It is considered the first postgraduate year of study.

For medical students who have decided to go into otolaryngology, the internship represents the first of two years of study in general surgery. Following the internship, physicians begin a residency. Physicians wishing to pursue a career in otolaryngology must first complete a second year of general surgery and then enter a three-year residency program in otolaryngology-head and neck surgery.

Throughout the surgical residency years, residents are supervised at all levels of training, with the attending surgeon ultimately responsible for the patient's care. Residents begin their training by assisting on and then performing basic operations. As the residency years continue, residents gain responsibility through teaching and supervisory duties. Eventually the residents are allowed to perform complex operations independently. At the end of this five-year postgraduate training, an ENT specialist who wants to subspecialize in an area, like Ira or Marcella, completes additional training through fellowships.

certification or licensing

In the United States, licensing is required before a doctor can practice medicine. In order to be licensed, doctors must have graduated from medical school, passed the licensing test of the state in which they will practice, and completed their residency.

The American Board of Otolaryngology (ABOto) was founded and incorporated in 1924 and is the second oldest of the 24 American certifying boards. The ABOto certifies physicians in otolaryngology and its subspecialty fields. In order to be considered a candidate for certification in otolaryngology, a physician must have successfully completed medical school and five years of required postgraduate specialty training. The specialty training must include one or more years of general surgery, and three or more years of otolaryngology-head and neck surgery in an approved residency program.

The certification process is in two parts. The first phase is a written qualifying examination. Candidates take the written exam in the fall. The second phase is an oral exam, which is offered in the spring. However, if candidates do not pass this written test, they are ineligible to take the oral exam.

To be a successful ENT specialist, you should

- Be a good clinician
- Pay close attention to detail
- Be imaginative and adaptable
- Enjoy helping and working with people
- Have good hand-eye coordination and manual dexterity
- Have respect for your patients
- Be able to listen and communicate well

scholarships and grants

Scholarships and grants are often available from individual institutions, state agencies, and special-interest organizations. Many students finance their medical education through the Armed Forces Health Professions Scholarship Program. Each branch of the military participates in this program, paying students' tuitions in exchange for military service. Contact your local recruiting office for more information. Lee chose to pay for medical school through this program. He fulfilled the equivalent of basic training at Fort Sam Houston in Texas. "I remember it was hot, and I remember the crickets," Lee recalls. "I had to get up at four in the morning just to go for a run."Just after his residency years in otolaryngology, Lee was assigned to Walter Reed Army Medical Center in Washington, DC. "I was lucky," he says. "I got Walter Reed. A buddy of mine got sent to Korea for two years on a hardship tour, which meant his family couldn't go." He stresses that he was grateful for the experience and the chance to attend medical school, but he cautions students against making a swift decision. "Your time is not your own."

The National Health Service Corps Scholarship Program also provides money for students in return for service. Another source for financial aid, scholarship, and grant information is the Association of American Medical Colleges. Remember to request information early for eligibility, application requirements, and deadlines.

Association of American Medical Colleges
2450 N Street, NW
Washington, DC 20037
202-828-0400
http://www.aamc.org

National Health Service Corps Scholarship Program
U.S. Public Health Service
1010 Wayne Avenue, Suite 240
Silver Spring, MD 20910
800-638-0824
http://www.fedmoney.org/grants/93288-00.htm

who will hire me?

The physician's qualifications and interests, as well as the community's needs, will influence or determine the scope and size of an individual's private practice. The broad challenges of the specialty allow ENT specialists to choose from many possible directions.

Many ENT specialists open their own private practice or join an existing practice. Still others work in a large academic/university setting, helping train medical students and residents, and handling a caseload of end-of-the-line patients—more like Marcella's university clinic than, say, Ira's private clinic.

where can I go from here?

Lee points out that once a surgeon no longer wants to operate, there are still options. "You can limit yourself to the office. A lot of otolaryngologists do that." ENT specialists advance in the academic field by publishing their case studies, developing and refining techniques, and ascending the departmental ladder, eventually chairing the department. In private practice, a good reputation among both patients and other physicians is the best way to advance one's career. Lee also stresses the importance of joining professional organizations and volunteer societies.

what are the salary ranges?

Average salaries of medical residents ranged from about $34,100 in 1998-99 for those in their first year of residency to about $42,100 for those in their sixth year, according to the Association of American Medical Colleges. Salaries vary depending on the kind of residency, the hospital, and the geographic area.

However, salaries for established otolaryngologists are considerably higher. In 1999, the median salary reported by members of the American Academy of Otolaryngology was $224,300. Members practicing on the East Coast were at the higher end of the earnings scale, with median earnings of $260,800, compared with members on the West Coast, whose median was $206,000. Other factors influencing individual incomes include type and size of practice, hours worked per week, and professional reputation.

what is the job outlook?

The expertise of the ENT specialist will always be in great demand. The specialty is gaining more and more attention, especially as more ENT specialists are appointed as the heads of medical schools and residency programs.

Overall, the health care industry is thriving and the employment of physicians in almost all fields is expected to grow faster than the average. Looking further ahead, the American Academy of Otolaryngology study indicates that on average, its respondents plan to retire at age 62, which will cause the supply of ENT specialists to drop by 2015.

how do I learn more?

professional organizations

Following are organizations that provide information on the profession of ENT specialist.

American Academy of Otolaryngology— Head and Neck Surgery
One Prince Street
Alexandria, VA 22314
703-836-4444
http://www.entnet.org

American Society for Head and Neck Surgery
203 Lothrop Street, Suite 519
Pittsburgh, PA 15213
412-647-2227

bibliography

Following is a sampling of materials relating to the professional concerns of ear-nose-throat specialists.

Bailey, Byron J. *Head and Neck Surgery-Otolaryngology*, 2nd Edition. Philadelphia, PA: Lippincott, Williams & Wilkins, 1998.

Corbridge, Rogan J. and William P. Hellier. *Essential ENT Practice: A Clinical Text.* New York, NY: Oxford University Press, 1998

Dhillon, R.S. *Ear, Nose, and Throat, and Head and Neck Surgery: An Illustrated Colour Text.* 2nd Edition. Kent, UK: Churchill Livingston, 1999.

Gates, George A., ed. *Current Therapy in Otolaryngology: Head & Neck Surgery.* St. Louis, MO: Mosby-Yearbook, 1998.

Jafek, Bruce W. and Anne K. Stark. *ENT Secrets.* Philadelphia, PA: Lippincott Williams & Wilkins, 1996.

Lee, K. J. *Essential Otolaryngology: Head and Neck Surgery.* New York, NY: McGraw-Hill Professional Publishing, 1999.

Lucente, Frank E. and Steven M. Sobol, eds. *Essentials of Otolaryngology.* 4th Edition. Philadelphia, PA: Lippincott Williams & Wilkins, 1999.

Electroneurodiagnostic Technologists

Definition

Electroneurodiagnostic technologists obtain recordings of the electrical activity in various body parts. They run tests like electroencephalograms (EEGs), electromyograms (EMGs), and electrocardiographs (ECGs). They prepare patients for tests, monitor equipment, note irregularities, and ensure the reliability of results.

Alternative Job Titles

END technicians
Electroencephalographic (EEG) technologists

High School Subjects

Biology
Chemistry
Physics

Personal Skills

Mechanical/manipulative
Technical/scientific

Salary Range

$22,000 to $32,000 to $46,000

Minimum Educational Level

Some postsecondary training

Certification or Licensing

Recommended

Outlook

Little change or more slowly than the average

GOE
10.03.01
O*NET-SOC
29-2012.00

Although the Neurodiagnostics Department at St. Vincent's Health Center has been computerized for nearly 10 years, Darlene Albrecht, R. EEG T., still works closely with patients. "That hasn't changed," she says. Darlene brings in the patient and offers a general explanation of the procedure, then asks about the patient's history. "We find out why they're being tested, what kind of medical problems they may have, medications, right-handedness, left-handedness, family history." Darlene then begins to prepare the patient for the procedure. "It takes probably a good 20 minutes to prepare and place the electrodes for monitoring."

The test is a 30-minute recording of the brain's electrical activity. "We do awake, drowsy, asleep, depending on what the physician is looking for. For instance, if someone comes in for a seizure disorder evaluation, we try to get as many states of consciousness as possible." But the technicians don't have a step-by-step process they follow; they must often rely on their instincts and understanding of the procedure. "I'd say that 95 percent of what we do, how we handle the recording, is at the tech's discretion."

what does an END technologist do?

Electroneurodiagnostic (END) technology is the branch of medicine that deals with using tracings (graphic recordings) of the brain's electrical waves in order to diagnose and determine the effects on the body of certain diseases and injuries, including brain tumors and accidental injuries, strokes, Alzheimer's, epilepsy, and various infectious diseases. By interpreting END test results, physicians are able to prescribe needed medicines or surgeries in the attempt to cure or relieve the suffering of a patient.

Electroneurodiagnostic (END) *technologists* are responsible for obtaining accurate tracings of the brain's electrical activity so that a doctor can use them in diagnosing patients. END

lingo to learn

Brainwaves: Patterns of wavy lines recorded by electroencephalographs (EEG machines) that result from electrical activity in the brain.

Cerebral: Of or having to do with the brain.

Electrocardiograms: Recordings of activity related to the heart.

Electroencephalograms (EEGs): Recordings of the electrical activity in the brain.

Evoked potentials: Recordings of the peripheral nervous system.

Neurologists: Physicians who specialize in the study of the brain and diagnosis and treatment of diseases in or relating to the brain.

Polysomnograms: Recordings of sleep processes.

Vascular: Of or having to do with the circulatory system.

technologists conduct a variety of electroneurological tests. Electrocardiograms (ECGs) are tracings of electrical activity associated with the heart ("cardio" refers to the heart). Electrooculograms are similar but have to do with the eyes, and electromyograms (EMGs) have to do with the muscles. The most common ones, electroencephalograms (EEGs), are tracings of the brain's electrical activity. END technologists generally perform some or all of these tests.

END technologists also administer newly developed tests like the Evoked Potential (EP), which records the electrical reaction from the brain, spinal nerves, and/or sensory perceptors in response to external stimuli. They might conduct the polysomnogram (PSG), an electroneurodiagnostic procedure that combines an EEG with other physiologic measures like heart rate, eye movements, and blood oxygen levels, in order to diagnose and treat sleep disorders.

All of these tests must be administered methodically and with close attention to detail. END technologists start by preparing a patient for a test. They write down the patient's medical history, listening carefully for family or personal illness that might influence either testing procedures or tracing interpretation and diagnosis. Next, they explain each step of the procedure to the patient so that he or she can remain calm throughout the test. Making the patient comfortable in this way is very important since his or her relaxation level can directly affect test results. Technologists must practice good "bedside manner," develop compassion for the patient's concerns, and learn to answer respectfully any questions the patient might have.

Next, the more technical part of the test begins. Technologists fasten electrodes to the patient's head or to other prescribed locations and connect them to the monitor. They make educated decisions about exact placement of electrodes and combination of machine settings, which they note in the patient's file. Once the machine is activated, it begins collecting data, which is amplified and recorded on moving strips of paper or on optical disks. The resulting graph is the "tracing" of the brain's electrical activity.

During the test or "study," technologists must keep an attentive eye on both the patient and the machines, taking notes about the patient's reactions and making any necessary adjustments to the equipment. They may keep track of vital signs like heart rate, blood pressure, and breathing, to make sure the patient stays out of danger. They are trained in basic emergency care in case something does go wrong with the patient during the test. If drugs have been prescribed, they are frequently responsible for administering them.

At the conclusion of the test, some technologists simply pass results on to the prescribing physician, while others evaluate them and note whether they are normal or abnormal. Still others might participate in the diagnostic process with the doctor by writing up a report summary. A technologist's degree of involvement in the interpretative process depends on the doctor who ordered the test originally and the education and experience of the technologist.

Although technologists do not necessarily interpret tracings, they are responsible for identifying abnormal brain activity and any extraneous readings collected by the machine during the test. In order to do so properly, they consider how an individual should perform on the test based on his or her medical history and current illness.

Technologists can also detect mechanical malfunction or human error in faulty recordings. They can fix some mechanical problems themselves but may have to call on the assistance of a supervisor or equipment technician.

what is it like to be an END technologist?

At the St. Vincent's Health Center in Pennsylvania, the Neurodiagnostics Department is a center for EEGs and other tests, such as all modalities of Evoked Potentials. The sleep lab, where tests for sleep disorders are performed, is shared between the Neurodiagnostic Department and the Respiratory Therapy Department. Darlene Albrecht, an EEG tech with St. Vincent's, has been in the career for 20 years. In her years of work, she has been involved in the conversion from paper and ink systems to digital, computerized EEG.

"We've all worked together for a long time," Darlene says of the techs at St. Vincent's, "and they're all pretty good at what they do, so they have the flexibility to run a test as to how they see fit. It's based on the individual patient."

Darlene's center administers sleep tests in addition to the EEG and Evoked Potentials. "We have a clinical polysomnographer who's the medical director, and we deal with all possible sleep disorders." A third shift comes in at 8:00 PM to work with patients. Hooking up the

patient for a sleep test is similar to that for an EEG. "Everything's glued on the body," Darlene explains, "and the patient basically sleeps in one of our bedrooms overnight. We do EEG monitoring during that time; there are eye monitors, sub-mental EMG; there are respiratory belts put across the chest and abdomen. We watch oxygen saturation throughout the night. It's pretty all-encompassing."

Though Darlene works closely with patients, she does spend a fair amount of time in a dark room administering the tests. "There are days when we all feel like moles," she says, "because even though we're responsible for our daily load of patients, we have to work independently."

That independence, however, is something Darlene often appreciates about the work. "You do have the independence to do the best for any given patient on an individual basis," she says. She also appreciates the variety. "We do infants, we do elderly. The variety of patients is incredible. Plus, we don't just do EEGs. Within the END field, we're doing Evoked Potentials. Some days I'm down in the OR." But Darlene hopes for the field to get more recognition within the health care industry. "I don't think it commands the respect that other disciplines do, because we've only been emerging. It's still considered an infant career. The whole organization nationwide has made strides, but it doesn't have the recognition that other areas, such as respiratory therapy and cardiology, have."

Ken Ashby has been an EEG technologist for 23 years, and currently works at the University of Utah. Ken's work is similar to Darlene's, and he works with about four or five patients a day. "The time we spend with patients varies," Ken says. "The minimum amount of time spent is probably about an hour." Preparing a patient for a test involves measuring the head, then applying the electrodes and ensuring they have good contact. "When something arises during a test," Ken says, "our job as a technologist is to make sure that's really brain-wave activity and not something else. Our position is not to interpret the recording; that's up to the neurologist."

When present in the operating room, Ken helps the surgeon by watching for signs of problems. "It's an early warning system," he says. "If they're working on the spinal cord and they damage an artery that supplies blood to the spinal cord, we'll see the signal from that." Because of this, a relationship with the others in the OR is important. "You have to build a rapport with the surgeon," he says.

Ken also witnessed the change from paper-generating machines to computers. "An EEG record would be about an inch thick," he says. "Now we archive all our EEGs to CD-ROM."

have I got what it takes to be an END technologist?

"You have to be very people-oriented," says Darlene. "That's the whole way to make it work: How you can establish a rapport with the patients." The ability to communicate effectively with people should be accompanied by quick thinking skills since technologists often have to change tasks abruptly. For example, if an emergency request is made for an EEG on a 30-year-old, a technologist might have to interrupt his or her work on a 65-year-old woman to do it. The technologist must then make rapid mental adjustments to accommo-date physical differences and test expectations of the new patient.

The best END technologists generally have strong manual dexterity, coupled with an aptitude for working with computers, good vision, and good abstract thinking skills. Technologists should have an eagerness to learn and the ability to learn quickly.

Technologists generally write observations, comments, and summaries in a report composed primarily of very technical language. Writing skills are thus very important for this job. Verbal communication skills are equally essential.

Working in a hospital or clinical laboratory can prove to be quite stressful, especially in the larger and busier ones. Just like their TV counterparts, doctors, nurses, and technologists of all specialties go in a million different directions and the effect can ruin concentration. Therefore, technologists should be good stress managers and should be able to perform well under pressure.

how do I become an END technologist?

Darlene trained on the job, under the guidance of a trained EEG tech. On-the-job training has continued at St. Vincent's in the years since. "There are so few formal schools out there," Darlene points out. "There are none in our area. Unfortunately, when you're in a working situation and learning at the same time, it becomes a little demanding."

Ken holds an associate's degree in general studies, and studied on his own for registration. "There are a lot of good techs who aren't registered," Ken mentions, "and there are probably a lot of techs who are registered who aren't very good."

education

High School
A high school diploma is required of all prospective END technologists. Science classes, especially biology, chemistry, physics, and anatomy, are particularly helpful, helping students to build a solid foundation in scientific knowledge, methods, and reasoning.

FYI

Sometimes, other more specialized diagnostic tests are needed to help a physician visualize the structure of the patient's brain and spinal cord. The CT scanner (for computed tomography) takes computer-generated X rays of different "slices," or areas, of the brain. For information on careers in this area of diagnostic testing, see the chapter "Special Procedures Technologists."

Mathematics courses should include at least algebra and are equally important since they encourage you to develop strong analytical and abstract thinking skills. Three or more years of both science and math are recommended.

English and speech courses provide good opportunities to enhance verbal and written communication. Social science classes, like psychology and sociology, help students begin to think about the affective, or emotional, needs of patients. This understanding leads prospective END technologists to develop a good "bedside manner."

In some high schools, vocational or technical courses dealing with mechanical and electrical equipment are offered. These courses can provide students with a head start on understanding END equipment and teach them how to approach and solve a technically oriented problem.

Postsecondary Training

There are two types of postsecondary training for prospective END technologists. The first is on-the-job training, and the other is formal classroom training at either a hospital, medical center, technical school, college, or four-year university. Often, intellectual ability is proven through completion of a postsecondary degree; it can also be proven through work and volunteering experience. As technology continues to change, however, it is generally considered preferable to pursue formal education.

On-the-job training usually lasts anywhere between three months and one year, depending on the nature and scope of the employer.

During on-the-job training, END technologists learn firsthand how to operate the equipment and carry out specific testing, maintenance, and repair procedures. They receive instruction from doctors and senior END technologists. They may be required to do some reading at home.

Formal training in electroneurodiagnostic technology consists of both academic course work and clinical practice. The length of formal programs varies between one and several years and results in either a certificate or an associate's degree. At the university level, curricula for a bachelor's degree in END technology is being developed in some areas, but degrees are already available in many related health professions. The American Society of Electroneurodiagnostic Technologists offers a nationally comprehensive list of formal educational programs in END technology (see "How Do I Learn More?"). Currently, there are 12

Advancement Possibilities

Electroneurodiagnostic technologist supervisors administer the more difficult or specialized lab tests and supervise other END technologists. They might also be involved in training new employees on testing techniques specific to the lab. They may share some administrative duties with the chief END technologist.

Chief electroneurodiagnostic technologists usually work directly under the direction of a neurologist, neurosurgeon, or other physician. They supervise or manage the END laboratory, establish lab procedures, make work and appointment schedules, keep records, and order supplies. They are also involved in teaching and training new employees from END technology education programs.

Electroneurodiagnostic technology educators or **researchers** teach in academic programs focused on END technology or in on-the-job training programs in hospitals and clinics. Researchers may work on improving, developing, and inventing electroneurodiagnostic procedures.

schools with accredited two-year END technology programs.

Academic instruction is usually concentrated on basic medical subjects, like human anatomy, physiology, neuroanatomy, clinical neurology, neuropsychiatry, clinical and internal medicine, and psychology. Courses specific to END technology include normal and abnormal pattern recognition, patient preparation, recording techniques, and electronics and instrumentation. The clinical practice incorporates what is taught in on-the-job training programs, but may do some of it in staged, not authentic, situations.

certification or licensing

Certification of END technologists is regulated at the state level and so varies from state to state. Past attempts at national certification programs have not been entirely successful, so now most END technologists are encouraged to obtain official registration instead. Individuals who have completed one year of on-the-job training or have graduated from a formal training program and been in the field for at least one year and completed a required number of recordings may apply for registration with the American Board of Registration of EEG and Evoked Potential Technologists, Inc. (ABRET) (see "How Do I Learn More?").

After application, the individual takes a two-part examination. The first part is written and the second oral. Only students who pass the written part may take the oral. Both sections comprehensively cover subjects related to the work of an END technologist.

ABRET offers two registrations: R.EEG T., or registered electroencephalographic technologist, and R.EP T., or registered evoked potentials technologist. Though not required for employment, registration is official acknowledgement of a technologist's expertise. It also makes advancement and financial promotion easier.

scholarships and grants

END technologists who receive on-the-job training are usually paid regular salaries, so tuition is not an obstacle. Those who pursue formal education in hospitals and medical centers should contact them directly about costs and financial aid opportunities. Technical school or university students should seek

To be a successful END technologist, you should

- Have strong manual dexterity skills and good vision
- Enjoy working with people of all ages and backgrounds
- Be adept at working with mechanical and electronic equipment and understanding technical data
- Communicate effectively, both verbally and in writing
- Possess good stress management skills

financial aid from their school's financial office. These offices usually maintain a complete list of available awards, as well as a profile of requirements. They should be contacted directly.

The American Society of Electroneurodiagnostic Technologists (ASET) sponsors conferences and continuing education courses; it offers some scholarships to ASET members for these courses.

If you are currently employed in a health- or medical-related business and want to pursue a degree in END technology, you may be eligible for tuition reimbursement programs offered by your employer. You should contact the company's personnel or benefits office.

internships and volunteerships

It is extremely difficult to find internships or part-time jobs in the field of electroneurodiagnostic technology since most clinics and labs are staffed by fully trained, full-time professionals. Prospective END technologists have to rely on the clinical practice that is part of both formal education and on-the-job training for in-depth exposure to daily routines. In some formal education programs, however, there may be some paid internships or co-op work (apart from regular clinical practice) organized by the school or clinic as part of the curriculum. Information about these kinds of opportunities can be obtained through the program administration.

Volunteerships are readily available at local hospitals, clinics, and medical centers. Experience of this type may be helpful for several reasons. First, as a hospital volunteer, you witness the everyday trials of hospital work and discover firsthand if a medical profession is right for you. Second, you may be allowed to specify that you would like to work in an electroneurodiagnostic area, which would provide a sort of direct, advanced training. Third, hospital volunteerships show employers and education program administrators that you are serious, interested, and enthusiastic about the health professions. Contact local hospitals and clinics for more information. ABRET and ASET may also have lists of specialized END labs across the country.

labor unions

There are no labor unions designated specifically for electroneurodiagnostic technologists. In some areas or certain hospitals and clinics, an allied health union may operate. If you are employed in such an area, you may be required to join the union.

who will hire me?

Darlene began working as a medical assistant in the cardiology department of St. Vincent's. At the time, the EEG department was part of the cardiology department, and Darlene learned a bit about the testing. When an EEG tech left, Darlene was invited to step into the position. Ken also began in another area of health care, working as a nursing assistant. He learned other forms of therapy, and eventually began working as an EEG tech.

Electroneurodiagnostic technologists work in any doctor's office, clinic, group medical center, health maintenance organization, urgent care center, emergency center, psychiatric facility, lab, or hospital that has the equipment necessary to perform END tests. Most END technologists, however, hold full-time positions in hospitals.

On-the-job trainees usually have no problem finding a job after training, since their employer/trainer hires them directly. END technologists who complete formal education in this field work closely with the placement office of the medical center, technical school, or university where they study. Such offices have long-standing working relationships with area employers and are often successful at placing graduates in full-time jobs.

For all END technologists, whether trained on-the-job or through formal education, newspaper and magazine classified ads are a good place to look for job openings in the area. You can also contact the personnel offices of the various medical facilities directly.

ASET sponsors a service called "Employment Exchange" which regularly provides subscribers with job listings. Membership in ASET provides the occasion to become part of a close-knit network of employed professionals, who may also be able to pass on information about job openings. Membership is beneficial in several ways, not the least of which is net-

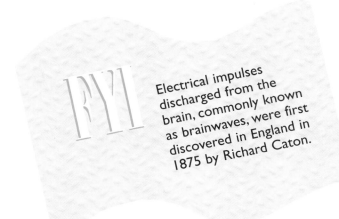

Electrical impulses discharged from the brain, commonly known as brainwaves, were first discovered in England in 1875 by Richard Caton.

working for employment opportunities. ABRET may also have job lists and job hunting ideas (see "How Do I Learn More?").

where can I go from here?

After registration and several years' experience, an electroneurodiagnostic technologist is eligible for promotion to a supervisory position. Supervisors generally perform the more complex tests or the regular tests on potentially problematic patients. They might also be called upon to conduct tests in emergency situations. Depending on the size of the lab, some supervisors may be involved with training new employees and have some administrative duties like job assignment, patient and employee scheduling, and supply ordering.

Supervisory positions may be followed by promotion to chief electroneurodiagnostic technologist. The chief technologist or lab director has much more immediate contact with doctors and hospital administration than do technologists; they may consult on the diagnosis of a case, offer input into the establishment of hospital regulations and policies, and manage the lab's budget. Although they still work with patients, they are in effect lab or departmental managers, with managerial and fiscal responsibilities.

Years of experience and a solid educational foundation put certain END technologists in a prime position to move into education. Some technologists may go to work for a manufacturing company, training their customers (medical END labs) in the proper use of END equipment. Others might teach in the on-the-job or formal training programs offered at medical centers and hospitals. People with advanced degrees might go to work in technical schools and universities.

what are the salary ranges?

According to the *Occupational Outlook Handbook*, END technologists had median annual earnings of $32,070 in 1998. Those in the lowest 10 percent earned less than $22,200 a year, while those in the highest 10 percent earned more than $46,620.

END technologists working in hospitals generally receive full benefits packages that may include health insurance, paid vacations, and sick leave. In some locations, benefits may also include educational assistance, pension plans, and uniform allowances. Technologists working outside the hospital setting usually receive benefits as well, though they vary in content with different employers.

what is the job outlook?

The U.S. Department of Labor estimates that the number of positions in electroneurodiagnostic technology will grow more slowly than the average for all other occupations. Increasingly sophisticated equipment requires fewer technicians to operate it. Also, technicians in other areas of care will be trained to work with END technology.

One area of growth will be in surgical units. Surgical teams find it more and more useful to have an END technologist, prepared to do an EEG, in the operating room for the duration of certain surgeries. END testing is proving to be an effective way to monitor the patient's condition and reactions to various surgical procedures.

Private neurologists' offices and neurological clinics were formerly predicted to be the area of greatest increase in demand for END technologists. However, this will certainly not be the case. The initial prediction was based on a trend in the medical community of doctors buying or leasing their own END equipment. This meant that if a doctor ordered an EEG, the patient would be able to have the test performed on the doctor's premises instead of going to the hospital or a specialized lab.

Recent legislation in Congress makes this process of self-referral illegal. The concern was that since the END tests are so expensive to the patient and insurance companies and profitable to the doctors, the latter might tend to order tests when they were not really needed. Prospective END technologists should pay attention to health-related legislation at both the federal and state levels, since it can have an enormous impact on employment growth and outlook.

how do I learn more?

professional organizations

For information on registration, contact:
American Board of Registration of EEG and EP Technologists
PO Box 916633
Longwood, FL 32791
407-788-6308

For a career brochure and information about scholarships and educational opportunities, contact:
American Society of Electroneurodiagnostic Technologists
204 West 7th Street
Carroll, IA 51401-2317
712-792-2978
info@aset.org
http://www.aset.org/

For information on accredited training programs, contact:
Joint Review Committee on Electroneurodiagnostic Technology
Route 1, Box 63A
Genoa, WI 54632

bibliography

Following is a sampling of materials relating to the professional concerns and development of electroneurodiagnostic technologists and technicians.

Careers in Focus: Medical Technicians. 2nd Edition. Chicago, IL: Ferguson Publishing Company, 2001.

Rumack, Carol M. *Diagnostic Ultrasound.* St. Louis, MO: Mosby-Year Book, 1998.

Sherry, Clifford J., and Robert S. Ledley. *Opportunities in Medical Imaging Careers.* Lincolnwood, IL: NTC/Contemporary Publishing Company, 2000.

Emergency Medical Technicians

Definition

Emergency medical technicians give immediate first aid treatment to sick or injured persons both at the scene and en route to the hospital or other medical facility. They also make sure that the emergency vehicle is stocked with the necessary supplies and is in good operating condition.

Alternative Job Title

Paramedics

High School Subjects

Biology
Health

Personal Skills

Helping/teaching
Technical/scientific

Salary Range

$12,000 to $20,000 to $45,000

Minimum Educational Level

Some postsecondary training

Certification or Licensing

Required

Outlook

Much faster than the average

GOE
10.03.02
O*NET-SOC
29-2041.00

At 6:45 AM Kelly Richey clocks in, says hello to the EMTs going off duty, and goes to the soda machine for her first Diet Coke of the day. It is half gone when the first call comes in, and 15 minutes later she is inside a crumpled black Camaro, placing an oxygen mask on a critically injured teenager.

"Are you still in school?" she asks him as she works over him. "What grade? Senior?" She is trying to determine his level of consciousness, and she has to speak in a near-shout because the fire department is cutting the roof off the car while she works. As soon as the roof comes off, she and her co-worker must work quickly to get the patient out of the car and on the way to the hospital. He has injuries to the chest and both legs and is losing blood quickly. If he doesn't reach surgery within an hour, his chances for survival are greatly diminished. In the ambulance, Kelly continues to talk to the young man, taking his vital signs every four to five minutes. She calls in to the hospital emergency room to notify them that they have a serious trauma patient coming in. "We have a 17-year-old patient, conscious and alert," she begins. "Involved in a single-vehicle accident. Patient has chest wounds and injuries to both legs. Vital signs are stable. We have an ETA of five minutes."

At the hospital, she and her partner unload the patient, deliver him to the emergency staff, and give a brief report to the doctor who will be on his case.

Kelly gets a blank "run report," and her second Diet Coke, and starts to document the first run of her day.

lingo to learn

Amkus cutter: A handheld rescue device, similar to scissors, used to free trapped victims by cutting through metal.

Amkus rams: A handheld rescue device used to free trapped victims by pushing or pulling obstructions, such as dashboard and seats, away from the victim.

Amkus spreader: A handheld rescue device used to free trapped victims by pulling crumpled metal apart.

Backboard: A long, flat, hard surface used to immobilize the spine in the case of neck or spinal injury.

Cardiac arrest: The complete stoppage of the heartbeat.

Defibrillator: An apparatus consisting of alternating currents of electricity, with electrodes to apply the currents to heart muscles in order to shock the muscles into operation. Requires the operator to interpret the heart rhythms and apply the shock at the proper time.

Endotracheal intubation: The insertion of a tube into the trachea, or windpipe, to provide a passage for the air, in case of obstruction.

IV or intravenous: Administered by an injection into the vein.

what does an emergency medical technician do?

If you are sick or hurt, you usually go to a doctor; if you are very sick or hurt you may go to the emergency room of a local hospital. But what if you are alone and unable to drive, or you are too badly injured to travel without receiving medical treatment first? It often happens that an accident or injury victim needs on-the-spot help and safe, rapid transportation to the hospital. *Emergency medical technicians* are the ones who fill this need.

Emergency medical technicians, or EMTs, respond to emergency situations to give immediate attention to people who need it. Whether employed by a hospital, police department, fire department, or private ambulance company, the EMT crew functions as a traveling arm of the emergency room. While on duty, an EMT could be called out for car accidents, heart attacks, work-related injuries, or drug overdoses. He or she might help deliver a baby, treat the victim of a gunshot wound, or revive a child who has nearly drowned. In short, EMTs may find themselves in almost any circumstance that could be called a medical crisis.

Usually working in teams of two, they receive their instructions from the emergency medical dispatcher, who has taken the initial call for help, and drive to the scene in an ambulance. The dispatcher remains in contact with the EMT crew through a two-way radio link. This allows the EMTs to relay important information about the emergency scene and the victims and to receive any further instructions, either from the dispatcher or from a medical staff member. Since they are usually the first trained medical help on the scene, it is very important that they be able to evaluate the situation and make good, logical judgements about what should be done in what order, as well as what should not be done at all. By observing the victim's injuries or symptoms, looking for medic alert tags, and asking the necessary questions, the EMTs determine what action to take and begin first aid treatment. Some more complicated procedures may require the EMT to be in radio contact with hospital staff who can give step-by-step directions.

The types of treatments EMTs can give depend mostly on the level of training and certification they have completed. The first and most common designation is *EMT-Basic* or

EMT-Ambulance. A basic EMT can perform CPR, control bleeding, treat shock victims, apply bandages, splint fractures, and perform automatic defibrillation, which requires no interpretation of EKGs. They are also trained to deal with emotionally disturbed patients and heart attack, poisoning, and burn victims. The *EMT-Intermediate,* who has finished the second level of training, can start an IV, if needed, or use a manual defibrillator to apply electrical shocks to the heart in the case of a cardiac arrest. A growing number of EMTs are choosing to train for the highest level of certification—the *EMT-Paramedic.* With this certification, EMTs are permitted to perform more intensive treatment procedures. Often working in close radio contact with a doctor, they may give drugs intravenously or orally, interpret EKGs, perform endotracheal intubation, and use more complex life-support equipment.

In the case where a victim or victims are trapped, EMTs first give any medical treatment, and then remove the victim, using special equipment such as the Amkus Power Unit. They may need to work closely with the police or the fire department in the rescue attempt.

If patients must be taken from the emergency scene to the hospital, the EMTs may place them on a backboard or stretcher, then carry and lift them into the ambulance. One EMT drives to the hospital, while the other monitors the passenger's vital signs and provides any further care. One of them must notify the hospital emergency room, either directly or through the dispatcher, of how many people are coming in and the type of injuries they have. They also may record the blood pressure, pulse, present condition, and any medical history they know, to assist the hospital.

Once at the hospital, the EMTs help the staff bring in the patient or patients, and assist with any necessary first steps of in-hospital treatment. They then provide their observations to the hospital staff, as well as information about the treatment they have given at the scene and on the way to the hospital.

Finally, each run must also be documented by the EMTs for the records of the provider. Once the run is over, the EMTs are responsible for restocking the ambulance, having equipment sterilized, replacing dirty linens, and making sure that everything is in order for the next run. For the EMT crews to function efficiently and quickly, they must make certain that they have all the equipment and supplies they need, and that the ambulance itself is clean, properly maintained, and filled with gas.

> You have 23 hours, 15 minutes of total boredom and 45 minutes of uncontrollable excitement.

what is it like to be an emergency medical technician?

Kelly Richey is a calm, soft-spoken woman who may save a life as a routine part of a day's work. Kelly works for the hospital in an average-sized Indiana city as an EMT. Although her father had been an EMT for years, Kelly had no intention of working in Emergency Medical Services when she first took the training course. "I just took the course for knowledge," she says. "I didn't really plan to do it as a job." However, during the training course clinicals, when she got the opportunity to actually go on runs, she changed her mind. "I just kind of got the fever," she says, laughing. "I decided it was something I wanted to do. I decided it was something I could do, and I thought if I can do this and I can save a life, I should maybe make this my profession."

Kelly's unit gives its EMTs the option of working two 24-hour shifts or one eight-hour and two 16-hour shifts each week. Kelly has done both, but prefers the shorter hours, which she currently works. This number of hours is fairly common for employees of ambulance firms and hospitals. EMTs who work for fire and police departments may be scheduled for as many as 56 hours per week.

EMT work can be physically demanding. EMTs often work outside, in any type of weather, and most of their time on a run is spent standing, kneeling, bending, and lifting. It is also stressful and often emotionally draining. "I'm pretty tired at the end of a shift," Kelly says. The sort of shift an EMT has depends almost entirely on how many and what type of calls come in. Some shifts are incredibly busy—up to 15 runs, according to Kelly, although not all of those are emergency runs. Her ambulance is frequently dispatched to carry nursing home patients to and from the hospital for treatment, as well as to transport stable patients from the local hospital to the larger medical complex an hour away for scheduled surgeries. Other shifts are considerably slower, with maybe only seven runs in the entire 16 hours.

At Kelly's hospital, the average length of a run is an hour and a half from dispatch till return to ready status. The location of the emergency and its seriousness greatly affect that time frame, however. There is a perception among many people that most calls involve life-or-death situations. That is not really the case, in Kelly's experience.

"On a monthly basis, only about 10 to 15 percent of my runs are actually life-threatening," she says. Other calls run the gamut from serious injury to cut fingers. "You wouldn't believe the stuff I've been called out for," Kelly says. "I've gotten calls for things you could put a Band-Aid on and go right about your business."

No matter what the call, the EMTs must respond. Each team of two has a certain area of the city that it is assigned to, but any team will take any call, if the designated team for that area is already out. Kelly's hospital employs approximately 70 EMTs and paramedics, including several who work on a part-time schedule, and it staffs up to five ambulances during the busiest parts of the day.

All the EMTs in Kelly's unit are required to take a driver training program when they are hired, so they are all qualified to drive. Kelly says that she usually drives on every other run, alternating turns with her partner. The team schedule is set up in such a way that the same partners always work together. That way, they get used to working as a team and communicating with each other. Also, they are able to become accustomed to each others' techniques and work habits and are able to function more efficiently.

Not every emergency requires that a patient be taken to the hospital. If it isn't necessary, or if the patient refuses to go, the EMTs give treatment on-site and return to await the next call. If a patient does need further attention, he or she is transported to the emergency room and unloaded by Kelly and her partner. The attending doctor is briefed on the case and the treatment. Whether a patient is transported or not, each run must be documented on a state-issued form called a run report.

Between calls, Kelly and her co-workers wait in the crewhouse. Complete with a kitchen, living room with TV, and two sleeping rooms, it has a comfortable, homey atmos-phere. The ambulances are kept in an adjoining garage, and during each shift, if time allows, the crew is responsible for washing its vehicle and making sure it is fully stocked and ready to go. "Some people like to restock after every run," Kelly says. She and her partner prefer to take stock at the end of their shift and make sure everything is replaced. "That way you know you're leaving it in good shape for the shift coming on."

Ree Braham is an EMT in Texas and, like Kelly, she feels particularly close to the work. "I believe the work is something that's in your blood," Ree says. "It's an addictive job. When I was seven years old, I just decided I wanted to work on an ambulance." Ree thrives on the gratification she gets from coming to the rescue. "Don't expect any thank-yous," she says, "you're not going to get them. You don't make money, and you can't pay your bills. You're away from your family for 24 hours at a stretch. You do this for the love of helping people. If you want to help somebody, and you've got a compassionate heart, you get gratification."

Ree's work schedule consists of 24 hours on the job and 48 hours off, answering anywhere from two to 24 calls a shift. "Idiot permitting," Ree says, meaning that many of her calls are the result of careless accidents, drinking, and other avoidable mishaps. "It depends on the moon," she says. "On a full moon, you can pretty much count on running around a lot."

Following a particular format, Ree prepares the injured patient for the ambulance ride. "We do everything that an emergency room does, but we're on wheels." The ambulance is stocked with drugs, splinting, bandaging, a defibrillator, oxygen, trauma gear, and other first aid. "A lot of what you do is common sense. If it's bleeding, make it stop. If it's broken, splint it. You can't fix what's broken, but hopefully you can eliminate some of the pain." But Ree is quick to point out that every case is different. "There are no textbook cases. You're going by your wits. It's a lot of improvising, a lot of hair pulling. Meanwhile, you've got family members crying on your shoulder, or they're mad at you because they swear up and down that you've done something wrong."

The TV series *ER* offers a good representation of the work, Ree says. "You see the EMTs bringing the patients in, and you hear them giving the report to the nurses and doctors. You're wheeling in and, depending on how critical your patient is, you're talking while you're wheeling and you're giving compressions and bagging the patient. If they're bleeding out, you've got IVs going, and you're holding pressure." Ree has seen many dramatic situations over the years, and recalls a particularly frightening car accident which involved an infant, icy roads, and drunk driving. "The mother was dead and the baby had been ejected from the car seat out of the vehicle. We found the car seat upside down out in a field, probably 100 feet from the car. When we finally got up to it, there was no noise. We flipped the seat over. The baby was sleeping. We worked the baby up from head to toe and transported, and the hospital released him. There was nothing wrong with him." Fortunately, not every day is filled beginning to end with drama. "You have 23 hours, 15 minutes of total boredom," Ree says, "and 45 minutes of uncontrollable excitement."

have I got what it takes to be an emergency medical technician?

EMTs regularly encounter situations that many people would find upsetting. Because they are faced with unpleasant scenes, crises, and even death, they need a certain emotional capability for coping. They must have stable personalities and be able to keep their heads in circumstances of extreme stress.

The stress level is the hardest thing about the job for Kelly. She also warns that the potential EMT must be able to deal with death. "There have been times when the family members have hung out in the E.D. [Emergency Department] after we brought patients in and that really gets to me," she says. "I feel like they're looking at me and saying 'Why didn't you do more?' when I know I've done everything I could do." At Kelly's hospital, the staff has initiated a debriefing process to help EMTs work through a bad experience on a run. It's important that the EMT be able to cope with such bad experiences without suffering lasting negative results. The stress and the emotional strain can take its toll; there is a high turnover rate in the Emergency Medical Services field.

"You're holding people's lives in your hands," Ree says. "You've got to have a strong mind set because some of your patients are going to die. You can't save everyone. We're the first on the scene, we make all the decisions. When we're the only ones there, we're the difference between life and death."

Such responsibilities can often be difficult to handle. "You can get burned out," Ree says.

"They used to say the average longevity for someone in the job was seven years. I'm on year eight." Ree relies on the camaraderie of her co-workers in tough times. "The people you work with are a very tight-knit family," she says, "which can be hard on your own family members, because you start confiding more in your co-workers. A lot of marriages break up in this career field. Families don't always understand why at 3:00 AM you're willing to dart out of your bed to go help someone else."

how do I become an emergency medical technician?

All states offer EMT training programs consisting of 100 to 120 hours of training, usually followed by 10 hours of internship in a hospital emergency room. To be admitted into a training program, you must be 18 years old, be a high school graduate, and hold a valid driver's license. Exact requirements do vary slightly in different states and in different courses.

Ree has been through a Basic-EMT course and an Intermediate-EMT course, as well as a semester of paramedic school. The course work and registry has proven extremely important to Ree. "You've got to be able to handle anything that comes your way," she says. "The classes are very compact for what we do. You've got to pay attention."

education

High School

A high school diploma, or its equivalent, is required for admission into the EMT training program. While most high school studies will not yield experience with emergency medical care, health classes may offer a good introduction to some of the concepts and terms used by EMTs. It may also be possible to take courses in first aid or CPR through the local Red Cross or other organizations. This sort of training can be a valuable background, giving you advance preparation for the actual EMT program. Some science classes, such as biology, can also be helpful in helping you become familiar with the human body and its various systems.

Driver's education is recommended as well for anyone who is interested in a career as an EMT. The ability to drive safely and sensibly in all different types of road conditions, and a firm knowledge of traffic laws is essential to

To be a successful emergency medical technician, you should

- Have a desire to serve people
- Be emotionally stable and clearheaded
- Have good manual dexterity and agility
- Have strong written and oral communication skills
- Be able to lift and carry up to 125 pounds
- Have good eyesight and color vision

the driver of an ambulance. English is a desirable subject for the potential EMT, since it is important to have good communication skills, both written and verbal, along with the capacity to read and interpret well. Finally, depending on what area of the country you might work in, it might be very helpful to have a background in a foreign language, such as Spanish, to assist in dealing with patients who speak little or no English.

Postsecondary Training

For the high school graduate with a strong interest in Emergency Medical Services, the next step is formal training. The standard training course was designed by the Department of Transportation and is often offered by police, fire, and health departments. It may also be offered by hospitals or as a nondegree course in colleges, particularly community colleges.

The program teaches you how to deal with many common emergencies. You learn how to deal with bleeding, cardiac arrest, childbirth, broken bones, and choking. You will also become familiar with the specialized equipment used in many emergency situations, such as backboards, stretchers, fracture kits, splints, and oxygen systems.

If you live in an area that offers several different courses, it might be a good idea to research all the options, since certain courses may emphasize different aspects of the job. After completing the basic course, there are training sessions available to teach more specialized skills, such as removing trapped victims, driving an ambulance, or dispatching.

EMTs who have graduated from the basic program may later decide to work toward reaching a higher level of training in the EMS field. For example, the EMT-Intermediate course provides 35 to 55 hours of further instruction to allow the EMT to give more extensive treatment, and the EMT-Paramedic course offers an additional 750 to 2,000 hours of education and experience.

certification or licensing

After you have successfully completed the training program, you have the opportunity to work toward becoming certified or registered with the National Registry of Emergency Medical Technicians (NREMT). (See "How Do I Learn More?") All states have some sort of certification requirement of their own, but 39 states accept registration in NREMT, in place of their own certification. Applicants should check the specific regulations and requirements for their state.

Whether registering with the NREMT or being certified through a state program, the applicant for an EMT-Basic title will be required to take and pass a written examination, as well as a practical demonstration of skills. The written segment will usually be a multiple-choice exam of roughly 150 questions. After passing the exam, EMTs usually work on a basic support vehicle for six months before certification is awarded.

While it is not always required in every state that EMTs become certified or registered, certification, at least, is a common requirement for employment in most states. It certainly is recommended, as it will open up many more job possibilities. The higher the level of training an EMT has reached, the more valuable he or she will become as an employee.

EMTs who are registered at the Basic level may choose to work on fulfilling the requirements for an EMT-Intermediate certification. After the mandatory 35 to 55 hours of classroom training, as well as further clinical and field experience, your must take and pass another examination. To earn paramedic status, you must already be registered as at least an EMT-Basic. You must complete a training program that lasts approximately nine months, as well as hospital and field internships, pass a written and practical examination, and work as a paramedic for six months before receiving actual certification.

All EMTs must renew their registration every one to two years, depending upon the state's requirement. In order to do so, you must be working at that time as an EMT, and meet the continuing education requirement, which is usually 20 to 25 hours of lecture and practical skills training.

labor unions
~ɅⱯ~ɅⱯ~

Some EMTs may have the opportunity to join a union when they become employed. The unionization of this industry has been fairly recent and is not yet widespread. Therefore, membership in a union will not likely be a requirement for employment, and may not even be offered as an option. However, the

Related Jobs

The job of EMT is similar to many other positions in the medical field in that there are very specific procedures and treatments that EMTs are trained and authorized to perform. The U.S. Department of Labor classifies Emergency Medical Technicians under the headings *Patient Care* (GOE) and *Healthcare Practitioners and Technical* (O*NET-SOC). Also under these headings are people who work under the supervision of a doctor or registered nurse to assist in medical treatment in a variety of areas. The areas of specialization that these medical assistants, or aides, could work in include orthopedics, psychiatry, optometry, dentistry, occupational therapy, physical therapy, podiatry, and surgery.

Specific related jobs include:
Ambulance attendants
Chiropractor's assistants
First-aid attendants
Licensed practical nurses
Nurse's aides
Occupational therapy aides
Optometric assistants
Physical therapy aides
Podiatric assistants
Psychiatric aides

EMT unions are growing rapidly, particularly in the public sector.

One of the principal unions of EMTs and paramedics is the International Association of EMTs and Paramedics, which is a division of the National Association of Government Employees, AFL-CIO. The other is the National Emergency Employee Organization Network.

EMTs with membership in a union pay weekly or monthly dues, and receive in return a package of services designed to improve working conditions, which include collective bargaining for pay and benefits, governmental lobbying, and legal representation.

who will hire me?
~ɅⱯ~ɅⱯ~

Kelly was lucky when she started to look for a job as an EMT. "I just went to the hospital and filled out their application," she says. "They called me in for an interview and I got the job. I didn't even have to apply anywhere else." Not everyone will be lucky enough to get a job on the first try, but currently the statistics are in the favor of EMTs. The demand exceeds the number of persons trained to do the work.

After serving in the Air Force, Ree went to work on a county ambulance in Idaho. "In Idaho," she says, "you could be a driver for an ambulance if all you had was CPR certification. But you couldn't do anything more than drive." Meanwhile, she enrolled in school and took the courses required for EMT work.

Nearly one-half of EMTs work in private ambulance services. An estimated third are in municipal fire, police, or rescue departments, and one-fifth work in hospitals or medical centers. Also, there are many who volunteer, particularly in more rural areas, where there often are no paid EMTs at all.

Because new graduates will be in heavy competition for full-time employment, it may be easier to break into the field on a part-time or volunteer basis. By beginning as a volunteer or part-timer, the new EMT can gain hours of valuable experience, which can be useful in landing a paid, full-time position later. The competition is also stiffer for beginning EMTs in the public sector, such as police and fire departments. Beginners may have more success in finding a position in a private ambulance company. There are also some opportunities for work that lie somewhat off the more beaten path. For example, many industrial plants have EMTs in their safety departments,

and security companies sometimes prefer to hire EMTs for their staff. Most amusement parks and other public attractions employ EMTs in their first aid stations, and in many cities there are private companies that hire EMTs to provide medical coverage for rock concerts, fairs, sporting events, and other gatherings.

One good source of employment leads for an EMT graduate is the school or agency that provided his or her training. Job openings may sometimes be listed in the newspaper classifieds under "Emergency Medical Technician," "EMT," "Emergency Medical Services," "Ambulance Technician," "Rescue Squad," or "Health Care." Many professional journals, and national and state EMS newsletters list openings. Finally, the National Association of Emergency Medical Technicians (NAEMT) provides members with a professional placement service and a bimonthly newsletter featuring employment information. (See "How Do I Learn More?")

It is also a good idea to apply directly to any local ambulance services, hospitals, fire departments, and police departments. The best approach is usually to send a current resume, complete with references, and a letter of inquiry. The letter should consist of a brief description of your situation and interests, and a request for an application. Most agencies have specific applications and employment procedures, so the resume and cover letter alone is not necessarily adequate. It is important to remember that most employers will accept applications to keep on file even if there is no specific job open at the time.

Joe Connelly worked as a paramedic in the Hell's Kitchen neighborhood of New York City for nearly 10 years, then wrote of his experiences in the novel *Bringing Out the Dead*. The novel was also made into a film by Martin Scorsese, starring Nicolas Cage. Both the book and the film have been praised by many EMTs as realistic portrayals of the demands of the work.

where can I go from here?

Kelly decided that she wanted to pursue more advanced levels of training shortly after she started working as an EMT. At present, she has already passed the paramedic training course and is getting ready to test for her certification. Eventually, she says, she might like to get into EMS education and train EMTs to do the job she does now.

Moving into the field of education and training is only one of several possible career options. For an EMT who is interested in advancement, usually the first move is to become certified as a paramedic. Once at that level, there are further opportunities in the area of administration. Moving into an administrative position usually means leaving field-work and patient care for a more routine office job. An EMT-Paramedic can pursue such positions as supervisor, operations manager, administrative director, or executive director of emergency services. Or, like Kelly, he or she may be interested in a career in education and training. Also, several new areas of specialization in EMS have recently received more emphasis. Quality control, safety and risk management, communications, and flight operations are some examples of these up-and-coming administrative areas.

Some EMTs move out of health care entirely and into sales and marketing of emergency medical equipment. Often, their experience and familiarity with the field make them effective and valuable salespersons. Finally, some EMTs decide to go back to school and become registered nurses, physicians, or other types of health workers. Kelly has seen EMTs take many different paths. "One woman who was a paramedic when I started at the hospital is a doctor now," she says, "so you can see how far you can go with it."

what are the salary ranges?

According to the *Occupational Outlook Handbook*, median annual earnings for EMTs were $20,290 in 1998. Those in the lowest 10 percent made less than $12,700, while those in the highest 10 percent earned more than $34,480.

Emergency Medical Services, a journal of emergency care, published data in 1999 compiled from all 50 states, including salary estimates. In New Jersey, a Basic-EMT made between $12,000 and $23,000, while a paramedic made between $20,000 and $30,000. In South Carolina, the annual salary for a Basic-EMT was between $16,000 and $22,000; for an Intermediate-EMT, between $17,000 and $23,000; for a paramedic, between $19,000 and $27,000. Indiana reported annual salaries of $10,000 to $22,000 for Basic-EMTs; $10,000 to $24,000 for Intermediate; and $12,000 to $40,000 for paramedics. In Washington state, the salaries ran from $21,000 to $47,500 for both Basic- and Intermediate-EMTs, while paramedics made between $31,000 and $52,000.

The most significant factor in determining salary is whether the EMT is employed in the private or the public sector. Private ambulance companies and hospitals traditionally offer the

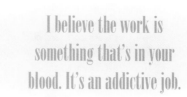

lowest pay, while fire departments pay better. Benefits may include life insurance, major medical insurance, uniform allowance, retirement or pension plans, and paid seminars and conferences.

what is the job outlook?

Employment opportunities for EMTs are expected to grow much faster than average for all occupations, according to the *Occupational Outlook Handbook*. One of the reasons for the overall growth is simply that the population is growing, thus producing the need for more medical personnel. Another factor is that the proportion of elderly people, who are the biggest users of emergency medical services, is growing in many communities. Finally, many jobs will become available because, as noted earlier, the EMT profession does have a high turnover rate.

The job opportunities for EMTs will depend partly upon the community where you wish to work. In the larger, more metropolitan areas, where the majority of paid EMT positions are found, the opportunities will probably be best. In many smaller communities, financial difficulties are causing many not-for-profit hospitals and municipal police, fire, and rescue squads to cut back on staff. Because of this, there are likely to be fewer job possibilities in the public sector. However, since many of the organizations suffering cutbacks opt to contract with a private ambulance company for service to their community, opportunities with these private companies may increase.

The trend toward private ambulance companies, which have historically paid less, is an important one, since it is likely to influence where the jobs will be found, as well as what the average pay is. One reason for the growth of the private ambulance industry is the growth of managed-care systems. The reason this affects the EMT profession is that medical transportation is one of the major services typically contracted for by managed-care providers. As managed care gains popularity, there is a greater need for the private ambulance contractors.

Because of America's growing concern with health care costs, the person considering a career as an EMT should be aware of the fact that health care reforms may affect all medical professions to some extent. Also, as mentioned before, the increase and growth of private ambulance services will almost definitely change the face of the emergency services field. In looking at a future as an emergency medical technician, both of these factors are worth keeping in mind.

how do I learn more?

professional organizations

For a list of accredited educational programs and general information on the health care industry, contact:
American Medical Association
Division of Allied Health Education and
Accreditation
515 North State Street
Chicago, IL 60610
312-464-5000
http://www.ama-assn.org

To learn about union membership:
International Association of EMTs and Paramedics
159 Burgin Parkway
Quincy, MA 02169
617-376-0220
info@iaep.org
http://www.iaep.org

For information about educational programs:
National Association of Emergency Medical Technicians
408 Monroe Street
Clinton, MS 39056-4210
800-346-2368
info@naemt.org
http://www.naemt.org

To learn about national registration:
National Registry of Emergency Medical Technicians
Box 29233
6610 Busch Boulevard
Columbus, OH 43229
614-888-4484
http://www.nremt.org

bibliography

Following is a sampling of materials relating to the professional concerns and development of emergency medical technicians.

Aehlert, Barbara, and Garret Olson. *Aehlert's EMT Basic Study Guide.* New York, NY: Lippincott Williams & Wilkins, 1998.

Copass, Michael K., et al. *EMT Manual.* Kent, UK: W. B. Saunders, 1998.

Mistovich, Joseph J., et al. *Prehospital Emergency Care.* Paramus, NJ: Prentice-Hall, 1999.

Sanders, Mick J. *Mosby's Paramedic Textbook.* St. Louis, MO: Mosby, Inc., 2000.

Sheehy, Susan Budassi, and Gail Pisarcik Lenehan. *Manual of Emergency Care.* St. Louis, MO: Mosby-Year Book, 1999.

Emergency Room Doctors

Definition

Emergency room doctors give immediate care to critically ill or injured persons, usually in hospital emergency rooms.

Alternative Job Titles

Emergency medicine specialists

High School Subjects

Biology
Chemistry
Mathematics
Physics

Personal Skills

Helping/teaching
Technical/scientific

Salary range

$125,000 to $195,000 to $250,000+

Educational requirements

Medical degree

Certification or Licensing

Recommended (certification)
Required by all states (licensing)

Outlook

About as fast as the average

GOE
02.03.01
O*NET-SOC
29-1063.00

An ambulance arrives at the emergency room (ER) of Norwegian American Hospital, on Chicago's west side. In the vehicle is a man in his 50s who began having chest pains while playing basketball. The paramedics and orderlies are bringing in the patient when Dr. Joseph Cortez walks in. He makes a brief examination and speaks to the paramedics who brought the patient, Roland Davies, to the hospital. For a moment, everything is still as the emergency room staff waits for Dr. Cortez's instructions. Then he speaks. "OK, possible heart attack. Let's get an EKG going and alert the Cardiac Unit. Has someone called the family?" He turns to the patient. "Hi, I'm Dr. Cortez. Mr. Davies, are there any heart problems in your family?"

The man tells him that there is heart disease on his mother's side. The EKG confirms the doctor's worst fears: the man is having a heart attack.

"Nurse, start an IV, please, TPA [a blood-thinning drug]." He glances at Mr. Davies. He is pale and sweaty, in obvious pain. "Let's add 10 milligrams of Demerol, also."

Minutes pass. The Cardiac Unit calls down to say that they are ready to admit Mr. Davies. Dr. Cortez wants to make sure everything is under control before he sends his patient upstairs. He asks the technician running the EKG for the latest readings. The readings show that the electrical activity in Mr. Davies' heart is almost back to normal. The TPA has broken up the blood clot that caused the heart attack. There would be days in the hospital and a long rehabilitation for Mr. Davies, but he is out of danger now. With the crisis past and the patient resting comfortably, Dr. Cortez allows Mr. Davies to be transported to the Cardiac Unit. The ER team can relax—at least until the next patient comes through its doors.

what does an emergency room doctor do?

Emergency room doctors (ERDs) are specialists who treat victims of accidents or sudden illness. They are responsible for these persons from the time they come into the emergency room (or other facility) until they are medically stable and can be either admitted to the hospital or sent home.

In low-income neighborhoods, where people are less likely to have medical insurance or a family doctor, emergency rooms often function as non-emergency clinics. ERDs may see a baby with a bad cold, stitch up a cut lip, admit a person with chest pains, and treat a gunshot wound, all in the same day. Not all emergency rooms have the same capabilities. In every case, though, the ERD's job is the same—stabilize patients until they can be moved safely.

As important as emergency medicine is, it is relatively new as a distinct medical specialty. The first specialist residency program was established in 1970, and the American Board of Medical Specialists authorized the first certification tests in 1979. Emergency rooms need specially qualified doctors because external injuries may hide a life-threatening injury. Internal injuries to vital organs may be overlooked by a doctor not trained to spot them. Medical professionals call the first hour after an accident the "Golden Hour." If a patient can make it to treatment within that hour, his or her chances of surviving even the most serious medical problems increase dramatically. A web of highly skilled professionals, including emergency medical technicians and emergency room nurses, works to ensure the quickest possible transport and treatment of these cases. At the center of it all is the emergency room doctor.

ERDs do not just see dramatic cases. They also handle emergencies that are not life-threatening. There are many minor accidents requiring treatment that can be taken care of in the ER without having to admit the patient into the hospital. Sprained ankles are wrapped or splinted, cuts are stitched, and prescriptions are given for minor illnesses or for pain.

No matter what the patient's complaint, the ERD must make quick, accurate judgments about the nature of the problem and the correct treatment. This process includes taking the patient's medical history, ordering tests, and giving medication. In addition to these duties, ERDs keep a running account of everything that occurs in the ER: tests ordered, test results, drugs administered, and any changes in the patient's condition.

ERDs do not work alone, of course. They operate as the head of a team. While on duty, the ERD is responsible for everything that goes on in the ER. ERDs must be able to work well with others and inspire the confidence of the people working with them.

lingo to learn

Electrocardiogram (ECG/EKG): A diagnostic tool used to monitor the electrical activity of the heart.

Managed care: A philosophy of health care that tries to keep medical costs down through education and preventive medicine.

Outpatient: Patient treated at the hospital but not admitted for extended care.

Residency: The period that doctors work in hospitals after medical school to become specialists: three years for emergency room doctors.

Tissue plasminogen activator (TPA): A blood-thinning drug used to treat heart conditions.

Emergency room doctors must be able to work quickly and accurately under stress. The pressure can be intense. At times, several patients will be waiting for treatment at once and the doctor may have to move back and forth between them. Doctors must be ready to make decisions that can mean the difference between life or death. Communications with staff, patients, and family are critical. Instructions to staff must be clear. Patients are often the only source of such vital information as their medical history and the circumstances of their injury. The ERD must be able to gain their trust quickly so that no time is wasted. It is also the doctor's job to speak to the patients' loved ones, letting them know what is happening and why. In order to keep everything running smoothly, ERDs must balance all these responsibilities.

what is it like to be an emergency room doctor?

Television and movies have given people outside the medical profession a glimpse into the workings of the emergency room. The life and death nature of emergency medicine makes for dramatic, if not always accurate, entertainment. Dr. Joseph Cortez knows where these fictional accounts stray from the real story. "Sometimes they keep people in the ER for hours," he laughs. "By that time, we have them admitted and up on the ward, or we have treated them and sent them home. Our job is to stabilize emergency patients, treat them if possible, and move them on."

Ask Joseph what a typical day in the ER is like, and he has trouble coming up with a simple answer. "There really is no typical day," he says. "Each day brings new cases, and they are all different." For those drawn to the field, part of the attraction of emergency medicine is the variety of cases they will see. Emergency rooms are prohibited by law from denying treatment to anyone. As the health care provider of last resort, what Joseph calls "the safety net," emergency rooms doctors treat more different types of illness and injury than any other type of doctor.

Treating a variety of cases is just one of the many ways emergency room doctors' activities different from those of other doctors. For one thing, ERDs work set shifts of eight, 10, or 12 hours, depending on the hospital. The ER is staffed 24 hours a day, seven days a week, so some weekend and night shifts are required. In comparison, doctors with regular practices work very long hours, and surgeons and other specialists may be called in to the hospital at any time. "It's one of the nicest things about ER medicine," explains Joseph. "There is a lot of time off, and it's your time. No pagers going off in the middle of the night." According to Dr. Glenn Murakami, director of emergency services at Swedish Covenant Hospital in Chicago, a typical ERD works four or five shifts a week, depending on the length of the shift.

The work is physically demanding. The stress of making life and death decisions takes a physical and psychological toll. While the ERD's work schedule (the number of shifts a person works in a given week) is very predictable, the workload (the number of cases seen during a given shift) is not. "A busy day is a long day," says Joseph. "There are days where you're on your feet for the whole shift, always moving. Sometimes you don't even have time to eat."

The stress is great at times, and the volume of patients is high, but ER doctors tend to remain in emergency medicine for a long time. Dr. Murakami has been an emergency room doctor and administrator for 22 years. "The type of person that is attracted to it [emergency medicine] will usually continue and be committed," he states.

In addition to treating patients, ERDs are responsible for the running of the ER on their shift. It is not just a matter of giving orders. Nurses, technicians, and paramedics are highly trained professionals in their own right. No doctor can afford to be without their trust and confidence. The ERD is still the one in charge, but making the emergency room click takes leadership in professional knowledge and in behavior. "Everyone takes their cues from you," says Joseph.

The emergency room is often a place of high drama, which comes from the nature of emergency medicine, where lives hang in the balance. While this adrenaline-charged atmosphere makes emergency medicine unique and exciting, it also means that emergency room staff deals with death on a regular basis. Sometimes, the best efforts of the ERD and the medical staff are not enough. It is the doctor's duty to tell the person's loved ones that they have lost a son, a mother, or a friend. "It's hard sometimes," Joseph admits, "but you have to be compassionate and still maintain your composure. You can't allow one case to affect your whole day, not when there are other cases to treat."

Emergency room doctors see new patients every day. Many, like Joseph, thrive on the vari-

in-depth

Emergency Medicine

Though emergency medicine is one of the 24 recognized medical specialties, experts in the field say there is still work to be done educating the medical community and the public about the need for good emergency care. Emergency departments are expensive to run and maintain, and not every hospital needs to operate its own emergency room.

One way of ensuring adequate emergency service is to categorize emergency rooms by their capabilities. Level I ERs (also known as trauma centers) have surgeons on duty around the clock. They can handle the most seriously injured patients. Level II hospitals accept ambulance traffic but have to call in surgeons and specialists as needed. Level III units are designed to take "walk-ins," those who arrive on their own without calling an ambulance.

This cooperation allows for maximum coverage of emergency service with a minimum of cost. The system is not, however, universally accepted. Some hospitals use their emergency departments as drawing cards in competition with other hospitals for business. This can lead to overcapacity in areas where hospitals compete, like big cities.

Emergency care is still evolving. Economic and political factors, along with purely medical considerations, will determine what emergency care looks like in the next century.

ety. ERDs see patients for an hour or two at the most. There is no time to develop a relationship. Doctors who have family practices, doing checkups, giving shots, etc., get to know their patients over a period of years. They sometimes treat two or three generations of the same family. Doctors who want to develop long-term relationships with their patients will not be able to do it in emergency medicine.

The ER is medicine in motion. High volume, high stress, high speed, and to many, highly satisfying. "Sometimes you have to say, 'I don't know what the problem is,' so all you can do is make sure they are stable and admit them. The other specialists have to figure it out," says Joseph. "Other times it's instant gratification. The patient has a sprained ankle, put a splint on it, send them home. You see the whole process."

have I got what it takes to be an emergency room doctor?

Perhaps the most critical trait for those wanting to become doctors is a powerful drive to succeed. Demanding professions require exceptional individuals, and few professions are as demanding as emergency room medicine. Doctors first and foremost must be excellent students. They must master vast amounts of information, and the learning does not stop with graduation. They have to learn new information constantly. "You are always going back to school to learn about new techniques and equipment," explains Joseph. "It's a requirement for staying certified."

Hard work and a keen mind are only the beginning. As noted before, ERDs are subjected to enormous stress. How they deal with stress will determine how successful they are in the emergency room. They must project a calm, confident manner in a crisis, because the staff, the patient, and the patient's family are looking to the doctor for answers and support. They must remain calm in the midst of emotional turmoil, and be ready to make decisions without consulting with other physicians. ERDs must have fairly strong egos. They must believe in themselves and in their abilities. Emergency medical situations push doctors to the limit, and persons wishing to work in this atmosphere must be prepared to give their maximum effort.

Communication skills are an important part of any doctor's practice, but the special requirements of emergency medicine make them vital to the ERD. Whether giving instructions to staff, getting vital information from a patient, or consulting with family members, the ERD is always communicating. Half of communication is listening, so ERDs must be able to concentrate in the midst of confusion. According to Joseph, how you project yourself nonverbally is very important, especially when dealing with patients. "You don't have much time to get [medical] history, which you need to start treatment. It's important to get them comfortable, so that they trust you and start working with you right away."

how do I become an emergency room doctor?

Doctors are among the most highly educated professionals in the world. A high school diploma, four-year undergraduate degree, four years of medical school, and a three-year residency in emergency medicine are standard for becoming an emergency room doctor. Beginning with medical school, competition for available positions is tremendous. Many more applications are received by medical schools than there are positions available. For example, for the 2000 academic year, 37,092 people applied for acceptance to the 125 accredited medical schools in the United States. Of that number only 16,301 ended up enrolled in programs, according to the Association of American Medical Colleges. Residency programs for ERDs are also very competitive. The National Resident Matching Program (NRMP) reported that 23,981 individuals participated in the program in March of 2001. At that time 1,001 first-year emergency medicine positions were offered. Achieving excellent grades in college is your first step on the road to acceptance at the medical school of your choice.

education

High School

You can begin preparing for medical school studies while you are still in high school. Get a solid background in the sciences by taking core courses, including biology, chemistry, and physics. Remember, though, that no area of study should be neglected. Take mathematics

A sampling of numbers from around the country shows that strong competition for openings in medical schools isn't a myth. The Association of American Medical Colleges reported these statistics for the fall of 2000:

University	Applications	Enrolled	Percent
Stanford	5,946	86	1.4%
Texas A&M	2,294	64	2.7%
Yale	4,643	106	2.2%

classes such as algebra, geometry, and trigonometry, as well as history and computer science courses. English classes will help you develop those important communication skills. Unlike some professions, where high school merely gives a basis for later learning, medical students will use their science training continuously throughout their schooling and into their professional lives. "At each level, through the first two years of medical school, the emphasis is on science, science, science," says Joseph. This is not to say that academics are the only area you should concentrate on. You should strive to be well-rounded at all levels. Doctors have to really want to help people. The best students do not always make the best doctors, not if they cannot relate to their patients. Volunteering in a local hospital is a good way to see if medicine is the career for you, and it helps develop aspects of your personality that academic studies don't.

Postsecondary Training

It is not necessary for students to follow a premedical course of study in college. Many future doctors majored in liberal arts or other fields before going on to medical school. Nevertheless, you will need to take all the required sciences, including organic and inorganic chemistry, biology, microbiology, and anatomy. Again, it is important for students to maintain good grades. According to the Emergency Medicine Residents' Association (EMRA), some students interested in emergency medicine get a taste of the field by becoming emergency medical technicians while still in college. One requirement for entering medical school is to take the Medical College Admission Test (MCAT). Students often take the MCAT in their third year of undergraduate study. MCAT test scores, college transcripts, and letters of recommendation are sent in with their applications to medical schools. At least one interview with a member of the college is usually required. In addition to academics, medical schools consider factors such as personality, character, and extracurricular activities, such as volunteer work in health care settings.

Only a fraction of the tens of thousands of applicants who apply to American medical schools are accepted. Here is where being more than just a good student becomes critical. Joseph explains. "They don't want people who are just bookworms—anyone can do that. Medical schools and residency programs are looking for people that are diverse, [who are] well-versed in a variety of areas." He recommends getting involved in basic research while in college as one way of separating yourself from the crowd.

The first two years of medical school are devoted to classroom and laboratory work. Students study more science, including pharmacology, immunology, anatomy, and chemistry. In addition, they take classes in psychology, medical ethics, and law, and they learn how to recognize symptoms and take patient histories. In the third and fourth years, students continue classroom work, but they also begin seeing patients under the watchful eye of a teaching doctor. "The second half of medical school was both the hardest and the most fun," remembers Joseph. The new responsibilities of patient care were stressful but a welcome change from classroom and laboratory, he says. During this time, students work as interns in different areas of medicine: pediatrics, internal medicine, family practice, obstetrics and gynecology, psychiatry, and surgery.

To be a successful emergency room doctor, you should

- Work well under pressure
- Be able to make quick, accurate decisions
- Have excellent communication skills
- Be a good leader
- Be able to work well with a variety of people

certification or licensing

Certification, given by the American Board of Emergency Medicine (ABEM), is not currently required for this work, but it is highly recommended. With ABEM certification you will enhance your chances of getting the best jobs and advancing in the profession. In addition, some in the field feel that ABEM certification should be mandatory, and this is likely to happen in the future. To get certification, ABEM requires emergency room doctors to have completed a three-year residency and pass both written and oral exams. Currently, certification by ABEM is good for 10 years before you must renew, but starting in 2003 it will be on a seven-year cycle. Requirements for recertification include having a valid medical license, completing certain self-assessment tests, and passing the Continuous Certification (Con-Cert) exam. This is in addition to the continuing education requirements all doctors must satisfy. For the American College of Emergency Physicians, the largest organization of ERDs in the nation, this means 150 hours of approved education every three years.

All states require doctors to be licensed before they can practice. In order to be licensed, doctors must have graduated from medical school, passed the licensing test, and completed their residency.

scholarships and grants

Scholarships and grants are often available from individual institutions, state agencies, and special-interest organizations. Many students finance their medical education through the Armed Forces Health Professions Scholarship Program. Each branch of the military participates in this program, paying students' tuitions in exchange for military service. Contact your local recruiting office for more information on this program. The National Health Service Corps Scholarship Program also provides money for students in return for service. Another source for financial aid, scholarship, and grant information is the Association of American Medical Colleges. Remember to request information early for eligibility, application requirements, and deadlines.

Association of American Medical Colleges
2450 N Street, NW
Washington, DC 20037-1126
202-828-0400
http://www.aamc.org

National Health Service Corps Scholarship Program
11300 Rockville Pike, Suite 608
Rockville, MD 20852
800-638-0824
http://www.fedmoney.org/grants/93288-00.htm

Specific information on financial aid programs can be found at:
Financing Your Medical Education
http://www.aamc.org/students/financing/start.htm

How do medical students pay for school?

According to the Association of American Medical Colleges, approximately 81 percent of medical school students borrow money to help pay for their education expenses. For those graduating in 2000, the median amount of their debt was more than $95,000.

who will hire me?

For those able to withstand the rigors of becoming an emergency room doctor, there is probably a job waiting for them when they finish. "In your third year of residency, you start to get stacks of mail from recruiters," says Dr. Joseph. There are other ways to learn about job openings as well. The Illinois College of Emergency Physicians, for example, holds a combination seminar and job fair to help ERDs understand the hiring process and to let recruiters and doctors meet. There is more competition for choice locations in the West and Southwest, but for now, things look good.

Not surprisingly, most emergency medicine specialists work in hospital emergency rooms. They can either work directly for the hospital or for an outside organization that runs a hospital's emergency room on a contract basis. Emergency medicine is not practiced in hospitals exclusively, however. Any place where the potential for an emergency medical situation is high is a potential place of employment. The EMRA lists nursing homes and automobile racetracks as places employing its members.

where can I go from here?

Many emergency room doctors remain in the emergency room for years. Others, like Dr. Glenn Murakami, elect to move into administration. Administrators are responsible for the smooth operation of the entire emergency department, either for the hospital or for one of the growing number of contract operators. In fact, some doctors choose to go into business for themselves as emergency service providers to hospitals. Because of the high cost of providing such services, these entrepreneurs commonly pool their resources with other doctors to form partnerships. They then hire doctors to work the actual shifts. Another avenue is emergency services, which include the whole range of emergency medical planning, from arranging radio networks for ambulance-to-hospital communication, to coordinating plans in the event of a large-scale emergency, like a natural disaster.

Teaching or medical research is also an option. Senior doctors may take on responsibility for supervising residents while still working in the ER. Doctors also can advance by publishing their research in professional journals.

what are the salary ranges?

All doctors are well paid. Specialists, like emergency room doctors, are even more highly valued. According to a study commissioned by the EMRA, ERDs can expect to start at about $125,000 per year. The American Medical Association reports that the median annual income for those working in emergency medicine is $195,000. Top earners in this field may make $250,000 or more per year. These numbers are for doctors working as emergency room doctors. Salaries for administrators, emergency medical services planners, and teachers vary widely.

what is the job outlook?

In general, physicians can expect faster than average employment growth through the next decade, according to the U.S. Department of Labor. The Society for Academic Emergency Medicine reports that there are many opportunities for those entering the field of emergency medicine. The society estimates that there are more than 25,000 doctors currently working in emergency departments but only about half are board certified in emergency medicine. Each year approximately 1,000 residents graduate in this specialty, but this number is only enough to replace the number of retiring certified emergency room doctors. The society predicts that it will take several decades before all those without certification are replaced by certified emergency physicians.

Another factor that may influence employment outlook is the increasing control managed care has on the medical industry. Managed care companies run hospitals and insurance programs for a flat fee, then cut costs to make a profit. One area frequently targeted as in need of trimming expenses is the emergency room. Nevertheless, emergency room visits remain high. Keeping in mind that the National Center for Health Statistics reported that there were over 100 million emergency room visits in 1998 and that accidents are still the leading cause of death for people age 44 and under, the need for emergency medicine is clear. While there is no consensus as to the long-term effects of managed care on the industry, it is reasonable to project the job outlook for those in emergency medicine should be at least as fast as the average.

how do I learn more?

professional organizations

Following are organizations that provide information on a career as an emergency room doctor.

American College of Emergency Physicians
1125 Executive Circle
Irving, TX 75038-2522
800-798-1822
http://www.acep.org

Association of Emergency Physicians
127 Branchaw Boulevard
New Lenox, IL 60451
800-449-4237
aep@interaccess.com
http://www.aep.org

Society for Academic Emergency Medicine
901 North Washington Avenue
Lansing, MI 48906-5137
517-485-5484
saem@saem.org
http://www.saem.org

bibliography

Following is a sampling of materials relating to the professional concerns and development of emergency room doctors.

Aehlert, Barbara and Garret Olson. *Aehlert's EMT Basic Study Guide.* New York, NY: Lippincott Williams & Wilkins, 1998.

Copass, Michael K., et al. *EMT Manual.* 3rd Edition. Kent, UK: W. B. Saunders, 1998.

Handysides, Gail. *Triage in Emergency Practice.* St. Louis, MO: Mosby-Yearbook, 1996.

Meyer-Avian, Peter. *You are the ER Doc! True-to-Life Cases for You to Treat.* New York, NY: Cetacean Press, 2000.

Mistovich, Joseph J. et al. *Prehospital Emergency Care,* 6th Edition. Paramus, NJ: Prentice-Hall, 1999.

Rothrock, Steven G. *Tarascon Adult Emergency Pocketbook.* Loma Linda, CA: Tarascon Press, 1999.

Rothrock, Steven G. *Tarascon Pediatric Emergency Pocketbook.* 3rd Edition. Loma Linda, CA: Tarascon Press, 2000.

Sachs, Dan, ed. *Emergency Room, Lives Saved and Lost: Doctors Tell Their Stories.* Boston, MA: Little, Brown & Company, 1996.

Sanders, Mick J. *Mosby's Paramedic Textbook.* 2nd Edition. St. Louis, MO: Mosby, Inc., 2000.

Sheehy, Susan Budassi and Gail Pisarcik Lenehan. *Manual of Emergency Care.* 5th Edition. St. Louis, MO: Mosby Yearbook, 1999.

Sheehy, Susan Budassi et al. *Manual of Clinical Trauma Care: The First Hour.* St. Louis, MO: Mosby, Inc., 1998.

Zeigler, Edward. *Emergency Doctor.* New York, NY: Ivy Books, 1997.

Endodontists

GOE
02.03.02
O*NET-SOC
29-1022.00

Definition

Endodontists are dental specialists who treat the inside of the tooth. They remove inflamed and infected tissue, carefully clean and shape the inside of the tooth, and then fill and seal the space.

High School Subjects

Biology
Health
Mathematics

Personal Skills

Helping/teaching
Technical/scientific

Salary Range

$150,000 to $221,000 to $300,000+

Educational Requirements

Bachelor's degree; Doctor of Dental Surgery (D.D.S.) or Doctor of Dental Medicine (D.D.M.) degree; postgraduate specialty training

Certification or Licensing

Required by all states

Outlook

Little change or more slowly than the average

Scary is a common word used in describing a root canal. Everyone at work told Mary horror stories about the procedure, so even though her general dentist had told her to see an endodontist a year earlier, Mary had put off making the appointment. As a result, her throbbing tooth had gone from occasionally bothering her to giving her frequent headaches. Chewing foods had become impossible. Lately, her aching tooth was preventing her from sleeping soundly through the night, leaving her tired every day at work. Mary tried every pain reliever, and in desperation, even tried old prescription pain pills from when she broke her leg. Nothing worked. When the pain got so bad that she couldn't go to work, she dialed the endodontist's office. The receptionist told her to come down to the office as soon as possible.

When Dr. Jerome Pisano, D.D.S., M.S., entered the treatment room, he could see Mary was frightened. Her face was white as she tightly gripped the arms of the dental chair.

"Doctor, you've got to do something," Mary said glassy-eyed. "I can't take this pain anymore. Just please, whatever you do, don't hurt me."

Dr. Pisano sat down on the stool next to the dental chair, and looked Mary in the eye. "The most important thing is to get you out of pain, Mary. That's what we're going to do today. Whatever we do, you will not feel a thing because you'll be completely numb," he said.

After being treated, Mary stood up and gave Dr. Pisano a hug. "That's what I feared and put off for a year? I can't believe I was worried. It was easier than a teeth cleaning," Mary said with a smile.

Dr. Pisano returned the smile, put his hand on her shoulder and said, "There's a misconception and all kinds of jokes about root canals and how painful they are. The thing that hurt was your infected tooth. When you come to us, we don't give pain, we're the ones who take the pain away."

what does an endodontist do?

Endodontists save teeth. Without endodontic treatment, irreversibly damaged teeth must be extracted.

Toothaches are often caused by problems inside the tooth. The inside of a tooth contains tissue called dental pulp, made up of blood vessels, nerves, and connective tissue. This pulp can be damaged by deep decay, a crack or chip in the tooth, a physical blow to the mouth, or repeated dental procedures. As the damaged pulp becomes inflamed, the pressure against the nerves inside the tooth becomes great, causing pain. If left untreated, dental pulp dies and creates an infection. Pus builds up and spreads out the root end of the tooth, creating an abscess, or painful infection in the jawbone. To alleviate pain and eliminate the infection, endodontists must perform a root canal.

When an emergency patient comes to the office, an endodontist acts as a detective, listening for clues as the patient describes his or her toothache. The endodontist examines the patient's teeth by taking X rays and tests how each tooth responds to temperature changes, tapping, and electrical stimulation.

If a tooth is diagnosed as damaged and infected, the endodontist prepares the patient for a root canal. First, the doctor uses a local anesthetic to numb the tooth. If the patient seems tense or worried about the procedure, the endodontist may also give the patient an oral sedative or other mild anesthesia.

Next, the endodontist makes a small opening in the tooth. Because the canals inside teeth can be as fine as a hair, a tiny, thin instrument called a file is used to remove the inflamed or infected pulp. While removing the pulp, the file also smooths and widens the walls of the canal. After the tooth has been hollowed out, the endodontist washes out the canal with a disinfecting solution to kill germs and prevent infection. The drilled hole is temporary filled until the next visit to allow time for the tooth to drain. After this initial visit, the

lingo to learn

Abscess: A serious inflammation in the soft tissues and jawbone that occurs when infection spreads out the end of a tooth root from an inflamed or infected pulp.

Cementum: The tissue covering the outside of the roots of the teeth.

Crown: The portion of the tooth that is visible above the gum line. Dentists also fabricate artificial crowns, or "caps," which are put on top of teeth that have received root canal treatment.

Dentin: The calcified material that makes up the bulk of the structure of the tooth and supplies support and nourishment to the enamel.

Enamel: The hard, calcified material that covers the crown of a tooth. It is the hardest substance in the body.

Pulp: The soft tissue that forms the inner core of a tooth. It contains the blood vessels, nerves, and connective tissues of the tooth and provides nourishment to the dentin, enamel, and cementum.

Roots: The part of the teeth below the gum line. Each tooth has one or more roots, which attach the teeth to the jaws.

patient's pain should be gone. However, the endodontist may prescribe medications to help eliminate any lingering pain and to keep the patient comfortable as the tooth and surrounding tissue begin to heal.

During the next appointment or two, the endodontist removes the temporary filling and cleans and shapes the root canals so that they can be filled with a permanent filling material. Finally, after the tooth is fully repaired and filled, the patient returns to his or her general dentist, who installs a crown or other restoration on the outside of the tooth for protection.

While root canals are the primary procedures performed by endodontists, other services include apicoectomy or root-end resection. Though root canal treatment is highly effective, a small percentage of patients have pain in the same tooth months or years later. When this happens, endodontic surgery provides a second chance to save the tooth. Sometimes a tooth needs surgery because of new decay. Other times, it is needed because the crown or other restoration was not placed soon enough after the procedure or because the restoration cracked or broke off, allowing saliva and bacteria to enter the canal and cause a new infection.

During endodontic surgery, the doctor opens the gum tissue near the tooth to examine the surrounding bone and tooth root. Sometimes the endodontist will find a tiny fracture in the root needing repair or will discover calcified or infected tissue that needs to be cleaned out. The endodontist may perform an apicoectomy, removing the very end of the tooth's root and putting a filling in the root end.

In special cases, the endodontist may temporarily extract a tooth to work on it outside the mouth, and replant it back in the socket. Other difficult cases may require removing tooth root or even dividing a tooth in half before repairing it.

what is it like to be an endodontist?

Dr. Jerome Pisano has been an endodontist for 21 years and currently works as a partner in a private practice in Schaumburg, Illinois. His practice employs a staff office manager, three receptionists at the front desk, and three den-

> Today I had two emergency patients holding on the phone, two in dental chairs, and a 10-year-old who just came in after being hit in the mouth with a baseball bat.

tal assistants. To accommodate patients, the office is open six days a week, and each partner works 40 to 45 hours a week. Jerome has children while his partner does not, so he arranges to have most weekends off. In many offices, however, endodontists will alternate working weekends and being on call.

"Some days my partner and I overlap, other days only one of us is here. Because the nature of endodontics is emergency appointments, one of us is always on call—we alternate weeks. Luckily, I haven't gotten too many calls in the middle of the night because people tend to wait until morning. Once in awhile, we do get calls from people in tremendous pain as early as 6 AM, and we tell them that we'll meet them at the office in 45 minutes."

Jerome's regular office hours are 7:45 AM to 5:30 PM, but emergencies and paperwork sometimes extend the day. "Besides scheduled patients, we had six emergencies yesterday, so I was there until 7:30 PM. Tonight I left on time, but I have to spend 45 minutes in my home office writing diagnosis and treatment plan letters with a copies of radiographs to send to patients' general dentists," he says.

Besides performing endodontic procedures on patients, Jerome's other office activities include training and overseeing the staff, working with insurance companies to obtain payment for procedures, and making sure the office is in compliance with the federal Occupational Safety and Health Administration standards. He and his partner also try to repair minor equipment malfunctions when they occur, such as air leaks or water line leaks. However, they may have to call a service company to repair problems outside their capabilities.

Even though he has an accountant to help with taxes, Jerome is responsible for some bookkeeping and accounting duties. The office staff is in charge of accounts payable and receivable, but Jerome may have to step in when there is a problem collecting payment.

He also must keep track of staff members' time-cards, benefits, and Social Security and tax deductions, and helps determine salaries, raises, and bonuses.

Jerome says being an endodontist means being compassionate every day, all day, while maintaining concentration on the work. "People are in pain, so you must be compassionate, kind, and reassuring all day long. You also have to be good under pressure. Today I had two emergency patients holding on the phone, two in dental chairs, and a 10-year-old who just came in after being hit in the mouth with a baseball bat. In situations like that, you have to maintain an even keel and calmly but quickly direct your staff."

This may entail going from one patient to another to start with, just to get them out of pain—then returning to treat them one at a time. "A little stressful," Jerome admits, raising his eyebrows.

The job involves physical stress as well. Endodontists must lean over patients to see inside the teeth, working with tiny instruments inside a hole smaller than a pencil eraser. The dexterity and visual acuity needed to discern differences of half a millimeter requires intense focus and concentration.

"I can't stay up late and drink a lot of alcohol the night before or drink a lot of coffee in the morning. I need a steady hand," he says.

Jerome makes an effort to offset the sitting he does at work by exercising and leading an active lifestyle. During his workday, between patients, he tries to remember to get up and stretch. If he forgets, the positioning can cause a backache.

By the end of the day, Jerome is tired but happy. "It's the self-satisfying kind of tired, like after you've worked out. It's the type of fatigue where I feel a sense that I've accomplished something."

have I got what it takes to be an endodontist?

Endodontists must have good people skills. "You have to be a patient, compassionate person," Jerome says. "You have to listen carefully to what patients are saying, and you must communicate effectively. They need to know what you want to do and why, before you do it. All this helps to reassure patients that they can trust you."

Jerome considers himself a "self-starter." Without a supervisor, he is his own boss. He is responsible for getting to the office on time. He is in charge of the overall running of the business as well as performing clinical treatment in emergency situations. The day is not over until he has treated the last scheduled or emergency patient. For this reason, endodontists must be flexible in their schedules. When Jerome is on call, his family and friends must be understanding if he excuses himself and heads for the office at any given time.

Good hand-eye coordination and precision skills are critical. "I would liken endodontic procedures to fixing watches—it's that meticulous. In fact, I knew an endodontist whose hobby was repairing antique watches. But I like to take a break from that kind of detail and go to a hockey game or water ski."

how do I become an endodontist?

Jerome was trained first through dental school, then in his postgraduate studies to obtain a master's degree in endodontics. To refresh and hone his knowledge, training, and clinical skills, he takes continuing education courses. Although some courses are required to keep a dental license, he attends many more on his own as part of a personal commitment to provide the best treatment. By going the extra mile, Jerome also feels more confident in his own abilities.

education

High School
High school students interested in becoming endodontists should begin preparing for this career with a course load emphasizing math and science subjects. Courses such as algebra, trigonometry, calculus, physics, biology, chemistry, and health are all helpful to prepare for college course work.

Jerome adds, "But don't limit yourself to these courses only. High school is the time to explore and develop your abilities and talents. Try taking speech, psychology, drama, creative writing. It won't hurt anything and will round out your education and you as a person."

Business, accounting, and economics courses will also help if you decide to run a private practice later on in your career.

Postsecondary Training

Dental schools require students to complete at least two years of undergraduate college education. Most students, however, obtain their bachelor's degree before applying.

Maintaining a high grade point average is important while in college. Applicants to dental school typically have strong grade point averages, and as a result, the competition for entry into dental programs can be intense.

A discussion with your college advisor will help you determine the classes to take each semester or trimester. Suggested college courses are similar to those recommended for high school. Typically, those who plan to be endodontists pursue a bachelor of science (B.S.) degree. This involves math courses, such as algebra, calculus, trigonometry, and geometry, and science courses, such as biology, physics, anatomy, physiology, and microbiology.

Business courses, including marketing, business administration, economics, accounting, and finance, provide good instruction for owning and operating a future business.

Liberal arts courses such as psychology, sociology, English, and drama will help you become comfortable with communicating with others. They also may provide insight into patients' personalities, fears, and behavior.

Before being admitted to dental schools, college students must take the Dental Admissions Test (DAT). DAT scores help a dental school determine whether a student will succeed in a program in which courses are exclusively made up of advanced science, clinical, and laboratory technique course work.

Dental programs generally last four years. The first two years are spent mostly in the classroom and laboratory, studying the basic sciences. The last two years emphasize clinical treatment. Students begin supervised treatment of patients at university dental clinics. Upon graduation, students receive a Doctor of Dental Surgery (D.D.S.) or Doctor of Dental Medicine (D.D.M.) degree.

This degree would be sufficient to practice as a general dentist. However, to become a dental specialist, more schooling is needed. Each year, one-fourth to one-third of new dental school graduates choose to prepare for a dental specialty. Postgraduate programs in endodontics accredited by the American Den-

Early Endodontics

Evidence indicates endodontics may have been practiced as early as the second or third century BC. A bronze wire, believed to have been used as treatment for an infected pulp, was found in the tooth of a skull discovered in Israel's Negev Desert.

In addition, evidence shows that pulp chambers of teeth were drained to relieve pressure and pain as early as the first century AD.

tal Association Commission on Dental Accreditation last two to three years.

certification or licensing

All 50 states and the District of Columbia require dentists to be licensed before they can practice. Most states require that dentists graduate from an accredited dental school and pass written and practical examinations. Individual state licensing boards administer the tests for licensure.

Currently, 17 states require endodontists to obtain a separate specialty license. To be able to practice as a specialist, dentists must graduate from an accredited postgraduate program and pass additional state examinations. Many state licenses allow dentists to practice both in their specialty and in general dentistry.

Board certification available through the American Board of Endodontics (ABE) is independent of state licensing requirements. To achieve ABE diplomate status, endodontists must file an application with the ABE, be interviewed and approved as a candidate, pass written and oral examinations, and provide written endodontic case histories. To maintain their status, endodontists must renew their certification every 10 years. ABE diplomate status is sought voluntarily by endodontists to show excellence in their abilities.

All dentists, including endodontic specialists, must plan on taking courses to continue their education after entering private practice. Reading professional journals and attending workshops and seminars are necessary to stay licensed and keep abreast of changing trends in dentistry and endodontics.

scholarships and grants

Scholarships and grants are often available from individual institutions, state agencies, and special-interest organizations. Many students finance their medical education through military service. The Armed Forces Health Professions Scholarship Program and the National Health Service Corps Scholarship Program provide money for students in return for military service.

Another source for financial aid, scholarship, and grant information is the Association of American Medical Colleges. Remember to request information early for eligibility, application requirements, and deadlines.

National Health Service Corps Scholarship Program
Department of Health and Human Services,
4350 East-West Highway, 10th Floor
Bethesda, MD 20814
800-638-0824
http://www.fedmoney.org/grants/93288-00.htm

To be a successful endodontist, you should

- Be a compassionate, patient person
- Have excellent hand-eye coordination
- Be self-motivated
- Have dexterity for detail work

Armed Forces Health Professions Scholarship Program
Air Force: http://hp.airforce.com/training/financial.html
Army: http://www.sirius.com/~ameddet/hpschps.htm
Navy: http://nshs.med.navy.mil/hpsp/default.htm

Association of American Medical Colleges
2450 N Street, NW
Washington, DC 20037-1126
202-828-0400
http://www.aamc.org

who will hire me?

According to the American Association of Endodontists, there are approximately 5,700 active endodontists in the United States—the majority working in private practice. Endodontists may own their own practice, work as an associate, or act as partner in a group practice. Setting up as private practice demands considerable financial resources and expertise.

Other opportunities for endodontists include teaching at universities, either full-time, or part-time while still practicing. Many private practitioners also volunteer their time as teachers in dental schools. Students interested in academic careers are advised to contact the endodontic department of university dental schools for more information.

Some endodontists choose to work as researchers for dental schools or for industry. Researchers may test new endodontic procedures and materials by working on models or animals.

Other endodontists may combine clinical practice, teaching, and research by working with the Federal Dental Health Services. These endodontists are found in the air force, navy, army, veterans' hospitals, and public health services. In the public health services, endodontists often work with underserved populations, such as on Native American reservations or in nursing homes or low-income communities.

where can I go from here?

The primary career path for most endodontists in private practice is to build their reputation. As their practice becomes recognized by general dentists in the surrounding community, referrals will increase and their patient base will become larger. An endodontist who can effectively communicate with a patient's general dentist and facilitate easy coordination of treatment is more apt to have a thriving practice.

Endodontists can advance their status by becoming active in organized dental associations, endodontic associations, and study clubs.

Some endodontists working full-time choose to practice or teach part-time during or close to their retirement years.

what are the salary ranges?

The U.S. Department of Labor reports that dentists earned a median annual salary of $110,160 in 1998. Self-employed dentists in private practice earn more, averaging $147,850 a year.

Specialists, because of the additional training and skills required, earn more than those working in general dentistry. According to the American Dental Association, the average net income for independent specialists in private practice was $221,510 in 1998.

The location of an endodontist's practice may play a role in determining income. In general, dentists in southern states have lower incomes than those in other regions of the country. Incomes are also affected by how many other endodontists are working in the immediate vicinity. In an area with few or no other specialists, an endodontic practice has a "corner on the market" and obtains referrals more easily than practices with more competition.

Earnings are also dependent upon years in the business, professional status, and size of a practice.

what is the job outlook?

The U.S. Department of Labor projects the demand for endodontists to grow slower than the average for all occupations. Most jobs will arise from the need to replace endodontists who retire or leave the occupation.

However, some factors will aid in the employment of endodontists. Because of the emergency nature of endodontic services, the nation's economic status has little impact on the job. When endodontic treatment is needed, patients have little choice but to seek medical attention. For those who may need help financing medical care, some offices may refer the patient for a loan or government assistance. Other offices work out payment plans as long as a substantial down payment is made at the onset of treatment.

Another factor that will help boost endodontics is the fact that people are living longer and, as a result, requiring more dental procedures. People are retaining their teeth longer and realize the importance of dental care. The practice of maintaining and restoring original teeth (as opposed to pulling diseased teeth and installing dentures) is on the rise—demanding more root canals and other endodontic procedures.

how do I learn more?

professional associations

Following are organizations that provide information on dental careers, accredited schools, and employers.

American Association of Endodontists
211 East Chicago Avenue, Suite 1100
Chicago, IL 60611-2691
800-872-3636
info@aae.org
http://www.aae.org

> You have to listen carefully to what patients are saying, and you must communicate effectively.

American Dental Association
211 East Chicago Avenue
Chicago, IL 60611
312-440-2500
http://www.ada.org

bibliography

Following is a sampling of materials related to the professional concerns and development of endodontists.

Arens, Donald E. et al. *Practical Lessons in Endodontic Surgery.* Chicago, IL: Quintessence Publishing, 1998.

Beer, Rudolf et al. *Endodontology.* New York, NY: Thieme Medical Publishing, 1999.

Freeman, Marsha. *Specialized Operating Procedures for Endodontists.* New York, NY: Dental Communication Unlimited, 1998.

Harty, F. J. and T. R. Pitt Ford, eds. *Endodontics in Clinical Practice.* 4th Edition. Newton, MA: Butterworth-Heinemann, 1997.

Walton, Richard E. and Mahmoud Torabinejad. *Principles and Practice of Endodontics.* 2nd Edition. Kent, UK: W. B. Saunders, 1995.

Epidemiologists

Definition
Epidemiologists study the causes and spread of disease in groups of people.

High School Subjects
Biology
Health
Mathematics

Personal Skills
Helping/teaching
Technical/scientific

Salary Range
$27,000 to $45,000 to $90,000+

Educational Requirements
Master's degree; post-doctorate work

Certification or Licensing
None available

Outlook
About as fast as the average

DOT
NA*
O*NET-SOC
19-1041.00

*Not Available. The DOT does not classify the career of epidemiologist as such but includes it in the larger category of statistician.

Phones rang futilely on the desks of staff epidemiologists in North Dakota and Minnesota in the spring of 1997. For the most part, no one was around to answer them—they were out in the field, called out in the aftermath of the terrible flooding of the Red River from the melting of the winter's record snows.

With the filthy river water covering three-fourths of Grand Forks, North Dakota, and most of East Grand Forks, Minnesota, the potential for public health problems was high. Rising waters had shut down the municipal water system and sewage system. There were only scattered portable bathrooms and water stations in the dry part of town. The risk of becoming of sick from tainted water was high.

"Sanitary conditions are primitive at best," a spokesperson from the National Guard was quoted as saying. As city officials contemplated using an eight-mile hose to bring in clean water, state epidemiologists were busy monitoring the site, taking samples, and checking on any outbreaks of illness among the 2,000 people evacuated to the nearby Grand Forks Air Force Base. Only late in the day, weary and loaded down with data and samples, did they return to their offices. There were reports to write, samples to analyze, and vital information to be sent to the Centers for Disease Control and Prevention in Atlanta.

what does an epidemiologist do?

Epidemiology is a branch of medical science that studies the cause, spread, and control of infectious and noninfectious diseases in human groups or communities. *Epidemiology* comes from the word *epidemic* and is concerned with diseases affecting a large number of people.

Armed with research, statistical analysis, field investigations, and laboratory techniques, *epidemiologists* determine the cause of disease, its distribution (by region, group, or environment), how it spreads, and what can be done to control and prevent it. Their work is important to the medical community and to public health officials who use their information to determine public health policies.

Epidemiology is a fairly complex field, and different epidemiologists focus on different things. *Infectious disease epidemiologists* focus on diseases caused by bacteria and viruses, such as botulism and chicken pox. *Chronic disease epidemiologists* focus on noninfectious diseases such as heart disease, lung cancer, breast cancer, ulcers, and other illnesses resulting from genetic predisposition, lifestyle, and other factors. Epidemiological work is even done on such epidemics as rising teen suicide rates and deaths by firearms.

Throughout the United States, there is a government-employed epidemiologist for every state and territory. These epidemiologists work for departments that usually are part of the state public health service. Local communities and counties also may employ epidemiologists. State and territorial epidemiologists work closely with the Centers for Disease Control and Prevention (CDC) on epidemiology, surveillance, and prevention activities. By law, states must report specific diseases in their populations to the CDC on a regular basis. For example, they report on new cases of AIDS, outbreaks of influenza, or incidences of food poisoning.

The CDC itself employs many epidemiologists. Along with the Agency for Toxic Substances and Disease Registry, the CDC is a kind of clearinghouse for national public health information. It helps states exchange information about disease control and prevention and makes recommendations for public health policies.

The CDC backs up its recommendations with research. Epidemiologists work in different branches of the CDC, focusing on a specific disease or public health practice area.

Beyond this, epidemiologists teach and research in universities. Others work for research organizations like the World Health Organization or the AIDS Institute. Epidemiologists even work in hospitals; typically, they

lingo to learn

Biostatistics: The design and analysis of biomedical research in humans and in laboratory experiments.

Chronic diseases: Noninfectious diseases, such as heart disease, breast cancer, and other illnesses resulting from genetic predisposition, lifestyle, and other factors.

Epidemic: Outbreak or incidence of disease that affects a large number of people.

Infectious diseases: Diseases caused by microorganisms such as bacteria, fungi, protozoans, and viruses. Examples include diphtheria, meningitis, scarlet fever, syphilis, tuberculosis, typhoid fever, amebic dysentery, malaria, AIDS, chicken pox, hepatitis, polio, and rabies.

Morbidity ratio: The ratio of sick people to well people in a given population.

Mortality ratio: The rate of deaths in a given population.

Statistics: Collecting and classifying data by numerical characteristics to make inferences and predictions.

Vectors: Carriers of disease such as animals or insects (including bacteria, fungi, protozoans, metazoans, and viruses).

are medical doctors researching a chronic or infectious disease.

"We don't sit! Part of our day is spent in the office, part out in the community," emphasizes Joanna Buffington, acting chief of the Epidemic Intelligence Service (EIS) of the CDC. Joanna helps run the two-year epidemiology training program at EIS for people interested in health and health prevention. About 350 people apply each time for about 65 available positions.

"Epidemiologists not only research, collect data, and systematically analyze it," she stresses, "but also share their information with the community."

what is it like to be an epidemiologist?

Bella Shiferaw, M.D., M.P.H., is an epidemiologist for the state of Oregon, working in the acute and communicable disease department. Oregon has a fairly large staff of epidemiologists, each focusing on specific diseases, such as HIV. Bella's specialty is food-borne poisoning—the bacterial contamination, such as by E. coli or salmonella, of food.

Bella's work is important because food poisoning is serious business. It can make you wretchedly ill—even kill you. State and county public health officials care about stopping such outbreaks in the interest of public safety.

Bella does a combination of research and field investigations. "We go out in the field when there's an outbreak; otherwise, we work primarily in the office," explains Bella. In a typical outbreak scenario, someone reports an incidence or suspected incidence of food-borne poisoning to the county. For example, a doctor or a lab technician that has diagnosed and treated a patient with food poisoning will contact the local health department. By law, medical professionals must do this so that public health officials can take steps to prevent future cases. If the local department does not have the personnel to investigate the outbreak, officials call the state's public health department for help.

That's where Bella comes in. She and a team of investigators visit the suspected source of the outbreak and try to figure out what happened. Perhaps a restaurant employee did not wash his or her hands and passed E. coli onto customers. Perhaps the

restaurant served bad meat that made customers ill. "We try to get a list of the people who have eaten at the restaurant, interview them, and record what they ate," says Bella. The team inspects the restaurant's kitchen, talks to food preparers, and takes cultures of any leftover food. The food samples are sent to the state's lab facilities to determine if bacteria is present.

Once the cause of the poisoning is determined, Bella and her team make sure steps are taken to stop the problem. They order tainted food to be destroyed, for example, or make sure an employee doesn't go back to work until stool samples prove he or she is free of the contaminant. If necessary, they instruct restaurant personnel about how to prevent future food poisoning. "We teach them about the proper handling of food, for example," says Bella.

in-depth

Epidemiology

Epidemiology didn't really become possible until the development of statistics and statistical analysis methods in the 19th century. However, classical medical texts reveal that the ancients made connections between disease and environmental factors. For example, early Hippocratic writings connect specific disease to locations, seasons, and climates.

In 1622, an English statistician, John Graunt, wrote *Natural and Political Observations . . . .Made Upon the Bills of Mortality,* the first study to deal with population and mortality rates systematically. It examined the social distribution of death in London, particularly deaths from plague.

In the 18th century, medical professionals began to relate population data to birth, death, and disease statistics. They applied this information to help classify diseases and test the success of treatments for such epidemics as smallpox.

The 19th century Sanitary Movement developed as a result of an alarming rise in sickness and death rates in the city slums of Europe and the United States. Public health specialists called sanitarians collected data that showed clusters of morbidity and mortality in specific areas and theorized that the cause was miasma, foul emanations by air, water, and soil. Incorporating better sanitation procedures, such as modern sewage systems and the consumption of cleaner water, helped to cut sickness and death rates.

The development of sophisticated statistical methods was necessary for the success of the Sanitary Movement. Two other key figures who used statistics for public health purposes during this time were Louis Rene Villerme in France and William Farr in England.

Toward the end of the 19th century, infectious disease epidemiology—the study of organisms causing specific diseases—was born. In 1865, Louis Pasteur showed that a specific organism was causing an epidemic in silkworms. In 1882, German bacteriologist Robert Koch established the bacterial cause of diseases in humans, including tuberculosis. Koch also studied anthrax, conjunctivitis, sleeping sickness, and malaria. His research led to disease prevention methods such as vaccines, quarantines, and antibiotics.

Chronic disease epidemiology began around the end of WW II, focusing on the rise of peptic ulcer disease, coronary heart disease, and lung cancer. Chronic disease epidemiologists helped to discover the link between lung cancer and smoking, for example, and between coronary heart disease and serum cholesterol.

Gene epidemiology is one of the newer branches of the discipline. Other new developments involve global health patterns and the application of new computer technology to epidemiology.

Finally, Bella reports all of the data from her investigation to the CDC. She usually transmits this information electronically via computer.

In addition to investigating outbreaks, Bella is also involved in a research project on air-borne food poisoning in collaboration with other state and county epidemiologists. She and her colleagues have been working on this project for more than a year now and hope to publish the results soon for other state and international epidemiologists. "You want to share the information," she stresses. "[Epidemiology] is a collaborative business, involving a lot of trade of information."

have I got what it takes to be an epidemiologist?

Who could be an epidemiologist? "Not someone who doesn't want to get out and talk to people," emphasizes Joanna Buffington. You must be comfortable with the public and be responsive to the needs of people. In addition, epidemiologists must be good scientists and statisticians and have strong writing skills to handle the reporting aspects of the work.

People interested in health issues are good candidates for this field. Curiosity, determination, persistence, and drive are necessary for research. Epidemiologists cannot be intellectual lightweights. Because their field involves medicine, computers, and statistical analysis, future epidemiologists must be good at cracking the books and taking tests and earn good grades in school.

how do I become an epidemiologist?

Epidemiologists are highly credentialed medical specialists. Academic requirements for this field are rigorous, and there is tough competition to get into epidemiology programs at the top universities in the country. Such programs include Boston University, Columbia University (NY), Harvard University, University of California at Berkeley, University of Illinois at Chicago, and the University of North Carolina at Chapel Hill.

education

High School
In high school, students should follow a premed track. Classes such as biology, health, English, physics, and math (including statistics) are recommended. Social studies and geography also are relevant. In addition, take the opportunity to start developing your computer skills because epidemiology increasingly makes use of the latest information technology.

Postsecondary Training
A four-year bachelor of science degree is the minimum requirement to enter an epidemiology program. New York University, for example, requires a bachelor's degree in biological, physical, or engineering science for admittance to its graduate program. Many graduate programs are geared toward people who already have a medical degree. Cornell University, for example, requires an M.D. or an R.N. degree plus three years of work experience for entrance into its epidemiology program.

Graduate programs usually require you to take the GRE, GMAT, or MCAT and TOEFL tests for entrance. Some require a minimum grade point average. Degrees awarded vary depending on the school, the program, and your course of study.

Not every graduate school focuses on the same thing. Johns Hopkins University has programs of study in chronic disease epidemiology, clinical epidemiology, genetics, infectious diseases, and occupational and environmental epidemiology. Case Western Reserve offers a program in genetic epidemiology, while Emory University offers a program in quantitative epidemiology.

The type of program available depends in part on the focus of faculty research. At Harvard University, the focus of faculty research includes breast, kidney, and pancreatic cancer, Hodgkin's disease, and nutritional epidemiology. At Johns Hopkins University, research concentrates on AIDS epidemiology and control, diarrheal diseases, vaccine development, and immunization programs.

As a result, classes in an epidemiology program will vary depending upon the program and the faculty's research orientation. Core classes in the University of Illinois at Chicago's program include principles of epidemiology, quantitative methods, and the epidemiology of infectious and chronic diseases. Additionally, some programs include foreign language or computer courses in their curriculum and may require a final dissertation or research project.

While obtaining your degree, you should get practical experience in the field. As she was earning her M.D./M.P.H. in Atlanta, Bella Shiferaw had the opportunity to do some project work for the CDC in Atlanta.

Although most graduate programs last four years, two-year programs are also available. For example, Georgetown University offers a two-year program for those working in the field as medical professionals or technologists.

scholarships and grants

Tuition for these programs can be costly. Financial aid in the form of fellowships, research positions, or teaching assistantships are available to eligible students. For example, Boston University offers federal work-study arrangements, institution-sponsored loans, and epidemiology internships or fieldwork. Other schools offer full and partial tuition waivers and scholarships.

Scholarships and grants are often available from state agencies and special-interest organizations. Many students finance their medical education through military service. The Armed Forces Health Professions Scholarship Program and the National Health Service Corps Scholarship Program provide money for students in return for service. Another source for financial aid, scholarship, and grant information is the Association of American Medical Colleges.

Armed Forces Health Professions Scholarship Program
Air Force: http://hp.airforce.com/training/financial.html
Army: http://www.sirius.com/~ameddet/hpschps.htm
Navy: http://nshs.med.navy.mil/hpsp/default.htm

National Health Service Corps Scholarship Program
Department of Health and Human Services,
4350 East-West Highway, 10th Floor
Bethesda, MD 20814
800-638-0824
http://www.fedmoney.org/grants/93288-00.htm

Association of American Medical Colleges
2450 N Street, NW
Washington, DC 20037-1126
202-828-0400
http://www.aamc.org

who will hire me?

Joanna Buffington was well into her schooling before she decided on a career in epidemiology. "I've always been interested in health and in prevention," she says. "But when I was in med school for internal medicine, where the focus is one-on-one and on disease, I was saying to myself, 'Where are all the healthy people?' " During her residency, she met someone who told her about the Epidemic Intelligence Service, which soon became her first employer.

Epidemiologists are employed by local, state, and territorial health departments. They work at the Centers for Disease Control and Prevention and the Agency for Toxic Substances and Disease Registry. Other government agencies that employ epidemiologists include the National Immunization Program, the National Center for Environmental Health, the National Center for Health Statistics, and the National Institute for Occupational Safety and Health. Epidemiologists also work in hospitals, universities, and research institutes such as the World Health Organization.

Typically, epidemiologists use their graduate programs as a springboard for approaching employers. When looking for their first job, students highlight their area of specialization and research in hopes that they fit the employer's needs. Bella's specialty of food-born poisoning, for example, matched openings in the state departments of both North Carolina and Oregon.

If you are currently in high school, you can start exploring future employers in a number of ways. Write to your state's epidemiology department and ask for information about current projects. Contact graduate programs to find out about course descriptions and where faculty research has been published. To learn more about the Centers for Disease Control and Prevention, visit their Web site at http://www.cdc.gov.

where can I go from here?

According to Bella, advancement depends on your interest. "Some people like to teach. Advancement in the university would go from assistant professor of epidemiology up to full professor. Someone working for a state epidemiology department could go on to become the state epidemiologist in that state or another. Some people may go into international epidemiology, like with the World Health Organization." Bella plans to stay at the state level of public health for now but is interested in moving into international epidemiology later on in her career.

In many cases, advancement depends on the area of research. Epidemiologists involved in research in critical areas such as AIDS or cancer may be in great demand to any number of research or public health organizations.

what are the salary ranges?

Levels of schooling, research, experience, and qualifications all affect the epidemiologist's earning potential. According to the school of public health at the University of North Carolina at Chapel Hill, starting salaries generally fall in the range of $30,000 to $35,000 for most positions.

The University of Texas at Austin reports that with a master's degree, epidemiologists in the private sector earn on average between $40,000 and $50,000. With a public health or medical degree, they can earn between $60,000 and $90,000. Those in the federal government generally earn between $27,000 and $40,000 to start.

what is the job outlook?

Job prospects for epidemiologists are promising because there will always be a need to understand, control, and prevent the spread of disease. The Centers for Disease Control and Prevention have only been in existence since 1951, and the World Health Organization since 1948. Less-developed countries still have high rates of tuberculosis, syphilis, malaria, and other diseases. Even developed countries experience periodic recurrences of infectious diseases; organisms that cause illness sometimes become resistant to existing vaccines. In addition, new strains of diseases are discovered all the time, such as Lyme disease in 1975, the Hanta virus in 1976, and Legionnaires' disease in 1977.

Recent episodes calling upon the skills of epidemiologists include a 1993 outbreak in Milwaukee, Wisconsin, when the *Cryptosporidium* parasite tainted the water supply and infected over 400,000 people. Not long after, a strain of E. coli in undercooked meat made 300 people ill in the Northwest. In 1995, the Ebola virus, which causes massive hemorrhaging and terrible suffering in its victims, emerged in Africa for the first time in almost 20 years.

"We don't sit! Part of our day is spent in the office, part out in the community."

Developments in technology will drive epidemiological research to improve the understanding and prevention of disease. Biomedical techniques such as genetic recombination and imaging are revolutionizing the field. The use of new information systems will make global communication more comprehensive and efficient between nations.

The need to understand the social context of disease transmission will also create opportunities for epidemiologists. Medical professionals may know what causes a disease and work to prevent its spread, but it is the epidemiologist's job to work on identifying and changing negative social behaviors to keep outbreaks from ever starting.

how do I learn more?

professional organizations

Following are organizations that provide information on epidemiology careers, accredited schools, and employers:

Centers for Disease Control and Prevention
1600 Clifton Road
Atlanta, GA 30333
404-639-3311
http://www.cdc.gov

Epidemic Intelligence Service
Centers for Disease Control and Prevention
1600 Clifton Road
Atlanta, GA 30333
404-639-3311
http://www.cdc.gov/epo/dapht/eis

Council of State and Territorial Epidemiologists
2872 Woodstock Boulevard, Suite 303
Atlanta, GA 30341
770-458-3811
http://www.cste.org

Society of Healthcare Epidemiology of America
19 Mantua Road
Mount Royal, NJ 08061
856-423-7222
http://www.shea-online.org

bibliography

Following is a sampling of materials relating to the professional concerns and development of epidemiologists.

Gordis, Leon. *Epidemiology*. Philadelphia, PA: W. B. Saunders, 2000.

Herwaldt, Loreen A., ed. *A Practical Handbook for Hospital Epidemiologists*. Thorofare, NJ: Slack Incorporated, 1998.

Last, John M. and J. H. Abramson. *A Dictionary of Epidemiology*. New York, NY: Oxford University Press, 1995.

MacMahon, Brian and Dimitrios Trichopoulos. *Epidemiology: Principles and Practice*. 2nd Edition. Boston, MA: Little, Brown, 1996.

Rose, Geoffrey and D. J. Barker, eds. *Epidemiology for the Uninitiated*. 4th Edition. London, UK: BMJ Books, 1997.

Rothman, Kenneth J. and Sander Greenland, eds. *Modern Epidemiology*. Philadelphia, PA: Livingston Williams & Wilkins, 1998.

Steiner, David L. and Geoffrey R. Norman. *PDQ Epidemiology*. 2nd Edition. Hamilton, ON: B. C., Canada Decker, 1996.

Stolley, Paul D. and Tamar Lasky. *Investigating Disease Patterns: The Science of Epidemiology*. New York:, NY: W. H. Freeman & Company, 1998.

Teutsch, Steven M., ed. *Principles and Practice of Public Health Surveillance*. New York, NY: Oxford University Press, 2000.

Ergonomists

Definition
An ergonomist studies the environments in which people work, the ways they use tools and technology to do their jobs, or how they use products that they buy. Then the ergonomist tries to adapt the workspace or the product to better suit human capabilities and ensure safety and productivity.

Alternative Job Titles
Human factors engineers
Human factors specialists
Industrial/organizational psychologists

High School Subjects
Mathematics
Physics

Personal Skills
Helping/teaching
Technical/scientific

Salary Range
$30,000 to $42,000 to $80,000

Educational Requirements
Bachelor's degree for entry-level; advancement may require a master's or doctorate degree

Certification or Licensing
Recommended

Outlook
About as fast as the average

GOE
11.03.01

O*NET-SOC
NA*

*Not Available. The O*NET-SOC does not categorize the career of ergonomist.

Kevin Quaid goes to work every day, but he doesn't always end up at his office. Sometimes he drives in a triple-trailer truck down an interstate. Sometimes he works in a candy-making factory or a police station. Once in a while, he finds his way to the offices of his employers at Ergonomics, Inc., in Seattle, Washington.

Kevin works as an *ergonomist*, and, in a broad sense, he studies how people's environment affects them. He asks people what sort of injuries they have had on the job, observes how the work is done, and studies the workplace environment. He investigates the factors that lead to employee injury or inefficiency on the job so that he can discover what is causing the problem. Kevin's responsibility then is to come up with solutions, which may mean redesigning tools, moving workstations, or providing the worker with different equipment.

what does an ergonomist do?

An astronaut living in a totally weightless environment. A long distance truck driver on the last leg of a cross-country round trip. An administrative assistant entering data into a computer. A high school student trying out a new toothbrush with a rubberized wide grip and an angled head.

What do these people have in common? They are all possible subjects for an ergonomist to study. Ergonomists have a curious job—they watch other people work. They do this so that they can understand the stresses that a human body undergoes in a particular job or environment. They then design ways to adapt the environment, or the tool used for the job, so that it is more well-suited to the worker.

Ergonomists work anywhere that people come into contact with systems, equipment, or technology. They either modify an existing product or build new ones that are specially designed for a specific purpose. For instance, ergonomists have designed keyboards, computer desks, and workstations to alleviate injuries caused by the increased use of computers. To develop these products, ergonomists asked questions of people who used less well-designed products and found that the body had difficulty adapting to certain positions or environments that these products created. They noticed common problems, such as back pain, eye strain, neck tension, and repetitive use injuries such as carpal tunnel syndrome, which affects the tendons in the wrist. Then they tried to eliminate the aspects of the environment that caused the problem.

As a result, we now have articulating keyboards that separate typing hands and prevent undue flexing of the wrist; wrist rests that keep the hand and wrist in a neutral position rather than flexed all the time; and desks that allow a computer monitor to be inset, so that the user can be looking down instead of up. Ergonomists are often at other people's worksites, collecting data that will guide them toward a better design. They may make models for new equipment or they might adapt products that already exist.

The job of an ergonomist is not always limited to the workplace, either. Have you ever tried to pull open a door that had a "push" sign on it? Your body was simply reacting normally to what the door was telling it to do. "I tend to make a distinction between human factors and ergonomics," says Kevin, who has worked in the industry for about five years. Human factors, he feels, are concerned more with what a person in any given situation wants to do naturally. They include psychological factors as well as knowledge about how humans react in a given situation. "If you come to a door that you need to pull open, the door should have a hook-style thing to pull on. If there's nothing to grab onto, the natural reaction is to try and push the door. If you come to a door that needs to be pushed open, it should have a flat barlike thing." Observations like this have lead to ergonomically designed doors that are easy to understand. For instance, panic doors, which can be opened outward quickly by pushing on a bar, are often used for fire exits in public buildings. They are intended to prevent people in a panic situation from making the wrong choice about how the door should open because they operate on the body's natural decision to push the bar.

Ergonomics, on the other hand, is concerned more specifically with a person's environment at work. The word *ergonomics* comes

lingo to learn

Kinesiology: The study of muscles and movement, especially for physical therapy.

MSDs (musculoskeletal disorders): Environment related health problems involving muscles, nerves, spinal disks, joints, cartilage, tendons, and ligaments, most frequently occurring in the lower back, shoulders, arms, and hands.

Negative tilt keyboard: A computer keyboard positioned so that it is below the user's elbow height when seated and the keyboard base slopes gently away from the user making the key tops accessible when the hands are in a neutral, or relaxed, position.

Perpetuating factors: Those actions that make an injury worse once it has occurred.

Physiology: Functional process of an organism or any of its parts.

Repetitive motion: Strain or disorder affecting any muscle or tendon that is repeatedly or incorrectly used.

from the Greek *ergon,* meaning work, and *nomos,* meaning law. Despite its ancient roots, ergonomics is a fairly modern science that began in the first half of the 20th century. With the increase of industrial and other non-agricultural jobs, workers faced new stresses. These stresses were eventually attributed to repetitive movements, fatigue, and machinery whose designs were incompatible with the physical abilities of the people operating them.

"Human engineering got its big push during World War II, when it was found that many of the new and complicated weapons were useless because they exceeded the capacities of their human operators. . . . That is the challenge for human factors engineers . . . to redesign present equipment and devise new equipment so that human errors, accidents, and frustrations can be reduced and efficiency increased." This quote, attributed to Alphonse Chapanis and reported in a pamphlet released by the Human Factors and Ergonomics Society (HFES), gives a good idea of the objective of the ergonomist.

what is it like to be an ergonomist?

Kevin Quaid is a consulting ergonomist. That is, he works for a company that helps other companies make their workplaces safer and less stressful for their employees. The consulting ergonomist is something of a "gun for hire" because he or she is not limited to helping one company exclusively or even helping one kind of company. Although Kevin may not see the same kind of job site twice, he does encounter the same kinds of problems at many of his assignments: tendonitis, repetitive motion syndromes, sore necks.

"The first thing I do when I get an assignment is head to the worksite and find out what the problem is. I ask a lot of questions: 'What kind of pain do you have? Where do you feel it? Is it worse in the evening than in the morning? Is it worse on Friday than on Monday? What do you do all day? Have you changed your job recently?'" The more that Kevin knows about the situation, the more easily he can eliminate irrelevant factors and isolate the true causes. "You know, it might be something really obvious that they are overlooking or don't have the technical know-how to correct. People might say, 'I hate my chair at work, it's so uncomfort-

able,' and not realize that their chair is stressing their body to the point of potential injury until they have low back pain all the time."

More often than not, people don't have the awareness of their bodies' capacities so they can't make the logical connection between what they do at work and where they hurt. Kevin explains, "If somebody started a new typing job in September and they'd never had a typing job before in their life, and then they develop some sort of wrist or finger problem, it might not be immediately apparent to them that their new job is the problem. The symptoms show up after the stress has been ongoing, not usually the day the job starts." Ergonomy is equal parts detective work and common sense.

Some solutions that may seem obvious can be useless if Kevin has not gotten enough information about the client or if he has asked the wrong questions. Kevin relates the case of the woman who was a typist and who had tendonitis in both of her hands and her wrists. "We changed her workstation, but she still had pain in her hands. Well, we finally found out that, as a hobby, she was a pianist in an orchestra. All that extra stress on her hands and wrists, even though it was only something she did in her off time, was a perpetuating factor of her tendonitis."

After he asks questions, Kevin may reach a decision about the sort of modification that must take place. Does the client need a footrest or higher armrests? Should the machines workers are using have levers at a different angle to where they are standing? If Kevin can recommend a solution, he submits his findings to the company. Sometimes, the answer requires some brainstorming with co-workers. Most of this work is done from his own office, researching a particular injury or the solutions that other ergonomists may have already devised. He might need to design his own solution to whatever he thinks the problem is and then monitor the results to determine if he has correctly identified the cause of injury.

Corporate and consulting ergonomists do work reactively. That is, businesses come to them with an established problem and they try to correct it. Some ergonomists, however, are more concerned with product research, design, and development. They don't usually visit other peoples' worksites but rather work in controlled environments, such as laboratories, much like other industrial engineers. They experiment with whatever they are developing and obtain feedback from test subjects. These ergonomists focus on how to make the product

in-depth

What's Wrong With the Way I Sit?

Ergonomists help create environments that enable people to maintain a healthy, ergonomic position—also know as good posture. Problems attributed to sitting at computer work stations include muscle strain, eye strain, tension headaches and numerous other complaints. Often, each of these factors contributes to the worsening of the others, and chronic multiple symptoms appear. Muscle strain that occurs when the head is constantly held forward, for instance, is known as protracted head syndrome.

This syndrome might affect people who sit slumped in a chair while typing. Their spine curves outward unnaturally at the top, or thoracic, vertebrae. To keep their eye level, they then raise their head up past 45 degrees, which is the limit of normal, comfortable range of motion in the neck. This causes great stress on the supporting back muscles, and weakens the muscles in the chest and abdomen. It may also cause respiratory problems, poor circulation, and chronic fatigue. Imagine your head to be a 10-pound bowling ball (your head probably weighs a little more than that) standing on top of a stack of quarters, which would be the vertebrae of your spine. For every inch you hold your head forward from the center line of support, it doubles the weight of your skull on your spine! Now picture your bowling ball slipping forward on that stack of quarters. See how the quarters at the bottom start to slip backwards? Ouch! That's a tearing muscle, or a slipped disc. Ergonomic chairs are built so that the lumbar, or lower vertebrae, curve of your back is supported. It is still possible to slump in an ergonomically designed chair, but it is much easier not to than it is in a poorly designed chair.

they are working on as stress-free and as user-friendly as possible. They may work for manufacturers in areas such as the automotive industry, creating ergonomic seats and dashboards, or the aerospace industry, creating control panels that are easy to operate.

Many consumer products are being redesigned with ergonomics in mind—tea kettles, toothbrushes, aspirin bottles, and pop cans can all boast additions that make their use easier, more comfortable, and safer for their users.

Multiple stressors, as in the case of the typing pianist, make it difficult to prove an injury is caused solely by the work environment. Kevin is able to approach each injury with the assumption that it is legitimate. "At my job, the employee usually already has a medical doctor's diagnosis—yes, he has carpal tunnel, yes, she has tendonitis in her left wrist—so I don't have to worry about whether a person is faking the injury or not." This is an interesting aspect of ergonomy, and one that is increasingly necessary in court rooms and during investigations of workers compensation claims. Could the job that the person is doing have possibly caused the injury he thinks he has sustained? Did she injure herself some other way and wants to claim workers compensation to pay for it? Ergonomists in this field combine aspects of health care issues and labor laws to investigate claims made in workplace injury lawsuits. Ergonomists who deal with the law (known in the industry as forensics professionals) comprise one of 21 areas of specialization within the Human Factors and Ergonomics Society. They concentrate on developing the legal guidelines employers must follow to provide a safe and comfortable workplace. They also provide evidence and data to support legislation having to do with ergonomic issues.

have I got what it takes to be an ergonomist?

Being an ergonomist requires good observation and problem-solving skills: Can you see what the problem is? Do you know how to ask the right questions? Communication plays a key role in a job like Kevin's—if he can't get the information from the people he is trying to help, he won't be able to help them very much. Analysis is a large part; this may require being comfortable with mathematical data and scientific methods of inquiry. "I think that people who are good at this job can look at a situation or problem and see what is causing it," says Kevin, adding that suiting a solution to a problem becomes easier with experience but there is no replacement for a perceptive and logical approach to each situation.

In addition to an analytical aptitude, ergonomy requires a thorough understanding of physics and anatomy. Ergonomists must know what the human body can do and what it can withstand. They should also have the ability to work with many kinds of people in all kinds of settings. Staying up to date with trends in ergonomy is also very important. It allows the professional in this field to offer the most current solutions to the problems of his or her clients. An interest in labor law or workers' rights may be helpful.

The HFES, which has a membership of approximately 5,000, reports that the majority of its members have advanced degrees in psychology and engineering. A large number of people who enter ergonomy, however, come from other fields, some decidedly different that engineering. "The advantage that an engineering degree has given me," Kevin says, "was that I spent four years solving problems and being analytical. That really sharpened my skills. Plus, I don't have a math phobia . . . if I need to calculate how much stress the spine undergoes in lifting a box that weighs so much . . . that's an easy statistics equation for me."

Job satisfaction among ergonomists is higher than the average. "One of the only things I don't like about my job is that I watch other people working all day," Kevin laughs. "Sometimes I want to do some work!"

how do I become an ergonomist?

Kevin discovered ergonomy while in college, almost by accident. It was mentioned in a general engineering course but was not really explored in depth. No classes that dealt exclusively with human factors were offered at his university. He heard about it again in a psychology class. "My first real taste of ergonomy

was an internship as an assistant for a physical therapist at a large health care company in Schaumburg, Illinois. I had gone on a career week through the university with a quality control engineer. I think he was sort of disappointed that I didn't know anything about quality control, but I tagged along with him all week. Through him I met the head of the physical therapy department who had been in Texas helping workers who made pacemakers all day long. I thought, 'That guy's job is cool' and I ended up writing him until he let me intern with him."

education

High School
In general, the future ergonomist should take classes in health; mathematics, including algebra, geometry, and trigonometry; and science, including biology and chemistry. Physics is also an especially helpful course to take, as are courses in computer science and logic. Since communication and research are so important to finding out how other people experience situations, taking such courses as English and speech is also a good idea. Other useful courses for those interested in ergonomics include psychology, design, and sociology.

Postsecondary Training
A bachelor's degree is required to begin work as an ergonomist, and many colleges and universities offer degrees in ergonomy, human factors, industrial engineering with a focus on

ergonomy, and industrial/organization psychology. According to the HFES, there are now more than 75 human factors undergraduate and graduate programs in the country. The HFES Web site contains links to college and university student chapters, and visiting these links is one way to learn more about the programs offered (see Professional Organizations). HFES also publishes the *Directory of Human Factors/Ergonomics Graduate Programs,* with information on graduate programs nationwide. Other resources to use for locating schools include trade journals and professional organizations, such as the Institute of Industrial Engineers, which lists accredited industrial engineering programs on its Web site. Curricula in these programs might include psychology of architecture, industrial design, computer modeling and programming, and anatomy, as well as general engineering classes. Other useful knowledge may be gained from biomechanics/kinesiology, statistics, public health, and labor law. After college, further formal education can include research in a specific dimension of ergonomy.

certification or licensing

Certification in ergonomy is not mandatory, but it is highly recommended for anyone wishing to advance in the profession. The Board of Certification in Professional Ergonomics (BCPE) offers the designations Certified Professional Ergonomist (CPE) and Certified Human Factors Professional (CHFP). To receive either certification, you must have a master's degree in ergonomics, human factors, or equivalent educational experience; four years of professional experience working with

To be a successful ergonomist, you should

- Be a good observer and listener
- Enjoy solving puzzles
- Be analytical
- Enjoy working with a variety of people in a variety of settings
- Be comfortable with mathematical data

ergonomics; documentation of education, work, and project involvement; and a passing score on the written exam given by BCPE. The BCPE also offers the designations Associate Ergonomics Professional (AEP) and Associate Human Factors Professional (AHFP) for those who are working on completing their four years of work experience to get the CPE or CHFP.

Ergonomists who work for the government may need to pass a civil service exam. In order to keep up with industry developments, some ergonomists choose to belong to professional groups like the HFES and the National Society of Professional Engineers. Such groups publish journals containing information about the latest breakthroughs in the industry as well as spread awareness of ergonomy to the public.

internships and volunteerships

Internships are a great way to break into ergonomics. Many large industrial design firms and insurance companies have ergonomics departments. Contacting some of those companies in your area is one place to start your search. The Internet may be able to provide access to those companies through ergonomics and human factors Web sites.

Local chapters of the HFES or similar organizations may be able to help you find companies with internships in your area.

who will hire me?

Ergonomists have the luxury of choosing from among many different fields to work in. People with human factors training can be hired to work anywhere humans come into contact with technology or systems. The 21 areas of specialization within the HFES give some idea of the variety of potential employers. As mentioned earlier, commercial products and industrial design companies employ ergonomists to assist in the development of new, human-oriented versions of old standards. Firms like Ergonomics, Inc. have taken hold because they can troubleshoot a company's workplace without that company bearing the expense for a full-time ergonomics department. Employees are increasingly aware of the strain that work puts on their bodies, and as a result, are complaining of work-related repetitive strain injuries 770 percent more than just 10 years ago. Insurance companies often have ergonomic departments that can help companies reduce economic loss due to injuries, sick days, and fatigue in the workplace.

Makers of prosthetic devices and other aids for people with disabilities use ergonomics to study human factors when human capacity may be limited. Government agencies and the military are also major sources of employment. Academic research requires qualified individuals to validate claims made on behalf of workplace ergonomics legislation efforts. The HFES offers a job placement service to members, based on education, region, and other criteria.

Regulating agencies at the federal and state levels are also possible sources of employment for ergonomists. The Occupational Safety and Health Organization (OSHA), an agency of the U.S. Department of Labor, is responsible for creating mandatory job safety and health standards and enforcing these standards. In addition, a number of states have their own occupational safety and health programs that are monitored by OSHA and carry out these same duties. These agencies have the authority to fine employers who knowingly neglect unsafe or unhealthy worksites that may be improved with ergonomics. OSHA and state programs need ergonomists to make sure that employers are doing everything that they are required to do to keep their employees healthy.

where do I go from here?

Those who are working in government jobs may advance to higher salaries in the private sector by consulting or working in design. Academically, advancement usually involves a master's or doctorate degree in a related field. This may require time dedicated to exhaustive research on a specific topic to contribute to the general knowledge in the field.

Basically, experience and increasing specialization are the methods of advancement in the field of ergonomy. As a result of his experiences helping people eliminate the causes of their injuries, Kevin has become interested in the ways those injuries are healed. Learning physical therapy applications might give him a new perspective on his work and allow him to

offer a more holistic approach to affected workers. He believes that the best ergonomists have a very clear idea of what the body can do and what it is not designed to do. There isn't a job title yet for somebody who goes out to the workplace, observes the strenuous activity causing an injury, recommends ways to reduce the strain or redevelops the equipment being used, and offers suggestions for the clients' self-care and follow-up physical therapy. Perhaps Kevin will be the first "ergonotherapist." Ergonomy is still a very new field, and there is room for pioneers to create their own area of expertise.

what are the salary ranges?

Education is usually the most important determining factor of an ergonomist's salary; the more advanced a person's level of education is, the higher the salary. Those with a bachelor's degree in an engineering field have an average starting salary of approximately $45,888 per year, according to the National Society of Professional Engineers. Those with master's degrees start slightly higher than this. An ergonomist's level of experience is also a factor influencing income. A survey conducted by HFES found that its members had average earnings of approximately $70,175 per year. Those with certification, advanced education, and work experience can expect to have the highest earnings. Full-time employees receive benefit packages such as vacation, health insurance, and retirement plans. Private consultants, including self-employed ergonomists, charge a wide range of hourly fees, from $100 to more than $200, depending on skill level, type of job, and the market in which they are competing. At this pay rate, ergonomists working full-time would have yearly earnings of approximately $200,000 to $400,000. Self-employed workers, however, must provide their own benefits, such as health insurance and retirement plans. In addition, they may also face periods of unemployment, which will lower yearly earnings.

Kevin points out that starting salaries may be less in ergonomy than they would be for those starting out with engineering degrees in other fields, but adds that the job satisfaction can be much higher in ergonomy than in other engineering related fields. A study by HFES also asserts that, because of the high levels of independence, feedback, and variable tasks, ergonomists report higher than average job satisfaction among professional and technical positions.

what is the job outlook?

The employment outlook for ergonomists is good. As the public has gained an increased understanding of and appreciation for ergonomy and as numerous work environments have become more complex because of technology advances, ergonomists have found a steady demand for their services. Businesses will continue to use ergonomy to reduce worker injury, raise levels of production, and increase profits.

Kevin believes urban areas are more receptive to ergonomy because the majority of office and factory jobs that potentially cause problems are located there. He also thinks employers on the East and West coasts may be more aware of the need for ergonomy and of its cost-effectiveness. However, given the general trend of concern for health and safety in the work environment, jobs will be available in most places. Work in this field is not limited to the United States. The HFES is part of a worldwide federation called the International Ergonomics Association, which encourages the exchange of ideas and breakthroughs among member countries.

Nationwide ergonomic legislation has been held up by disagreements over what standards should be set and to whom they should apply. Although OSHA issued an ergonomics standard to address this issue (effective January 16, 2001), the standard was repealed on March 21, 2001 as too costly to businesses. Despite this lack of a nationwide ergonomics standard, however, the need for ergonomists remains strong. Employment should increase about as fast as the average because of the numerous areas of specialization, the opportunities to combine the practice of ergonomy with other fields, such as industrial engineering or psychology, and the relatively few number of ergonomists in the field. Human factors jobs are not expected to be affected very much by a weak economy, and they do very well in times of economic strength. As technology becomes an increasingly unavoidable part of our lives, there will be a demand for people who can make that technology easy, safe, and effective to use.

how do I learn more?

professional organizations

The following organizations provide general information about the field of ergonomics as well as information about education and certification programs.

Board of Certification in Professional Ergonomics
PO Box 2811
Bellingham, WA 98227-2811
360-671-7601
BCPEHQ@bcpe.org
http://www.bcpe.org

Human Factors and Ergonomics Society
PO Box 1369
Santa Monica, CA 90406-1369
310-394-1811
info@hfes.org
http://hfes.org

Institute of Industrial Engineers
25 Technology Park
Norcross, GA 30092
800-494-0460
http://www.iiienet.org

National Society of Professional Engineers
1420 King Street
Alexandria, VA 22314
703-684-2800
http://www.nspe.org

bibliography

Following is a sampling of materials relating to the professional concerns and development of ergonomist and human factors specialists.

Bridger, R. S. *Introduction to Ergonomics.* New York, NY: McGraw-Hill, 1995.

Chapanis, Alphonse. *Human Factors in Systems Engineering.* New York, NY: John Wiley & Sons, 1996.

Hollands, Justin and Christopher Wickens. *Engineering Psychology and Human Performance.* Upper Saddle River, NJ: Prentice-Hall, 1999.

Wickens, Christopher D., et al. *An Introduction to Human Factors Engineering.* Reading, MA: Addison-Wesley, 1997.

Gastroenterologists

Definition
Gastroenterologists are physicians who specialize in the treatment of the digestive system and associated organs, such as the liver and gall bladder.

Alternative Job Title
Internists

High School Subjects
Biology
Chemistry

Personal Skills
Helping/teaching
Technical/scientific

Salary Range
$42,000 to $150,000 to $186,000

Educational Requirements
Bachelor's degree, medical degree

Certification or Licensing
Recommended (certification)
Required by all states (licensing)

Outlook
Faster than the average

GOE
02.03.01
O*NET-SOC
29-1063.00

A 12-year-old boy has been prepped for surgery and as he is wheeled to the operating room, his parents walk alongside his bed. Earlier, the gastroenterologist, Dr. Steven Hanauer, explained how the surgery would help Jake so he didn't have cramps and diarrhea all the time and so that he could play soccer like he used to before he got sick. His illness, Crohn's disease, had caused swelling in his small intestine, and today Steven and his surgical team will remove the diseased portion of the small intestine and reconnect the two healthy ends of the intestine. Steven's nurse showed Jake a picture of the digestive system and pointed out the areas where the doctor would operate. Steven smiles as he remembers the boy's comment at some of the frightening information he was receiving. "If it helps me so I don't have to leave class to go to the bathroom all the time and I can play soccer again, I can do it."

Steven watches from the window where he scrubs for surgery as Jake is wheeled into the operating room. The anesthesiologist starts the intravenous drip that will keep Jake unconscious throughout the surgery. His parents squeeze his hand and leave the room as Jake goes to sleep.

The procedure will take a few hours; Steven will explore the small intestine to identify and remove only the diseased portions and then carefully perform the anastomosis (reconnecting the healthy segments of the intestine). After the surgery, Steven will grab a quick lunch in the hospital lounge before conducting hospital rounds with medical students.

lingo to learn

Antacid: A medication used to neutralize stomach acids.

Colonoscopy: A procedure that involves inserting a soft, bendable tube into the anus and advanced into the rectum and the colon, for cancer screening and to evaluate diarrhea, bleeding, or colitis.

Endoscopy: A procedure where flexible, lighted tubes are inserted into the body without surgery to help diagnose and treat gastrointestinal problems.

Gastritis: A condition in which the lining of the stomach is inflamed.

Helicobacter pylori: Also called *H. pylori*, these bacteria have been shown to have a significant effect on ulcers and their chances of recurring once treated.

Laparoscope: A type of endoscope used to examine the abdominal cavity.

Peptic ulcer: An open sore on the lining of the stomach, esophagus, or duodenum (the first part of the small intestine).

Polyp: Small growth in the colon and intestines that, if left untreated, can become cancerous. Polyps are now commonly removed using endoscopy.

what does a gastroenterologist do?

Gastroenterologists are internal medicine physicians who specialize in the treatment of the digestive system. They examine patients, prescribe drugs when needed, diagnose disease, and perform various procedures to treat those diseases.

Gastroenterologists confine their practice to diseases and conditions of the digestive system, a complex system that includes the esophagus, stomach, small and large intestines, colon, liver, pancreas, and gallbladder. Digestive problems are extremely common. Over 95 million Americans experience some kind of digestive problem, and over 10 million are hospitalized each year for gastrointestinal problems. All people are susceptible to digestive problems, and though many digestive problems are more common as people get older, children and young adults are also susceptible to illnesses such as Crohn's disease. Many digestive problems, such as mild heartburn or ulcer, can be treated by a family physician with drugs or a change in diet. However, there are many disorders of the digestive system that don't respond to diet or drug treatment alone. This is when most patients are referred to a gastroenterologist, who is specially trained in the many common, and not-so-common, disorders of the digestive system. Also, since many disorders of the digestive system share the same symptoms, a gastroenterologist may be needed to perform a diagnostic procedure such as endoscopy, which a family physician may not be qualified to perform.

An endoscope is a medical instrument that enables physicians to see organs and cavities in the body that are otherwise hidden from view. The endoscope is inserted through a natural opening, such as the mouth or rectum. It is a long thin tube with an optic viewing system that transmits images of the patient's body to a television monitor. Endoscopy is a commonly use by gastroenterologists for such things as flexible sigmoidoscopy (view of rectum to lower colon), colonoscopy (view of the entire colon from rectum to lower end of the small intestine), upper GI endoscopy (view of the esophagus, stomach, duodenum), and ERCP (view of the liver, gallbladder, pancreas, bile ducts).

Patients who undergo colonoscopy are most likely adults over age 50. A diagnosis of colon cancer or colorectal polyps (benign growths that occur on the lining of the colon and rectum that can become cancerous) can be confirmed through colonoscopy. Patients who undergo colonoscopy have generally been referred by a family physician who has performed other less invasive tests and suspects polyps or cancer. Only a gastroenterologist can perform a colonoscopy. If the cells removed during the colonoscopy prove cancerous, a gastroenterologist or other specialist such as a colon and rectal surgeon will perform surgery to remove the cancerous polyps and other malignant tissue.

Colon and rectal surgeons are just one of the many specialists gastroenterologists work closely with in treating diseases of the digestive system. Oncologists (cancer specialists), cardiologists (heart specialists), and other surgeons may collaborate to ensure the best possible care. The chronic nature of many gastrointestinal problems means that doctors often have patients for years, building long-term relationships. Patients who suffer from gastrointestinal problems generally experience some level of discomfort from their symptoms, which can include heartburn, nausea, vomiting, diarrhea, and bloating. They are especially appreciative when a gastroenterologist can relieve symptoms that have severely limited their lifestyle and quality of life, as in the case of the 12-year-old boy who couldn't play soccer and was embarrassed by his symptoms.

The field of gastroenterology goes back decades. The American College of Gastroenterology was founded in 1932. The study of the digestive system is as old as medicine, but in recent years there have been a number of important breakthroughs. Peptic ulcers, a common type of ulcer affecting millions of people, have been linked to the *Heliobacter pylori* bacteria. Through research, gastroenterologists learned that treating patients with antibiotics, along with the regular treatments given for ulcers, dramatically lowered the recurrence of the disease. Other advances are technological. Computers and fiber-optic technology have allowed gastroenterologists tremendous flexibility in the diagnosis and treatment of conditions that in the past would have required surgery.

what is it like to be a gastroenterologist?

Dr. Steven Hanauer is a professor of medicine and clinical pharmacology at the University of

Chicago's Center for Research in Inflammatory and Autoimmune Diseases. He is board certified in internal medicine and gastroenterology and a leader in his field in research on inflammatory bowel disease, irritable bowel syndrome, ulcerative colitis, and Crohn's disease. Though much of his time is spent teaching and in conducting clinical trials, he also sees patients on a regular basis and performs diagnostic and surgical procedures.

"I work harder than anyone else I know," he laughs. "I arrive at the hospital by 7 AM and don't leave until 7 PM five days a week. I work Saturday morning in the clinic and take care of writing and paperwork on Saturday afternoons." Along with a gastroenterologist at Johns Hopkins University, Steven is also the co-editor of the medical textbook, *Advanced Therapy of Inflammatory Bowel Disease*, written for physicians and surgeons.

One of the clinical trials he is currently conducting involves an antibody that may prevent certain cells in the body's defense system from causing inflammation and damage to the intestine, such as in Crohn's disease or ulcerative colitis. While many theories about what causes Crohn's disease exist, none have been proven. The most accepted theory is that the body's immune system reacts to a virus or a bacterium by causing ongoing inflammation in the intestine. If successful, this new therapy could prevent Crohn's disease and ulcerative colitis in some individuals.

Steven also spends considerable time traveling to conferences and meetings with colleagues. About one day a week he is traveling somewhere in the United States, he estimates, in addition to about six trips to Europe every year.

The fast-paced lifestyle he leads is not uncommon for doctors who are involved in teaching and research as well as patient care. Some gastroenterologists limit their work to seeing patients; others emphasize teaching and research. And while not all will keep the same hectic schedule Steven does, any physician can expect to work more than a 40-hour workweek, to be on call frequently, and to work long or odd hours. But most who enter this field are ambitious and thrive on the hard work.

"My motivation is to be a leader in my field. If you want to be at the top of your field you can't be afraid to work all the time," Steven comments.

have I got what it takes to be a gastroenterologist?

Physicians are among the most highly trained professionals in the world. For gastroenterologists there is up to 13 years of postsecondary training. Students who want to be doctors must have perseverance. They must also be excellent students, able to master the knowledge and skills necessary to practice medicine.

Gastroenterologists must be able to communicate effectively with other health care professionals and with patients. This includes being a keen listener. A large part of successful treatment is accurate diagnosis, which requires carefully taken patient histories and close analysis of symptoms.

Gastroenterologists must also be able to work with all types of people and have a deep sense of caring and compassion. Steven notes that one of the things that attracted him to the field was the opportunity to conduct research as well as maintain contact with patients through diagnostic procedures and surgery. Gastroenterologists see patients of all ages, since digestive system problems can occur in children, teenagers, and adults.

For Dr. Joseph Kirsner, another gastroenterologist with the University of Chicago Medical School, it is the degree of intimacy in the lives of a doctor's patients that makes gastroenterology unique. "A patient's life situation is very important," he explains. "The connection between emotions and gastrointestinal problems is well known. Fifty percent of my patients are caught up in the problems of living, and a gastroenterologist has to understand that."

how do I become a gastroenterologist?

education

High School
Medical training requires a very strong background in the sciences, so you should take as many science classes as you can. Biology and chemistry are most important, but physics, anatomy, and others are also helpful. Mathematics and humanities, especially English, will help prepare you for the rigorous academic demands encountered in college and medical school.

Postsecondary Training
Many people who want to go to medical school choose one of the basic sciences, like biochemistry, as their major field of study, but it is not required. Some students take a premed program, which includes many science courses, such as biochemistry, physics, and physiology. Some college students volunteer in hospitals to gain experience and to see if they enjoy a medical environment.

You must take Medical College Admissions Test (MCAT) at some point during your undergraduate studies. The exam covers four areas: verbal facility, quantitative ability, knowledge of the humanities and social sciences, and knowledge of biology, chemistry, and physics. All medical colleges in the country require the test for admission.

Medical schools admit about half of their applicants. Only the best candidates are accepted. College grades are very important, but there are many people with excellent grades who do not get in to medical school. MCAT scores are taken into consideration, as are the applicants' character, personality, and extracurricular activities.

The course of study in medical school is intense, with the first two years being devoted to laboratory and classroom study. In the second and third years the emphasis is on clinical experience.

After completing medical school, you must enter an internal medicine residency, which

Diseases Treated by Gastroenterologists

Cholecystitis: An infection of the gallbladder.

Cirrhosis: Permanent injury and scarring of the liver, causing harm to the structure of the liver and blocking the flow of blood through the organ.

Diverticulosis: Small pouches that bulge outward through weak spots in the colon. Each pouch is called a diverticulum. When the pouches become infected or inflamed, the condition is called diverticulitis.

Gastroesophageal reflux disease (GERD): A digestive disorder that affects the muscle that connects the esophagus with the stomach.

Hemorrhoids: Swollen blood vessels in and around the anus and lower rectum that stretch under pressure, similar to varicose veins in the legs.

Inflammatory bowel disease (IBD): A group of chronic disorders that cause inflammation or ulceration in the small and large intestines. IBD may be called ulcerative colitis, Crohn's disease, colitis, enteritis, ileitis, or proctitis.

Irritable bowel syndrome (IBS): Also called spastic colon or mucous colitis; occurs when bowel movements occur too slowly (constipation) or too quickly (diarrhea).

Lactose intolerance: The inability to digest significant amounts of lactose, the predominant sugar of milk.

Pancreatitis: A rare disease in which the pancreas becomes inflamed; damage to the gland occurs when digestive enzymes are activated and begin attacking the pancreas.

Ulcer: A sore or lesion that forms in the lining of the stomach or duodenum (upper part of the small intestine). Ulcers in the stomach are called gastric or stomach ulcers. Those in the duodenum are called duodenal ulcers. In general, ulcers in the stomach and duodenum are referred to as peptic ulcers.

---

lasts three years. Following residency, you must spend an additional two to three years in a gastroenterology fellowship. Competition for the available openings is fierce. According to Joseph, the University of Chicago receives 400 applications every year for its two or three openings.

At all points in your career as a gastroenterologist it is very important to keep up with the rapid advances in the field. Continuing education is paramount in providing the best possible care for patients. Taking postgraduate courses and remaining active in medical education are some of the ways to remain current in the field.

certification or licensing

After receiving your medical degree, you are required to take an examination to be licensed to practice. It is conducted through the board of medical examiners of each state.

Certification, offered by the American Board of Internal Medicine (ABIM), is not required but is recommended. It is a sign of professional excellence in the field and one that patients may look for in choosing a gastroenterologist. To become a board-certified gastroenterologist first requires certification in internal medicine. ABIM requirements for internal medicine certification are: graduation from an accredited medical school, three years of postdoctoral training, proven clinical competency, and passage of a comprehensive examination. Additional requirements for certification in the subspecialty of gastroenterology include three years of training in gastroenterology and passing a comprehensive subspecialty exam.

scholarships and grants

Most students borrow the money they need to go to medical school. Added to the debt many have from their undergraduate education, the amount can reach in excess of $100,000. There are scholarship opportunities offered by various government agencies. The Armed Forces Health Professions Scholarship Program provides recipients with tuition and a small salary in exchange for active service in the military. Doctors serve one year for each year they receive payments. Each branch of the military participates in this program, paying students' tuition in exchange for military service. Contact your local recruiting office for more information on this program.

Scholarships and grants are also available from individual institutions, state agencies, and special-interest organizations. The National Health Service Corps Scholarship Program also provides money for students in return for service in underserved or rural communities. Another source for financial aid, scholarship, and grant information is the Association of American Medical Colleges.

Armed Forces Health Professions Scholarship Program
Air Force: http://hp.airforce.com/training/financial.html
Army: http://www.sirius.com/~ameddet/hpschps.htm
Navy: http://nshs.med.navy.mil/hpsp/default.htm

Association of American Medical Colleges
2450 N Street, NW
Washington, DC 20037
202-828-0400
http://www.aamc.org

To be a successful gastroenterologist, you should

- Have a deep sense of caring for others
- Be a good communicator and keen listener
- Be able to work with a variety of people
- Have an abiding interest in science
- Have a great deal of perseverance
- Be committed to continuing education

National Health Service Corps
Scholarship Programs Branch
U.S. Public Health Service
4350 East-West Highway, 10th Floor
Bethesda, MD 20814
301-594-4410
http://www.fedmoney.org/grants/93288-00.htm

who will hire me?

Gastroenterologists, like all physicians, can work in different settings. The majority work in some type of office-based practice, such as a clinic or health maintenance organization; some are employed solely by hospitals, including teaching hospitals affiliated with university medical schools.

In the past, many physicians went into business for themselves, either by starting their own practice or by becoming a partner in an existing one. Today, fewer physicians are choosing to follow this path for a number of reasons. Often, the costs of starting a practice or buying into an existing practice are too high. Instead, more new physicians are taking salaried positions. Over one-third of all physicians are now salaried employees of provider groups such as hospitals, physician-hospital organizations, and large group practices. This caps the doctor's income, since salaried employees, unlike partners, do not receive a share of the profits in successful practices. On the positive side, many doctors are attracted to a guaranteed income and the freedom from the responsibilities of running a business.

where can I go from here?

Most gastroenterologists continue to see patients on a regular basis, even if they emphasize research or teaching in their career. Joseph has been a doctor for more than 60 years, and he is still treating patients and working with residents. These doctors may eventually run departments, as Steven does. Doctors who wish to move on have become hospital administrators, have organized their own medical service companies, or have joined pharmaceutical or bioengineering companies as researchers, consultants, or sales representatives. Some doctors return to school to become teachers in medical schools. They often decide to earn an advanced degree in a basic science, like biology.

what are the salary ranges?

Salaries during medical residencies ranged from about $34,100 to $42,100 in 1998-99, according to the Association of American Medical Colleges (AAMC). After completing a residency, internal medicine specialists average about $150,000 per year. Several factors influence earnings, including years of experience, geographic region of practice, and reputation. In general, those working in private practice earn more than those on staff at a hospital. The median salary in 1999-2000 for an assistant professor of gastroenterology at a teaching hospital was $134,000. After a few years' experience and advancement to associate professorship, the median salary rises to $163,000 and to $186,000 for those with full professorship at a teaching hospital, according to the AAMC.

what is the job outlook?

The job outlook for physicians as a whole is good. The U.S. Department of Labor predicts the field to grow faster than the average for all occupations. The demographics of the U.S. population bodes well for all physicians, as baby boomers age and come to need more medical services.

Still, gastroenterology is a very competitive field, and the demographics that are creating jobs for other physicians may not provide the influx of patients for gastroenterologists. Cardiologists and oncologists, for example, stand to gain patients as the population ages because diseases of the heart and circulatory system and cancers are more frequent with age. Diseases of the digestive system, however, range across all age groups.

Also, managed care companies stress preventive medicine by primary care physicians over treatments by specialists, which can be very expensive. In response to this financial pressure, more medical students are choosing

family practice residencies. Joseph, for one, believes the effect of this shift will be temporary, and that patient demands for the best possible care will create openings for specialists in the more distant future. Internal medicine is considered a primary care discipline and some gastroenterologists may be able to find work as internists.

how do I learn more?

professional organizations

Following are organizations that provide information on gastroenterologist careers.

For information on certification requirements, contact:
American Board of Internal Medicine
510 Walnut Street, Suite 1700
Philadelphia, PA 19106
800-441-2246
request@abim.org
http://www.abim.org

American College of Gastroenterology
4900 B South 31st Street
Arlington, VA 22206
703-820-7400
http://www.acg.gi.org

American Gastroenterological Association
7910 Woodmont Avenue, 7th Floor
Bethesda, MD 20814
301-654-2055
http://www.gastro.org/

exploring health care careers

bibliography

Following is a sampling of materials relating to the professional concerns and development of gastroenterologists.

Aliperti, Giuseppe, ed. *The Year Book of Gastroenterology.* St. Louis, MO: Mosby-Yearbook, 1999.

Brandt, Lawrence J. and Fredric Daum, eds. *Clinical Practice of Gastroenterology.* Kent,.UK: Churchill Livingstone, 1999.

Heuman, Douglas M., A. Scott Mills, and Hunter H. McGuire, Jr. *Gastroenterology.* Philadelphia, PA: W. B. Saunders Company, 1996.

Rigas, Basil. *Clinical Gastroenterology: Companion Handbook.* 4th Edition. New York, NY: McGraw-Hill, 2000.

Yamada, Tadataka and David H. Alpers, eds. *Textbook of Gastroenterology.* 3rd Edition. Philadelphia, PA: Lippincott Williams & Wilkins, 1999.

General Practitioners

Definition

General practitioners provide primary care to people of all ages. They diagnose and treat various common ailments.

Alternative Job Titles

Family practitioners
Primary care physicians

High School Subjects

Biology
Chemistry

Personal Skills

Helping/teaching
Technical/scientific

Salary Range

$34,000 to $136,000 to $250,000+

Educational Requirements

Bachelor's degree, medical degree (M.D. or D.O), residency training

Certification or Licensing

Required by all states

Outlook

Faster than the average

GOE
02.03.01
O*NET-SOC
29-1062.00

Dr. Warren Dollar is tired. He was on call last night, and his pager went off repeatedly. Now it is 8:30 AM, and his first patient of the day is waiting in an examining room. He sits at his desk, finishing a quick cup of coffee and looking over a log of phone calls.

"Dr. Dollar?" his nurse, Cynthia, appears at the door. "Dr. McCahn wanted to check with you on Emily Rohne's condition. She called last night?"

"She did, yes," Dr. Dollar replies. "I've got to get in to see this patient right now, but tell Jim I'll talk to him afterward."

"Okay," Cynthia says. "And I pulled all the charts you asked for. I'll bring them in for you."

"Thank you, Cyn." Standing up, Dr. Dollar reaches for a stethoscope that is lying on his desk. "And, hey, can you do me a favor? Make another pot of coffee?"

what does a general practitioner do?

Many physicians specialize in one particular aspect of medicine. Some, for example, specialize in treating a certain part of the body, such as the heart. Others become specialists in treating a particular disease, such as cancer. There is, however, a physician who treats all types of patients for a wide variety of diseases and injuries. These physicians are called *general practitioners,* or *primary care physicians.* They are usually the first health care professional their patients consult for a problem. They tend to see the same patients on a continuing basis, often for years. They may also be called *family care physicians,* because they treat all the members of a family.

General practitioners diagnose and treat any illness or injury that does not require the service of a specialist. When their patients need more extensive treatment than they can provide, general practitioners refer them to an appropriate specialist.

General practitioners perform routinely scheduled examinations on healthy patients as part of their preventive care. A routine examination might involve listening to a patient's heart and lungs with a stethoscope; checking the ear canal, throat, and eyes; testing range of motion and reflexes; and palpating the abdomen for signs of pain or discomfort. In addition to these diagnostic procedures, the doctor may ask the patient questions about his or her sleep patterns, diet, exercise routine, and other health-related issues.

After the exam, the general practitioner may order further diagnostic tests and procedures, such as urine or blood tests, electrocardiograms, or CAT scans, to analyze the patient's health in greater detail.

When treating a sick or injured patient, the general practitioner asks about current symptoms and performs an examination. If he or she diagnoses an illness or injury, the doctor then decides upon a course of treatment. This may involve prescribing medication or treatment, ordering further tests, or referring the patient to a specialist.

Unlike a specialist, general practitioners treat the whole patient, not just a specific body part or illness. They may offer advice on diet, lifestyle, and other methods for preventing disease or injury. They often follow their patients for years, monitoring their health and progress through various stages of life.

According to the American Academy of Family Physicians, general practitioners average 52 hours per week in practice; 96.4 percent of their time is spent in the office, seeing patients by appointment. In addition to office visits, they make hospital rounds, perform minor surgery (either at the hospital or at an outpatient surgery clinic), and, in some cases, visit patients in nursing homes or other residential facilities.

General practitioners who work in a physicians' group usually take turns being on call for questions and emergencies that arise outside normal office hours. Doctors who work in a solo practice must either remain on call constantly or coordinate with other physicians who can share the responsibility.

Depending upon a physician's working arrangement, he or she may be responsible for supervising office staff and running the business end of the practice. In larger physicians' groups, these duties are usually taken care of by an office manager.

lingo to learn

Electrocardiogram (EKG): A visible record of the electrical activity occurring as the heart beats.

Health Maintenance Organization (HMO): A network of doctors that provides comprehensive health care but limits the subscriber to referrals for care by outside specialists.

Managed care: A philosophy of health care that tries to keep medical costs down through education and preventive medicine.

Otoscope: A viewing instrument used to examine the outer ear canal and the eardrum.

Outpatient: Patient treated at the hospital but not admitted for extended care.

what is it like to be a general practitioner?

Dr. Warren Dollar has worked for 30 years in a practice that he owns with another physician. His staff consists of four nurses and three office workers who handle patient records and take care of the billing and insurance.

He starts his workday early. "I usually have a patient scheduled by 8:30," he says. "So I come in a bit earlier and take care of any paperwork, return phone calls—whatever needs to be done."

Warren sees a wide range of patients, from newborns to the elderly. Many of his patients have been coming to him their whole lives. "I don't deliver babies anymore, but I used to," he says. "Now I see these 'kids' that I delivered 25 years ago, coming in with their own kids."

The types of illnesses that Dr. Dollar sees are as varied as his patients' ages. "I see a wide variety of things," he says. "From kids with ear infections to seniors with arthritis."

Some patients come in with a medical problem that requires specialized treatment. In this case, Warren refers them to an appropriate doctor within a network of medical professionals. This network is called a HMO, or Health Management Organization. Patients who belong to the HMO select a primary care physician who is responsible for basic health care and medical referrals. For example, if a patient needs the services of a cardiologist, the HMO requires a written referral to the cardiologist from the patient's primary care physician. The primary care physician serves as a "gatekeeper" to medical services.

"Patients who see me under the HMO often come in and say, 'Dr. Dollar, I really think I need to see an ear, nose, and throat specialist,'—or whatever. If I agree that it's necessary, then I refer them."

Many cases do not involve another doctor. For more basic medical ailments, Warren decides upon a course of treatment, such as a prescription drug. Sometimes, he works with patients to help them improve their health without medication by simply modifying their lifestyles. Warren often advises patients on proper diet and exercise. "Patient education is a very big facet of this work," he says. "People need to know how their choices affect their health. They need to know what not to eat when they have gallbladder problems. They need to know how smoking affects their blood pressure. They need to know why exercise is important."

Some ailments require a bit more investigation before determining treatment. Warren routinely orders blood tests, urine tests, throat cultures, and other laboratory tests to help him diagnose the nature and extent of a patient's problem. In some cases, he may order X rays, CAT scans, electrocardiograms, or electroencephalograms.

While the bulk of his workday is spent seeing patients, Warren has certain other duties as well. Although the office staff takes care of much of the paperwork, he and his partner oversee the office finances. They authorize payments, salary increases, and equipment and supply orders.

> I don't think you could stand this job if you didn't like people. Really, it's all about people.

have I got what it takes to be a general practitioner?

A successful general practitioner should first and foremost like people. Because this type of physician must develop an ongoing relationship with his or her patients, good people skills are essential. "I don't think you could stand this job if you didn't like people," says Warren. "Really, it's all about people."

A general practitioner should have compassion for his or her patients and should be able to relate to them in an understanding way. "You've got to be sensitive to people's needs," Warren says. "Sometimes patients come in and they want to talk to you. They want some soothing. Whatever is wrong with them, you have to take it seriously."

In addition to compassion, general practitioners need a great deal of stamina to keep up with the many demands their jobs require. Physicians work long irregular hours, including instances when they may be called from their homes or offices to attend to emergencies. "It's not your regular nine-to-five job," says Warren. "You have to be willing to make it a really substantial part of your life."

Dedication is also necessary to keep up with the rigorous educational demands. "Med school is a grind, residency is a grind," he says. "It's well worth the effort, but believe me, it is an effort."

For Warren, as for many physicians, however, the career's rewards far outweigh its demands. Helping sick people become well is both gratifying and uplifting. "You know, when you help someone—when someone comes in feeling awful and you know you can make them feel better—that's just a wonderful feeling," he says. "That makes everything worthwhile."

how do I become a general practitioner?

Warren decided early on he wanted to be physician. In the seventh grade, a friend of the family influenced his career interests. "One of my dad's friends was a doctor in our town, and he was always telling me that I should consider medical school," he explains. "He really loved the career, and he piqued my interest. In fact, my current partner is his son."

more lingo to learn

Preferred Provider Organization (PPO): A network of medical professionals that are under contract with insurance companies to provide care to individual subscribers.

Preventive care: A type of medical care that stresses the prevention of disease by teaching patients better eating habits and other healthy lifestyle choices.

Residency: A period of advanced medical training and education that normally follows graduation from medical school.

Stethoscope: An instrument used for listening to sounds within the body, primarily in the heart and lungs.

education

High School

High school students who plan to become physicians need to take a basic college preparatory curriculum, including English, history, social studies, math, and foreign languages.

Specific high school classes that will be helpful to prospective physicians include biology, chemistry, physics, and physiology. English and speech classes are also useful because doctors need to develop good communication skills, both written and oral.

Finally, look into volunteer opportunities in local hospitals or other health care facilities. You can gain exposure to a medical environment and experience helping people, even if your job involves delivering flowers or filling water pitchers in patients' rooms. You can also benefit from simply talking to general practitioners about their work.

Postsecondary Training

In college, you should enroll in a program with a strong emphasis on the sciences, such as a premed program. You can also follow a liberal arts program and major in biology or chemistry. In general, students take classes in physics, biology, mathematics, inorganic and organic chemistry, as well as classes in the humanities and social sciences.

During the junior or senior year of college, students should arrange to take the Medical College Admission Test (MCAT). This test, which is given twice a year, evaluates students' ability in four areas: verbal facility, quantitative ability, knowledge of the humanities and social sciences, and knowledge of biology, chemistry, and physics.

Medical schools are highly competitive. In addition to MCAT scores, applicants must submit transcripts and letters of recommendation. In addition to academics, an applicant's character, personality, leadership qualities, and participation in extracurricular activities are also taken into account.

During the first two years of medical school, students spend most of their time in the laboratory or the classroom. They take courses such as anatomy, physiology, pharmacology, psychology, microbiology, pathology, medical ethics, and medical law. They also learn how to take medical histories, examine patients, and recognize basic symptoms.

The last two years are spent working with patients in hospitals and clinics under the supervision of practicing physicians. Students spend set periods of time, called "rotations," in internal medicine, family practice, obstetrics and gynecology, pediatrics, psychiatry, and surgery.

While remaining closely supervised, the medical student is actively involved in patient treatment as part of a hospital medical team. The student also continues to do course work. In addition to the clinical sciences, there may be work in business areas, such as decision analysis and cost containment.

Upon completion of medical school, students receive either the Doctor of Medicine (M.D.) or the Doctor of Osteopathic Medicine (D.O.) degree and continue their training through medical residencies. Residents are actively involved in patient treatment as part of a hospital medical team. The residency for a general practitioner usually lasts three years and involves long hours of demanding work and intensive study. According to the Association of American Medical Colleges, residents may work up to 80 hours per week, day or night.

certification or licensing

All states and the District of Columbia require physicians to be licensed. General practitioners seeking licensure must graduate from an accredited medical school, complete residency postgraduate training, and pass a licensing examination administered by their state's board of medical examiners. Some states have reciprocity agreements so that a physician licensed to practice in one state may be automatically licensed in another state without having to pass another examination.

Board certification is granted by the American Board of Family Practice. This credential, though voluntary, signifies that the physician is highly qualified in family practice. To be eligible to take the credentialing exam, applicants must have satisfactorily completed three years of residency training accredited by the Accreditation Council for Graduate Medical Education (ACGME) after receiving their medical degree from an accredited institution.

scholarships and grants

Medical school is extremely costly. According to the American Association of Medical Col-

The ancient Greek physician Hippocrates is credited with the belief that disease has physical, not magical, causes.

leges, annual tuition and fees at state medical schools in 1999 averaged $11,375 for state residents and $25,195 for nonresidents. At private schools, annual tuition and fees averaged $26,991 for residents and $28,733 for nonresidents. Over 80 percent of medical students borrow money to cover their expenses through grants or loans.

When evaluating medical schools, students should be sure to get information on the financial aid possibilities for each one. Some schools may offer scholarships, grants, or awards to qualified students.

There also are financial aid opportunities available from both government and private sources. The easiest way to explore these options is either to contact the source directly or do your own research through your college financial aid office or at your local library.

Loan programs available through the federal government include Pell Grants, Stafford Student Loans, and the National Direct Student Loan Program.

Students can also finance their medical education through military service. The Armed Forces Health Professions Scholarship Program and the National Health Service Corps Scholarship Program provide money for students in return for military service.

Another source for financial aid, scholarship, and grant information is the Association of American Medical Colleges. Remember to request information early for eligibility, application requirements, and deadlines.

**Armed Forces Health Professions
Scholarship Program**
Air Force: http://hp.airforce.com/training/
financial.html
Army: http://www.sirius.com/~ameddet/
hpschps.htm
Navy: http://nshs.med.navy.mil/hpsp/default.htm

Association of American Medical Colleges
2450 N Street, NW
Washington, DC 20037-1126
202-828-0400
http://www.aamc.org

**National Health Service Corps
Scholarship Program**
Department of Health and Human Services
4350 East-West Highway, 10th Floor
Bethesda, MD 20814
800-638-0824
http://www.fedmoney.org/grants/93288-00.htm

who will hire me?

When Warren finished his residency, he was approached by the same family friend who suggested he attend medical school and was offered space in his practice.

"Although I wasn't certain that I wanted to come back here after I finished college, I decided to try it," Warren says. "And here I am still."

After general practitioners complete their residency programs, they are ready to enter practice. They may choose to open a solo private practice, join a partnership or group practice, or take a salaried job in a clinic or man-

aged care (HMO or PPO) network. Salaried positions are also available with federal and state agencies, neighborhood health centers, and the military, including the Department of Veterans Affairs.

Many new physicians choose to join existing practices instead of attempting to start their own. Establishing a new practice is costly, and it may take time to build a patient base. In a clinic, group practice, or partnership, physicians share the costs for medical equipment and staff salaries, as well establish a wider patient base.

General practitioners who hope to join an existing practice may find leads through their medical school or residency. During these experiences, they work with many members of the medical community, some of which may be able to recommend them to appropriate practices.

Another approach would be to check the various medical professional journals, which often run ads for physician positions. Aspiring physicians can also hire a medical placement agency to assist them in the job search.

Physicians who hope to work for a managed care organization or government sponsored clinic should contact the source directly for information on position availability and application procedures.

The majority of physicians practice in urban areas, near hospitals and educational centers. Therefore, competition for patients is likely to be higher in these areas. In contrast, rural communities and small towns are often in need of doctors and may be promising places for young physicians to establish practices.

To be a successful general practitioner, you should

- Be committed to helping people
- Be compassionate and understanding
- Have the stamina to work long and irregular hours
- Have good communication skills
- Inspire confidence and trust

where can I go from here?

There are few advancement possibilities for general practitioners. Like most other physicians, these doctors stay in their field, building their practices until retirement. As they build their patient bases and reputations, their practices become larger and their incomes steadily increase. For those who work in a large group practice, advancement may come in the form of opening a private practice.

Some general practitioners decide to pursue a teaching or research career at a college or university. Generally, these doctors first earn a Ph.D. in the sciences.

what are the salary ranges?

Physicians, as a group, have among the highest annual earnings of all occupations. According to the American Medical Association, median income for all physicians was $164,000 in the late 1990s. The middle 50 percent earned between $120,000 and $250,000 a year.

However, salaries vary widely depending on specialty. The income of general practitioners, though lower than many other specialists, has been on the rise in the last decade, according to the Academy of Family Physicians. In 1997, the average net income for family physicians (not involved in obstetrics) was $136,002. Starting general practitioners generally earn more at the beginning of their career compared to other physicians. For this reason, most newly graduated practitioners are able to pay off their student loans quickly.

A general practitioner's earnings may be affected by several factors, such as location and type of practice. Income tends to increase with the size of the city in which a physician is located. However, some underserved communities offer high salaries to attract badly needed medical professionals. According to a 1997 survey by the American Academy of Family Physicians, those working in urban areas made an average of $137,900 a year, while those working in rural communities earned a bit more, at $140,800 a year.

Salaries for medical residents in 1998-99 ranged from $34,100 for first-year residents to $42,100 for sixth-year residents, according to the Association of American Medical Colleges.

A general practitioner's income increases with years of experience. According to an American Medical Association study, physicians' incomes tend to build gradually to a peak between the ages of 46 and 55.

Practitioners affiliated with a group practice make a higher net income than those in solo practice, but those who are self-employed earn considerably more than salaried employees.

Physicians who are self-employed must provide their own insurance coverage. Those who are employed by a clinic or managed care organization usually receive a benefits package that includes insurance and paid time off.

what is the job outlook?

Employment of all physicians is expected to grow faster than the average for all occupations through the next decade, according to the U.S. Department of Labor. One reason for this demand is population growth. People are also living longer, requiring more health care as they age.

Another reason for the growth is the availability of better health care. Physicians can perform more tests and treat conditions that were once untreatable. In addition, the widespread use of medical insurance plans help to make expensive procedures more affordable to patients.

According to the American Academy of Family Physicians, job opportunities are especially good for general practitioners. Efforts to control health care costs have increased the role of managed care systems. These networks employ many primary care physicians. In managed care, patients who might once have gone immediately to a specialist must now see their general practitioner first to get a referral for further treatment.

Because most physicians choose to practice in urban areas, these areas are often oversupplied and fiercely competitive. General practitioners just entering the field may find it difficult to enter a practice and build a patient base in a big city. There is a growing need, however, for physicians in rural communities and small towns. General practitioners who are willing to relocate to these areas should have excellent job prospects.

how do I learn more?

professional organizations

For more information on becoming a general practitioner, contact the following organizations:

American Academy of Family Physicians
11400 Tomahawk Creek Parkway
Leawood, KS 66211-2672
800-274-2237
http://www.aafp.org

American Board of Family Practice
2228 Young Drive
Lexington, KY 40505-4294
888-995-5700
general@abfp.org
htttp://www.abfp.org

American Medical Association
515 North State Street
Chicago, IL 60610
312-464-5000
http://www.ama-assn.org

American Osteopathic Association
142 East Ontario Street
Chicago, IL 60611
800-621-1773
http://www.am-osteo-assn.org

Association of American Medical Colleges
2450 N Street, NW
Washington, DC 20037-1126
202-828-0400
http://www.aamc.org

bibliography

Following is a sampling of materials relating to the professional concerns and development of general practitioners.

Braunwald, Eugene et al. *Harrison's Principles of Internal Medicine*. 15th Edition. New York, NY: McGraw-Hill, 2001.

Chan, Paul D. et al. eds. *Medicine*. 2001 Edition. Laguna Beach, CA: Current Clinical Strategies, 2000.

Ferri, Fred F. *Practical Guide to the Care of the Medical Patient*. St. Louis, MO: Mosby, Inc. 2001.

Haist, Steven A. *Internal Medicine on Call*. New York:, NY: McGraw-Hill, 1997.

Most people in the United States can expect to live well into their 70s. In 1850, however, the average life span was only about 40 years. Lengthened life span is largely the result of centuries of medical advances.

Hirsch, Jeffrey G. *Family Medicine*. 2nd Edition. New York:, NY Springer-Verlag, 1996.

Huang, Elbert et al. *Internal Medicine: Handbook for Clinicians, Resident Survival Guide*. Arlington, VA: Scrub Hill Press, 2000.

Lederman, Robert J. and James S. Winshall. *Tarascon Internal Medicine & Critical Care Pocketbook*. 2nd Edition. Loma Linda, CA: Tarascon Press, 2000.

Rakel, Robert E. *Conn's Current Therapy, 2001: Latest Approved Methods of Treatment for the Practicing Physician*. Kent, UK: W. B. Saunders, 2001.

Schrier, Robert W., ed. *The Internal Medicine Casebook: Real Patients, Real Answers*. Philadelphia, PA: Lippincott Williams & Wilkins, 2000.

Sloane, Philip D. *Essentials of Family Medicine*. 3rd Edition. Philadelphia, PA: Lippincott Williams & Wilkins, 1998.

Taylor, Robert B., et al. eds. *Family Medicine: Principles and Practice*. 5th Edition, London, UK: Springer Verlag, 1998.

Tierney, Lawrence M., et al. eds. *Current Medical Diagnosis and Treatment 2001*. New York, NY: McGraw-Hill, 2000.

General Surgeons

Definition
General surgeons provide preoperative, operative, and postoperative care in surgery for almost any part of the body. They also typically work with trauma victims and the critically ill.

High School Subjects
Biology
Chemistry
Health

Personal Skills
Helping/teaching
Technical/scientific

Salary Range
$175,000 to $204,000 to $300,000+

Educational Requirements
Bachelor's degree, medical degree, residency

Certification or Licensing
Required by all states

Outlook
Faster than the average

GOE
02.03.01

O*NET-SOC
29-1067.00

Emergency room doors slide open as a medical technician calls out vital signs to the on-duty surgeon. A child and his mother have been in a car accident. The child lies bleeding and unresponsive on a gurney. In a matter of moments, the surgeon has decided which case is more urgent and begins to work on the small boy. While the chief resident and two medical students attend to the mother, the surgeon works with a team to try to stabilize the child. The surgeon discovers that a piece of metal has pierced the boy's appendix and arranges for an immediate appendectomy.

As orderlies transfer the child to an operating room, the surgeon asks, "What's next?" It is a drive-by shooting victim, wounded in the chest, abdomen, and leg. "Here we go again," the surgeon sighs. It is another typical night for a surgeon on duty in the ER.

what does a general surgeon do?

General surgeons perform operations to repair injuries, remove diseased or deformed organs, and prevent disease. They are trained to perform surgery on almost any part of the body. Because of their broad knowledge, general surgeons also usually oversee emergency room trauma victims and critically ill patients.

The general surgeon must be able to surgically treat any patient that comes through the emergency room. To do this, the surgeon learns the core knowledge and skills common to all surgical specialties. Through clinical training, the general surgeon acquires knowledge and technical skills treating conditions affecting the head and neck, chest, skin, abdominal wall, extremities (hands and feet), and physiological systems such as the vascular system. General surgeons must also know when to refer patients to specialists. They use a variety of diagnostic techniques to detect problems, including endoscopy, which uses fiber-optic instruments to closely examine organs.

The work of general surgeons varies according to the area in which they specialize. For example, a general surgeon who specializes in trauma care often works in a large urban hospital, spending a great deal of time performing emergency procedures in the operating room. On the other hand, a general surgeon who specializes in hernia repair can expect a more predictable work schedule and spends most of the time in an ambulatory (outpatient) surgery center.

A general surgeon is responsible for the diagnosis of a patient, for performing operations, and for providing patients with postoperative surgical care and treatment. In emergency room situations, the patient typically comes in complaining of severe pain. If the patient needs surgery, the on-duty general surgeon will schedule the surgery. Depending on the urgency of the case, surgery may be scheduled immediately or for the following day.

A general surgeon may treat gunshot, stabbing, or accident victims. Other cases that often involve emergency surgery include appendectomies (removal of the appendix), splenectomies (removal of the spleen), or removal of kidney stones. When problems such as a kidney stone or an inflamed appendix are diagnosed at an early stage, the general surgeon can perform nonemergency surgery.

There are four areas of subspecialization in general surgery: general vascular surgery, pediatric surgery, hand surgery, and surgical critical care. General vascular surgery involves the blood vessels, excluding those of the heart, lungs, or brain. Pediatric surgery involves surgical procedures on premature and newborn infants, children, and adolescents. Hand surgery covers procedures done to the hand and wrist. Surgical critical care involves overseeing critically ill patients, especially trauma victims. These surgeons typically work in emergency rooms, intensive care units, trauma units, or burn units.

lingo to learn

Drape: Sterile cloth used to surround and isolate the actual site or location of the operation on the patient's body.

Endoscope: An instrument used to visually examine the interior of a hollow organ.

Esophagus: The muscular canal that extends from the pharynx (throat) to the stomach.

Forceps: An instrument that looks like cooking tongs; used by surgeons to hold back skin or other soft tissue.

Hernia: Condition in which an organ pushes through the muscle wall of the cavity surrounding it. Hernias can be surgically repaired.

Scrubbing: The cleaning of the hands, wrists, and forearms of the surgeon and all surgical staff before surgery to kill germs and harmful bacteria.

Sterile field: The sterile area in which the surgery takes place; any object or person entering this area must be sterilized, or completely free of germs and bacteria.

Sutures: The stitches used to close a wound or surgical incision.

Vascular: Having to do with the blood vessels.

what is it like to be a general surgeon?

"I'm never, ever bored," says Dr. Kathryn D. Anderson, surgeon-in-chief at a children's hospital in Los Angeles, California. In addition to the surgical procedures she regularly performs, Kathryn is particularly interested in cases involving lungs and the esophagus.

Many of her cases are babies born prematurely. They often have difficulty breathing and need time for their lungs to heal or recover. "We put them on a heart/lung machine for several days," explains Kathryn. "The machine drives the oxygen through their lungs for them, giving their lungs a chance to heal."

She has also become an expert at replacing or reattaching a child's esophagus. "We take eating for granted—these kids don't," she says. "Children swallow lye, or household products, and destroy or damage their esophagus. And some children are born without an esophagus or with the esophagus not joined to the stomach," she explains. "Usually, you can join them, either with a piece of the large intestine or with a part of the stomach."

The parents of ill children seek her out because of her expertise in these areas, but she remains humble. "You become an expert by doing something well," she says simply.

Kathryn's work keeps her in the operating room, on the average, two days a week, for most of the day. She arrives at the hospital at 6:30 or 7 in the morning and does not leave until 7 or 8 that night. The rest of her week is spent seeing patients, teaching, and running the departments and divisions that she heads.

Some surgeons relinquish much of their roles as active surgeons once they acquire additional administrative responsibilities. However, Kathryn feels that continuing to practice surgery is essential. "I think one is more credible as an administrator if one is practicing," she says.

Ever since she was a young child, Kathryn wanted to be a doctor. Through determination and family support, she advanced in a career that was at the time extremely difficult for women to enter. "When young women look at me today, they think I had an ambition to be chief surgeon from the start, but it wasn't like that, really," says Kathryn. "I always segmented my ambitions, and this was true of medicine, as well. I took it in small bites. That way, I

> When young women look at me today, they think I had an ambition to be Chief Surgeon from the start, but it wasn't like that, really.

could always tell myself, if I die right now, I've done all I've planned to do." She recommends this approach for anyone going into medicine, since it helps to focus on the task at hand instead of being overwhelmed by the years of study ahead.

have I got what it takes to be a general surgeon?

Discipline and stamina help medical students and residents get through their education and training, but discipline also comes in handy throughout an entire medical career. Many physicians, like Kathryn, juggle a number of different responsibilities. Kathryn is the administrative head of surgery in a large children's hospital, the head of the pediatric surgery division, and the director of the operating room. In addition to these large administrative duties, she sees about 300 patients, operates, and teaches. "I'm always working very hard," she says, "but it's not work when you enjoy it."

Kathryn is proud to be both an administrator and an educator. "I supervise the premier training program in the country—I'm proud of that," she says. "If they do well," she says of her students, "I do well."

General surgeons, like all surgeons, must possess excellent dexterity and be able to make and execute decisions promptly. Although all surgeries are structured, the degree of planning varies according to the situation. Emergency surgeries, for example, are planned differently from elective surgeries. Regardless of the situation, surgeons must always be prepared for the unexpected, such as a sudden drop in blood pressure, an inex-

"Today's medical students are a bit more cynical," says Dr. C. Everett Koop, a former surgeon general of the United States. "But I excuse that. They're being taught in the same time-span 20 times what we were taught."

Dr. Koop is now senior scholar and the Elizabeth DeCamp McInerny Professor of Medical Ethics at Dartmouth Medical School in Hanover, New Hampshire. In this position, he works to shape the medical educational system of tomorrow. In a traditional medical program, a medical student spends the first two years in the classrooms and libraries of the school—without patient contact. A main activity is the memorizing of facts, names, descriptions, and symptoms—a lot of memorization. The last two years of the program are spent gaining clinical experience. It is in these clinics that the student first works with patients.

This traditional program has long been criticized for segregating the clinical experience from the scientific process. Dr. Koop believes that the traditional structure needs to change as medicine and technology change. "I loved medical school," he says. "Even the drudgery of anatomy was stimulating. But I do want to make medical school more meaningful to students."

Dartmouth's integrated medical curriculum, called New Directions, has medical students working with patients from the very first day. "The new curriculum isn't separated," explains Dr. Koop. "For example, there is no lecture on glucose in the first year. You deal with it in your third year while treating diabetes. The idea is to try and integrate the basic science of medicine with the problems of the clinic." Dr. Koop believes this integrated curriculum will be adopted by most of the medical schools in the United States within a decade.

Another innovative feature of the new curriculum is the videotaping of patient/physician sessions, from the medical student's first encounter with a patient until his or her last. "The difference is comical," says Dr. Koop.

The program also encourages medical students to improve their communication skills by participating in a project called Partners in Health. This project teams pairs of first- and second-year medical students with area elementary teachers to teach basic health care issues to children. By teaching, med students improve their communication skills, establish ties to the communities they serve, and experience the reward of serving people as health professionals.

Computers, Dr. Koop notes, already play a large role in the study of medicine. "A med student up late studying might have a question. Instead of having to wait until the next day, that student can tap right into the medical library and find an answer," he says.

Another technology learning tool is Dartmouth Medical School's Interactive Media Laboratory (IML). IML is a system that combines computer, media, and communication technologies to produce medical simulations for learning. The technology has been used to train medical students, doctors, nurses, and rural emergency medical technicians. Realistic situations are simulated so that the trainee gets critical lifelike experience before having to make important decisions on the job.

As for the medical students of the future, Dr. Koop says, "We're looking for the student who is apt to learn . . . who is a communicator, who has sensitivity and compassion, and who has a drive to help others. The individual who has a genuine drive to help others has been doing it all along. They delivered Meals on Wheels in high school."

To be part of this medical future, you might want to start hitting the books and volunteering now. Getting into medical school is a competitive business. Good luck!

plicable reaction to anesthesia, or complications with the surgical procedure itself. Surgeons must be able to cope with these crises as they occur.

Another essential quality in surgeons is a genuine concern for people. Surgeons treat the whole individual, not merely the condition requiring surgery. Therefore, those who aspire to be general surgeons must be able to deal compassionately with patients and their families and address any fears, questions, or needs they might have.

As a career, surgery requires a lifelong commitment to learning, physical and emotional stamina, and the ability to deal with stress. When Kathryn was in medical school, female surgeons were still a rare sight in operating rooms. "It was difficult for women to go into surgery in 1964. So, I took a year in pediatrics," she says. "I liked it, but not enough. I decided I did want to try surgery, so I did my first residency in general surgery. And then I followed that with a fellowship in pediatric surgery."

Kathryn notes that throughout her residency and fellowship years she faced subtle discrimination. "I was often mistaken for a nurse. Of course, you have to realize," she says, "there were no female role models. You had only yourself."

Kathryn says she was fortunate enough to have had the support of her husband, also a doctor. "Don't settle for second best," she advises. "Try and do exactly what you want to do and be willing to work extremely hard to accomplish it."

How does anesthesia affect your body?
Did you know that when you have general anesthesia for a surgery, the anesthesia affects your whole body? The anesthesia, which is either breathed in or taken through an intravenous injection, circulates through the bloodstream to reach all areas of your body, such as your brain, heart, and lungs. During an operation, your blood pressure, breathing, temperature, and heart rate are continuously monitored for signs of possible side effects from the anesthesia. Following surgery, side effects such as a queasy stomach are not uncommon.

how do I become a general surgeon?

education

High School

High school students interested in becoming general surgeons should take college preparatory classes. Important courses to take include biology, chemistry, physics, algebra, geometry, and trigonometry. These science and math classes will allow you to determine both your aptitude and interest in these areas. Courses in computer science are a must, as well, since technology is changing medicine—from the way it is taught to the way it is practiced. English classes that emphasize writing and researching skills will help prepare you for your undergraduate and graduate education. In addition, social studies and foreign language classes can make you a well-rounded and appealing candidate for admission into a college or university.

Postsecondary Training

College is the next step on the path to becoming a surgeon. Kathryn began her studies in medicine at England's Cambridge University and then finished up in the United States at Harvard. "In England," she explains, "you go straight from high school into medical school." This arrangement is similar to the six- and seven-year medical school programs available in the United States. Some universities offer accelerated programs, combining undergraduate and medical school education. High school students interested in these accelerated programs should see their school guidance counselors for more information. Applying early to these programs is highly recommended.

Students intending to attend medical school after college often major in a science field, such as biology. Course loads generally include math, biology, chemistry, anatomy, and physics. Classes in the humanities, such as English, ethics, and government, are also important and will help you later in your career.

There are 125 medical schools in the United States; admission into all of them is competitive. Applicants are considered for admission based on their grade point averages, scores on the Medical College Admission Test, interviews with the admissions staff, and recommendations from professors. Schools also look at personality, leadership skills, and participation in extracurricular activities. Most students apply to several medical schools early in their senior year of college. Only about one-third of those who apply to medical school are accepted.

In order to earn the Doctor of Medicine (M.D.) or the Doctor of Osteopathic Medicine (D.O.) degree, a student must complete four years of medical school. For the first two years, students attend lectures and spend time doing research in laboratories. Courses include anatomy, biochemistry, physiology, pharmacology, psychology, microbiology, pathology, medical ethics, and laws governing medicine. Students learn to take patient histories, per-

form routine physical examinations, and recognize basic symptoms.

In their third and fourth years, students are involved in more practical studies. They work in clinics and hospitals supervised by residents and physicians and learn acute, chronic, preventive, and rehabilitative care. They go through what are known as rotations (brief periods of study) in different areas, such as internal medicine, obstetrics and gynecology, pediatrics, psychiatry, and surgery. Rotations allow students to gain exposure to the many different fields within medicine and to learn firsthand the skills of diagnosing and treating patients.

After graduation from an accredited medical school, prospective surgeons complete a transition year, called an internship, to gain further clinical training and help select an area of specialization. Kathryn's internship was in pediatric medicine.

Following the internship, physicians begin what is known as a residency. Those wishing to pursue general surgery must complete a five-year residency in general surgery according to requirements set down by the Accreditation Council for Graduate Medical Education.

Throughout the general surgery residency, residents are supervised by attending surgeons at all levels of training. Residents begin their training by assisting in basic operations, such as the removal of an appendix. As the residency years continue, residents gain responsibility through teaching and supervisory duties. Eventually the residents are allowed to perform complex operations independently. Residents often work 24-hour shifts, easily putting in 80 hours or more per week. Although these are busy years filled with work and stress, they are also filled with inspirational moments that can help shape careers.

To be a successful general surgeon, you should

- Be able to think quickly and act decisively in stressful situations
- Enjoy helping and working with people
- Have strong organizational skills and be able to give clear instructions
- Have good hand-eye coordination
- Be able to listen and communicate well

certification or licensing

Licensing of general surgeons is mandatory. In order to be licensed in the state they plan to practice, surgeons must graduate from an accredited medical school, complete residency training, and pass a licensing test administered by the state.

Board certification in general surgery is administered by the American Board of Surgery (ABS). While certification is a voluntary procedure, it is highly recommended. Most hospitals require surgeons to be board certified. Many managed care organizations and other insurance groups will not make referrals or payments to surgeons without board certification. Also, insurance companies are not likely to insure a surgeon for malpractice if he or she is not board certified.

To be eligible to apply for certification in general surgery, a candidate must have successfully completed medical school and residency training in general surgery and be licensed to practice. Once a candidate's application has been approved, he or she can take the written and oral examinations.

Certification in general surgery is valid for 10 years. To obtain recertification, general surgeons must supply the ABS with documentation proving their continued medical education and the operations and procedures they have performed. They also must submit to a review by their peers and pass a written exam.

scholarship and grants

Scholarships and grants are available from individual institutions, government agencies, and special-interest organizations. Your high school or college career counselor can help you find sources of financial aid. Your local library is another source of information about funding for medical school.

Many students finance their medical education through military service. The Armed Forces Health Professions Scholarship Program and the National Health Service Corps Scholarship Program both provide money for tuition in return for service.

In addition, another source for financial aid, scholarship, and grant information is the Association of American Medical Colleges. Remember to request information early for eligibility, application requirements, and deadlines.

Armed Forces Health Professions Scholarship Program
Air Force: http://hp.airforce.com/training/financial.html
Army: http://www.sirius.com/~ameddet/hpschps.htm
Navy: http://nshs.med.navy.mil/hpsp/default.htm

Association of American Medical Colleges
2450 N Street, NW
Washington, DC 20037-1126
202-828-0400
http://www.aamc.org

National Health Service Corps Scholarship Program
Department of Health and Human Services
4350 East-West Highway, 10th Floor
Bethesda, MD 20814
800-638-0824
http://www.fedmoney.org/grants/93288-00.htm

who will hire me?

There are two basic career paths in general surgery. Surgeons either can practice with an emphasis in general surgery or specialize in one of its subspecialties: vascular surgery, surgical critical care, pediatric surgery, or hand surgery. General surgeons with a practice in one of the subspecialties usually work in urban areas where there is a large enough population to support their specialized practice. The general surgeon working in a rural or smaller suburban community, on the other hand, usually performs a variety of medical procedures.

General surgeons may work in private practice, either independently or with a group of medical professionals. They also may be employed by university hospitals, performing surgeries, teaching, and taking part in administration. Other general surgeons work in ambulatory care centers, military hospitals, or in other clinical care facilities.

General surgeons often work in the emergency room, burn unit, or trauma center in hospitals of all sizes. However, because ambulatory surgery can be performed in a variety of settings, the general surgeon working in this field may work in a variety of locations. Whether in a large city or suburban community, outpatient surgery may be performed in the surgeon's office, in a surgical department within a hospital, in a center independent from the hospital, or in an independently owned center run by a private practice.

where can I go from here?

Not every general surgeon can expect to become surgeon general of the United States or even the chief of surgery for a large children's hospital, such as Kathryn. General surgeons can, however, advance by keeping current with advanced technologies, improved medications, and new techniques. They can also enhance their medical skills through researching, teaching, and participating in practical clinical experience.

General surgeons who do not specialize in one of the four subspecialties may develop an area of expertise by concentrating their practices on an area and gaining extensive experience. This can raise a surgeon's professional status, and in turn, raise his or her earning potential.

Publishing articles in respected medical journals, such as *JAMA* (*Journal of the American Medical Association*), is another avenue for professional enhancement. Many general

Related Jobs

Optometrists

Oral and maxillofacial surgeons

Oral pathologists

Orthodontists

Pathologists

Prosthodontists

Teacher, medical school

Veterinary pathologists

Veterinary surgeons

surgeons also grow professionally by combining research and teaching with a private practice. General surgeons who work as professors at universities and at teaching hospitals can advance to become department heads or heads of hospitals. Many general surgeons aim to become the chiefs of their surgical divisions or the chief of surgery for the entire hospital, but these appointments are extremely competitive.

what are the salary ranges?

Salaries will vary depending on the kind of surgical practice, the hospital, and the geographic area in which the general surgeon works. Other factors influencing earnings are professional status, amount of hours worked, and level of surgical experience. According to the U.S. Department of Labor, the median net income of all surgeons was $217,000 in 1997.

Salary.com reports that surgeons working in the United States earned a median base salary of $ $203,999 in 2000. Half of all surgeons earned between $175,788 and $251,160.

what is the job outlook?

General surgeons will always be in demand, regardless of whether or not they practice a subspecialty. The health care industry, in general, is among the fastest growing in the United States. According to the U.S. Department of Labor, the demand for all physicians is expected to grow faster than the average for all other occupations in the next decade.

The health care industry is enjoying strong growth for a number of reasons. Technological developments are allowing surgeons to undertake more extensive procedures and treat diseases that were once thought untreatable. Also, the U.S. population is growing older and living longer. General surgeons will be needed to perform additional surgical procedures required by this expanding population.

In addition, the number of physicians in medical school has begun to level off, reducing the competition for jobs. Though many jobs are found in urban areas, good job prospects can be found in rural locations where communities are in need of medical professionals.

Surgeons willing to relocate to these areas will have ample employment opportunities.

Although employment of physicians in general is on the rise, the number of available surgical positions will be smaller. Many surgeons practice well into their 60s, limiting the number of openings available due to retirement. However, the demand for general surgeons is expected to be higher than in specialty surgery because their talents are more widely applicable.

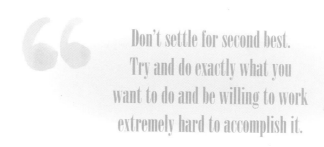

"Don't settle for second best. Try and do exactly what you want to do and be willing to work extremely hard to accomplish it."

how do I learn more?

professional organizations

For more information on becoming a general surgeon, contact the following organizations:

American Academy of Orthopaedic Surgeons
6300 North River Road
Rosemont, IL 60018-4262
847-823-7186
http://www.aaos.org

American Association of Neurological Surgeons/Congress of Neurological Surgeons
5550 Meadowbrook Court
Rolling Meadows, IL 60008-3852
847-378-0500
http://www.neurosurgery.org

American Board of Plastic Surgery
1635 Market Street, Suite 400
Philadelphia, PA 19103-2204
215-587-9322
http://www.abplsurg.org

American Board of Surgery, Inc.
1617 John F. Kennedy Boulevard, Suite 860
Philadelphia, PA 19103
215-568-4000
http://www.absurgery.org

American College of Surgeons
633 North St. Clair Street
Chicago, IL 60611
312-202-5000
postmaster@facs.org
http://www.facs.org

Association of Women Surgeons
414 Plaza Drive, Suite 209
Westmont, IL 60559
630-655-0392
info@womensurgeons.org
http://www.womensurgeons.org

Society of Thoracic Surgeons
401 North Michigan Avenue
Chicago, IL 60611-4267
312-644-6610
sts@sba.com
http://www.sts.org/

bibliography

Following is a sampling of materials relating to the professional concerns and development of general surgeons.

Greenfield, Lazar and Michael Mulholland, eds. *Essentials of Surgery: Scientific Principles and Practice.* 2nd Edition. Philadelphia, PA: Lippincott Williams & Wilkins, 1997.

Jacocks, M. A. *General Surgery.* 2nd Edition. New York, NY: Springer-Verlag, 1996.

Lawrence, Peter F. et al. eds. *Essentials of General Surgery.* Philadelphia, PA: Lippincott Williams & Wilkins, 2000.

Morris, Peter J. and Ronald A. Malt, eds. *Oxford Textbook of Surgery.* 2nd Edition. New York, NY: Oxford University Press, 2000.

Niederhuber, John E. *Fundamentals of Basic Surgery.* New York, NY: McGraw-Hill, 1998.

Polk, Hiram C., Jr., Bernard Gardner, and H. Harlan Stone. *Basic Surgery.* 5th Edition. St. Louis, MO: Quality Medical Publishing, 1995.

Schwartz, Seymour I. et al. eds. *Principles of Surgery.* 7th Edition. New York, NY: McGraw-Hill, 1998.

Selzer, Richard. *Mortal Lessons: Notes on the Art of Surgery.* San Diego, CA: Harvest Books, 1996.

Sherris, David A. and Eugene B. Kern. *Basic Surgical Skills.* Rochester, MN: Mayo Clinic Scientific Press, 1999.

Souba, Wiley W. and Douglas W. Wilmore, eds. *Surgical Research.* Albany, NY: Academic Press, 2001.

Taylor, Irving, and Stephen Karran, eds. *Surgical Principles.* London, UK: Edward Arnold, 1999.

Youngson, Robert M. *The Surgery Book: An Illustrated Guide to 73 of the Most Common Operations.* New York, NY: St. Martin's Press, 1997.

Genetic Counselors

Definition

Genetic counselors are health care professionals who work with individuals who may be at risk for a variety of inherited conditions or who have family members with birth defects or genetic disorders.

Alternative Job Titles

Genetic social workers
Medical geneticists

High School Subjects

Biology
Mathematics

Personal Skills

Helping/teaching
Technical/scientific

Salary Range

$23,000 to $46,000 to $75,000

Educational Requirements

Master's degree

Certification or Licensing

Recommended

Outlook

Much faster than the average

GOE
10.01.02
O*NET-SOC
19-1020.01

The meeting would be difficult. Ann Happ Boldt, a certified genetic counselor, carefully reviews her file before seeing the Hagans. Last night, she called the expectant parents to tell them that genetic testing had confirmed that their unborn child had achondroplasia, a skeletal dysplasia or dwarfing condition. Now it's time for Ann to meet with the Hagans to explain the condition in detail and outline their options. Ann knows it will be emotionally stressful for the parents to learn that their child will have special needs. She will explain that children with achondroplasia have normal intelligence but are significantly below average in height and have very short limbs. Then she will guide the Hagans through the process of deciding what to do with this information.

Ann explains that the parents in this case have three options. "They could continue the pregnancy and raise their baby. They could continue the pregnancy and put the baby up for adoption. Or, they could terminate the pregnancy. My role is to provide information to help the parents make the choice that is right for them."

what does a genetic counselor do?

Genetic counselors translate technical information about inherited health disorders into language that can be understood by the average person. They explain health disorders, the available options for testing for or treatment of these

lingo to learn

Amniocentesis: Sampling of the amniotic fluid contained in the uterus during pregnancy.

Chromosomes: Threadlike structures of nucleic acids and protein that carry genes.

Down syndrome: A chromosome disorder that results in abnormal physical development. Many people with this condition are mildly retarded.

Genes: The units of heredity that are transmitted from parents to offspring and control or determine a single characteristic in the offspring.

Huntington's disease: A hereditary disease that causes progressive brain-cell degeneration, resulting in spasmodic body movements and mental confusion.

Muscular dystrophy: A group of hereditary diseases characterized by the wasting away of muscles.

Teratogens: Agents that cause malformation in developing embryos.

Ultrasonography: The process of creating an ultrasound image of structures deep within the body. Ultrasound images can be used for fetal monitoring and to show fetal development.

disorders, and the risks associated with each option. They also help patients come to terms with the emotional and psychological aspects of having an inherited disorder or disease.

Cate Walsh Vockley, a genetic counselor at the Mayo Clinic in Rochester, Minnesota, describes the role of a genetic counselor as "providing information to help the patients arrive at the best decision for them."

Individuals turn to genetic counselors for a wide variety of reasons. The Hagans were originally referred to Ann by their physician because the expectant mother was over 35. "Advanced maternal age is associated with chromosome abnormalities, such as Down syndrome," Ann explains. The genetic counselor reviews the patients' risks and available options. "When they came to see me the first time, I discussed their testing options and explained the risks associated with the testing."

One method of obtaining genetic information is through amniocentesis, a procedure in which a physician withdraws a small amount of amniotic fluid from the womb to test for chromosome abnormalities. There is a 1 in 200 risk of miscarriage associated with this test. The Hagans decided to take the test, which came back with normal results. An ultrasound, however, indicated that their baby's limbs were significantly shorter than normal. The couple turned to Ann for information, referrals, and support.

Expectant parents are among the many families who may benefit from genetic counseling. Other couples who already have one child with an inherited disorder or whose families have a history of an inherited disorder may want information about the probability of having another child with that disorder. Individuals whose families have a history of inherited disease, such as Huntington's disease or muscular dystrophy, may want to know whether they have inherited the genes that give rise to these diseases. Individuals whose families have a high incidence of cancer may want to find out whether they have an inherited susceptibility to the disease. Members of specific geographic or ethnic groups in which a genetic disorder is common may want to determine what their risk is for developing the disorder.

When an individual schedules an appointment, the genetic counselor usually asks the patient to gather as much specific information about the past two generations of his or her family as possible. The counselor may ask for physicians' records, photographs, and anecdotal information. If a patient is concerned about inherited cancer, for instance, the physician wants to know how frequently the disease has occurred in the family, what types of cancer occurred, and at what age family members developed the disease. All of this information provides the genetic counselor with important clues about the patient's genetic probability of inheriting a disease.

Before going any further, the genetic counselor explains the risk associated with genetic counseling and testing. Some genetic testing presents physical risks, like those associated with amniocentesis. Others present emotional and psychological risks. If a patient discovers, for instance, that he or she has inherited the genes for Huntington's disease, how will he or she cope with knowing that this disease will develop at some later time? What if a patient wants to obtain genetic information about his or her family, but other siblings do not want this information and refuse to participate in its discovery? Genetic counselors want patients to be aware of and prepared for these situations. Genetic counselors also inform patients that genetic testing may threaten their insurability. "If," Cate explains, "an insurance company discovers that a patient has inherited a genetic susceptibility for cancer, that person may have a very difficult time getting coverage or may be charged outrageous premiums."

If a patient decides to proceed with testing, the genetic counselor interprets the test results, discusses treatment options, and explains the risks, both physical and emotional, associated with the various treatment options. To help the Hagans make their decision, for example, Ann arranged for them to meet with several members of Little People of America, an organization for people of short stature. This meeting gave the Hagans a better understanding of what achondroplasia would mean for their child and helped them decide whether they were equipped to raise a child with special needs. Since Little People of America maintains a list of couples who are willing to adopt infants with skeletal dysplasias such as achondroplasia, the meeting also helped the Hagans evaluate their options.

Throughout the counseling process, the genetic counselor must remain supportive of the patient's choices. "A genetic counselor cannot be judgmental. The patient's agenda must be addressed," Cate notes.

In addition to their counseling responsibilities, genetic counselors often assume administrative or teaching responsibilities. They also discuss test results with laboratory technicians and answer physicians' questions. Some supervise graduate students who are training

to become genetic counselors. Because the available genetic information is increasing so rapidly, all genetic counselors must read extensively and attend conferences to learn about new developments in genetic research. Many also strive to educate the public and physicians about the availability of genetic counseling. "There is a lack of public awareness about our services," Cate notes. "A significant number of patients who could benefit from genetic counseling are not currently being referred to a genetic counselor."

what is it like to be a genetic counselor?

Cate describes her career as a great way to combine a love of science with a desire to work with people. "Genetic science is advancing rapidly, and genetic counselors are in the perfect position to translate all the new information for patients. This is a truly fascinating field," says Cate.

Cate specializes in adult genetic disorders, particularly cancer. Before each appointment, she does quite a bit of preparation, to be sure that she has as much information as possible to offer the patient. Most appointments are at least two hours in length. Some days Cate sees as many as three patients. Other days she devotes entirely to administrative work, reading scientific journals, and interacting with other medical professionals. As a member of the National Society of Genetic Counselors (NSGC), Cate also serves on task forces that explore the many ethical issues surrounding genetic research and testing. These task forces provide information to legislators who must develop laws regarding genetic research, testing, and insurability.

In her work as a prenatal specialist at St. Vincent Hospital in Indianapolis, Ann worked with parents who had learned that their unborn or newborn child was either at risk for or had a genetic disorder. Because time is a critical factor for parents who must make decisions about testing or treating a developing fetus, prenatal specialists must react quickly. Their schedules tend to be less predictable, and there may be little time to gather family information before meeting with parents. After an initial meeting, Ann generally notified parents before their next meeting. "If I have difficult news to deliver as a result of an amniocentesis, I try to call in the evening when there is a better chance that both parents will be home together. I believe that parents need some time to get past the initial emotional shock. We then meet the next day, when they are better prepared to ask questions and to comprehend the information I give them."

Genetic counselors regularly encounter tragic situations. Helping families cope with frightening information and painful decisions can be extremely stressful. "This also can be the most rewarding part of being a genetic counselor, though," Ann reflects. "Families engage in a great deal of soul searching when they are faced with difficult choices. These experiences, although very challenging, can offer the families tremendous opportunities for growth. It can be very fulfilling to help a family deal with a painful situation in a positive manner."

The Hagans, for example, ultimately decided to place their baby for adoption. When their baby was born, family members gathered to hold the baby and take pictures. "It was their way of saying goodbye," says Ann.

have I got what it takes to be a genetic counselor?

Genetic counselors wear two hats: they are scientists, and they are counselors. As scientists, genetic counselors must be able to think critically. They must be intellectually curious and read constantly to stay abreast of the ever-changing information in this field. As counselors, they regularly interact with people who may be undergoing the most difficult and painful experiences in their lives. Genetic counselors must be compassionate, and they must be able to convey complex information clearly and concisely. Genetic counselors also must be able to deliver unpleasant news gently but directly. "This is not the job for someone who needs to make people feel good all the time," notes Cate. "Genetic counselors are often called upon to deliver bad news."

Above all, members of this profession must be able to deliver information without trying to influence their patients' decisions. "Genetic counselors must understand themselves very well," says Cate. "We all have certain biases. Genetic counselors must be aware of their own biases and must prevent them from influencing the way they impart information to patients."

Finally, to succeed in this profession, genetic counselors must be able to distance themselves somewhat from the suffering they encounter. Cate observes, "You must be compassionate, but you can't internalize your patients' pain to the point that it disrupts your personal life."

how do I become a genetic counselor?

education

High School

If you are interested in this career, you should begin by taking college preparatory courses in high school. Such classes as biology, physiology, chemistry, and statistics will help you determine your aptitude in these areas as well as prepare you for college. Since counseling skills are as important to the performance of this job as understanding genetics, you will also benefit from classes in sociology and psychology. English classes will help you develop your written communication skills and speech will help you gain confidence in speaking.

Volunteer experience is also extremely useful to individuals considering a genetic counseling career. Although experience in a medical setting is ideal, volunteer opportunities exist in many settings, such as at nursing homes, private clinics, and programs for the disabled. By exposing yourself to working with a wide variety of people with different needs and backgrounds you may develop communication skills, problem-solving strategies, and insight, and compassion.

Postsecondary Training

Getting your bachelor's degree is the next step to becoming a genetic counselor. Although no specific major is required, students entering this field typically have a degree in biologic science, social science, or a related field. Important college courses to take include general biology, developmental biology, genetics, chemistry, and statistics and probability. Other helpful courses include psychology, English, and ethics.

Following college, you must complete a two-year master's degree. At present there are 25 graduate schools offering programs in genetic counseling in the United States. To obtain a list of these programs and contact information, contact the American Board of Genetic Counseling (see Professional Organizations for address). Graduate school studies in genetic counseling typically include classes in client-centered counseling, issues in clinical genetics, medical genetics, biochemistry, human anatomy and physiology, and clinical medicine. All programs require field experience in clinical settings.

certification or licensing

Licensing is not required for genetic counselors. Certification is also not required, although it is highly recommended. Most employers will expect a genetic counselor to be certified. The American Board of Genetic Counseling (ABGC) offers certification in the United States through an exam offered every three years. Candidates must successfully complete both the general and specialty certification examination. In addition, they must have a graduate degree in genetic counseling, clinical experience in an ABGC-approved training site or sites, and a log book of 50 supervised cases. The ABGC reports that 72 to 74 percent of candidates taking the test pass it successfully.

who will hire me?

In its biannual survey of members in 2000, the NSGC found that 44 percent of genetic counselors are employed by university medical centers. That number is slowly decreasing though, as private and public hospitals, health mainte-

nance organizations (HMOs), diagnostic laboratories, and physicians in private practice are hiring more genetic counselors. Only 2 percent work in their own private practices, independent of a physician. Data published by the NSCG suggests that an increasing number of genetic counselors are working in genetic research.

where can I go from here?

Genetic counselors can advance by assuming teaching and administrative responsibilities. Research opportunities are available for individuals who earn a doctoral degree. Ann estimates that the available genetic information doubles every 18 months. As scientists and doctors learn to use the information provided by the mapping of the human genome, even more information will be available. "The mapping of the human genome truly will revolutionize the way we practice medicine," Ann notes. Professionals in this field are constantly learning, which may explain why 89 percent of genetic counselors describe themselves as "satisfied" or "very satisfied" with their careers.

Ann, a former president of the NSGC, now devotes much of her professional time to her work on the U.S. Secretary of Health and Human Services Committee on Genetic Testing. She was one of 13 persons nationwide appointed to the committee, which was created in 1999 to advise lawmakers and government agencies on policy issues associated with the flood of new genetic information and its implications for patients and the medical community. She makes frequent trips to Washington, DC, for meetings and is able to do some private, independent genetic counseling because of her years of experience.

what are the salary ranges?

According to the NSGC 2000 survey of members, genetic counselors with a master's degree working full-time receive a mean salary of $46,436. Entry-level salaries were as low as $23,575, but after a few years experience, salaries increase to just over $30,000. Those with 10 to 15 years of experience receive an average salary of $53,272. Those with significant experience may earn as much as $75,000.

Genetic counselors whose primary focus is adult genetics, neurogenetics (nervous system disorders), or cancer genetics tend to earn more than those who concentrate on specialty disease counseling or teratogens (agents that cause malformation in developing embryos). Those who specialize in prenatal or pediatric genetic counseling receive salaries that fall somewhere in the middle.

The same study indicated that, except at the highest levels, genetic counselors who are employed by the private sector, such as HMOs or private hospitals, generally are paid more than those who work for university medical centers or public hospitals. Genetic counselors who work in a physician's private practice are paid only slightly less than those who work in private hospitals. Those who practice independently, however, make significantly less than other counselors.

what is the job outlook?

This field is expected to grow much faster than average for many years to come. Scientific developments in understanding adult genetic disorders and in reproductive technologies have created new opportunities for treatment and testing. The data produced by the Human Genome Project (the mapping of human DNA) will create new ethical dilemmas as new genetic tests become available. This, in turn, will create an increased need for individuals who can help patients understand the options these developments present, as well as their associated risks.

how do I learn more?

professional organizations

Following are organizations that provide information on genetic counseling careers and accredited schools.

American Board of Genetic Counseling
9650 Rockville Pike
Bethesda, MD 20814
http://www.agbc.net

American Society of Human Genetics
9650 Rockville Pike
Bethesda, MD 20814
http://www.faseb.org/genetics

Genetics Society of America
9650 Rockville Pike
Bethesda, MD 20814
http://www.faseb.org/genetics

National Society of Genetic Counselors
233 Canterbury Drive
Wallingford, PA 19086
nsgc@aol.com
http://www.nsgc.org

bibliography

Following is a sampling of materials relating to the professional concerns and development of genetic counselors.

Baker, Diane L. et al. eds. *A Guide to Genetic Counseling.* New York, NY: Wiley-Liss, Inc., 1998.

Bennett, Robin L. *The Practical Guide to the Genetic Family History.* New York, NY: John Wiley & Sons, 1999.

Eanet, Karen and Julia B. Rauch. *Genetics and Genetic Services: A Child Welfare Worker's Guide.* Washington, DC: Child Welfare League of America, 2000.

Fisher, Nancy L., ed. *Cultural and Ethnic Diversity: A Guide for Genetics Professionals.* Baltimore, MD: Johns Hopkins University Press, 1996.

Gelehrter, Thomas D. et al. *Principles of Medical Genetics.* Philadelphia, PA: Lippincott Williams & Wilkins, 1998.

Gormley, Myra Vanderpool. *Family Diseases: Are You at Risk?* Baltimore, MD: Clearfield Company, 1998.

Harper, Peter S. *Practical Genetic Counseling.* Newton, MA: Butterworth-Heinemann Medical, 1998.

Ott, Jurg. *Analysis of Human Genetic Linkage.* Baltimore, MD: Johns Hopkins University Press, 1999.

Strachan, Tom and Andrew P. Read. *Human Molecular Genetics.* New York, NY: John Wiley & Sons, 1999.

Weil, Jon. *Psychosocial Genetic Counseling.* New York, NY: Oxford University Press, 2000.

Young, Ian D. *Introduction to Risk Calculation in Genetic Counseling.* New York, NY: Oxford University Press, 1999.

Geriatricians

Definition
A physician with specialized knowledge in the diagnosis and treatment of disorders common to old age.

Alternative Job Titles
Gerontologists
Geriatric specialists

High School Subjects
Biology
Chemistry
Mathematics

Personal Skills
Helping/teaching
Technical/scientific

Salary Range
$95,000 to $115,000 to $150,000+

Educational requirements
Bachelor's degree, M.D., fellowship in geriatrics

Certification or Licensing
Recommended (certification)
Required by all states (licensing)

Outlook
Much faster than the average

GOE
NA*

O*NET-SOC
NA*

*Not Available. The U.S. Department of Labor does not classify geriatrician as such, but rather classifies the geriatrician's primary profession (e.g., doctor of internal medicine).

No one could get near her. Even though she was lying down, the 97-year-old woman cleared a wide path around her hospital bed in the intensive care unit as she swung an old, black purse through the air. "Barely conscious, delirious with fever, she kept swinging that purse around," remembers Stephanie Studenski, then an intensive care unit nurse, now a doctor and director of the Center for Aging at Kansas University Hospital in Kansas City. "She was afraid, confused, and combative," Dr. Studenski says. "It was difficult to care for her." The old woman had been flown in from a remote, rural area after apparently passing out. "Her heartbeat was irregular. She needed a pacemaker," says Stephanie. "Right then, while she was swinging that purse around, she was just a sick old woman in a bed. But a few days later, when she was better, she talked to me and was a different person."

As a geriatrician and director of the Center for Aging, Stephanie works hard every day to make sure that patients "don't lose themselves." In talking with her patient, Stephanie learned that the woman had emigrated from Sweden to the United States as a child with her family. They had eventually settled on a farm in rural, western Kansas. Now, so many years later, the woman was alone and frightened. "She said she'd never been sick a day in her life," Stephanie said. "When she stood up, she was six feet tall, a physically strong woman with insight and history. She only looked small in that bed. I realized then that she had turned back into herself with good care. I wanted to make sure she didn't lose herself. That's my goal now," Stephanie says. "To keep patients composed, calm, well. Unafraid."

lingo to learn

Acute care: Intense care, usually given in a hospital setting, for a serious illness or trauma and lasting until recovery.

Cataract: Abnormal condition in which a film forms on the lens of the eye. It typically occurs after the age of 50.

Chronic: A condition that develops slowly in a patient and lasts for a long period, often the lifetime of the patient.

Degeneration: The gradual deterioration of cells and loss of function.

Dementia: A progressive disorder marked by mental confusion, loss of memory and judgment abilities, and personality changes. Alzheimer's disease is a specific type of dementia.

Hypertension: Persistent and abnormally high blood pressure.

Hypotension: Persistent and abnormally low blood pressure.

Incontinence: The inability to control the elimination of body wastes, sometimes caused by aging.

Insomnia: The chronic inability to sleep or to sleep throughout the night.

what does a geriatrician do?

A *geriatrician* is a physician, such as a physician of internal medicine, a general physician, or a psychiatrist, with specialized knowledge in the prevention, diagnosis, treatment, and rehabilitation of disorders common to old age. The term *geriatrics* refers to the clinical aspects of aging and the comprehensive health care of older people. It is an area of medicine that focuses on health and disease in old age.

Formal training in geriatrics is relatively new. Today, life expectancy continues to advance and geriatricians are faced with medical and ethical challenges: What is aging? What distinguishes aging from diseases of the aging? Can life be extended, and for how long? What can be prevented? And what can be cured?

Geriatricians spend most of their time with patients, taking patient histories, listening to their comments or complaints, and running any of a number of diagnostic tests and evaluations, including physical examinations. They work in a number of environments, from private offices to hospitals to nursing homes.

Geriatricians face unique challenges in each patient, mainly because the health problems of older patients are typically complex and involve social and psychological problems as well as physical ones. As a result, geriatricians often work with other physicians to diagnose and treat multiple problems. For example, an elderly man's complaint of fatigue could signal one or more of a large number of disorders, and diagnosis may be complicated by the coexistence of physical and mental problems, such as heart disease and dementia (mental confusion). The geriatrician might consult or work with a psychologist to treat the dementia. If the patient was living alone, the geriatrician might also enlist the support of a social worker, neighbor, or relative to make certain that heart medication was routinely administered.

Often, there is no cure for the patient's condition. In such a case, the geriatrician must devise some way of helping the patient cope with the condition.

what is it like to be a geriatrician?

"Putting the pieces of the puzzle together," says Dr. Jason Karlawish. "That's what I do." A fellow in geriatrics at the University of Chicago's Pritzker School of Medicine, Jason divides his time among duties at the clinic, hospital, and nursing home where he works.

When Jason works at the clinic he sees outpatients. They may already have been treated for some condition or disorder, or they may be coming to the clinic for the first time. The most common problems that Jason sees among his patients are dementia, heart disease, high blood pressure, and diseases of the joints. Often the patient is accompanied by a family member who has sensed a problem and brings the patient in for a checkup. Jason explains, "Something's wrong, but they're not sure what. 'Mom used to do this and now she doesn't.' The challenge is to work with the family member and the patient to come to an understanding of what's wrong and what we can do about it."

Juggling the needs of both patient and family members can be frustrating as well as beneficial. "Many elderly patients have concerned family members, and they expect you to work with them. This can be emotionally demanding, as well as time-consuming," says Dr. Stephanie Studenski. "Often, I'll be talking about a diagnosis or treatment with one sibling who lives in New York, and another sibling will call up who lives on the other coast—while I'm still on the phone with his sister." The geriatrician's time is best spent getting the patient the needed care, but with so many elderly people living alone, geriatricians are glad to have family members actively involved.

Taking the patient's history is the first step in the diagnosis of any problem. "Truly, the patient's history is the centerpiece of the clinical encounter. You really have to listen to the patient," Jason says. The patient history is supplemented by a physical examination, including structured tests to assess how well the patient is functioning—mentally, emotionally, and physically.

The patient in a nursing home or other long-term care facility has unique needs. For example, a 72-year-old man who lives in a nursing home and has severe dementia, kidney problems, and diabetes has different needs than someone who can live independently. The nursing home patient would likely have difficulty remembering to watch his diet, to take his medication, and perhaps even when to eat. Therefore the course of treatment for this man is highly regulated. "Half of the folks in nursing homes have dementia. They're ill from advanced diseases plus they have dementia," says Jason. "The sad thing is that almost everyone in the nursing home could be living in their own community, but unfortunately, health care services are not universally available to them, so they end up in a home."

The patients seen by a geriatrician in a hospital are often very sick. The care and treatment of these patients also differs from those in a nursing home and those seen on an outpatient basis. In addition to treating life-threatening conditions, the geriatrician tries to make the hospital patient as comfortable as possible. "Discussions frequently revolve around issues of death and dying," Jason says.

In all three settings—clinic, long-term care facility, and hospital—the geriatrician works closely with other physicians and health professionals to provide the best care possible for each patient. "It's very team-oriented, very collaborative," says Stephanie.

Part of the geriatrician's specialized knowledge includes an understanding of a patient's tolerance levels in everything from stress to medications. "Nothing is more fun than taking a 90-year-old person who's doing pretty well and keeping that person well," says Stephanie. "That patient is really vulnerable. He tolerates mistakes less well than a 30-year-old in worse health. The same pill you give a 20-year-old could make that 90-year-old pass out. Older people are more vulnerable physically and emotionally. You have to be accurate and perfect in your health care."

have I got what it takes to be a geriatrician?

The career of geriatrician is both intellectually and emotionally demanding. A good geriatrician needs to be able to effectively manage all aspects of a patient's problems. Older patients often have complex cases due not only to disease or disorders, but also to social and emotional issues. Such factors as poor living conditions or the mental confusion of a spouse complicate the situation and limit treatment possibilities. "We have very creative problem-solving strategies," says Stephanie. "You have to—in order to manage diabetes in the face of heart problems, poor vision, and arthritic fingers."

Such demanding work, however, can also be fulfilling. "It's really fun to do what I do," says Stephanie. "I constantly come away from clinic feeling rewarded. The patients just give back to you a lot of love, warmth, humor, and history. They're so appreciative. Not all physicians get to have that." Stephanie also adds, however, that there are difficult aspects to the job. "It's sometimes sad," she says. "For example, I care for a lot of people with dementia. It's harder to establish a relationship with someone who's no longer capable of making personal contact. They just can't respond. I have a hard time with those patients," she says. "That's not all you do, at all, as a geriatrician. It's the hard part."

Jason notes that when he is able to connect with a patient suffering from dementia, the reward is well worth the effort. "The greatest pleasure I take from my job is when I can communicate in a meaningful way with someone who is frail, elderly, and suffering from dementia. Not even necessarily communicating about medicine, but about them as a person—that's so satisfying," he says. "But that's almost what defines the geriatrician: the desire to work with the terminally ill, or those with dementia, rather than with those who are only acutely ill and who may be able to be cured."

Geriatricians need to have a general interest in aging and the problems related to aging. "The hardest thing for me," says Jason, "is coping with the fact that aging is a social problem as much as a medical problem. Sometimes you can't help much because the root of a problem lies in the way society chooses to value or devalue a person's problems." Stephanie

agrees and believes the system often works against the patients. "Elderly patients have complicated medical and social problems. The current health care system and Medicare is based on a 30-year-old with a headache. It is not set up to efficiently and expertly care for patients who need longer visits," she says, adding, "the profession is working to change the system and to create strategies for sensible solutions." One possible trend, according to Stephanie is using teams of doctors to get the work done.

To help their patients, geriatricians work with other health care workers, such as social workers. And, because of the requirements of Medicare and private insurance companies, there are forms to be completed and signed, releases and prescriptions to write. "We work with all the community agencies and medical specialties," says Stephanie. "There is a lot of paperwork."

how do I become a geriatrician?

education

High School

If you are interested in pursuing a medical degree, a high school education emphasizing college preparatory classes is a must. Science courses, such as biology, chemistry, and physics, are necessary, as are math courses. These classes will not only provide you with an introduction to basic science and math concepts but also allow you to determine your own aptitude in these areas. Since college will be your next educational step, it is also important to take English courses to develop your researching and writing skills. Foreign language, history, and computer classes will also help make you an appealing candidate for college admission as well as prepare you for your future undergraduate and graduate education. As a high school senior you may want to consider applying to colleges or universities that are associated with a medical school. Jason knew when he was in high school that he wanted to be a doctor. He applied to one such accelerated program at Northwestern University in Evanston, Illinois.

FYI

The term geriatrics comes from the Greek geras, meaning old age, and iatrikos, meaning physician.

Postsecondary Training

Stephanie entered the field of medicine by first attending nursing school, graduating in 1976 from the University of Kansas. "I soon realized," she says, "that I needed to know what doctors knew, but that I would continue to act like a nurse, in terms of closeness to my patients."

Jason was admitted to Northwestern University's seven-year medical school program. There he spent three years as an undergraduate at Northwestern University in Evanston, then he continued his studies at the university's downtown Chicago medical school campus for the next four years. This educational approach has its advantages and disadvantages. Although Jason's first three years were devoted to the basic requirements that any student would need to enter medical school, he was also able to experiment a bit by taking classes outside the sciences. "The virtue of the seven-year med program," says Jason, "was that I didn't have to worry about the perfect grade point average the way the typical premed student does. I was free to follow a path of study that might put your grade point at risk."

On the other hand, Jason says, the major drawback to the six- or seven-year med program is pretty obvious. "You were committed to medical school. So, you were stuck if you changed your mind."

A bachelor's degree from an accredited university or college is required for entrance to medical school. Commonly, students considering medical school receive their degrees in the science areas. Typical college courses for a student in either a regular or an accelerated premed program include biology, organic and inorganic chemistry, physics, psychology, and mathematics. Other courses such as English, ethics, and government are also beneficial and will prepare you for a people-oriented career. Medical schools look to admit candidates with a well-rounded background. Working or volunteering at a local nursing home or hospital will add to your experience in dealing with old people.

Medical school is the next step after you receive an undergraduate degree. Admission is competitive, and applicants undergo a fairly extensive and difficult admissions process that takes into consideration grade point averages, scores on the Medical College Admission Test, and recommendations from professors. Most students apply to several medical schools early in their senior year of college.

In order to earn the degree doctor of medicine (M.D.), a student must complete four years of medical school study and training. For the first two years of medical school, students

attend lectures and classes and spend time in laboratories. Courses include anatomy, biochemistry, physiology, pharmacology, psychology, microbiology, pathology, medical ethics, and laws governing medicine. They learn to take patient histories, perform routine physical examinations, and recognize symptoms. "I was unsure of myself at first, as far as basic sciences, because of my nursing background," says Stephanie. "But I didn't have to be worried. I was fine. But there is a high volume of learning. It was helpful to me to get organized. I set up steady study schedules, so that I wasn't waiting until the last minute."

"It was a lot like going back to first grade," says Jason of his medical school years. "Small groups all doing the same thing, working together. It was a camaraderie-building experience. The pressure of grades is relaxed," he says. "The stress isn't in making the grade, but in getting the material in. The volume of material is so great."

In their third and fourth years, students are involved in more practical studies. They work in clinics and hospitals supervised by residents and physicians. During this time they learn acute, chronic, preventive, and rehabilitative care. They go through what are known as rotations (brief periods of study) in a particular area, such as internal medicine, pediatrics, dermatology, and surgery. Rotations allow students to gain exposure to the many different fields within medicine and to learn the skills of diagnosing and treating patients.

Upon graduating from an accredited medical school, physicians must pass a standard examination given by the National Board of Medical Examiners. Most physicians complete an internship, also referred to as a transition year. The internship is usually one year in length and helps graduates to decide on their area of specialization.

Following the internship, the physicians begin what is known as a residency—additional training and study in particular area. Both Stephanie and Jason ended up specializing in internal medicine. It was during their residencies that each decided to subspecialize in geriatric care. "During my residency in internal medicine I discovered I was not interested in episodic or crisis care. I realized I wanted to help with chronic cases and get to know the patients and their families," Stephanie says.

Following the residency period, geriatricians receive formal training through geriatrics fellowships. Fellowships are available through departments of family practice, internal medicine, and psychiatry. Often, several different departments share the responsibility of administering these fellowship programs. There are over 100 geriatrics fellowship programs in the United States and Canada. The length of these programs varies, ranging from 12 months to four years, depending on the type of fellowship and the goal of the individual. Someone wanting to become a clinical educator, for example, will have two years of training and then become a full-time medical school faculty or clinical faculty member.

The American Geriatrics Society offers guidelines on fellowship training that were used, in turn, by the Accreditation Council for Graduate Medical Education as the basis for their requirements for fellowship training programs. The Association for Gerontology in Higher Education (AGHE) offers the *Directory of Educational Programs in Gerontology and Geriatrics,* which has information on more than 750 programs at several educational levels, including fellowship programs.

To be a successful geriatrician, you should

- Be able to work as part of a team
- Be a creative problem solver
- Be able to work on complex cases with multiple problems
- Enjoy working with old people
- Be patient
- Be an effective communicator and listener

certification or licensing

A Certificate of Added Qualifications in Geriatric Medicine or Geriatric Psychiatry is offered through the certifying boards in family practice, internal medicine, osteopathic medicine, and psychiatry for physicians who have completed a fellowship program in geriatrics.

Licensing is a mandatory procedure in the United States. It is required in all states before any doctor can practice medicine. In order to be licensed, doctors must have graduated from medical school, passed the licensing test of the state in which they will practice, and completed their residency.

scholarships and grants

Scholarships and grants for those pursuing careers in the field of geriatrics are available from several sources. The American Federation for Aging Research (AFAR) administers 10 grant programs a year, including the John A. Hartford/AFAR Academic Geriatrics Fellowship Program and the Glenn/AFAR Scholarships for Research in the Biology of Aging. The AGHE also provides information on scholarships and fellowships in the field.

An excellent source for financial aid, scholarship, and grant information for medical school is the Association of American Medical Colleges. Contact these organizations early for information on eligibility, application requirements, and deadlines.

American Federation for Aging Research
1414 Avenue of the Americas, 18th Floor
New York, NY 10019
212-752-2327
http://www.afar.org

Association for Gerontology in Higher Education
1030 15th Street, NW, Suite 240
Washington, DC 20005-1503
202-289-9806
aghetemp@aghe.org
http://www.aghe.org

Association of American Medical Colleges
2450 N Street, NW
Washington, DC 20037-1126
202-828-0400
http://www.aamc.org

Specific information on financial aid programs can be found at:
Financing Your Medical Education
http://www.aamc.org/students/financing/start.htm

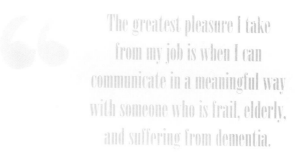

The greatest pleasure I take from my job is when I can communicate in a meaningful way with someone who is frail, elderly, and suffering from dementia.

who will hire me?

Geriatricians work in a number of medical environments. Geriatricians may practice as a primary caregiver in any of the following settings: private practice, ambulatory (outpatient) care, or long-term care. They may also work at private clinics, hospitals, or nursing homes or other long-term care facilities. Or, like Jason, they may combine a number of these settings in their practice. Geriatricians also work in research universities and clinics where they may provide clinical care, teach, or conduct research. Still other geriatricians move into administration, directing long-term care facilities, such as nursing homes, life/care communities, home care programs, and other chronic care facilities. Flexibility in the work setting is one of the main benefits to physician who specializes in geriatrics.

where can I go from here?

Geriatricians will find numerous professional opportunities awaiting them. Career advancement can be found as a geriatrics consultant, medical director of a long-term care facility, or full professorship at a university. Increasingly, search committees seeking a well-qualified candidate to be the chair or president of a medical center are turning to geriatricians to fill these key roles.

The future also holds a great deal of promise for those geriatricians working as community or health-systems leaders in geriatrics. These geriatricians might head the geriatric or long-term care divisions of an HMO or a large group practice, developing and managing systems of care for the elderly. Possibilities include providing consultative geriatrics in a variety of settings, including clinical assessment and nursing home patient services.

Research about issues that affect or directly involve health care for the aging is also a growing area. Jason is very aware of the importance of research in clinical geriatrics. He spends a lot of time reading and writing papers on bioethics and other issues involving the aging community, as well as learning techniques for conducting clinical research.

what are the salary ranges?

According to the Association of American Medical Colleges, the average annual salary for first-year residents is approximately $34,100. Once a doctor has completed all of his or her training and begun professional practice, salaries rise dramatically. Specific information on salaries for those working in geriatrics is limited; however, a review of salary ranges for those in related areas will provide a general idea of earnings in this field. According to a 2000 salary survey by the recruiting agency Physicians Search, starting salaries for those in internal medicine—both Jason's and Stephanie's specialty—ranged from approximately $95,000 to $145,000, with an average income of $115,000. After several years of working, the average salary for those specializing in internal medicine was approximately $150,200.

Because geriatricians must spend a fair amount of time with each patient, they may be able to serve fewer clients then doctors who can schedule appointments 20 minutes apart. This often results in earnings that are slightly lower than the specialty's average. Incomes are also influenced by geographic region, years in practice, area of practice (private, hospital, or administrative, for example), and the "people friendly" reputation of the individual doctor. In addition, as our population ages and the special skills of geriatricians are in greater and greater demand, salaries for these specialists may rise.

what is the job outlook?

The U.S. Department of Labor predicts job growth for all physicians to be faster than the average through the next decade. This outlook should be especially true for those working in geriatric medicine. Today approximately 35 million Americans are age 65 or older. This number is expected to increase to 70 million by 2030. As the large generation of Baby Boomers ages, more physicians will be needed to treat their specific needs. According to an article in the *Chicago Tribune,* published in July 2000, only 100 to 150 physicians each year decide to work in geriatrics. This small number of incoming specialists means the field will continue to offer numerous employment opportunities. The outlook for geriatricians should remain faster than the average for some time to come.

how do I learn more?

professional organizations

Following are organizations that provide information on aging issues, geriatrician careers, accredited schools, and employers.

Alzheimer's Association
919 North Michigan Avenue, Suite 1100
Chicago, IL 60611-1676
800-272-3900
http://www.alz.org

American Association for Geriatric Psychiatry
7910 Woodmont Avenue
Bethesda, MD 20814-3004
301-654-7850
Main@aagponline.org
http://www.aagpgpa.org

American Federation for Aging Research
1414 Avenue of the Americas, 18th Floor
New York, NY 10019
212-752-2327
http://www.afar.org

American Geriatrics Society
The Empire State Building
350 Fifth Avenue, Suite 801
New York, NY 10118
212-308-1414
Info@americangeriatrics.org
http://www.americangeriatrics.org

Association for Gerontology in Higher Education
1030 15th Street, NW, Suite 240
Washington, DC 20005-1503
202-289-9806
Aghetemp@aghe.org
http://www.aghe.org

bibliography

Following is a sampling of materials relating to the professional concerns and development of geriatricians.

Abrams, William B. et al. eds. *Merck Manual of Geriatrics.* Whitehouse Station, NJ: Merck & Company, 2000.

Cantor, Marjorie H. and Mark Brennan. *Social Care of the Elderly: The Effects of Ethnicity, Class and Culture.* New York, NY: Springer Publishing, 2000.

Gallo, Joseph J. et al. eds. *Handbook of Geriatric Assessment.* Gaithersburg, MD: Aspen Publishers, Inc., 2000.

Gallo, Joseph J. et al. eds. *Reichel's Care of the Elderly: Clinical Aspects of Aging.* 5th Edition. Philadelphia, PA: Lippincott Williams & Wilkins, 1999.

Hazzard, William R. et al. eds. *Principles of Geriatric Medicine and Gerontology.* New York, NY: McGraw-Hill, 1999.

Kane, Robert L. et al. *Essentials of Clinical Geriatrics,* 4th Edition. New York, NY: McGraw-Hill, 1999.

Lueckenotte, Annette Giesler. *Pocket Guide to Gerontologic Assessment.* 3rd Edition. St. Louis, MO: Mosby, Inc., 1998.

Maddox, George L., ed. *The Encyclopedia of Aging: A Comprehensive Resource in Gerontology and Geriatrics.* New York, NY: Springer Publishing Company, Inc., 2001.

Pritchard, Jacki. *Working with Elder Abuse: A Training Manual for Home Care, Residential and Day Care Staff.* London, UK: Jessica Kingsley Publishers, 1996.

Reuben, David B. et al. *Geriatrics at Your Fingertips.* Dubuque, IA: Kendall/Hunt Publishing Company, 2001.

Grief Therapists

Definition

Grief therapists offer therapy for people mourning the death of a family member or close friend. They help patients confront feelings of anger, resentment, or sadness and guide them towards acceptance of the loss of their loved one.

Alternative Job Title

Bereavement counselors
Grief counselors

High School Subjects

Psychology
Sociology

Personal Skills

Communication/ideas
Helping/teaching

Salary Range

$35,000 to $45,000 to $100,000

Educational Requirements

Master's degree

Certification or Licensing

Required by certain states

Outlook

Faster than the average

GOE
10.01.02
O*NET-SOC
19-3031.03

Four Lopez brothers, one sister, and one stepmother squeeze into Darcie Sims's office; one chooses to stand, while the others sit in chairs, on the couch, or on the floor. The brothers are quiet and almost seem disinterested while the stepmother wails and rocks, and pulls tissue after tissue out of the box next to her. The sister rolls her eyes—an act that catches Darcie's attention.

"You know that everyone grieves in different ways," explains Darcie. "Not one type of grieving is considered better, or more important. So you just have to express yourself and your grief the way that feels most comfortable. Now, how is everyone doing with their journals? Anyone care to share?"

Surprisingly, the quietest brother, the one uncomfortable with the idea of a group session, writes the most passionate entries. He recalls fond memories of his father, the feeling of anger when he learned of his father's fatal car accident, and calling his dad stupid after identifying the body at the morgue.

"Why did you call your dad that?" asks Darcie.

The quiet brother hesitates. "Because that is what my dad would say when he realized he didn't have control of the situation."

"Just like you didn't have control over your dad's accident and death?" counters Darcie. Now it is the brother's turn to cry and reach for the tissues. The stepmother stays quiet; the sister rolls her eyes.

lingo to learn

Abnormal grief: A prolonged, difficult response to traumatic loss.

Acute mourning: A grieving stage of disorientation, dulled senses, denial, and yearning.

Anniversary reaction: A worsening of grieving on anniversary dates of the loss.

Bereavement: Process of grieving.

Chronic grief syndrome: An abnormal grief reaction to the loss of a deeply dependent relationship.

Delayed grief: Bereavement that occurs years or decades after the loss.

Grief work: A bereaved individual's efforts to accept the reality of a loss.

Hidden grief: Solitary mourning; a grieving pattern common to men.

Mourning ritual: A formalized expression of bereavement.

Normal grief: A grieving process that lasts less than six months; resolves without treatment.

Survivor guilt: Self-blame for surviving after the loss of a loved one.

Thanatology: The study of death, dying, bereavement, and grief.

Unfinished business: Personal concerns that need to be resolved before death.

what does a grief therapist do?

A *grief therapist*, also known as a *grief counselor* or *bereavement counselor*, offers therapy for people who are mourning the death of a family member or friend. Grief counseling is a rather new specialty. It was unheard of just 30 years ago, but today it is in great demand. According to Dr. Dana Cable, Professor of Psychology at Maryland's Hood College and a licensed psychologist and certified grief therapist, "Grief therapy is a growing area because of the nature of many deaths today. There are many more issues to be worked through when we lose young people to violent deaths and diseases such as AIDS. In addition, there is some movement away from organized religion where people used to find comfort when they lost a loved one." The stigma once attached to counseling has also diminished, as people become more understanding of and tolerant to its benefits.

Grief therapists may specialize in bereavement and death issues or may incorporate them as part of their counseling practice. Their main objective is to help the surviving person to accept the death of their family member or friend. Feelings of fear, guilt, or anger are identified, confronted, and resolved. A counseling session may be one-to-one, a small group, or as part of a larger support group.

Many therapists use the four basic tasks of mourning as identified by J. William Worden, a psychologist and author of *Grief Counseling and Grief Therapy: A Handbook for the Mental Health Practitioner.* The first task is to accept the reality of the death of a loved one; the second, to fully experience emotions connected to the loss; third, to adjust to life without the loved one; and fourth, to relocate the memory of the deceased in one's mind so that progress is possible.

Grief therapists may be self-employed, or part of a counseling practice; they may work in a clinical setting such as a hospital, hospice, funeral home, nursing home, assisted care facility, or any other facility that deals with the sick and dying. Grief therapists are often called to the scene of disaster and violence by airlines, communities, businesses, and schools. Some therapists may choose to become grief and bereavement educators and teach at colleges or universities, or conduct research regarding grief issues. They may also educate people who work in professions that deal with the sick and dying.

The Association for Death Education and Counseling (ADEC), formed in 1976, is the oldest organization promoting the field of dying, death, and bereavement. ADEC promotes the research, knowledge, and practice of thanatology. The association is also known and respected for its certification program for grief and death education.

what is it like to be a grief therapist?

Personal experience was what drew Darcie Sims into grief therapy. "Our son died 24 years ago," she says. "While there was a lot of support during his illness, we found very little support after his death." Darcie was already employed as a professional counselor but "wanted more than self-help." There was some bereavement help available from several hospices, but since their son did not die in a hospice setting, Darcie and her husband found the support really did not fit their case. Darcie ended up delving into the topic of grief and eventually earned a doctoral degree.

According to Darcie, a grief therapist in private practice or employed at an agency usually schedules four to five clients a day. Private practitioners have the freedom of lengthening a session or changing their schedules. Therapists employed by agencies tend to be more rigid about their schedules. During the first consultation, also called an intake, Darcie asks the patient basic questions—name, reason for the visit, concerns—in order to get an idea of the problem. Most sessions last about an hour, including 50 minutes of client time and 10 minutes of charting. On busy days, she sees patients back-to-back, leaving little time for lunch or a coffee break. Hours depend on the type of clients she sees. Darcie has hours during the day and also some evenings; Saturday hours are a must for patients who work or are in school during the week.

In addition to treating patients, private practitioners also have the worries associated with running a business, such as paying rent on office space, ordering office supplies, supervising support staff, and billing. In fact, Darcie pinpoints paperwork, especially that associated with patient billing, as the least rewarding aspect of the job. "Many times you spend hours going back and forth with insurance billing," Darcie says, "It takes away from the real job." For that reason, many therapists choose to employ someone specifically to bill patients and their insurance plans or delegate the responsibility to outside medical billing companies.

People grieve in different ways; some are very vocal with their grief, while others are very subdued. Many times the type of grief people express is similar to their personalities. If a person is very shy and quiet, then most likely they will express their grief in the same manner. Darcie does not try to erase a person's grief through therapy but rather teaches different skills and tools to ease the pain. Anger management may be needed if feelings of resentment or guilt come into play. Personal relaxation is taught to help eliminate panic. Other techniques include reading or writing poetry, keeping a journal, or painting.

The length of treatment depends on the patient and his or her situation. "The grieving issue is complex," explains Darcie. "Everyone needs different amounts of time. Some patients need three to four visits, some six to eight, others need two to three." The patient and the therapist mutually decide when to stop therapy. A tentative date is picked, and if both parties feel comfortable at the time, then the sessions are ended. Darcie usually sends a card or note on the anniversary of the trigger event to make sure the patient is feeling fine and to open up lines of communication should the patient need to talk.

have I got what it takes to be a grief therapist?

Becoming a good therapist takes more than years of schooling and training. Darcie says, "You should be a good listener. Don't just listen to the words, but also to the emotions and what is not being said out loud. Pay attention to the body language." Grief therapists should also be able to express themselves clearly and sensitively.

Darcie makes it a point not to allow the patient-therapist relationship to develop into anything more. "I can't be friends with my patients either during or after our sessions" states Darcie, calling any such friendship unprofessional. "I know too much about their lives, while they know nothing about mine, except what I offer during sessions."

This job is very much people-oriented. "You must be comfortable with different types of people," warns Darcie. "You need to work without judging the person you are trying to help." It's also important to feel at ease with dealing with the sick and dying, as well as with those working in the health, religious, and legal professions.

Darcie is quick to point out the rewards of the job. "I really love watching and helping people to grow. It's quite rewarding to see patients conquer pain and discover their inner strengths. You can't help but take that awareness and use it in your own life."

how do I become a grief therapist?

Anyone can offer to counsel the bereaved, but not everyone can legally call himself or herself a counselor or therapist. Traditionally, a professional counselor—one that has met the academic and practical training in the field of

To be a successful grief therapist, you should

- Be a good listener
- Have an interest in helping others
- Be very comfortable with yourself
- Be nonjudgmental
- Be organized and patient
- Be able to express your thoughts clearly

death, grief, and bereavement—gives grief therapy. Many grief therapists have master's degrees or even doctorates in counseling, social work, or psychology, with an emphasis in thanatology—the study of death and the personal ways of dealing with it. Counselors also seek certification before offering their services in grief therapy.

education

High School

It's important to be a well-rounded person for a career in counseling. You should consider classes in psychology, sociology, history, literature, music, and art. Also, since communication is a big part of therapy, you should take speech, communication, English, and a foreign language. Check with your school counselors about any recommendations they may have on your curriculum.

Volunteering can also give you a wealth of experience in dealing with people from different social and economic backgrounds. Try places such as your local hospice center, nursing home, or day care center.

Postsecondary Training

The educational road to becoming a grief therapist is a long one. While in college, a major in psychology, sociology, or premedicine is a good choice. Afterwards, you need to earn a master of science degree in counseling, social work, or psychology. A doctoral degree in psychology is highly recommended, with a major or minor in thanatology. You may also choose to study medicine and emphasize in psychiatry.

certification or licensing

According to Donna Schuurman, first vice-president of the ADEC, the certification program is currently undergoing renovation to include two levels of credentialing. Among the requirements for the first level is a master's degree, work experience, successful completion of a comprehensive exam, recommendation, and required credits of approved continuing education classes. The second level, an eight-module certificate program, will be open to those without a master's degree. The goal of ADEC is to replace the designations of certified grief therapist, counselor, or educator with certification in the field of death, dying, and bereavement. ADEC hopes to complete its new certification program in 2002. You can periodically check its Web site listed (see address at the end of this article).

Some states require a license to practice grief therapy counseling with particular requirements varying from state to state. For information, check with the state in which you plan to practice or with the American Counseling Association.

who will hire me?

Don't plan on working as a grief therapist right out of school. After graduating from a master's program, most therapists practice general counseling before specializing. Even then, most states have strict requirements for practicing grief therapy.

There are several employment possibilities. Some grief therapists work with other therapists as part of a group practice offering a variety of counseling and therapy services. If you choose to work in a more clinical setting, then you may be employed at a hospice organization, hospital, nursing home, funeral home, or any facility or organization that deals with the sick and dying. Large corporations may employ grief therapists as part of their Employee Assistance Programs. Airlines, schools, businesses, and communities also hire grief therapists to help in crisis situations. The Red Cross in 1995, for example, brought disaster debriefing teams, including grief therapists, to the Alfred P. Murrah Federal Building, site of the Oklahoma bombing incident, to deal with victims and their families. Other nonprofit organizations that are present during times of tragedy include the Salvation Army, the National Organization for Victim Assistance, and the Center for Mental Health Services.

You may also find employment in a state run program. Darcie, for example, once worked as director of Family Support in her state's coroner program. She and her team helped families identify bodies of victims of foul play, fires, or accidents.

E-therapy

The Internet has opened up a whole new side to therapy. Today, it is possible to attend grief therapy sessions, as well as other counseling sessions in other fields, without leaving the comfort of your own home. Called e-therapy, people can talk about their feelings in a chat room, or have one-to-one sessions with a therapist via email. In fact, there is now an association, the International Society for Mental Health Online, devoted to e-therapy. But patients beware: make sure everything is legit before baring your soul.

where can I go from here?

While Darcie enjoyed working in a mental health clinic and in private practice she feels most satisfied with her career presently. "I teach and write extensively about grief. I also [give] keynote [addresses] all over the world and have several books published, as well as video and audiotape programs," says Darcie proudly.

Though clinical work is the path most grief therapists take, your choices are vast. If you excel in administrative work, you could start and direct programs for hospice centers, mental health hospitals, or disaster teams. Writing, speaking, and educating others about thanatology issues is another option; your audience could range from college students, funeral workers, and counseling professionals to the general public. Darcie gets much satisfaction from teaching others about grief issues and different techniques for handling them.

what are the salary ranges?

The salary range for grief therapists is generally the same as for other therapists and counselors. Beginning therapists can expect to make around $35,000. More experienced counselors can make about $45,000, with some earnings reaching $60,000. Some counselors in private practice and those who become directors of facilities may earn considerably more. For example, a counselor in private practice holding a Ph.D. can earn $100,000 a year. However, much of that is invested in office overhead—rent, secretary's salary, billing, and other expenses. Also, those employed by agencies and clinics are usually offered a benefits package, while private practitioners must arrange for their own health insurance and retirement plans.

what is the job outlook?

According to the *Occupational Outlook Handbook,* employment opportunities for counselors overall is expected to grow faster than the average for all occupations. Demand should be especially strong for counselors specializing in rehabilitation and mental health, the latter including grief therapy.

Our population is aging and experiencing grief at the death of family members and friends. Violence in schools, churches, workplaces, and sports arenas—places that were once considered safe—can raise questions of fear and anger. Car accidents, airline crashes, and the rise of AIDS-related and drug-related deaths can cause feelings of guilt and depression. Natural disasters, such as tornadoes, floods, and earthquakes, can also bring about feelings of disbelief and helplessness that grief therapists can help address. Also, grief is not strictly associated with death and disaster. Grief can be felt during any time of change, such as divorce, unemployment, and illness.

As the idea of counseling becomes more accepted as a valuable tool for dealing with life's problems, the demand for counselors, including grief therapists will rise. In 2001, about 500 grief therapists and counselors have been certified through ADEC, a large increase over the 262 certified therapists and counselors in 1999. ADEC's membership is about 2,000 and growing.

how do I learn more?

professional organizations

Following are organizations that provide information about a career as a grief therapist.

American Counseling Association
5999 Stevenson Avenue
Alexandria, VA 22304-3300
703-823-9800
http://www.counseling.org

Association for Death Education and Counseling
342 North Main Street
West Hartford, CT 06117-2507
860-586-7503
http://www.adec.org

bibliography

Following is a sampling of materials relating to the professional concerns and development of grief therapists.

Browne, Sylvia and Nancy Dufresne. *A Journal of Love and Healing: Transcending Grief.* Carlsbad, CA: Hay House, 2001.

Goldman, Linda. *Breaking the Silence: A Guide to Help Children with Complicated Grief: Suicide, Homicide, Aids, Violence, and Abuse.* Bristol, PA: Accelerated Development, 1996.

Leick, Nini and Marianne Davidsen-Nielsen. *Healing Pain: Attachment, Loss and Grief Therapy.* New York, NY: Routledge, 1991.

Malkinson, Ruth. *Traumatic and Nontraumatic Loss and Bereavement: Clinical Theory and Practice.* Madison, CT: Psychosocial Press, 2000.

Worden, James William. *Grief Counseling and Grief Therapy: A Handbook for the Mental Health Practitioner.* 2nd Edition. Springer Publishing, 1991.

Health Advocates

Definition
Due to the complex nature of today's insurance and health industries, patients turn to health advocates for help. Health advocates work on behalf of patients on issues ranging from insurance coverage to hospital intervention. Advocates are employed by hospitals and nonprofit groups, or work as independent contractors.

Alternative Job Titles
Consumer health advocates
Patient representatives

High School Subjects
Biology
Health
Speech

Personal Skills
Communication/ideas
Helping/teaching

Salary Range
$30,000 to $45,000 to $60,000

Educational Requirements
Bachelor's degree

Certification or Licensing
Voluntary

Outlook
Faster than the average

GOE
NA*

O*NET-SOC
NA*

*Not Available. The U.S. Department of Labor does not categorize the career of health advocate.

Eileen Raia was just about to take a short lunch break when her pager went off. A look at the pager's gray screen gave Eileen her next destination—the oncology floor. She raced to the specified room and found a distressed patient, and equally distressed family members. "Hello, my name is Eileen Raia, and I am a patient representative here at the hospital. Is there a problem?"

"Yes!" exclaimed a very agitated family member. "My mother is suffering and the nurse won't give her anything for the pain. Why is she not helping us?" A quick discussion with the charge nurse gave Eileen a different side of the story.

"Mrs. Evans," said Eileen to the patient, "your doctor did prescribe pain medication, which the nurse already gave you." Eileen further explained in a tactful way that the nurse was only following orders. In fact, the nurse was trying to reach the doctor to see if more medication can be safely given. That seemed to ease both Mrs. Evans and her daughter.

After documenting the case, detailing the complaint and its resolution, Eileen was again thinking about a quick lunch. Just then the phone rang. It was the fourth floor asking for advance directive papers and someone to explain the procedures. By the way, could Eileen find a Korean interpreter for the patient? Eileen smiled and shuffled through her Rolodex.

lingo to learn

Advance directive: A written communication to your family and health care providers stating your wishes about treatment if you are dying or no longer able to make health care decisions.

Claim: A request by an individual (or his or her health care provider) to an insurance company to pay for services of a health care provider.

Denial of a claim: Refusal by an insurance company to pay a claim submitted to them by a health care provider on behalf of an insured individual.

Durable power of attorney for health care (DPAHC): A legal document that allows a trusted family member or friend to act as an individual's proxy in making health care decisions.

Living will: A type of advance directive in which you put in writing your wishes about medical treatment should you be unable to communicate at the end of life. State laws may vary on when the living will goes into effect, and may limit the treatments to which the living will applies.

Patient Self-Determination Act (PSDA): An act passed by Congress In 1991that requires all health facilities that receive federal funds to inform patients of their rights to accept or refuse treatment and to prepare advance directives.

what does a health advocate do?

Today's health care system has become so complex; many patients often have difficulties navigating though the maze of insurance plans and their limitations. *Health advocates,* using their health care and medical expertise, work on behalf of patients and their interests. Patients may try to resolve problems and insurance denials themselves; appeals may go on for several months or even years. Many times, health advocates give a case an air of authority, which in turn expedites approval for treatments and medications, physician referrals, and reimbursements.

Primarily, there are three types of health care advocates. Those that are employed by large companies such as hospitals, insurance companies, large physician groups, and other health organizations are often called *patient representatives,* or *consumer health advocates.* The second category of health advocates works primarily for nonprofit organizations that deal with a wide variety of medical and insurance concerns, or they might work for a group that targets a particular illness or disease, such as cancer or lupus. The third group of health advocates works for private advocacy firms.

Many hospitals have seen the need and benefits of having a team devoted to resolving complaints of patients and their families and watching out for the interests of the patients as well as of the hospital. Patient representatives receive complaints from the patient or the family and work towards a resolution to the problem. The problem may range from issues between two patients sharing a room, to miscommunication between the patient and medical staff, to misplaced personal items. For example, if a patient felt mistreated by a hospital staff member, the patient representative must hear both sides of the case, determine if the claim is valid or a misunderstanding, and hopefully work out a peaceful and satisfactory resolution.

Patient representatives also document patients' concerns and experience with the hospital and its staff. Complaints and the method of resolution are recorded to help in future cases. Measuring and recording patient satisfaction are important because the hospital uses this information in finding areas to improve. Another important role of representatives is to interpret medical procedures or unfamiliar medical terms and to answer patients' questions in regards to hospital procedures or health insurance concerns. They also educate patients, as well as the hospital staff, about the patients' bill of rights, advance directives, and issues of bioethics. Sometimes they handle special religious or dietary needs of the patient or personal requests, such as commemorating a birthday.

While patient representatives work for the patients' well-being as well as their employer's best interests, health advocates employed by nonprofits act as the patient's champion against insurance companies, employers, and creditors. Many times patients are denied much-needed medical treatments because insurance companies consider them to be experimental. Certain drugs might be denied because of the way they are taken. Health advocates provide assistance in getting these issues resolved. They help identify the type of health insurance and the depth of coverage the patient has and organize paperwork and referrals from physicians and hospitals. Sometimes patients also need help composing letters to insurance companies explaining their situation. Health advocates also make phone calls to physicians and insurance companies on behalf of the patient.

Patients sometimes encounter job discrimination because of an existing illness or extended medical leaves, and this is another area in which health advocates can help. Many nonprofit groups also have lawyers on staff who provide legal counsel. Also, with any serious illness, financial concerns are likely. Health advocates can offer suggestions on how to get the most from a patient's insurance coverage, negotiate with physicians and hospitals to lower costs, and work with pharmaceutical companies in providing expensive medications at a lower cost.

Health advocates may choose to work independent of a hospital, group, or organization. Such advocates act as consultants and may have their own private practice or work for an advocacy firm. Their cases usually involve patients with a variety of issues and concerns. They usually charge a flat fee per case.

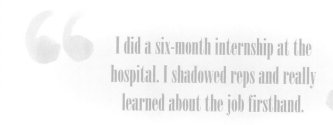

I did a six-month internship at the hospital. I shadowed reps and really learned about the job firsthand.

what is it like to be a health advocate?

Eileen Raia's background was in education and she was already working as a teacher, but her sister's long illness triggered an interest in advocacy, especially helping those unable to help themselves. After inquiring with the Society of Healthcare Consumer Advocacy, she was led to Northwestern Memorial Hospital. "I did a six-month internship at the hospital," says Eileen, " I shadowed reps and really learned about the job firsthand." After the internship, she was hired full-time as a patient representative.

The Patient Representative Department is housed within the hospital itself. Each representative has a private office with a computer terminal and has access to a workroom and larger meeting room for conferences with patients and their family members. Weekly meetings are held one-on-one with the department manager to keep him informed of ongoing cases. Monthly departmental meetings are scheduled to compare cases and discuss new developments in the hospital.

"Each day is different," says Eileen. Some days may be inundated with new caseloads, which means Eileen must spend a great deal of time assessing the complaint or problem. To do this, she must interview the patient either over the phone or more likely in person. If another party is involved, whether a staff member or another patient, she must also get their side of the story. Most disagreements stem from a lack of communication. The identification of the problem and proposed solution or resolution is called service recovery. Afterwards, all case notes must be documented for future reference. Other days may be spent interpreting a hospital bill or intervening with a patient's insurance carrier.

Another important part of Eileen's job is to measure patient satisfaction. Usually, prior to discharge or soon afterwards, patients are contacted and surveyed about their hospital stay. They answer questions regarding such topics as the quality of medical service and attention given to the patient. Information is interpreted in order to gauge any needed changes in hospital procedure, as well as to bring a sense of patient awareness to the medical staff. At times, Eileen makes presentations to hospital staff members regarding the patient's bill of rights and tries to promote a better environment that supports these rights.

Eileen also informs patients about advance directives and answers any questions they may have. In some cases, she obtains translators for those who do not speak English or sign language interpreters for the hearing impaired.

What is Eileen's favorite case? She fondly remembers orchestrating a wedding in the hospital. "The bride's mother was hospitalized and couldn't attend her daughter's wedding," recalls Eileen. "We accommodated the family by re-enacting the wedding as best we could. We had decorations, cake, and a little ceremony so the mother could, in a way, be part of the occasion."

have I got what it takes to be a health advocate?

The most important quality to have in this field is an intense desire to help others. As a health advocate, your central goal is to put the interest and needs of patients first. Being a good and compassionate listener is also important because you have to identify the patients' problem or fears before you can help them. You must also be prepared to interact with a variety of people, many times from different social and economic backgrounds. It is also important to have good communication skills. You must be able to effectively convey the patients' needs to insurance and pharmaceutical companies, but also be able to explain situations to patients clearly.

You must be aggressive and assertive. If the insurance company says no to a much-needed treatment, advocates need to find ways around the situation. The answer "no" must never be a deterrent. In these situations, having a health background may help give you an air of authority.

how do I become a health advocate?

education

High School

Classes such as writing or public speaking help in this field. Health advocates spend a majority of their time talking with patients and employees of big organizations like major insurance companies. It's important to know how to express your message in a clear and concise manner. You may want to study biology or other health-related classes to get an understanding of the medical field. Although a medical background is not an

FYI Advocates encourage patients to be organized. It's important to keep copies of all paperwork connected with health care, including medical records, test results, physician referrals, documentation, and correspondence from hospitals and insurance companies. They suggest organizing paperwork according to subject matter and keeping all information in one binder. Having all information on hand makes the advocate's job and the patient's case easier to complete.

absolute prerequisite, it is helpful to be familiar with common medical terms, diagnoses, and treatments.

If you want to gain work experience while in high school, you may find volunteer opportunities at your local nursing home or hospital. Time spent at a nursing home, for example, can prepare you to interact with the elderly. You may be asked to run errands or perform small tasks such as writing letters for those without relatives living nearby.

Many nonprofit advocacy groups welcome volunteers to do a variety of tasks. You may be assigned to collate informational flyers or participate in a fundraiser instead of heading an actual grievance case; however, the work experience and industry contacts are invaluable.

Postsecondary Training

There are no nationally recognized education standards for health advocates. Most advocates have bachelor's degrees and experience in human services, communications, supervision, management, or conflict negotiation. Experience in health care is also important, including familiarity with medical terminology. Some advocates have degrees in social work or psychology and some are registered nurses. A few universities offer undergraduate courses in patient representation and a few, such as Sarah Lawrence College in New York, have master's programs in health advocacy.

certification or licensing

There is no one nationally recognized certification program offered for this field. Certification is available in social services or oncology. Continuing education classes are offered throughout the year for those already in the field. For example, Eileen must attend seminars covering topics such as hospital ethics, changes in Medicare or Medicaid, and computer training, as part of her job.

who will hire me?

Your future employment depends on what field of advocacy you wish to pursue. Do you want a regular Monday through Friday schedule, a hospital environment, and a customer-

The bride's mother was hospitalized and couldn't attend her daughter's wedding. We accommodated the family by re-enacting the wedding as best we could.

service work setting? If so, then your main employers will be hospitals, specialty practices, and managed care organizations. For example, Northwestern Memorial Hospital, Eileen's employer, has a six-member Patient Representative Department. They handle about six to seven cases per week. This large hospital had a total of almost 43,000 admissions for 2000. In addition to regular grievance cases, each representative is responsible for data management (documentation) for patient satisfaction with both inpatient and outpatient services. They also are responsible for educating staff on how to better serve patients.

Nonprofit organizations, such as foundations dealing with a particular illness like cancer or a special group such as the elderly, hire advocates to handle patients' treatment needs or financial difficulties. The Patient Advocate Foundation (PAF), for example, is a national nonprofit organization that acts as a liaison between patients and their insurance carriers, employers, or creditors to resolve issues ranging from nonpayment for necessary treatments to fundraisers to help defray medical costs. Eighty percent of its cases involve insurance problems. PAF employs about 25 to 30 full-time employees including caseworkers, managers, and other administrative employees. PAF, with over 150 lawyers in its legal department, also offers legal support to patients. In 1999 PAF resolved almost 30,000 cases through mediation and negotiation—not one case went to court.

If you want a career in health advocacy, but are undecided which route to take, consider an internship. Families USA Foundation, for example, offers several paid internships to college students, graduate students, and recent graduates. Prerequisites include a strong academic background and an interest in public education, advocacy, and media relations.

Interns work on projects such as monitoring government policy changes on Medicare and Medicaid and preparing educational information on health and welfare issues for community leaders and the public.

where can I go from here?

Advancement possibilities also depend on what type of work environment you desire. Eileen's position gives her a global view of how a hospital functions. Her work experience and diplomatic skills could easily earn a transfer to other departments within the hospital or a nonprofit foundation.

A goal of Eileen's is to be more involved with staff training at the hospital. Topics such as hospital services, patient awareness, and advance directives are presented periodically to different departments.

With solid work experience and expertise in a particular field, you may be a candidate for advocacy work on a national level. High-profile advocates travel extensively, giving speeches or seminars or familiarizing members of Congress on a particular cause. The PAF, for example, recently held its annual Patient Congress in Washington, DC. During this congress, PAF representatives met with members of Congress, cancer research experts, and cancer survivors to discuss the latest developments in the detection and treatment of cancer.

To be a successful health advocate, you should

- Want to help others, especially those who can't help themselves
- Be able to interact with people from a variety of social and economic backgrounds
- Be a good speaker
- Be a good listener
- Be strong willed and aggressive
- Be organized

what are the salary ranges?

Advocates working for hospitals, insurance companies, or large group practices earn between $40,000 to $60,000 a year. Those employed in the private sector also enjoy benefits such as paid vacation and sick time, some overtime pay, health insurance, and retirement plans. Since most nonprofit groups are without the financial means of private corporations, most advocates working for nonprofits tend to earn much less.

Independent health advocates have opportunities that employed advocates do not—working solely for the benefit of the patient, setting their own hours, and working from home. However, independents also do not have the stability of job security or a regular monthly salary. Self-employed health advocates usually work for consultant fees that range from $75 to $150 per case. After analyzing insurance statements and identifying any savings for the patient, that amount is split evenly between the patient and the advocate. Though many self-employed advocates enjoy a good salary, it is certainly unpredictable; independents may have many clients and referrals one year and a slow year with little earnings the next.

what is the job outlook?

The U.S. Department of Labor expects that as many as 2.8 million jobs will be created in health care services in the next decade, listing it as one the fastest growing major industry groups. Although health advocacy is only a small part of this industry, it would be safe to assume that employment of health advocates will also grow. As insurance, hospital, and medical services become more advanced and complex, patients' needs for advocates will increase as well.

Beth Darnley, from the Patient Advocacy Foundation, definitely sees this field expanding on a nationwide level. As insurance issues become more complicated, people will turn to experts to interpret the legalese and show results. Health advocates can provide this guidance and get attention paid to their patients' cases, especially from big bureaucracies like Medicare and other insurance giants. As the number of health advocates grows, there will be more regulations, and perhaps a national standard of certification and training will develop to better establish the field of health advocacy.

how do I learn more?

professional organizations

For internship opportunities, contact:
Families USA
1334 G Street, NW
Washington, DC 20005
202-628-3030
info@familiesusa.org
http://www.familiesusa.org/

For career information, the latest news in health care reform and publications dealing with patient advocacy, contact:
National Patient Advocate Foundation
753 Thimble Shoals Boulevard, Suite A
Newport News, VA 23606
800-532-5275
action@npaf.org
http://www.patientadvocate.org

For career information, contact:
Society for Healthcare Consumer Advocacy
1 North Franklin
Chicago, IL 60606
312-422-3726
http://www.shca-aha.org

bibliography

Following is a sampling of materials relating to the professional concerns and development of health advocates.

Bateman, Neil. *Advocacy Skills for Health and Social Care Professionals.* London, UK: Jessica Kingsley Publishers, 2000.

A Patient's Bill of Rights

The American Hospital Association created this bill of rights to ensure a safe and comfortable hospital stay and the best medical treatment possible. It is used as a guide for quality patient treatment at many hospitals and organizations. Highlights of the Patient's Bill of Rights include:

You, as the patient, have the right to considerate and respectful care.

You have the right to know your diagnosis, treatment, and prognosis. You also have the right to know the identity of those treating you.

You have the right to advance directives—living will, power of attorney, and health care proxy.

You have the right to privacy, including medical records, test results, and examinations.

You have the right to refuse treatment, as well as the right to be informed of alternative care options.

For a complete listing of the American Hospital Association's Patient's Bill of Rights, check its Web site: http://www.aha.org/resource/pbillsofrights.asp.

Teasdale, Kevin. *Advocacy in Health Care*. Boston, MA: Blackwell Science, Inc., 1999.

Phillips, Lauren B. *In the Name of the Patient: Consumer Advocacy in Health Care*. Chicago, IL: American Hospital Association, 1995.

Health Care Managers

Definition

Health care managers run hospitals and other health care organizations that provide patient care.

Alternative Job Titles

Department managers
Hospital administrators
Nursing home administrators

High School Subjects

Business
English
Mathematics

Personal Skills

Helping/teaching
Leadership/management

Salary Range

$28,000 to $48,000 to $88,000

Educational Requirements

Bachelor's degree; Master's degree strongly recommended

Certification or Licensing

Required for certain positions

Outlook

Faster than the average

GOE
11.07.02

O*NET-SOC
11-9111.00

Bustling as usual, the emergency department at Christ Hospital and Medical Center never closes. Located in Oak Lawn, Illinois, the hospital is a Level I trauma center, providing emergency services to a wide range of medical emergency patients. Ambulances deliver patients all day and night. Other patients arrive by car with family members or friends. The hospital emergency department treats critically ill and injured patients who come from miles away seven days a week, 24-hours a day. The patient mix is diverse—adults, children, senior citizens, workers injured on the job, and gang members. They come from all walks of life, and all ethnic backgrounds. Some have insurance; some do not. The emergency department physicians treat a wide range of medical problems, from chest pain, to fractures, to bullet wounds.

In her office, Joyce Woytek checks the time. As the hospital's administrative director of emergency services, she has put in another 10-hour day. She looks at her calendar to see what is scheduled for tomorrow. Meetings, meetings, and more meetings—but that is how managers get their job done.

"People think all we do is go to meetings," Joyce says. "But the meetings are all important. We have to maintain contact with both our staff and our colleagues. It doesn't sound exciting, but it's necessary."

Joyce's duties in health care management may not seem as exciting as those of some of her subordinates who treat emergency patients, but her job is a critical part of providing patient care.

lingo to learn

Ambulatory care: A facility that treats patients on an outpatient basis.

HMO (Health Maintenance Organization): A prepaid managed care plan where members pay a fixed amount of money in exchange for most of their medical needs.

Hospice: A facility that provides health care, especially pain control and emotional support, to terminally ill patients and their families.

Managed care: A system for organizing many health care providers within a single organization to control health care costs.

Nursing home: A facility that provides living quarters and care for persons unable to look after themselves, such as the elderly or chronically ill.

PPO (Preferred Provider Organization): A managed care medical plan that contracts with doctors, hospitals, and other providers to obtain discounts for care. Providers agree on a predetermined list of fees for all services.

Rehabilitation center: A facility that uses therapy, education, and emotional support to help patients regain health to lead useful lives.

what does a health care manager do?

Health care managers oversee health care facilities or individual departments within them. Management positions range from middle-management department heads to senior-level managers. Health care managers are accountable for the financial side of the business. Similar to other business managers, health care managers plan, organize, supervise, budget, and direct staff. They develop and implement programs and services, manage their employees and physical facilities, identify and solve problems, and develop budgets. Health care managers are responsible for establishing fees and billing procedures, planning space needs, purchasing supplies and equipment, and providing mail, phone, computer, laundry, and other services needed by patients and staff. Working with other medical staff and department heads, they may also develop and implement training programs for staff members.

To accomplish their many duties, health care managers meet regularly with staff members and colleagues to discuss pressing issues, expectations, and recent accomplishments. They also may be actively involved in the community, attending meetings or making speeches to community groups and professional organizations. Managers may be required to travel to their organization's regional facilities or to out-of-town meetings.

Health care organizations are varied, ranging from single hospitals to multi-hospital systems, nursing homes, clinics, hospices, health maintenance organizations, medical group practices, mental health centers, ambulatory care facilities, and rehabilitation centers. In small facilities, health care managers usually handle all the management responsibilities, taking a more direct role in daily operations. In large facilities, the chief executive officer (CEO) in charge of managing the entire organization delegates duties to other administrators. For example, a CEO may assign personnel matters to the facility's human resources manager.

Christ Hospital and Medical Center, a teaching hospital with more than 800 beds, is part of the Advocate Health Care system, which includes eight hospitals, two children's hospitals, a home health care company, long-term care services, and retirement housing. As administrative director of emergency services, Joyce Woytek reports to one of the hospital's two co-administrators. "I have overall fiscal and operational responsibility for the hospital's emergency services," she says.

These services include emergency medical services (including paramedic training), the cast room, and the emergency department. Last year, she assumed additional responsibility for medical records, medical affairs, and performance improvement. She has also become involved in strategic planning, working with architects to plan the addition of two new spaces in the emergency services area. "The nonclinical areas that I am responsible for do not take care of patients, but they support patient care," she says.

Health care managers may be generalists (in charge of an entire facility) or specialists (in charge of specific clinical departments or services). Examples of areas within health care facilities that have specialized managers include clinical areas such as surgery, nursing, physical therapy, and psychiatry and administrative areas such as finance, security, maintenance, and housekeeping.

Generalists have broader managerial responsibilities and, as a result, require a more comprehensive background. On the other hand, specialists must be trained and educated in the area they manage. For example, nursing administrators generally have worked as staff nurses before advancing into management. Similarly, most medical records administrators hold a bachelor's degree in medical records administration.

Hospital administrators are generalists who work with the institution's governing board to develop long-range plans and policy. Administrators are accountable for the success of business plans, such as proposals to expand health care services or implement a fund-raising campaign. Administrators set the overall direction of the organization. They deal with government regulation, reimbursement, and community issues.

Department managers are responsible for staff, budgets, programs, and policies for their specific area. They may coordinate activities with other managers.

Group medical practice managers work closely with the physician owners. Office managers usually handle business matters for small group practices, while physicians make policy decisions. However, large medical group practices often hire a full-time health care administrator to manage the business operation and delegate responsibilities to assistants.

Health maintenance organization (HMO) managers have responsibilities similar to managers in large group medical practices but may have larger staffs. They also may put more emphasis on preventive care.

The health care field has undergone tremendous changes over the past several years. These changes include the merging and restructuring of health care institutions. The number of stand-alone hospitals has decreased, while the number of hospital systems continues to grow. Health care managers are (and will continue to be) involved in the restructuring of health care organizations; they must have concern for both fiscal management as well as patient care.

Though similar in nature to other administrative or management positions, health care managers have the rare opportunity to help improve the health of the communities in which they serve. They accomplish this by researching the demographics of the communities, determining their needs, providing relevant services, and promoting these services in the community.

what is it like to be a health care manager?

Joyce Woytek works in a hospital that serves a large population in a major metropolitan area. She has to make decisions every day and resolve problems as they come up. "Whether dealt with at the basic supervisory level or at the chief executive officer level of management, operational issues take up a manager's time and usually are unscheduled," Joyce says.

Her weeks are filled with meetings. She has weekly meetings with the hospital's Administrative Council, the senior management team that runs the hospital and reports to the two co-administrators. The council discusses operational issues and policy at their meetings.

Joyce meets every other week for one to three hours with the managers who report to her. "It is time-consuming but necessary to communicate and maintain contact with your managers," she says. She also holds full-staff meetings in order to communicate with all her employees. All together, more than 300 people report to her.

Joyce brings an operations perspective to her meetings with physicians. These meetings are important to share the knowledge of hospital operations among staff. Joyce is also involved with many specialized hospital committees, such as the Disaster Committee and the Safety Committee.

Like many health care managers, Joyce is actively involved in community and professional activities. She serves on the board of the local chamber of commerce, where she represents the hospital as the largest employer in town. She also is involved with a homeless shelter program and the Crisis Center for South Suburbia, which cares for victims of domestic violence.

The health care field is constantly under pressure from businesses, insurance companies, and the government to cut costs. Providing high quality patient care with shrinking resources is one of the major challenges that health care managers face. "The challenges of maintaining financial viability are overwhelming," Joyce says. "We are challenged to look at everything we do and determine how to do it better—for less money."

Health care managers typically work in an office. Physical demands are light but health care managers need stamina and concentration to withstand long workdays. Because organizations such as hospitals and nursing homes are open 24-hours a day, managers work long and irregular hours.

Joyce and the hospital's other senior managers work a minimum of 10 hours a day. "Many of us also work at home on job-related business," she says. "This is a very demanding and consuming role. You can't do it in 40 hours a week. It's laden with responsibilities."

have I got what it takes to be a health care manager?

Health care managers spend much of their time working with people and must have good communication skills, both written and oral. They must be able to develop and present reports and proposals.

Health care managers must be able to work effectively with people at all levels in the organization—governing board members, medical staff, senior management, other managers, subordinates—as well as patients and their families, community leaders, and vendors. Their many responsibilities require tact and good judgment.

"The single biggest factor in managerial effectiveness is people skills," Joyce says. "It's the hardest thing to teach, and it's the single, most critical factor to learn. People can learn the other things, such as budgeting. People skills—knowing how to get the best out of people—are a manager's key to success."

Health care managers require administrative skills such as the ability to train, delegate, evaluate, and negotiate with staff. In addition, they must be able to coordinate a variety of functions concurrently. "You can manage people who are not trained the same as you are. You don't have to have similar backgrounds in education," Joyce says. "One of our administrators is a nurse. We're breaking some molds."

Leadership skills are also necessary to inspire and motivate others. Health care managers have to weather some disappointments occasionally. "Disappointment can occur when people—whether staff members or colleagues—let you down," Joyce says. "Failures in the system can be dealt with, but when the people piece falls apart, it's more disappointing."

Managers must also have analytical skills to be able to understand and solve problems quickly. However, at other times, they must show patience and thoroughness when a decision needs more thought and careful research. To solve many of their problems, health care managers must understand financial management, information systems, human resources, public relations, marketing, and organizational behavior.

Finally, they must also be interested in health care and in management. "I like the opportunity I have to work for a large group of people in their effort to deliver high-quality patient care," Joyce says. "Knowing that you can impact the quality of care is weighty."

how do I become a health care manager?

Joyce's initial interest in nursing gave her a start in health care. After working as a hospital staff nurse for many years, Joyce decided to move into management. After 21 years of being out of school and in the workforce, she went back to college for her master's degree. When she was close to completion, she moved into a management position at Christ Hospital. It was there that opportunities opened up for her. Joyce's nontraditional career path is one that an increasing number of people are following. Many health care management programs are marketing their programs to mature students who have many years of work experience and are looking for further advancement or a career change.

education

High School

Students considering a career in health care management should take science, math, and business courses. Since both oral and written communication skills are required, English and speech classes are recommended.

Postsecondary Training

Health care managers must hold a minimum of a bachelor's degree for entry-level positions in smaller facilities or departments. Entry-level health care managers move into higher positions through work experience or after obtaining additional education.

Most senior management positions require a master's degree in health services administration or public health, although some managers are entering the field with graduate degrees in medicine, business, public administration, and other fields. "A master's degree is almost the accepted standard here now," Joyce says.

According to the Accrediting Commission on Education for Health Services Administration, 67 schools offered two- and three-year graduate programs in health services administration in 1999. To earn a master's degree, students complete course work in areas such as hospital organization and management, marketing, human resources, accounting, strategic planning, and health information systems. In addition, most programs require that students complete an internship or residency, and possibly write a thesis.

Some programs allow students to specialize in a particular type of organization, such as hospitals, nursing homes, mental health facilities, health maintenance organizations, or ambulatory care facilities. Other programs provide a generalist approach to health care administration.

During the supervised internship or residency, students can apply the theories and principles they learned in class to the type of health care setting in which they want to work. The administrators with whom the students work closely serve as their mentors. Some pro-

grams may also include a fellowship, which involves additional supervised work.

"If I were to do it again today, I'd consider getting my master's in hospital administration or business administration, which would be more pertinent to my position. However, [nursing] worked for me," Joyce says. "If students are looking for an administrative position, courses in health care administration and health care finance will better prepare them for an administrative position in a hospital. These types of courses give you the perspective of health care as well as teach you the rudiments of business management."

Health care managers who want to teach, consult, or conduct research may be required to hold a Ph.D.

certification or licensing

Managers working as nursing home administrators are required to be licensed by the state in which they practice. Requirements vary depending on the state, but generally, nursing home managers must obtain a bachelor's degree from an accredited college or university, complete a state-approved training program, and pass a licensing examination. They must also complete continuing education courses and renew their license yearly or every two years.

State licensing is not required for other health care managers. Certification, offered by the American College of Health Care Administrators, is voluntary. Managers may choose to obtain certification to improve their professional credibility and opportunities for advancement.

scholarships and grants

Scholarships and grants are often available from individual institutions, state agencies, and special-interest organizations. Ask your high school college counselor for information about financial aid opportunities; your local library may also be a good resource.

If you decide you want to become a physician first and eventually get into health care administration, you may want to consider financing your medical education through programs that exchange military service for tuition coverage. The National Health Service Corps Scholarship Program and the Armed Forces Health Professions Scholarship Program are two opportunities that help pay for medical school.

Another source for financial aid, scholarship, and grant information is the Association of American Medical Colleges. Remember to request information early for eligibility, application requirements, and deadlines.

Armed Forces Health Professions Scholarship Program
Air Force: http://hp.airforce.com/training/financial.html
Army: http://www.sirius.com/~ameddet/hpschps.htm
Navy: http://nshs.med.navy.mil/hpsp/default.htm

Association of American Medical Colleges
2450 N Street, NW
Washington, DC 20037-1126
202-828-0400
http://www.aamc.org

National Health Service Corps Scholarship Program
Department of Health and Human Services
4350 East-West Highway, 10th Floor
Bethesda, MD 20814
800-638-0824
http://www.fedmoney.org/grants/93288-00.htm

who will hire me?

Health care managers work in a variety of settings. Besides hospitals and hospital systems, positions can be found in ambulatory care facilities, hospices, nursing homes, health maintenance organizations, medical group practices, mental health organizations, universities, public health departments, consulting firms, and health care associations. In addition, health care managers work in home health agencies, dentists' offices, medical and dental laboratories, and offices of allied health professionals.

Most universities have placement offices that offer their students and graduates information about career opportunities as well as specific job openings.

Many people learn about job openings by joining professional membership organizations. Membership allows managers to network with other members and find out about conferences, continuing education, and other professional activities. The American College of Healthcare Executives (ACHE) offers a student associate membership with a reduced membership fee. These student chapters invite guest speakers, elect officers, and undertake community service and fundraising projects.

ACHE's *Career Link* is a good source for job leads, available to members by subscription or by visiting its Web site, http://www.ache.org. H*ospital & Health Networks* and *Modern Healthcare* are other publications that carry job leads and professional information.

Job openings can also be found in the classified advertising sections of newspapers in major cities. In addition, executive search firms that recruit for the health care field may help in locating management positions. In many cases, the employer pays any applicable fees to the recruiter.

where can I go from here?

Advancement in health care management usually depends on a combination of a person's education and experience and the organization's size and complexity. A health care manager's first job may be an entry-level to mid-level management position in a specialized area such as patient care services, medical staff relations, or finance. Once they have experience, health care managers can move into positions with higher levels of responsibility, such as chief executive officer, administrator, assistant administrator, vice president, or department manager. Those with master's degrees have better opportunities for advancing into higher-level positions. Knowledge of and experience in finance, budgeting, information systems, strategic planning, patient care, and staff management are valuable.

Keys to advancement are keeping informed of the changes in the field and staying flexible to take advantage of opportunities when they appear. One way to advance your career is to take on greater responsibility.

"Opportunities in health care are opening up all over," Joyce says. "Health care has expanded beyond our wildest dreams. Health care is dealing increasingly with preventive care. Managed care is also growing. Many career opportunities have opened up outside the hospital."

Joyce believes educational credentials and work experience are both important to advancement. She also advises those interested in upper management positions to work their way up. "You don't start at the top," she says. "Get some real experience. Opportunities will open up to you. You have to be flexible."

what are the salary ranges?

Earnings of health care managers vary according to levels of experience, responsibilities, and the type, size, and location of facilities. According to the U.S. Department of Labor, the 1998 median salary for health care managers was $48,870. The lowest paid 10 percent earned less than $28,600; the highest paid 10 percent earned over $88,730 a year.

Health care managers who work in individual departments within hospitals or other facilities earn different salaries. A 1998 survey by *Modern Healthcare* magazine reports the following median earnings by department: respiratory therapy, $57,700; home health care, $62,400; ambulatory and outpatient services, $66,200; radiology, $66,800; clinical laboratory, $66,900; physical therapy, $68,100; rehabilitation services, $73,400; and nursing services, $100,200.

what is the job outlook?

The health care field today is dynamic and growing, offering a wide range of opportunities and challenges. Employment for health care managers is expected to grow faster than the average for all occupations, according to predictions by the U.S. Department of Labor. The health care industry is expanding because of the growing aging population, advances in medical technology, increasing emphasis on disease prevention, and growing pressures from business, government, insurance companies, and patients to hold down health care costs.

Organizations are being restructured for cost economies, and traditional patient care is changing. There are fewer stand-alone hospitals and more hospital systems. There is greater emphasis on ambulatory care and managed care. As the health care field diversifies, many health care services are being provided outside of the traditional hospital setting.

Job opportunities are available at a variety of organizational levels, from chief executive officer to department head. Health care managers with strong business and management skills will find the best job opportunities. Those with graduate degrees will also have an edge.

Competition for top jobs is intense, but because of the expansion and diversification of health care services, employment will grow in nontraditional areas that provide patient care. The best opportunities for health care managers will be in home health care and long-term care. In addition, health maintenance organizations are being marketed to elderly citizens to supplement or replace Medicare programs. Growth in this market will increase the need for qualified health care managers. In addition, job prospects are increasing in ambulatory care as patients receive more health care services on an outpatient basis. Finally, the long-term care segment of the industry is expanding to meet the needs of the rapidly growing elderly population. Patients are demanding (and receiving) more specialized high-quality services geared to their individual needs. This demand has lead to the growth of patient care services specifically designed for the elderly, women, and children.

how do I learn more?

professional organizations

For information about academic programs and careers in health care management, contact the following organizations:

American College of Healthcare Administrators
1800 Diagonal Road, Suite 355
Alexandria, VA 22314
info@achca.org
http://www.achca.org

American College of Healthcare Executives
1 North Franklin Street, Suite 1700
Chicago, IL 60606-3491
312-424-2800
http://www.ache.org

Association of University Programs in Health Administration
730 11th Street NW, 4th Floor
Washington, DC 20001-4510
202-638-1448
aupha@aupha.org
http://www.aupha.org

bibliography

Following is a sampling of materials relating to the professional concerns and development of health care managers.

Field, Shelly. *Career Opportunities in Health Care.* New York, NY: Facts on File, 1997.

Gift, Robert G. and Catherine F. Kinney, eds. *Today's Management Methods: A Guide for the Health Care Executive.* Chicago, IL: American Hospital Publishing, Inc., 1996.

Ginter, Peter M. et al. *Strategic Management of Health Care Organizations.* Oxford, UK: Blackwell Science Publishers, Inc., 1997.

Kaluzny, Arnold D. et al. eds. *Health Care Management: Organization Design & Behavior.* Albany, NY: Delmar Publishers, 1999.

Kovner, Anthony R. and Alan H. Channing. *A Career Guide for the Health Services Manager.* 3rd Edition. Ann Arbor, MI: Health Administration Press, 1999.

Nowicki, Michael. *The Financial Management of Hospitals and Healthcare Organizations.* Ann Arbor, MI: Health Administration Press, 1998.

Zelman, William N. et al. *Financial Management of Health Care Organizations: An Introduction to Fundamental Tools, Concepts, and Applications.* Albany, NY: Delmar Publishers, 1998.

Health Physicists

Definition

A health physicist is a radiation safety professional whose work entails protecting other workers, the public, and the environment from the harmful effects of ionizing radiation while promoting its beneficial uses.

Alternative Job Title

Radiation safety officers

High School Subjects

Chemistry
Mathematics
Physics

Personal Skills

Communication/ideas
Technical/scientific

Salary Range

$26,000 to $82,000 to $147,000

Educational Requirements

Bachelor's degree, master's degree recommended, doctorate required for most positions in medicine, education, and research

Certification or Licensing

Recommended

Outlook

Little change or more slowly than the average

GOE
05.01.02
O*NET-SOC
29-9011.00

After starting out in college studying fashion design, then switching to a premed curriculum, Kathy Pryor wound up employed as chief engineer (senior health physicist) at Battelle Pacific Northwest Laboratory. "I found this field by mistake," she explains. "I was looking for a graduate program to fill in my time while I waited to reapply for medical school, and I wanted to stay at the University of Washington, where I had done my undergrad work. I opened up the catalog and it happened to fall open to the page on radiological sciences. I knew nothing about radiological sciences except what I'd absorbed from B movies on nuclear holocausts and the resultant mutant grasshoppers, etc. However, the program had an option in radiation biology, and when I talked to the program adviser, he explained that everyone got multiple job offers before graduation (this was 1979). I enrolled in the program and really enjoyed the courses. I never went back to applying for medical school and have never regretted my choice of careers."

what does a health physicist do?

Health physicists are radiation safety professionals. They are responsible for protecting other workers, the public, and the environment from the possible hazards of ionizing radiation while at the same time promoting its beneficial uses. Ionizing radiation is used in the diagnosis and treatment of diseases, in scientific research, and in generating electrical power. But exposure to excessive amounts can be hazardous to people, animals, plants—in fact, all living organisms. There are potential hazards, too, if it is used in an unsafe manner. Caution must be exercised whenever dealing with nuclear reactors, particle accelerators, X-ray machines, radiation therapy, and nuclear weapons as well as during the manufacture and disposal of radioactive materials. And this is where the health physicist comes in.

Kathy spells out the responsibilities of a health physicist: "We evaluate the potential for workers to be exposed to radiation in a variety of work settings—commercial nuclear power, hospitals and medical centers, industrial uses, and research institutions. We calculate potential doses to workers from radiation sources and specify ways to reduce doses through the use of shielding, more efficient work practices, substitution of sources, reduction of sources, use of automation and remote handling tools, etc. We also conduct radiological surveys to measure radiation fields in the workplace and the environment and use dosimeters to measure doses received by workers and the environment. We develop procedures to implement federal and state regulations and guidelines for the safe use of radioactive materials and help workers to use these procedures correctly through training and assessments in the workplace."

Secondarily, Kathy says, "We get involved in emergency preparedness and response in the event that an accident occurs involving a loss of control of radioactive materials. Some health physicists also deal with nonionizing radiation sources, such as lasers, microwaves, and radiofrequency radiation."

Health physicists may work in any of several different areas. Some concentrate on research, studying the effects or levels of radiation. Others become educators, training future health physicists in colleges, universities, or laboratories or teaching the general public about radiation.

Power reactor health physicists work at reactor sites, where they oversee everything having to do with radiation protection, such as the selection, purchase, and maintenance of equipment. They are trained to deal with the rare radiation accident that does occur. Other responsibilities may include supervising a staff of technicians, analyzing radiation records and dosimetry data, and examining survey and laboratory results to make sure that the reactor is operating properly.

Nuclear weapons health physicists are the ones who make sure that defense sites take proper precautions in storing and putting together nuclear weapons. They are responsible for keeping the workplace safe for the weapons technicians by determining the appropriate protective equipment to be used,

lingo to learn

Decommission: Act of shutting down a nuclear facility and then reducing remaining radioactive materials to such a level that the facility can be used without restrictions.

Decontamination: Reduction or removal of contaminating radioactive materials from a person, place, or thing.

Dosimeter: Instrument that measures and records doses of radiation received by people or the environment.

Industrial hygienist: Worker responsible for assessing, eliminating, and managing occupational health hazards and diseases.

Ionizing radiation: High-energy radiation that produces ions as a result of displacing electrons from atoms or molecules. Examples are alpha and beta particles, X rays, and gamma radiation. Examples of nonionizing radiation are infrared radiation, microwaves, visible light, and lasers.

teaching them about radiation safety in terms of handling nuclear weapons, and compiling and approving safety procedures.

Medical health physicists can be found working in facilities where radiation sources are used in the treatment or diagnosis of disease. Some of these places are hospitals, health care clinics, and medical centers. It is the responsibility of these professionals to make sure the facility is safe for patients and workers. Sometimes the medical health physicist functions as the facility's *radiation safety officer (RSO)*. According to Kathy, "A health physicist and a radiation safety officer are similar. Most radiation safety officers are health physicists by profession and training. Some aren't, but it makes their job much more difficult. Radiation safety officers are specifically listed on a radioactive materials license from the regulatory body [the National Regulatory Commission] or an agreement state [state agency that has an agreement with the NRC], and they are responsible for ensuring that radioactive materials are used in a safe manner according to the terms and conditions of their license. They are responsible for the radiation safety program at the licensee's facilities, which includes inventory and control of radioactive materials, performing radiological surveys of facilities, providing radiation dosimetry and bioassay (to determine amount of exposure) to radiation workers and interpreting the results of these measurements, providing training to users of radioactive materials, and providing for the safe packaging and disposal of radioactive wastes. Larger programs have an RSO and a number of health physicists and technicians working for them. Smaller programs may just have the RSO to do all of the above activities."

Regulatory enforcement health physicists devise and enforce the rules and regulations concerning radioactive materials. *Occupational safety health physicists* work with the private sector to ensure that safety procedures are not only in place but being followed. *Industrial* or *applied health physicists* make suggestions to management about the radiological equipment or methods that would be most suitable in their particular situations. They may also help to design new radiation facilities or control programs.

Environmental health physicists are responsible for protecting not only the environment but also the public from exposure to manmade or natural radioactivity. They may conduct radiation surveys and laboratory analyses in the decontamination and decom-

The hardest part of my job is explaining radiation protection regulations to a researcher who feels that the rules are interfering with his or her ability to get work done.

missioning of former facilities, or they may focus on the study of radon in the home, doing analysis, testing protocols, and developing guidelines.

"I took my first job as a rotational engineer with Westinghouse Hanford Company in Richland, Washington," remembers Elaine Marshall, now safety coordinator at Fermi National Accelerator Laboratory. "WHC was a prime contractor at the Hanford Reservation. In that position, I had the opportunity to transfer to different positions for a period of up to two years. This allowed me to try out several different things. I was involved in the isotope development program and development of irradiation experiments. I then moved to review irradiation experiments for the Fast Flux Test Facility. From there, I was involved in conceptual facility design. I finally landed a position as a technical health physics liaison with the analytical chemistry laboratory. I learned about this position through a job fair at a conference that I attended while still in college."

Kathy describes some of her early experiences in health physics: "I worked in a radioecology laboratory at the University [of Washington] preparing soil samples from Enewitok for radiochemical analysi) and in the university's Radiation Safety Office. At the Radiation Safety Office, I collected and packaged radioactive waste and performed radiological surveys in the labs. I also had a U.S. Public Health Service grant to do my research in radiation biology in the lab. I removed liver cells from rats, irradiated them, cultured them and looked at changes in DNA and protein metabolism relative to dose."

About her first job, at Southern California Edison as a junior health physics engineer, Kathy says, "I was given a project to develop an in-house radiation dosimetry processing capability using commercially available dosimetry readers and dosimeters. I also provided dosimetry support during plant outages, did evaluations of ways to minimize worker doses on specific jobs and evaluated systems and ways for minimizing radioactive waste generation. I had to work about 60 hours a week during outages, but I got lots of good experiences during that time."

"My job scope has changed somewhat as I took a transfer to provide me with some more practical experience in the areas of environmental and occupational health to support my master's degree," Elaine shares. "I oversee my organization's radiological program, writing procedures, auditing, training, and evaluating work for radiological controls, surveys and other measurements. Besides the radiological aspect, I am responsible for evaluating workplace hazards and implementing appropriate controls."

what is it like to be a health physicist?

The work of a health physicist is highly technical in nature. Health physicists deal with radiological equipment, analyze data, and devise guidelines. Much time may be spent in a laboratory. Something Elaine Marshall enjoys yet finds to be challenging is that the work varies daily. Plus, she says, "I get to work with various individuals on various levels." That, too, comes with its drawbacks, in that it "involves negotiation among people and organizations," which at times may prove difficult. Much of her day is spent in front of her computer. "However, I do get to get out into the field. Travel is limited, usually to training courses."

"I've worked at two nuclear power plants, as the radiation safety officer for USC health sciences campus, and now, for nearly nine years, at the Pacific Northwest National Lab," says Kathy Pryor, who is currently working on a design project as the lead radiological engineer. "We are designing a facility to be built for the Department of Energy at the Savannah River Site to disassemble nuclear weapons and convert the plutonium to a form that cannot be used in nuclear weapons. My job is basically a desk job and currently involves a lot of travel. We are subcontracted to an architect/engineering firm in Denver, so I spend about half my time in Denver and half in Richland, Washington, where Battelle Pacific Northwest Laboratory is located. I am responsible for calculating potential doses that workers will receive in this facility, specifying shielding and automation to reduce doses, reviewing facility layouts and process descriptions to identify radiological impacts, and evaluating the cost of dose-saving measures versus the dose that can be saved over the design life of the facility. I do a significant amount of work on the computer, and the people on my task run Monte Carlo computer codes to model areas of the facility and calculate radiation dose rates."

Kathy comments, "I enjoy the process of evaluating worker doses and determining ways to reduce those doses. I have also, in my previous job as a manager of the Radiological Control Technical Support group, done work in counseling pregnant radiation workers and in translating regulations and guidelines into reasonable work practices for the workplace. I enjoy writing, and a large part of my job involves written communications."

According to Kathy, "One of the less desirable parts of my job is the result of a very heavily regulated workplace—radiation safety regulations tend to be very prescriptive and more costly to implement than is really necessary. This is due to the difficulties involved in setting a safe level of exposure for workers and the public. Regulatory entities, the scientific community, and the public do not necessarily agree on a safe level of exposure, which has a lot to do with the level of risk that people are willing to accept on the job and in the environment."

"The hardest part of my job," continues Kathy, "is explaining radiation protection regulations to a researcher who feels that the rules are interfering with his or her ability to get work done. This requires good communication skills and the ability to successfully adapt regulatory requirements to the workplace."

have I got what it takes to be a health physicist?

Good communication skills, both written and verbal, will be a definite asset in such areas as teaching, supervising, resolving issues with colleagues, and documenting research. "I have good written and verbal communication skills," remarks Kathy about her strengths, "and I try to look for ways to compromise and adapt requirements to the unique situations found in a research environment. I also need good communication skills when working with the design engineers on my current pro-

Health Physics Pioneers

Karl Z. Morgan (1907-1999) was a founder of health physics as well as the Health Physics Society. In 1942, upon creation of the first nuclear reactor, Morgan was among those to insist upon the institution of safety measures, marking the unofficial beginnings of health physics.

In 1943 Morgan worked on the Manhattan Project, along with Enrico Fermi and other scientists, to develop the world's first atomic bomb. Morgan served as director of health physics at Tennessee's Oak Ridge National Laboratory (ORNL) from 1944 to 1972.

A prominent figure in the field of nuclear science, Morgan recognized the potential dangers posed by unsafe or excessive uses of radiation and worked tirelessly to ensure radiation safety. At times he even became critical of the nuclear power industry. In fact, he testified on behalf of parties that claimed to have been harmed by exposure to radiation. One of these cases involved Karen Silkwood, who was exposed to radiation while working in a nuclear facility. (This incident and Silkwood's subsequent activism for worker safety were dramatized in the movie *Silkwood*, starring Meryl Streep in the title role.) Morgan's memoirs were published in the 1999 book *The Angry Genie: One Man's Walk through the Nuclear Age*.

Another founder of the Health Physics Society was Elda E. Anderson (1899-1961). This pioneer in health physics earned a master's in physics in 1924 and a doctorate in 1941. In between those years she taught physics and chemistry classes. In 1943 she, too, became a member of the team developing the atomic bomb. After this experience, Anderson became chief of education for the ORNL Health Physics Division. Anderson wrote *Manual of Radiological Protection for Civil Defense* (1950), documenting her research at ORNL. Every year, the Health Physics Society bestows the Elda E. Anderson Award on a young HPS member for achievements made in the field of health physics.

ject in order to ensure that radiation safety features are designed into the new facility."

Health physicists who train other technicians or the public in radiation safety issues should be patient and enjoy teaching. Team players will do well in this field because it takes a number of people working together to develop and maintain radiation safety. On the flipside, "a person who likes to make an individual contribution and get credit/recognition for the work that he or she does" might be unsuitable for a job in health physics, according to Elaine.

"Generally," Kathy observes, "people who are inflexible will have trouble with this type of job. The application of radiation safety to the workplace requires the ability to deal with shades of gray rather than blindly prescribing black-and-white rules."

Since health physicists are responsible for assessing the effects of radiation and then coming up with safety solutions, good problem-solving skills will be beneficial. Elaine notes other attributes to be self-motivation and the ability to handle shifting priorities.

how do I become a health physicist?

education

High School

Health physics is an interdisciplinary science, combining aspects of biology, chemistry, and physics along with statistics, ecology, and toxicology. Because of this, you should take a lot of science courses in high school to be sure you get a solid foundation in basic science. Elaine found math in addition to science classes in particular to be helpful in preparing her for a career in health physics. Kathy agrees, saying, "I did take four years of math, through pre-calculus, and two years of science—biology and physics. I would recommend taking calculus in high school, as well as classes in physics, biology, and chemistry." According to Kathy, you will need that "good solid background in math, physics, and biology in order to understand the mechanisms of interaction of radiation with matter and living systems."

Kathy attended a private girls' school in Hawaii that "focused on humanities and the arts. Even though I took a lot of math and science in college, I think that my [high school] classes in English and writing helped develop my communications and people skills. Many of my fellow health physicists had much more exposure to science in high school than I did."

Postsecondary Training

The *Health Physics Education Reference Book* (available online at the Health Physics Society Web site) lists and describes degree programs in the United States. Some schools may not specifically offer a health physics program; instead, you may get your degree in nuclear engineering, environmental engineering sciences, or physics with a health physics emphasis or option.

As an undergraduate, you'll probably want to get your degree in science, engineering, or health science, being sure to take classes in physics, mathematics, chemistry, and nuclear engineering. If you plan to become certified, check with the American Board of Health Physics (ABHP) for educational requirements. A majority of health physicists go on to get a master's degree. A graduate degree will most

likely be required for health physicists in medicine, education, and research.

Elaine received a bachelor's degree in nuclear engineering with a bioengineering option at the University of Illinois. "UIUC has since expanded their program to include radiological engineering. I had to make it up as I went. I then received an M.S. in environmental and occupational health from Washington State University."

Earning a master of science in radiological sciences from the University of Washington, in her opinion a very rigorous and research-oriented course of study, Kathy had an emphasis in radiation biology. "I also took a bunch of nuclear engineering courses. I started a Ph.D. in radiation biology, but my adviser lost his funding. I elected to enter the workplace at that point."

The paths these two women took to enter the field of health physics were not entirely direct. As mentioned earlier, Kathy didn't go to college expecting to become a health physicist. "I started out at the University of Hawaii in fashion design! After my freshman year, I decided that I'd never make a decent living in fashion design and switched to a premed curriculum . . . but did not get admitted to medical school. I was planning to reapply to medical school the following year and started a graduate program in radiological sciences (radiation biology). I liked it so much that I never reapplied to medical school."

Elaine, like Kathy, wound up studying health physics by accident. "I started out in nuclear engineering wanting to focus on plasma research. I soon learned that I was more of a people person and research and I didn't get along. I was then going to transfer to a pre-med major. My adviser told me that biology degrees were prevalent on medical school applications. If I stayed in engineering I would have something that would stand out and something that would pay the bills if I didn't get into medical school. By chance, I landed in health physics."

According to Kathy, necessary job training might change one of these days since "there is some discussion about seeking accreditation for health physics programs in the future, but this is still being discussed by the Health Physics Society and the heads of the programs."

Health physicists must continue to keep on top of developments and news in the industry. Elaine does this by regularly reading the Health Physics Society's journal *Health Physics and Newsletter* as well as the American Nuclear Society's *Nuclear News*. Kathy also

To be a successful health physicist, you should

- Have superior problem-solving skills
- Be a team player
- Be able to adjust to changing priorities
- Have good written and verbal communication skills
- Be self-motivated
- Be proficient in computer usage

reads HPS and ANS publications. She explains, "The HPS publications [the newsletter and *Operational Radiation Safety*] are very important to my job. The HPS journal is less important, but is good for staying current in the field."

Both Kathy and Elaine view their memberships in professional organizations as being invaluable to them in their careers. The two belong to the Health Physics Society and the American Nuclear Society. Kathy is also a member of the American Academy of Health Physics. She says, "It's important to develop a network of professional colleagues to consult if you have questions." Elaine says, "Being a member of the HPS allows me to stay current with regulations and practices in the field. It helps in networking and problem solving."

Kathy urges students to explore the HPS Web site to learn how to get involved. "The HPS has student chapters and sponsors student papers at our annual conference. We also provide some travel support to students and give awards for the best student papers." The American Nuclear Society offers membership to those students who are enrolled in a science or engineering program at a qualifying institution.

certification or licensing

Kathy is certified in the comprehensive practice of health physics by the American Board of Health Physics. As vice chairperson of the ABHP, she has firsthand knowledge of the process. "The certification process consisted of meeting the academic and experience requirements and successfully passing a multiple choice exam and a calculational/essay exam." According to the ABHP, an applicant must have at least a bachelor's degree from an accredited college or university. Acceptable fields of study are physical science, engineering, health physics, or a biological science with a minor in physical science or engineering. "I think that the process is generally a good one," Kathy continues, "and gives candidates a chance to demonstrate both academic knowledge and practical application of health physics to situations found in a variety of workplaces."

Also a certified health physicist, Elaine shares additional information: "The certification process involved examination and a review of my work, in addition to references. The first part can be taken immediately out of school, but the second part cannot be taken until you have a specific combination of education and work experience." The ABHP specifies that an applicant must have a minimum of six years of experience in health physics before taking the second part of the exam. "After that," Elaine goes on, "you must be recertified every four years, which requires a review of the continuing education that you have completed during that time period and your current work scope. I think the process does ensure that only qualified individuals are certified. However, I do also think there are a number of excellent health physicists out there who never have been certified. Certification is not necessary to perform this work. Most individuals pursue the certification out of a personal desire, not because it changes their job or the pay."

It's Elaine's opinion that "more and more employers are asking for certification or eligibility for certification. We may see certification take on a different role. Many employers are also asking for formal training/education in the field."

scholarships and grants

You can find information on scholarships, fellowships, assistantships, grants, and so on in the *Health Physics Education Reference Book*.

internships and volunteerships

You might want to volunteer at a hospital or other medical facility just to gain exposure to the health care field and perhaps even to learn about the use of radiation therapy in medical treatments. "I did volunteer work at the local children's hospital," remembers Kathy, "which helped to get me interested in the health care field." She continues, "I did work in the university Radiation Safety Office, which, while not specifically an internship, was directly applicable to my subsequent jobs. There are internships available through the Department of Energy and the Nuclear Regulatory Commission, as well as through a number of the utilities."

In addition to those opportunities, Kathy states that "high school kids in our area can participate in internships with the Pacific Northwest National Laboratory and can assist researchers in the labs," although there may be special requirements applied to students when using radioactive materials.

who will hire me?

Health physicists may find employment in commercial or governmental nuclear power facilities, medical centers, defense plants, and university research laboratories as well as various industries where there are radiation safety concerns.

"There are both government and private sector employers," says Elaine. "Within the government, you have the Department of Energy and the Nuclear Regulatory Commission. The NRC has entered into several agreement state arrangements and those states, such as Illinois, then have their own state agencies. There are many DOE contractors. I work for one [Fermilab]. Oak Ridge, Hanford, Los Alamos, Brookhaven, and Argonne are all examples of others. Within the private sector, you have academic institutions; hospitals; research laboratories, especially those affiliated with pharmaceutical development; consulting firms; and nuclear power plants. Your employers will either be regulated by the DOE or the NRC. It is difficult to transfer between the two. For example, if your first job is with a national laboratory or weapons site regulated by the DOE, you will find it very difficult to find employment with an organization regulated by the NRC, like a power plant."

According to Kathy, "The main employers are hospitals and academic institutions, the government [DOE and NRC], government contractors [operators of national laboratories and other DOE facilities], nuclear utilities, and certain types of industries that use radioactive materials or radiation-generating devices, like X-ray machines and accelerators."

You won't find too many health physics jobs advertised in the newspaper classified section. Instead, some of the avenues you might want to explore when conducting a job search are job fairs, placement agencies, and college placement offices. "It is my understanding that there are a number of placement agencies that advertise in the technical journals," states Elaine. "However, most individuals hear about their positions through word of mouth after they land their first."

In addition to those resources, Kathy recommends checking academic programs for openings. Certain professional organizations (such as the Health Physics Society and the American Nuclear Society) post job listings online. Frequently you'll have to be a member of an organization in order to access details. Another online resource is the Idaho State University Radiation Information Network's employment listing.

where can I go from here?

About advancement possibilities currently available to her, Elaine says, "Our company structure is pretty flat and much of the movement is lateral in nature. I hope to continue to expand my experience in different areas." Certain opportunities will be open to you only if you participate in additional training programs or take more classes. Elaine explains, "The position that I am in currently expounds upon industrial safety and industrial hygiene. I have had to take training in OSHA regulations and other general safety courses." Her goal is to move into a management position.

Kathy states, "I have been up through the ranks in management as far as serving as the University of Southern California radiation safety officer and as a manager of a technical support group of engineers at both the Trojan Nuclear Plant and at PNNL. You can generally advance to positions such as director of environment, safety, and health, or positions in operations for a facility."

For personal reasons, Kathy prefers not to go into an upper-level management position because of the extra hours demanded. "I would prefer to stay in an individual contributor role or as a first line manager," she comments. "I enjoy applied health physics and radiation safety program development."

If you want to focus your efforts on conducting research, Kathy advises that you get a Ph.D. Having certification will be a definite advantage should you want to advance in engineering or management.

what are the salary ranges?

The Oak Ridge Institute for Science and Technology conducted a salary survey (June 1999) of health physicists in utilities and nonutilities (private-sector organizations and DOE facilities). Ranges were given for workers with 0 to 10 years of experience who had received a bachelor's or master's degree or a doctorate. In utilities, the range was a low of $33,300 for a worker holding a bachelor's degree and no experience up to $81,000 for someone with a Ph.D. and 8 to 10 years of experience. In nonutilities, that range was $26,000 to $86,600.

For its 2000 salary survey, the American Association of Health Physicists (AAHP), in conjunction with the Health Physics Society, collected data on certified health physicists (CHPs). The report indicates that the salary range for CHPs (working in health physics) with a bachelor's degree earned a minimum of $37,500 and a maximum of $107,500, with $72,500 being the median. Those with a master's degree made a minimum of $32,500 and a maximum of $147,500, with $82,500 the median. Finally, those with a Ph.D. made a minimum of $32,500 and a maximum of $137,500, with $87,500 the median.

"Government salaries are based on the grade of the employee and are consistent nationwide," reports Elaine. Kathy says that salaries are "heavily influenced by the geographical region and type of industry that you are employed in. Academic and government regulatory agencies pay a bit less and nuclear utilities tend to pay more."

Both Elaine and Kathy report that their compensation other than salary is the usual benefits package: paid vacation and sick days, some kind of pension or 401-K plan, medical and dental insurance, tuition reimbursement, and long-term disability. Their employers also have flexible work hours as well as flexible spending or reimbursement accounts, which might be used for child care.

what is the job outlook?

Although it does not include data specifically pertaining to health physicists, the *Occupational Outlook Handbook* reports that employment for physicists and astronomers will result in little change through the next decade. This is because many physicists and astronomers work on defense-related research projects, the funding for which is seeing little or no growth. Budget cuts by the federal government in the funding of research projects will likely have an impact on employment prospects as well. There has also been an ongoing slowdown in the growth of civilian physics-related research.

Health Physics on the Web

For definitions of terminology used in the field of health physics, check out these sites:
Borders' Dictionary of Health Physics
http://www.hpinfo.org

The U.S. Nuclear Regulatory Commission's Glossary of Nuclear Terms
http://www.nrc.gov/NRC/EDUCATE/GLOSSARY/index.html

This Web site has a collection of images of and details about objects contained in the Oak Ridge Associated Universities museum, such as dosimeters, electroscopes, ionization chambers, and survey instruments.
Health Physics Historical Instrumentation Museum Collection
http://www.orau.com/ptp/museumdirectory.htm

The Web site of this DOE-funded project features an in-depth timeline covering the history of radiation research as well as a detailed glossary of terminology.
U.S. Department of Energy Low Dose Radiation Research Program
http://lowdose.org

RadSafe is a mailing list focused on discussion of health physics-related topics.
RadSafe
http://www.vanderbilt.edu/radsafe

Elaine surmises that the above scenario is true in the field of health physics, too. "Over the last several years," she says, "the field in general has been slowly declining. However, with the expansion of nuclear medicine and other technologies and the retirement of many of the field's pioneers, jobs have been available."

"I'd say that the future is steady right now," Kathy comments. "Growth is shrinking, but we need to replace retiring health physicists. There is some push to be multidisciplinary and have some industrial hygiene and environmental training."

"I think with the growing energy crisis and the positions of the current administration regarding nuclear energy, health physics will again be a promising career," Elaine asserts. But in her opinion it remains to be seen which areas of the United States hold more promise than others for employment in the field. "This one has to play out since nuclear energy is such a political hot potato," Elaine says. Kathy, too, realizes that public opinion is a factor: "If nuclear power rebounds in the United States, this will be a good area to get into."

"Currently the DOE sites are employing a lot of health physicists," notes Kathy. "These areas are in eastern Washington state [Hanford], Colorado, South Carolina [Savannah River], and Tennessee [Oak Ridge]. If you concentrate on commercial nuclear power, then you need to be located near nuclear power plants in the Northeast, Midwest, and South."

Continuing, Kathy says, "I think that the best opportunities for health physics exist in health care (as a medical physicist or medical health physicist) and in decontamination and decommissioning of existing facilities. Depending on the resolution of the current power crisis, nuclear power may become more attractive and the outlook for power plant HPs may improve significantly. Many of the current health physicists are retiring, and we are not graduating many replacements for them. So, I think that the outlook is generally good."

how do I learn more?

professional organizations

Following are organizations that provide information on careers in health physics.

American Academy of Health Physics

1313 Dolley Madison Boulevard, Suite 402
McLean, VA 22101
703-790-1745 X25
aahp@BurkInc.com
http://www.hps1.org/aahp

American Industrial Hygiene Association

2700 Prosperity Avenue, Suite 250
Fairfax, VA 22031
703-849-8888
infonet@aiha.org
http://www.aiha.org/pr/radiatn.html

American Nuclear Society

555 North Kensington Avenue
LaGrange Park, IL 60526
708-352-6611
nucleus@ans.org
http://www.ans.org

Health Physics Society

1313 Dolley Madison Boulevard, Suite 402
McLean, VA 22101
703-790-1745
hps@BurkInc.com
http://www.hps.org

National Council on Radiation Protection and Measurements

7910 Woodmont Avenue, Suite 800
Bethesda, MD 20814-3095
301-657-2652
ncrp@ncrp.com
http://www.ncrp.com

Together, the Idaho State University Health Physics Program, Health Physics Alumni Association, and ISU HPS Student Chapter host an employment listing for professionals in health physics.

Radiation Information Network

http://www.physics.isu.edu/radinf/listing.htm

bibliography

Following is a sampling of materials relating to health physics.

Bevelacqua, Joseph John. Basic *Health Physics: Problems and Solutions.* New York, NY: John Wiley & Sons, 1999.

Cember, Herman. *Introduction to Health Physics.* New York, NY: McGraw-Hill, 1996.

Jayaraman, Subramania. *Clinical Radiotherapy Physics: Basic Physics and Dosimetry.* Boca Raton, FL: CRC Press, 1996.

Martin, James E. *Physics for Radiation Protection.* New York, NY: John Wiley & Sons, 2000.

Ramesh, Chandra. *Nuclear Medicine Physics: The Basics.* Philadelphia, PA: Lippincott Williams & Wilkins, 1998.

Hematologists

Definition

Hematologists study and/or treat diseases of the blood and the blood-forming tissues. Some hematologists are physicians (M.D.s) who specialize in blood diseases; other hematologists are medical scientists (Ph.D.s) who do research on blood diseases but do not treat patients.

High School Subjects

Biology
Chemistry
English
Mathematics

Personal Skills

Helping/teaching
Technical/scientific

Salary Range

$43,000 to $53,000 to $72,000+ (Ph.D.s)
$147,000 to $164,000 to $269,000+ (M.D.s)

Educational Requirements

Bachelor's degree, M.D. or Ph.D.

Certification or Licensing

Recommended (certification for M.D.s)
Required by all states (licensing for M.D.s)

Outlook

About as fast as the average

GOE
NA*
O*NET-SOC
NA*

*Not Available. The U.S. Department of Labor does not classify hematologist as such, but rather classifies the hematologist's primary profession (e.g., doctor of internal medicine).

Unlocking the mysteries of erythropoietin (EPO), the hormone that stimulates the body's production of red blood cells, has the been the goal of Dr. Steven Sawyer for many years. Bone marrow cells need EPO to develop into red blood cells—a lack of this essential hormone causes anemia and leukemia.

As a hematologist at the Medical College of Virginia, Steven is doing important research that he also finds fascinating. Working with mice that were injected with the leukemia virus, he is trying to discover how EPO binds ("sticks") to the cell's receptor proteins. Unless this binding takes place, the bone marrow cell will die.

hematologists

what does a hematologist do?

Hematologists study and/or treat diseases of the blood and blood-forming tissues—the spleen, bone marrow, and lymph nodes. (*Hema* is Greek for blood.) There are several types of blood diseases, including anemias (which are characterized by a deficiency of hemoglobin), leukemias (which are malignant overproduction of white blood cells), and leukosarcomas (which are malignant white blood cell tumors, such as Hodgkin's disease).

Some hematologists, like Dr. Steven Sawyer, have Ph.D.s (usually in biochemistry) instead of medical degrees. They work as medical scientists who do blood-related research, but they do not treat patients. Other hematologists have M.D.s and are licensed physicians who have chosen to specialize in working with blood diseases. Some physicians in hematology concentrate on work with patients, while others are more research oriented. A few students who plan to focus on medical research choose to do a joint M.D./Ph.D. program.

Hematology is classified as a subspecialty of *internal medicine* (the branch of medicine that studies and treats, usually by nonsurgical means, diseases of the body's internal organs). Hematology is closely connected with oncology, the internal medicine subspecialty dealing with tumors; hematology and oncology are often combined into a single department in medical schools and hospital residency training programs. Some doctors specialize as *pediatric hematologists/oncologists,* working exclusively with children who have blood disorders and/or cancer.

Hematology is an exciting high-tech field in which medical research has made dramatic advances in recent decades. Many forms of leukemia that would formerly have meant death for the patient within a few months of diagnosis are now curable. Progress has also been made in treating other blood-related cancers. In addition, there are now effective treatments available for hemophilia patients who formerly faced the threat of bleeding to death from very minor injuries.

Bone marrow transplants offer exciting possibilities for treatment of a number of conditions. Research results that are still experimental suggest that bone marrow transplants will eventually offer a cure for sickle-cell anemia—a hereditary anemia in which abnormally shaped cells block the capillaries and prevent the body's tissues from getting the blood and nutrients they need.

Dr. Mark Koury, a hematologist at Vanderbilt Medical School, does leukemia-related research. In one of his projects, he is trying to discover why people who previously had a deficiency of the folate vitamin continue to be at a greater risk of developing leukemia even after the vitamin deficiency has been corrected. How a folate deficiency causes anemia is understood, but it is still not clear what happens to create the predisposition to leukemia. In another of Mark's projects, he is testing the chemosensitivity of the cells of leukemia patients in an attempt to determine which drugs these individuals will respond to in treatment. The goal is to be able to accurately predict the course of treatment in advance.

lingo to learn

Anemia: A deficiency of hemoglobin in the blood; the condition may be caused by acute or chronic blood loss, destruction of red blood cells, or the failure of the bone marrow to produce enough red blood cells.

CBC: Complete blood count, a procedure done to determine the number of red blood cells, white blood cells, and platelets per unit volume of blood.

Enzymes: Proteins that act as biochemical catalysts in living organisms.

Erythrocytes: Red blood cells.

Hemoglobin: The protein contained in red blood cells that carries oxygen from the lungs to the various tissues of the body and also brings carbon dioxide back to the lungs for removal.

Internal medicine: The field of medicine that deals with the diagnosis and, usually, nonsurgical treatment of diseases of the internal organs; hematology is a subspecialty of internal medicine.

Leukocytes: White blood cells.

Oncology: The study and treatment of tumors; oncology is a subspecialty of internal medicine that is closely related to hematology.

what is it like to be a hematologist?

What it is like to be a hematologist depends, in part, on whether one is a research scientist or a medical doctor. In the case of a doctor, it also depends on whether one is primarily involved in research or in patient treatment. The work setting makes another difference: Hematologists are employed in medical centers, university medical schools, blood banks, and private research centers.

Steven has his Ph.D. in biochemistry and works in an academic research setting. His principal responsibility is carrying out his research, a task that also includes running his lab, supervising the people who work in it, and writing grants to get federal money for funding the lab. He holds the position of associate professor at the Medical College of Virginia in Richmond. As an associate professor, one of his responsibilities is to give lectures to graduate and professional students in pharmacology, toxicology, and dental hygiene. He has also begun doing some undergraduate teaching.

In addition to this work, Steven reviews research grant proposals and manuscripts for the American Academy of Science and the American Heart Association.

Research and teaching are the parts of the job that he enjoys the most. When asked what he finds most difficult about his work, he replies without hesitation, "The many hours spent on grant writing." The uninitiated might assume that a grant proposal is a simple page or two summarizing one's research project. A typical grant proposal, however, is an 80-page (single-spaced) document. Steven has to raise $130,000 annually from the federal government to run the lab and cover the 25 percent of his salary that is not paid by the state of Virginia. When he was an assistant professor at Vanderbilt, he had to raise $200,000 a year from the government and from the Leukemia Society.

A lifelong interest in science led Steven to hematology. At first, he had thought of becoming a chemist, but he found that he did not have much interest in "making molecules." What did fascinate him was the cell—the most fundamental unit of living matter—and how it worked. While he was an undergraduate, his father developed kidney failure. He learned a lot about medicine from helping his mother

FYI

Rh Factor

The Rh factor is a hereditary substance found in the red blood cells of 85 percent of all human beings. A person who has this substance in the blood is said to be *Rh positive*. People who lack it are *Rh negative*. The presence of the Rh factor was first detected in 1940 by mixing a sample of human blood with the blood of rhesus monkeys. The term Rh comes from *rhesus*.

handle his father's home dialysis treatment; Steven also discovered that he did not want to become a medical doctor, primarily because he does not feel comfortable around critically ill people.

After earning his Ph.D. in biochemistry, Steven went to Vanderbilt for a two-year post-doctoral fellowship working with Dr. Stanley Cohen, who was doing research on the development of cells. Dr. Cohen received a Nobel Prize in 1986 for the discovery of epidermal growth factor (EGF).

Later, a member of the hematology department invited Steven to join the EPO research project. One of the benefits to emerge from the study of EPO is that EPO injections can now be given to those patients with kidney failure who develop anemia because they cannot produce the hormone on their own. This outcome is especially gratifying for Steven.

While he was still in medical school, Mark realized that he wanted to go into research because there was so much in medicine that was not yet scientifically explainable. He was drawn to the field of hematology partly because, as he says, "the research material is so readily available. Blood cells are easily accessible without surgery."

Although Mark still sees patients and teaches at Vanderbilt Medical School, his work is primarily research oriented. Like Steven, he also has to devote much time to the administrative side of running a lab, especially the problem of raising the necessary funds.

in-depth

Some Diseases of the Blood

Leukemia is any of several types of cancer of the blood-forming tissues; these cancerous tissues cause white blood cells to vastly increase in number.

Granulocytopenia occurs when there is a decrease in the number of white blood cells to fewer than 5,000 cells per cubic millimeter. It is usually caused by chronic overdoses of certain drugs. It often leads to susceptibility to bacterial infections and ulcers.

Polycythemia, a disease in which there is an excess of red blood cells, occurs most often in males over 60 years old. It is characterized by the development of fibrous tissue in the bone marrow.

Anemia is a deficiency in the number of red blood cells, in the amount of hemoglobin in the red blood cells, or both.

In *hemophilia,* a hereditary disease, there is excessive bleeding and inability of the blood to clot. The symptoms are limited to males, but only females can transmit the disease to their children.

Blood poisoning, or *septicemia,* is caused by the presence in the blood of bacteria that become lodged in certain parts of the body, setting up local points of infection. It is termed *toxemia* when caused by toxic substances in the blood.

Malaria, spread by mosquitoes, is caused by a parasite that attacks the red blood cells.

Intense radiation produced by nuclear reactions damages the blood. Injured white blood cells cannot fight bacteria. Blood platelets also are destroyed, leading to uncontrolled bleeding.

have I got what it takes to be a hematologist?

Students do not usually discover the specific field of hematology until they are in medical school or are doing graduate work, so the question for a high school student would really be: "Have I got what it takes to be a doctor or medical scientist?"

The most important quality for anyone going into scientific research is curiosity—a lifelong commitment to the process of asking questions and searching for the answers. You need to love doing laboratory research. Since a hematologist needs to earn an M.D. or a Ph.D. (and sometimes both), academic ability, especially in the sciences, and strong motivation are also essential qualities.

Anyone going into medical practice, especially in a field that involves serious blood diseases, needs to develop the ability to be comfortable with critically ill and dying people. Pediatric hematology-oncology can be particularly distressing in that respect. If you are strongly drawn to medicine but do not like to work with sick people, then you should consider going into medical research.

Medical research requires patience and the ability to be a team player; research projects often last for many years before significant results begin to emerge. The financial realities of scientific research today also require the patience and writing ability to produce detailed and persuasive grant proposals.

Other paper work includes filling out forms for the use of research animals, for compliance with biosafety regulations, and for accountability in the spending of money. Good oral communication skills are important as well for teaching and presenting papers.

how do I become a hematologist?

education

High School

Future scientists and physicians should take a good college preparatory course in high school. The laboratory sciences (biology, chemistry, physics) and mathematics (algebra, geometry, trigonometry) are especially important as the foundation for more advanced work later, but you also need to take English, a foreign language, history, and other courses in the humanities and social sciences. Doctors and scientists should not forget to develop good communication skills, both written and oral.

It is also important to gain experience working in a medical setting. This does not mean you have to find work analyzing the blood of mice, but you should try to get volunteer work at a hospital, lab, or even nursing home. Also, talk with some physicians and scientists about their work. One hematologist remarked recently that most scientists are glad to show visitors around the lab, because they welcome an opportunity to let the public see that scientists really are normal people.

Postsecondary Training

If you plan to go to medical school and your college offers a premed program, you should take advantage of this and major in premed. If there is no premed program at your school, or if you are thinking of attending a Ph.D. program instead of medical school, then chemistry or biology are appropriate undergraduate majors. Some colleges also offer the option of undergraduate majors in biochemistry, microbiology, or genetics.

Whatever your major, your undergraduate work should include biology, chemistry, physics, biochemistry, mathematics, statistics, and computer science. You should also take courses in English, humanities, and social sciences as part of a liberal arts education.

Students planning to apply to medical school need to take the Medical College Admission Test (MCAT), which is required by all U.S. medical schools. The exam tests verbal and quantitative (mathematical) ability, general knowledge of the humanities and social sciences, and knowledge of the laboratory sciences (biology, chemistry, and physics). Students planning to apply to graduate school need to take the Graduate Record Exam (GRE), which is required by virtually all graduate programs. The GRE covers verbal, quantitative, and analytical ability; you may also need to take a GRE achievement test in your major subject area. MCAT and GRE scores are among the factors considered by medical school and graduate school admissions committees, in addition to undergraduate grades, letters of recommendation from professors, and other criteria.

Where do hematologists work? According to the American Society of Hematology, of its members approximately

- **58%** work at an academic medical center
- **13%** belong to a group practice
- **12%** are in private practice
- **8%** work at research institutions
- **3%** work in other institutions

You should apply to at least three medical or graduate schools to increase your chances of acceptance. The Association of American Medical Colleges provides helpful information about medical schools and the American Medical College Application Service offers students the opportunity to use its centralized application processing service when applying (see the end of this article for contact information). Competition for spots in medical schools is keen. Less than half of all qualified applicants are accepted each year. Those wanting Ph.D.s should keep in mind that admission to good graduate programs is also highly competitive.

Medical school lasts four years; Ph.D. programs in the biomedical sciences generally take at least four years. A combined M.D./Ph.D. program usually takes six to seven years. During the first two years of medical school, students take human anatomy and physiology, biochemistry, pathology, microbiology, pharmacology, and human behavior. They may also begin supervised work with patients—learning to take a medical history, to perform a physical exam, and to make a diagnosis.

The last two years of medical school are devoted to the clinical sciences, giving students an opportunity to gain experience in all the major areas of medicine—internal medicine, surgery, obstetrics, gynecology, psychiatry, pediatrics, and family practice. The student is actively involved in patient care as part of a hospital medical team. There is also likely to be course work in areas of current concern such as medical ethics, primary care, and health-care-cost containment. There may be opportunities for electives in areas of medicine that the student is contemplating as his or her future specialty.

Ph.D. programs, such as in the field of biochemistry, require several years of course work and laboratory experience, followed by comprehensive exams and the writing of a dissertation based on original research. After completing the Ph.D., students generally spend several years in postdoctoral research fellowship positions. These "postdocs" provide the opportunity to build up an area of research expertise that can be turned into a successful grant proposal later. It is hard to find a research position above the postdoc level unless you bring your own grant money with you.

After graduating from medical school, students spend at least two years (and usually longer) in hospital residency programs. The length of the residency period depends on the specialty chosen. Nearly all physicians warn that the residency years are physically, intellectually, and emotionally exhausting and can put a severe strain on family and social life.

Because hematology is a subspecialty of internal medicine, future hematologists do a three-year residency in general internal medicine, followed by two years of training in a hematology or hematology/oncology program. Those going into medical research often do a postdoc afterward.

certification or licensing

Hematologists who are medical doctors can receive certification at two levels from the American Board of Internal Medicine (ABIM). Requirements for being certified as a Diplomate include completing three years of clinical

To be a successful hematologist, you should

- Have academic ability, especially in the sciences
- Love doing laboratory research
- Have the discipline to spend long hours writing grant proposals
- Have an inquiring mind
- Have the patience and ability to be a team player
- Be comfortable with critically ill people

training in an accredited internal medicine program and passing an exam administered by the ABIM. After achieving the Diplomate designation, physicians also can be certified in the subspecialty of hematology. To receive subspecialty certification, they must complete additional training, show verification of their clinical competence, and pass another exam administered by the ABIM. Although certification at either level is voluntary, it is highly recommended and demonstrates a commitment to the field. Certification is valid for 10 years; recertification requirements include completing continuing education and passing another exam.

After graduating from medical school, students must pass the licensing examination administered through the board of medical examiners in the state where they plan to practice. For medical scientists who are not M.D.s, the Ph.D. is generally considered one's "license."

scholarships and grants

There are many sources of financial aid for undergraduate students planning careers in science or medicine. Consult the financial-aid office of the institution you plan to attend for information about scholarships, grants, loans, work-study programs, and other possibilities. Also, there are some scholarships and other financial-aid opportunities targeted specifically for members of ethnic/racial minorities. In addition to consulting the financial-aid offices of schools, those planning on attending medical college should contact the Association of American Medical Colleges for information on grants, scholarships, and financial aid. (See the end of this article for contact information.)

Students applying to graduate programs in the sciences should consult their academic department as well as the university financial-aid office. Research and/or teaching assistantships are widely available for Ph.D. students in the sciences and usually pay enough to live on. Since there are fewer sources of financial aid for medical school, most medical students need to take out educational loans. Although heavy debt loads can look alarming, medical students should remember that they will be earning high incomes in the future.

who will hire me?

Hematologists are employed at medical centers, university medical schools, private research institutes, and blood banks. Hematologists who are physicians have a wider range of employment opportunities than scientists without the M.D. Physician hematologists have the option of working in clinical practice in addition to, or instead of, research.

Hematologists find out about job openings in their field through personal contacts and professional journals. Sometimes a postdoctoral fellowship turns into a permanent job. The competition for research positions at prestigious institutions is keen; there can be hundreds of applicants for one job.

As previously noted, the ability to attract grant money for one's lab and all or part of one's salary plays a major role in a hematologist's employability. Occasionally, it is even necessary to raise one's own funding for a postdoctoral position.

where can I go from here?

Hematologists advance by developing and carrying out research that is recognized as significant by their professional peers and that has the ability to draw grant money from the federal government and private foundations. Some hematologists move into administrative positions and become directors of major research projects.

Those in academic positions advance by moving from assistant professor to associate professor to full professor. In a field like hematology, the most important criteria for academic promotion would be research achievements and publications. Academic hematologists can also advance their standing by joining professional associations and serving on their committees. Hematologists (or hematologists/oncologists) who are involved in clinical work advance in their profession as more patients are referred to them for specialized treatment.

A medical researcher responsible for a major breakthrough in the advancement of scientific knowledge could be a candidate for a Nobel Prize.

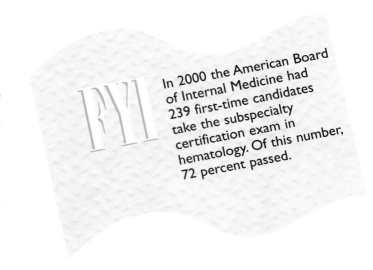

FYI
In 2000 the American Board of Internal Medicine had 239 first-time candidates take the subspecialty certification exam in hematology. Of this number, 72 percent passed.

what are the salary ranges?

According to the Association of American Medical Colleges, first-year medical residents had an average annual salary of approximately $34,000 in 1998-99. Postdoctoral fellows general earn less than this, with salaries ranging from the $20,000s to the $30,000s. According to a 1998-99 salary survey conducted by the American Association of University Professors the average yearly earnings for professors (regardless of discipline) was $72,700. The survey also found that associate professors averaged $53,200, while assistant professors averaged $43,800. Hematologists holding Ph.D.s and working at schools, such as Steven, may have yearly incomes within this range.

Physicians earn considerably more than these amounts. The American Medical Association reported the median income for M.D.s in 1997 was approximately $164,000 after expenses. Those in internal medicine, of which hematology is a subspecialty, had a median income of $147,000. A salary survey conducted by Physicians Search, an employment service company, found that those working in hematology/oncology and with three or more years of experience had an average annual income of $269,298. Salaries for these doctors ranged from $155,475 to $473,000. As for any career, salaries will vary depending on factors such as geographic location, size of employer, and the worker's years of experience in the field. Physicians in clinical work, however, generally have higher salaries than those who concentrate on research and are dependent on grants for funding.

what is the job outlook?

Although there are many blood-disease questions still to be answered, the future of research depends on the availability of funding. As legislators work to trim government budgets, medical research funding decreases. Some hematologists also note that other subspecialties are taking over some of the areas previously handled by hematologists. The relationship between hematology and oncology is growing closer, which could result in hematology eventually being absorbed into oncology. In another shift, those working on coagulation problems are increasingly from the specialties of cardiology and neurology. Cardiologists and Neurologists are interested in this area because of the role clotting plays in heart disease and strokes.

Nevertheless, physicians continue to have one of the lowest unemployment rates of any profession. The U.S. Department of Labor predicts employment for physicians in general to be faster than the average for all occupations. Given factors such as those mentioned above, it is reasonable to expect the outlook for hematologists to be about as fast as the average.

how do I learn more?

professional organizations

To learn more about the field of hematology, contact the following organizations.

American Board of Internal Medicine
510 Walnut Street, Suite 1700
Philadelphia, PA 19106-3699
800-441-2246
http://www.abim.org

American Society of Hematology
1900 M Street, NW, Suite 200
Washington, D.C. 20036
202-776-0544
http://www.hematology.org

American Society of Pediatric Hematology/Oncology
4700 West Lake
Glenview, IL 60025-1485
info@aspho.org
http://www.aspho.org

Association of American Medical Colleges (AAMC)
2450 N Street, NW
Washington, DC 20037-1126
http://www.aamc.org

The hematology subspecialty page has specific information on training and certification for this field.
American Board of Internal Medicine
http://www.abim.org/subspec/hem.htm

For information on medical school applications, visit:
American Medical College Application Service
http://www.aamc.org/audienceamcas.htm

Specific information on financial aid programs can be found on the AAMC site at:
Financing Your Medical Education
http://www.aamc.org/students/financing/start.htm

bibliography

Following is a sampling of materials relating to the profession of hematologists.

Bain, Barbara. *A Beginner's Guide to Blood Cells.* Cambridge, MA: Blackwell Science, 1996.

Beutler, Ernest et al., eds. *Williams Hematology.* New York, NY: McGraw-Hill, 2000.

Carr, Jacqueline H. and Bernadette F. Rodak. *Clinical Hematology Atlas.* Philadelphia, PA: W. B. Saunders Company, 1999.

Hoffbrand, A. V. et al. *Essential Hematology.* 4th Edition. Cambridge, MA: Blackwell Science, 2001.

Hoffman, Ronald. *Hematology: Basic Principles and Practice.* 3rd Edition. Kent, UK: Churchill Livingstone, 2000.

Lee, G. Richard. *Wintrobe's Clinical Hematology.* Philadelphia, PA: Lippincott, Williams & Wilkins, 1999.

Stiene-Martin, E. Anne, ed. *Clinical Hematology: Principles, Procedures, Correlations.* Philadelphia, PA: Lippincott, Williams & Wilkins, 1998.

Histologic Technicians

The patient lies unconscious on the operating room table under a blaze of lights, surrounded by doctors and nurses. The chief surgeon peers at the patient's exposed stomach, looking for evidence of disease. She thinks cancer has caused the patient's symptoms, but she needs confirmation. She has taken a biopsy of the tissue, and the operation cannot be completed until the results come back from the laboratory.

Meanwhile, in the clinical pathology department of the large hospital, Jim Pond works swiftly with his cryostat, a special medical instrument that cuts the tissue sample into slices only three to six microns thick. He has stabilized the sample by freezing it. Now he arranges the paper-thin slices of tissue on microscope slides and quickly, carefully adds a chemical stain. Like magic, the stain turns some components of the specimen a different color. What was invisible suddenly becomes apparent. Jim passes the specimen to a pathologist, who examines the tissue under a microscope and verifies the surgeon's suspicions. The results are rushed to the operating room, and the surgery proceeds.

As a histologic technician, Jim sometimes works under pressure, but he handles it well. "I thrive on that," he says. "Sometimes we must work quickly, and sometimes we have more time, but we're always careful and pay close attention to detail. Patients depend on our work."

what does a histologic technician do?

When a physician or researcher takes a tissue sample from a human, animal, or plant and sends it away for analysis, a team of laboratory workers prepares the specimen and studies it under a microscope. Cancer, leprosy, bacterial infections, and many other disorders can be detected in this way. The professional who performs basic laboratory procedures to prepare tissues for microscopic scrutiny is a *histologic technician*. Workers in this field use delicate instruments, which are often com-

lingo to learn

Biopsy: Removal of a section of tissue for medical examination and diagnosis.

Embedding: Placing prepared tissues into blocks of wax so that they may be cut and examined more precisely.

Fixing: Preserving tissue specimens from deterioration using special laboratory techniques.

Histology: The branch of science that deals with the structure and function of normal and abnormal tissue.

Microtome: Laboratory machine used to cut thin sections of tissue.

Pathology: The study of the nature of disease, its structure, and the changes produced by disease.

puterized. They also perform quality control tests and keep accurate records of their work.

After a tissue sample is taken, the first step in preparing it for study, known as "fixation," is usually performed by a pathologist or scientist. The specimen is examined, described, trimmed to the right size, and placed in special fluids to preserve it.

When the fixed specimen arrives at the histology lab, the technician removes the water from it. The water is replaced with melted wax, which moves into the tissue and provides support for the delicate cellular structure as it cools and hardens. Then the technician places small pieces of wax-soaked tissue in larger blocks of wax, a step called "embedding." Without the wax, the tissue would collapse during the next step of the process.

The technician sections the specimen by mounting it on a microtome, a scientific instrument with a very sharp blade. The microtome cuts thin slices of tissue, often only one cell thick, a procedure that requires precision, patience, and a steady hand. The technician cuts many sections of tissue, usually one after another so they form a ribbon, which is placed in warm water until it flattens out. Then the prepared sections are laid on microscope slides.

Next, the technician stains each tissue specimen by adding chemicals and places a coverslip over the sample to protect it. Different stains highlight different tissue structures or abnormalities in the cells, which helps pathologists, researchers, and other scientific investigators diagnose and study diseases.

A second, quicker technique is used to prepare samples and make diagnoses while the patient is still in the operating room. In these cases tissue specimens are frozen instead of being embedded in wax. It's important for a technician to work swiftly and accurately and to cooperate well with the rest of the team during this procedure, because the surgery cannot be completed until the test results are delivered.

Histologic technicians are part of a team of workers. They may be supervised by *histotechnologists*, who have more education; they perform complicated procedures, such as the staining of antigenic sites inside tissues. Some histotechnologists specialize in electron microscopy, which involves the precision cutting of tissues on such a small scale that the work is done under a microscope. Cytotechnologists are highly skilled and educated professionals who determine the presence of disease by studying slides prepared by histologic technicians; they sometimes supervise or educate technicians. *Pathologists* are medical doctors who interpret and diagnose the effect of disease on tissues, often by examining slides prepared by histologic technicians. The technician may also work closely with other physicians and researchers.

A laboratory team may include workers in other areas of specialization, such as medical and clinical laboratory technologists, who perform a variety of complex tests. For instance, they examine blood and other bodily substances under microscopes; make cultures to detect the presence of bacteria, fungi, and other micro-organisms; type and cross-match blood samples for transfusions; and determine a patient's cholesterol level. *Clinical chemistry technologists* prepare specimens and analyze the chemicals and hormones in bodily fluids. *Microbiology technologists* examine and identify micro-organisms such as bacteria. *Blood bank technologists* collect blood, determine its type, and prepare it for transfusions. *Immunology technologists* study the way the human immune system protects itself from disease by responding to viruses and other foreign bodies.

what is it like to be a histologic technician?

"My job as a histologic technician is never dull," says Jim Pond. "Just when I think I've seen it all, something new comes along, something medical or technical, and I get a chance to experience that. It may be working with large mechanical parts when I fix a problem with a machine, or it may be doing something new with tissue from a heart biopsy. Sometimes the specimens histologic technicians work with are so tiny that there's almost no room for error. When I'm able to solve a problem, big or small, that gives me pride in what I do."

Jim typically begins his day by receiving specimens and keeping track of the patient's identification number. "Then I process the tissue specimens and cut thin sections, using the microtome. Next, depending on the physician's instructions, I stain the tissue so that a diagnosis can be made," Jim says. He pauses and nods his head. "The true histologic technician is able to do many things. Sure, we work with a lot of machines—robotic stainers, tissue

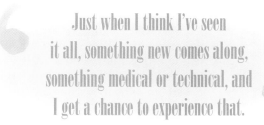

processors, cover slippers—but in this lab, if every machine crashed tomorrow, we could do it all anyway. It would take longer, but we could do it."

A large part of Jim's day is spent working with people, often resident physicians in training, who are just learning about histopathology. "This hospital is part of a teaching institution," he explains, "so we get asked to do more stains and a larger variety as well, simply because the residents are learning which techniques work best."

Orders for histology procedures on common tissue specimens might include sampling gall bladders, tonsils, cardial sacs, and some of the more typical cancers. Rarer cancers might need an electron microscope workup, while unusual diseases like leprosy might need special stains.

"You have to know what you're doing in this job and be tactful, too," says Jim. "Over time, you gain a lot of experience and information as a histologic technician. Sometimes a resident will ask me to do a certain silver stain and I'll think that it's because he's searching for signs of a fungus, since we usually do silver stains for fungus. Then the resident might mention that he's concerned about the possibility of Alzheimer's disease, and so I might suggest that we try another stain, too.

"There are lots of ways to approach taking tissue samples, and each one provides a different kind of information. For instance, histologic technicians can take multiple samples at a certain level within the tissue, or we can reorient the tissue completely, or we cannot reorient it at all. Then there are all those different types of stains. One stain helps us look for infectious agents in the lungs, for example; another highlights connective tissue troubles; another tracks down inflammation in the blood vessels. The doctors make their diagnoses based on the information you and your techniques provide for them. Histologic technicians, through tact and craft, help physicians find out what's causing problems and confirm suspicions so that accurate diagnoses can be made."

Histologic technician Carol Bischof, directs the program at Fergus Falls Community College in Fergus Falls, Minnesota. Part of her day is spent working with students, either in the classroom or as they gain clinical experience in area hospitals. "I love it when I can get into the laboratory with students," she says. "Some of the stains histologic technicians use are so beautiful. Tri Chrome stain, for instance, is very pretty. Its colors could be used to design a quilt."

Carol explains that there is a significant amount of technique involved in staining tissue. "Your artistic abilities come out when you do this," she says. "Some stains need to be added gradually or removed slowly in order to bring out the correct details. Some stains differentiate between connective tissue and muscle tissue; others differentiate between brain and spinal tissue. It's a complex and beautiful procedure."

This is a fascinating and satisfying career, but it does have a few drawbacks. When histologic technicians work for large laboratories, they may spend a great deal of time standing or sitting in one position and performing one type of operation, but most are able to rotate the type of work they perform. Increasingly, they also must deal with governmental regulations designed to insure quality control in laboratory work. A part of each day is spent complying with these rules. Some histologic technicians, especially those working for large hospitals, may work rotating shifts, including weekends and holidays.

FYI

In 1664, Robert Hooke, an English scientist, used his penknife to slice pieces of cork. He placed these thin sections under the microscope. A few years later, the Dutch naturalist Anton van Leeuwenhoek used his shaving razor to carve thin sections from flowers, a writing quill, and a cow's optic nerve. Both men wanted to observe the microscopic structure of objects. Because of their investigations, the science of histology was born.

have I got what it takes to be a histologic technician?

Lee G. Luna, a pioneer in histotechnology, said that histologic technicians need to be three things: scientist, mechanic, and artist. They need an interest in anatomy, biology, chemistry, and physics; an ability to repair equipment malfunctions; and an artistic eye for pattern, detail, and color. It's also important to have manual dexterity, patience, and the ability to work quickly and with precision.

As in most professions, histologic technicians tend to do a better job if they're willing to learn new techniques and concepts. Jim Pond remarks, "It helps to know when to ask questions, how to listen for answers, and how to store up information. Good pathologists will encourage histologic technicians to ask questions, and they will help them gain a bigger knowledge base so that the laboratory team can function even more efficiently."

As part of a team, technicians must also develop a sense of professional integrity. "It's essential, too, that you be professionally honest," says Eileen Nelson, former director of the University of North Dakota's histologic technician program at Grand Forks. "Sometimes the work is quite repetitive, and if you make a mistake, you don't cover it up. When you cut a slice wrong or misplace a piece of tissue, you have to say so. People's lives may depend on how well you do your job."

A lot of the work histologic technicians do uses standard procedures and is almost like following a recipe. Sometimes histologic technicians who work in larger laboratories may repeat the same part of a procedure all day long. Workers at a huge clinic might do cutting only, for example, or embedding only. This can be boring. Histologic technicians generally report that they are more satisfied with their jobs when they can spend time alternately cutting, staining, and charting tissues.

Histologic technicians work in laboratories that are well ventilated, and most of the tissue processors that they use are enclosed. This minimizes problems with odors and chemical fumes. Sometimes histologic technicians work with hazardous chemicals, but they wear protective clothing, as well as badges that will indicate overexposure and allow workers to seek immediate medical treatment should accidents occur. Histologic technicians also face the possibility of coming into contact with disease through tissue samples, but several of the steps involved in preparing specimens generally kill any living organisms.

how do I become a histologic technician?

Carol Bischof's path to histotechnology began with college in Mississippi and Ohio and led to a job in Minnesota. "While working on my master's degree in zoology, I did research for the Environmental Protection Agency," she says. "I studied how substances in paints and plastics affected rats and watched as histologic technicians processed and embedded the rodent tissues that we used. Then a friend called and said that the lab where she worked needed someone to do histology. I was familiar with laboratory techniques and so I got the job. Later on, I went back to school and got my certificate as a histologic technician."

education

High School

Biology, chemistry, and other science courses are necessary if you wish to enter a histotechnology program after graduation. Mathematics and computer science courses are also important.

Postsecondary Training

There are three ways to become a histologic technician. It's possible to enter the profession with a high school diploma and on-the-job training only, but a college degree or formal training through an institution such as a hospital is becoming more generally recommended.

On-the-job training is still an acceptable entry into the field, according to Sumiko Sumida, a histologic technician and histotechnologist. Sumiko is technical director of the histology laboratory at the University of Washington Hospital Pathology Department in Seattle. She says, "Many laboratories will train people. It's an exciting field, because it has a lot of opportunities for people at the time they're just getting out of high school and maybe don't have the money to go to college. Most of the hospitals do require some college

Advancement Possibilities

Histotechnologists perform more complicated procedures than histologic technicians, such as enzyme histochemistry, electron microscopy, and immunofluorescence. Histotechnologists can teach, become laboratory supervisors, or become directors in schools for histologic technology.

Cytotechnologists analyze stained tissue samples for subtle clues that indicate disease. A cytotechnologist with more education and experience may advance to become a specialist and will typically supervise or educate other employees.

Categorical technologists focus on one field instead of rotating through various departments of the laboratory. They may be certified in microbiology, chemistry, blood banking, immunology, or hematology.

Pathologists are medical doctors who study the nature, cause, and development of diseases, and the structural and functional changes caused by them.

background, but opportunities do exist for on-the-job training," especially in rural areas.

The second way to enter the field involves completion of a one- to two-year certificate program at an accredited institution, usually a hospital. The certificate program includes classroom studies along with clinical and laboratory experience.

The third method involves earning an associate's degree from an accredited college or university and includes supervised, hands-on experience in clinical settings. General course work for histologic technicians includes classes in organic and inorganic chemistry, biochemistry, general biology, mathematics, medical terminology, and medical ethics. Additional classes include histology, quality control, instrumentation, microscopy, records and administration procedures, and studies in fixation, processing, and staining. College programs may also require core curriculum classes such as English, social science, and speech.

certification or licensing

Certification is not required for entry-level histologic technicians. Some states do require that technicians be licensed. Histologic technicians become certified by passing a national examination offered by either the Board of Registry of the American Society of Clinical Pathologists (the main certifying organization) or by the National Certification Agency for Medical Laboratory Personnel. Applicants can qualify for the Board of Registry exam in three ways. They can complete an accredited program in histotechnology, earn an associate's degree from an accredited college or university and combine it with one year of experience, or have a high school diploma and two years of experience. Starting in January 2005, however, the high school/on-the-job training route will be discontinued, so an accredited program will become even more important for histologic technicians.

scholarships and grants

Most colleges and universities offer general scholarships. The National Society for Histotechnology is the main source of information for scholarships specifically for students of histotechnology (see "How Do I Learn More?"). Several scholarships and awards are available each year through this organization. Occasionally, employers will provide educational funding for general laboratory workers who wish to enter the field of histotechnology.

To be a successful histologic technician, you should

- Have good color vision
- Be attentive to detail
- Be able to concentrate well
- Be patient
- Be able to work under pressure and to work quickly when necessary
- Be honest and willing to admit mistakes

---

who will hire me?

Jim Pond worked at three hospitals before deciding to study histotechnology. First, he had a job as a clerk. Then he moved to laboratory work in phlebotomy. His third job involved basic hematology and chemistry work. At each hospital, pathologists would note the quality of his work and encourage him to get additional schooling so that he could advance into a position of more responsibility within the laboratory. "Finally, I listened to what they were recommending," Jim says. "The hospital where I was had a school for histologic technicians, and when the hospital said that they'd even pay me while I learned more about the field, I decided to give it a try."

A histologic technician has the opportunity to work in many fields of medicine and science. Most are employed by hospitals or by industrial laboratories that specialize in chemical, petrochemical, pharmaceutical, cosmetic, or household products. Some work for medical clinics, universities, or government organizations. Many biomedical companies hire histologic technicians to aid in research projects. Immunopathology, forensic medicine, veterinary medicine, marine biology, and botany are just a few of the options.

Sumiko Sumida says that people who have training in both histology and cytotechnology are in demand, especially in rural areas, which tend to have greater difficulty in attracting qualified technicians. That's partly due to the fact that salaries are often lower there. In addition, many histologic technicians are women, and it's sometimes hard for them to move their families to rural areas.

If you'd like to work part-time in the field while you go to school, consider a job with a regional laboratory for large health systems. Histology is one of many fields that have been consolidated in recent years as health groups have pooled their resources to save money. For example, the average hospital used to employ a team of three to six histologic technicians, and smaller facilities often had only one. Now, many of these institutions have combined their resources. The result is laboratories with teams of perhaps 30 to 50 histologic technicians. Because these facilities operate seven days a week, 24 hours a day, there's a good chance you could be assigned to shifts that would not interfere with your classes at college.

Employers sometimes schedule recruiting visits to schools that offer histologic technician programs. You can also find leads on employment in professional journals.

where can I go from here?

Some histologic technicians become supervisors. Others specialize in certain areas of histotechnology, such as orthopedic implants or diseases of the lungs.

"If you have an interest in science, you can grow with the field and use it as a jumping-off point for the future. It's a field you can use as a stepping-stone to go in any direction. It's really up to the individual to take the plunge, take some risks," says Sumiko Sumida.

She suggests that a young person without much money could work as a histologic technician for a few years while attending college part-time or completing a training program at a hospital, then use that experience and training to advance to a high-paying position as a pathologist's assistant. She strongly recommends taking a certification examination after working in the field for two years.

Technicians who have more education and experience are more apt to be promoted. With some employers, no matter how good your job skills might be, your chances of advancement are significantly smaller if you don't have formal training, including some college study. In the future an associate's degree will likely become the standard requirement for entering the field and being promoted. Returning to school, earning a bachelor's degree, and becoming a histotechnologist will boost your career even further and will probably increase your salary.

"If you go on to college, there are a lot of opportunities," Sumiko says. "You can go into management or become a technical representative." You could also earn an advanced degree and teach sciences.

what are the salary ranges?

Geographic location, experience, level of education, employer, and work performed determine the salary ranges for histologic technicians. According to a 1998 wage survey conducted by the American Society of Clinical Pathologists (ASCP), pay rates were highest in the Northeast and Far West.

Beginning histologic technicians had median hourly wages of $10.90 (or $22,672 annually for full-time work). The average annual salary was $28,080, and the top salary was $32,240. Histologic technologists had higher wages: beginning technologists had median annual earnings of $24,960. The average earnings were $32,448, and top earners made around $36,800. Histologic supervisors had annual earnings of between $30,900 and $44,300.

Full-time technicians can expect benefits packages that include health insurance, paid vacation, and 401 (k) plans.

Related Jobs

The U.S. Department of Labor classifies histologic technicians under the headings *Laboratory Technology: Life Sciences* (GOE) and *Healthcare Practitioners and Technical* (O*NET-SOC). Also under these headings are medical technologists, polygraph examiners, farm production technicians, clinical chemists, and medical laboratory technicians.

Specific related jobs include:
Biological aides
Clinical chemistry technologists
Cytotechnologists
Dental hygienists
Laboratory technicians
Microbiology technologists
Pheresis specialists
Phlebotomy technicians

what is the job outlook?

According to the *Occupational Outlook Handbook,* employment of clinical laboratory workers is expected to grow about as fast as the average for all other occupations. As director of a histology program, Carol Bischof has seen the job market improve over the last few years. "There's going to continue to be a strong demand for well-trained histology technicians," she says. "There are many hospitals that have been giving sign-on bonuses, because there's a shortage of technicians. They want to hire them before they're even done with their clinical." The 1998 wage and vacancy survey conducted by ASCP calculated the ratio of job openings to full-time histologic technicians and found that there were more job openings than people to fill them. The study found that histology had the highest vacancy rate of all the laboratory careers surveyed, with 14.4 percent of positions unfilled. Though the vacancy rate for histologic technicians saw a slight decrease from 1996 to 1998, the rate increased from 5.3 percent to 10.3 percent for histotechnologists. The most substantial increase of the vacancy rate was in the position of histologic supervisor: the rate doubled, from 10 percent in 1996 to 20 percent in 1998.

"Right now, because of the consolidations that health care has been seeing in the last year or so, it's been pretty stable," Sumiko Sumida comments, but she adds, "There will probably be a huge outflux of people within the next five years," because a large number of professionals in the field are nearing retirement age.

how do I learn more?

professional organizations

For career and certification information, and information about accredited programs, contact:
American Society of Clinical Pathologists
2100 West Harrison Street
Chicago, IL 60612
info@ascp.org
http://www.ascp.org

For career information, and information about accredited programs, contact:
National Accrediting Agency for Clinical Laboratory Sciences
8410 West Bryn Mawr Avenue, Suite 670
Chicago, IL 60631
info@naacls.org
http://www.naacls.org

For a free career brochure about histotechnology, contact:
National Society for Histotechnology
4201 Northview Drive, Suite 502
Bowie, MD 20716-2604
301-262-6221
histo@nsh.org
http://www.nsh.org

bibliography

Following is a sampling of materials relating to the professional concerns and development of histologic technicians.

Carson, Freida L. *Histotechnology: A Self Instructional Text.* 2nd Edition Includes techniques. Chicago, IL: ASCP Press, 1997.

Cormack, David H. *Essential Histology. An introductory book to the field.* Philadelphia, PA: J. B. Lippincott Company, 1993.

Kessel, Richard G. *Basic Medical Histology: the Biology of Cells, Tissues, and Organs.* New York, NY: Oxford University Press, 1998.

Zhang, Shu-Xin. *An Atlas of Histology.* New York, NY: Springer-Verlag, 1999.

Home Health Aides

Definition
Home health aides provide medical services to elderly, disabled, sick, or recovering persons in their own homes instead of in a health care facility.

Alternative Job Titles
Homemakers
Home attendants

High School Subjects
Family and consumer science
Health
Psychology

Personal Skills
Communication/ideas
Helping/teaching

Salary Range (per hour)
$5.73 to $7.58 to $10.51

Educational Requirements
High school diploma; some postsecondary training required in some states

Certification or Licensing
Voluntary

Outlook
Faster than the average

GOE
10.03.03
O*NET-SOC
31-1011.00

Joanna Kolaczynski finishes putting away the groceries she just bought for Mr. Nelson, who is sitting in his wheelchair reading the newspaper. She clears his breakfast dishes from the tray beside him and loads them into the dishwasher.

"Thank you, Joanna. But I really would rather have something more interesting to eat tomorrow than oatmeal," he tells her.

"Now, Mr. Nelson, you told me you love oatmeal and that you wanted me to make you some, so that's what I made you," Joanna says in a stern but soothing voice. "I'll make you some pancakes tomorrow, OK?"

"Oh, well, all right. But they'd better be good," Mr. Nelson says.

Joanna lets the last comment slide. "Now you know your daughter will be here after she gets off work to make you dinner and help you into bed. And I'll be back tomorrow morning to help give you your bath and make you breakfast." Joanna squeezes Mr. Nelson's hand and tells him goodbye, then walks outside to her car. "Mr. Nelson was really crabby today," she thinks. "I hope he's in a better mood tomorrow."

She looks at her watch. It's 11 AM; she has 15 minutes to get to Mrs. Elliot's, a woman in her mid-fifties, recovering from cancer surgery. Joanna gets into her car and reminds herself that Mrs. Elliot, a widow whose only child lives six states away, will need her to do laundry and clean around the house, as well as help her to take a bath.

Tomorrow she will spend the morning with Mr. Nelson and the afternoon with Mr. Keating, who is in his eighties and has been very depressed since his wife died a few months ago. Mr. Keating is physically able to do most things for himself, but Joanna knows that her challenge will be motivating him to do something active since he has been spending most of his time watching TV. She makes a mental list of possible activities to engage him in as she pulls in front of Mrs. Elliot's house.

lingo to learn

Chronic: A disease or disorder that lasts a long time or that has frequent recurrences.

Gerontology: The branch of medicine concerned with aging and the problems of elderly people.

Hospice care: A program that provides a variety of medical and nonmedical services to terminally ill patients and their families in a home or in a health care facility.

Infection control: Precautionary methods, such as the use of disposable gloves, gowns, and masks, to avoid the spread of germs.

Long-term care: A program that provides care and encouragement to chronically ill or disabled patients in the home or residential care facility.

Vital signs: The pulse rate, breathing rate, and body temperature of a person.

what does a home health aide do?

Today's medical technology has enabled more and more elderly, disabled, and sick persons to live comfortably in their own homes rather than in a hospital or institution. In addition, medical professionals have found that elderly or ill people are happier and may be more likely to thrive in their own homes as opposed to an institution. However, these individuals still need help with household work or personal care. The work involved in caring for them may be too complicated for friends or family members to provide. Some individuals need help every day; others need assistance only one or two days a week.

Home health aides provide this assistance by visiting people in their homes and doing basic housework, such as cooking, grocery shopping, and laundry. Home health aides also assist clients with personal care. For example, an elderly woman may need help taking a bath or shower, getting dressed, brushing her teeth, doing her hair, or clipping her nails. Other clients, such as those with AIDS or cancer, may be too weak to move or walk without help. In these cases, home health aides help clients move from their bed to other locations, such as the bathroom or kitchen. Clients who are ill or recovering from an illness also may need home health aides to check vital signs and fluid intake, assist with exercises, and provide other therapy. Home health aides may also change nonsterile dressings, assist with medication routines, use special equipment such as hydraulic lifts, or help clients with braces or artificial limbs.

Home health aides may also visit with children whose parents are ill or disabled to help them plan and prepare nutritious meals, teach good hygiene, and help with schoolwork.

A home health aide's daily (and often weekly) routine can vary. One week he or she may visit a single client for eight hours a day, six days a week. Another week, the aide may visit several different clients a day, caring for some of them for months or even years, and others for only a short time. Typically, however, home health aides visit three or four clients in one day.

Some home health aides are self-employed, but most work for home care agencies, nursing homes, hospitals, and social service agencies. Generally they report to a registered nurse who supervises the home health aides in the organization. Often home health aides are part of a team that cares for a specific client, in which case they may work with a physical therapist or a social worker who gives them specific duties.

The home health aide's supervisor may drop in to a client's home once a month, or more frequently when the aide is new to a specific assignment. However, home health aides generally work without direct supervision. They are responsible for their own transportation and any transportation costs incurred to and from clients' homes. Most agencies will work to accommodate a home health aide who must rely on public transportation by assigning them to accessible clients.

Because home health aides help other people, it is essential that they have strong interpersonal skills. Working in clients' homes allows home health aides time to get to know their clients and their individual needs. This can be both emotionally rewarding and very challenging. Some homes are messy and depressing; others are tidy and cheerful. Some clients are pleasant and cooperative; others are more difficult, possibly feeling angry, confused, depressed, abusive, or in pain. To handle these varying situations and temperaments, home health aides must be patient, understanding, sensitive, and assertive. At the same time, they must provide a warm and nurturing environment, and a sense of humor doesn't hurt.

Sometimes a client's emotional needs may demand more attention than their physical needs. Clients may simply want someone to listen to their problems. Or perhaps they just want company—someone to accompany them on a walk through the park or to the doctor's office. Home health aides must be willing to provide this emotional support or comfort.

Home health aides work in the client's home, so they do not have access to the same equipment and facilities that are available in a hospital. As a result, they need to be flexible and creative in order to provide care using the basic resources in the client's home. Their work is often physically demanding, so aides should be in good physical shape and have the strength and stamina to perform household chores.

Because supervision is minimal, even home health aides who are not self-employed operate as if they were independent. They have a lot of flexibility in their scheduling and most often work alone with their clients.

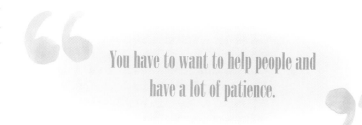

You have to want to help people and have a lot of patience.

what is it like to be a home health aide?

A home health aide's typical workday, or even a typical workweek, is hard to define. Joanna Kolaczynski has worked as a home health aide for four years, both on a self-employed basis and with agencies and nursing homes. Most recently, she assisted an 84-year-old woman with household chores and personal care. She spent eight hours a day, six days a week with the client, leaving no time to see other clients. While she enjoys her job, Joanna admits that it presents challenges. "It can be hard at times, but most people are just lonely and very nice, even if they seem crabby," she says.

Other home health aides might see four or five patients in one day. It all depends on what kind of schedule an aide wants to maintain. "I like getting to know one person. I can give them better care because I know what they need when I see them all day," Joanna explains. Other aides prefer getting experience with a variety of clients with different needs.

An average day for Joanna with her most recent client consisted of helping her out of bed and, every other day, into the shower. The client was able to bathe herself, so while she was in the shower, Joanna usually prepared breakfast. After breakfast, Joanna spent time with the woman, whether by going on a walk or just watching TV together. "Mostly, we would just spend time together. She wanted company," Joanna says.

"You have to want to help people and have a lot of patience," Joanna says. She adds that the job can often be tiring because so much physical labor is involved, from cleaning to helping the client move around the house. Another tiring aspect of the job is the time spent traveling long distances to reach a client.

Because home health aides often work with clients who are ill or susceptible to illness (such as AIDS clients), they may have to wear a sterile gown and gloves. This is done both for the benefit of the client and the caregiver. "Health care professionals know that HIV is spread only through exchange of fluids, so the gloves and gown are to protect the patient," says Dawn Golek, a former home health aide. "But there's also the chance that if someone has the flu or a cold that you can get that, too. So it's important to wash your hands a lot."

Although the aide's job is full of emotional challenges, they are usually offset by emotional rewards. "Even if they don't say it or are unable to tell you, you always get a sense of appreciation from a client. They are glad that you are there, because most of the time you may be all they have," Dawn says.

have I got what it takes to be a home health aide?

Home health aides must like working with and helping people. They also must be willing to work hard and be responsible to handle the large responsibilities of the job. Clients depend on them to lead happier, healthier lives. Dawn says, "It's important that you are a friendly person. You have to earn their trust, because after all, you are going into their home."

She adds that good communication skills are also necessary. "The elderly in particular are very wise people. They've got a lot of history to share, and you have to be able to have a conversation with them. They have so much to tell, and being able to carry on a conversation also makes them feel special. I talk a lot, so it was easy for me."

Home health aides must be in good physical shape to perform household tasks and lift clients if necessary. "I helped my patient get out of bed and take a bath. It's physically demanding to lift another person and have them leaning their entire body weight against you," Dawn points out.

Home health aides also must be patient, compassionate, and emotionally stable. Clients may be in physical pain, which in turn may make them irritable or depressed. Or they may be lonely, causing them to act needy. "One woman I was helping was really missing her family and she didn't want to do anything but watch TV," Dawn relates. "I had to come up

with things to keep her busy. She wouldn't go outside with me, so I got her to do some crossword puzzles. It took a lot of persuasion."

Clients' varying physical and emotional needs often require the home health aide to stay flexible and be willing to change plans at any moment. "[Clients] can completely change your schedule, and you have to be creative and willing to do something else," Joanna says.

An even temper is another important attribute of home health aides. They must keep their emotions under control at all times, even if a client is crabby, unreasonable, or rude. Instead, aides must be able to provide comfort, warmth, and assertiveness, no matter how difficult their client may be.

Because clients may need to follow a regimented health plan, it is important that home health aides follow instructions closely and stick to prescribed medical plans. Unless a home health aide also happens to be a registered nurse, he or she cannot administer or help administer medication. Home health aides follow the treatment given by the client's physician, therapist, or social worker.

how do I become a home health aide?

Most home care agencies and nursing homes prefer aides who have at least basic nurse aide training. If you are unsure that a job as a home health aide is right for you but are interested in exploring the field, consider volunteering. Many aides start out by volunteering at social service agencies, which can provide an inside look at the type of work required for the job.

On the other hand, if you are more certain about the career, start by requesting information from local agencies and schools about their home health care training programs or employment guidelines. Check to see if any of the agencies sponsor open meetings in your community. If they do, attend one to learn more about the specific organization and the role they serve. Most agencies are listed in the yellow pages under "nursing homes" or "social service organizations."

Nursing homes, public and private health care facilities, and local chapters of the Red Cross and United Way are likely to hire entry-level home health aides. Contact them directly for more information about job opportunities and to inquire about necessary qualifications.

education

High School

While in high school, prospective home health aides should take classes in health and family and consumer science (specifically cooking, sewing, and meal planning). Dawn advises that history classes will also be helpful. "These people often have lived through world wars and the Depression. It's good to have knowledge about historical events so you can relate to the things they might talk about."

Courses that focus on family living, psychology, home nursing, nutrition, and child development are also good preparation. "Psychology is helpful because it helps you understand why a person is acting a certain way," Joanna adds.

Obtaining any experience that relates to home health care is a good way to get your foot in the door. A job at a nursing home, even as a dishwasher, can provide you with contact and social experience with the elderly. Volunteering at a nursing home, hospital, or social service agency will give you a closer look at the work aides perform and the patients they assist.

Postsecondary Training

A college degree is not necessary for a job as a home health aide. However, a college background with courses in family living, home nursing, nutrition, health care and child development will give you an advantage when looking for a job.

Some states require home health aides to have formal training in the form of classroom and supervised practical instruction. This training can be sought through a formal college program or through home health care agencies that provide training to newly hired employees.

The length of training varies depending on state requirements and whether the person can train full- or part-time. Most aides receive at least 75 hours of classroom and supervised work experience before beginning a job.

Dawn completed her training in about six weeks. "It took up most of my week, but the work itself was not that difficult," she recalls. She had class two times a week and completed her clinical work in a hospital three days a week.

Home health care began in the 19th century when visiting nurses checked on patients who lived far from town or who lacked transportation for medical visits. These nurses discovered that the needs of the patients went beyond medical care. Patients were grateful for the company of another person in their homes, having someone to read to them or do errands for them. As the demand for this kind of home care grew, the profession of home health aide was born.

certification or licensing

Aides who work for organizations that receive Medicare reimbursement are required to pass a state competency test that covers such areas as communication skills; observation, reporting, and documentation of patient status and care; reading and recording vital signs; basic infection control; recognition of and procedures for emergencies; and basic nutrition.

Before aides can take the test, they must complete at least 75 hours of classroom and practical training supervised by a registered nurse. Once training is complete, aides take the state competency test. Dawn found the proficiency test much easier than the final exam she took to complete her classroom work.

Besides meeting your state's individual training requirements, there are no additional licensing or certification requirements needed to become a home health aide. Even though it is voluntary, Dawn recommends becoming certified anyway. "[Certification] gives you a comprehensive background and makes you more qualified," she explains. The National Association for Home Care offers the Certified Home/Hospice Care Executive (CHCE) program for home health aides. Visit its Web site, http://www.nahc.org, for more information.

scholarships and grants

Many opportunities exist to obtain financial assistance while seeking educational and practical training. Many home health agencies fully pay for the training they give their new hires. Community college programs may also offer financial aid. Contact individual institutions for more details. State and federal scholarships, loans, and grants are also available. School counselors may be of assistance if you are considering applying for government-sponsored aid.

volunteerships

Because many social service agencies and nursing homes are nonprofit organizations with limited funding, they rely on volunteers to help provide companionship to patients in nursing homes or hospitals or to make house calls. Social service organizations that work with the physically or mentally disabled also need volunteers. Opportunities to volunteer are plentiful. Check your local yellow pages for names of social service agencies or nursing homes to find out more information.

who will hire me?

Dawn had just finished training to become a certified nursing assistant (CNA) when a family friend asked her to take care of an elderly relative for a month. This experience led her to take other jobs as a home health aide.

She advises those interested in becoming a home health aide to first build a medical foundation and obtain certification. Her background as a CNA became a good source of prospective jobs. "There's no column in the classified ads called home health aides," she says, "so you really can get ahead if you get certified."

According to the U.S. Department of Labor, home health and personal care aides hold approximately 750,000 jobs. Home health aides work for home care agencies, visiting nurse associations, nursing homes, hospitals, community volunteer agencies, and temporary help firms. Some aides are self-employed, which means that they find their own clients, arrange their own schedules, and set their own fees.

However, most home health aides start with an agency or medical institution. Dawn recommends using the yellow pages to find employers you might be interested in working for and calling them directly to inquire about available opportunities.

where can I go from here?

Home health aides often start out by performing household duties, such as meal preparation, laundry, and cleaning. As they gain experience and training, they may help with medical equipment and physical therapy. The career path for home health aides who want to continue working directly with clients is limited. They may want to acquire more specialized training or education to focus their care on those with special needs, such as clients with Alzheimer's disease or

To be a successful home health aide, you should

- Sincerely be interested in helping people
- Be even-tempered and patient
- Be cheerful, friendly, and flexible
- Be a good communicator
- Be compassionate
- Be physically strong

AIDS. Working with more demanding cases usually results in pay increases as aides take on more responsibilities.

Home health aides may also decide to pursue a nursing degree, enabling them to work in a clinic or hospital.

Another option for advancement is to pursue a different job that draws upon home care skills. For example, after working as an aide for many years, Dawn now works as an activity assistant at Norwood Park Home in Norwood Park, Illinois. Her job draws on the communication and people skills she used as a home health aide. She is responsible for motivating patients at the home to participate in activities that she plans.

what are the salary ranges?

The average salary for home health aides varies. They may be paid hourly or per visit or receive an annual salary. According to the U.S. Department of Labor, the median hourly salary for home health aides was $7.58 in 1998. The lowest paid 10 percent earned less than $5.73 an hour; the highest paid 10 percent earned over $10.51 an hour.

A 1999 compensation survey by the National Association for Home Care reports that the median hourly pay for home care workers was $11.88. Depending on levels of experience and their job responsibilities, aides generally earn between $11 and $13 per visit.

Home health aides are paid only for the time they work in the home. Generally, they are not paid or reimbursed for travel time or expenses. In addition, most do not receive health care or retirement benefits since they are usually employed on an on-call basis.

what is the job outlook?

Job opportunities for home health aides are increasing and employment is expected to grow faster than the average through the next decade, according to the U.S. Department of Labor. Several factors are responsible for this strong growth. First, the number of senior citizens in this country is expected to continue rising, which in turn increases the need for health care assistance.

Second, hospitals are trying to control rising health care costs, often by moving patients out of hospitals as quickly as possible. This trend has increased the number of patients who need assistance in their homes. Besides cutting treatment costs, medical professionals now recognize that patients tend to respond to treatment more readily if they are treated in their homes rather than in a hospital. Finally, because a home health aide's job is so physically and emotionally challenging, job turnover in the profession is high. Job openings for people who have the necessary skills and experience will be plentiful to replace workers who leave the field.

how do I learn more?

professional organizations

For more information about home health aide careers, contact the following organization:
National Association for Home Care
228 Seventh Street, SE
Washington, DC 20003
202-547-7424
http://www.nahc.org

bibliography

Following is a sampling of materials relating to the professional concerns and development of home health aides.

Burton, Marti. *Prentice-Hall Health's Survival Guide for Long-Term Care Nursing Assistants.* New York, NY: Prentice-Hall, 2001.

Chestnut, Mary Ann. *Maternal-Child Home Health Aide Training Manual.* Philadelphia, PA: Lippincott Williams & Wilkins, 1998.

Fuzy, Jetta. *The Home Health Aide Handbook.* Albuquerque, NM: Hartman Publishing, Inc., 2000.

Gingerich, Barbara Stover and Deborah Anne Ondeck. *Pocket Guide for the Home Care Aide.* Gaithersburg, MD: Aspen Publishers, Inc., 1998.

exploring health care careers

355

Gish, Jim. *Home Health Aide Exam.* New York, NY: Learning Express, 1997.

Graves, Lou Ebrite, ed. *Prentice-Hall Health Outline Review for the Home Health Care Aide.* Paramus, NJ: Prentice-Hall, 2001.

Huber, Helen, and Audree Spatz. *Homemaker Home Health Aide.* 5th Edition. Albany, NY: Delmar, 1997.

Marrelli, Tina M. et al. *Home Health Aide: Guidelines for Care: A Handbook for Caregiving at Home.* Englewood, FL: Marrelli and Associates, 1996.

Smith, Doris. *Home Care Aide.* St. Louis, MO: Mosby-Year Book, 1995.

Straight, Eileen. *Mosby's Textbook for the Home Care Aide.* St. Louis, MO: Mosby-Yearbook, 1996.

Zucker, Elana. *Being a Homemaker/Home Health Aide.* 5th Edition. New York, NY: Prentice-Hall, 1999.

Related Jobs

The U.S. Department of Labor classifies home health aides under the headings *Child and Adult Care* (GOE) and *Healthcare Support* (O*NET-SOC). Also under these headings are social service workers and people whose jobs involve personal contact to help or instruct others, sometimes within a private household. Workers in related jobs include attendants in children's institutions, childcare attendants in schools, child monitors, companions, nursing aides, nursery school attendants, occupational therapy assistants, physical therapy assistants, playroom attendants, and psychiatric aides.

Homeopaths

Definition
Homeopaths use specifically prepared natural substances to treat a variety of ailments.

Alternative Job Title
Homeopathic practitioners

High School Subjects
Biology
Chemistry

Personal Skills
Helping/teaching
Technical/scientific

Salary Range
$30,000 to $60,000 to $150,000

Educational Requirements
Two to three years of training in a school that offers a program in Homeopathy; college or graduate studies in nursing, traditional or naturopathic medicine is highly recommended

Certification or Licensing
Recommended (certification)
Required by certain states (licensing)

Outlook
Little change or more slowly than the average

GOE
NA*
O*NET-SOC
NA*

*Not Available. The U.S. Department of Labor does not classify homeopath as such. Generally homeopaths are classified with naturopathic physicians.

Bloodletting, purging, and large doses of toxic "medicines" like arsenic were common treatments for disease used at the end of the 18th century. Samuel Hahnemann, a German doctor, opposed this sort of treatment and searched for new, more effective ways to treat disease. His studies led him to experiment with substances that, given in large enough doses, would mimic the effects of certain diseases. He eventually created a system based on the idea that "like cures like"; that substances that produce symptoms of a disease will cure that same disease if they are given in small enough doses. For instance, a small dose of quinine, made from a certain tree bark, is used to treat malaria, but a large dose of it will cause the symptoms of malaria in an otherwise healthy person. (The term *homeopathy* comes from the Latin root *homo,* meaning same.)

Homeopathy was popular at the end of the 19th century in the United States, but as advances were made in traditional medicine, homeopathy fell out of favor. Within the past 20 years, as alternative medical treatments have become more accepted, homeopathy has begun to reemerge. There are approximately 3,000 homeopathic practitioners in the United States.

lingo to learn

Allopath: As opposed to a homeopath, an allopath treats disease with remedies that produce effects differing from those of the disease treated. For instance, treating a blood clot with a blood-thinner, is an allopathic remedy. Most Western medicine is based on allopathic principals.

Constitutional type: The general personal characteristics, acquired or inherited, that indicate to a homeopath which remedy will be most effective for a client. Constitutional types are determined by the questions asked a client in an initial consultation, including temperament, physical appearance, emotional history, previous ailments, and preferences about food. Constitutional type may change as a person ages, and a person may be a combination of different types.

Holistic: Looking at the whole system, instead of the parts. This describes the way homeopaths view disease-causing agents, by looking at a whole person, not just symptoms.

Naturopath: A physician trained in natural, non-drug oriented treatments for conditions and illnesses.

Remedy: In homeopathy, a remedy is the dilute mixture of alcohol, water, and drug that is given as treatment for illness. Paradoxically, the more dilute a remedy is, the more powerful it is.

what does a homeopath do?

Homeopaths look at illness differently than traditional doctors. They view sickness as a symptom of a larger problem and they try to look for the underlying cause of this larger problem. In order to discover the reasons for sickness, homeopaths begin with a very involved interview process. Many different types of people come in looking for relief, and symptoms of the same disease might vary from person to person. Good communication skills are vital.

Homeopaths have to be very attentive to detail because the right cure depends on every aspect of the patient's situation. They spend up to two hours with each of their patients, asking questions and listening to complaints and comments. They take note of every detail of a person's problems, probing for information about every aspect of the person's life, not just the illness. This is to get an idea of what type of person the patient is. Homeopaths classify people in many categories (called constitutional types) according to personality: what kinds of food they like, how they react to the weather, and many other traits. The type and strength of medicine they use to treat a person depends on all of these personal details as well as the physical symptoms of their illness.

The medicines that homeopaths use are specially prepared. Remedies begin as plant, animal, or mineral extracts. There are remedies made from toxic substances, such as snake venom, and others made from common foods, such as oats or onions. The raw material is dissolved in a mixture of alcohol and water, then diluted several times and shaken vigorously. A principle of homeopathy is that the more dilute a remedy is, the more powerful its effect.

After consulting a patient, homeopaths begin the research process. It can take a long time to look through all the reference material. There are times when the symptoms of a patient point to an obvious cure, but not always. Homeopaths can spend a good part of their day at the office looking through their books and notes.

After a remedy is chosen, homeopaths usually ask their patients to come back for a follow-up visit in a few weeks. At this time they look for signs of improvement, and sometimes choose a different remedy if the patient has not responded. Usually only one remedy is given at a time. They are trying to stimulate the body's natural defenses with a minimal amount of medicine.

Since most homeopaths work in private practice, as opposed to a large hospital with a support staff, they also have to handle all of the paperwork and administrative tasks that a doctor in private practice would. Homeopaths who are also licensed physicians have to understand and manage their own malpractice insurance, their patients' insurance, and run an office. Some homeopaths pursue an advanced degree as a doctor of naturopathic medicine (N.D.). N.D.s must be licensed to practice in 11 states; in addition, N.D.s must register in order to practice in the District of Columbia. Homeopaths who are not licensed physicians or N.D.s work in a legal grey zone in most states. There have been some homeopaths without medical degrees who have been fined for practicing medicine without a license. The Federal Drug Administration classifies homeopathic remedies as drugs and therefore regulates how they are produced. Companies manufacturing these drugs follow guidelines from the Homeopathic Pharmacopoeia of the United States. The legal details involved in practicing homeopathy can be puzzling, but these issues do not stop homeopaths who are truly committed to helping people.

This commitment has lead many homeopaths to seek funding for research because they want to prove the effectiveness of homeopathic remedies to the established medical community in the United States. The National Center for Homeopathy holds a yearly conference where homeopaths from all over the world come to share the research they have done. There are several organizations in the United States for homeopaths interested in meeting their colleagues, but there are even more international groups because of homeopathy's greater acceptance abroad.

what is it like to be a homeopath?

At her homeopathic practice in Chicago, Dr. Tony Bark estimates that she sees from six to 10 people a day, depending on how many new patients she has that day. "In my old practice, I saw over 40 people a day. Now I spend about an hour and a half with new patients, and about half an hour with the follow-up visits." Compared to traditional doctors, homeopaths

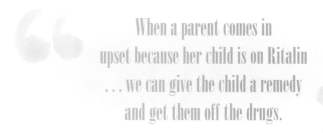

When a parent comes in upset because her child is on Ritalin …we can give the child a remedy and get them off the drugs.

spend far more time in personal contact with their patients.

Homeopaths spend a lot of time listening. Many times, people come to a homeopath as a last resort, when they have become frustrated with doctors, nurses, and the side effects of powerful drugs. Sometimes new patients are skeptical and a homeopath will have to spend time explaining what they do, trying to convince new patients that homeopathic remedies actually work. Homeopathic remedies are commonly prescribed in France and England, but in the United States, homeopathy is less well-known.

Many homeopaths find themselves defending their work or trying to educate other health professionals about homeopathy. Tony lectures at local universities and hospitals on a regular basis. Like most homeopaths, she is also a member of several societies for homeopaths, so she travels to meetings and conferences all over the country.

Tony is also a licensed doctor, so her patients can sometimes have their insurance cover her treatments. If a patient comes in with asthma, she will try to find out if there were any emotional or psychological stresses that may have triggered this kind of illness. "I ask people about their dreams, what they eat, whether they are usually cold or hot. I look for information about their emotional state when the illness began."

After the interview process, a single dose of a remedy is prescribed. The most rewarding thing about homeopathy is when this process works perfectly the first time and the patient's symptoms are relieved. The stories that homeopaths tell of their successes sound like small miracles. "It's wonderful when it works," says Tony, "when a parent comes in upset because her child is on Ritalin and antidepressants and we can give the child a remedy and get them off the drugs." Many of the patients who go to a homeopath are just not comfortable using a lot of prescription drugs and prefer to be treat their illnesses more naturally.

Just because homeopaths do not work the same way as most traditional doctors does not mean that they don't know about traditional medicine. Tony notes that "it takes a lot of studying, even if you don't go through medical school. You have to have a background in disease so that you can understand the symptoms."

have I got what it take to be a homeopath?

Homeopathy is a career for inquisitive, people-oriented types. The ability to communicate is key; this enables the homeopathic practitioner to explain homeopathic practices to different types of people (some of whom may have never encountered homeopathy before), and then to obtain the information needed from the client. Tony says that "you have to be interested in the psych aspect of it." Homeopaths are in many ways like psychologists: they have to be curious about how people think, work, and react. They generally split their time between talking to their clients and researching remedies, so it helps to enjoy both personal contact and solitary work.

It is important to be academically motivated. As any doctor can tell you, it takes serious dedication to go through medical school and homeopathic training is no different. Most homeopathic training programs involve more than two years of study. Also, many homeopathic practitioners have credentials in other areas of health care that have required extensive education and training, including nurses, traditional medical physicians, and naturopathic physicians. As with most health care professions, continuing education in homeopathic practices is necessary after the initial training period.

Besides academic motivation, homeopaths also need to have initiative. There are fewer homeopathic programs than there are medical programs, so it requires some effort to look for training. It also takes a certain amount of courage and optimism to work in a field that is only recently attaining validity and followers in the United States. Homeopaths choose to work outside the mainstream medical community.

how do I become a homeopath?

Tony worked as a traditional doctor before she began her training in homeopathy. There are programs for homeopaths at several schools in the United States and there are many programs for people without medical training.

education

High School
To become a homeopath you will need a solid background in sciences; therefore, you should take high school classes in biology, chemistry, and physics. You should also take classes in mathematics, psychology, and sociology. English courses will help you develop communication skills. Courses in business and computer science are also recommended. The basics that you learn in high school allow you to become familiar with standard medical knowledge and to use this information as a foundation for in-depth study of homeopathic practices.

Postsecondary Training
Until recently, organized homeopathic curricula was almost nonexistent, and the most common way to become a homeopath was by learning the trade under a practicing one. Today that is no longer the case.

Most homeopaths study a health-related field, such as nutrition, biology, or nursing, in college. From there, you can go on to a traditional medical school or to a naturopathic

Related Jobs

Acupuncturist
Aromatherapist
Ayurvedic doctor
Chiropractor
Herbalist
Holistic dentist
Holistic physician
Hypnotherapist
Massage therapist
Naturopath

Profile

Dr. Samuel C. Hahnemann, founder of homeopathy, was born in Meissen, Germany, in 1755. He began medical studies in 1775 in Leipzig and later studied at Vienna and Erlangen, earning a medical degree in 1779. Afterward he practiced medicine in several locales, finally settling in Dresden.

Hahnemann soon became disillusioned with the medical practices of the time and began investigating other methods of treating illness and disease. His interests turned to chemistry, and he published several academic papers on chemistry during 1787-92.

In 1796 Hahnemann published a paper that later became the foundation for homeopathy. In later papers he refined his theory and put forward the idea that a drug that produces a response similar to the primary symptom of a disease will be likely to produce a reaction in the body to overcome the disease.

Hahnemann's reputation grew and in 1812 he joined the faculty at the University of Leipzig to teach his theory of medicine. He was later forced to resign after the death of an Austrian prince who had been under his care.

Despite this setback, his reputation continued to grow, and he continued to develop theories and methods for the new practice of homeopathic medicine. In 1835 he moved to Paris, where he developed a large medical practice and worked until his death in 1843.

school that offers beginning courses in homeopathy. The Council on Naturopathic Medical Education has accredited three schools in the United States: Bastyr University in Kenmore, Washington; the National College of Naturopathic Medicine in Portland, Oregon; and the Southwest College of Naturopathic Medicine & Health Sciences in Tempe, Arizona. In addition, the College of Naturopathic Medicine in Bridgeport, Connecticut, has gained candidacy status and is being reviewed for accreditation. Some homeopaths choose to earn their doctorate in naturopathic medicine. Others pursue training in special programs for homeopathy at several institutions all over the country.

While it is easier to practice homeopathy if you are also licensed to practice traditional or naturopathic medicine, there are programs in homeopathy for non-medically trained people. These programs can demand as much time from their students as traditional medical schools do. There are programs offered on a part-time basis for people who need flexible class hours. For those interested in studying abroad, they may look into international homeopathic schools. England, India, and France have schools for classical homeopathy. Foreign language classes may benefit the future homeopath by providing avenues for sharing knowledge with international colleagues.

certification or licensing

A number of professional organizations offer certification for those practicing homeopathy. Some organizations, such as the American Board of Homeotherapeutics, offer different types of certification. The Diplomat designation given by this board is available only to licensed medical or osteopathic doctors, while its Homeopathic Primary Care Certification is available to licensed physicians, advanced practice nurses, and physician assistants. The Homeopathic Academy of Naturopathic Physicians offers certification only to N.D.s. All professionals are able to apply for certification from the Council for Homeopathic Certification. Certification indicates that a homeopath has met the organization's standards for education and knowledge.

Licensing requirements for homeopaths vary by state. According to the National Center for Homeopathy, three states—Arizona, Connecticut, and Nevada—have licensing laws specifically for homeopaths. Additionally, 11 states license N.D.s, who may use homeopathy in their practices. Finally, any medical or osteopathic doctor, physician assistant, dentist, or other licensed health care professional may be able to use homeopathy within the scope of their license, depending on their state's regulations. It is important to know that it is possible for a person to be a certified homeopath but still not be licensed to practice medicine.

scholarships and grants

There is no federally funded student aid for programs in homeopathy, but some of the societies for homeopaths offer scholarships. "We all donate—I just donated. It's part of being involved in this field," notes Tony. People involved in homeopathic societies are generally enthusiastic supporters of others who are interested in the career. Those considering a career in homeopathy should contact any homeopathic practitioners in their area or homeopathic national societies for information about scholarship funds and requirements. (See How Do I Learn More? for contact information.)

who will hire me?

Because homeopathy is only recently gaining acceptance in the United States, hospitals and other health care organizations do not hire

To be a successful homeopath, you should

- Have an inquisitive personality
- Be committed to natural health care and able to take criticism well
- Have very good interpersonal communication skills
- Be a careful listener
- Enjoy solving a mystery
- Be academically motivated

homeopathic practitioners. Homeopaths practice their trade on their own in solo practice or with a partner. Tony works at the Comprehensive Chiropractic and Alternative Medical Center in Chicago with a partner. Working with a partner makes practicing easier because the costs of running an office are shared. Also shared are the administrative tasks that are associated with running a business, such as bookkeeping and record keeping.

It is easier to practice homeopathy in some areas of the United States such as the West Coast, but Tony points out that she has colleagues practicing all over the country, in rural and urban areas. As interest in homeopathic medicine and its effects take root in the medical community, it is possible that homeopaths will be needed to help test homeopathic principles in controlled environments. Trained homeopaths may also tour lecture series, symposiums, and health fairs to help teach the public about the benefits of homeopathy. Private practice, however, is the norm for most homeopathic practitioners.

where can I go from here?

Advancement comes with building a solid reputation. Many homeopaths are active promoters of the discipline—becoming involved in various media, including writing articles for journals or magazines and presenting information on homeopathy in public forums, such as radio and television. Some homeopaths pursue research into homeopathic treatments, presenting their findings to colleagues at conventions or publishing their work in the press.

what are the salary ranges?

Homeopaths who are licensed medical doctors can make almost as much as their traditional counterparts. According to the American Medical Association, the median yearly income for traditional doctors is approximately $164,000. Other professionals, such as chiropractors and dentists, who use homeopathy generally earn somewhat less than their traditional counterparts. The U.S. Department of Labor reported the median yearly earnings of salaried chiropractors as $63,930 and salaried dentists as $110,160 in 1998. Keeping these figures in mind, the salary range for health care professionals using homeopathy may be from $60,000 to $150,000 or more. A non-doctor homeopathic practitioner will definitely make less, beginning around $30,000.

A practitioner's salary also depends on factors such as years of experience, location, and the size of the practice. Homeopaths often see fewer patients than traditional counterparts. As Tony noted, she may only see up to 10 patients a day. Her consultations last about an hour and a half to two hours and cost around $220. Although this sounds like a lot of money, she must pay the typical overhead that any doctor does, such as carrying malpractice insurance. Some homeopaths supplement their income by teaching or lecturing.

what is the job outlook?

Alternative medicine is gaining popularity in the United States as people look for new ways to deal with illness. People who suffer from chronic diseases like asthma and arthritis are often uncomfortable depending on prescription drugs, both because of their cost and their side effects. People who are tired of dealing with the often confusing and impersonal system of hospitals and insurance companies can go to a homeopath if they want a doctor who will take the time to listen to them about their problems and who will view their mental and emotional states as important contributors to their physical health. Because of the recent interest in alternative medicine, homeopathic practitioners may find that more people are willing to try their remedies. However, those wanting to practice only homeopathy will find that this is a very small field. Most practitioners have combined the practice of homeopathy with traditional medical jobs, such as those of doctors and nurses. These "combined" practitioners will have the best opportunities, although they will be slower than their traditional counterparts. One reason for this is that insurance companies often do not pay for homeopathic treatments. Overall, the growth of homeopathy as a career is expected to show little change.

There is research currently being conducted that may validate the findings of successful practicing homeopaths. If this research were to reveal any insights into the benefits of homeopathy, business for those who are already established in the business may grow more than expected.

As homeopathy becomes more widespread it will be helpful to have a medical degree to be competitive in the market. Now, there is a spirit of cooperation among homeopaths as they work for recognition, so competition is not an issue.

how do I learn more?

professional organizations

Following are organizations that have information about the field of homeopathy and about careers as a homeopathic practitioner.

American Board of Homeotherapeutics
801 North Fairfax Street, Suite 306
Alexandria, VA 22314
703-548-7790
http://www.homeopathyusa.org/specialtyboard

American Institute of Homeopathy
801 North Fairfax Street, Suite 306
Alexandria, VA 22314
888-445-9988
http://www.homeopathyusa.org

Council for Homeopathic Certification
1060 North Fourth Street
San Jose, CA 95112
408-971-5915

Homeopathic Academy of Naturopathic Physicians
12132 Southeast Foster Place
Portland, OR 97266
hanp@igc.apc.org
http://www.healthy.net/pan/pa/homeopathic/hanp

Homeopathic Educational Services
2124B Kittredge Street
Berkeley, CA 94704
510-649-0294
http://www.homeopathic.com

National Center for Homeopathy
801 North Fairfax Street, Suite 306
Alexandria, VA 22314
703-548-7790
info@homeopathic.org
http://www.healthy.net/nch

homeopaths

North American Society of Homeopaths
1122 East Pike Street, Suite 1122
Seattle, WA 98122
206-720-7000
http://www.homeopathy.org

The following Web site offers numerous links to sites that provide more information on homeopathy:
Homeopathy Home
http://www.homeopathyhome.com

bibliography

Following is a sampling of materials relating to the professional concerns and development of homeopaths.

Bailey, Philip M. *Homeopathic Psychology: Personality Profiles of the Major Constitutional Remedies.* Berkeley, CA: North Atlantic Books, 1996.

Cummings, Stephen. *Everybody's Guide to Homeopathic Medicines: Safe and Effective Remedies for You and Your Family.* New York:, NY: J. P. Tarcher/Putnam Publishing, 1997.

Grandgorge, Didier. *The Spirit of Homeopathic Medicines: Essential Insights to 300 Remedies.* Berkeley, CA: North Atlantic Books, 1998.

Hersoff, Asa. *Homeopathic Remedies: A Quick and Easy Guide to Common Disorders and Their Homeopathic Treatments.* New York, NY: Avery Penguin Putnam, 2000.

Jones, Rosemary. *Educational and Career Opportunities in Alternative Medicine: All You Need to Find Your Calling in the Healing Professions.* Roseville, CA: Prima Publishing, 1998.

Lockie, Andrew. *Encyclopedia of Homeopathy: The Definitive Home Reference Guide to Homeopathic Self-Help Remedies & Treatments for Common Ailments.* New York, NY: DK Publishing, 2000.

Lockie, Andrew. *Complete Guide to Homeopathy: The Principles & Practice of Treatment.* New York, NY: DK Publishing, 1995.

Rowe, Todd et al. *Homeopathic Methodology: Repertory, Case Taking, and Case Analysis: An Introductory Homeopathic Workbook.* Berkeley, CA: North Atlantic Books, 1998.

Steinfeld, Alan. *Careers in Alternative Medicine.* New York, NY: Rosen Publishing Group, 1999.

Weiner, Michael. *The Complete Book of Homeopathy: A Comprehensive Manual of Natural Healing.* New York: Fine Communications, 1997.

Hospice Workers

Definition

Hospice is a special kind of care that provides support for patients in the final stage of a terminal illness. Hospice workers include a wide variety of specially trained health care professionals who help these patients live comfortably in their last days or weeks of life.

High School Subjects

Health
Psychology
Religion
Speech

Personal Skills

Following instructions
Helping/teaching
Technical/scientific

Salary Range

Varies according to position

Educational Requirements

Varies by profession

Certification or Licensing

Varies by profession

Outlook

Faster than the average

GOE
10.01.01
O*NET-SOC
NA*

*Not Available. The O*NET-SOC does not classify hospice workers as such, but rather classifies the worker's primary profession (e.g., registered nurse).

An urgent message has sent Jane Merritt hurrying through traffic. Her newest hospice patient is in a crisis. The women has terminal pancreatic cancer and is scared and exhausted. The attending nurse has told Jane that the woman is anxiously calling for someone to end her pain, to be her "Dr. Kervorkian." "This isn't the goal of hospice," Jane says to herself. "Hospice is about making the best of what time is left, reducing the symptoms and pain of an incurable disease. It's about trying to die with dignity and peace."

The woman is bone-thin and can barely raise her hand to greet Jane as she enters the room. Her eyes are sunken and glassy, her breathing labored, then calm again. She is very alert, though. The sound of children playing and of passing cars seeps through the windows of the den where her bed is set up. An oxygen machine puffs and chugs in the background. "Are you comfortable? Can I adjust your bed?" The woman nods and Jane presses a button to elevate the head part of the bed. "How about some water?" Jane listens as the women pours out her fears, worries, and grief, holding her hand and occasionally offering a reassuring smile. She knows that there are no easy answers, that a terminal illness cannot be healed with words, that she is not the one suffering. Her training and experience have taught her to be a good listener, to know when and when not to talk. After Jane prays with her, she notices that the woman is starting to calm down. Sometimes sick people just need to know that someone cares, that they are not alone in the world.

what does a hospice worker do?

Hospice workers help patients who have a variety of terminal illnesses, and who can no longer benefit from curative treatment. Typically, a hospice patient has less than six months to live. Care is primarily provided in the patients' homes, but may also be provided in nursing homes and hospitals, with the intent to make patients as comfortable and pain free as medically possible during the final days of their lives.

Hospice uses a team approach to plan and coordinate care for the patient. This team includes the patient, family, and the hospice team, all working together. Family or primary caregivers can call for the help of a hospice team member 24 hours a day, 7 days a week, and a team member will respond whenever needed.

Hospice workers' job responsibilities are related to their profession. A listing of specific hospice careers follows:

Hospice medical directors may be licensed physicians who oversee the medical program and advise the hospice care staff.

Field supervisors, supervisors of home health care aides, and *supervisors of rehabilitation services* oversee the activities of their particular hospice team. They ensure that each patient is properly attended to by the various hospice specialists.

Registered nurses may be responsible for seeing that a member of the hospice team meets the patient's needs. Registered nurses and *licensed practical nurses* also visit patients to monitor their emotional and physical symptoms.

Nurse assistants and *home health care aides* assist the family in the personal care of the patient such as bathing, grooming, and changing the bed linens.

Physical, occupational, and *speech therapists* help patients with daily living tasks that have become difficult or impossible to perform.

Social workers help the patient and family deal with the emotions surrounding the illness. They also help locate personal and community resources that may assist the patient or the family.

What is hospice?

Hospice is a form of care for the terminally ill. The hospice health care environment concentrates on palliative treatment, in effect, treating and addressing pain and other symptoms of an incurable disease. Patients enter hospice programs at their own request. A physician's referral indicating a prognosis of no more than six months of life is usually required.

Hospice patients have a wide variety of terminal illnesses. According to the Hospice and Palliative Care Association of America, 69.7 percent of hospice patients in 1995-96 had cancer. Other conditions include diseases of the circulatory system, and parasitic diseases, infectious diseases (including HIV), diseases of the nervous system and sense organs (including Alzheimer's, Parkinson's, meningitis, and others), and diseases of the respiratory system. Hospice programs emphasize quality, not length of life, and treat dying as a normal process. While hope is never lost for a remission of a terminal disease or even a cure—the goal of hospice is to help patients live comfortably and productively in their last days or months in an environment filled with peace and dignity.

Hospice care is usually provided in a patient's home, but may also be provided in a hospital, a nursing facility, or in a freestanding facility. Hospice is covered nationwide by most private insurance policies as well as by Medicare and Medicaid in 43 states.

Volunteer coordinators are responsible for organizing and directing the volunteer program and for training the volunteer workers.

Chaplains provide religious support to the patient and family in accordance with their specific religious beliefs.

Music therapists use music to provide comfort and relaxation to the patient.

Grief therapists help the family deal with the death of their loved one and cope with their grief.

Most hospice workers visit terminally ill patients in their homes or in the homes of their caregivers so the work environment can be as varied as their patients' lifestyles. Some workers are on call 24 hours a day and may be required to travel to homes in all areas of a city or rural area to provide medical and supportive care. Patients and family members can be very tense during this stressful period in their lives, and they may be unpleasant and uncooperative at times. As with any health care profession, there is the possibility of exposure to contagious diseases; however, proper precautions and training diminish this risk.

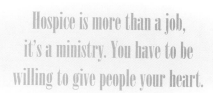

"Hospice is more than a job, it's a ministry. You have to be willing to give people your heart."

what is it like to be a hospice worker?

Jane Merritt has worked as a hospice chaplain in the Chicago area for one year. Before getting involved with hospice she was a religious teacher for many years. Jane has also been an Adrian Dominican nun for the past forty years, but notes that not all hospice chaplains are nuns. She states, "We are nondenominational and are not out to proselytize." In addition to her religious background, Jane is a licensed clinical professional counselor as well as a licensed marriage and family therapist.

After a number of years teaching, Jane felt that she needed a new challenge. She realized that she had always enjoyed interacting with students and their families, and felt that she had a natural affinity for listening to the problems and troubles of others. So she decided to return to school and "retool" for a career as a pastoral counselor. After earning a degree in pastoral counseling, she served as pastoral counselor for a number of local churches. "I dealt with many other issues, in addition to dying, as a pastoral counselor for the churches."

On most mornings, Jane heads straight from home to her first patient. "I try to sched-ule four patient visits a day." Jane spends about three hours a day driving from case to case. She visits most of her patients in private homes. "I spend about one hour with each patient unless a special circumstance arises. I see where the person is at emotionally, see if there is anything in particular that they want to talk about. If there are any medical problems, I page the patient's case nurse. We also use voice mail to inform one another what's going on with a patient on a daily basis. The nurse or other members of the team will do the same if they feel that emotional counseling is necessary." She offers emotional and spiritual support to each of her patients. "If the patient is interested in prayer, I will pray with them. I leave that open to them as an option."

The average workday for Jane and other hospice workers is extremely demanding. As a result, she tries to stay highly organized. "I tend to be a planner," she explains, "so I try to schedule my day so that I can make the best use of my time, but in some instances you have to go with the flow." Sometimes situations arise that cannot be scheduled. Jane must respond to any emergency calls that she receives in the course of her day. "If a patient has died, if the family needs me, I change my schedule, go to the family, and stay with them until the funeral director arrives." Emergency calls usually deal with the death of a patient or a patient very near death.

Jane works a standard workweek, but is expected to work overtime if needed. "If you are with a patient and family, and the patient is dying, you can't look at your watch, and say it's five o'clock and I have to go home," she explains. "Hospice is more than a job, it's a ministry. You have to be willing to give people your heart."

Jane spends every Tuesday in the office. This is her team day, where the entire interdisciplinary team meets to discuss the patients and any issues that have arisen relating to their

in-depth

Volunteers

Hospice volunteers are an integral part of the hospice experience. According to the Health Care Financing Administration, there were almost 90,000 people involved in Medicare-certified hospices in 1998; and over 46,000 of these people were volunteers. Hospice volunteers offer various services to patients and their families such as running errands, light housework, meal preparation, and a variety of other tasks. Sometimes volunteers will stay with the patient so that the primary caregiver can take care of errands and appointments or simply rest or relax.

Hospice volunteers undertake rigorous training—an average of 22 hours—before they are assigned to work with a patient and his or her family. Many volunteers have had a personal experience with a friend or family member who has had a life-ending illness. This allows them to be especially supportive and helpful as a volunteer. "If you care about other people, and you hurt when other people hurt, you'll probably end up sometime as a worker or volunteer for a hospice," says Eleanor Maynard, a hospice volunteer for 20 years.

care and the team's work in general. The remaining days of the week are spent almost entirely in the field. Occasionally, Jane may stop back at the office at the very end of a workday to file paperwork.

An important part of her duties is working as part of the interdisciplinary hospice team. She likes hospice because "you can use your counseling skills in a collaborative way with other members of a team." She works closely with social workers and music therapists to address the emotional and psychological needs of patients. "Oftentimes, with a new patient, the social worker and I make the initial visit together so as not to overwhelm a new patient." (For a new patient the first week of care is often overwhelming, as various nurses, nurse assistants, and other workers make their initial visits.) Jane likes her close working relationship with the social worker. "We back each other up a lot, and constantly update each other on the emotional and physical condition of our patient."

It is important to note that hospice patients have the right to refuse counseling service (though they may not refuse medical service under the terms of the hospice agreement), but this rarely happens. "Sometimes people think that we might come in quoting scripture, waving our arms, but it is not like that. We as chaplains do not represent a particular denomination." If a patient feels this way Jane may ask for one visit and state that she

has no agenda or intent other than a supportive visit. This usually works. Conversely, if a patient would like her to make additional visits, she will fit them into her schedule.

Jane performs other duties in addition to those in the field. "There is always office paperwork connected to the job." She is required to fill out a team conference summary, a spiritual assessment for each patient, and an interdisciplinary progress report, which covers what occurred during her visit with the patient. They may describe the patient's mood, which family members were present during her visit, and any special requests the patient made, such as for prayer.

She also compiles a record of her itinerary, which details where and how much time she spent on each call. Finally, she submits a tentative schedule for the following week's activity. It is important that she be accurate and thorough in her paperwork since, as she explains, "all forms we fill out are subject to scrutiny by Medicare and the state."

Hospice care has been covered by Medicare since 1982. As a result, her program, like all other Medicare-funded programs, is periodically audited to ensure that everything is in order.

Jane's duties do not end with a patient's death. "I also perform bereavement follow-up calls to see how the family is doing after a death. I see if the family needs to talk, if the spouse needs a visit, or if they need grief counseling." Other types of bereavement service include group or private counseling and memorial services.

Jane is also responsible for obtaining the wake and funeral information and relaying it to the other team members so that they may, if time permits, express their sympathies to the patient's family.

Jane will be undertaking two new responsibilities in the near future. First, she will visit terminally ill people and their families who are not involved with hospice and educate them about the benefits of hospice. If they so choose, she will sign them up to enter the program. She will not perform any type of medical assessment, but will try to ascertain the psychological state of the patient. Second, Jane's hospice is starting an on-call program for which she will carry a beeper and—during specified times—be available for emergency situations with patients and their families.

No discussion of what it is like to be a hospice worker can be complete without a frank discussion of death and dying. Some terminally ill patients are very comfortable talking about their own death; others are in denial and are not able to speak openly about the subject. In her experience, Jane feels that the majority of her patients are comfortable talking about their illness and dying. "Our goal," Jane explains, "is not to take away their feelings of denial but get to know them, visit with them frequently, build trust, and if and when their condition begins to deteriorate, sometimes they open up and discuss dying with us."

Many may feel that working with the terminally ill must be especially hard and stressful. "It is draining emotionally to work in this field, but I like giving comfort to others," Jane says. "I do not find it depressing; I find it energizing. Being with the patient and their family gives me energy. Of course when a patient dies, especially one you got to know well, you feel sad."

To offset the natural stress that is part of dealing with patients and their families in such deep crises, Jane is a member of a support group of other hospice professionals. "We meet every other week to encourage and support one another."

In order to perform her job well, Jane tries to stay current with issues in pastoral counseling and hospice in general. Jane reads *Hospice Journal*, which is published by the National Hospice and Palliative Care Organization (NHPCO). It covers physical, psychological, and pastoral care issues. She is also a member of a variety of organizations, including the

NHPCO, the American Association of Family Therapists, and the American Counseling Association.

Jane feels very strongly about her work as a hospice chaplain. "I like it very much. I meet all kinds of people. I like to think of it as holy work. It's a ministry with people at a very serious, intimate moment in their lives. I can't think of a more intimate time in someone's life than when they are dying."

have I got what it takes to be a hospice worker?

If you are planning to become involved in hospice care, you should be able to work as a member of a team to provide the support and care that is needed by terminally ill patients and their loved ones and caregivers. You should be compassionate, patient, sensitive, and well organized. You should also feel comfortable dealing with the sick and dying.

Hospice workers must be willing to work overtime and be flexible about their schedule. "You can't be a clock watcher in this field," Jane explains. She recounts a story of a newly hired nurse that constantly glanced at her watch as she went about her duties. "She didn't last very long at our hospice. You just can't look upon this as simply a job."

Finally, a sense of humor is very important in this field. People that are very ill or dying may use humor as an outlet to relieve pain and stress. "You need to be able to laugh with a patient and their families if they laugh," Jane comments. Jane and her colleagues sometimes share a light moments during their weekly team meetings. "We need to remind ourselves not to always take things so seriously."

how do I become a hospice worker?

education

Jane received her bachelor's degree from Siena Heights College in Siena, Michigan. She has earned master's degrees from Catholic University in Washington, DC, and Loyola University in Baltimore, Maryland. In addition, she has earned post-doctoral certificates from Loyola University in Baltimore and the Family Institute of Chicago.

High School

Persons wishing to obtain a college degree in one of the professions employed by hospice organizations should take a well-balanced college preparatory course in high school, with a good foundation in the sciences. Obviously, biology, chemistry, and psychology are important courses. You should take anatomy and physiology if your high school offers these courses. You should also take courses in the humanities and social sciences, as well as classes that improve communication skills.

High school diploma requirements vary with hospice organizations and the volunteer responsibilities. Some volunteer work does not require a diploma of any kind, for example, answering the phones, cleaning, or maintaining grounds. However, a high school diploma would probably be required for any volunteer position that involves patient contact.

Postsecondary Training

The degree program you should pursue depends on the role you hope to play in the hospice programs. Some positions require a bachelor's degree and others a medical degree or other specialized degree. Although only a few colleges and universities offer specialized hospice degrees, many hospitals do offer medical rotations in hospice care to physicians, nurses, and other professionals involved in training.

To be a successful hospice worker, you should

- Have a strong desire to help people
- Be a good listener and communicator
- Be compassionate
- Have strong interpersonal skills
- Be a good team player
- Be comfortable with people who are sick or dying

certification or licensing

The certification or licensing requirements are determined by the medical specialty or professional career that you wish to pursue. The hospice itself is usually licensed by the department of health of each state (44 states licensed hospice programs in 1999), and certified by Medicare and Medicaid.

who will hire me?

Hospice organizations hire hospice workers and also welcome hospice volunteers. As of March 2001, there were 3,139 hospice programs in all 50 states, the District of Columbia, and Puerto Rico.

If you are interested in pursuing a career as a hospice worker, you should consider doing volunteer work at a hospice center, hospital, or nursing home when in high school. This will give you an insight into the hospice environment and its career possibilities.

If you choose to complete professional training, a placement office associated with your degree program may help you locate employment opportunities. In addition, contacts you made in clinical settings while training or volunteering may also be helpful. Applying directly to hospices and other health care agencies and answering ads in professional journals can also produce employment opportunities.

where can I go from here?

Advancement opportunities include director and supervisor positions within the hospice program. Other opportunities may exist with government agencies and organizations associated with hospice and home health care programs. An advanced degree may be required to advance to some positions.

what are the salary ranges?

Salaries for hospice workers are similar to those of their counterparts in a more typical medical setting and are generally are based on the position, the educational requirements for that position, and the level of experience of the worker. According to a survey conducted by the Hospital & Healthcare Compensation Service in 1999, the salary range for an executive director was $50,662 to $75,000 with the median salary being $62,000. The median salary for a director of social work and counseling was $41,900, while the median salary for a director of nursing/clinical services was $51,497. The survey also reported the following average hourly rates by hospice profession: registered nurse, $18.77; licensed practical nurse, $13.74; social worker, $17.93; home care aide, $8.94; and physical therapist, $25.64.

Hospice chaplains, music therapists, and grief therapists earn salaries that range from $20,000 to $35,000 annually.

Fringe benefits are usually similar to those of other full-time health care workers and may include sick leave, vacation, health and life insurance, and tuition assistance.

what is the job outlook?

Hospice participation has grown at a dramatic rate, especially among those involved with Medicare. According to the National Association of Home Care, from 1984 to 1998, the total number of hospices participating in Medicare rose from 31 to 2,287—nearly a 75-fold increase. The NHPCO estimates that 700,000 patients were served by hospice or home care organizations in the United States in 1999. This number is expected to increase as the population ages and health care costs rise. In addition, according to the NHPCO, families and medical professionals are choosing hospice care because of its holistic, patient-family, in-home centered philosophy.

A few factors may affect the glowing future of hospice. Holistic, patient-centered hospices are facing increasing challenges as managed care providers jump on the hospice bandwagon. Many hospitals and nursing homes are entering the hospice market in pursuit of increased revenue, creating fears that the home-based, patient-centered, interdiscipli-

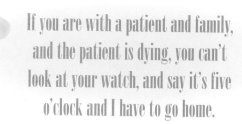

If you are with a patient and family, and the patient is dying, you can't look at your watch, and say it's five o'clock and I have to go home.

nary philosophy of hospice will become a thing of the past. Traditional hospice agencies are being forced to merge or affiliate with other programs, increase community awareness, and develop other new strategies in order to compete with the big business trends in health care delivery. The increasing role of insurance companies and government programs in health care have led to fears that hospices may begin to value profit over the individual needs of the patient.

"There is a fear in hospice," Jane explains, "a danger, that the psychosocial spiritual aspects of patient care will be overlooked, and not given as much attention." Many feel that the role of psychosocial workers might be reduced in the interest of cost-cutting and budgetary control. "This is why," Jane explains, "it is especially important to monitor and encourage the interdisciplinary approach in this era of downsizing. If you cut out social workers, chaplains and the other interdisciplinary parts of hospice, it is no longer hospice. There is a need for continuing education regarding hospice, and its role in the health care system, in order to keep hospice philosophy intact."

how do I learn more?

The best way to get hands-on experience in hospice is to serve as a volunteer at a hospice, nursing home, or hospital in your community. This experience will help you get a sense of what it is like to be around sick people. You can also contact associations for hospice and ask them to send you further information. You may also consider asking a teacher or guidance counselor to set up an interview or presentation by a hospice chaplain or other hospice professional. Since serious issues of illness and death are dealt with everyday in hospice, you will need to have a willingness to grow psychologically, spiritually, and intellectually as you gain experience with those suffering terminal illnesses.

professional organizations

The following organizations provide information on hospice careers:

Hospice Education Association
190 Westbrook Road
Essex, CT 06426-1510
800-331-1620
hospiceall@aol.com
http://www.hospiceworld.org/

National Association for Home Care
228 Seventh Street, SE
Washington, DC 20003
202-547-7424
http://www.nahc.org

National Hospice and Palliative Care Organization
1700 Diagonal Road, Suite 300
Alexandria, VA 22314
703-837-1500
info@nhpco.org
http://www.nhpco.org/

bibliography

Following is a sampling of materials relating to the professional concerns and development of hospice workers.

Beresford, Larry. *The Hospice Handbook: a Complete Guide*. Boston, MA: Little, Brown & Company, 1993.

Buckingham, Robert W. *The Handbook of Hospice Care*. Amherst, NY: Prometheus Books, 1996.

Elisabeth Kubler-Ross, Elizabeth. *On Death and Dying*. Reprint Edition. New York, NY: Collier Books, 1997.

Lattanzi-Licht, Marcia John J. Mahoney and Galen Miller. *The Hospice Choice: In Pursuit of a Peaceful Death*. New York, NY: Fireside Press, 1998.

Ray, M. Catherine. *I'm Here to Help: A Guide for Caregivers, Hospice Workers, and Volunteers*. New York, NY: Bantam Books, 1997.

Human Services Workers

Definition

Human services workers help people handle problems of daily living through education, counseling, and assistance. They generally work under the direction of other professionals such as nurses, psychiatrists, physical therapists, or social workers.

Alternative Job Titles

Adult day care workers
Client advocates
Family support workers
Group activities aides
Social worker assistants

High School Subjects

Psychology
Sociology

Personal Skills

Communication/ideas
Helping/teaching

Salary Range

$13,000 to $21,000 to $33,000+

Educational Requirements

Some postsecondary training; Bachelor's degree recommended

Certification or Licensing

Required for certain positions

Outlook

Faster than the average

GOE
11.05.02
O*NET-SOC
21-1093.00

Releasing pent up emotions, Angela began crying. She was crying, but she was also smiling. Alina Garza, an intern working to become an alcohol and drug counselor, remembered how different Angela had been just a few weeks before. On her first day in the group, Alina tried to put Angela at ease.

"Before we get started, I wonder if you would tell everybody your name and a little bit about yourself," said Alina.

"My name is Angela. You people can talk all you want. I got nothin' to say," she said, sitting rigidly with her arms folded, her eyes focused on the floor.

"That's fine, Angela. Just listen, and when you have something to add, jump in," Alina calmly responded, not wanting to antagonize the woman further. She knew that it took some people longer to get comfortable in the group setting. There would be time for talking once Angela loosened up.

The days passed. Alina watched as Angela slowly opened up. As the other members of her group talked of their struggles with life and addiction, Angela's aggressive body language began to dissolve. Finally, after two weeks, her story began to unfold. She had suffered several devastating losses. Three people close to her had been murdered. Unable to cope, Angela had turned to drugs to escape. She gave up custody of her children when she realized that she wanted to die.

Alina helped her to make sense of her feelings and to see that in using drugs, she was grieving, though destructively, for the loss of her friends. Alina got Angela to talk about her children and her hopes for the future. Most importantly, Alina listened. By the end of the six-week session, Angela wanted to work toward getting her children back. Alina knew Angela had only started to put her life back together, but with new hope and caring professionals to help her, she had a good chance to make it.

what does a human services worker do?

The field of human services is a broad one, encompassing social work, alcohol and drug abuse counseling, family therapy, mental health awareness, and other services. A good definition of the general duties of *human services workers* comes from the National Organization for Human Service Education: "The pri-

mary purpose of the human services worker is to assist individuals and communities to function as effectively as possible in the major domains of living."

Human services workers give comfort, counseling, advocacy, and education to people in need. Working under the supervision of psychologists, sociologists, medical professionals, and social workers, human services workers lead drug and alcohol addiction groups, help people obtain access to government services, and provide food and shelter for the homeless—to name a few of their many tasks. Wherever there is a population in need, they are there to help.

Human services workers provide the most direct line of social service, working directly with their clients. The tasks they perform and job titles they hold are as varied as the populations they serve. *Residential counselors* work with abused and neglected children in institutional settings, like state or private shelters. Other human services workers are *community outreach workers*, who sponsor programs or run activities at community centers and park districts. *Gerontological aides* help the elderly with household tasks, such as grocery shopping, cleaning, or transporting clients to and from doctor appointments. Some individuals require more attention, needing the help of *adult day care workers*, who closely monitor clients' medical needs, diets, and mental well-being.

Human services workers deal with specific social problems, as well. *Drug and alcohol abuse counselors* lead groups struggling with addictions and their associated problems. Some human services workers are *halfway house counselors*, helping people recently released from prisons, mental health facilities, or inpatient substance abuse clinics to successfully rejoin society. Human services workers also may be *family support workers*, helping to educate parents in such matters as the necessity of immunizing children or working out conflicts peacefully. *Eligibility counselors* act as a liaison between citizens and the government agencies that distribute medical, employment, and financial aid benefits. *Youth workers* work with troubled or endangered children and may organize anti-gang and anti-drug abuse efforts.

In addition to their duties with clients, human services workers must keep accurate records of client progress, track expenditures, and communicate with supervisors and government agencies. They must keep up with advances in their fields and stay abreast of changes in relevant areas of law and government regulation.

lingo to learn

Advocacy: In human services, this refers to the assistance given to disadvantaged people moving through courts, government agencies, or other large bureaucracies.

Group therapy: Therapy in which people who share a common problem, such as drug abuse, meet with a counselor to share ideas and support.

Relapse: The failure to maintain a certain type of behavior, like sobriety.

what is it like to be a human services worker?

Alina Garza works part-time as an assistant teacher while going to school to become a Certified Alcohol and Drug Counselor (CADC). She works for Leyden Family Services and is doing an internship through Proviso Family Service/ProCare Center. Angela was a member of a group Alina led as part of her CADC internship.

"There was a total change in attitude from the first meeting to the last," Alina says of Angela. "It was amazing to see the transformation." Though it can be difficult to juggle studies, work, and an internship, Alina has managed to stay on top of things.

Alina's first experience with counseling was working with rotating groups of people who met three hours a day, four days a week, for six weeks. "We call these groups intensive outpatient," explains Alina. "They still need the constant support of the group. They are very vulnerable to relapsing [into their addictive behavior] right after they get out of rehab."

She plans to work exclusively with women during the next phase of her internship. "I could have stayed with the intensive group," she says, "but I wanted to experience a different kind of group."

In addition to Alina's group discussions, specialists are invited from other areas of the center to give seminars on different topics. "People come in and talk about things like AIDS/HIV awareness or relapse prevention," Alina explains. "Afterward we talk about the lecture and I try and answer their questions."

The remaining time is spent in what are called process groups, where clients have an opportunity to discuss their lives and the problems they may be having. Alina acts as a supporter and guide, not as a preacher. "Mostly I just listen and let the clients work on the problems themselves," she says.

In addition to her duties during sessions, Alina must update her clients' paperwork. "I add a group note and an individual note to each client's chart after each session," she says.

Alina also works part-time as an assistant teacher at Our Place Drop-in Center, where parents can come in with their children to learn parenting skills and share experiences. "The kids have a place to play while their parents interact and learn from each other," Alina says. "I read to the children or just watch them play. It's very informal."

Alina works regular daytime hours. However, not all human services work can be done during the day. Heather Bradley is a unit supervisor at a children's shelter in Chicago. Abused and neglected children come to the shelter when their emotional and psychological problems are too severe for traditional foster care. Since there must be supervision of the children at all times, these residential counselors work some nights and weekends.

have I got what it takes to be a human services worker?

Human services work requires a great deal of commitment. The work is very demanding and the pay is relatively low. Those interested in the field must have a strong desire to help people. Clients are sometimes resentful of or even openly hostile to the very people who are trying to help them. For this reason, patience and an even temper are crucial attributes. In addition, human services workers must maintain a healthy distance from their clients' difficulties. If they do not, they cannot remain objective in their counseling work and may risk getting overwhelmed and burned out.

"When I first started working with the group, I was surprised how much of an emotional toll it takes on you," Alina recalls. She quickly realized she had to adapt if she was going to continue in the profession. "I started working out regularly, meditating, and just paying more attention to self-care," she says.

Many of the clients Alina works with are not there voluntarily, having been referred to the program after trouble with the law. "Working with addicts can be frustrating. They don't want to give up their high," Alina says.

Sometimes the reluctant ones can be reached, as was the case with Angela. But not everyone can be helped. Alina remembers one client who snorted heroin during a break and came back to the group high. "He was nodding out in the middle of group," she recalls.

Heather's work with troubled children can be similarly trying. "Working with other human beings is always difficult, and people are in treatment for their deficiencies," she says. "You have to be able to keep things in perspective. That kid that just slapped you or called you filthy names . . . you just can't take it personally."

in-depth
Pioneer in Human Services: Jane Addams and the Settlement House Movement

In the 19th century, poverty was a much debated topic, but little was accomplished in terms of relieving it. At best, aid to the poor consisted of handouts from wealthy individuals. Some went so far as to say that the poor deserved to be poor, reasoning that sobriety and hard work could lift anyone out of a wretched condition.

Jane Addams thought differently. Copying the settlement house concept begun in England, she established Hull House on Chicago's West Side in 1889. Hull House was unique in that instead of simply distributing charity, Jane and her "residents" moved into a slum neighborhood to attack the problems of poverty at their roots. They became members of the community and worked to provide new facilities such as a local library, theater, playground, and gymnasium. By 1906, the Hull House and its neighborhood outreach projects were second only to the University of Chicago in the number of facilities built dedicated to a single purpose.

Jane went on to champion a number of other social causes including child labor laws and women's suffrage. In recognition for her life of work on behalf of the less fortunate, she was awarded the Nobel Prize in 1931.

Self-awareness is also important. Heather says, "Ideally, people who work with other people should be asking themselves, 'What is my motivation? Am I being objective?' You have to be reflective, self-critical."

While it is true that human services work can be daunting, it offers rewards that are not found in many other jobs. "I really like knowing that I have helped someone," Alina says.

Heather also gets great satisfaction from helping people. "The best part is that you do make an impact on people. You will have an impact on the world," she says.

Heather notes that some people enter residential counseling thinking it will be an easy job, but they rarely last very long. "It can be hard, but if you like children and if you're challenged by the work, it keeps you there," she says.

how do I become a human services worker?

Like many other fields, jobs in human services that were once available to high school graduates now require at least some postsecondary training. The more education and training you have, the better your chances of getting hired and commanding a higher salary.

education

High School

Those interested in human services work can begin preparing during high school by taking courses in sociology, psychology, speech, and English. Human services work requires a broad range of skills, so students should strive to be well-rounded, both academically and socially. Generally speaking, high school students should take a wide range of classes in anticipation of further study in college.

Postsecondary Training

There are a number of different courses of study depending on the area of human services work you wish to enter. Alina is pursuing an associate's degree in applied sciences, which can be applied towards her certification as a substance abuse counselor. Her classes include psychology (abnormal and social), physiology, anatomy, and more specialized courses on issues of addiction, such as intake assessment and the effects of drugs and alcohol on families. In addition to her classroom work, she must complete 600 hours of clinical observation and an intern experience. "I've always been good at school. School is easy. Internship challenged me," she admits.

For those interested in residential counseling, Heather recommends obtaining at least a bachelor's degree. "A lot of people come into residential counseling with generic [non-specialist] bachelor's degrees, but sociology or psychology would be the best," she explains.

certification or licensing

Certification is required for some human services jobs. Alina must pass a test given by the state of Illinois before she can become certified as an alcohol and drug counselor. Candidates for the test must graduate from an accredited program before they can take the test. Certification as an alcohol/drug abuse counselor is good for five years; those wishing to renew must complete a specified number of continuing education credits.

Hiring requirements for larger organizations are often more stringent than smaller agencies. Large employers may require applicants to be certified in the field they are working, pass drug and/or alcohol screenings, or submit to a criminal background investigation before consideration for a job.

internships and volunteerships

For some positions, employers require applicants to have past experience through a human services internship. Even if not required for a job, some form of pre-professional experience is highly desirable to potential employers.

The good news is that opportunities for experience abound. There may be no field with more chances for volunteer experience than in human services. Community organizations, hospitals, nursing homes, church groups, and hundreds of other social service organizations are always looking for volunteers. In addition to helping out your community, participating in an internship can help you discover whether you have the motivation and skills to do human services work. Also, volunteering is an excellent way to network for a job.

It is never too early to start checking around for opportunities. Contact your local school, church, hospital, or nursing home directly to ask about positions. You may also want to look into options with local, state, or federal government agencies. The U.S. Department of Health and Human Services offers a variety of summer internships to students. Check out its Web site, http://www.hhs.gov, for more information.

Heather's advice to prospective human services workers is clear: "Volunteer as early as you can, and as often as you can."

who will hire me?

According to the U.S. Department of Labor, there are approximately 268,000 human services workers employed in the United States. They can be found in many different settings. A large number of them are employed with federal, state, and local government agencies; private agencies for adult day care, substance abuse, crisis intervention, and counseling; halfway houses; and hospitals or community health centers. Many job openings are listed in the classified sections of newspapers. Alina learned of her internship opportunity by word of mouth while she was working as a receptionist at the Leyden Family Service.

Heather might be considered an expert on what employers are looking for since she is in charge of hiring residential counselors for the children's shelter. She gives great weight to past volunteer history. "More than academics, I want to see if they've been around kids, do they like kids," she says.

where can I go from here?

Advancement beyond entry-level positions is closely tied with levels of formal education. Those who wish to move into management or into more specialized forms of human services should plan on getting a master's degree in their related field, such as psychology, social work, counseling, rehabilitation, or human services management. Heather began her career in human services with a bachelor's degree in fine arts and then went on to earn her advanced degree in counseling. Alina plans to get her master's degree in social work and a Ph.D. in psychology to advance her career.

what are the salary ranges?

Because the field encompasses so many jobs, exact salary figures are hard to estimate. The U.S. Department of Labor reports that in 1998, the median annual salary for human services workers was $21,360. The lowest paid 10 percent earned less than $13,540, and the highest paid 10 percent earned over $33,840 a year.

Median 1997 salaries of workers employed with the largest employers are as follows: social services (not elsewhere classified), $20,200; health and allied services (not elsewhere classified), $20,600; hospitals, $21,200; local government, $23,500; and state government, $25,600.

what is the job outlook?

According to the *Occupational Outlook Handbook,* employment for human services workers is expected to grow faster than the average for all occupations. The U.S. population is aging, requiring more workers in residential care facilities and private adult day care agencies. Another reason for the employment growth is that the public is gaining a better understanding of issues such as substance abuse, illiteracy, and child abuse. These social problems cost society a great deal, both in terms of the money spent and the human potential squandered. Improved public awareness has sparked an increase in the demand for professionals such as addiction counselors, crisis intervention workers, and family counselors.

Managed medical care has also made an impact on the field of human services. As private insurers look for ways to cut costs, new treatment methods and counseling programs have come about. Preventing health problems is much cheaper than treating them once they occur, and the work of many human service workers aims to do just that—deal with existing addictions, crises, and hardships before they further compromise the health of an individual.

Another factor aiding employment is purely financial. As health care and government social service budgets have been trimmed, more

human services workers will be needed to perform jobs once carried out by more highly educated (and higher paid) social workers.

Finally, the need to replace workers in human services occupations will bring about many job openings. Due to the difficult nature of the work and the relatively low pay, the field of human services has a high turnover rate. Qualified applicants should have ample opportunities for employment.

how do I learn more?

professional organizations

For more information on careers in human services and educational and training requirements, contact the following organizations:

American Counseling Association
5999 Stevenson Avenue
Alexandria, VA 22304
http://www.counseling.org

National Organization for Human Service Education
http://www.nohse.com

U.S. Department of Health and Human Services
200 Independence Avenue, SW
Washington, DC 20201
http://www.hhs.gov

bibliography

Following is a sampling of materials relating to the professional concerns and development of human services workers.

Brill, Naomi I. *Working with People: The Helping Process.* 6th Edition. Reading, MA: Addison-Wesley, 1997.

Harris, Howard S. and David C. Maloney, eds. *Human Services: Contemporary Issues and Trends.* 2nd Edition. New York, NY: Allyn & Bacon, 1998.

Martin, David G. and Allan D. Moore, eds. *Basics of Clinical Practice: A Guidebook for Trainees in the Helping Professions.* Prospect Heights, IL: Waveland Press, 1998.

Wallner, Rosemary. *Human Services Worker.* Mankato, MN: Capstone Press, 2000.

To be a successful human services worker, you should

- Have a strong desire to help people
- Be patient and even-tempered
- Have good interviewing skills
- Interact well with a variety of people
- Have good problem-solving skills
- Be a good listener and communicator

Hypnotherapists

Definition

Hypnotherapists help people to enter a hypnotic state in order to increase their motivation or change behavior.

Alternative Job Titles

Hypnocounselors
Hypnotists

High School Subjects

Biology
Psychology
Sociology

Personal Skills

Communication/ideas
Helping/teaching

Salary Range

$50/hour to $45,000/year
to $100,000+/year

Educational Requirements

Some postsecondary training

Certification or Licensing

Recommended (certification)
Required by certain states (licensing)

Outlook

About as fast as the average

GOE
10.02.02
O*NET-SOC
NA*

*Not Available.
The O*NET-SOC does not categorize the career of hypnotherapist.

Winning his matches was a major problem for Albert, a high school wrestler. He had good skills. He did well in practice. But when it came to matches, he was blocked. He wasn't beating the opponents he should have. So Albert started seeing a hypnotherapist. After a few sessions, he started winning more matches. His confidence grew.

After that, Albert didn't need to see the hypnotherapist anymore. But he did call him once, toward the end of the season. "Tomorrow's the biggest match of the season," Albert said anxiously. "I think I'm pretty nervous." "Don't worry, Albert," the hypnotherapist told him reassuringly over the phone. "Let's just talk together for a few moments, and then we'll go over that self-hypnosis technique I taught you...."

what does a hypnotherapist do?

Hypnotherapists induce (bring about) a hypnotic state in others in order to increase motivation or change behavior. They may also train people in self-hypnosis techniques. Hypnotherapists don't "cast a spell," gain control of their clients' minds, or do anything else that's magical or strange. Instead, they use hypnosis to help people tap the power of their own minds so that they can help themselves.

Hypnosis has been proven to work in literally hundreds of different ways, from helping people to stop smoking to easing the pain of childbirth. While there's been a lot of research on it, including U.S. government research that goes back to World War II, exactly how hypnosis works is still being explored.

A hypnotic state is a sleep-like condition in which a person's brain waves have slowed and that person is much more relaxed than normal. The hypnotized subject is aware of and sensitive to the environment—he or she is not asleep. But when a subject's fully alert mind might break in and stop the acceptance of a suggestion—saying, for example, "No, I can't win that wrestling match!"—in the hypnotic state, suggestions seem to bypass these doubts. The brain appears to more readily accept the idea, whether it is "I am not afraid to fly," or, "I will experience less pain."

The hypnotized subject is always in control in the hypnotic state—he or she won't do or say anything that he or she wouldn't normally do or say. "It's a myth that you can get someone to do something against their morals or ethics," stresses Dr. Dwight Damon, president of the National Guild of Hypnotists (NGH). Founded in 1951, NGH is one of the oldest and largest organizations for hypnotherapists, with more than 6,000 members worldwide. "I could tell you, 'Go stand on your head in the corner,' and if you wouldn't do it normally if I suggested it, you wouldn't do it under hypnosis."

A typical session with a hypnotherapist takes place in his or her office and starts with a brief discussion. Clients tell the hypnotherapist what they want to accomplish—stop smoking, eat less, experience less pain, or whatever. They also may answer questions about their background and lifestyle. "Then we explain to the patient what hypnosis is—or really, what hypnosis is not, because people have a lot of misconceptions about it," says Dwight. "They think it's sleep, or that they're going to reveal some deep dark secret, or that someone's going to get control over their mind. But none of these is true."

Next, the hypnotherapist does conditioning or susceptibility tests—checking to see how open to suggestion the clients are and which hypnosis method or methods are likely to work best. There are many such methods. For example, the hypnotherapist could have one client look steadily at an object while the therapist speaks in a monotone. Sounds like ocean waves, a ticking clock, or an air conditioner may help another client relax and focus. "I might have you look at a spot on the wall and say to you, 'Your eyelids are getting heavy, drowsy, tired. . . . But do not close your eyes yet; look at the spot on the wall. . . . Your eyelids are getting heavy, drowsy, tired. . . . But do not close your eyes yet; look at the spot on the wall,'" Dwight says. Guided by these suggestions, clients become more and more relaxed, drifting into a hypnotic state.

Under hypnosis, the clients' attention is very concentrated on the hypnotherapist's voice. If he or she suggests something that is acceptable, such as, "you want to quit smoking," the client's mind will be highly responsive to the suggestion and accept it. "How long the process takes depends on what you're doing, but you usually don't need a lot of time," says Dwight. One of the phenomena of hypnosis is that subjects often think they've been "under" for a shorter time than they actually have, he says. "People may think they've been hypnotized for a few minutes, when actually it was 20."

Sometimes it takes a few sessions before hypnosis works—before the hypnotherapist is

lingo to learn

Hypnotherapist: A person trained to use hypnosis to help people.

Hypnotic state: A sleep-like condition in which your brain waves have slowed and you are much more relaxed than normal.

Induce: Bring about; cause to happen

Pastoral counselor: Minister, priest, rabbi; clergy.

Psychosomatic: A physical disorder that has its origins in an emotional disturbance.

Suggestibility: The degree to which you are open to suggestion.

able to help a client enter a hypnotic state. This is because the client is becoming conditioned in how to enter the state.

Hypnosis also is used in medical or clinical settings and even in emergency situations. "Many of our people are training EMTs [emergency room technicians] and paramedics in hypnosis," adds Dwight. These workers may use hypnosis to help people under their care slow down the flow of blood, control breathing, and reduce pain and anxiety through positive suggestions.

Many mental health professionals also use hypnosis in the course of treating patients. In the hypnotic state, people may be more open to remembering past events that have affected them traumatically. Once these events are remembered, a psychologist or other mental-health professional can help patients deal with them through therapy. In addition, hypnotherapy can help people replace negative thoughts with positive ones or deal with their fears (such as agoraphobia).

Hypnosis has been used in the treatment of depression, schizophrenia, sleep disorders, anorexia, panic, neuroses, attention deficit disorder, asthma, allergies, heart disease, headaches, arthritis, colon and bowel problems, dental procedures, and more. Experimental research is testing its use with cancer. Young children, for example, have been taught to picture good white blood cells eating cancer cells like Pac-Men.

what is it like to be a hypnotherapist?

Gary Elkins, Ph.D., ABPP, ABPH (American Board of Professional Psychologists, American Board of Psychological Hypnosis) is a health psychologist and associate professor of psychiatry and behavioral science at the Scott and White Clinic of Texas A&M University in Temple, Texas. Gary is that relative rarity—someone who practices clinical hypnosis within the medical establishment. He divides his time between teaching and clinical practice, handling all different types of cases. A person is not a clinical hypnotist, Gary emphasizes. "One uses clinical hypnosis. Just as a surgeon might use a scalpel, he or she might use clinical hypnosis as part of their practice."

At the Scott and White Clinic, Gary and his colleagues take a team approach to a patient problem—looking at psychology, physical therapy, anesthesiology, and other aspects of the patient's case all together. "We address the 'bio-psycho-social cycle of care,'" he says, which means the patient's body, mind, and environment.

All are important to treatment. "For example, with chronic pain, many factors may be involved," Gary explains. "That includes the patient's perceptions, attitudes, beliefs, [and] lifestyle" as well as the physical problem. Gary's work reflects the established medical community's growing interest in how the mind's power can be harnessed to help in healing. "For example," he says, "relaxation has been shown to reduce pain."

In a typical day, "I might begin by conducting a seminar for psychiatry or family practice residents," says Gary. The topic might be sleep disorders, medical hypnosis, or behavioral approaches to treating sexual disorders. Next come grand rounds, or case consultation. A physician presents a case and several other physicians, psychiatrists, and psychologists provide feedback and suggestions.

Next, Gary sees patients. He'll know beforehand what cases he'll see and will have talked them over with the physicians and others involved with the case prior to visiting the patient. His largest category of patient cases are probably those involving chronic pain, tension headaches, and migraines.

"With such patients," says Gary, "I might evaluate psychological factors for chronic pain, such as back pain," asking questions about the patient's lifestyle and background that might provide clues to what's contributing to the pain besides the physical reasons. "I might use clinical hypnosis and biofeedback for tension headaches or migraines," following basically the same sort of process that Dwight and other hypnotherapists use.

Other cases also allow Gary to apply hypnosis techniques. For example, says Gary, "I might use behavioral hypnosis for a patient with irritable bowels. See children with psychosomatic problems, such as abdominal pain from fear. Help patients stop smoking or lose weight. Reduce anxiety connected with surgery or other medical procedures. There's lots of needle phobia out there, for example. That can be difficult, especially with diabetics," many of whom must inject themselves daily with insulin.

Where Do You "Go" When You're Hypnotized?

To understand where you "go" when you're hypnotized, it's helpful to understand levels of brain activity. At the beta level, you're fully awake and active. At the alpha level, your brain waves slow. Your mind relaxes. The theta level is similar to the alpha level, except deeper—the brain waves are even slower; you're even more relaxed. At the delta level, you're in a state of deep and relaxed sleep (or you have a brain injury).

When you're hypnotized, you're at the alpha, or sometimes theta, level. (Suggestions don't work at the delta level.) How deep you go depends on the hypnotherapist's ability and on your willingness to "let go." The feeling of being in the alpha level is like that half-awake, half-asleep stage in the morning when you're first emerging from sleep. Hypnosis helps you get to this level.

Who Can Be Hypnotized?

It's believed that up to 90 percent of all people can be hypnotized. This includes children, as long as they're not too distractible. (In fact, children are usually highly hypnotizable, says Dwight Damon.) Generally, the more intelligent the person, the more likely and the faster he or she can be hypnotized. People with very, very low IQs tend not to be hypnotizable.

Other reasons why some people are not hypnotizable: They may be easily distracted. They may be afraid of revealing a dark secret. Or they may believe that allowing themselves to be hypnotized would show weakness or low intelligence. You can't know beforehand who will or will not be hypnotizable. Sometimes, it may take a few tries before hypnosis works. The person is becoming conditioned to the experience. Some research has shown that hypnotizability peaks between ages 14 and 30.

have I got what it takes to be a hypnotherapist?

A hypnotherapist should be patient, credible, and able to interact well with all different types of people. He or she also should have integrity. Hypnotherapists must be able to inspire trust and build rapport with others. You need to be able to reassure people who may feel nervous about disclosing information about themselves or being hypnotized.

Those who plan to use hypnosis as part of a clinical practice should be able to handle the rigors of a medical education. You should be capable of studying fairly complex subjects like psychology and be able to grasp basics about the workings of the mind and body.

A potential candidate "would be someone oriented to a people-helping type of career" such as teaching or counseling, says Dwight.

"If you're antisocial, this would not be a good job for you." It's also possible to do hypnosis as something ancillary to another career, he notes. For example, he says, "in the Chicago area, we have a licensed pastoral counselor who works in a hospital with patients with cancer—not to cure them but to help with the side effects of radiation," with pain and with anxiety. Others, as noted earlier, may also make use of hypnosis in their work.

how do I become a hypnotherapist?

"Forty years ago, the average person learned from a stage hypnotist or lay hypnotist," recalls Dwight Damon. Today, the simplest way to become a hypnotherapist is to earn a high school diploma or equivalent and then follow the training required by one of the many professional hypnotherapy associations. Those who wish to train in clinical hypnosis will have a more rigorous education path to follow.

Gary Elkins, for example, is highly credentialed and part of the ongoing professionalization of hypnosis within the traditional medical community. "Hypnosis has struggled for acceptance within the medical establishment," says Gary. "But I see that as progressively changing as more is understood." As evidence of this change he points to the publication of two major medical journals devoted to clinical hypnosis, the *American Journal of Clinical Hypnosis* and the *International Journal of Clinical and Experimental Hypnosis*.

education

High School

If you're planning to make hypnotherapy your career, take a general course of study in high school for a broad-based educational background. Your studies should include science classes, such as health and biology, as well as sociology and psychology. English classes will help you develop the important communication skills you will need in this line of work. Those who are considering using hypnosis as part of another career must do course work pertaining to their future field. In addition to the previously mentioned classes, future doctors, dentists, psychologists, and other medical professionals should take advanced courses in science and math, such as chemistry, algebra, geometry, and trigonometry.

Postsecondary Training

If you wish to work only as a hypnotherapist (not combining hypnotherapy with the practices of another profession) you do not need a four-year college degree. You will, however, need some postsecondary training. Many schools across the country offer training in hypnosis, but it will be a key factor in your future success to attend a respected and accredited program. Look for a school or program that has been accredited by a professional organization, such as the American Council of Hypnotist Examiners (ACHE) or the NGH, as well as approved by the state's department of education. Right now, some areas of the country have more state-approved schools than others. (Sparsely populated states like

North and South Dakota, for example, don't have as many choices in schools.) If you attend a program without these credentials, you will have difficulty getting certification or licensing later on. Course work tends to vary from school to school. NGH-certified instructors, however, teach a standard curriculum. Dwight Damon explains that this way the association knows its students are getting the same basic education no matter where they're located in the world. "The core curricula is a work in progress; we keep adding to it," says Dwight. It is built on what he describes as a "basic, classic approach to hypnosis," including study of and practice in hypnosis techniques, such as progressive relaxation, introduction to psychology, introduction to ethics, and practical information about running your own business. You are not taught how to be a psychologist or psychiatrist or counselor per se, Dwight emphasizes, but must be able to refer people to these professionals for serious problems.

If you want to use hypnosis with a medical, dental, psychological, social work, religious, or other profession, you will first need to earn your college and, in some cases, advanced degree in the particular field that interests you and then pursue training in hypnosis. Some medical and dental schools now offer courses in clinical hypnosis, although, again, this is still relatively rare. The major professional associations also provide certification in clinical hypnosis.

Healthy psychology—Gary Elkin's field—is a postdoctoral specialty within psychology that has been growing since the late 1970s. After earning a Ph.D., you may pursue further studies in health psychology through postdoctoral training such as a fellowship in behavioral medicine or health psychology.

certification or licensing

A number of associations offer certification, but the two best-known certifying groups are ACHE and NGH. ACHE offers three levels of certification: Certified Master Hypnotist, Certified Hypnotherapist, and Certified Clinical Hypnotherapist. To attain the Certified Master Hypnotist designation, you must have completed at least 150 hours of instruction from an approved school, pass a written exam, and hold a business license (if applicable). The other designations require the completion of more education. NGH also offers certification at several levels. The basic requirements are the completion of two semesters of approved hypnotherapy training as well as 15 hours of continuing education per year. Certification is highly recommended because it demonstrates both to your peers and your clients that you have received thorough training and are keeping up with developments in the field.

While most states do not license hypnotherapists, legislation for licensure is being considered in many states. You will need to check with your state's licensing board for specific requirements in your area. In addition, hypnotherapists who run their own businesses will need a business license.

who will hire me?

"I was a hypnotist and then a chiropractor," says Dwight Damon. He started learning about hypnosis at around age 14, mostly from books. "I didn't really know how to do it myself, though, until I was attending Emerson College in Boston and went to a free lecture-demonstration" in hypnosis given by a prominent psychiatrist at a large Boston Hospital. Dwight then signed up for a 10-week course given by this psychiatrist, who became his mentor, and started working with him part-time at the Hypnotism Center in Boston before enlisting in the service. "In the service, hypnotism was a very good skill to have," Dwight says. "I was able to entertain the other men and pull some good duty!"

After the service Dwight enrolled at the Palmer College of Chiropractic in Davenport, Iowa. He taught hypnosis to help pay his way. "I taught some of the teachers I had during the day in my hypnosis classes at night," he recalls.

To be a successful hypnotherapist, you should

- Be able to interact well with a variety of people
- Have an interest in helping others
- Be a patient individual
- Be able to inspire trust in others
- Have the ability to grasp the basics about the workings of the mind and body

Then, as a chiropractor, Dwight always used hypnosis as a tool in his practice. He did not accept patients just for hypnotherapy, however, because he did not have the time.

Gary Elkins says he got into clinical hypnosis "through a gradual procedure," starting back when he was an intern at an air force medical center. His interest in mind-body connections in health led him to pursue training in the health psychology specialty, and he was hired by the Scott and White Clinic out of school.

Most people who practice hypnotherapy are not hired by someone else—they set up and run their own business. After becoming certified as a hypnotherapist and getting a business license, they rent office space (or work out of their home) and start advertising for business. They may network with doctors, dentists, and psychologists to develop a client base. They may arrange to speak to community, religious, or professional groups to educate the public and attract clients. They also may advertise in local newspapers, distribute brochures, or mail letters to people in the community.

It also may be possible to rent space in a doctor's, dentist's, or psychologist's office suite and build a clientele on the physician's patients.

Those who will use hypnosis as part of another career will be hired by employers in that field. Clinics and hospitals like Gary's, that emphasize the body-mind-environment in patient treatment, are the most likely to make use of doctors with clinical hypnosis skills. The American Society of Clinical Hypnosis and the Society for Clinical and Experimental Hypnosis are two groups to contact for information about such hospitals and clinics. Scientific research in the field continues, with great interest in the potential use of hypnosis in treating biogenic diseases.

Teaching or association work are other possible paths for those interested in hypnosis and hypnotherapy. "I have a friend who teaches it to premed and pre-dental students," notes Dwight. Dwight himself now has a 12- to 15-hour-a-day, seven-day-a-week job as the president of NGH. "We're trying to become separate and distinct from other healing arts," ensuring that hypnotherapy can be practiced by more people than just licensed medical, dental, or psychological professionals. Besides editing the Guild's newsletter and magazine, Dwight travels around the country working with state legislators and medical groups, speaking to interested groups about hypnosis, and meeting with fellow hypnotherapists.

Associations are the best sources of information about potential employers. The Academy of Scientific Hypnotherapy, for example, has both placement and referral services, as does NGH and other association groups.

where can I go from here?

Hypnotherapists with their own business can build on their knowledge and skills. Research in the field continues, and hypnotherapists need to make sure they know all the latest techniques. They can learn about and become certified in more counseling or healing arts practices. And they can market their services more aggressively. All of these things can help bring in more business.

Those in the medical or other fields also need to keep their skills up to date. They can study hypnosis techniques at the doctorate or postdoctorate level and potentially earn more money because of their expertise in a specialty. The Association of Master Hypnotists, founded in 1995, and some other associations now award advanced credentials and recognition to exceptional hypnotherapists. This includes awards for outstanding contributions to the field.

what are the salary ranges?

Salaries for people who do hypnosis for a living vary so widely that it is difficult to give a range. A hypnotherapist in a large urban area may charge from $50 an hour to $150 an hour, depending on his or her experience and ability. Annual salaries vary widely, particularly since many people do hypnotherapy as a part-time work, while others combine it with another job. According to the Hypnotherapy Academy of America, an ACHE-approved school, a certified hypnotherapist can earn $45,000 or more per year. Average salaries for medical professionals like doctors or dentists are well over $100,000 per year.

what is the job outlook?

As Gary Elkins noted, there is growing acceptance of hypnotherapy by the conventional

The British Medical Association accepted hypnosis as a valid treatment in 1956. The American Medical Association followed suit in 1958. Among those today who may use hypnosis in their work are pastoral counselors (ministers, priests, rabbis), social workers, police officers, private investigators, and motivational experts.

medical establishment. Gary also sees much greater acceptance from the public within the past 15 years. "Across the country, people are more health conscious," he says. "There's been a growing trend toward people becoming more actively involved in their own health." This involvement is a key aspect of behavioral medicine, and it is an important trend in the acceptance by the public of hypnosis techniques.

According to the government's *Occupational Outlook Quarterly* (*OOQ*), the best opportunities in hypnotherapy are for those who add hypnosis skills to other medical or therapeutic skills, such as dentistry or psychology. People trained only in hypnotherapy generally have a more difficult path. Working for themselves, they need to advertise their services and develop a client base. It can take time to build up a business to the point where it can support its owner. Competition also may be tough, especially in California. (The *OOQ* says about 4,000 hypnotherapists advertise in the yellow pages in the United States, about half of these in California.) The *OOQ* states that hypnotherapists with limited training often drop out of the field. In addition, legislation by the states will have an impact on the extent to which hypnotherapy can be practiced and who can practice it.

how do I learn more?

One way to learn more is to experience hypnosis yourself. Look in the yellow pages for an accredited hypnotist or hypnotherapist and make an appointment for a session. (This may not be possible in some smaller towns or rural areas, however, because none may work there.) You also can contact some of the many professional organizations for hypnotherapy and/or clinical hypnosis and ask for referral information. Some organizations even post listings of accredited members on their Web sites.

professional organizations

For information on certification and approved programs, contact:

American Council of Hypnotist Examiners
700 South Central Avenue
Glendale, CA 91204
818-242-1159
http://www.sonic.net/hypno/ache.html

For information about certification and training as well as information on states' legal requirements for practitioners, contact:

National Guild of Hypnotists
PO Box 308
Merrimack, NH 03054-0308
603-429-9438
http://www.ngh.net

Other associations to contact:

American Association of Professional Hypnotherapists
AAPH Headquarters
4149-A El Camino Way
Palo Alto, CA 94306
650-323-3224
http://www.aaph.org

Related Jobs

The U.S. Department of Labor classifies hypnotherapists under the heading *Therapy and Rehabilitation* (GOE). Also in this category are people who do magnetic resonance imaging technology procedures, physical therapists, acupuncturists, dialysis technicians, musical therapists, athletic trainers, physical education instructors, dental hygienists, occupational therapists, nuclear medicine technologists, and others.

American Society of Clinical Hypnosis
130 East Elm Court, Suite 201
Roselle, IL 60172-2000
630-980-4740
info@asch.net
http://www.asch.net

Society for Clinical and Experimental Hypnosis
Central Office
Washington State University
PO Box 642114
Pullman, WA 99164-2114
509-332-7555
sceh@pullman.com
http://sunsite.utk.edu/IJCEH/scehframe.htm

bibliography

Following is a sampling of materials relating to the professional concerns and development of hypnotherapists.

Barber, Joseph, ed. *Hypnosis and Suggestion in the Treatment of Pain: A Clinical Guide*. New York, NY: W. W. Norton & Company, 1996.

Gafner, George and Sonja Benson. *Handbook of Hypnotic Inductions*. New York, NY: W. W. Norton & Company, 2000.

Hogan, Kevin L. *Hypnotherapy Handbook: Hypnosis and Mindbody Healing in the 21st Century*. Eagan, MN: Network 3000 Publishing, 1999.

James, Tad et al. *Hypnosis: A Comprehensive Guide*. Alpine, TX: LPC Publishing, 2000.

Olness, Karen and Daniel P. Kohen. *Hypnosis and Hypnotherapy with Children*. 3rd Edition. New York, NY: Guilford Press, 1996.

Overdurf, John et al. *Training Trances: Multi-Level Communication in Therapy and Training*. 3rd Edition. Portland, OR: Metamorphous Press, 1995.

Temes, Roberta, et al. eds. *Medical Hypnosis: An Introduction and Clinical Guide*. London, UK: Churchill Livingstone, 1999.

Udolf, Roy. *Handbook of Hypnosis for Professionals*. 2nd Edition. Northvale, NJ: Jason Aronson, Inc., 1995.

Zimmerman, Katherine. *Hypnotherapy Scripts*. Vol. II. Sacramento, CA: Trance Time Publishing, 1996.

Kinesiologists

Definition

Kinesiologists are health care workers who plan and/or conduct therapeutic exercise programs designed to help individuals, many with disabilities, develop or maintain endurance, strength, mobility, and coordination. Kinesiologists also work with patients who are recovering from injuries or illnesses and need help keeping their muscle tone during long periods of inactivity.

Alternative Job Title

Kinesiotherapists

High School Subjects

Biology
Physical education
Psychology

Personal Skills

Communication/ideas
Helping/teaching

Salary Range

$20,000 to $28,000 to $54,000

Educational Requirements

Bachelor's degree

Certification or Licensing

Recommended

Outlook

About as fast as the average

GOE
NA*
O*NET-SOC
NA*

*Not Available. The U.S. Department of Labor does not categorize the career of kinesiologist.

"**I chose to** focus my studies in kinesiology on the prevention and care of injuries as an athletic trainer," says Jennifer Hurst, lecturer in kinesiology at the University of Illinois at Chicago. She enjoyed athletic training, but something seemed to be missing for her in that particular area of kinesiology. "Sometimes the root of an athlete's problem is not physical, but a manifestation of stress or something psychological. No, a trainer is not a psychologist, but he or she does need to be able to recognize warning signs and problems so they can be referred to qualified personnel." Her subsequent training and research in sport psychology has armed her with a firmer understanding of what it takes to treat the whole person and not just the symptoms.

This holistic approach is an important, albeit tricky, aspect of kinesiology, which essentially is the study of muscles and anatomy with the purpose of better understanding the mechanics of human movement. Kinesiologists use muscle testing and physical therapy to evaluate and improve the state of various bodily functions in their patients, taking into account all body systems when treating a patient. With the aim being to treat the whole person and not to simply correct a physical problem, kinesiologists allow patients to work through a disability or disorder.

what does a kinesiologist do?

"Kinesiology is a very broad field that encompasses a variety of professions and activities," says Jennifer. "If I were to give a general definition of a *kinesiologist,* it would be an individual who is knowledgeable in the study, practice, and instruction of movement and its effect on the physical, social, and spiritual well-being of various populations. This is a very broad definition and incorporates several areas of study [physical education, athletic training, fitness

lingo to learn

Anatomy: The science of the structural composition of the body and its organs.

Biomechanics: The study of the mechanical principles by which the musculoskeletal system functions and moves.

Exercise physiology: The study of the functions and responses of the human body during (or deprived of) exercise as well as how exercise affects the human body.

Holistic: Relating to the treatment of the whole person, both mind and body, rather than individual parts.

Pedagogy: The science or profession of teaching.

Sport psychology: The study of how psychological issues affect a person's participation in exercise and sport as well as how a person's participation in exercise and sport affects that individual's psychological makeup.

and wellness, exercise physiology] that deal with many different populations of people [athletes, children, persons with disabilities, the general population]. Yet one thing ties all of these professions together, and that is the use of movement to achieve a certain end."

She acknowledges, "It is confusing. Kinesiologists are really identified more by their specializations than the general field of kinesiology. Yes, I could be called a kinesiologist, but it is a bit misleading because there are areas of kinesiology that I am not as familiar with. There really are very few, if any, people that refer to themselves as kinesiologists. Professionals are mainly referred to by their area of specialization.

"I'm a faculty member in the Department of Kinesiology [University of Maryland], which is the name by which most departments like mine prefer to be known," says exercise physiologist Marc Rogers. "In the old days our departments were called health and physical education, sometimes now called exercise and sports sciences, or health sciences. I'm an exercise physiologist by training and refer to myself as such. Very few folks call themselves kinesiologists. The discipline of kinesiology has many subdisciplines: exercise physiology, sports psychology, motor development, sports history and sociology, pedagogy or the science of teaching, biomechanics, sports management, motor behavior, athletic training, etc."

What this boils down to is that there are many diverse career opportunities open to those who study kinesiology. Some become physical education or dance teachers, coaches of sports teams, health and fitness consultants, athletic or personal trainers, or researchers in such areas as biomechanics, exercise physiology, or sports psychology. For the purposes of this article, the broader interchangeable terms kinesiologist or kinesiotherapist will be used except for those cases when information deals specifically with a particular specialty.

Working as members of medical teams, kinesiologists treat and educate a wide range of people, both individually and in groups. Their clients may be disabled children or adults, geriatric or psychiatric patients, the people with developmental disabilities, or amputees. Some may have had heart attacks, strokes, or spinal injuries. Others may be affected by such conditions as arthritis, impaired circulation, or cerebral palsy. Kinesiologists also work with people who were involved in automobile accidents, have congenital birth defects, or have sustained sports injuries.

First, physicians describe the kind of exercise their patients should have, and then the kinesiologists develop programs to meet the specific needs of the patients. Kinesiologists do this by assessing a client's physical ability and aptitude in such areas as muscular strength, functional mobility, flexibility, and cardiovascular fitness. Additionally, kinesiologists consider a client's psychosocial characteristics including appropriateness of behavior, task-planning capability, patient-family interaction, and motivation. Kinesiologists then teach clients whatever exercises or activities have been drawn up as part of the client's individual treatment plan.

The work is often physically demanding. Working with such equipment as weights, pulleys, bikes, and rowing machines, kinesiologists demonstrate exercises so their patients can learn to do them properly. Kinesiologists also may teach members of their patients' families so they are able to help the patients exercise. They may work with their patients in swimming pools, whirlpools, saunas, or other therapeutic settings. When patients are very weak or have limited mobility, kinesiologists may help them exercise by lifting them or moving their limbs.

Other responsibilities may include teaching patients to use artificial limbs or walk with canes, crutches, or braces. Kinesiologists may help visually impaired people learn how to move around without help or teach patients who cannot walk how to drive cars with hand controls. For mentally ill people, kinesiologists may develop therapeutic activities that help them release tension or teach them how to cooperate with others.

These professionals work to help their clients be more self-reliant, enjoy leisure activities, and even adapt to new ways of living, working, and thriving. Although kinesiologists work with their patients physically, giving them constant encouragement and emotional support is also an important part of their job.

Based on their findings, kinesiologists write reports on patients' progress, describing the treatments and their results. These reports provide necessary information for researchers or other members of the medical team, which may include nurses, psychologists, psychiatrists, social workers, massage therapists, physical therapists, acupuncturists, and vocational counselors. In certain cases, kinesiologists may refer a patient to another specialist for additional treatment.

The best part of my job is the fact that each day I have the opportunity to help someone to learn something and discover his or her own potential.

Kinesiologists do not do the same work as physical therapists, orthotists, or prosthetists. Physical therapists test and measure the functions of the musculoskeletal, neurological, pulmonary, and cardiovascular systems and treat the problems that occur in these systems. Orthotists are concerned with supporting and bracing weak or ineffective joints and muscles, and prosthetists are concerned with replacing missing body parts with artificial devices. Kinesiologists focus instead on the interconnection of all these systems.

what is it like to be a kinesiologist?

"Even within the field of athletic training there is a variety of jobs that one can pursue," reports Jennifer Hurst. "Only a small number of athletic trainers work with elite and professional sports. The traditional athletic trainer works in either a high school, college, or university setting caring for student athletes or in a clinic setting working with both athletes and other rehabilitation populations. There are also athletic trainers who work with both injured and healthy populations in industrial wellness and fitness centers and as independently contracted providers of athletic training services. I used to practice as a traditional athletic trainer in both a high school and a college, but now I bring that practical experience to a university classroom. I teach the next generation of athletic trainers the knowledge and skills that they will need to be successful within the profession."

Regarding her role as a lecturer in kinesiology, Jennifer describes her main responsibilities: "My primary duties are to teach my classes and to help the students learn the material. I do this not only with what I do in the classroom, but also with extra study sessions and observing the students while they work with the athletic teams. My secondary duties include serving on committees, attending faculty meetings, doing research, and providing service outside the university." In a typical week she will prepare and teach six to eight class sessions. Additionally, she spends time working on current research projects and presentations as well as attending professional meetings.

Marc Rogers explains his duties as an instructor: "I teach graduate courses in muscle physiology, metabolism, and laboratory research techniques in exercise physiology, and do research in exercise and aging, specifically the effects of aging on skeletal muscle." Plus he advises graduate students on research projects and courses for their programs, writes grants for research, serves on departmental and college committees, and reviews manuscripts and books for publication.

"As a traditional trainer," Jennifer says, "I would be responsible for covering practices and competitions. Preparing the athletes for practices and competitions, administering first aid to those that got hurt, and supervising rehabilitation programs were some of the things I would do on a daily basis. I would also maintain the training room, inventory supplies, assist with equipment issues, monitor playing conditions and environment, and educate athletes when necessary on a variety of issues."

In this capacity, Jennifer would frequently work 60 to 70 hours per week, which she says is typical for a traditional trainer. As an instructor, she now works a mere 50 hours per week, "but it is with a variety of activities that all center around my academic field and teaching."

Marc works long hours, too, often getting to the office around 8:30 AM and staying as late as 7:30 PM. Some of his activities at the office include handling email and phone correspondence, preparing upcoming course lectures, reading articles in professional scientific journals, meeting with students, and grading lab reports or papers for class. And this is all before lunch! After lunch he edits and revises manuscripts, helps students rewrite theses or dissertation drafts, conducts business for a university committee on human subjects, and reviews slides for a graduate lecture course. Practicing what he preaches, Marc manages to fit in 60 to 90 minutes of exercise late in the day. Then he returns to the office and works another hour or so writing or reading assignments for the next day's class.

What Marc likes about his profession is having a "flexible schedule, time off in the summer if you want it, respect of one's peers, freedom to do the kind of research that one wants, ability to interact and train students." But the positives don't come without a price. He reports some of the cons as being low pay, the lack of income during the summer, the stress associated with publishing and getting grant money, and too little time for much of a social life. In fact, getting grants and "trying to get everything done on time" are most difficult.

Jennifer says, "The best part of my job is the fact that each day I have the opportunity to help someone to learn something and discover his or her own potential. Ironically, this is also the hardest part of my job, because as a teacher, you come to realize that you will not be able to do this for all of your students. That is the hardest thing for me to accept about my job, but it is those times when I can see someone's face light up with understanding that keeps me going."

Kinesiologists who work in hospitals and clinics usually work a typical 40-hour workweek, with hours somewhere between 8 AM and 6 PM, Monday through Friday. Some may work evenings and weekends instead in order to accommodate their clients' schedules. Because of the long-range, rehabilitative nature of the work, most kinesiologists work a set schedule and generally don't have to be available for emergency situations.

The number of patients the kinesiologist works with usually depends on the size and function of the facility. When leading a rehabilitation group, the kinesiologist may work with three to five patients at a time, helping them work on their own and as part of a team. They may see their patients in hospitals and other health centers, or they may visit patients in their own homes or arrange for rehabilitative outings. Their clients may be confined to beds, chairs, or wheelchairs. Exercises are often performed in pools or on ramps, stairways, or exercise tables.

have I got what it takes to be a kinesiologist?

Kinesiologists must have maturity and objectivity and should be able to work well with patients and other staff members. You must have excellent oral and written communication

History Lesson

Kinesiology studies how the principles of mechanics and anatomy affect human movement. *Kinesio* is derived from the Greek word *kinesis,* meaning motion. Kinesiology literally means the study of motion, or motion therapy. Kinesiology is based on the idea that physical education is a science.

Scientists throughout the centuries have studied how the body works: how muscles are connected, how bones grow, and how blood flows. Kinesiology builds on all that knowledge. The practice of kinesiology (or corrective therapy, as it was known originally) developed during World War II, when physicians in military hospitals saw that appropriate exercise could help wounded patients heal faster and with better results than they'd had before. This exercise therapy proved particularly useful for injuries to the arms and legs.

By 1946 Veterans Administration hospitals were using prescribed exercise programs in rehabilitation treatment. Before long, other hospitals and clinics recognized the benefits of kinesiology and instituted similar programs. Within a few years the new therapy was an important part of many treatment programs, including programs for chronically disabled patients.

In the 1950s a number of studies indicated that European children were more physically fit than American children were. To decrease the gap in fitness levels, the U.S. government instituted physical fitness programs in schools. This practical application of kinesiology to otherwise healthy children boosted the field dramatically. In 1987 the term *corrective therapy* was changed to kinesiotherapy, also known as kinesiology.

Today, the study of physical fitness and the movement of the body is illustrated in countless fields. Although kinesiologists have historically worked with injured or disabled patients, as humans move toward a more computerized, less active lifestyle, kinesiologists and other health care professionals will be in demand to help people of all abilities maintain good health and fitness.

---

skills so you can explain the exercises in such a way that patients can understand your instructions and perform the exercises properly. Communication skills also help you write accurate, understandable reports for colleagues.

Furthermore, kinesiologists need stamina to demonstrate the exercises and help patients with them. An ample supply of patience is also essential since many exercise programs are repetitive and carried out over long periods. A good sense of humor helps to keep up patient morale. You also must know how to plan and implement your programs, and you must stay current on new developments in the field. Certification usually requires continuing education courses.

Jennifer, in describing personal qualities that make her good at her job, says, "First and foremost, I like to work with people and have the patience to do it." She credits her "curiosity and excitement for human anatomy and physiology and how it relates to sports and injury" with being assets in her career. "Yet, I think what helped me the most in finding my niche within the athletic training field was spending the time to explore all the possibilities and then deciding what my particular talents lent me toward and where I found the most enjoyment," she continues. "Though I liked and could work with athletes, watch practices, travel with teams, and do rehabilitation programs, it was not what excited me the most or what I did the best. It was only with time and a little trial and error that I realized that it was in the teaching of athletic training that I really did well and enjoyed myself the most."

Marc thinks that those who are successful in his field have these characteristics: "calmness, sense of humor, basic level of intelligence, ability to work as a member of a team and to get along well with others, not taking oneself too seriously, working until the job is done." In his opinion, "Someone who wants a 9 to 5, someone who values money above all else" would not be suited for a career in this field.

"The potential in this field," Jennifer says of athletic training, "is very good for those willing to work and put in the effort. Athletic trainers do not make big money and it tends to be a rather thankless job. Trainers are people who love and appreciate sports, want to make a difference, and like to help people—that is why we do what we do."

how do I become a kinesiologist?

If you are thinking about pursuing a career in kinesiology, you should check out the resources offered by professional organizations in your area of interest. Both Jennifer and Marc agree that membership in professional organizations is important to their jobs. Jennifer explains, "The athletic training organizations are a vital network of people who exchange ideas, provide support, and work to uphold and develop the standards by which all trainers work. It is our professional organizations on the national, district, and state levels that work to pass legislation, develop educational opportunities, and raise and organize resources to carry on the activities to develop the profession."

education

High School
If kinesiology interests you, you should take a strong college preparatory course load. Classes

To be a successful kinesiologist, you should

- Enjoy working with people
- Have good written and oral communication skills
- Be patient
- Be physically fit
- Have stamina

in anatomy, chemistry, biology, mathematics, and physics will give you the basic science background you will need to study kinesiology in college. Health, psychology, and social science will also be very helpful. Be sure to take physical education classes in order to gain a better appreciation for the nature of movement and muscles. Marc lists chemistry, biology, anatomy and physiology, health science, and cell biology as being the high school courses that best prepared him for his job.

Jennifer's experience was a little different: "There were no particular classes I had in high school that helped me to prepare for my job. What did help, however, was learning how to study effectively while I was in high school, so it was not so difficult to make the transition to college level work."

You can get experience in several ways. Basic physical education courses as well as team sports, like volleyball or track, will help you gain an appreciation for the possibilities and limitations of the body, enabling you to learn about kinesiology from an inside perspective. Plan and carry out exercise programs or instruct others in proper exercise techniques. Exercise classes are offered at community centers and by organizations such as the YMCA and YWCA.

Marc suggests that you might want to "join a science club in high school, volunteer to help out in a research project in a local college or university, do projects in the science fair at school, or try to find a summer job in a research lab at a hospital or medical school."

Jennifer's ideas are mainly geared toward students wanting to become an athletic trainer. "If your school has an athletic trainer, see if you can spend some time observing him or her. If there is any opportunity to work with that person, do it. There are summer camps that are held at some universities, designed for high school students to explore the field of athletic training and get a taste for it; try to find one of these. Look on the National Athletic Trainers' Association (NATA) Web site at http://www. nata.org to get more information about the profession and different programs."

Postsecondary Training
In order to become a registered kinesiotherapist, you will need to earn a bachelor's degree from a four-year program at an accredited school. Some kinesiologists major in physical education and have kinesiology as a specialty, but a growing number of institutions in the United States are starting to offer undergraduate degrees in kinesiology. Master's degrees in

kinesiology and related programs are offered at more than 100 institutions; you can find doctoral programs at some 55 universities. Kinesiology programs include classes in education, clinical practice, biological sciences, and behavioral sciences. Specific courses may have titles such as Recognition and Evaluation of Athletic Injuries, Biological Factors Influencing Exercise Performance, Statistical Evaluation in Kinesiology, Quantitative Procedures in Exercise and Sport Sciences, Biomechanics, Measurement of Motor Behavior, Exercise Physiology, and Exercise and Health Psychology.

"If you really know you want to pursue athletic training, then find an accredited program and go there," advises Jennifer. "Be prepared to work hard and to take a lot of classes that are grounded in anatomy, exercise physiology, and kinesiology."

Reflecting back on her schooling, Jennifer comments, "I really enjoyed all of my athletic training classes and I really enjoyed my anatomy and physiology classes. The professor that taught the anatomy and physiology classes was wonderful. In fact, when I think of why I became a teacher, she was part of the reason. I also enjoyed my sport psychology class in my graduate training. That class helped me to redirect the focus of my career and better understand a component of my profession that is severely lacking. I always felt that something was missing when I would treat the athletes I would work with, and I realized I was ignoring the whole athlete and focusing on the hurt part. The focus of my research these days is surrounded around the psychology of sports injuries."

Exercise physiology was one of Marc's favorite postsecondary courses. "I was always active and in sports, and I enjoyed learning about the mechanisms of how the body works." Nutrition was another because, he explains, "I began to understand that diet and exercise played a big role in determining one's health status both now and in the future. Quality of life was important to me as was quantity of life."

You should enjoy learning and being in school because you may wind up spending quite a few years completing your education, as did Marc. "I would say I spent four years in undergrad school, three years on a master's, five years on a Ph.D., and three years in a postdoc. I was 30 years old before I made more than 10 grand a year." (Keep in mind that this was probably a decade or so ago.) He continues, "It is a competitive life and not that con-

ducive to having a young family. Do it because you love the discipline, not for the money."

The American Kinesiotherapy Association sponsors continuing education programs for registered kinesiotherapists.

certification or licensing

Although certification is not mandatory for every job, it is highly recommended, given that certification requirements are starting to become more regulated. The certification requirements and process may vary depending on your specialty and where you practice. To become a registered kinesiotherapist requires a bachelor's degree in specified courses accredited by the Commission on Accreditation of Allied Health Education Programs (CAAHEP), 1,000 hours of clinical practice under the supervision of a registered kinesiotherapist, and successful completion of the registration examination administered by the Council on Professional Standards for Kinesiotherapy. Graduates from schools having CAAHEP Approved Integrated Curriculum in Kinesiotherapy need take only the written part of the examination, whereas other applicants must take both the written and the oral/practical parts.

After meeting the basic requirements and passing the examination, candidates become nationally certified kinesiologists. If you have earned undergraduate degrees in physical education, you also may become state-certified physical education teachers after meeting the certification requirements for the state in which you plan to work.

The American College of Sports Medicine offers certifications for health and fitness instructors and directors and also for exercise leaders. Athletic trainers are certified by NATA's Board of Certification. According to Jennifer, who is both nationally certified and state licensed, "National certification consists of satisfying the programmatic and competency requirements through an accredited program to be eligible to sit for the certification test. The test is a three-part test that is designed to evaluate your knowledge base and clinical skills."

Marc is not certified but thinks that mandatory certification is a great idea, saying that "the profession will benefit if we ever get to the stage and have licensure . . . just like M.D.s, nurses, P.T.s, etc."

internships and volunteerships

Opportunities for volunteer, part-time, or summer work may be available at facilities that have kinesiology or kinesiotherapy programs, such as hospitals, clinics, nursing homes, and summer camps for disabled children. Health and exercise clubs also may offer summer work or part-time jobs. In addition, you may be able to visit kinesiology departments at health care centers to talk with staff members and see how they work.

who will hire me?

Kinesiologists work in many types of organizations and settings. They work for the government in the Department of Veterans Affairs, public and private hospitals, sports medicine facilities, health and fitness clubs, chiropractic clinics, and rehabilitation facilities. Learning disability centers, elementary and high schools, colleges and universities, and health clubs also employ kinesiologists. Other kinesiologists work in private practice or as exercise consultants. Kinesiologists can also find employment with sports teams, or they may write for or edit sports, rehabilitative, and other medical journals. Many kinesiologists also teach in the field or do research.

Most colleges and universities offer job placement assistance for their alumni, so that's a good place to get further guidance. Many kinesiologists find employment by networking with other professionals in the field. Some professional organizations and associations—for example, the American College of Sports Medicine, the NATA, and the National Collegiate Athletic Association (NCAA)—maintain listings of positions open in various locations. Sometimes these listings are available to members only.

Beginning kinesiologists may gain paid employment with a facility if they start out doing volunteer work. Some organizations prefer to hire therapists with some work experience, and volunteer work gives the new kinesiologist a great opportunity to learn more about the field and a particular organization.

where can I go from here?

Kinesiologists often start as staff therapists at hospitals, clinics, or other health care facilities. After several years, they may become supervisors or department heads. Some move on to do consultant work for health care facilities. Some kinesiologists use their practical experience to do more research in the field, or they may teach at a kinesiology program. They may write for field newsletters or journals, reporting on their progress in rehabilitating a particular patient or in treating a specific disability.

Marc got his start as a college professor at Michigan State University. He says, "I began to really get interested in exercise physiology/kinesiology when I became a competitive distance runner back in the early 1980s. The physiological and nutritional knowledge that I gained was very helpful in assisting me in reaching my athletic goals. From there I became interested in exercise and aging and the role that physical activity plays in successful aging."

Jennifer remembers her first job working for a hospital as what is called an outreach trainer. "I worked for the hospital but was contracted out to various high schools that wanted athletic training coverage. I would cover competitions and some practices depending on the contract the school had with the hospital."

Jennifer advises, "Some job openings are posted in newspapers. A lot are by word of mouth, so it is important to get exposure and meet people through professional meetings and volunteer work. I have found in this field that people like to hire people that they know somehow, either personally or through someone else's recommendation. Most jobs are also posted on the NATA Web site or the NCAA Web site."

With advanced training, experienced kinesiologists may go on to more senior positions at health care centers, clinics, colleges, and related facilities. These positions might include going from assistant to head athletic trainer, directing a research lab, or becoming a full professor with tenure, chairperson of a kinesiology department, or dean of a college of kinesiology. Jennifer notes, "The profession is getting to the point where a master's degree is becoming more desirable. In the academic arena, a Ph.D. is very helpful for advancement."

About his goals, Marc says, "I'd like to be promoted to full professor in the next three to four years and get another NIH [National Institutes of Health] grant for my muscle research."

what are the salary ranges?

The American Kinesiotherapy Association reports the average projected starting salary for registered kinesiotherapists is $28,000 per year. This, of course, depends on the experience of the kinesiotherapist and the location of the job. Since kinesiology is a relatively new field, few reliable salary sources exist, but salaries are probably comparable to related health professions.

According to the *Occupational Outlook Handbook,* the median salary for occupational therapy assistants was about $28,690 in 1998. The median for physical therapist assistants was about $21,870 per year in 1998. Those working in hospitals tended to earn less than those in private practice. Physical therapists earned approximately $56,600. Kinesiologists' salaries are likely to be somewhere in those ranges.

NATA publishes a salary survey broken down into numerous categories (e.g., district, sex, NATA membership type and length of membership, age, education, employment settings, employment status). Data covers both part-time and full-time workers. The 1998 survey range begins at under $20,000 annually (likely the result of the inclusion of part-time respondents) and goes up to more than $50,000. The estimated average for someone having a bachelor's degree is $31,588, a master's is $36,448, and a doctorate is $54,183.

Depending on their employers, most kinesiologists enjoy a full complement of benefits, including vacation and sick time as well as holidays and medical and dental insurance. Kinesiologists who work in a health care facility usually get free use of the equipment.

what is the job outlook?

The employment outlook for kinesiologists is expected to grow about as fast as the average for the next few years. The demand for their services may grow somewhat because of the increasing emphasis on services for disabled people and patients with specific disorders, as

FYI

Select Areas of Specialization in Kinesiology

Athletic Training

Biomechanics

Exercise Physiology

Fitness and Wellness

Motor Behavior

Motor Development

Physical Education

Sport History and Sociology

Sport Injury Management

Sport Pedagogy

Sport Psychology

well as the growing number of older adults. Plus, kinesiology has the potential to grow as a profession as more is learned about the field and also as the importance of physical activity in our society increases.

On the other hand, until more individuals in our society not only recognize the importance of physical activity but also embrace and regularly put into practice a more physically active lifestyle, the employment outlook could show little change.

As health care costs rise, the importance of outpatient care is expected to increase as well. Many insurance companies prefer to pay for home health care or outpatient care instead of lengthy, expensive—and often unnecessary—hospital stays. Part-time workers in the field will also see increased opportunities.

Jennifer thinks that the field of athletic training is growing. "I see trainers continuing to fill their traditional roles in schools and clinics but also branch out into some other areas. Independent contracting will start to grow as more park districts and private sport groups will need professional coverage for events. Those individuals with some business know-how and background will be able to capitalize on this growing area. The need for more Ph.D.s is evident as the education of trainers is becoming more stringent. The field will need more women as they will start to fill roles in female sports' coming of age."

Marc's take is that the field will remain steady but that "people with expertise and interest in genetics and cell biology will be in demand in our field in the future."

how do I learn more?

professional organizations

Following are organizations that provide information on kinesiology careers.

American Academy of Kinesiology and Physical Education
c/o Human Kinetics
PO Box 5076
Champaign, IL 61820-2200
humank@hkusa.com
http://www.aakpe.org/

American Kinesiotherapy Association
One IBM Plaza, Suite 2500
Chicago, IL 60611
http://www.akta.org/

American Physiological Society
9650 Rockville Pike
Bethesda, MD 20814-3991
http://www.the-aps.org/

American Society of Biomechanics
Mechanical Engineering Department
Stanford University
Stanford, CA 94305-3030
http://asb-biomech.org/

Association for the Advancement of Applied Sport Psychology
Centennial Conferences
4800 Baseline Road, Suite A112
Boulder, CO 80303
http://www.aaasponline.org/

Commission on Accreditation of Allied Health Education Programs
35 East Wacker Drive, Suite 1970
Chicago, IL 60601-2208
caahep@caahep.org
http://www.caahep.org/

This organization, dedicated to health and fitness, has information on kinesiology and related fields.

American Alliance for Health, Physical Education, Recreation and Dance
1900 Association Drive
Reston, VA 20191-1598
703-476-3400 or 800-213-7193
aahperd@aahperd.org
http://www.aahperd.org/

For members only, NATA's placement listing service features employment opportunities for athletic trainers.

National Athletic Trainers' Association (NATA)
2952 Stemmons Freeway
Dallas, TX 75247-6916
214-637-6282 or 800-879-6282
http://www.nata.org/

This University of Illinois at Urbana-Champaign Web site provides links to many kinesiology-related resources.

The Kinesiology Forum
http://www.kines.uiuc.edu/kinesforum/

For employment opportunities, visit the NCAA Web site.

NCAA
http://www.ncaa.org

bibliography

Greene, David P., and Susan L. Roberts. *Kinesiology: Movement in the Context of Activity.* Chicago, IL: Year Book Medical Publishers, 1999.

Hoffman, Shirl J. and Janet C. Harris, eds. *Introduction to Kinesiology: Studying Physical Activity.* Champaign, IL: Human Kinetics Publishing, 2000.

Lippert, Lynn S. *Clinical Kinesiology for Physical Therapist Assistants.* Philadelphia, PA: F. A. Davis Company, 2000.

Mow, Van C. and Wilson C. Hayes, eds. *Basic Orthopaedic Biomechanics.* Philadelphia, PA: Lippincott Williams and Wilkins, 1997.

Smith, Laura K., Elizabeth Lawrence Weiss, and L. Don Lehmkuhl. *Brunnstrom's Clinical Kinesiology.* Philadelphia, PA: F. A. Davis Company, 1996.

Licensed Practical Nurses

Definition

Licensed practical nurses administer direct patient care under the supervision of physicians or registered nurses in hospitals, clinics, private homes, schools, and other similar settings.

Alternative Job Titles

Home health nurses
Vocational nurses

High School Subjects

Biology
Chemistry
Health

Personal Skills

Following instructions
Helping/teaching

Salary Range

$20,000 to $26,000 to $37,000

Minimum Educational Level

Some postsecondary training

Certification or Licensing

Required by all states

Outlook

About as fast as the average

GOE
10.02.01

O*NET-SOC
29-2061.00

Part of Debra McFadden's day as a

licensed practical nurse (LPN) at a correctional facility may involve working the doctor's line, which means she sees patients who have requested to see the nurse because of illness. "It's like doing a kind of triage," she says. "We go in and assess them for these various ailments. If we want, we can have them go see the doctor. 'Doctor's line' is getting these people prepared to see the doctor, something like how an office nurse does."

Debra finds the work to be fast-paced and very educational. "You really do learn about the vast majority of illnesses," she says. "I never knew of all the different medications. It really is quite interesting."

what does a licensed practical nurse do?

Licensed practical nurses are trained to provide quality, cost-effective nursing care wherever patient care is needed. Work sites include hospitals, nursing homes and long-term care facilities, rehabilitation facilities, doctors' offices, health maintenance organizations (HMOs), clinics, schools, and private homes. LPNs may also be recruited as members of the military services. Their duties vary according to each state's Nurse Practice Act and the place of employment but generally involve basic patient care. The LPN might also participate in the planning, implementation, and evaluation of nursing care. LPNs provide for the emotional and physical comfort and safety of patients: observing, recording, and reporting to the appropriate people any changes in the patient's status. LPNs can also perform more specialized nursing functions, such as administering medications and therapeutic treatments, as well as assisting with rehabilitation.

In the hospital setting, LPNs usually work under the supervision of registered nurses (RNs), performing many basic nursing duties of bedside care, particularly those that are routine or performed regularly. They take vital signs, keeping checks on temperature, pulse, and blood pressure readings; prepare and administer prescribed medicines to patients (in most states); help prepare patients for examinations and operations; collect samples from patients for testing; and perform routine laboratory procedures, such as urinalysis. They also observe patients and report any adverse reactions to medications or treatments. One of an LPN's main functions is to ensure that patients are comfortable and that their personal hygiene needs are met. They are on hand to give alcohol rubs or massages or to help patients bathe or brush their teeth, and to respond to patients' calls and answer their questions. The LPN may work in any unit of the hospital, including intensive care, recovery, pediatrics, medical-surgical, and maternity, with varying duties according to the demands of the department. For instance, in the obstetrics department, an LPN helps in the delivery room and may feed and bathe newborns, as well as give basic care to recovering new mothers. Some LPNs direct nursing aides and orderlies and may also have clerical duties.

In nursing or retirement homes, LPNs often serve as *charge nurses,* taking over many of the responsibilities that RNs would have in a hospital setting. Because much of the care provided in nursing homes is of the routine variety, LPNs are used extensively and are often in charge of an entire floor, with responsibility for the hands-on care of many patients. In addition to providing routine bedside care, LPNs in nursing homes (fast becoming the largest employer of LPNs after hospitals) may also help to evaluate residents' needs, develop care treatment plans, and supervise nursing aides. In addition, they are charged with contacting doctors when necessary, completing any associated paperwork, and reporting to doctors or RNs on patients' status. Doctors and RNs often depend on detailed reporting from LPNs to accurately maintain patient records and treatment courses. LPNs frequently act as supervisors of nursing assistants in nursing homes.

LPNs working in clinics for physicians and dentists, including HMOs, help prepare patients for examination and even help the

lingo to learn

Anatomy: The science of the structure of the body and its organs.

Catheter: A rubber, plastic, or glass tube used to insert into the bladder in order to withdraw urine; or a tube for passage into a structure for the purpose of injecting or withdrawing a fluid into or out of the body.

Charge nurse: The nurse in charge of a particular floor or unit of a hospital, nursing home, or other health care setting.

Clinical rotation: Time spent working on a floor or unit of a health care facility, usually as part of required training for medical health care professionals.

Geriatrics: A branch of medicine that deals with the problems and diseases of old age and aging people.

Inpatient: A hospital patient who receives lodging and food as well as treatment.

IV: Abbreviation for intravenous—going into a vein.

physician conduct the exam. They apply dressings, explain prescribed treatments or health measures, schedule appointments, keep records, and perform other clerical duties. LPNs who work in home health care as private duty nurses prepare meals for their patients, keep rooms orderly, and teach family members simple nursing tasks as part of patient care.

what is it like to be a licensed practical nurse?

Debra McFadden works as a licensed practical nurse in a county prison, where her primary responsibilities include leading the intake process to gather medical information on those people entering the system. Her day begins with preparing medications, then going into the cell block area and passing them out. "After that I go to the quarantine units," she says. "New people just coming in go to a quarantine unit until they've had their medical intake done. Basically, the intake process involves asking them health-related questions: illnesses, diagnoses, whether or not they're withdrawing from any drugs or alcohol. I take their vitals, and I give them a TB test. We also draw blood for syphilis testing."

The area of the jail in which Debra works is like a small hospital. "We have routine medication orders," she says, "and emergencies. Anything from somebody trying to clean out his ears with a Q-tip and getting it stuck, to overdose, broken bones, people attempting suicide. We have a medical unit for those who are in medical distress of any type. It all runs the gamut, from colds to HIV. We do have emergencies—guys getting into fights. It can sometimes be just like an ER, with somebody bleeding. Anybody in immediate distress, we have to send out. We also have a psych ward for those the psychiatrist is following closely, for those we are concerned about, or who have verbally stated that they were going to try to commit suicide."

Debra also prepares "rewrites" for people with long-standing illnesses such as cardiac problems or diabetes. "They get medication on a routine basis every day, but we're only allowed to have a 30-day order. So every 30 days we have to go back and do a rewrite—get the doctor to re-sign for those medications. A lot of times in nursing homes, the pharmacies just send you new med sheets. We have to do that ourselves, so we get the patient's chart out, write down all the medications they're getting on an ongoing basis, and the doctor signs off on that."

Most of Debra's patients are men, though there is also a small unit for women at the prison. Working in corrections requires that Debra be aware of certain aspects of the work not common to LPNs of other facilities. "You learn about the security issues," she says. "We have a lot of people who come in and are withdrawing from drugs. They try to manipulate you to get medications they don't really need." Though Debra hasn't had much problem with the transition into correctional nursing, she has watched some nurses leave the work. "Some people can't stand the sound of the door closing and locking. Some are very intimidated by the whole penal system. But it is an interesting option for nurses. Part of traditional nursing is working with people who are infirm and elderly; you have so much more with prison nursing. It covers everything."

Karen Hanson has worked as an LPN in different kinds of facilities, including long-term care. "You provide the best care possible," Karen says. "If they are an Alzheimer's patient, or forgetful, you reorient them to the time and place, and help them to maintain their sense of independence. It's not that they can't do for themselves; you just must remind them of how to do things."

Karen assures that her patients are without pain and that they're comfortable. "This includes medicating the patient as per doctor's orders; turning the patient if they're unable to do so on their own, to prevent the bedsores that can cause more pain and infection; cleaning the patient and providing proper skin care if they are incontinent of stool or urine. You have to assist them with eating. If they're not eating and they're losing weight, that opens the door for dehydration and infection."

have I got what it takes to be a licensed practical nurse?

"In correctional nursing," Debra says, "you definitely have to know right from wrong. Most people get into nursing because of their compassion. You still must have that, but you must also not be gullible, you must know where to draw the line. Even though you may do much for a drug addicted person, that person may always want more."

Karen emphasizes patience. "In a long-term facility you really must care," she says. "The patients become like your family. You're with them all the time, and you assure that they're being taken care of. But you need to know how to let go, as well. You are usually with these patients until they pass on."

Licensed practical nurses, and virtually anyone opting for a career in patient care, should also possess physical and mental stamina and endurance. While LPNs should possess a compassionate nature, they sometimes need to be thick-skinned when it comes to occasional unkind treatment from others. Doctors, nurses, and others who supervise LPNs, particularly in a hospital setting, are often under a lot of pressure and may take their frustrations out on those standing shoulder to shoulder with them in providing patient care.

In any case, focusing on the higher goal of contributing to the health and well-being of people can counter the stresses of being on your feet all day or being the recipient of unkind remarks from anguished patients or overburdened and frustrated doctors or supervisors. These qualities, along with good communication skills and the ability to follow directions, will help LPNs achieve a workable balance in their chosen field.

how do I become a licensed practical nurse?

education

High School

To become an LPN, you must first complete an approved practical nursing program in your state. Nearly all states require a high school degree to enroll in the program. Several states in the country, however, require only that applicants complete one or two years of high school. And some high schools even offer a practical nursing program that is approved by a state board of nursing or other regulatory body.

Generally, students with a broad-based educational background and wide-ranging interests will be well prepared to adapt to the academic work and clinical practice required for the LPN training program. Although many practical nursing schools do not require specific high school courses for admission, high school students interested in more focused nursing career preparation will find science and mathematics courses helpful, including biology, chemistry, and physics. Because communication skills are critical to effective nursing, English and speech courses are also a good idea. But perhaps most important are the intangible benefits of possessing a caring, sympathetic nature, a sincere desire to contribute to the health and well-being of people, and the ability to follow oral and written directions.

According to statistics gathered by the U.S. Census Bureau and the American Health Care Association, 34.6 million Americans, or 13 percent of the population, are 65 years old or older. It is estimated that this number will rise to 62 million, or 20 percent of the population, in 25 years. In 1999, there were 1.6 million people living in the approximately 17,000 nursing homes in the United States. This number is expected to quadruple to 6.6 million by 2050.

Postsecondary Training

To be eligible to take the examination required for licensing, students must graduate from an approved school of practical nursing. (A correspondence course in practical nursing does not qualify you to take the state licensing examination.) The length of this program varies from state to state, depending on the individual state's admission requirements. Most programs run for 12 months, although some are as long as 18 months, and a few are less than a year. The trend now is toward an 18-month or two-year program leading to an associate's degree. The trend of expanded education speaks to the growing need for all nurses to have a broader base of knowledge. More complex technologies and the desire to minimize liability risks are reasons why. Many nursing students are opting for a four-year degree because of the accompanying increase in job status and opportunities.

LPN programs are generally offered through two-year colleges and vocational and technical schools. Some programs are offered in high schools, hospitals, and colleges and universities. Men and women 18 years of age or older are eligible to apply, and some programs actually have an upper age limit. Students go to school five days a week, for six to eight hours a day. Participation in a practical nursing program is a full-time commitment. Students who must work a part-time job while enrolled should consult the program director in advance to work out an arrangement.

Although practical nursing programs are no longer strictly hospital-based and contain more theory than clinical practice, they are generally affiliated with a hospital and include a clinical rotation along with classroom instruction. Classroom study covers basic nursing concepts, anatomy, physiology, medical-surgical nursing, pediatrics, obstetrics, psychiatric nursing, administration of drugs, nutrition, and first aid. Clinical practice usually takes place in a supervised hospital setting, but may include other settings as well. Students practice nursing techniques on mannequins before moving on to human patients. After successfully completing the program, students receive a diploma or certificate and may then sit for the state board licensing exam in the state where they plan to work.

Some schools have waiting lists for their practical nursing education programs. It is wise to plan early by obtaining and completing all application forms, beginning this process approximately one year ahead of intended enrollment. Interested students should write

more lingo to learn

Obstetrics: The branch of medicine dealing with childbirth.

Occupational health nurse: A nurse who provides nursing services to employees at their workplace.

Outpatient: A patient who does not sleep overnight in a hospital, but who visits a clinic or dispensary connected with it for diagnosis or treatment.

Pediatrics: A branch of medicine dealing with the development, care, and diseases of children.

Physiology: The science dealing with the study of the function of tissues or organs.

Psychiatric nursing: A nursing specialty that deals with psychiatry, that is, mental, emotional, or behavioral disorders of patients.

Public health nurse: A nurse working for a community or government health organization stressing preventive medicine and social science.

Registered nurse: A degreed nurse who has been licensed by a state authority after qualifying for registration.

to several schools in the desired area and ask for their brochures, financial aid information, and application forms. Make sure the practical nursing program you select is approved by your state's board of nursing. For information on practical nursing education and accredited programs, see "How Do I Learn More?"

certification or licensing

After graduating from an approved school of practical nursing, applicants must then pass an examination to become licensed. All states and the District of Columbia require practical nurses to be licensed and to renew that license every two years. The state board of nursing issues the practical nursing license (or the vocational nursing license in California and Texas) once the National Council Licensure Examination for Practical Nurses, a written exam, is passed. Legal minimum requirements for the license are set by each state through its board of nursing, so these may vary from state to state. LPNs in one state wishing to practice nursing in another state must apply to the board of nursing in that state. Although requirements vary slightly, it is generally not difficult to obtain another license and may not even require a written examination. Licensed practical nurses can identify themselves by putting the initials LPN or LVN (in Texas and California) after their names.

scholarships and grants

Students interested in pursuing a scholarship should contact the counselor or program director working directly with the school or educational program where they are seeking entry. Applicants are urged to write for this information well in advance of starting the term.

labor unions

Although hospitals often have unions that medical employees are eligible to join, LPNs don't necessarily benefit much from member-

ship. Hospital unions often group professional employees with other employee groups whose interests do not converge with those of professional nurses. Consequently, union membership does not benefit those without the greatest voice. Membership with a professional association that has the interests and issues of the LPN at its core is often more beneficial.

who will hire me?

Newly licensed LPNs frequently step into part-time or full-time jobs with the hospitals where they did their training. Networking among staff may uncover other job leads worth exploring. While VA hospitals still employ a large number of LPNs, continued growth for LPNs working in hospitals generally is not expected to continue. This is due largely to the decreasing number of inpatients, which is related to cost concerns: it has become too costly for hospitals to care for patients for a prolonged recovery period.

Although the latest available statistics show the major employer of practical nurses still to be hospitals (32 percent), nursing homes are employing about 28 percent of LPNs. Nursing homes will offer the most new jobs for LPNs as the number of aged and disabled persons in need of long-term care rises rapidly with the aging Baby Boomer population. Nursing homes will also be called on to care for the increasing number of convalescing patients who have been released from hospitals but are not recovered enough to go home.

Job seekers may apply at local employment agencies, although newspaper want ads may be the best avenue. Openings for LPNs are usually advertised in the classified section of the paper under headings such as "Nurses," "Licensed Practical Nurses," "LPNs," "Health Care," "Hospitals," "Private Duty," or "Temporary Nursing." LPNs can also apply directly to hospitals, public health agencies, or nursing homes. Targeting a major hospital with acute care facilities may offer greater growth potential, and veteran's hospitals in particular use a large number of LPNs to meet their ongoing need for basic, hands-on patient care. Applicants can send their resumes, with a short cover letter, directly to the personnel directors of health care facilities. With the shortage of qualified people, calls for interviews should quickly follow. Nurses' associations and professional journals sometimes offer job leads

To be a successful licensed practical nurse, you should

- Be mature, alert, and tactful, displaying patience and emotional stability
- Maintain an objective point of view
- Be able to follow detailed instructions and take correct action, particularly in a crisis
- Have a caring, sympathetic nature and the flexibility to adapt to diverse situations
- Possess good communication skills and the ability to assume responsibility
- Be in good health and have physical stamina

and should be contacted individually (see "How Do I Learn More?").

Rapid growth for LPN employment is also expected in such residential care facilities as board and care homes and group homes for the mentally disabled. In-home health care will also have high demand. Those interested in private duty nursing may be able to sign up with a hospital registry or with a physician's office. Employment is projected to grow rapidly in physicians' offices and clinics as well, including HMOs. Again, newspaper want ads are a good place to begin the job search, along with employment agencies. Large cities generally have employment agencies that specialize in jobs in the health care industry.

where can I go from here?

Licensed practical nurses can advance to higher-paying careers as medical technicians and registered nurses, and many do. Forty percent, in fact, use their LPN designation as a stepping-stone to greater pay and more responsibilities. There are several ways for an LPN to climb the ladder. One is to locate similar positions in larger or more prestigious facilities where higher salaries are offered. It is also possible, by accumulating experience, to obtain supervisory duties over nursing assistants and nurses aides. Another way to advance is to complete the additional education (usually two years at a community college) necessary to become a registered nurse.

But regardless of specialty or career ambition, LPNs must keep their skills current; participation in ongoing self-education is critical to job performance and advancement.

Participating in continuing education courses is a good way to stay current with the technological advances and growing complexity of patient care techniques and procedures. Some states even require a minimum number of continuing education hours before they will renew the practical nursing license every two years. Continuing education programs may be sponsored by a variety of organizations, including community colleges, government agencies, vocational-technical institutes, private educational firms, and local, state, and national health associations. LPNs must assess the educational opportunities available in their communities and determine which are the most relevant for maintaining their practice skills.

Advancement Possibilities

Nurse anesthetists administer anesthesia to patients before and during surgery to desensitize them to pain, also working with pain management and respiratory management of patients.

Physician assistants provide health care services to patients under the direction and responsibility of a physician and may perform comprehensive physical examinations, compile patient medical data, administer or order diagnostic tests, and interpret test results.

Surgical technicians, also known as **operating room technicians,** perform any combination of tasks before, during, and after surgery, including arranging instruments and supplies in the operating room, maintaining supplies of fluids for use during an operation, handing instruments and supplies to the surgeon, and performing other tasks as directed by the surgeon during the operation.

Another method of improving skills and growing in the field is to take advantage of in-service educational programs that many employers are offering. These may include seminars, workshops, and clinical sessions on relevant work topics. Taking advantage of these in-house opportunities will help LPNs accumulate additional skills and may even lead to more specialized and higher-paying careers. Some hospitals offer programs that teach LPNs to do kidney dialysis or to work with patients in cardiac or intensive care units, which may lead to more specialized job titles.

what are the salary ranges?

Nursing2000, a monthly journal, conducts an annual salary survey. According to the results, LPNs earned $11.65 per hour on the average, with the highest averages in the New England ($14.42 per hour) and Pacific ($13.28) regions of the country. The mean salary for staff LPNs was reported as $26,000 annually. According to the *Occupational Outlook Handbook,* the median annual salary for LPNs was $26,940. Those in the lowest 10 percent earned less than $20,210, while those in the highest earned more than $37,540. In hospitals and other health care institutions, LPNs usually receive paid vacations, hospital and health insurance, and pension benefits.

For accurate information on wage scales for LPNs in the community where you want to work, call a hospital in the area, ask for the personnel department, and inquire about salaries for newly licensed LPNs. Other sources include registries, long-term care facilities, or the visiting nurse associations, which can provide specific details on LPN wage scales.

what is the job outlook?

The job outlook is excellent for LPNs and anyone choosing a medical health care profession. As the number of students graduating from practical nursing schools continues to rise, so does the demand for their services. The general growth in health care and the long-term health care needs of an aging population help ensure the continued need for LPNs and other health care professionals. The nursing workforce is also aging, and experts predict a severe shortage of registered nurses as they retire. LPNs will likely be needed to help deal with this shortage.

However, employment of LPNs is expected to increase only as fast as the average for all occupations, according to the U.S. Department of Labor. This is because hospital LPNs mostly work with inpatients, and the number of those patients is not expected to increase. Some in the medical field have been concerned that health maintenance organizations (HMOs) negatively affect nursing employment. Cost-cutting measures by HMOs result in fewer hospital patients and the replacement of registered nurses with unlicensed assistive personnel. In staff reductions, LPNs are believed to be more affected than registered nurses.

As mentioned previously, most new jobs for LPNs will be in nursing homes and long-term care facilities that cater to the growing aging population. These agencies will also house recovering patients released from hospitals but not yet well enough to return home. State and federal regulations on nursing homes are requiring them to hire more LPNs in lieu of other so-called "health aides," who may be given minimal training, are unlicensed, and often underqualified to administer patient care. A similar demand for LPNs will occur in physicians' offices and clinics, including HMOs, concerned with liability issues. New rules and regulations set out by insurance companies shortening the length of stay allowed for patients in a facility will create a great demand for private duty nurses. Rapid growth is expected in board and care homes and group homes for the mentally disabled as well.

how do I learn more?

professional organizations

Following are organizations that provide information on licensed practical nursing careers, approved practical nursing programs, and employers.

National Association for Practical Nurse Education and Service, Inc.
1400 Spring Street, Suite 330
Silver Spring, MD 20910
301-588-2491

National Council of State Boards of Nursing
676 North St. Clair Street, Suite 550
Chicago, IL 60611-2921
http://www.ncsbn.org

National Federation of Licensed Practical Nurses
893 U.S. Highway 70 West, Suite 202
Garner, NC 27529
http://www.nflpn.org

bibliography

Following is a sampling of materials relating to the professional concerns and development of licensed practical nurses.

Hill, Signe S., and Helen A. Howlett. *Success in Practical Nursing: Personal and Vocational Issues.* 3rd ed. Philadelphia, PA: W. B. Saunders, 1997.

Wallner, Rosemary. *Licensed Practical Nurse.* Mankato, MN: Capstone Press, 2000.

Massage Therapists

Definition
Massage therapists use several different massage techniques and therapies to relax muscles, improve blood circulation, reduce stress, and help clients avoid injuries.

Alternative Job Titles
Bodyworkers
Massotherapists

High School Subjects
Biology
Health
Physical education

Personal Skills
Helping/teaching
Mechanical/manipulative

Salary Range
$13,000 to $36,000 to $62,000

Educational Requirements
High school diploma, Some postsecondary training

Certification or Licensing
Recommended (certification)
Required by certain states (licensing)

Outlook
About as fast as the average

GOE
09.05.01

O*NET-SOC
31-9011.00

The athletes have trained years for this one day: the Olympic trials. Between each qualifying heat they must remain at their highest performance level. Mark McNeill, an accredited massage therapist, is there to see that they do just that. By using the massage techniques incorporated into pre-event and post-event massage, he will keep the athletes limber and ready for their next race.

For massage therapists specializing in sports massage, working with elite world-class athletes can offer tremendous challenges and pressures. It can also provide opportunities for therapists to see the immediate effects of their work—perhaps even to see someone fulfill a lifelong dream to compete in the Olympics.

what does a massage therapist do?

Massage therapists use their hands as tools of healing. By stimulating blood circulation through various massage techniques and therapies, they help the body heal, relax muscles, and prevent injuries. The results of massage therapy can be seen almost immediately. As the therapist begins working on a client, the client should start to relax and breathe properly.

There are many different forms of massage therapies, and new ones are being developed all the time. Some therapies concentrate on local muscle groups, while others are best suited for a full-body massage. Well-trained massage therapists will use a combination of these therapies to achieve the best results for their clients.

One of the best-known massage therapies is the **Swedish Massage.** A Swedish Massage is a full-body massage that uses long sweeping strokes to help a client relax and reduce muscle tension.

Trigger Point Therapy [sometimes called **Myotherapy** [see the article Myotherapists] or **Neuromuscular Therapy**] is used when a client feels pain in one part of the body that is actually being caused by a trigger point somewhere else. For example, a headache felt in the forehead may actually be caused by a trigger point in the neck. Once the massage therapist finds the trigger point, he or she will apply pressure to the area and release the pain.

Deep Muscle Massage releases muscle tension by applying pressure to contracted muscle groups in the body. The massage strokes can go with or against the direction of the muscles.

Oriental methods of massage, such as **Shiatsu** and **Acupressure,** are based on the philosophy that there are invisible energy channels that flow through the human body. Clients feel pain when these channels, or meridians, are blocked. To relieve this pain, massage therapists will apply finger pressure massage to the blocked areas, releasing the body's energy and returning it to a balanced state.

In addition to being trained in the use of traditional massage techniques and therapies, *sports massage therapists* are required to take classes in anatomy, physiology, and kinesieology. The additional training helps a sports massage therapist to quickly identify sports-related injuries, such as ligament damage. Sports massage therapists can choose to specialize in one sport and concentrate on those muscle groups most affected during that event or work with many different athletes across the spectrum of sporting events.

Sports massage techniques can be divided into maintenance, pre-event, and post-event massage. Maintenance massage therapy is used on a regular basis while an athlete is in training. With regularly scheduled sessions, massage therapy will soften and lengthen tissue, which helps keep muscles healthy. Another benefit of regularly scheduled visits is that a therapist can identify early signs of muscle strain, allowing athletes to adjust their training schedule and avoid an injury.

Pre-event massage techniques are used immediately prior to an athletic event to help the athlete warm-up. Massage becomes even more valuable during sporting events that require athletes to maintain their performance levels through several qualifying heats.

Post-event massage techniques are used immediately following the event. They help the body to begin recovery as soon as possible from any trauma experienced during the athletic event. By healing faster, athletes can return to their normal training schedule much earlier than without post-event massage. Using a technique called lymphatic drainage, which is lightly and gently massaging the skin, the healing time required by athletes can be greatly reduced.

lingo to learn

Effleurage: A long gliding stroke technique that relaxes muscles.

Friction: A strong circular stroke used to reach deep into muscle fibers.

Petrissage: A light circular stroke used to lift or knead muscles.

Tapotement: The short percussive movements created with the sides of the hands.

what is it like to be a massage therapist?

Massage therapists usually work in a relaxing, tranquil environment. The equipment needed is very minimal. Basically, all a therapist needs is a padded table or chair, some lotions or oils, and a quiet space. The padded table is used for full-body massages, while the seating chair is used for shoulder and neck rubs. Most therapists will play soothing music in the background to help clients relax.

The first thing clients must do before beginning massage therapy is to fill out a form explaining their health status. Massage therapists must be aware of any potential health problems. If a client has any medical problems that are not covered by the scope of massage therapy, the therapist will advise him or her to see a specialist. Massage therapists typically begin a session by talking to clients to find out why they are using massage therapy. However, experienced therapists can sometimes feel with their hands the stress and tight muscles that are the cause of the pain before clients can explain it for themselves.

As more and more people spend their day in front of a computer, for up to 40 hours a week, bad posture has become something of a classic complaint for many people visiting massage therapists. Rounded shoulders and a forward head are telltale signs of stress in the shoulders and neck. By the end of a session therapists may be able to see the positive effects of their work just by helping clients loosen their shoulders and take a full, deep breath.

Mark McNeill has been an accredited massage therapist for over three and a half years. He became interested in massage when he received one after participating in a triathlon. As he continued receiving therapeutic massages, Mark had his two best years of training. Furthermore, the massages left him feeling healthier than ever. Today, Mark teaches sports massage at the Chicago School of Massage Therapy.

In addition to his teaching responsibilities, Mark works with the athletic department of Northwestern University in Evanston, Illinois. During the football season he travels to the university twice a week. The sessions are pretty intense because he will treat up to six players over a two-hour period. As a therapist to a football team, the ailments Mark sees most frequently include stress in the upper neck, chronic hamstrings problems, and muscle tightness.

Mark also works with Northwestern's swimming team. He attended this year's Big Ten Swimming Championship and could see for himself the growing acceptance of sports massage therapy. "You go to the meets and almost every team has a therapist." In fact, a special area was cordoned off for the massage

The Commission on Massage Therapy Accreditation has accredited or approved 70 massage training programs in the United States.

therapists, with 14 or 15 therapists working in the space. However, Mark has found that traveling with the team can be demanding. While working at big meets Mark keeps a rigorous schedule. He can work six days in a row with barely a break between each race.

Massage has found more acceptance not only in sports but by the general public as well. It has become so popular that it can even be found at some local malls. A new chain of massage stores called The Great American Back Rub is one such facility.

Therapists are also making massage more accessible for busy office workers by bringing the massage to them. For an on-site massage the therapist typically brings a special massage chair to a client's office; sometimes the therapist will also bring soft music to play. Clients are able to take a break from their daily routine by sitting in the chair and having a 15 to 20 minute massage, an experience that transforms the stressful office environment into a serene and peaceful haven.

have I got what it takes to be a massage therapist?

The most important requirement for success as a massage therapist is compassion. People will instinctively know if a massage therapist cares about their problems and is giving them full attention. A successful massage therapist takes the time to discover the combinations of massage techniques and therapies that are just right for each client. This nurturing, compassionate quality automatically helps clients to relax and begin to feel comfortable.

Massage therapists must have great communication skills and be able to listen attentively to each of their clients. Stress and muscle tension can be expressed in a patient's posture, muscle tone, and voice. The therapist needs to be able to understand and recognize these clues to treat a client effectively.

Because therapists will work with many different people all day long, having an outgoing personality and enjoying working with people are essential. Therapists need to face their last client of the day with the same level of enthusiasm they had when they saw their first client in the morning.

Therapists need an appreciation for continuing their education after graduation, both to keep up with new therapies and also to keep their certification. For this reason, therapists who have long and successful careers also have a natural curiosity and inquisitiveness.

A massage therapist needs to be in good physical shape. Because of the hours they spend on their feet, some massage therapists can develop a bad posture of their own. Successful therapists develop the ability to combine the strength to manipulate muscles with a gentle touch.

how do I become a massage therapist?

Self-motivation can play an important role in acquiring a first job as a massage therapist. For example, after Mark graduated from massage school he happened to notice the massage equipment at the local YMCA. He found out they were looking to hire a therapist. He

applied and was hired, beginning a career as a massage therapist.

education

High School

A high school diploma or a GED equivalent is a requirement to enter an accredited massage school. Because a thorough knowledge of the human body's musculature and cardiovascular systems is a requirement, you should take science courses, such as biology, anatomy, and physiology, while you are in high school. In addition, health courses will also teach you about the human body and how it functions.

If you are interested in specializing in sports massage, you should also take physical education classes. They will you teach you about staying physically fit and also give you a firsthand experience of the strains and aches sports activities can cause. This knowledge will help you when you begin treating clients.

If you are interested in working as a self-employed therapist, enroll in basic math, business administration, and marketing classes. Self-employed therapists are responsible for their own bookkeeping, which includes invoicing clients and paying bills and taxes. Furthermore, to break into the field and begin to build a successful client base, self-employed therapists must know how to market themselves.

You should consider enrolling in English and psychology classes. These classes will help you develop the interpersonal communication skills needed to work with many different people.

Postsecondary Training

Regulations covering instruction for massage therapy differ from state to state. Some programs demand as little as 120 hours of training with differing requirements for graduation. Such programs, however, are not very helpful for those serious about a career in massage therapy. Instead, you should get a more thorough education at an accredited massage school. The Commission on Massage Therapy Accreditation (COMTA), which is affiliated with the American Massage Therapy Association (AMTA), currently accredits or approves a total of 70 training programs. COMTA's Web site (http://www.comta.org) can provide you with more information about programs and accreditation.

FYI David Palmer, the father of on-site massage, first had one of his specially designed chairs sold in 1986. Today, he estimates that over 100,000 massage chairs based on this design have been manufactured and sold worldwide.

Besides having a high school degree, many accredited programs require prospective students to undergo an interview as part of the admissions process. The interview serves two purposes. First, it is an opportunity for prospective students to meet with a school representative and discuss their goals. Second, it allows admissions officers to gauge the prospective student's personality and expectations. Massage therapy is physically and emotionally demanding work, and schools seek mature, well-balanced candidates to take on the responsibilities of the profession.

You should look for an accredited program that consists of at least 500 hours of classroom instruction, including a minimum of 300 hours of massage theory and technique and 100 hours of anatomy and physiology. In addition, you will be required to enroll in 100 hours of additional courses, including CPR and first aid. For hands-on experience, most programs require their students to participate in elective clinics, which allows them the chance to practice their techniques through volunteering massage services to outreach programs such as hospices, hospitals, and shelters. The requirements of individual schools can be even more demanding than those listed here. For example, the Chicago School of Massage Therapy requires that their students take a minimum of 612 classroom instruction hours and 50 community outreach hours. Finally, be aware that states have varying licensing requirements for massage therapists. Make sure the school you choose will help you meet your state's requirements.

certification or licensing

Massage therapists can receive a nationally recognized certification from the National Certification Board for Therapeutic Massage and Bodywork (NCBTMB). In order to obtain the designation Nationally Certified in Therapeutic Massage and Bodywork, candidates must show proof of education, including the completion of a certain number of hours in several subjects such as anatomy and physiology, and pass an exam administered by NCBTMB. Certification is highly recommended. Not only does it demonstrate to your clients and employer the thoroughness of your education and commitment to the field, but it may also make you eligible for more jobs and advancement.

The ancients knew about and practiced the art of massage, which comes from the Arabic word *massa*, to stroke. The first written records of massage date back 3,000 years to China. Other civilizations, including the Egyptians, Greeks, Persians, Romans, and Pacific Islanders, have used massage in their healing regimens.

Modern massage can trace its roots to the early 19th century. That is when Peter Heinrik Ling, a Swedish doctor, educator, and athlete, developed a hands-on technique that is known today as Swedish massage.

As mentioned earlier, licensing requirements vary from state to state. According to AMTA, over 25 states and the District of Columbia currently regulate the practice of massage therapy. Some states require therapists to be licensed, while others require therapists to register. Candidates may be required to show they have completed a certain amount of education and to take an exam administered by the state. You will need to check with your state's licensing board to determine the specific requirements for your area. It is important to do this early in your career preparation so you know that your education will fulfill your state's regulations.

internships and volunteerships

In states where there is very little regulation governing massage therapy it is fairly easy to find an internship. However, interns should speak directly with the person supervising the internship to discuss what their responsibilities will be. Several internship opportunities for massage therapy are informal with little or no supervision and take the form of volunteering. It takes a certain amount of self-motivation but many students can learn of volunteer or internship opportunities by speaking to the managers of spas or health clubs, or trainers at athletic departments.

who will hire me?

The growing acceptance of massage as a legitimate form of therapy is creating a great demand for competent accredited therapists. In fact, the Chicago School of Massage Therapy keeps a job placement listing of potential employers who have called the school looking to interview recent graduates.

Mark began his career as a sports massage therapist at Northwestern University when the new athletic trainer came to the massage school looking for a therapist. Having used massage therapy at two previous universities, the trainer recognized its value and insisted that the department begin using massage therapy at Northwestern. He inquired at the Chicago School of Massage Therapy for a therapist with a background in sports. Mark began to work at Northwestern as a volunteer and eventually was hired.

Besides working on staff at hospitals, nursing homes, spas, and health clubs, massage therapists can work with physical therapists and chiropractors. When working on staff, the responsibilities of massage therapists can vary greatly. At some spas the therapist will be responsible for cleaning the room and preparing it for the next client. The exact responsibilities of therapists should be negotiated before they begin their employment.

Some massage therapists prefer to work on a contractual basis at spas or health clubs. In these instances therapists work for themselves but use the facilities of a spa or health club. In return, they may pay either rent or a percentage of their income to the management.

To be a successful massage therapist, you should

- Have an outgoing personality
- Be physically fit
- Be a good listener and observer
- Have a natural sense of compassion and a desire to heal
- Have the ability to market yourself
- Be naturally curious and inquisitive

Therapists who are self-employed can provide massages in their own homes. However, self-employed therapists will often go where they are needed, either to an office for an on-site massage or to a client's home. Self-employed therapists enjoy the freedom of deciding their own schedules and can choose to work as many or as few hours as they like.

where can I go from here?

Once massage therapists graduate from an accredited school and receive certification and any needed licensing, they are required to attend continuing education classes to maintain their credentials. By keeping up with the latest techniques and developments in massage therapy, they can increase their skills and offer their clients a greater variety of services. This can increase their client base and raise their salary. Continuing education is available through the AMTA's Speaker's Tour and National Learning Center. In addition, AMTA holds an annual convention. These are excellent opportunities for massage therapists to learn about the latest developments in massage therapy, meet experts in their field, and find out about any potential employment opportunities.

Therapists who decide to specialize in one area of massage, such as sports massage, must constantly refine their skills. However, by becoming an expert in their specialty they can build a loyal and regular client base.

Therapists who have worked on staff at a spa or health club for several years can build a strong client base. At some point they may consider opening up their own place of business and become their own boss.

what are the salary ranges?

Salaries for massage therapists vary widely. Incomes are influenced by such factors as location and number of steady clients. According to the AMTA, therapists in large metropolitan areas may charge between $35 and $60 per hour. Usually, though, therapists do not work 40-hour weeks because of the physical strain of the job. Some therapists will only see four to five clients a day in a four-day workweek, which would make for a maximum of 20 billable hours. A therapist charging $35 per hour and working 20 hours a week, therefore, could expect a yearly income of about $36,400. At $60 per hour under these circumstances, a therapist's annual income would be $62,400. AMTA also notes, however, that therapists working away from large metropolitan areas tend to earn less per hour, between $25 and $50. In addition, many work part-time, which is considered 10 or fewer hours per week. A therapist working 10 hours at $25 per hour will have an annual income of about $13,000. Naturally, those who are self-employed must pay for their own equipment, space, marketing, insurance, and other business expenses. These expenses will lower therapists' take-home pay.

Experience is also an important factor in determining how much a therapist can earn. A therapist who is just beginning in the field may be paid as little as $10 an hour. Hourly rates, however, may be as high as $75 an hour for someone who is self-employed with a large and loyal clientele in an extremely affluent community.

what is the job outlook?

Because of the continuing acceptance of massage therapy by the medical community, athletic departments, and the public at large, the job outlook for accredited massage therapists is good.

This growing acceptance is illustrated by the willingness of some insurance companies to reimburse clients for the cost of massage therapy.

Athletic trainers and coaches have seen the positive results of massage therapy and are using therapists more and more to keep their players healthy and give to their team a winning edge.

Also, as the baby-boom generation ages and seeks out new ways to stay in shape and feel better, the demand for accredited massage therapists will grow even higher. The AMTA reports that consumers visit massage therapists approximately 114 million times a year. In addition, traditional medicine has become more accepting of alternative therapies such as massage. Over 75 of the 125 medical schools in the United States now offer courses in alternative medicine.

All of these facts point to a healthy employment future for massage therapists.

Research studies have found many health benefits of massage. Among these are:

Reduction of heart rate and blood pressure

Reduction of muscle soreness after exercise

Improvement of weight gain in premature infants

Significant reduction of premenstrual symptoms

Relief for tension headaches and eyestrain

how do I learn more?

professional organizations

Following are organizations that provide information on massage therapy, education, certification, and employment.

American Massage Therapy Association
820 Davis Street, Suite 100
Evanston, IL 60201
847-864-0123
http://www.amtamassage.org

Associated Bodywork and Massage Professionals
271 Sugarbush Drive
Evergreen, CO 80439-9766
800-458-2267
expectmore@abmp.com
http://www.abmp.com

**Commission on Massage Therapy
Accreditation**
820 Davis Street, Suite 100
Evanston, IL 60201-4444
847-869-5039
cellis@amtamassage.org
http://www.comta.org

**National Certification Board for Therapeutic
Massage and Bodywork**
8201 Greensboro Drive, Suite 300
McLean, VA 22102
800-296-0664
info@ncbtmb.com
http://www.ncbtmb.com

Related Jobs

The U.S. Department of Labor classifies massage therapy under the headings *Attendant Services, Physical Conditioning* (GOE) and *Healthcare Support* (O*NET-SOC). Also under these headings are people who work in the service industry. The responsibilities and educational requirements for these occupations vary greatly, but they all have in common working in the service of others. Related jobs include: cooling-room attendants, electrologists, manicurists, salon attendants, and weight reduction specialists.

bibliography

Following is a sampling of materials relating to the professional concerns and development of massage therapists.

Beck, Mark F. *Milady's Theory & Practice of Therapeutic Massage.* 3rd Edition. Albany, NY: Milady Publishing Corporation, 1999.

Biel, Andrew R. *Trail Guide to the Body: How to Locate Muscles, Bones & More!* Boulder, CO: Andrew R. Biel, 1997.

Cassar, Mario-Paul. *Handbook of Massage Therapy: A Complete Guide for the Student and Professional Massage Therapist.* Newton, MA: Butterworth-Heinemann Medical, 1999.

Frita, Sandy. *Mosby's Fundamentals of Therapeutic Massage.* 2nd Edition. St. Louis, MO: Mosby-Year Book, 1999.

Fritz, Sandy et al. *Mosby's Basic Science for Soft Tissue and Movement Therapies.* St. Louis, MO: Mosby-Year Book, 1999.

Juhan, Deane and Ken Dychtwald. *Job's Body: A Handbook for Bodywork.* Barrytown, NY: Barrytown, Ltd., 1998.

Tappan, Frances M. and Patricia J. Benjamin. *Tappan's Handbook of Healing Massage Techniques: Classic, Holistic, and Emerging Methods.* New York, NY: Prentice-Hall, 1998.

Werner, Ruth and Ben E. Benjamin, eds. *A Massage Therapist's Guide to Pathology.* Philadelphia, PA: Lippincott, Williams & Wilkins, 1998.

Medical Assistants

Definition
Medical assistants help physicians keep their offices and clinics running smoothly. They maintain medical records, assist with the examination and treatment of patients, and perform routine office duties so doctors can spend more time working directly with patients.

High School Subjects
Biology
Computer science
Health
Mathematics

Personal Skills
Helping/teaching
Technical/scientific

Salary Range
$14,000 to $20,000 to $28,000+

Minimum Educational Requirements
Some postsecondary training

Certification or Licensing
Voluntary

Outlook
Much faster than the average

GOE
10.03.02

O*NET-SOC
31-9092.00

Around three o'clock in the afternoon, Donna Bolton, CMA (certified medical assistant) greets Marie and begins to prepare her for a treadmill test. Eighty-three-year-old Marie had called the Kalispell Diagnostic Clinic first thing that morning. She'd been feeling tired lately, run-down, and barely had the motivation to get out and sell her Avon products. She thought something might be wrong with her heart.

Donna took Marie's call when it came in. Experience had taught Donna not to mess around with heart complaints. "Have you had any shortness of breath, dizzy spells, or pains up and down your arms or in your chest?" she asked Marie.

"No," Marie answered slowly. "I'm just tired."

"Better come right in," Donna told her, checking the appointment log. "We can see you this afternoon." After hanging up, Donna discussed

Marie's call with the doctor, who prescribed a treadmill test for Marie.

Now Donna weighs Marie, takes her blood pressure and temperature, then prepares her skin for the electrodes soon to be attached to her chest. She tells her patient about the test, explaining to her how to walk on the machine and to be sure and let the doctor know right away if she feels dizzy or has any arm or chest pain. After a few minutes, the doctor enters the room to monitor Marie's test, and Donna stays to assist.

"Marie stayed on the treadmill for a full five minutes, and her heart was strong the whole time," Donna says. "She did great. She's tired because she's 83. Sometimes, it's hard to accept that you're slowing down."

lingo to learn

Aseptic technique: Any procedure used to prevent microorganisms from contaminating equipment, rooms, or people.

Dialysis: A process that is used to purify the blood of persons whose kidneys have stopped functioning.

Electrocardiogram (ECG): This test registers, in wave patterns, the electrical currents from heart muscle contractions.

Lavage: The French term for washing, especially the therapeutic washing out of an organ. An ear lavage washes out the ears with very warm water, usually to dissolve excessive wax buildup that could be causing pain and hearing loss.

Medical transcription: A typed record of a physician's dictated material concerning a patient's medical record.

Physician assistant: A person who is certified to diagnose, treat, and prescribe medication under the direct supervision of a licensed physician.

Vitals: These are the signs of life. To take someone's vitals is to measure blood pressure, temperature, respiratory rate, and pulse.

what does a medical assistant do?

Medical assistants are trained to do both clerical and clinical duties. Often, depending on the size of the office, they do both. The larger the office, the greater the chance the medical assistant will specialize in one type of work. In smaller offices or clinics with only one doctor and one registered nurse, for example, the medical assistant may find herself, or himself, doing everything it takes to run the practice, from making appointments to greeting patients to billing them.

The clinical duties of a medical assistant are those tasks that are patient-centered. Assistants take the medical histories of patients and record them in patient files. They find out what a patient's current symptoms are and what concerns to share with the doctor. Assistants help physicians by preparing patients for examination and treatment. They may check and record a patient's blood pressure, pulse, and temperature. Medical assistants help with the preparation of diagnostic tests and procedures, including educating the patient about what to expect during the test. They also educate patients about medication, special diets, and instructions about their treatments. Assistants prepare patients for X-rays, electrocardiograms (ECGs), and treadmill tests; some may administer ECGs. Assistants can give injections, apply or change dressings, remove sutures, draw blood, and collect specimens for laboratory tests, such as Pap smears.

"Injections," says Donna, "are one of the most controversial procedures. Some states restrict medical assistants from giving injections, other states allow it. Here in Montana, CMAs can give injections. In other states, only a registered nurse or doctor can." Other procedures are likewise prohibited in some states and allowed in others. Invasive procedures, such as setting up intravenous tubes, are the most controversial. "We definitely don't put patients through dialysis in this state, either," says Donna.

Medical assistants are usually the ones who prepare the examination rooms for patients, keeping them clean and orderly. After each examination, they straighten up the room, dispose of the used linen and medical supplies, then restock the room. They sterilize the instruments and equipment used during examinations, and order new supplies and keep track of inventory.

An assistant's administrative duties vary depending on how many other employees staff the office. Medical assistants type case histories and surgery reports and keep patients' files, X-rays, and other medical records up to date. This includes the financial records, too, preparing and sending the bills and receiving payment when it comes in. Assistants answer the phone, greet patients, fill out insurance forms, schedule appointments, take care of correspondence, and arrange for patients to be admitted to hospitals for treatment and tests when necessary. They call in prescriptions to pharmacies and authorize drug refills as instructed by the doctor. Assistants do many of these tasks by computer. Some offices have medical secretaries and medical receptionists who perform these administrative duties, but they rarely do the clinical tasks of a medical assistant.

Medical assistants can specialize in specific medical fields. *Ophthalmic medical assistants* help ophthalmologists with eye exams and treatments. They give eye drops and use special equipment to test eyesight and check for disease. They show patients how to use eye dressings, protective shields, and safety patches and how to use and care for contact lenses. They maintain and sterilize the optical and surgical equipment and could assist during eye surgery. An *optometric assistant* prepares patients for examination and helps them select their eye wear. A *chiropractic medical assistant* works with patients with muscular and skeletal problems. And a *podiatric medical assistant* exposes and develops X-rays, makes castings of feet, and assists podiatrists in surgery.

what is it like to be a medical assistant?

"I walked in the door this morning and was handed a chart before I even got my coat off," says Donna. "I had to phone in a prescription for a patient who called, checking it with the doctor first." After that was done, Donna sat down with the doctor to discuss a few problems that had cropped up. "I didn't get a chance to talk with her the day before, so I wanted to do it first thing." By that time, the first patient of the day had arrived for a tread-

mill test, and Donna needed to prep him and get all of his information into the computer.

Donna works in a large and busy practice. There are six doctors, five certified medical assistants, and one registered nurse (RN). Two of the medical assistants are *coders*. They handle the billing, and one does strictly office billing while the other does hospital billing. One CMA is the *records clerk*, gathering all the patient's information such as previous tests, X-rays, and hospital stays. The other two medical assistants, Donna included, are clinical. "We do everything you've ever been to a doctor's office for," says Donna.

After the morning's treadmill test, Donna noticed a Holter Monitor scheduled before lunch. "A Holter Monitor runs off batteries and is designed to give us a true picture of what is happening with the heart," Donna explains. It is the size of a large calculator, a box about six inches by three inches, that fits into a pouch with a strap that goes over the shoulder. It monitors the heart through electrodes. "Each electrode has a little pad that sticks to your skin. Conducting gel is in the pad, and the gel picks up the electricity your heart puts out," says Donna. "We give people a diary to record the times they feel dizzy or have pain in the chest or arms, anything irregular. When they feel this, they push a button on the monitor. We later read the printout and the diary to get a truly accurate picture of what's going on." Doctors may order the monitor kept on for 24 to 48 hours, depending on the patient's situation. "I get them hooked up properly, educate them about the diary and using the monitor correctly, and chart the visit. The doctor reads and interprets the printout."

After lunch, Donna calls in all her prescriptions. As the afternoon's patients come in, Donna grabs their chart, greets them, and shows them into an examination room where she learns the reason for their visit. She charts this information and passes it on to the doctor, saving the doctor valuable time to work directly with the patient. Donna then preps the patients for the doctor's exam, taking their vitals and weighing them.

One patient needed an ear lavage (washing). "I normally do several ear lavages a day," says Donna. She usually has several ECGs (electrocardiograms) to do in a day as well, but this particular day there weren't any scheduled. "It's just as well," says Donna, "because we have four men from the fire department coming in unexpectedly for routine treadmill tests. They needed to have it done today for their certification, and they're all due after three o'clock. The rest of the day is going to be busy." Most of Donna's days are. "I'm never bored," says Donna. "I'm a people person and I love working with the patients. I make them feel more comfortable, and it's gratifying."

Donna works a 40-hour week, 8:00 AM to 5:00 PM, Monday through Friday. "If you want to be in the medical profession, this is a nice schedule if you have a family," says Donna. "Nursing shifts in hospitals are long, late hours that make it hard to spend time with your children."

have I got what it takes to be a medical assistant?

"We're there for the patient," says Donna. "Above all, a medical assistant must be able to work well with people." Good medical assistants have patience, a friendly disposition, and empathy and compassion for all people. They recognize and respect cultural diversity. Putting patients at ease is essential. "You can't shy away from people," says Donna.

Medical assistants must be able to explain complicated procedures and doctors' instructions to patients as well as explain patients' symptoms to doctors. "Medical assistants are the go-between, the liaison, for patient and doctor," says Donna. Assistants are responsible to keep accurate records and charts of everything that happens to a patient. Therefore, good communication skills, both verbal and written, are important. This includes phone skills. Medical assistants spend a lot of time on the phone, talking with patients and making appointments, calling in prescriptions, and collaborating with hospital and laboratory staff. Assistants should be able to recognize and respond to emergency situations and think well on their feet. Donna never hesitates to bring someone in if they have an ear infection. "You don't mess around with ear infections. You could end up with a ruptured eardrum."

Medical assistants should have solid organizational skills. They are called upon to perform many different tasks, and they must know how to prioritize and manage their time effectively. They are required to have a neat appearance and be professional at all times. Respecting patient confidentiality, following instructions, and complying with complicated policies and procedures are all part of the professional conduct of a medical assistant.

Donna believes medical assistants need to have lots of energy and be able to deal with tragic situations. "You have to leave your patients' problems at the office. You can't take it home with you," says Donna. "If you do, you won't last long as a medical assistant. You'll go crazy."

how do I become a medical assistant?

Donna was planning to be a registered nurse when she met her future husband, "a handsome Marine who swept me off my feet." Donna married in the 1950s, and her husband was shipped off first to Korea, then later Vietnam. "I began to think that I needed a career so I could support myself and my children, in case something happened to my husband. The possibilities were very real." Donna saw an ad on television for a medical assisting program. "It looked like a solid career choice. It was faster than becoming a nurse, two years as opposed to four, and I liked the hours better." Donna has never been sorry. "For 10 years we moved all over the place, and I was never without a job."

FYI In a dialysis machine, blood is circulated on one side of a porous layer of tissue while dialysis fluid—containing matter necessary to the body and closely matching the composition of blood— is circulated on the other. Waste products such as urea, the main solid component of urine, are diffused through the tissue into the dialysis fluid and are discarded, while the diffusion of substances needed by the body is prevented.

education

High School

Most medical practices and clinics will not hire a medical assistant without a high school diploma or its equivalent. Some medical assistants are trained on the job, but this is becoming less common than it was in the past.

If you're interested in becoming a medical assistant, you should take health, biology, computer science, and business courses. Because being a medical assistant is a combination of administrative and clinical work, it is important to have a background in both. Bookkeeping, typing, and other office practices are essential to learn. Most of your record keeping will be done by computer, so don't neglect computer science, either. Advanced math classes, especially algebra, are also important. If you decide to enter into a two-year CMA program or move into nursing or some other related job, you'll have the required math and science.

High school is a good time to begin volunteering in the medical profession. Working in hospitals, nursing homes, and other health care facilities is one way to determine if the medical field is right for you. Another way is to join clubs or organizations, such as Future Nurses of America.

Postsecondary Training

The majority of doctors' offices and other health care facilities prefer medical assistants to complete a two-year associate's degree program or some other formal training program. Two agencies recognized by the U.S. Department of Labor accredit medical assisting training programs: the Commission on Accreditation of Allied Health Education Programs (CAAHEP) and the Accrediting Bureau of Health Education Schools (ABHES). In 1999 there were about 590 accredited medical assisting programs recognized by either of these two boards. The Committee on Accreditation for Ophthalmic Medical Personnel accredited 14 programs in ophthalmic medical assisting. South Dakota is the only state that requires medical assistants to be graduated from an accredited medical assisting program.

Formal training to become a medical assistant is available at trade schools, community colleges, junior colleges, and universities, and can last anywhere from nine months to two years. A two-year associate's degree can be applied to a nursing degree if you want to con-

tinue on someday. In medical assisting programs, you do course work in biology, anatomy, physiology, and medical terminology. You learn all nine systems of the body as well as how to draw blood, take vitals, expose and develop X-rays, and administer an ECG and other medical tests and procedures. "Medical assistants work with all the instruments, learning their names and how to use them," says Donna. For the administrative end of the job, you study computer science, record keeping, transcribing and typing, and other office procedures.

During your formal training, you also do what is called an externship, working three months in the field practicing a variety of clinical and administrative duties. Schools usually help arrange a student's externship with nearby health care facilities, doctors' offices, and clinics. Although you're not graded, the facility where you work sends in a report on how well you did. According to Donna, a well-rounded externship is crucial. The CAAHEP requires it for certification, and future employers look closely at it. "It may be your only experience out in the field before your first job, so it counts a lot," says Donna.

For more information about CAAHEP-accredited programs and a list of ABHES-accredited programs, write The American Association of Medical Assistants (AAMA) or the Accrediting Bureau of Health Education Schools (see "How Do I Learn More?").

certification or licensing

Although there is no required state or national licensing or certification for medical assistants, there is voluntary certification. And some states require medical assistants to receive additional training or certification for specified tasks, such as exposing and developing X-rays. The American Association of Medical Assistants awards the Certified Medical Assistant (CMA) credential, and the American Medical Technologists awards the Registered Medical Assistant (RMA) credential. The Joint Commission on Allied Health Personnel in Ophthalmology awards the Certified Ophthalmic Assistant, and the American Society of Podiatric Medical Assistants awards the Podiatric Medical Assistant Certified credential.

The CMA national certification exam is given twice a year, in January and June, to students who graduate from a CAAHEP-accredited medical assisting program. The exam consists of 300 questions covering clinical, administrative, and general material. In order to retain your certification, you must have 60 hours of continuing education credits, or take a recertification exam every five years. The RMA is given to students who graduated from an ABHES-accredited program. RMA recipients automatically become members of the American Medical Technologists association and must pay yearly dues to renew their certification. Annual continuing education credits are voluntary but recommended.

Donna, who is a Montana state representative for the AAMA, believes being a member of a professional medical assisting organization offers medical assistants a great support system. "If your right to practice is being questioned, the help you receive is invaluable," says Donna. "Being a member gives you the opportunity to communicate with others in your field at the local, state, and national level." In addition to a bimonthly publication titled *PMA* (Professional Medical Assistant), members of the AAMA can attend an annual convention with continuing education credits available. They also have access to a toll-free information line.

scholarships and grants

The AAMA offers the Maxine Williams scholarship once a year to a medical assisting student attending a CAAHEP-accredited school. The scholarship is for $1,000. To apply, call or write the AAMA (see "How Do I Learn More?").

To receive financial assistance to attend a school with a postsecondary medical assisting training program, contact the school's financial aid office for information about the availability of grants and scholarships.

internships and volunteerships

The externship done in conjunction with medical assisting training programs is a nonpaid learning experience considered part of your overall course work.

Volunteering in a hospital, clinic, or other health care facility is a good way to see if being a medical assistant is right for you. Many facilities offer volunteer opportunities and welcome the extra help and personal touch that volunteers bring. Donna suggests volunteering with children, too, to test your ability to be a medical assistant, as many practices are exclusively pediatric or serve children. To explore these opportunities, contact hospitals, nursing and residential care facilities, child care centers, and state and county health services near you for more information about their volunteer programs.

To be a successful medical assistant, you should

- Have good communication skills
- Have a friendly disposition
- Be accurate and well organized
- Have excellent phone skills
- Be able to recognize and respond well to emergencies
- Have lots of energy

who will hire me?

Most jobs for medical assistants are found in immediate care facilities, such as physicians' offices. Sixty-five percent of all medical assistants work in private doctors' offices, and another 14 percent work in optometrists' and chiropractors' offices. The remainder work in hospitals, clinics, and other medical facilities, like nursing homes and physical therapy practices.

If you're in a postsecondary medical assisting training program, your supervised clinical experience may lead you to a job. In fact, students are often asked to stay on and offered permanent positions when their externship is over. "That's how I got my first job in California," says Donna. School career placement offices usually list jobs available in the field, and high school guidance counselors may also have information about possible job openings. Calling local doctors' offices and health care facilities, checking out the want ads, and registering with state employment agencies are all good methods of finding out about medical assisting positions near you.

For information about career opportunities in medical assisting, you can write the American Association of Medical Assistants and the American Medical Technologists (see "How Do I Learn More?"). For information about careers in ophthalmology, write the Joint Commission on Allied Health Personnel in Ophthalmology (see "How Do I Learn More?").

where can I go from here?

Donna has been a medical assistant for 29 years and still loves it. "It's where I belong," says Donna, "although working with children is not my forte. I could never stand to stick them and hear them cry." Donna plans to retire in just a few years.

Although Donna is content where she is, many medical assistants must change occupations in order to advance. Medical assistants can move into managerial or administrative positions without further education, and as more clinics and group practices open up, the need for office managers will increase. These positions could easily go to experienced, well-qualified medical assistants. As with most jobs on the market today, the better your computer skills, the greater your chances of moving into a management position. Teaching medical assisting courses at a training program is also a possibility for advancement that may appeal to you. However, if you think you may someday want to advance into an occupation with more clinical responsibilities, such as nursing or physician assisting, or a more technical position such as respiratory therapist and technician, you will need to return to school. Donna believes being a medical assistant gives you the background to go just about anywhere in the medical field.

History

In 1903, the first practical electrocardiograph (ECG) for measuring the activity of the heart was developed by W. Einthoven. The electrocardiograph is the instrument that records the electrical output occurring during a heartbeat, and the electrocardiogram is what registers the wave patterns of the heart on a light-sensitive film recording. Deviations in the normal height, form, or duration of the wave pattern indicate specific disorders, and the ECG is an important aid in diagnosing heart disease.

The ECG is also referred to as an EKG after its European spelling. In 1923, Einthoven was awarded the Nobel Prize in medicine for his efforts.

what are the salary ranges?

The earnings of medical assistants vary widely, depending on experience, skill level, and location. According to the *Occupational Outlook Handbook*, median annual earnings for medical assistants were $20,680 in 1998. The highest 10 percent earned more than $28,640 a year, while the lowest 10 percent earned less than $14,020. In 1997, medical assistants earned the following median annual salaries by industry: offices of osteopathic physicians, $19,600; hospitals, $20,400; and offices and clinics of medical doctors, $20,800.

Medical assistants at Kalispell Diagnostic start at $6.50 to $7.50 an hour, depending on experience. Wages in Montana, however, are among the lowest in the nation.

Whether or not a medical assistant receives health insurance benefits, a pension plan, and paid vacation and sick leave is usually up to the individual employer. Some doctors' offices and clinics have excellent benefit packages for medical assistants; others tend to hire part-time employees who are excluded from the benefits package.

what is the job outlook?

Job prospects for medical assistants look particularly good in the years to come. Jobs in all areas of medical assisting are expected to increase much faster than the average for all other occupations as the health care industry grows to meet the needs of a large population of elderly people. Replacements for medical assistants leaving the field are expected to make up the bulk of the new job openings.

According to the U.S. Department of Labor, medical assisting is one of the fastest growing occupations. It predicts that employment will grow by 58 percent from 1998 to 2008. Employment will be driven by the number of new clinics, group practices like the one where Donna works, and health care facilities that need a higher proportion of support staff to run efficiently. The more flexible you are as a medical assistant, able to handle both clinical and administrative duties, and the better trained you are, the more likely you will be to find a job. Those with formal education, and particularly certification, will be the best candidates.

Related Jobs

The U.S. Department of Labor classifies medical assistants under the headings *Nursing, Therapy and Specialized Teaching Services* (GOE) and *Healthcare Support* (O*NET-SOC). Also under these headings are nurses, dental assistants, physician assistants, physicians, cardiovascular technologists, dental hygienists, nuclear medicine technologists, physical therapists, respiratory therapists and technicians, and emergency medical technicians.

Workers in other medical support occupations include medical secretaries, hospital admitting staff, pharmacy helpers, and medical record clerks. With more training, medical assistants can shift to other medical careers with more clinical responsibilities, such as nursing and physician assisting. There are plenty of positions in the field of medical technology, as well as the option to become a doctor, dentist, optometrist, ophthalmologist, chiropractor, physical therapist, or pharmacist.

how do I learn more?

professional organizations

The following organizations provide information on career opportunities, medical assisting certification and certification exams, accredited schools and training programs, and medical assisting programs in ophthalmology.

Accrediting Bureau of Health Education Schools
803 West Broad Street, Suite 730
Falls Church, VA 22046
abhes@erols.com
http://www.abhes.org

American Association of Medical Assistants
20 North Wacker Drive, Suite 1575
Chicago, IL 60606-2963
http://www.aama-ntl.org

American Medical Technologists
710 Higgins Road
Park Ridge, IL 60068-5765
http://www.amt1.com

Joint Commission on Allied Health Personnel in Ophthalmology
2025 Woodlane Drive
St. Paul, MN 55125-2995
jcahpo@jcahpo.org
http://www.jcahpo.org

bibliography

Following is a sampling of materials relating to the professional concerns of medical assistants.

Clement, J. E. *Review Questions for the Medical Assistant Examination.* New York, NY: Parthenon Publishing Group, 2000.

Palko, Tom, and Hilda Palko. *Prentice Hall Health Question and Answer Review for the Medical Assistant.* 5th Edition. *Appleton & Lange Review Series.* Upper Saddle River, NJ: Prentice Hall, 2000.

Primm, E. Russell. *Medical Assistant (Careers Without College).* Mankato, MN: Capstone Press, 1998.

Sacks, Terence J. *Opportunities in Physician Assistant Careers.* Lincolnwood, IL: VGM Career Horizons, 1995.

Medical Ethicists

Definition
Medical ethicists are consultants, teachers, researchers, and policy makers in the field of medical ethics, the branch of philosophy that addresses the moral issues involved in medical practice and research.

Alternative Job Title
Bioethicists

High School Subjects
Biology
Psychology

Personal Skills
Helping/teaching
Technical/scientific

Salary Range
$33,000 to $71,000 to $100,000+

Educational Requirements
Master's degree

Certification or Licensing
Voluntary

Outlook
About as fast as the average

GOE
NA*
O*NET-SOC
NA*

*Not Available. The U.S. Department of Labor does not categorize the career of medical ethicist.

Dr. Christine Caron taps on the patient's door and enters his room. Earlier in her office, she had looked over his charts and learned the patient is 84 and suffers from chronic heart failure, with symptoms of fatigue, loss of appetite, irregular heartbeat, dizziness, poor circulation, difficulty breathing, and overall weakness. His wife, 82, cares for him at home, with help from their son, who lives nearby. His symptoms have worsened considerably over the past week, and he was admitted yesterday afternoon.

Christine touches the man's frail hand and sits next to his wife and introduces herself. "I'd like to talk about what you've been going through the past week and help you decide how you want us to help you," she says.

The patient's voice is quite weak, and he doesn't open his eyes throughout their brief conversation. After learning he does not wish to be kept alive artificially, such as with the assistance of a machine or through a feeding tube, Christine tells the couple about what can be done to keep him comfortable. She will return later with the appropriate legal document, an advance directive, that will state the patient's wishes for his end-of-life care.

Christine leaves the room and checks the time. One more patient to see, and then on to a staff meeting on genetic counseling at 9:00 AM. Today is going to be a busy day.

what does a medical ethicist do?

Medical ethics as a distinct field arose in the 1960s, although, of course, the realization that an ethical code is an essential aspect of the practice of medicine goes back to ancient times. Physicians throughout the Western world traditionally took the Hippocratic oath (named for the Greek father of medicine) in which they pledged to put the patient's well-being ahead of all other considerations and to observe confidentiality in all doctor-patient transactions. They promised to respect human life and refused to perform abortions or assist in suicides.

By the middle of the 20th century, however, the explosion in medical technology had made ethical decision-making far more complex. At

lingo to learn

Active euthanasia: Mercy killing, also called physician-assisted suicide.

Advance directive: An individual's instructions (also called a living will) concerning his or her wish not to be kept alive by means of artificial life-support systems in the case of terminal illness or injury with no possibility of recovery.

Bioethics: The study of moral problems in the fields of medicine, health, the life sciences, and the environment. Bioethics includes (but is not limited to) medical ethics.

Cloning: The production of genetically identical cells or organisms, all descended from a single ancestor.

Competency: The capacity to give informed consent to medical treatment.

the same time, patients were demanding the right to be actively involved in making decisions about their medical treatment; they were no longer willing to passively accept the paternalism of the traditional "doctor-always-knows-best" model of health care.

Recognition of the urgent need for a new emphasis on medical ethics had already been triggered by the revelations of the post-World War II Nuremberg trials in which the world learned of the appallingly inhumane medical experiments carried out by Nazi physicians on human beings. During the next few decades, accounts of unethical medical research projects in the United States also emerged; one notorious case was the Tuskegee Syphilis Study in which medical treatment for syphilis was deliberately withheld from a group of black men so that the progress of their disease could be studied.

Dr. Richard Zaner directs the Vanderbilt University Center for Clinical and Research Ethics, where Christine Caron served her fellowship. Recalling the early days of his career, Richard says, "Doctors were desperate for help with the issues involved in the new technology of the 1960s. So they turned to philosophers as the people who know ethics, and I was one of the people called." Richard had begun his academic career as a professor of philosophy with strong interdisciplinary interests. As the field developed, medical ethics became the focal point of his work as an educator, clinical consultant, and writer.

Medical ethics addresses the complex questions involved in modern medical treatment and research. Medical breakthroughs in recent decades have saved lives but have also created new dilemmas.

In the past, people were considered dead when they stopped breathing and the heart stopped beating. Now, however, brain-injured persons unable to breathe on their own can be kept alive indefinitely in a persistent vegetative state by means of artificial ventilators that breathe for them and artificial alimentation (feeding). Is this life? Who has the right to decide? What would the patient want? What about the people waiting for transplants who would benefit from the organs of the person being kept alive on the ventilator?

The questions are endless: How is competency to make life-or-death decisions for oneself defined? What if parents want to withhold lifesaving treatment from their severely handicapped newborn baby? How do we decide who gets organ transplants? What about the use of fetal-tissue transplants to treat Parkinson's disease and other conditions? When people are suffering intense pain from incurable illness, should physician-assisted suicide be allowed? What are the implications of high-tech reproductive developments—in vitro fertilization, artificial insemination, surrogate motherhood? What about gene splicing and cloning?

The identification of all 30,000 genes in human DNA as part of the Human Genome Project has created a new world of possibilities —and dilemmas—that *medical ethicists* will help doctors and patients confront.

Who should have access to information about an individual's genetic makeup? Should it be available to insurance companies that might refuse to insure people with potential genetic problems?

The Patient Self-Determination Act (PSDA), which took effect in 1991, requires hospitals, hospices, and nursing homes to inform competent patients that they have the right to accept or reject treatment and to draw up a living will or other advance directive making their wishes clear. The PSDA obviously provides some parameters for the rights of individuals but leaves many questions unanswered. More and more, patients, family members, physicians, and other medical personnel are turning to medical ethicists for assistance in clarifying the issues and making decisions. Medical ethicists acting in this role are known as *ethical consultants*.

what is it like to be a medical ethicist?

Most medical ethicists are involved in some combination of teaching and research in an academic setting: a medical school, seminary or divinity school, or the department of philosophy and/or religion at a college or university. Some hold academic positions and also have a private practice as ethical consultants for local health care institutions. A small but increasing number of medical ethicists work full-time as consultants in private practice (without a teaching position). Others are employed as researchers and policy developers by federal, state, and private agencies.

For Richard Zaner, a typical workweek includes about 10 to 15 hours of teaching classes or holding private conferences with students. His classes typically attract students from a wide range of professional programs

(law, medicine, nursing, and religion) as well as graduate students in ethics.

Richard works to make his classes reflect practical issues that he encounters as a medical ethicist. One such class is Life Before Birth, a course that hadn't been offered for a few years but that is drawing renewed interest because of recent scientific developments. The class covers the latest developments in the Human Genome Project and the ethical and social issues it raises, such as privacy and commercial use of genetic information and issues in genetics research, counseling, clinical use, and engineering.

On the average, Richard spends about eight hours a week in individual ethics consultations with patients or staff members at Vanderbilt Medical Center. An ethics consultation can be called by any patient or hospital staff member. Some requests are quite simple—a patient wanting to talk about making a living will, for example. Others are more complex, involving a patient's refusal of treatment or disagreements between doctors and family members about treatment options.

Although competent adults have the right to refuse treatment, a life-or-death decision should not be made without serious discussion. In many cases, competency to make an informed decision is a difficult matter to determine. When the patient is clearly not competent (an infant or a person in a coma) and has not left an advance directive (a living will or assignment of durable power of attorney), ethical problems multiply. And what happens if a patient's condition becomes critical but the person to whom he or she has given durable power of attorney cannot be located?

While Richard is called in at one time or another by all hospital departments, his assistance is most frequently requested by the ICU (intensive care unit) or in connection with organ transplants, premature births, and difficult pregnancies. In addition to about eight hours of consulting at Vanderbilt Medical Center, a typical week includes about two hours of external consulting with other hospitals or local individuals.

Another two to four hours a week of Richard's time is devoted to hospital and university committees, dealing with such matters as possible conflicts of interest: for example, are researchers who are being funded by industry manipulating their data to produce the results their sponsors want to see? As director of the Center for Clinical and Research Ethics, he also has to spend time attending to administrative duties, such as planning budgets.

Research, writing, and participation in professional organizations are also important parts of Richard's work. One of the books he has published, *Troubled Voices: Stories of Ethics and Illness,* is a personal account for general readers of some of his experiences as a medical ethicist. At the same time he was writing *Troubled Voices,* he was preparing to participate in a nationwide teleconference on end-of-life issues and to lecture on clinical ethics in a meeting of the Society for Law, Medicine, and Ethics.

more lingo to learn

Gene splicing: The transfer of genetic material from one organism to another by splitting DNA strands at certain key points; this procedure is also called recombinant-DNA formation.

Genetic engineering: Human intervention in the reproductive and/or hereditary processes of organisms by such techniques as gene splicing, cloning, artificial insemination, in vitro fertilization, and hybridization.

Passive euthanasia: The termination of life-sustaining treatment.

Hippocratic oath: The oath that summarizes the physician's ethical code; it promises to observe confidentiality and to respect human life.

After earning her Ph.D. in religion with a specialty in biomedical ethics, Christine Caron splits her time between teaching and serving as an ethical consultant at Saint Thomas Hospital. Christine also works with community outreach teams—helping home health care agencies, hospices, and other community-based organizations to develop policies and procedures for dealing with ethical issues. She gained her clinical consulting experience in Vanderbilt Medical Center's trauma, obstetrics, neonatal, and pediatrics departments.

have I got what it takes to be a medical ethicist?

When asked what personal qualities are important for a medical ethicist, Richard Zaner puts "wonderful listening skills" at the head of the list. "You need to have flexibility and a balanced temperament, the courage to explore the unknown, and the ability to live with moral uncertainty." He has coined the term *possibilizing* to sum up the essential imaginative quality of "thinking for the possibly otherwise."

"The hardest part of the job is wondering if you're really helping or just complicating things," reflects Christine. "I wonder if I have asked the right questions, if I have been fair." The rewards, however, are also great. Christine finds a deep satisfaction in being able to work with people in their decision-making processes and seeing the sense of peace and understanding that they eventually reach.

Medical ethics is not the right profession for people who expect to find easy, clear-cut answers or prefer to avoid dealing with the tough questions of life and death. Clinical consulting in medical ethics also requires the patience and emotional maturity to work day after day with people who are suffering and in pain.

Since a career as a medical ethicist often requires a Ph.D., or at least a master's degree with some clinical and/or life experience, it is obviously essential to have good academic skills and to enjoy studying. Learning does not stop when one's formal education is over. In a rapidly developing field like medical ethics, this is even truer than in most professions. Medical ethicists today are confronting issues created by technological advances that would have been dismissed as science fiction not long ago.

how do I become a medical ethicist?

education

High School

To become a medical ethicist, you should take a well-balanced college preparatory course in high school—science, math, history, literature, and languages. Richard Zaner emphasizes the importance of including courses that encourage the development of imagination and creativity, such as literature, art, and music. Good communication skills are also important.

Sometimes it is possible for high school students to get personal exposure to the work of medical ethicists. On several occasions, Richard has arranged for an interested high school student to spend a few weeks shadowing him—accompanying him on hospital rounds, attending his classes and committee meetings, and sitting in on discussions with patients and doctors. Perhaps there is a medical ethicist in your community who would be willing to offer you a similar educational experience. If not, there may be opportunities to do volunteer work at a hospital, which would give you an idea of the kinds of issues that arise in medical settings. You might be able to interview the chair of a hospital ethics committee or other people who are involved in the field. Reading newspapers and magazines will acquaint you with the latest developments and controversies in medical ethics.

Postsecondary Training

Students with many different college majors go into the field of medical ethics. Most people working in medical ethics today got their formal training not in medicine or bioethics, but in law, medicine, philosophy, religion, or sociology.

While Christine Caron was enrolled in a pre-med program, she took a course called Law, Medicine, and Ethics. She "fell in love" with ethics and eventually decided to get a Ph.D. in religion with a bioethics specialty instead of going to medical school. A good liberal arts program that includes laboratory sciences, social sciences (especially psychology and sociology), and humanities (philosophy, religion, history, and literature) provides a solid foundation for graduate work in ethics. Richard recommends philosophy or religious studies as the best undergraduate majors for studying the human experience and traditions of ethical reflection.

A medical ethicist usually earns a Ph.D. from a department of religion or philosophy, with a concentration in medical ethics. At Vanderbilt, for example, ethics is one of the fields within the graduate department of religion. Some programs, like Vanderbilt's, emphasize the clinical side of medical ethics (hands-on experience doing ethical consultations with patients and medical staff); others, most notably the University of Chicago, have a policy-development orientation.

Because medical ethics is a newly emerging field and is highly interdisciplinary, it is important not to focus solely on issues of medical ethics in one's graduate work. You need to get a broad base in the entire field of ethics, as well as doing work in such areas as psychology and sociology.

Many medical ethicists approach their work from the perspective of a commitment to a particular religious tradition (some ethicists are ordained clergy), but this is not necessary.

Whether a medical ethicist has a secular or religious perspective, however, it is essential for him or her to develop the ability to demonstrate sensitivity and understanding toward people who may have strong convictions that differ from the ethicist's own views.

Feminist and multicultural issues are just beginning to emerge in medical ethics as more women and members of minority groups enter the profession, observed Christine recently.

Richard Zaner and Christine Caron emphasize the importance of getting supervised clinical training during one's graduate program. "You need that experience at a hospital bedside talking with patients and doctors," says Dr. Zaner. (Analyzing ethical problems in a seminar room is very different from being involved in actual life-and-death situations.)

In addition to clinical experience, your Ph.D. program will require several years of course work beyond the master's degree, comprehensive exams (also known as qualifying exams), reading exams in (usually) two foreign languages, and the writing of a dissertation based on original research.

certification or licensing

There is no universal certification or licensing entity for medical ethicists. Most medical ethicists have at least a master's degree; many have a Ph.D. and several years of experience in a clinical, academic, or theological setting. Because medical ethicists come from such varied backgrounds and fill varied roles, there is not yet a consensus in the field on who should be allowed to serve as a medical ethicist.

One organization does certify ethicists who work as part of Institutional Review Boards. The Applied Research Ethics National Association (ARENA) is a national membership organization that offers a certification exam to candidates with a bachelor's degrees plus two years of relevant IRB experience. IRBs approve biomedical and behavioral research protocols for clinical trials, help hospitals and universities consider the rights of patients, and guard against scientific misconduct, such as may occur when commercial entities sponsor research.

scholarships and grants

There are many sources of financial aid for graduate and undergraduate students. Consult the financial aid office of the institution you plan to attend for information about scholarships, grants, loans, work-study programs, and other forms of assistance.

Graduate students should also contact their academic department for information about fellowships and teaching or research assistantships. Funding may also be available through the National Institutes of Health, National Endowment for the Humanities, and various private foundations.

To be a successful medical ethicist, you should

- Have the courage to explore the unknown
- Be able to ask the tough questions about life and death
- Be a perceptive and compassionate listener
- Have a solid background in the social sciences and humanities
- Have the ability to deal with moral uncertainties

internships and volunteerships

The National Institutes of Health, through its Clinical Center Bioethics Program, offers short- and long-term internships and has visiting fellows and scholars. The Scientific Freedom, Responsibility and Law Program of the American Association for the Advancement of Science offers internship opportunities for undergraduate and graduate students to "experience firsthand how issues at the intersection of science, ethics, and the law are addressed in a policy setting." It is currently an unpaid internship but may offer course credit. Call 202-326-6600 for more information. When applying for any kind of financial aid, always be sure to get all the paperwork in well ahead of the deadline.

who will hire me?

Most medical ethicists are employed by academic institutions and university-related medical centers. Typically, they teach at medical and nursing schools, colleges, universities, seminaries, and divinity schools. They often do consulting at university-related and/or local health care facilities as part of a hospital ethics committee or IRB. For most, ethical consulting is part of their academic jobs, but some maintain private consulting practices along with their teaching positions. A new and growing trend in the field of medical ethics is to become a full-time private entrepreneur with a clientele made up of various local hospitals and health care agencies, now that all hospitals are required to have ethics committees.

Other medical ethicists, generally those who are more interested in research and policy development than in direct involvement with the clinical aspects, work for federal agencies. For example, one of Richard Zaner's colleagues is employed by the Department of Energy for its radiation-exposure study.

Some medical ethicists work for the National Institutes of Health on the Human Genome Project. The Ethical, Legal, and Social Implications Program of the Human Genome Project considers ethical dilemmas presented by new genetic knowledge. State agencies usually do not hire medical ethicists for full-time positions, but this may change in the near future. There are also employment opportunities for medical ethicists at private agencies, institutes, and foundations, such as the Rockefeller or Lilly Foundations.

Medical ethicists learn about job openings through personal contacts, professional journals, and listings published by professional organizations, such as the American Philosophical Association and the American Academy of Religion. Students looking for their first professional position in medical ethics should turn to their graduate school professors (especially their dissertation committee members) for advice on current job openings.

where can I go from here?

Medical ethicists in academic institutions advance by being promoted from assistant professor to associate professor to full professor, as they demonstrate increased professional achievement (success in teaching, research, writing, consulting). Some medical ethicists become directors of major research projects or of centers for ethical study (in university settings, government agencies, or private foundations). Advancement for consultants in private practice means winning wider recognition for one's expertise and being called upon by more clients.

Richard Zaner, plans to retire next year. He will spend a leave-of-absence year with full pay from Vanderbilt University to finish the books he has been working on and travel to lecture on medical ethics. Christine Caron has also left Vanderbilt to help establish the new Center for Ethics and Public Policy at Seattle University, where she will also teach medical ethics courses. The center will serve as a resource for health care agencies and biotechnology companies and universities engaged in research.

what are the salary ranges?

Starting salaries for faculty members in universities and medical schools range from $33,390 to $71,360; the medical schools tend to pay more than other academic institutions. Medical ethicists who are employed as consultants for hospitals have comparable incomes. Upper-level salaries for medical ethicists are usually more than $100,000.

what is the job outlook?

Medical ethics has been a growth industry for the last 10 years, and this trend will probably continue. The sheer quantity of issues demanding attention from medical ethicists will undoubtedly continue to expand as advances in technology, like the mapping of the human genome, are made.

Despite the bioethics boom, related jobs remain relatively few in number. Only a select few will make medical ethics a full-time career in the near future; most will supplement their work teaching or consulting in their area of expertise, such as law, religion, or medicine. The advent of managed health care has made it difficult for most institutions to hire full-time medical ethicists. Also, as more universities offer master's level and certificate-level programs, people already employed by hospitals and universities can receive medical ethics training rather than providing openings for new staff members.

While many medical ethicists are employed by a college or university, the academic sector alone cannot provide jobs for everyone entering the field. Medical ethics jobs in the government sector continue to hold promise, according to a recent article in the multidisciplinary magazine *The Scientist*. Government staff positions include working with congressional health committees, state and legislative health subcommittees, and executive branch policy-related committees.

IRBs are also providing more jobs for medical ethicists, according to *The Scientist*. IRBs have grown in number as both the amount of research being conducted and the regulatory demands on that research continue to increase. Most IRBs are affiliated with hospitals or universities, but some independent IRBs offer consulting on new drug and device reviews.

Because medical ethics is an exciting field that is often in the news, it is attracting many students, and there is a lot of competition for jobs.

how do I learn more?

professional organizations

For more information about the field of medical ethics, contact the following organizations:

American Society for Bioethics and Humanities
4700 West Lake
Glenview, IL 60025-1485
847-375-4745
http://www.asbh.org

National Institutes of Health Clinical Center Bioethics Program
Building 10, Room 1C116
9000 Rockville Pike
Bethesda, MD 20892
301-496-2496
http://www.cc.nih.gov/

Public Responsibility in Medicine and Research Applied Research Ethics National Association
123 Boylston Street, 4th Floor
Boston, MA 02116
617-423-4112
arenainfo@aol.com
http://www.primr.org/arena.html

Operated by the University of Pennsylvania's Center for Bioethics, this Web site offers links to graduate programs, news and issues, and career information.
Bioethics.Net
http://www.bioethics.net

bibliography

Following is a sampling of materials relating to the professional concerns and development of medical ethicists.

Beauchamp, Tom L. and Leroy Walters, eds. *Contemporary Issues in Bioethics.* 5th Edition. Belmont, CA: Wadsworth Publishing Co., 1999.

Crigger, Bette-Jane, ed. *Cases in Bioethics: Selections from the Hastings Center Report.* 3rd Edition. New York, NY: Bedford Books, 1999.

Friedman, Emily. *The Right Thing: Ten Years of Ethics Columns from the Healthcare Forum Journal.* Alexandria, VA: Jossey-Bass, 1996.

Howell, Joseph H. et al. eds. *Life Choices: A Hastings Center Introduction to Bioethics.* 2nd Edition. Washington, DC: Georgetown University Press, 2000.

Jecker, Nancy S., Albert R. Jonsen, and Robert A. Pearlman. *Bioethics: An Introduction to the History, Methods, and Practice.* Sudbury, MA: Jones & Bartlett Pub, 1997.

Jonsen, Albert R. *The Birth of Bioethics.* New York, NY: Oxford University Press, 1998.

Jonsen, Albert R. et al. *Clinical Ethics: A Practical Approach to Ethical Decisions in Clinical Medicine.* 4th Edition. New York, NY: McGraw-Hill, 1998.

King, Nancy M. P. and Jane Stein. *Beyond Regulations: Ethics in Human Subjects Research.* Chapel Hill, NC: University of North Carolina Press, 1999.

Kuhse, Helga and Peter Singer, eds. *Bioethics: An Anthology.* Osford, UK: Blackwell Science Publishers, 1999.

Little, Miles. *Humane Medicine: A Leading Surgeon Examines What Doctors Do, What Patients Expect of Them, and How the Expectations of Both Are Not Being Met.* New York, NY: Cambridge University Press, 1995.

Mappes, Thomas and David Degrazia. *Biomedical Ethics.* 5th Edition. New York, NY: McGraw-Hill, 2000.

Pence, Gregory E. *Classic Cases in Medical Ethics: Accounts of Cases that Have Shaped Medical Ethics.* 3rd Edition. New York, NY: McGraw-Hill, 1999.

Shannon, Thomas A. *An Introduction to Bioethics.* 3rd Edition. Mahwah, NJ: Paulist Press, 1997.

Veatch, Robert M. *The Basics of Bioethics.* New York, NY: Prentice-Hall, 1999.

Medical Illustrators and Medical Photographers

Definition

Medical illustrators and medical photographers create visual materials intended to communicate information about anatomy, biology, physiological conditions, and medical procedures.

High School Subjects

Art
Biology
Computer science

Personal Skills

Artistic
Communication/ideas

Salary Range

$28,000 to $37,000 to $64,000+

Educational Requirements

Master's degree (medical illustrators)
Associate's degree (medical photographers)

Certification or Licensing

Recommended

Outlook

About as fast as the average (medical illustrators)
Little change or more slowly than the average (medical photographers)

GOE
01.02.03
02.04.02
O*NET-SOC
27-4021.02

Ankle and foot bones lie on the desktop. Pat Thomas studies them and adjusts a surgical instrument, trying to recreate the angle an orthopaedic surgeon would use when performing surgery on this part of the human body. Finally satisfied with the arrangement, Pat reaches for her sketchpad and pencils and begins sketching the delicate bones of the human foot. When she has completed the sketch, she will send it to the orthopaedic surgeon for review. "I'm working on illustrations for a foot and ankle textbook," Pat says. "The surgeon will study the sketches and tell me whether the angle of the instrument should be a bit higher or whether the insertion point should be further back on the foot. We'll go back and forth a few times—there are always revisions. That's why illustrators start with pencil sketches!"

what does a medical illustrator or a medical photographer do?

Medical illustrators and *medical photographers* share the same challenge: They must communicate very complex medical or scientific information in a visual format. They work with such diverse subject matter as skeletal systems, organs, surgical procedures, and illnesses or injuries. Visual communication is used to convey scientific and medical information in textbooks, professional journals, advertisements, brochures and pamphlets, instructional videotapes, computer-assisted instruction, exhibits, lecture presentations, television, and even courtrooms.

Because the uses for medical and scientific visual communication can vary as greatly as the subject matter, medical illustrators and photographers must tailor their techniques to meet the objectives of each project.

When an illustrator prepares a drawing for a brochure intended to explain a condition or procedure to a patient, for example, he or she might use a very simple style of illustration, such as using cartoon drawings. If an illustration will be used to describe a new surgical procedure to physicians, the illustrator might strive for extreme realism and detail. An illustrator who is preparing a cover for a medical journal might use fairly realistic, but dramatic coloring. In a diagram illustrating the flow of blood through the circulatory system, the illustrator might instead use color as a kind of code to distinguish, for example, the oxygen-rich blood leaving the heart and the oxygen-poor blood returning to the heart.

Like illustrators, photographers can vary their style depending on the purpose of a photograph. Photographs that are used to document a patient's condition before and after surgery, for instance, must be technically proficient, but need not use space or lighting in an interesting way. Photographs for brochures or advertising materials, on the other hand, are often highly stylized and dramatic. Photographers use lighting, camera angles, and design principles to create different effects in their photographs.

Many photographers and illustrators today work in media and communications departments and must be able to perform a variety of tasks, including computer illustration and animation, writing, editing, page design, and project management.

lingo to learn

Airbrush: A tool that uses compressed air in supplying a fine spray of paint.

Animation: A movie made by photographing a changing succession of inanimate objects, such as puppets or drawings.

Anterior: Front view.

Cartooning: Drawing, usually characterized by simplicity or humor, used to convey a message.

Cross section: A piece of tissue, organ, or bone that is cut at a right angles to its surface.

Dorsal: Back view.

Fixed specimen: Tissue that has been coated or soaked in a substance that makes it firm and unchanging.

Lateral: Side view.

Perspective: In drawing or photography, the arrangement of objects to give the proper sense of depth and distance.

Stock photography: Photographs that are in stock, that is, part of a permanent collection owned by a department such as a hospital's medical photography department.

what is it like to be a medical illustrator or a medical photographer?

Because medical illustrators and photographers can work in such a wide variety of settings, it is difficult to generalize about their experiences. Pat Thomas, for example, is self-employed. She works in an office in her own home and can set her own hours. Pat is a very disciplined individual, who is able to concentrate for long hours on her work. "A person who works at home has to be very self-motivated," Pat comments. "It's pretty easy to get distracted by household chores and errands."

Pat rarely uses live models for illustrations. She relies on her knowledge of anatomy, reference materials, and physicians' descriptions. Pat also studies the human skeleton she keeps in her office. She hastens to add that, "It isn't from a real person. It's made out of plastic." Although she is sometimes called upon to meet with a physician or observe a procedure, Pat usually spends many hours a day working in solitude.

"I'm from the old school," Pat says of her work. "Although I now do quite a bit of work on the computer, I became a medical illustrator before [computers] were as important to illustration as they are today. I am well versed in the traditional media, such as pen and ink, airbrush, and water color." She adds, "The computer is really just another tool in illustration, though. Illustrators who rely on computers still must have extensive training in design and drawing. And even illustrators who work almost entirely on the computer begin by making sketches."

An individual who works in a hospital, on the other hand, may interact with a large number of different people each day. Joe Baraby describes his days as a medical photographer for a large hospital as filled with variety, excitement, and a certain amount of chaos. On a typical day, Joe arrives by 8 AM and begins catching up on production work, such as copying and printing photographs. At 9:30 or so, he might meet with a member of one of the hospital's many departments to discuss a brochure project. He then might spend several hours on location, taking photographs for the brochure. "My work is not all scientific," Joe explains. "If the hospital needs a brochure about its pediatric wing, for instance, I may spend several days taking photographs of children or of staff members."

At any point in his day, Joe might be called up to document a surgical procedure. "When I get called into a surgery, I can't hold up the procedure. I have to grab my equipment, run up to surgery, put on a surgical gown and cap, and get in there."

Once he is in the operating room, Joe must work swiftly but carefully. "I have to be very careful not to touch anything," says Joe. "If I accidentally bump an instrument tray, the surgical team will have to replace it with a sterile tray. They don't appreciate interruptions like that, so you learn to be extremely cautious."

Because pooling blood makes the site of a surgical incision very difficult to see, let alone photograph, the surgical team usually must swab the area that is being photographed. Joe then tries to find a good perspective for the photograph without leaning directly over the patient.

When documenting a surgical procedure, Joe may have to be in and out of the operating room all afternoon. "I don't stay in the operating room throughout a procedure," he comments. "I might take one shot at 1:30, then run down to do some production work in my office. At 2 PM, I might run back up to take a shot of the next step in the procedure, then run down to photograph a ribbon-cutting on a new wing, then run back up for the final stage of the surgery. It makes for an exciting day."

Illustrators who work in a hospital setting usually do not cover as many miles in a day as a photographer. Richard Doering, who is a medical illustrator in the communications department of a large urban hospital, spends most of his day creating graphic illustrations, charts, and graphs on a computer. Unlike Joe, Richard rarely works with live subjects. Instead, he relies on reference books and stock photography. Richard often scans existing photographs or illustrations into his computer and then alters them to illustrate particular conditions or procedures.

The challenges that Richard faces are similar to those faced by designers and communications professionals in many other settings. He must satisfy clients, obtain approvals from hospital management, and meet very tight printing schedules. He also must keep meticulous records. "We have to charge departments within the hospital for our time," he explains, "so we have to keep track of the time and materials we devote to each project. The paperwork can be time consuming and tedious." It is, however, a necessary part of the job.

> The computer is really just another tool in illustration, though. Illustrators who rely on computers still must have extensive training in design and drawing.

in-depth

Technology Plus Art

Leonardo da Vinci (1452-1519 AD), a leading figure of the Italian Renaissance period, kept busy by painting, sketching, inventing mechanical objects, and deducing that the arrangement of leaves on a plant allowed for their maximum exposure to sunlight—among other things. Possessing both an artistic and a scientific mind, was he a medical illustrator? Perhaps. Leonardo da Vinci did extensive studies of the human body (both alive and dead) and affected the artistic and medical communities with his highly detailed and accurate sketches of the body and various organs. Even today his work is recognized for combining the interests of these two communities. In fact, the illustration at the beginning of every chapter in this book is based on his drawing, Vitruvian Man.

Artists throughout the centuries have made use of new technologies to enhance their work. The development of oil-based paints, prestretched canvases, and photography are only a few innovations that have changed how an artist creates. Today medical illustrators and photographers make use of the computer to help with the design and refinement of their works. Illustrators may employ computer drawing programs for detail. Photographers may use scanning devices and thermal imaging systems (that actually portray the heat from a person's body as a color) to create unique photographs showing a new and interior perspective.

have I got what it takes to be a medical illustrator or a medical photographer?

To succeed as either a medical illustrator or a medical photographer, an individual must have a talent for art and a keen sense of design, as well as an interest in science. "Medical illustration was the perfect way for me to combine my love of art with my interest in science," says Richard.

Although both professions require a dual interest in art and science, they also require some very different skills. Medical illustrators must be able to sit very still for hours at a time. They must have exceptional concentration skills and meticulous attention to detail. Most medical illustrators today also must be able to use a variety of computer software programs, as well as traditional media, such as pen and ink, watercolors, and airbrushes.

Medical illustrators also must be creative, but technically precise. "Although medical illustration must be accurate, it is actually a very subjective process," Pat says. "A medical illustrator is trying to convey information, not to recreate exactly what you would see if you looked into an incision in a human body. If an illustration is to be useful, the illustrator must carefully select its content to communicate essential information and ignore irrelevant details."

Medical photographers also must have an appreciation for design and extensive knowledge of anatomy. In addition, they must understand lighting and they must be able to work skillfully but quickly. Because they often must photograph individuals who are ill or injured, they must be able to project a professional demeanor under emotionally charged circumstances.

how do I become a medical illustrator or a medical photographer?

Both medical illustrators and medical photographers must spend years studying art and science. Medical illustrators must complete a master's program that includes an assortment of art courses as well as many of the science courses taken by medical students. Medical photographers must complete an associate's or a bachelor's degree program that emphasizes art, photography, and science.

education

High School

If you are interested in becoming a medical illustrator, you should concentrate on art and science courses in high school. Art and graphics classes that teach the principles of design are essential for you to take. Concentrate on drawing courses, particularly those that focus on drawing live models, as well as classes that focus on different media, such as pen and ink drawing, watercolor, sculpture, or computer illustration. In addition, you should take science classes, such as biology, chemistry, health, and anatomy. Since you will need a college education, take other classes that are college preparatory, including math, history, and English.

If you are interested in becoming a medical photographer, your high school course work should be similar to that of those interested in medical illustration. Naturally, though, you should concentrate on developing your photography skills by taking photography classes. Don't limit yourself only to those available at your high school. Often local museums will offer workshops or weekend classes in different types of photography. Gain additional experience by taking photographs for the school yearbook or newspaper or by joining after-school photography clubs. In addition, take as many science classes as possible. Any class that gives you the opportunity to perform dissections or study anatomy will be beneficial. Again, like those wanting to be medical illustrators, round out your education with math, history, and English classes.

Finally, whether you want to become a medical illustrator or medical photographer, you should take computer science courses. You will use computers not only to create artwork but also to keep records in your business.

Postsecondary Training

The next step for the future medical illustrator is to get a bachelor's degree from an accredited college or university. In your undergradu-

ate studies you should continue to focus on art and science courses. Those who enter this field typically have bachelor's degrees either with an art major and a science minor or a science major and an art minor. In either case, important classes to take include drawing, advanced life drawing, color theory, design, computer graphics, and photography. Science courses should closely follow a curriculum designed to prepare you for medical school. These courses usually include general biology, zoology, anatomy, embryology, physiology, and chemistry.

After college, you will need to get a master's degree from a program accredited by the Commission on Accreditation of Allied Health Education Programs. Currently there are five such programs in the United States and one in Canada. These programs generally accept between three and 12 students per year, so competition is intense. Graduate programs in medical illustration are usually two to three years in length and include extensive art courses, medical science courses, and some business management courses.

After high school, the next educational step for the future medical photographer is to get a degree in photography. According to the BioCommunications Association (BCA), the leading organization for medical photographers, the only school in the country that currently offers a degree specifically in biomedical photography is the Rochester Institute of Technology (RIT) in New York. Through its school of Photographic Arts and Sciences, RIT awards a bachelor's degree in biomedical photographic communications. Course work covers topics such as photography, digital photography, human biology, and medical terminology. (For more information, visit the Institute's Web site at http://www.rit.edu.) The Brooks Institute of Photography, located in California, offers a bachelor's degree in industrial/scientific photography, and students may choose to concentrate on medical photography. (For more information, visit the Institute's Web site at http://www.brooks.edu.) Unfortunately, few other colleges and universities have medical photography programs. Many schools, however, offer photography degrees, either at the associate's or bachelor's level. If you attend a general photography program, be sure to supplement your course of study with as many science classes, such as anatomy and biology, as you can. Also, while you are in school, try to get a summer photography job or internship in a medical setting, for example, at a local hospital.

certification or licensing

The Association of Medical Illustrators (AMI) offer the professional designation Certified Medical Illustrator (CMI). To receive this designation, an illustrator must have graduated from an accredited medical illustration program or have five years of professional medical illustration experience and have completed a dissection course in human anatomy. In addition, the illustrator must pass a written exam and portfolio review of his or her medical illustrations. Certification is valid for five years and to renew, illustrators must complete continuing education requirements.

The BCA offers medical photographers the designation Registered Biological Photographer (RBP). To receive this designation, photographers must pass written and oral exams as well as a practical exam. The practical exam consists of assembling and submitting a portfolio of medical photography demonstrating the individual's impressive skills and understanding of the field.

Medical photographers who specialize in ophthalmology can also receive certification from the Ophthalmic Photographers' Society, Inc. Requirements for obtaining the Certified Retinal Angiographer (CRA) designation include submitting a photography portfolio, passing written and performance exams, and having an up-to-date Cardio-Pulmonary Resuscitation (CPR) certificate.

Certification is not mandatory for either medical illustrators or photographers, but it can be extremely helpful in establishing credibility and obtaining employment. Licensing is not required in either field.

To be a successful medical illustrator or a medical photographer, you should

- Enjoy doing detailed work
- Be creative and able to communicate ideas visually
- Enjoy art, design, and working with your hands
- Have patience
- Enjoy working with technology

who will hire me?

Both medical illustrators and medical photographers are employed by hospitals and academic institutions. Others are employed by biological laboratories, pharmaceutical manufacturers, schools of dentistry, schools of osteopathy, or schools of veterinary medicine. A few are employed by organizations that publish medical literature or textbooks. Many professionals in both fields are self-employed, and they work as consultants for medical facilities, academic institutions, individual doctors, publishing companies, and law firms.

Professional organizations, such as the AMI and the BCA, can be very helpful for individuals who are just starting out in either field. In addition to posting information about available positions, these organizations create opportunities for professionals to share information with one another about new techniques, technologies, and trends.

where can I go from here?

Medical illustrators and photographers who work for large hospitals or teaching institutions can become managers of media and communications departments. Those who are successful in management positions are willing to do administrative work and have excellent interpersonal skills.

Other members of these professions shape their careers by specializing in a particular area, such as ophthalmology. Still others who want to have a greater variety of work, more control over their projects, and higher profits choose to form their own businesses. In addition to the skills necessary to produce effective illustrations and photographs, these individuals also must be able to market themselves in order to draw in new clients, have the self-discipline to manage schedules and adhere to their own deadlines, and have strong record keeping and accounting skills.

what are the salary ranges?

The Economic Research Institute reported that the average annual salary for medical and scientific illustrators just starting out in the field was $28,040 in 1999. An illustrator's income usually grows with his or her experience. Those with five years of experience earned an average of $37,363, while those with 10 years of experience averaged a salary of $44,932. According to the U.S. Department of Labor, the highest paid 10 percent of visual artists, including medical illustrators, made more than $64,000 annually in 1998. A very few illustrators earn between $100,000 and $200,000 per year. These individuals, however, are at the very top of their field and may be heads of departments, administrators, or combining freelance work with full-time positions.

Illustrators who work for academic institutions usually make less than those who work for major hospitals. Self-employed illustrators can earn more or less than a person with a full-time position, depending on the number of hours they work, the reputations they have established in the field, and the nature of their clients' work. Publishing companies, for example, usually pay less than law firms who hire illustrators to create illustrations that will be used as evidence in a trial.

According to the U.S. Department of Labor, photographers had median yearly earnings of $20,940 in 1998. The highest paid 10 percent made more than $43,860 per year. These salary figures are for all photographers, and medical photographers may have higher annual incomes than these median amounts. Medical photographers, however, may earn slightly less than medical illustrators with the same amount of experience.

what is the job outlook?

The demand for medical illustrators is fairly constant. Because of factors such as the small size of this profession, the highly selective nature of graduate schools offering medical illustration programs, and the small number of people entering the field each year, new graduates should have little trouble finding positions. The outlook will be best for those willing to relocate. Employment in this area should grow about as fast as the average.

The demand for medical photographers, on the other hand, has actually slowed in recent years. As health care providers cut costs to remain competitive, more institutions are purchasing and altering stock photography rather than hiring photographers to produce

There are five accredited graduate programs in medical illustration in the United States. They are:

Johns Hopkins School of Medicine
The Medical College of Georgia
University of Illinois at Chicago
University of Michigan at Ann Arbor
University of Texas Southwestern
  Medical Center at Dallas

original pictures. Some physicians also take photographs for themselves or rely upon members of a media or communications department to take them. In addition, the U.S. Department of Labor predicts employment for photographers in general to increase more slowly than the average in the next decade.

Not everyone, however, believes that this downward trend will continue. Dan Patton, a registered biological photographer who works for the Ohio State University College of Veterinarian Medicine, comments, "Although the demand for medical photography has been declining in the past few years, I believe that it will begin to increase in the very near future. Because there are so many important new developments in the scientific world right now, the scientific and medical communities will need photographers to help communicate all this new information to physicians, medical students, and the public."

how do I learn more?

professional organizations

Following are organizations that provide information on careers and schools for medical illustrators and medical photographers.

Association of Medical Illustrators
2965 Flowers Road South, Suite 105
Atlanta, GA 30341
770-454-7933
http://medical-illustrators.org

BioCommunications Association
Central Office
115 Stoneridge Drive
Chapel Hill, NC 27514
919-967-8246
http://www.bca.org

This Web site has additional information about ophthalmologic photography.
Ophthalmologic Photographers' Society, Inc.
http://webeye.ophth.uiowa.edu/ops

bibliography

Following is a sampling of books and periodicals relating to the professional concerns and development of medical illustrators and medical photographers.

Burns, Stanley. *A Morning's Work: Medical Photographs from the Burns Archive & Collection, 1843-1939.* Santa Fe, NM: Twin Palms Publishers, 1998.

Gilman, Sander L. *Picturing Health and Illness: Images of Identity and Difference.* Baltimore, MD: Johns Hopkins University Press, 1995.

Hansen, Julie V. et.al. *The Physician's Art: Representations of Art and Medicine.* Durham, NC: Duke University Press, 2000.

Kemp, Martin and Marina Wallace. *Spectacular Bodies: The Art and Science of the Human Body from Leonardo to Now.* Berkeley, CA: University of California Press, 2000.

Levin, Meryl. *Anatomy of Anatomy.* New York, NY: Third Rail Press, 2000.

Medical Illustration Sourcebook. 13th Edition. Atlanta, GA: Association of Medical Illustrators, 2000.

Saine, Patrick J. and Marshall E. Tyler. *Ophthalmic Photography: A Textbook of Fundus Photography, Angiography, and Electronic Imaging.* Newton, MA: Butterworth-Heinemann Medical, 1997.

Sherry, Clifford J. *Opportunities in Medical Imaging Careers.* Revised Edition. Lincolnwood, IL: NTC/Contemporary Publishing Co., 2000.

Stack, Lawrence B. *Handbook of Medical Photography.* Philadelphia, PA: Hanley & Belfus, 2000.

Related Jobs

Did you know that there are a number of jobs related to medical illustrators and medical photographers?

The U.S. Department of Labor classifies medical illustrators and medical photographers under the headings *Commercial Art* (GOE), *Life Sciences* (GOE), and *Art, Design, Entertainment, Sports, and Media* (O*NET-SOC). Other professionals in this category include art directors, exhibit designers, industrial designers, fashion artists, cartoonists, creative directors, fashion artists, graphic designers, photographers, photojournalists, photographic reproduction technicians.

Medical Laboratory Technicians

Definition

Medical laboratory technicians perform routine tests and laboratory procedures. They collect and prepare specimens of body fluids, tissues, and cells for use in diagnosis and treatment of disease. They also analyze blood, urine, spinal fluids, and other body fluids.

Alternative Job Titles

Clinical laboratory technicians
Laboratory technicians
Laboratory assistants
Medical technicians

High School Subjects

Biology
Chemistry

Personal Skills

Helping/teaching
Technical/scientific

Salary Range

$21,000 to $26,000 to $30,000

Minimum Educational Level

Associate's degree

Certification or Licensing

Required by certain states

Outlook

About as fast as the average

GOE
02.04.02
O*NET-SOC
29-2012.00

"**Because I work** in the health center at a large university, a lot of the people we see are not very sick," says Cheryl Montoya, a medical laboratory technician. "Most students are in pretty good shape. They have colds, the flu, sports injuries . . . minor things mostly." Cheryl shakes her head and adds, "But that's not always the case. One time a student came in for a routine physical, and when we did his blood work, his white cell count was very low. Results like that scare us. The laboratory supervisor called upstairs to the doctor. He ordered more blood tests, and after we finished they rushed the student to the hospital. He had leukemia.

"That was a few months ago," Cheryl says. "The student is finished with his chemotherapy treatment now and his hair's growing back, too. Sometimes he comes to visit us in the laboratory, and he's doing just fine."

what does a medical laboratory technician do?

In the early days of medicine, healers knew that certain herbs would cure rashes and that the bark of certain trees would reduce fevers. They observed that drinking poor water and eating bad food contributed to ill health. However, they could only guess about how the human body really worked and about what actually caused disease. Over time, people began to solve these mysteries.

A huge step occurred with the development of the microscope. For the first time, doctors and scientists could observe microorganisms like bacteria and viruses within the human body. They could study the structure of tissue, watch blood coagulate, and see cells divide.

As the science of medicine progressed, physicians began to search for assistants to help them. The career of nursing was born during the Crimean War in the mid-1850s, but physicians still needed skilled workers to perform routine laboratory tests and procedures.

lingo to learn

Blood bank: The lab area responsible for drawing donor blood and separating, identifying, and matching its components to allow safe transfusions.

Cytology: The study of cells, their origin, structure, and function.

Hematology: The lab area that counts, describes, and identifies cells in blood and other body fluids.

Histology: The study of the structure and function of normal and abnormal tissue.

Immunology: The branch of medicine dealing with the body's ability to cope with infections.

Pathology: The study of the nature of disease, its structure, and the changes produced by disease.

Virology: The study of viruses and viral diseases.

In the United States, most physicians taught their own laboratory assistants until the mid-1930s when attempts to standardize training began. Today, *medical laboratory technicians* aid physicians in a variety of ways.

Medical laboratory technicians may be either generalists or specialists. Generalists do several different kinds of laboratory tasks, while specialists concentrate on performing one type of activity. All laboratory technicians are part of a medical team that helps detect, diagnose, and treat disease. General medical laboratory technicians collect samples of blood, body fluids, and tissues as directed by physicians. They use these specimens to perform standardized medical tests. Medical laboratory technicians follow detailed instructions. They may employ precision equipment or perform the tests manually. They may use computers to retrieve, record, or relay patient information. Medical laboratory technicians also conduct routine quality control checks and restock laboratory equipment and supplies.

Medical laboratory technicians often are supervised by *medical laboratory technologists.* Medical laboratory technologists are sometimes known as *clinical laboratory technologists,* while medical laboratory technicians are sometimes known as *clinical laboratory technicians.*

Medical laboratory technologists hold a bachelor's degree and are able to perform a wider range of laboratory tests. They may be responsible for interpreting laboratory results for physicians, and they may recommend additional testing, depending on the results of the initial procedures.

Like medical laboratory technicians, medical laboratory technologists may be either specialists or generalists. Areas of laboratory specialty for both medical laboratory technicians and medical laboratory technologists include histology, cytology, immunology, phlebotomy, blood bank technology, microbiology, chemistry, and urinalysis. *Histologic technicians* prepare tissue specimens for microscopic examination. They mount tissues on slides and stain them using special dyes so that tissue structure is more visible (see chapter "Histologic Technicians"). *Cytotechnologists* study cells. They collect cells, prepare slides, and use the microscope to search for abnormalities in order to diagnose disease (see chapter "Cytotechnologists"). *Immunology specialists* examine the components and responses of the body's immune system. In particular, they may conduct tests for sexually transmitted diseases, rheumatoid arthritis, and lupus.

Phlebotomy technicians draw blood for testing or for use in donor banks. They process, label, and secure the blood (see chapter "Phlebotomy Technicians").

Microbiology specialists study specimens in order to detect viruses, fungi, bacteria, and parasites. They may isolate and grow additional microorganisms in order to facilitate identification and help physicians make diagnoses. *Chemistry specialists* test body fluids and blood for the presence and level of many substances, including drugs, poisons, sugar, albumin, and acetone. Using chemical analysis, they help detect illnesses such as diabetes, heart disease, and kidney and liver malfunctions. Medical laboratory technicians who specialize in urinalysis perform tests on urine to check for pregnancy, the presence of various infections, or the presence of liver, kidney, and other diseases.

what is it like to be a medical laboratory technician?

Cheryl Montoya works in the student health center at University of Arizona in Tucson. Although she's a general medical technologist, she ends up doing a lot of hematology, or blood work. In this procedure, she draws blood from patients and runs the controls on the machine that does the complete blood count, or CBC, for each person.

"Drawing blood is where I make the most contact with people," she says. "I like that, especially at the university, because people come here from all over the world. Sometimes the diseases they have are very unusual. Mostly I perform routine procedures and work with the machines in the laboratory, however."

At the beginning of each day, Cheryl is also responsible for checking to make sure that each machine is functioning properly. She also makes sure that all liquids in the laboratory are full and that other supplies are stocked adequately. "Sometimes it can get very busy in here," she says, "and you don't want to have to take time out to refill a container."

Even though she does a lot of blood work, Cheryl also conducts other types of tests. To check for strep throat, for example, she swabs the patient's throat. Then, in the microbiology section of the laboratory, the specimens are

> *I like working in the laboratory. I like using the equipment, running tests, working with chemicals, drawing blood, and swabbing throats.*

examined for the presence of bacteria. Urine specimens are tested first with a dipstick and studied for any change in color. Depending on the results, additional urine samples may be mixed with chemical reagents. A cloudy mixture can represent the presence of certain kinds of proteins and indicate infection.

"It's really neat working in the chemistry part of the laboratory," she says. Testing stool specimens is another of the tasks medical laboratory technicians perform. Small amounts of the specimens are planted in purple or green agar, a gelatinous base made from seaweed that is used to grow colonies of bacteria. The specimens are covered and placed in incubators for 24 hours. "If, a day later," Cheryl says, "the colonies are still the same color, that's fine. However, black or clear-colored colonies growing on purple or green agar may indicate the presence of salmonella or shigella bacteria. That's not good. Salmonella can indicate food poisoning and shigella can be a sign of dysentery.

"I like working in the laboratory," Cheryl says. "I like using the equipment, running tests, working with chemicals, drawing blood, and swabbing throats. Where I work though, it's the people that are the best part of the job. I enjoy my co-workers as well as the patients."

have I got what it takes to be a medical laboratory technician?

Anne Loving, director of the Felician College training program in Lodi, New Jersey, points out that medical laboratory technicians may not always work in the lab. "In hospitals, you're running up to the floors to take samples or talking to nurses in order to get information. A good medical laboratory technician has to be able to work under pressure and enjoy working with people. He or she has to be a good communicator and a good listener, too."

Medical laboratory technicians who work in very large labs may find themselves repeating the same procedure over and over again. The fundamental role of medical laboratory technicians is to perform routine testing and complete basic laboratory procedures wherever they are employed.

Nevertheless, the majority of medical laboratory technicians work in much smaller facilities where they are able to rotate the type of work they do from day to day or from week to week. Medical laboratory technicians work under supervision and follow the orders of physicians. New technologies are developed in the medical field all the time, and technicians have opportunities to learn many new things, resulting in a variety of responsibilities.

Because medical laboratory technicians work in medicine, they run a slight risk of infection from disease. However, the technicians wear protective clothing such as lab coats, gloves, and when necessary, face masks, to help minimize risk.

how do I become a medical laboratory technician?

Cheryl Montoya grew up in a small mining town in Arizona. In high school, she knew that she wanted to work in the medical field, but she didn't think she wanted to be a nurse. A special program at the university, Med Start,

Severe diarrhea is sometimes caused by tiny parasites that may contaminate drinking water or food. Based on the microscopic study of patient specimens by medical lab techs, these tiny parasites are identified and the infection diagnosed.

helped her learn about other kinds of health careers. Med Start combined in-class studies with on-the-job experience.

She worked for three months as a volunteer at Planned Parenthood and then decided to make medical laboratory technology her career. She went to technical school in Phoenix, passed the state board examination, and has worked in the field ever since.

education

High School
Biology, chemistry, mathematics, English, and computer science are helpful for students wishing to enter medical laboratory technician programs after graduation.

In addition, students should also be sure to fulfill the entrance requirements of the college or technical school they plan to attend. Check with your school guidance counselor and with the admissions departments of various schools well in advance of graduation to give yourself plenty of time to prepare.

Postsecondary Training
Both degree and certificate programs are offered for medical laboratory technicians. Degree programs are two years long and provide both in-class study and clinical experience. Students earn an associate's degree. A few organizations, such as the Accrediting Bureau of Health Education Schools (ABHES) and the National Accrediting Agency for Clinical Laboratory Sciences, offer accreditation to medical laboratory technician programs.

Medical laboratory certificate programs are from one to two years in length. They also offer in-class study and clinical experience. The trend in the education and hiring of medical laboratory technicians is toward two-year, degree-granting programs rather than certificate programs.

Classes for medical laboratory technicians include study of the circulatory, urinary, central nervous, endocrine, digestive, skeletal, and muscular systems; first aid; computer literacy; basic chemistry; inorganic biochemistry; cell biology and genetics; virology; urinalysis and body fluids; immunology; serology; immuno-hematology; microbiology; parasitology; transfusion medicine; blood-banking; laboratory office procedures; medical terminology; anatomy and physiology; psychology; phlebotomy; statistics and quality control; pathology; injections; cardiopulmonary resuscitation; and patient communications. Students wishing to specialize as phlebotomy technicians or histologic technicians need additional course work in these subjects (see chapters "Histologic Technicians" and "Phlebotomy Technicians").

certification or licensing

Certification is available from American Medical Technologists. An applicant must hold an associate's degree in medical technology from an accredited two-year college. The American Society of Clinical Pathologists (ASCP) also offers certification for medical laboratory technicians. Most employers require certification, and it is especially important for advancement within the field. Some states require licensing as well; technicians can check with their state's department of health for licensing requirements.

scholarships and grants

Most colleges and universities offer general scholarships. Institutions with specific medical laboratory technician programs are most likely to have scholarships available for students interested in this field. Colleges, along with professional organizations, are sources of information for work-study, grants, and scholarships (see "How Do I Learn More?").

labor unions

Some medical laboratory technicians are unionized. Participation varies according to employer and state of residence.

who will hire me?

Mary Anderson, the program director for the medical laboratory technology program at the Wichita Area Vocational Technical School in Kansas, mentions that health care seems to be

Specialize and You Won't Be Sorry

Experts say developing a specialty as a medical laboratory technician is a great career move, especially for those people interested in working at big-city hospitals. While rural areas tend to need more generalists in all areas of health care, most larger hospital laboratories are divided into sections, according to the type of testing performed.

The **hematology** department analyzes blood and bone marrow. Patients with anemia, leukemia, and other blood infections are diagnosed and monitored here.

Workers in **serology** perform tests for syphilis, rheumatoid arthritis, and lupus.

Microbiologists cultivate and identify bacteria, viruses, and fungi which cause disease.

In the **urinalysis** department, technicians check urine for infections, kidney or liver disease, and pregnancy by detecting the presence and amounts of certain chemicals.

moving out of the metropolitan areas and into rural areas. "The demand is very high," she says, "and the money is very good." Her graduates are finding better opportunities in the areas outlying the city of Wichita.

Most medical laboratory technicians work for hospitals. Others work in doctors' offices, blood banks, or in reference laboratories. Some work as veterinary laboratory assistants (see chapter "Veterinary Technicians") and many work for industry. Industries that hire medical laboratory technicians include chemical and petroleum plants, food producers, and cosmetics manufacturers.

Many of the publications serving health professionals carry job advertisements. In addition, some employers actively recruit graduating students through visits to accredited programs.

where can I go from here?

Though Cheryl began working at the student health center as a medical laboratory technician, she recently took the state boards to become a medical technologist. Her work responsibilities haven't really changed, but payment for technologists is typically higher than that for technicians.

Other medical laboratory technicians become histologic technicians, cytotechnologists, or specialists in blood bank technology or enter other associated four-year degree programs.

what are the salary ranges?

A 1998 survey of pay and vacancy rates conducted by ASCP found that medical laboratory technicians had beginning hourly wages of $10.40 (or $21,600 for full-time employees). The average wage was $12.90 an hour ($26,800), and the top wage $14.90 an hour ($30,992). The survey also found that the pay was best in the Northeast and Far West regions of the country. According to the American Society for Clinical Laboratory Science, the

average starting salary in 2000 for clinical laboratory technicians was between $20,000 and $26,000. Full-time employment generally includes benefits such as retirement and health and life insurance.

what is the job outlook?

According to the *Occupational Outlook Handbook,* employment of clinical laboratory workers is expected to grow about as fast as the average for all other occupations. Demand for medical laboratory technicians will continue to grow, especially as the population of the country ages and more people are in need of health care. The 1998 vacancy survey conducted by ASCP found that the average vacancy rate for medical laboratory technicians was 11.1 percent, with the highest vacancy rates in the Northeast and West South Central (Arkansas, Louisiana, Oklahoma, and Texas) regions of the country.

"The need is higher than the supply," Mary Anderson says of the workforce. "We have a smaller student population than we have had at times in the past." Changes that she has noticed in the career include better developed computer systems for laboratories. "The smaller labs now have laboratory information systems, and that used to be something that was only a component of a large laboratory." These systems typically provide a database and direct linkage between the lab computer systems, the instruments that are doing the testing, and the hospital's main system, allowing for more networking of information.

Another factor influencing job growth is the cost of health care. As hospitals seek to control salary expenses, medical laboratory technicians are sometimes hired instead of more costly medical laboratory technologists, especially when both are able to perform the same basic procedures. Increased automation within the medical field may slow the demand for medical laboratory technicians somewhat. However, this slowing most likely will be offset by advances in new testing technologies that will require additional workers.

To be a **successful medical laboratory technician, you should**

- Be patient
- Be conscientious and precise
- Be able to follow orders
- Not be squeamish about dealing with bodily fluids
- Be a problem solver
- Be able to work under pressure
- Have good manual dexterity and good color vision

how do I learn more?

professional organizations

For a list of accredited schools offering programs for medical laboratory technicians, contact:

Accrediting Bureau of Health Education Schools
803 West Broad Street, Suite 730
Falls Church, VA 22046
703-533-2082
abhes@erols.com
http://www.abhes.org

For information on the latest health issues and archived JAMA issues, contact:

American Medical Association
515 North State Street
Chicago, IL 60610
312-464-5000
http://www.ama-assn.org

For information about certification, contact:

American Medical Technologists
710 Higgins Road
Park Ridge, IL 60068
847-823-5169
http://www.amt1.com

For career information, contact:

American Society for Clinical Laboratory Science
7910 Woodmont Avenue, Suite 530
Bethesda, MD 20814
ascls@ascls.org
http://www.ascls.org

For a career brochure, job listings, and information about publications and workshops, contact:

American Society of Clinical Pathologists
2100 West Harrison Street
Chicago, IL 60612
info@ascp.org
http://www.ascp.org

For information on accredited and approved educational programs in the clinical sciences, contact:

National Accrediting Agency for Clinical Laboratory Sciences
8410 West Bryn Mawr, Suite 670
Chicago, IL 60631
info@naacls.org
http://www.naacls.org

Advancement Possibilities

Program directors teach at universities, hospitals, and laboratories, instructing students in both theoretical and technical areas. They also plan and coordinate the students' clinical training, advise new students, give guidance during their school years, and assist them in finding jobs upon graduation.

Medical researchers use their investigative skills to help develop new products or explore new directions in medicine. They use computers and other instruments to gather data, and then they study and experiment with the data to learn and test new theories about diseases, laboratory methods, or products.

Cytotechnologists are laboratory specialists who study cells under microscopes, searching for cell abnormalities such as changes in color, shape, or size that might indicate the presence of disease.

bibliography

Following is a sampling of materials relating to the professional concerns and development of medical laboratory technicians.

Careers in Focus: Medical Technicians. 2nd Edition. Chicago, IL: Ferguson Publishing Company, 2001.

Linne, Jean Jorgenson, and Karen Munson Ringsrud. Clinical Laboratory Science: The Basics and Routine Techniques. Chicago, IL: Year Book Medical Publishing, 1999.

Marshall, Jacquelyn. The Medical Laboratory Assistant. Indianapolis, IN: Macmillan, 1999.

Related Jobs

The U.S. Department of Labor classifies medical laboratory technicians under the headings *Laboratory Technology: Life Sciences* (GOE) and *Healthcare Practitioners and Technical* (O*NET-SOC). Also under these headings are *special procedures technologists* who aid physicians in the process of cardiac catheterization, *ultrasound technologists* who operate equipment to provide two-dimensional ultrasonic recordings of internal organs, *pheresis specialists* who collect blood components and provide therapeutic treatments, and *radiation therapy technologists* who prepare and operate equipment to provide radiation therapy as prescribed by physicians.

Specific related jobs include:

Audiometrists
Cardiology technologists
Dental hygienists
Dialysis technicians
Electrocardiograph technicians
Electroneurodiagnostic technologists
Electroradiograph technicians
Health service coordinators
Medical records technicians
Nuclear medicine technologists
Occupational safety and health specialists
Optometric and ophthalmic technicians
Orthotists and prosthetists
Radiologic technicians
Radiologic technologists
Surgical technologists and technicians
Transplant coordinators

Medical Laser Technicians

Definition

Medical laser technicians test, service, operate, and install laser systems in medical or research environments.

Alternative Job Titles

Equipment technicians
Biomedical equipment technicians
Minimally invasive surgeons

High School Subjects

Computer science
Technical/shop

Personal Skills

Mechanical/manipulative
Technical/scientific

Salary Range

$33,000 to $40,000 to $53,000

Educational Requirements

High school diploma, associate's degree

Certification or Licensing

Voluntary

Outlook

About as fast as the average

GOE

05.03.05

O*NET-SOC

NA*

*Not Available. The O*NET-SOC does not categorize the career of medical laser technician.

Medical history may be in the making as Adam Palmer adjusts the strength of the laser in the operating room. Adam then looks across the length of the patient's body at the surgeon holding the laser and waits for any signal that will indicate he should lower the laser's power. A probe equipped with lights and a camera illuminates tiny glowing areas inside the patient's prostate. All members of the surgical team watch a monitor that captures the probe's image. The glowing areas have been magnified several times; these are cancerous cells. Armed with the laser, the surgeon directs the precise beam of light toward these cells. Adam, the medical laser technician assisting on the surgery, watches the monitor as, one by one, the small glowing areas wink out as they come into the laser's range.

The patient on the operating table suffers from prostate cancer. Two days earlier the patient was injected with a special drug that cancerous cells retain for a long time. When the light from a laser reaches the drug within the cancerous cells, it creates a chemical reaction that in turn produces a toxin, or poison, within the cancerous cell. This toxin destroys the cancerous cell completely and instantly.

This special photodynamic therapy is part of an ongoing research project at the Goldman Laser Institute at the Jewish Hospital in Cincinnati, Ohio. If this therapy is proven successful, Adam will be part of the medical team that developed a new way to treat prostate cancer.

what does a medical laser technician do?

Medical laser technicians help design, test, install, and repair laser systems and fiber-optic equipment. Medical laser technicians work with medical and research equipment and instrumentation. They routinely perform tests and take measurements using lasers and electronic devices. Medical laser technicians gather data, perform calculations, and prepare reports based on the data they have accumulated. In addition, they must be able to read and interpret shop drawings, diagrams, schematics, and sketches. Based on these drawings, medical laser technicians might build parts or direct the assembly of components.

Medical laser technicians follow safety precautions when they use or service lasers, and when they clean and maintain the lasers they use. They may perform regular alignment procedures on optical systems that use lasers, in order to document the reliability of their measurements and to safeguard against inaccuracies in their measurements or testing. Medical laser technicians may also repair lasers and troubleshoot technical problems as they arise during the use of a laser or fiber optics system in a surgery or other medical situation.

While all medical laser technicians do not necessarily perform every one of the tasks just described, many different jobs require that a medical laser technician be able to perform any number of them. Much depends on where in the medical community the medical laser technician works and what type of position he or she holds. In the past, the use of lasers in the medical world was primarily restricted to the surgical environment. Today, lasers are used in nearly every medical specialty at locations as varied as hospitals, clinics, and the offices of solo medical practitioners. Lasers and fiber optic technology is used in the medical world for surgery, ophthalmology, dermatology, and research.

lingo to learn

Laser: An acronym for Light Amplification by Stimulated Emission of Radiation. This is the scientific description of the process that creates laser light.

Monochromaticity: Light that is made up of a single color.

Directionality: Light with little radiation.

Coherence: Light waves in step.

Excitation mechanism: A laser's source of energy, such as an electric current or flashlamp.

Active medium: Usually a solid or gas that produces light by stimulated emission.

Feedback mechanism: In laser, a pair of mirrors aligned to reflect the laser light back and forth through the active medium.

Output coupler: A partially transparent mirror that allows some coherent light to leave the laser device in the form of the output beam.

what is it like to be a medical laser technician?

"We do about a hundred laser surgeries a month," says Adam Palmer, a medical laser technician at the Goldman Laser Institute. "On a typical day, I'm at the hospital by 7:00 AM and in surgery by 7:30, where I may be for the rest of the day." Adam is one of two medical laser technicians employed by the hospital. His preparations for surgery include readying the lasers that will be used during the operation. "Some lasers need to heat up, some need to cool down," Adam explains. "While I warm up or cool down the laser, I make sure that all the necessary accessories, attachments, and materials are in the operating room."

Tim Putnam, director of Laser/Advanced Surgery at St. Mary's Medical Center in Evansville, Indiana, underscores the impact lasers have had on the medical field. "Fifteen years ago, if you walked into an operating room it looked more like a carpenter's shop. There was hardly anything high tech in the room, with the exception of the anesthesia machine. The same operating room, today, looks more like people getting ready to launch the space shuttle."

Increasingly, physicians and surgeons are turning to less invasive methods of surgery and other treatments to cure their patients' problems, and lasers are among the most promising solutions. Medical laser technicians provide support to surgeons and other physicians who use lasers and fiber optic equipment. Before getting into the medical field, Tim worked as a laser technician in other areas, including field service and research.

"Working as a field service laser technician is very different from being part of team in an operating room," he says. "Laser technicians are the technical experts during the operation and must respond quickly and efficiently to any problems."

As Tim explains it, the physician or surgeon is the expert on the patient's needs, while the medical laser technician is the expert on the technology being used. So, while the doctor is the only person who actually uses a laser instrument and has direct contact with the patient, the medical laser technician has to be there to make recommendations; to fine-tune the many attachments, instruments, and machines; and to assist the physician in the event that a technical problem occurs.

Just as a golfer uses many different clubs to hit a ball, depending on the situation, a surgeon needs to choose among many different instruments. Not only do lasers have a multitude of functions, but there are many different ways to deliver a laser to a patient's body. A surgeon might use several different methods during one surgery. A surgeon, for example, could choose to deliver lasers through a microscope, through a fiber-optic tube, or through a contact tip that transfers the energy to the patient's tissue in the form of heat. The surgeon knows what cut to make and where to make it. Medical laser technicians advise how to use laser equipment to make the surgery possible. In addition, medical laser technicians help set up reflection devices, similar to

"Every day is usually different in the operating room. I like that there are always new things to learn, new types of procedures to master."

mirrors, which are used to aim the laser beam in very hard-to-reach spots.

Once the surgery is in progress, Adam notes, the medical laser technician monitors the laser, sometimes advising the surgeon on a particular power setting or suggesting the best attachment to use to achieve whatever the surgeon wants to do. Frequently, this means helping direct the laser beam to access a hard-to-reach site inside the patient's body. An example of such a surgery is in the case of an enlarged prostate. The surgeon and medical laser technician carefully position the laser to vaporize a portion of the prostate so that urine is allowed to pass through to the bladder.

In addition to helping assist the surgeon with the laser, the technician has a number of other duties. While the laser is in use, the medical laser technician makes certain that everyone in the operating room, including the patient, is protected from the laser by safety goggles. If there are any windows in the operating suite that the laser can penetrate, the windows are covered and "laser in use" signs are posted on all doors and windows of the operating room suite. Finally, the medical laser technician is responsible for filling out special forms that record the lasers used during the surgery, the strength and other settings for the lasers, and any changes made to those settings either by the medical laser technician or the surgeon. Billing notes are also taken down on these forms, including the use of additional materials or surgical drapes. These records then become part of the patient's surgical file. Should there ever be a question about the surgery, the medical laser technician will have a complete record of everything he or she did during the operation.

As the director of a unit, an average day for Tim means checking the operating room schedule first thing in the morning to make certain that a medical laser technician and nurse are covering all of the laser/advanced surgery cases. "If they're not covered," Tim says, laugh-

in-depth

What Exactly Is a Laser?

An acronym for Light Amplification by Stimulated Emission of Radiation, the laser is a precisely controlled light beam that is narrowly focused and aimed at a minute target. In each laser, various frequencies of light are converted into an intense beam of a single wavelength, or color. Because it is the color that determines how the beam will interact with particular kinds of tissue, different lasers or strengths are used for different types of surgery. Lasers may function continuously or in pulsed bursts. The type of laser determines the number of pulses per second, the duration of the pulses, and whether the light will be used to cut through, vaporize, or seal tissue.

Various lasers take their names from the different substances that produce the beam.

The carbon dioxide laser, with a wavelength in the far infrared spectrum, penetrates tissue to a depth of 1 millimeter. It has been used widely to treat some types of cancer, gynecological disorders, and brain tumors.

The argon laser, functioning in the blue-green frequencies, reacts with the color red and will penetrate the skin until it comes in contact with blood. Because it readily coagulates with blood in the area of the incision or operation, the argon laser has been particularly useful in the fields of ophthalmology, plastic surgery, and dermatology.

The YAG laser, with a wavelength in the near infrared spectrum, is used to cook or vaporize tissue that will then be removed from the body. The most invasive of all surgical laser devices, the YAG laser can penetrate 4 to 5 millimeters.

Dye lasers can be tuned to react to different wavelengths of light, simply by adding or diluting the dye. The free-electron laser, also tunable, uses magnets to stimulate pulsed light from a stream of electrons.

The excimer laser breaks up intermolecular bonds and decomposes matter, allowing precise surgery through holes so small no stitches are necessary. When certain gases are stimulated and combined and then returned to a disassociated state, their electrons emit photons of light in ultraviolet wavelengths. For example, patients undergoing excimer laser surgery to repair corneal damage do not experience the thermal effects of shock waves of conventional lasers. Without even touching the cornea, the excimer vaporizes the molecular links that bond the tissue with cool ultraviolet light.

ing, "that's where I am all day—in surgery." Normally, he divides his day between assisting in surgery, working with new instrumentation, handling administrative tasks, and reading up on new techniques and instruments.

Adam's days are divided among his many responsibilities: he might be in the operating room, scheduling cases, making certain equipment is tested and ready to be used, repairing and maintaining laser equipment, taking stock of necessary accessories and ordering them when needed, or working on a research project with a surgeon or research team.

"The research projects vary," explains Adam. "A doctor may see a technique and want to conduct his own study to see if widespread use of the technique is really warranted, or if it's just a lot of hype. For example, I might work on a blind study examining whether or not lasers should be used to treat wrinkles. Half of the participants' upper lips would be treated with dermabrasion, a method commonly used by plastic surgeons to reduce wrinkles, and the other half of the participants' upper lips would be treated with lasers."

The project described at the beginning of this article is another research project Adam is involved in. It combines laser-and-drug therapy for cancer treatment. This process is used to treat many types of cancer, but is now being approved for prostate cancer treatment. "The photodynamic therapy project is at least 15 years old, but it's taken that long for an interesting reason. The FDA has its procedures for approving drugs, and it has its procedures for approving techniques. But this case is one of the first times a drug and a technique [together] have been approved by the FDA," says Adam.

have I got what it takes to be a medical laser technician?

Having a calm demeanor and good judgment are important qualities for this field. "You definitely have to have a special type of personality to work in the medical field," Adam says. "Doctors can be extremely arrogant. I think they're not used to having their instructions and ideas questioned or challenged by others. They're used to giving orders, no questions asked," he explains. "Sometimes I think they like to test you, to see what your breaking point is. So, in order to work with them, you have to let a certain amount slide off you, but you also need to stand up to doctors to let them know you won't just sit back and take it all the time." Adam gives a short laugh, "You have to know when to stand up for yourself and when to let things slide."

Adam warns prospective medical laser technicians about the communication difficulties inherent in the medical field. "I don't know of any other field or industry that's like this. For example, in industry, if you have an idea, you can just go up to the engineer and tell him your idea. It's strange, but in medicine, you have to really think about how you bring things up. You have to be clever about it. You can't just go up to the surgeon and say, 'I think it could be done better this way.' Unfortunately, things don't work that way. Sometimes it might even come down to letting the surgeon think it was his idea." Adam doesn't believe in kidding people about how tough-skinned you need to be to survive in the field. "If your feelings are easily hurt, this isn't the best place to work."

On the other hand, Adam loves the variety of his job. "Laser techs working in industry often get stuck doing the same thing, day in and day out. Every day is usually different in the operating room. I like that there are always new things to learn, new types of procedures to master."

Medical laser technicians can always expect some degree of stress, pressure, and even danger. Tim clearly states how these three elements combine in his work. "If equipment fails or a physician is using it incorrectly, it is the laser technician who has the responsibility to intercede—even during an operation—if the patient could be in jeopardy."

Laser technicians working in the medical field also need to be able to work efficiently in a variety of circumstances. Tim's job requires him to work with very little discussion while in surgery. Later, however, working with the same doctor on an experimental instrument, Tim may have to voice his opinion without feeling intimidated by the doctor. He agrees that laser technicians working in the medical field need to feel comfortable around surgeons. "A surgical team operates with very little conversation. Familiarity with procedures and with the physicians is necessary to respond to any situation that might occur with the equipment," Tim says. "The laser technician is a liaison between the physicians and the equipment."

how do I become a medical laser technician?

Tim received an associate's degree in lasers and optics from Vincennes University in Vincennes, Indiana. After graduating, he went to work in research at a hospital in Cincinnati, Ohio, where he received a lot of practical, on-the-job experience.

"A lot of the technology involving lasers was just blossoming when I began in research," Tim says. "I was lucky, in that sense, because it was an incredibly dynamic field then. It still is a very dynamic field, but recent pressures to keep the costs down for insurance purposes have made the field tighten up a bit, in terms of spending money on research."

education

High School

If you are interested in becoming a medical laser technician, you should start preparing for this highly technical field while still in high school. Important classes to take include four years of English, two years of mathematics (including algebra), and at least one year of physical science (preferably physics) with laboratory instruction. Computer programming and applications, machine shop, basic electronics, and blueprint reading are also useful. Any class that explores systems and the ways in which they work will help you understand lasers.

Postsecondary Training

The best way to become a medical laser technician is to enter a two-year program at a technical school or community college. There are 11 such programs in the country, according to Dave Tyree, associate professor and chairman of the laser department at Vincennes University in Indiana. Laser training programs have grown in recent years, but there is still room in most programs for new students. At Vincennes University, the program could accommodate up to 40 students, but there are only 20 currently enrolled.

"Most programs are relatively small, but that's changing. This year the graduating class has 10 graduates," Dave says. "It's tough to get high school students interested in this area or any area of high tech. It's not as glamorous as law enforcement or other fields. A lot of students tend to see the old stereotype of the computer geek; they don't view it as a cool job."

To be a successful medical laser technician, you should

- Be able to successfully communicate ideas and disagree when necessary
- Be able to work with others
- Be interested in technology and be willing to learn new systems as they come along
- Have good hand-eye coordination

A laser technician career is attractive because it is a field with a relatively high starting salary for only a few years of schooling. "I'm sure the heavy demand for graduates will generate more interest in the career, leading to larger classes," Dave says.

The average course of study in lasers includes intensive technical and scientific study with more hours in a laboratory or work situation than in the actual classroom. This hands-on experience is combined with other first-year courses in mathematics, physics, drafting or drawing, diagramming and sketching, basic electronics, electronic instrumentation and calibration, introduction to solid-state devices, electromechanical controls, introductory computer programming, and English composition.

The second year of study includes an introduction to lasers, geometrical optics, digital circuits, microwaves, laser and electro-optic components, devices and measurements, vacuum techniques, communication skills, technical report writing, microcomputers, and computer hardware.

Completing special projects is often a requirement of the second year, and this work can help students to narrow the field in which they plan to use their laser technician degree. At other times, a job simply opens up and presents the technician with an opportunity, as in Adam's case. His lab partner in school told him about an opening and, in his words, "I just fell into medicine. My training had zero to do with the medical field. Most laser technician programs have a real slant towards industry because that's where the majority of the jobs are. Basic laser instruction is the same from laser to laser, it's the application that differs, what you use that laser to do—cut skin or cut metal—and that you have to learn on the job."

At his first job, Adam was a bit of a pioneer since he was the first to hold this position. Adam recalls, "I was the first laser tech hired by the hospital where I first worked, so there wasn't anyone to train me or show me the ropes. Learning on the job can be tough, but it's also the best teacher." Adam also recommends taking classes in anatomy and physiology to ease the learning process: "Anything that will help you understand the terms and references to the body."

Further training after employment is almost always required and is usually paid for by the employer. This training helps laser technicians advance their knowledge and expertise.

certification or licensing

Currently, there are no mandatory certification or licensing requirements for medical laser technicians. The National Council on Laser Excellence is working to establish a minimal competency and quality assurance program for Excellence in Laser Service. Candidates with a two-year certificate and/or experience in laser technology would take an examination to be LSE (Laser Service Excellence) certified. The NCLE currently offers voluntary Laser Operator and Medical Laser Safety Officer certification.

You should know, however, that some employers require their medical laser technicians to take and pass qualifying or certifying examinations on a particular machine or program.

scholarships and grants

Scholarships and grants may be available from individual technical schools or community colleges. You should contact these institutions for specific information, such as requirements and deadlines. Currently, the national associations do not offer scholarships specifically for medical laser technicians.

internships and volunteerships

Summer or part-time work in areas where lasers are used, such as manufacturing plants, hospitals, medical research facilities, and construction sites, can help to give the aspiring laser technician valuable contacts, information, and experience.

who will hire me?

Many laser technicians now graduating from a two-year technical school or community college will probably obtain their first jobs through interviews on campus. "For our students graduating with a technical degree, we feel that one of the main parts of our job is

Lasers have three special light properties: monochromaticity, directionality, and coherence.

Monochromaticity is useful in photochemistry, atomic isotope separation, and spectroscopy.

Directionality gives laser light the ability to travel great distances while remaining intense, which makes the laser helpful with drilling and welding.

The *coherence* of laser light helps surveyors to accurately measure distances and helps the military to track missiles.

placement," remarks Dave Tyree of Vincennes University. Fortunately, he says, his job is made that much easier by the fact that companies are coming to him. "The job market has really taken off," he says. "I've got companies calling me who want every single graduate I've got!" He adds, "And head hunters—they usually only search for executives—are calling me for laser technicians."

While it is true that most of the recent interest has been from nonmedical employers, Dave says the medical field is doing just fine. As lasers gain approval for everything from treating kidney stones to cancers, patients are demanding these less invasive treatments and more insurance companies are covering such procedures. Another relatively new avenue of employment for laser technicians is through employers such as LaserVision Centers Inc., which hires laser engineers and operators to install and maintain transportable lasers and assist physicians in laser vision correction procedures. The Laser Institute of America also provides a list of employers.

Many colleges provide students with lists of companies and resume assistance. Colleges often work closely with hospitals and companies involved in medical research, as in the case of Idaho State University's Laser Electro-Optics Program, which involves a Corporate Advisory Committee of six to 12 companies. This advisory committee is active in hiring graduates as well as in giving advice on curriculum.

Former graduates of the college are frequently valuable resources in placement. "Our first graduating class was in 1975, and whenever any of them needs to fill positions, they call us," Dave says.

The U.S. Armed Forces provides another entry for the medical laser technician. Military training is not always compatible with civilian requirements, however, so those entering the civilian field may need additional training.

History of the Laser

Originally commissioned by industry leaders in the 1960s to study the effects of lasers and radioactivity on employees who used lasers in their work, Dr. Leon Goldman, a dermatologist, saw untapped potential for the new technology in the field of medicine. Dr. Goldman followed his vision far beyond the scope of his original study, and today he is considered the father of laser surgery.

While at the Jewish Hospital in Cincinnati, Ohio, Dr. Goldman treated hundreds of patients, pioneered countless treatments and procedures involving lasers, and trained doctors from all over the world in his techniques. The Goldman Laser Institute at the Jewish Hospital is named for him and continues to research and introduce new procedures that take advantage of laser technology. For example, the Institute pioneered the use of a flashlamp-pumped dye laser in the treatment of birthmarks and spider veins.

Dr. Goldman's research and resulting procedures have forever altered medical history. Today lasers are used in a variety of specialties, including ophthalmology, otolaryngology, plastic surgery, urology, neurosurgery, vascular surgery, general surgery, dermatology, and gynecology. The Goldman Laser Institute has conducted research in arthritis, bladder cancer, cervical cancer, gastrointestinal cancer, dermatology, orthopedics, lung cancer, head and neck cancer, and vascular welding.

where can I go from here?

There are many possibilities for advancement, although the primary ways are through on-the-job experience and by keeping up with technological changes and developments in the field.

Obtaining a supervisor or director position is one way to advance in this field. After 10 years of experience as a laser technician, Tim is now a director of other technicians. He still has technical duties in the surgical room, but now he is also responsible for supervising the department's caseload and personnel and for shaping the future of laser surgery at St. Mary's. "It's definitely possible to advance by learning all you can and getting all the experience you can," Tim says.

Many employers designate levels of employment according to experience, education, and job performance. By working through these levels, medical laser technicians can advance to supervisory positions. It is an essential skill for the supervisor or director to be able to balance many responsibilities. Part of what Tim enjoys most about his work is his variety of duties as technician, administrator, and perpetual student of new technology. "New instrumentation develops rapidly in this field. As best I can, I stay up to date."

Some medical laser technicians may advance to become teachers in laser technician education programs. Also, laser technicians who work in the medical field can always pursue work in other fields and industries. "One company called me looking for laser technicians to work on government optical systems, specifically the repair systems for the Hubble spacecraft," Dave says.

Tim agrees about the diversity of the field. "If I got together with the rest of my graduating class and talked about what we were each doing," he comments, "we'd have almost nothing in common."

Another avenue for advancement is to work as a consultant. Consultants work closely with clients to define their needs or problems by conducting studies and surveys to obtain data. They analyze data and recommend solutions to the client's problems.

Constant training in the safety and use of lasers is necessary for all types of laser technicians to keep up with the industry. Many companies pay for employee training. There are also several opportunities for continuing education available through the Laser Institute of America.

what are the salary ranges?

Salaries for medical laser technicians vary greatly in different parts of the country and for different educational backgrounds and applications. The job market has taken off and, as a result, salaries have risen dramatically in a few short years. Although the medical field is currently experiencing slower growth than the other fields that utilize the talents of laser technicians, the starting salaries of medical laser technicians have continued to move upward alongside those of nonmedical laser technicians.

In order to remain competitive, hospitals and private clinics have had to continue to match the salaries of nonmedical laser technicians or face losing their technicians to other fields. Medical laser technicians can expect to start at about $33,000, Dave Tyree says. "But most can expect to earn $40,000 or better after three to five years of experience." For advanced, supervisory, sales, service, or private consulting positions, medical laser technicians may earn $49,000 to $53,000 or more.

In addition to good salaries, most medical laser technicians can expect a wide array of benefits, including insurance, paid holidays and vacations, and retirement plans. Many employers offer opportunities for continuing education.

what is the job outlook?

The job growth for laser technicians entering the medical field should remain about average. Vincennes University boasts nearly 100 percent placement for its laser technician graduates entering all fields. "Last year," says Dave, "we had companies who could not fill all of the positions that they had open, so this year they're back to hire our graduates."

The majority of jobs available for laser technicians are in industry and areas other than medicine, but jobs do exist for laser technicians who wish to work in the medical field. "You really have to go to a pretty big laser center, say a hospital with at least eight to 10 lasers," Adam advises. "A hospital with only two

or three lasers will just send a nurse through a training program to learn how to operate the lasers. But in a hospital with 10 or 15 lasers, it's just too much for one person to try and keep up with. Then it becomes cost-effective for the hospital to hire a laser technician."

Calvin Christiansen, instructor/coordinator for Idaho State University, also reports a high job placement rate, but says, "Some who don't find jobs are just not willing to go where the jobs are." For the best entry-level jobs, graduates must sometimes relocate to large, urban centers.

Depending on the strength of the economy, laser technicians who want to work in research areas may have a greater challenge locating a position. On the whole, however, the medical field remains a viable option for laser technicians.

how do I learn more?

professional organizations

Following are organizations that provide information on careers, schools, and possible employers for medical laser technicians.

American Society for Laser Medicine and Surgery
2404 Stewart Square
Wausau, WI 54401
715-845-9283
information@aslms.org
http://www.aslms.org

Laser Institute of America
13501 Ingenuity Drive, Suite 128
Orlando, FL 32826
407-380-1553
http://www.laserinstitute.org

National Council on Laser Excellence and Laser Training Institute
PO Box 522379
Marathon Shores, FL 33052
800-435-3131
http://lasercertification.org

bibliography

Following is a sampling of materials relating to the professional concerns and development of medical laser technicians.

Arndt, Kenneth M. et al, eds. *Laser in Cutaneous and Aesthetic Surgery.* Philadelphia, PA: Lippincott Williams & Wilkins, 1997.

McGhee, Charles et al, eds. *Excimer Lasers in Ophthalmology, Principles and Practice.* Newton, MA: Butterworth-Heinemann Medical, 1997.

Rosen, Arye and Harel D. Rosen, eds. *New Frontiers in Medical Device Technology.* New York, NY: John Wiley & Sons, 1995.

Sarnoff, Deborah S. and Joan Swirsky. *Beauty and the Beam: Your Complete Guide to Cosmetic Laser Surgery.* New York, NY: Griffin Trade Paperbacks, 1998.

Slade, Stephen G. et al. *The Complete Book of Laser Eye Surgery.* Naperville, IL: Sourcebooks Trade, 2000.

Medical Record Technicians

Definition

Medical record technicians compile, code, and maintain medical records to document patient diagnoses and treatments. They also tabulate and analyze data from the records to assemble reports.

Alternative Job Titles

Certified coding specialists
Health information technicians
Medical records clerks

High School Subjects

Biology
English

Personal Skills

Following instructions
Technical/scientific

Salary Range

$16,000 to $30,000 to $50,000

Minimum Educational Level

Some postsecondary training

Certification or Licensing

Recommended

Outlook

Much faster than the average

GOE
07.05.03
O*NET-SOC
29-2071.00

The intensive care unit of Saint Patrick Hospital is crowded with doctors, nurses, and visitors as Susan Lucchesi examines a patient's medical chart and writes in her notepad every diagnosis, procedure, and comment that has been added since she reviewed the data two days ago. She jots down a few questions that come to mind, points of clarification that she will call to the attention of the attending physicians. After discussing the chart with one of the nurses, she adds another comment to her notes. Although the patients in intensive care probably have no idea who she is, and she might not recognize their faces, she's familiar with each of them, because she studies their charts regularly. As a records technician, she makes sure that the details of their stay at the hospital are documented with impeccable thoroughness and accuracy.

When she returns to her quiet, pleasant office in the medical records department, she enters information from her notes into the hospital's computer system, prints it, keeps a copy for the patient's medical records folder, writes out her questions for the doctors, attaches them to a second copy of the printout, and sends it back to intensive care for the doctors to review. She'll repeat the procedure every two or three days until the patient is moved to another department, where a different medical records technician will take over.

lingo to learn

Abstracting: Removing pertinent information from a patient's medical record for use in a larger study or survey.

Coding: In medical records, assigning numbers for systematic classification.

CPT (Common Procedural Terminology): The numerical classification system used in the medical records field to code procedures and treatments.

DRG (Diagnosis-Related Grouping): A system used by Medicare and many insurance companies to classify medical patients' care and treatment.

ICD (International Classification of Diseases): The numerical classification system used in the medical records field to code diagnoses.

Source-oriented chart order: A system of organizing patient charts by grouping information into sections based on different health care departments, such as nursing, radiology, or attending physician.

Stat: Immediately.

Terminal Digit Order: A numerical filing method emphasizing the last two digits, which is the most effective use of filing space, as well as the most effective method of insuring patient privacy.

Transcription: Making written copies of orally dictated material.

what does a medical record technician do?

If you've ever spent time in a hospital, either as a patient or visitor, you may remember the steady parade of nurses and doctors in and out of the patients' rooms for one thing or another. They might check body temperature, blood pressure, heart rate, or frequency of labor pains, give medication, check incisions, or test range of motion in a damaged limb. They're always writing on that little chart at the foot of the bed, generating an amazing amount of data for each patient at every hospital. If you've wondered what happens to all that information when the patient goes home, you have wondered about the job of the *medical record technician*.

An individual's medical record consists of all the information noted by any health care workers who have dealt with the patient. Along with the patient's medical history, it may include admission date, diagnoses, progress notes, surgical procedures, X-rays, lab reports, prescribed medications or treatments, and discharge assessment. Medical record technicians assemble and organize records, make sure they're accurate, and prepare them for the use of doctors, insurance companies, or other authorized agencies or individuals. The technician also may compile statistical reports from groups of records. Hospital administrators, public health agencies, health program planners, and others use these reports to analyze trends and patterns or to see if a treatment is effective.

In smaller organizations, with fewer records to manage, the technician may work in all areas of the medical records department. In larger institutions there may be separate departments for each phase of the work, with each technician having very specific responsibilities.

Technicians who specialize in assigning a numerical code to every diagnosis and procedure are called *medical record coders* or *coder/abstractors*. To determine the correct codes, these technicians use specialized computer software, a coding reference guide, medical dictionaries, and the *Physician's Desk*

Reference. Most hospitals in the United States use a nationally accepted coding system, which makes the data easier to handle and analyze in the records department and by organizations that pool information from many institutions. A coded record can be cross-referenced and sorted by its various components, such as physician, patient, diagnosis, or treatment. The technician may also assign the patient to a diagnosis-related grouping (DRG), which helps the Medicare system and insurance companies determine the amount to reimburse the hospital for the patient's stay. At some institutions patients are assigned to DRGs by technicians who specialize in using computers to analyze patients' charts.

In larger facilities some records technicians work in a release-of-information department that does nothing but release medical records to doctors, insurance agencies, state and federal organizations, law enforcement agencies, attorneys, and the patients themselves. These technicians prepare and release information for authorized use only. Maintaining confidentiality of patient records is a priority, not only for this department but for all medical records technicians.

Finally, the medical record must be filed away for storage and easy retrieval, either on computer, paper, or microfilm. In some institutions the medical record technicians supervise other personnel, such as *medical records clerks*, who perform the storage and retrieval work.

Most medical records technicians have more advanced training than medical records clerks, but not all have passed certification exams. Those who hold an associate's degree and certification are called *accredited records technicians*. They ensure the accuracy of medical records, create disease registries for research, and submit data to insurance companies, which then reimburse the health care facility.

Registered records administrators hold a bachelor's degree and certification. They are managers who also interpret data, do research and statistical reports, and ensure the privacy of health information.

Certified coding specialists have taken seminars or college classes in coding, along with on-the-job experience, and they are certified. The credential, *certified coding specialist physician-based*, is for technicians who specialize in coding for physician services in facilities other than hospitals.

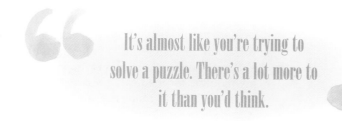

"It's almost like you're trying to solve a puzzle. There's a lot more to it than you'd think."

what is it like to be a medical record technician?

As a medical records coder at Saint Patrick Hospital in Missoula, Montana, Susan Lucchesi spends most of the day at her computer in the medical records department assigning a numerical code to each diagnosis and procedure on patients' charts. She works in cooperation with a team of coders, a transcriptionist, and the clerks in the office next door; the clerks maintain an entire room full of records documented on paper, neatly stored in filing cabinets. "We all help each other out. We work together, and no one person gets the credit for anything. We're a very close team," she says.

Like many technicians in her field, Susan used to see little of the doctors, nurses, and other health care professionals who perform the work summarized in the medical charts. Thanks to a new program at the hospital, however, Susan now spends a few hours each day reviewing charts in the intensive care unit. The other coders on her team have different departments to visit; Susan has the option of covering the intensive care unit for one year and then rotating to another department.

She still communicates with doctors by notes, email, and phone calls from the medical records department, but she has enjoyed the chance to see how the intensive care unit operates. "I've made a lot of friends with doctors and nurses on my floor. That's been a learning experience," she says.

By tracking each patient's progress and assigning codes that help identify the main reason the person was admitted for treatment, Susan helps the doctors zero in on the patient's most pressing health problems and possible remedies. "It's almost like you're trying to solve a puzzle," she says. "There's a lot more to it than you'd think."

Some medical records technicians are more involved in following up after the patient has been discharged and the paperwork has been done. Terri Young works in the release-of-information department in another hospital. She also works as part of a team that processes many requests for medical information every day. One technician mans the special phone line, known as the "stat line," which receives calls mainly from emergency rooms. Information for those calls may be given over the telephone or by fax after the technician has verified the patient's name and birth date; all other requests must be in writing and include either the patient's authorization or a court order.

Requests are logged into the computer and prioritized. Terri's hospital strives to send out the information within two weeks of receiving it, but medical requests always receive priority over insurance requests. For each request, Terri gets the patient's medical record number from the computer, uses it to locate the chart, looks for the requested information in her records, and locates any specialized information in other areas of the hospital, such as the X-ray department. When she has found everything to complete the request, she fills out a worksheet, indicating what items need to be copied, and turns the file over to a medical record clerk.

Other technicians in the medical records department perform other duties. There are coding and abstracting technicians, most of whom have taken special training in coding. They spend their days almost exclusively at computer terminals. "You have to be able to concentrate," says Terri. "You have to be able to sit and sit and keep your mind on what you're doing."

There's a data entry team, the first technicians to work with patient records. They visit each floor of the hospital daily, pick up the charts for patients discharged the day before, assemble each chart in a specific order, and enter the information into the hospital's computer system.

There's a chart analysis team, which puts each patient's diagnoses in the correct time sequence and uses a computer software package to assign the patient to one of hundreds of diagnosis-related groupings. The groupings determine how much the hospital will be reimbursed by Medicare and insurance companies for the patient's stay. Accuracy is essential for the chart analysis team. Terri explains, "Medicare is so picky that if diagnoses aren't sequenced properly, it may make thousands of dollars difference in what they pay."

Because the hospital's records department never closes, some of the technicians work second and third shifts, as well as some weekends and holidays. Terri works Monday through Friday, 7:00 AM until 4:00 PM. The 40-hour workweek is standard for most medical record technicians.

have I got what it takes to be a medical record technician?

The medical record technician is responsible for keeping accurate records for the benefit of the hospital, the physician, and the patient. Sloppy work could cause serious problems; the hospital might not receive proper payment, and inaccuracies in the records could affect the patient's health care in the future. The technician must develop precise and fastidious work habits to ensure as complete and correct a job as possible. Susan says a medical record technician should be detail oriented, interested in medicine, and adaptable. "It can be stressful sometimes," she adds. "There are so many federal regulations."

The technician needs to handle heavy workloads, pressure to get things done rapidly, and constant interruption. "It's stressful," Terri Young says, "because people want things immediately. They don't take no for an answer." The phone rings constantly, she says, with requests to have records retrieved, prepared, copied, and faxed. It is also important for the technician to be able to deal with sometimes trying personalities. "Doctors get frustrated," Terri says, "and tempers flare at you, even if it's not your fault." She adds that technicians need to react in a professional manner and avoid taking things personally.

What Terri likes most about her job is that it is challenging. She enjoys the detailed work and the opportunity for growth. "I have learned a great deal by working here," she says. She has worked in several different capacities since she started in the medical records department. The department itself has become more computerized and automated. Terri agrees with Susan that being adaptable to change is very important for a technician.

She also thinks it is important to have a strong interest in the medical field. "I think that a lot of people have a desire to work in the medical field, but they don't want to deal with the actual patients," she says. "This job would fulfill that need." Discretion and tact are also a must, Terri cautions. Medical records are confidential, and maintaining a patient's privacy is an important aspect of this job. "If it's in a file, it's confidential, no matter what," says Terri. "You have to remember that you heard it here, not on the street corner."

how do I become a medical record technician?

Susan became interested in the medical records profession soon after she left high school. She heard that job openings were plentiful in this occupation, so she enrolled in a two-year medical records program at a vocational school. After earning an associate's degree, she completed several internships, which gave her experience in various aspects of the profession.

To prepare for a career in medical records, Susan recommends taking high school classes in computers, anatomy, physiology, medical terminology, and pharmacology. She didn't take specific preparatory classes in high school, because at that time she hadn't decided what career she wanted to pursue, but her classes in biology, chemistry, and computers proved helpful.

Terri Young became interested in health information management because two of her older cousins were record technicians. "They just loved it," she says. "They were always talking about their jobs." Terri decided when she was still in high school that she wanted to be a medical record technician. She earned an associate's degree from a junior college that offered an accredited program, then took the test to become accredited. She says her classes were challenging and enjoyable, good preparation for the examination.

education

High School
Students contemplating a career in medical records should take as many high school English classes as possible, because technicians need both written and verbal communication skills to prepare reports and communicate with other health care personnel. Basic math

Advancement Possibilities

Tumor registrars compile and maintain records of patients who have cancer to provide information to physicians and for research studies.

Medical record administrators plan, develop, and administer health information management systems for health care facilities; develop procedures for documenting, storing, retrieving, and processing patient information; supervise staffs; and analyze patient data.

Utilization-review coordinators analyze patient records to determine legitimacy of treatment and the patient's hospital stay to comply with government and insurance reimbursement policies. They also review applications for patient admission, abstract data from records, maintain statistics, and determine patient review dates.

Medical billing service owners use special software to help doctors and other health care professionals get payment for services. They send bills to patients, private insurance companies, Medicare, and other insurers. Most billers work from their home offices, though some work in the offices of doctors and clinics.

or business math is very desirable because statistical skills are important in some job functions. Biology courses help by familiarizing the student with the terminology that medical record technicians use. Other science courses, computer training, typing, and office procedures are also helpful.

Postsecondary Training
Most employers prefer to hire medical record technicians who have completed a two-year associate's degree program accredited by the American Medical Association's Commission on Accreditation of Allied Health Professions (CAAHP) and the American Health Information Management Association (AHIMA). There are approximately 175 of these accredited programs available throughout the United States, mostly offered in junior and community col-

leges. They usually include classroom instruction in such subjects as anatomy, physiology, medical terminology, medical record science, word processing, medical aspects of record keeping, statistics, computers in health care, personnel supervision, business management, English, and office skills.

In addition to classroom instruction, the student is given supervised clinical experience in the medical records departments of local health care facilities. This provides you with practical experience in performing many of the functions learned in the classroom and with the opportunity to interact with health care professionals.

certification or licensing

Medical record technicians who have completed an accredited training program are eligible to take a national qualifying examination to earn the credential of Registered Health Information Technician (RHIT). Most health care institutions prefer to hire individuals with an RHIT credential as it signifies that they have met the standards established by the AHIMA as the mark of a qualified health professional.

Technicians who have achieved the RHIT credential are required to obtain 20 hours of continuing education credits every two years in order to retain their RHIT status. These credits may be obtained by attending educational programs, participating in further academic study, or pursuing independent study activities approved by the AHIMA.

AHIMA also offers the following certifications for technicians who complete advanced education and pass a national certification

To be a successful medical record technician, you should

- Be extremely thorough and detail oriented
- Feel confident in dealing with medical staff, administrators, and insurance agencies
- Be able to concentrate for long periods of time
- Be able to handle a heavy workload
- Feel comfortable working with computers

examination: Registered Health Information Administrator, Certified Coding Specialist, and Certified Coding Specialist-Physician Based.

scholarships and grants

AHIMA has a foundation that offers scholarships and loans to health information management students. Undergraduate applicants may qualify for loans up to $2,000. The foundation also bestows a number of scholarships, ranging in amount from $1,000 to $5,000. For details, contact AHIMA (see How Do I Learn More?).

who will hire me?

When Terri Young graduated from her two-year college program, she put together a resume and started to look for a job. She responded to an ad in her hometown newspaper for a medical record technician's position at the local hospital. After two interviews and a nerve-wracking two weeks, she was offered the job. Her first duty was to transfer some of the older records to microfilm for storage. "I worked way in the back," she says, "and never even saw any current records at first."

More than half of the medical record technicians in the United States work in hospitals. Most of the rest work in other health care settings, such as nursing homes, group medical practices, health maintenance organizations, outpatient clinics, surgery centers, or veterinary hospitals. There are also technicians who work for insurance companies and accounting and law firms that deal with health care issues. Public health care departments also use medical record technicians to help collect and research data from health care institutions.

If you're graduating from an associate's degree program, your school placement office might help you find a job. You may also want to apply directly to the personnel departments of local hospitals, nursing homes, and outpatient clinics. Checking newspaper classified ads is also a good idea, since they often list medical record technicians' job openings.

Some publications geared especially to the health information management field carry classified advertising, including job listings. Also, the American Health Information Management Association (AHIMA) offers a resume referral service to its members. The technician can send the AHIMA office a resume, which will be kept on file and faxed to employers who have notified AHIMA of job opportunities (see How Do I Learn More?).

where can I go from here?

"The jobs are there, everywhere," says Susan. "You can go overseas. You could go to Saudi Arabia for a year, or Hawaii. There's a lot you can do with this degree."

She explains that medical records technicians have the option of working for companies that assign them to temporary jobs almost anywhere in the nation or in other countries, with travel and lodging allowances included. Some technicians work as consultants, teaching other technicians how to do coding and other tasks that require specialized skills. Others are assigned to temporary, contract jobs. Some freelance, typically coding records on a hospital's computer system.

Susan has worked at Saint Patrick Hospital for about a year and says the hospital's progressive medical records department offers her an excellent opportunity to learn the latest technology, a real advantage if she ever wants to make a career move elsewhere. "This is my first real coding job," she comments. "I really like it. I could leave here and get a job almost anywhere."

In contrast, Terri has spent seven years in the medical records department of her hospital and has worked in almost every phase of the record-keeping process. She feels she may have exhausted the new frontiers available within the department and is currently taking classes in transcription. She plans to run a doctors' transcription service from her home eventually.

For the technician who works in a large health care facility, advancement may mean becoming a *section supervisor* and overseeing the work of the others in the section. Another way to climb the ladder is to specialize in an area such as coding.

Better advancement and higher pay are possible for the technician who goes back to school. Those with a bachelor's degree in medical record administration, along with AHIMA accreditation, can become department directors or assistant department directors. Because of the shortage of medical record administrators, hospitals often make it easy for techni-

Related Jobs

The U.S. Department of Labor classifies medical record technicians under the headings *Record Preparation and Maintenance* (GOE) and *Healthcare Practitioners and Technical* (O*NET-SOC). Also under these headings are insurance policy processing clerks, stenographers, file clerks, shorthand reporters, and people who maintain and file records for aircraft, insurance agencies, and personnel departments.

The profession of medical record technician requires a strong clinical base; although technicians are not involved with actual patient care, they must be familiar with medical terminology, anatomy, and physiology. Positions in the medical field that require a similar background include medical secretaries, transcriptionists, writers, and illustrators.

cians to get their bachelor's degree by giving them financial aid and time off to go to class.

what are the salary ranges?

According to a 2000 membership survey by the American Health Information Management Association (AHIMA), 67 percent responding earned between $20,000 and $39,000 annually. A little over 11 percent of the respondents earned between $40,000 and $49,000, while 6.7 percent earned between $50,000 and $74,999. The *Occupational Outlook Handbook* reports that health information technicians had median annual earnings of $20,590 in 1998. Those in the middle 50 percent earned between $16,670 and $25,440 annually.

Most full-time positions in health information management include a benefits package. Health care insurance, paid vacations and holidays, pension plans, and sick leave are commonly offered.

what is the job outlook?

Employment prospects for medical record technicians are excellent. The U.S. Depart-

exploring health care careers

ment of Labor predicts that employment in this field will grow by 44 percent in the next decade. The demand for well-trained medical record technicians will grow rapidly and will continue to exceed the supply. This expectation is related to the health care needs of a population that is both growing and aging and the trend toward more technologically sophisticated medicine and greater use of diagnostic procedures. It is also related to the increased requirements of regulatory bodies that scrutinize both costs and quality of care of health care providers. Because of the fear of medical malpractice lawsuits, doctors and other health care providers are documenting their diagnoses and treatments in greater detail. Also, because of the high cost of health care, insurance companies, government agencies, and courts are examining medical records with a more critical eye. These factors combine to ensure a healthy job outlook for medical record technicians.

Technicians with associate's degrees and RHIT status will have the best prospects, and the importance of such qualifications is likely to increase.

how do I learn more?

professional organizations

For information on earnings, careers in health information management, and RHIT accreditation, contact:
American Health Information Management Association
233 North Michigan Avenue, Suite 2150
Chicago, IL 60601-5800
312-233-1100
info@ahima.org
http://www.ahima.org

For a list of schools offering accredited programs in health information management, contact:
Commission on Accreditation of Allied Health Education Programs
American Medical Association
35 East Wacker Drive, Suite 1970
Chicago, IL 60601-2208
312-553-9355
caahep@caahep.org
http://www.caahep.org

bibliography

Following is a sampling of materials relating to the professional concerns and development of medical record technicians.

Careers in Focus: Medical Technicians. 2nd Edition. Chicago, IL: Ferguson Publishing Company, 2001.

Goldberg, Jan. *Medical Record Technician (Careers Without College).* Mankato, MN: Capstone Press, 1999.

Rudman, Jack. *Amra Medical Record Technician National Registration Examination.* Susosett, NY: National Learning Corporation, 1997.